LONG◎SHOTS

*Stories of Unexpected People,
Places, and Adventures*

Colonel D. D. Behrens, USAF ret

Copyright © 2023 Colonel D. D Behrens, USAF ret
Long Shots: Stories of Unexpected People, Places, and Adventures

Third printing

All rights reserved. No part of this publication may be reproduced, distributed, or transmitted in any form or by any means, including photocopying, recording, or electronic or mechanical methods, without prior written permission by the author, except in cases of brief quotations embodied in reviews and certain other non-commercial uses permitted by copyright law.

ISBN: 978-1-7352249-8-5   PCN

Printed in the United States of America

LONG ⊕ SHOTS

Table of Contents

Notes to the Reader 11
Acknowledgements 13
Foreword 15

I — Early Days

Earliest Memories 21
Murder in Iowa 30
Santa Paula 32
Two Boys and Three Guns 37
Boy Scouts of America 40
Jobs 43
Three Friends 56
The Flying Stetson 58
Riding Shotgun with the Sheriff 61
Automobiles 66
Wanderlust 70
Hitchhiking through Europe 1958 74
Going to College 83

II — Military

In the Army Now	99
Air Force	106
Vietnam Background	121
Arriving in Vietnam	123
The Tet Offensive	128
Close Calls	138
A Dangerous Mistake	142
The Three Year Hochzeitsreise (Honeymoon)	147
Assignments After Ramstein	168
Never Go Back	171
The Pentagon	194
Not Again, or, The Five 4-Star Flag Officers	205
Air Force Retirement and Coming Home	225

III — Hunting

I am a Hunter	251
A Black Bear Hunt, Lake Velesk, Alaska Range	270
Pheasants in England	273
Pheasants in Belgium	276
Land of the Morning Calm	280
Quail	288
Hunting in Italy	307
Driven Bird Shoots	309
Women Shooters and Hunters	319
No Good Deed Shall Go Unpunished	323
Argentina	328
African Adventures	339
Professional Hunters and Friends	377
Expedition Adventures, Inc.	390

IV — Teams

Air Force Rifle Team	417
Earning Bragging Rights	430
A Shocking Win	452
The Longhorn and the Carrot	467
Western Music and the Swagger Stick	472
Air Force Shotgun Team	473
Modern Pentathlon	483
World Championships 1993 to 2002	496
World Military Games	512

V — FAMILY AND FRIENDS

Family Tree	543
Loretta	552
Mother	571
My Father Hit Me	576
Brother Bob	583
Bunker Club	587
My Boys, My Guys, My Kids	592
The Big Three	611
Goofs, Comeuppance, Stupid, and Other Embarrassing Moments	620
Honorables	633
Reflections	653

VI — BACKWORD

Flashbacks from "DDB's Boys" by Col Rolf Smith	679
Appendix	705
Index	717

Notes to the Reader

THIS BOOK IS NOT MEANT TO BE AN AUTOBIOGRAPHY. It is a collection of stories and vignettes as I remember them. They were written at different times and are not necessarily presented in chronological order. Many will overlap and cover the same period. It is meant to be suitable reading for family members of all ages and therefore some language has been slightly altered, and I'll let the reader's imagination make mental adjustments. For the most part, Air Force abbreviations are used for military ranks and grades of the services except for the Navy.

Acknowledgments

MY WIFE HAS SUFFERED THE MOST; SHE HAS READ ALL THE STORIES and corrected my most egregious mistakes, sometimes reminding me, Who shot John, and what year it happened. Who encouraged me the most was Col Rolf Smith, a friend for nearly 60 years. He wrote an excellent, seriously academic book himself which is in its sixth printing. He's been needling me for years to put some stories together. Another person who must take some of the credit or blame is my friend and trusted partner Gordon White. He wrote a delightful little book, *Field Notes from Wild Places,* recalling his early hunting adventures, that is just a pleasure to read. His enjoyable and well-crafted book inspired me. The question was, if not now, when?

My faithful ladies, Mindy Reed and Diane Pollard, carried the early load. Mindy was the first reviewer and organized the marrying up of stories, print, index, and photos. Diane was my guardian for making sense. She has neither a military nor a hunting background and very rightly challenged me when she found something that was not clearly understood. I loved her questions. They made me think and reminded me who the audience would be. Carroll Wilson my proofreader aided me in tidying up the writing. Col Rolf Smith did a final review that got me over the hump. Thanks also to Rebecca Byrd for the photo and book design. Two other friends who must be recognized are Jeff Julig from San Antonio, Texas, and Max Jungk from Germany. They got me out of trouble every time (which was often) I jammed up or crashed my computer. They kept the train moving night and day.

The last chapter, Backword, was an add-on after the book was written. Rolf Smith was the architect and the reason it is included. He suggested input from "my boys, my guys, my kids." Originally, I dismissed the idea as being too egotistical, but now I am delighted he persisted and collected the narratives. What pleases me most is not the overly generous and handsome accolades; it is a testament to the character of the fine young men I've had the honor of accompanying me on my life's journey. Thank you, Col Smith. And finally, I must thank my family, friends, fellow service members, hunters, and acquaintances who gave me the fabric and inspiration to put my memories on paper. Some will appear in this text and some not, but thanks to each and every one.

Foreword

THIS IS NOT JUST A STORY ABOUT ME. IT IS AN ACCOUNT OF THE people, places, and experiences that made me. The people include parents, family, bosses, subordinates, contemporaries, mentors, teachers, friends, acquaintances, and all the incredible people I have met in my sojourn through the first 89 years of my life. We are each a product of the experiences that shape us and mine have been good. The narratives in this book reflect my memories of the events and people who allowed me into their lives which made mine so much richer. Some accounts will tell of lives that I may have helped shape, but make no mistake, those individuals also shaped my life.

When I was looking for a title for this book, I thought maybe Lucky Boy would be a good description as I feel like a lucky boy, or perhaps, The Many Lives of Dennis Behrens, since I've had so many different experiences. Then I thought I should describe how I got where I am today, which might better be described as WHAT HAPPENED? In the end it seemed like Long Shots would be the most descriptive title. I believe that will be confirmed as you read on.

How did I have such a wonderful, exciting, adventurous, and fulfilling journey in this life? There was no master plan worked out for me, nothing like growing up in a family that mapped out private schools, college, business, West Point, a professional career, and a total life plan. I could hardly have planned to have such perfect parents and to be born in such a wonderful country. I didn't think about going to college until it was upon me. And then, it was by luck we lived close to Ventura Junior College so I could also work and live at home. Going on to Fresno State College was in part because three of my high school buddies decided to go along with me.

Teaching school was never in the plan but offered a great experience. Joining the Air Force was rather a fluke as I was drafted in the Army but was looking more favorably on the Marine Corps. I certainly never expected to make military service a lifetime career, much less make full colonel. Only by chance did I become the officer in charge of the Air Force High-Power Rifle Team. I was just a lieutenant on the only USAF Rifle Team to ever beat the Army and Marine Corps for the United States National Championship, which was a real long shot.

Going on a full-blown African safari was beyond my dreams, but it happened, and I followed it with 62 additional safaris. Whoever thought I would be invited to shoot with lords and ladies in Europe, hunt Argentina more than 100 times, hunt on five continents, see the Aurora Borealis from the top of the world and watch the Southern Right Whales calve in Hermanus Bay at the bottom? How did that happen? Who would ever dream I could travel the world visiting over 79 countries?

Working in the Pentagon was an adventure and challenge in and of itself, but being military assistant to five different four-star generals and admirals has to be a world record. Starting my own business, Expedition Adventures, was just a natural result of taking friends on adventuresome trips. Why did I start working with Modern Pentathlon and all those fine young athletes? How did they win the world championship and also the Military World Games? That was a long shot, too. How did I get to work for or with so many outstanding people? How did I end up with champion shooting and pentathlon teams? Who would've thought I could carry our beautiful American flag officially as chief of mission of our sports teams to so many countries?

How did all this happen? I can't adequately answer. Certainly, I was not just a blowing tumbleweed. I worked hard at everything, set self-imposed goals along the way, and always did the very best I could with what I had. I have to admit that often there was luck involved.

Yogi Berra was famous for saying: "When you come to a fork in the road, take it." Somehow, I managed to take the right trail most of the time. My life has been more of a winding journey than traveling to an established destination. Above all, it was my good fortune to catch the right woman for a wife and lifetime partner.

This collection of thoughts, recollections, and stories is meant for family and a few good friends. While it won't be elegant prose, it is true and you will hear my voice. It was my good fortune to know my grandparents, my great-grandmother, numerous great-uncles and great-aunts, uncles and aunts, and flocks of cousins. They all had stories, but most are now gone (some cousins are still alive) with little evidence left behind and memories lost. I'm eternally sorry not to have gotten more history from my grandmother, Marie Ables, who came from the Netherlands through Ellis Island. She lived from horse and buggy days to a man on the moon. My great-grandmother, Eva Thomas, from another part of the family, lived in Kansas when Indians were still dangerous and told me how scared she was when they came into their sod house while her parents were absent. Her ancestors fought in the American Revolution, our Civil War, and the Spanish-American War where we lost my great uncle James Thomas. Our family also fought for our country in WW II and Vietnam. My mother was a Rosie Riveter during World War II and I can remember that, but I know little about her life growing up. Nor do I know much about my father's and uncles' early years.

"Privileged" could describe my upbringing, not by wealth or in a powerful family but by love, safety, stability, and super role models. I consider myself a lucky boy indeed to have had so many experiences and to have been enabled to do so many things. I lived many lives, from growing up in Santa Paula, California, to living and working on farms in Iowa, to competitive rifle and shotgun shooting, and hunting all over the world. I had a wonderful and rewarding Air Force career. I led Modern Pentathlon teams, traveled in many lands, and shot in the National Shooting Championships at Camp Perry. Belonging to the Masons, the Bunker Club, the Grand National Quail Club, and the California Indians expanded my circle of friends and broadened my perspective. This is not just a story of accomplishments. Rather it is accumulated memories of the dozens and dozens of wonderful friends who guided and propelled me on my life's journey.

I have tried always to act upon the square, and to work toward things of greater worth, but I have not been immune to the frailties of human nature. Sinless, I cannot claim. I am not a perfect person, for sure. Some lessons were learned the hard way. I hope my multiple errors and flaws of intolerance, impatience, and being too quick to judge, will be outweighed by some good. So many people have enriched my life in so many ways that it would be impossible to recount them all. A great number of mentors taught me without my realizing it at the time—and maybe they did not realize it either. They were dignified, striving always to do the right thing, even if it was painful for them. The experiences and adventures I enjoyed have been larger than I could've ever imagined as a schoolboy. And most of all, how was it even possible to establish friendships with so many outstanding people? Few multimillionaires can match me in that arena.

The quote from Luke 12:48, "To whom much is given, much will be required," begs reflection as I was given much. My point is that none of this was ever directed in any long-term family plan. I'm happy to report I came from a hard-working American family that moved from low economic status to a higher economic and social class. They supported me and urged my success, but no one directed or molded me in any specific direction. That lack of intervention made me self-reliant, disciplined, independent, and a self-starter. And I feel my life has been much richer and more fulfilling because of it.

I am still wondering, *WHAT HAPPENED?* A lifetime cannot be captured in a few hundred pages. Hopefully the little vignettes offered in this text will be of interest and at least record a very small speck of history. From the Latin proverb: *Vox audita perit littera scripta manet,* "The heard voice perishes, but the written letter remains."

I
Early Days

Earliest Memories

Iowa became the 29th State in the Union in 1846. I didn't come along until 1937 when Iowa and, more specifically, the people of Iowa, played a huge part in my development and upbringing. Both my mother and father were born in Iowa, and I lived there the first three years of my life. My first distinct memory is being in a crib at my Grandmother Marie Sykes' farmhouse with my aunts playing with me. I remember one telling me she was my mother, but I knew better. My Grandfather Clarence Sykes, known as Jack, rented a farm in central Iowa near the small town of Blairsburg, which is about an hour north of Des Moines, Iowa, and 30 minutes east of Webster City. The farm was a quarter section. It was located a mile south of Blairsburg off a gravel main road with wide ditches on both sides. The country was more rolling than flat, but well suited for farming, corn, soybeans, oats, and alfalfa. My grandfather also had dairy cows, pigs, and Hereford cattle.

Our family moved to San Fernando, California, in 1940. We had an upstairs room in a hotel right on Main Street, which was also the main Highway. I can remember the stairs led down directly to the street. For some reason we moved around the corner to another hotel which was across the street from a movie theater. One afternoon I managed to get away from my folks, crossed the street, walked into the theater, and watched a cowboy movie. I guess I was small enough that no one in the ticket counter saw me and there must not have been anybody taking tickets at the door. My mother was frantic looking for me and upon returning to the apartment I was told I couldn't go to the movies by myself. I don't remember the hotel room being particularly small, but it had a Murphy bed which folded into the wall when not in use. We had a shared bathroom down the hall. I do remember using my father's shoes as toys. One was a police car, and another was a fire engine, but I don't remember ever having any real little kid toys.

I never felt deprived. Of course, there was no yard, but my folks took me to the San Fernando Franciscan Mission which offered nice lawns and grounds for me to run and play. Those were fond memories and I suppose the reason I am such a proponent of parks and playgrounds. Later we moved to a duplex at 1202 3rd Street; that was after Pearl Harbor. I remember an air raid warden knocking on our door one night to tell my mother he could see light coming from one of our windows. The street lights were on but were painted black on top. Housing must've been very tight as I recall servicemen staying with us a night or two. One was an Army Air Force flyer who stayed with us several times. While I didn't fully understand it, my folks were upset when he stopped coming—they never saw him again. After the war my father liked to go to drag races and particularly midget auto races and he took me with him, which was big time. We even got to have a pop at the races. Most of the kids were like me. They did not care about watching the races—what they wanted to do was play with other kids, and that is what we did under the grandstands.

My Aunt Shirley took me back to Iowa on the train during the early part of WW II to stay with my grandparents in Blairsburg. I suspect my mother wanted to get rid of me as she was working full-time and probably couldn't get or afford a babysitter. I recall hearing on the Blairsburg School bus that President Franklin Roosevelt died. Before all the farms had electricity, one of my jobs was filling the kerosene lamps. I do recall some of them were quite pretty, mostly amber- or orange- colored. There was no running water in the house at that time, but the windmill was right outside next to the front porch. A large milk can full of water sat next to the windmill and a tin dipper hung on its side so people could dip in for a drink of water. The large white two-story farmhouse was built on a slight rise a couple hundred yards off the county road at the end of a nice lane, which was fenced on both sides. In summertime, the house was surrounded by beautiful green fields of corn, soybeans, and alfalfa with oat fields turning a golden color signaling harvest time. The house had a screened porch stretching halfway along the front entrance. The wide front yard was fenced in, which made a great playground for kids, but I suspect it was mainly meant to keep unwanted farm critters from invading the house. All the bedrooms were upstairs; the bottom floor contained a large kitchen and large dining room. Another large sitting-living room made up the ground floor. Those rooms were well furnished, and I remember lace curtains. The kitchen had a table that served as a dining room on normal days so naturally it was the most active room in the house.

It was an old house but was kept in very good condition. The house had a large basement where my grandmother stored a mountain of potatoes and other vegetables during the winter. The basement also served as a place to take a bath (using a large tin tub) in wintertime. In the summertime, my uncle and I took baths in large tin tubs placed in the front yard early so the sun could warm the water. One could call the house comfortable; however, it was built before electricity was common on Iowa farms and people still used outhouses. There was a large red barn facing the house and just down a slight slope there were some cow pens and other red farm buildings, including a chicken house and a large building for pigs, plus a couple of large round corn cribs.

My recollection of the farm before moving to California is dim. Going back to Iowa during World War II it is a little brighter. I can also remember the golden light that flowed into the kitchen at sunset. One memory that stands out vividly is having my first dog. Of course, the dog wasn't mine, he just belonged to the farm, but I thought he was mine, and he was with me whenever I was outside. I begged my grandmother to let Champ come in the house with me. Dogs and cats were better than barn animals, but they were not allowed in the house. My grandmother finally gave in, and I got Champ inside. He really wasn't comfortable in the house. We were playing on the kitchen floor, and he had a sore infected ear. Somehow in playing, I managed to hit that spot and he gave me a little nip. My grandmother saw this and threw a pan she was holding at him. Champ was immediately and unceremoniously evicted from the house along with the proverbial "kick in the rear with a frozen overshoe." I was crying because I thought it was so unfair because Champ didn't mean to nip, and I was the one who caused the ruckus. I begged Grandmother to let Champ back in but to no avail. He was banished for life.

Another story about Champ that I am advised was told many times by my aunts and uncles: They were never allowed in my grandfather's car unless he was with them and then only with their very best clothes on. I don't recall any special reason but somehow I managed to be out of the house in the springtime when there was still snow on the ground. I walked down the lane with Champ and then walked the County Road to the neighbor's farm which was probably 1,000 yards from my grandfather's lane. I had just started back when I saw my grandfather's car coming toward me. Apparently, the neighbors Mr. and Mrs. Oakland, whose house was close to the county road, saw me and called my grandmother. My grandfather drove up and told me to get in the car, but I didn't want to leave Champ, being afraid he might get lost, so I got stubborn and wouldn't get in the car unless Champ could get in also. It was a standoff. Why my grandfather didn't just come around the car, grab me, and stick me in remains a mystery. He reluctantly agreed but Champ knew better and didn't want to get in the car. I finally coaxed him in, and he sat on the floor in the backseat with me holding him. I guess Granddad's kids gave him a lot of good-natured ribbing about a dog riding in his beautiful black Chevrolet sedan.

I recall making homemade ice cream. Not an easy thing. Of course, we had plenty of milk and cream, but we had to get ice from town. The ice cream was made in a metal container with something like a Mixmaster blade used to churn butter. The metal container was put in in a wooden bucket holder lined with ice. Salt was added to the ice to get some of the ice melted, and the metal container was turned by winding the handle. It was a lot of work but fun and the ice cream was super. My grandmother churned butter but that was a different process entirely.

I can also remember going to a movie in Blairsburg. They didn't have a theater, but they stretched a large screen that looked like a white sheet between two buildings, and we sat on folding chairs in the open air. I don't recall the movie, but I remember it was a fun time.

Long Shots — Early Days

My grandmother had a huge garden so big that my grandfather plowed it with his team of Belgian Draft Horses. He also used that team to mow the grass on the sides of the lane leading to the house. It wasn't unheard of, but few farmers still had teams of horses. It requires more than just the horses. My grandfather had horse collars, blinders, reins, harnesses, and all the leather rigging hanging up in the barn near the horse stalls. He still had all the farm implements designed to be pulled by horses, but he just used the team around the house and occasionally for pulling wagons. My Uncle Joe did all the heavy work, and I never saw my grandfather drive a tractor, which is a little strange since he owned one of the first steam tractors, a Nichols and Shepard steam engine from 1914. That engine is on the cover of the *Iron Man Album Magazine* of July/August 1983. My uncles John and Joe Sykes are shown on the engine. A long row of raspberries formed one side of Grandma's garden with rows of string beans, potatoes, radishes, lettuce, tomatoes, and all manner of other vegetables filling nearly an acre.

A fun thing was watching my uncle milking the cows. Barn cats would all come around faithfully to get a little bowl of milk. They waited patiently and my uncle would often squirt milk at them directly from the cow. The cats would often catch that milk in their mouths, so they were game players.

Everybody worked hard on the farm including the ladies, but they did have their social lives also. I can remember neighboring farm ladies coming to the house and all sitting around the table stitching on the same quilt with bits and pieces of different cloths. One of the favorites was cloth cut from seed sacks as they were very colorful. I am lucky to have inherited a couple of those handstitched quilts.

My grandfather smoked a pipe and used Velvet tobacco, which came in a pocket-sized red flat tin can. I still have the image in my mind of empty red Velvet tobacco cans perched upside down on the top of metal fence posts as crowns.

One memory that sticks in my mind is picking up rocks, and my grandfather paid me five cents per bucket. It took a long time to fill a bucket, and it is doubtful there was much value in my efforts. It was most likely to keep me busy and out of my grandfather's hair. Another interesting job was trapping gophers in the lane and along the county road, but my grandmother put a stop to that when I finally caught a skunk. Grandmother Sykes was a marvelous cook, not fancy food but really just mouthwatering solid meals. Her pot roasts and fried chicken just can't be duplicated. Her pies were legendary with a crust light as a croissant. Of course, they cooked with a lot of lard in those days. We had rhubarb growing in the front yard, and if you've never had combination rhubarb and raspberry pie, you've missed out.

Most astonishing of all: Grandma did all her cooking on one of those large cast-iron stoves using corn cobs for fuel. In addition to filling kerosene lamps, it was my job to keep the cob bucket next to the stove filled from a large cob pile at the side of the house. She was still baking bread in her 90s, and what a delicious aroma that produced. Sadly, none of her daughters, including my mother, inherited or bothered to learn or continue her cooking skills. They all seem to have abandoned the farm as quickly as possible for other careers.

I did visit my Behrens grandparents, who lived in the Iowa countryside but no longer farmed. They were older than my Sykes grandparents, and while they were kind to me there was nothing for me to do at their house, so I was not there often. The first time I recall my parents taking me to visit them was in the early 40s when I was still a little guy, maybe five. Two large geese that did not like visitors patrolled the front yard. One exercised his authority and gave me a dutiful hard bite. Don't laugh, it hurt, and I nearly cried. That may be the reason my favorite hunting is for birds.

The world was different in those days, and I traveled for summer farm visits from California to Iowa and back by myself on Greyhound buses starting when I graduated from the fifth grade. The big draw in Iowa was being on my grandfather's farm, outdoors all day long with lots of activities and some important duties, feeding pigs and yearling calves, helping to collect the eggs, and chopping the heads off fryers for my grandmother. Neither one of the jobs with chickens was much to my liking. Some of those old hens were quite intimidating to a young kid, and they pecked hard. Chopping the heads off a dozen fryers produced headless dead chickens running around with blood spurting everywhere. I also bottle-fed a couple of young lambs and brought them back to good health and I helped my grandmother pick her strawberries and raspberries. But the most fun was driving the tractors. While I loved my grandparents, the biggest draw was playing and being with my cousins. There were three sets of brothers all about the same age as I was. The closest and therefore the ones I was with the most were Duane and Vernon Behrens, the sons of Clifford and Velma Behrens, who lived in the town of Williams, which is only about five miles east of Blairsburg. Clifford was my father's older brother. They lived in town, but Clifford also leased a small acreage for farming. He had a truck and hauled grain for farmers. We had all kinds of fun fishing, shooting, and just tomfoolery. Dale and Larry were sons of Elmer and Lucille Wagner. Lucille was my mother's oldest sister. They lived on a farm on the other side of Webster City, so I wasn't around them as much. Still, we had plenty of time together for play and work. On their farm they had to milk cows and had many other chores to perform. They had a pony and a four-wheeled antique carriage that we hooked up to tour the county gravel roads. The pony normally trotted, but Larry carried clods to add speed. He would throw them and hit the pony in the rump; that would put her into passing gear. Of course, he would only do this when we were far from the house and his dad couldn't see us.

Another set of cousins were Melvin and Gordon, sons of Leo and Neta Evans. Neta was my father's sister. They were rough and tumble; their father was a tough master who kept them working most of the time. They lived farther away so we had less playtime. Twenty-five years later I met a fellow Air Force officer who went to school with them. He told me they would fight anyone in school. And if no one wanted to fight they would fight each other. I believed him. All my cousins had younger siblings but, of course, at our ages we wouldn't play with girls or little kids.

By the time I took the bus back to Iowa the second time, I was old enough to work and really be of some help. My grandfather was still active in the community and was well-known. He was a long-standing member on the Blairsburg School Board, which was consolidated, with school buses picking up students at all the farms. He took me to my first concert. I must admit it was a high-school band playing on a white bandstand in the little town park. Still, it was pretty neat being there with my grandfather, who was obviously somebody important. Another time, I remember my grandfather taking me with him to a sale barn near Webster City where farm animals were auctioned. It was an indoor arena with a dirt floor and bleachers on the side. We sat in the bleachers and as my grandfather swatted a fly and removed his pipe, he made a sudden move with his hand that was somehow taken as a bid by the auctioneer. He was surprised to hear he won the bid. He didn't argue and said to me we need a few more heifers anyway. Watching and hearing an auctioneer for the first time was worth the trip. And, of course, being with my grandfather was a treat.

My Uncle Joe was the youngest son. He stayed on the farm and did most of the work. He eventually took over that farm and even bought another close acreage when my grandfather retired. Joe was a happy guy. I never saw him down about anything or anybody. That just seemed to be the norm with all my uncles. He worked hard all the time from early morning milking to the evening milking before supper time. The norm for those hard-working farmers was five meals a day. Breakfast was served just after morning milking. What was called lunch came around 9:30 or 10:00 a.m. and was a sandwich and a cup of coffee. Dinner was served around the noon hour, and it was big, the main meal of the day. Another lunch would come around 3:30 or 4:00 p.m. and then supper, which was a light meal, sometimes just leftovers from dinner, came after milking was done at night. Farmers in those days did hard physical labor all day every day. Work is never finished on the farm. Even if the animals are taken care of and the crop is brought in there are still fences to fix, corrals to take care of, buildings to repair, gates to fix, ditches that need cleaning, and all manner of other things. It's not an easy life, for sure. Even the women who worked constantly cooking and taking care of kids had daily outside chores. Carl Hamilton's book *No Time at All* provides an insightful view of farm work before World War II. I witnessed much the same in the 1940s and early '50s.

My grandmother was in charge of eggs and the new batch of fryers (young chickens). She also did most of the harvesting from her vast garden. In summer and fall she was busy canning fruits and vegetables from the garden. It's a wonder how they did it. Much of my help was just driving the tractor pulling a wagon or trailer. When harvesting alfalfa, it first must be cut and then raked into rows. That would be followed by a baler pulled by a tractor, which would pick up the rowed alfalfa, compress it into square bales and tie the square bales, dropping them on the ground. Those bales would then have to be picked up and loaded on a trailer to be driven to the barn. Then they would have to be unloaded and stacked in the barn. Lots of hard labor, I can tell you.

My granddad had two tractors. The most powerful was a green John Deere Model A. The other tractor was a red Farmall Model H. I learned to drive on the John Deere because it had a hand clutch and at eleven or twelve, I wasn't big enough to reach the foot clutch on the Farmall. Neither was I skilled enough or maybe not yet trustworthy to do any cultivating the first summer, but the second year I got pretty handy and was turned loose to cultivate soybeans on the Farmall, which was only equipped with a two-row cultivator, while the John Deere with a four-row cultivator was used by my Uncle Joe. None of the tractor driving was yet considered work by me because it was fun to drive. My grandfather even let me drive his black Plymouth sedan but only around a mowed alfalfa field with him in the car. That was really big stuff because even my uncle didn't drive my grandfather's car.

Going to town on Saturday night was a big event. Joe and I would take a bath in the front yard in tin tubs that had been sitting in the sun to warm the water. Immediately after milking we would head to Webster City: Grandpa, Grandma, and me in the Plymouth. Joe would take his own car and go his own way. When we got to town, Grandpa and Grandma had things to do. Grandma would be taking eggs to a seller and then they would visit around and buy whatever they needed. I got a quarter and could spend it any way I wanted. My routine started with a hamburger that cost a dime. It was nothing like a hamburger today with lettuce and tomato and all the trimmings. It was simply a patty of meat with a bun, but you put on ketchup, mayonnaise, and relish as desired. Then I would go to a movie in a real movie theater which cost another dime. The last nickel was then splurged on a pop. Big time in the big town of Webster City.

Murder in Iowa

Murder in Iowa? How could it be in a sleepy farm community? But it was true, for sure. It was the summer of 1948 on Grandfather's farm about a mile south of Blairsburg. The marauding killer was vicious and without mercy. He attacked his helpless victims' throats, and his dastardly deeds were a bloody mess. Worse yet, he ambushed his prey in their beds. The country was terrorized and rightly so with such a grisly murderer on the loose. I was an enthusiastic volunteer to help my Uncle Joe to put a stop to the violent mayhem. A plan was hatched. Uncle Joe went armed with a 12-gauge humpback Browning—a formidable weapon to confront and dispatch the murderer. My job was lookout, but also backup with my grandfather's trusty H&R .410 single-shot shotgun. Uncle Joe placed a feed wagon at a strategic point to act as a blind to intercept the evil culprit in the early morning hours. My grandfather agreed, and we were up in the dark hours of the early morning.

We crept silently to our blind and waited, eyes peeled, silent without movement, much like the *Field & Stream* articles reported on leopard hunting. The night dragged on until finally some pink showed up in the east. We waited, hoping beyond hope, to stop the wanton killing. I remained ready for a follow-up shot. Nothing, and then the sun was shining brightly. Our mission was interrupted so Uncle Joe could get to morning milking. The killer was still at large and a horror throughout the community—especially to my precious grandmother. It was hoped the murderer had moved on. Uncle Joe determined further stakeouts were not necessary since no killing had happened in the last 24 hours. I was devastated. My chance of being an 11-year-old member of the Roundtable was lost forever. My protests to set up another stakeout fell on deaf ears. There would be no further crusade. Dreams of being a hero were now lost.

It happened in the early hours of the next morning when I awoke, needing to make a toilet trip. The outhouse was located about 30 yards from the back door, which was open for good ventilation because it was a warm summer night. Only the screen door was closed.

Long Shots — Early Days

I did my business but thought I could smell an intruder in the yard. The sun was still hidden, but it was light enough to see all was clear. Still, it seemed prudent to arm myself in case the killer was prowling about. The .410 was retrieved from behind the kitchen door. Ammo was obtained and the .410 was loaded. Quietly and still barefoot, I made my way to the back door. And then there he was—I was face-to-face with the wicked killer! I could feel the cold steel barrel in my hands and knew what must be done. The killer had left blood and feathers all over my grandmother's henhouse. Her precious layers and eggs were destroyed. I must not fail. The killer moved, and I fired instinctively. I don't remember even aiming. He was hit hard, and I knew he was finished. The egg money would be saved. The report from my trusty .410 resounded through the farmhouse. My grandfather was first on the scene, and he pronounced the killer dead, dispatched by me. In my zeal to save the poor hens in the heat of battle I forgot about the screen door, which was now no longer bugproof. Not much was said about the screen door, but my grandfather dictated that there would be no more firing from inside the house. It could not be absolutely confirmed that the skunk was the hen killer; however, it was too late to call a grand jury. Vigilante justice had been dispensed. There was no more killing in the henhouse.

    A noteworthy experience in my life that cannot be repeated today was participating in a threshing ring. This is where a group of farmers get together to bring the grain crop (oats in this case) to a threshing machine, which separates the grain from the stems and chaff. The threshing machine I saw used was powered by a tractor running a leather belt to a wheel on the threshing machine. Originally they were powered by steam engines. Again, it was a very labor-intensive effort. First the oats had to be cut, second, the oats had to be raked into rows, then they had to be gathered into shocks and tied together with binder twine. After that they were loaded by pitchfork onto the wagons pulled by tractors and sometimes teams of horses that were then driven to the threshing machine, and once again pitchforks were used to throw the crop into the threshing machine, which spit out the oats into a waiting truck while blowing the chaff away into a pile. I was too inexperienced on my first summer to drive one of the tractors, but I did get to hold the reins of the horses in the field on a straight line. My uncle climbed back on the wagon and took the reins to make the turns. He commanded the horses by calling "hee" and "haw," "whoa," and sort of a clicking noise for the horses to move forward, as he walked alongside and pitched shocks of grain into the wagon. Combines were not yet common and far out of the price range for small farmers. That changed rapidly and even the small farms began to hire combine crews.

Dinner on these threshing runs was something to see. The farmers' wives would get together to cook and prepare the meal. It would be served in two shifts since a threshing machine and harvesting was going the full day and there was no stopping. The food was stacked high in different dishes: fried chicken, pot roast, steaks, and mountains of mashed potatoes with bowls of gravy, numerous vegetables, and salads. And all of that was followed by a ton of pies and cakes. I loved it. Those visits to Iowa and being around great-grandparents, grandparents, great uncles, uncles, aunts, and cousins gave me very strong close feelings for the country and people in agriculture.

Santa Paula, California

The small town (about 12,000) of Santa Paula, California, is located on the Santa Clara River, which is really just a stream most of the year. It is ten miles east of the Pacific coastal city of Ventura and ten miles west of Fillmore. It's a beautiful area nestled between South Mountain, which are high hills with the highest elevation at 2,313 feet, and North Mountain, which is a part of the California Coastal Mountain Range with Santa Paula Peak at 4,957 feet. The foothills are mostly brush or high chaparral with a few scrub oaks scattered about and enough native grass to run small cattle operations. The area receives only about one foot of rain per year so the hills are mostly dry and brown, but often golden brown in the morning or afternoon sunlight.

The valley floor is lush green, packed tightly with lemon, orange, and avocado groves, called ranches. Why they were called ranches with no cattle or livestock remains a mystery to me. They are beautiful, tidy orchards that reflect different shades of green with oranges and avocados deeper green than the brighter lemons. Sometimes these forests of citrus are tinged with orange or yellow from the citrus fruit ready for the picking crews with their waiting ladders and canvas collection bags. These ranches were often no more than 20 or 30 acres, but they produced the very best quality citrus fruit in the world, which was shipped worldwide. No better oranges could be found. The lemons were of the same quality as were the avocados. Santa Paula was the center of the citrus belt between Ventura and Piru with the best Valencia oranges grown on the west side and the best navel oranges on the east side. The lemons were raised mostly on the west side of town, but avocados were scattered about east and west. Most of these ranches were privately owned with the owners living and working the ranch.

Teague McKevitt and Limoneira Ranches were both large acreages jointly or corporately owned. To my knowledge, the Limoneira is still the largest lemon ranch in the world. The folks who owned the ranches usually did their own irrigation and the cultivation between rows of trees. The fumigation or spraying of trees was contracted out. Picking of the fruit was done by Mexican laborers in the Bracero program. Packing houses, which were mostly co-ops, sorted and prepared fruit for shipping. Sunkist was one of the leaders in marketing. Don't mistake the picture of dust storms and sod farmers from the Depression with these California citrus ranchers. They were educated, sophisticated, and traveled people, conservative and modest without McMansions. One of my mentors and a great role model (also the father of my best high school girlfriend), Charles Leavens, owned and operated a 20 or 30-acre ranch. He was a graduate of Stanford University, and his daughter also became a Stanford graduate.

What a great city to grow up in in the 1940s and 1950s. I mentioned Santa Paula in some of my stories, but I want to tell you more about this wonderful city, which I had the great fortune to be part of in my formative years. It was quite a pretty and clean little town. The downtown buildings were no higher than two stories except for the town clock, which reached four stories on top of the Odd Fellows

Lodge. Santa Paula didn't have any heavy industry but thrived on agriculture, mostly citrus and avocados, with a small amount of oil activity. Not 100% accurate, but Norman Rockwell's paintings reflect much of the images that remain in my mind. The town was small enough that nearly everyone was connected one way or another, and if nothing else, at least knew each other by facial recognition. The population was about evenly divided between Anglo and Mexican ancestry. The largest employers were the fruit packing houses.

A volunteer fire department was still in use, but we had a full- time Police Department, City Hall, and all the other city government departments, plus several schools for kids of all ages. The small hospital on West Main Street was more of an infirmary and not manned 24 hours by medical doctors. Additionally, we had a fulltime county fire department unit along with some Ventura County agricultural departments. The U.S. Forest Service had a small station and, of course, we had a post office. The *Santa Paula Chronicle* was a daily newspaper.

Main Street, where angle parking was still used, held nearly all the commercial businesses: three movie theaters, two major grocery stores, three banks, two pool halls, the Odd Fellows, Moose and Masonic lodges, Rotary Club, barbershops, pharmacies, three quality men's stores, J C Penney, and furniture, flower, and jewelry stores. Dealers for all the major car manufacturers were on or close to Main Street. Cafés, bars, and churches were scattered around town. We had a small but well-known airport used for some crop dusting but mainly for recreational flying. The actor Steve McQueen rented a hangar for his bi-wing and vintage motorcycles, and because of the motorcycles he and my father became coffee drinking buddies. He was well liked.

Santa Paula could be described as a vibrant small city at that time with parades, Western days, and high school homecomings. The schools were excellent, and the teachers were well-respected. In those days, they dressed like professionals: coat and tie for the men and skirts or dresses for the women. My teachers were good from the fourth grade, when I started school at McKevitt Elementary, through high school.

Long Shots — Early Days

This little memoir is too short to include all the schools, so I'll cover just our high school. It was a beautiful California mission-style campus and remains quite handsome today. It was located part way up the hill on the north side of town with a view of the Santa Clara River Valley facing South Mountain but also with a view of the Pacific Ocean 10 miles to the west. Agriculture was my main interest and area of study. Later I found it was a bad mistake, missing the prep courses needed for college. My parents came from farming families without any higher education, but they encouraged study, and my father bought an encyclopedia set for me when I was in middle school. That was kind of a big deal. They were expensive but were a quick reference to any number of subjects and hopefully excited interest for the student to dig deeper. This was long before home computers and cell phones that provide instant information. Nevertheless, my parents didn't know how to guide me scholastically. The teacher for agriculture was Mr. Woods. He was good and would not tolerate any nonsense. I liked him and got along well in his classes.

History was my favorite subject. It was taught by Mr. Jennings, who was new to Santa Paula and lived in the Price Apartments just down the hill below our house. He was a World War II veteran, and I suspect his first teaching job was in Santa Paula High School. We started together in 1952. He was strict and allowed no shenanigans in his classroom, but he was interesting and well liked. He once showed me his military medals when I was in his apartment—no other kid ever saw them to my knowledge. I believe one was a Silver Star. Mr. Ricards was another favorite. He taught science and was popular with students. He took us on fun field outings, even camping trips to the high desert where we caught trapdoor tarantulas. Mr. Forney was our principal.

Our teachers set high standards and were good examples to emulate. They were certainly mentors. Sadly, Mr. Jennings died before I got around to thanking him, but I was able to thank Mr. Ricards on one of my trips home before he died. I was also fortunate to catch Mr. Woods and his wife as they were moving out of their home near the high school. They were going to the high desert to be near their children and grandchildren. He was elderly by then but still sound in mind and body. We had fun remembering his classes and my classmates. I was a full colonel by that time, and it was clear he appreciated me telling him of the fine example he set for all of us. He deserved high praise. High school was fun for me, but I must admit I didn't work at it very hard. Having said that, I did win the Bank of America award as best student in agriculture in 1956 and the highest standing award from the Future Farmers of America so it wasn't just all fun.

I didn't play on any of the high-school sports teams nor did I participate in the various clubs and after-school activities (other than the Future Farmers of America), which I realize now was a mistake as I missed so many school experiences. However, I had afterschool jobs, which gave me income, but more importantly, taught me about work, people, the value of a dollar, and the adult world. The truth is I didn't have to work—my mother and father both worked, and they provided housing, food, clothing, and anything I needed. But they were children of the Great Depression and believed there was reward in work even beyond monetary gains. They didn't push me, but I caught the same work disease. Really too much work, but I was still able to do Boy Scout activities, camping trips, and shooting matches so I can hardly complain. Both my mother and father encouraged and supported me in all those activities or, for that matter, any interest I pursued.

It is with trepidation that I name some friends from high school—too many to name all. Please forgive me for anyone who is left out. Doug Udall was my best friend followed by Wayne Bailey, Byron Edde and John Randall. Others were Jim Gofourth, Butch Moore, Manny Vanegas, John Brock, Bud Foster, Billy Herrera, Alex Villa, Robert Uffen, Richard Hyde, George Dabney, Steve Bingham, Lou Grivetti, and Randall Best. John Brock and Don Williams were in the junior class but hung around with us. Kurt Meissner from Wels, Austria, was our exchange student. My girlfriend during our senior year was Charla Leavens. We had a number of really great girls in our class: Irene Fort, Joan Fulton, Joan Habbick, Anita Bustillos, Kathleen Hawthorne, Yolanda Salazar, Nadyne Davison, Mary Ann Ellis, Julie Revill, Lillian Rust, Diane Rieger, and Gloria Jones.

The graduating senior class of 1956 was 134 students, and many came through grade and middle school together, so we knew each other pretty well. We didn't have gangs or conflicts between those of Mexican or Anglo heritage. In fact, I can hardly remember any serious fights at all.

By today's standards, our graduation party would no doubt be called crummy, but we thought it was neat. Our class represented the normal sins of a teenager at the time: drinking, smoking, etc. Fear of teenagers drinking and driving loomed large at the time, so I suspect much of the graduation party was to head that off. The graduation ceremony was held on a beautiful June night on the lawn in front of our school. Immediately after the graduation, we had a dance at the school gym and then went swimming at the school pool. Following that, we went to a midnight movie at a new fancy theater on Main Street. We ended up with breakfast at daybreak. No drunk driving on graduation night. And certainly, no school trip to Hawaii.

The excitement, commerce, and charm of Main Street have sadly disappeared. The three fine men's stores have closed, and only one bank remains. All the car dealers are gone along with the grocery stores. The jewelry stores, ladies' shops, and furniture store have closed. Still, the town remains somewhat of an attraction for a day's getaway for those in crowded regions as it is only an hour's drive North of the Los Angeles metropolitan area. For my money, Santa Paula has the best weather of any place in the world, and I have fond memories every time I visit.

Two Boys and Three Guns

Duanne and Vernon were the sons of my uncle and aunt, Cliff and Velma Behrens. They lived in the small town of Williams, Iowa, less than a half hour from my Grandfather Sykes' farm in Blairsburg. They were great playmates, for sure. We had lots of fun, and I spent a large part of my summer visits in Iowa with them.

They had all kinds of animals: rabbits (which we watched procreate with interest and enthusiasm), chickens, pigeons, and all manner of cats and dogs. They also had a young pet goat that I decided would be a fun playmate. Of course, my cousins egged me on, and I quickly learned not to butt heads with a goat. I certainly saw stars! I can tell you that even young goats can be dangerous.

Duanne was our chief and a few years older than Vernon and me. He was already in high school while we were just starting in the middle school. Duanne even had a part-time job working at the Massey Ferguson farm equipment dealership. He also smoked—more or less openly—but not at home. Duanne was practically an adult in our eyes and smoking with him was a high privilege. We only did that in the small garage barn behind their house and certainly not on the street.

Vernon was 10 and I was 11 years old that summer when the circus came to Williams, and we were thrilled. Word was out they needed help setting up their big tent as well as some rides and booths. Payment in exchange for helping was a free ticket. Vernon and I were there early. Neither one of us could sling a sledgehammer, but we held ropes and did other odd jobs. By noon, everything was set up. We got our free tickets and were proud as peacocks and felt like we'd been on an adventure.

We were minor delinquents at night with Duanne leading us around the little town—nothing serious—small-scale shenanigans, but no real nefarious deeds. One night, we snuck into the school, which was closed for the summer. They had installed a new fire escape from the second floor to the ground. It was like a big, enclosed slide. We managed to crawl up the slide and, "wahoo," we were inside. A daring adventure for sure. Even Sherlock Holmes would not have found us out.

My Uncle Clifford did not have a car at that time, so he just used his dump truck for all his driving. After work one day he and Aunt Velma took us on a picnic to a large pond where we could fish. Duanne, Vernon, their little brother Gene, and I rode in the truck bed. It was great fun riding in the back of that big dump truck. At the pond, to our delight, we caught a bucket full of bullheads (a catfish). No one wanted to leave. Finally, it got too dark to fish, but then the truck would not start. I wondered what we were going to do. Uncle Cliff said it was too late and dark to walk, so Aunt Velma and Gene slept in the cab while Uncle Cliff, Duanne, Vernon, and I slept in the truck bed. It probably seems strange that no one thought about where we were or if something had happened to us. It was sort of a mini adventure for us kids.

That same summer, Uncle Clifford was growing cucumbers for the pickle market and had 30 or 40 acres under cultivation just outside the city limits of Williams. Pheasants had been seen on the property, so Vernon and I hatched a plan to shoot one. Never mind that it was not pheasant season. We reasoned the pheasant would be dinner so that probably made it okay. Neither of us had experience hunting pheasants but we made plans to be successful. Our decision was to take two shotguns and also a .22 rifle in case we could not get close enough to use the shotguns. I'm sorry to admit that at that time I thought it was a good plan. Of course, since there was no cover around the cucumbers, we did not get close to a pheasant, so the mission was altered, and we amused ourselves by sniping at abandoned cans and bottles. Stupid set in quickly, and rather than laying shotguns on the soil, we each held our own shotgun but took turns awkwardly shooting the rifle. It was a .22 single-shot bolt action. Vernon held the shotgun in his left hand while he held the rifle in his right hand. He loaded the chamber and then closed the bolt with the muzzle that rested on the top of his shoe. The rifle was old and the trigger too light, so the firing pin hit the bullet primer when he closed the bolt. The bullet went through his shoe and then his big toe. "I got me!" he shouted. I already knew that.

Vernon took off his shoe, and we viewed the damage: He was bleeding but not bad. He put the shoe back on, and we started trekking back to town. It happened that Uncle Clifford came along to check his cucumbers before we got very far, and he stopped and took us to the doctor's office in Williams. It was upstairs over one of the few stores in town. The doctor examined the wound and cleaned it a bit. The bullet messed up his toenail, but skirted the bone. He gave Vernon a tetanus shot and that was that.

Uncle Clifford said, "Only one gun per boy in the future." There was no lecture. He may have said for us to be more careful, but I don't remember even that much. Different times, for sure.

Boy Scouts of America

Boy Scout Troop 301 was sponsored by the Presbyterian Church in Santa Paula where my family worshiped. They met in the basement of the church once a week. I joined the troop when I started middle school and stayed in Scouting until my high-school graduation. By the time we were in high school, most of us moved into Explorer Scouts (still part of the Boy Scouts), which was for older guys whose interests were camping, backpacking, and shooting. It was a wonderful experience and great fun. My best Scouting friends were Doug Udall, John Randall, Jim Gofourth, and Byron Edde. It is unfortunate that we didn't work much on merit badges or making Eagle Scout. While merit badges were part of the Scout program, my friends and I were more interested in outdoor activities. We could have and should have paid more attention to becoming Eagle Scouts. My badges ranked me as a Life Scout. I only had two or three more badges to go for Eagle when work and college ended my Scouting pursuits—a mistake on my part. I did not recognize it at the time but Scouting molded much of my later life and strengthened what my parents projected, such as following the Boy Scout oath and just being a good, honest person. Much of the value was gained unconsciously by watching and copying the fine role models of the senior Scouts, our strong Scout leaders, and the many parents and businessmen who helped the troop in so many ways, including driving us to camps and events, helping to organize our activities, and providing funds when appropriate, such as bankrolling our annual Christmas tree sales.

We had wonderful campouts. One was up Piru Creek long before the building of the Piru Dam. It was a hike-in with backpacks that carried all our gear and food. We used World War II surplus equipment so our tents were made by connecting two shelter halves, teaming up two Scouts. Another camping trip was up Santa Paula Creek behind the Ferndale Ranch. These were wonderful experiences on how to get along in the backcountry. We learned to bring what we needed and not the extra weight of what would just be nice to have. The Boy Scout permanent camp, Frazier Park in the Los Padres

National Forest, was another excellent experience. We didn't camp as buildings were already there, but we had all kind of outdoor events and woodsman training, plus nightly campfires for marshmallows, singing, and telling tall tales. And best of all, U.S. Marines taught target shooting. They were and still are extremely impressive and second to none in rifle training and inspiring young Scouts.

Two of my favorite Scoutmasters were Mr. Moose Miller and Mr. Onstatt. They took three of us, Doug Udall, Jim Gofourth, and me on a marvelous camping trip on the east side of the Sierra Nevada Mountains. Mr. Miller drove us from Santa Paula to the Owens Valley and then north to the little town of Independence in his rather hard-used Chevrolet sedan. We had all our gear and food for five people on a week-camping trip loaded in the trunk. It's a steep climb up the Sierra Nevada from the small Onion Valley. As we climbed, a packer came riding down the trail leading six mules that had been used to carry the gear and food up for a previous party. We thought, what luxury. Our climb ended at the Kearsarge Pass with an elevation of 11,823 feet. Mount Whitney at 14,505 feet is the highest peak in the Sierra Nevada and the lower 48 states. We weren't after more climbing. What we wanted was a chance for golden trout in the cold crystal-clear waters of the Sierra. Success was ours, but I have to admit, while we used fly rods, the goldens were caught using small spinners. Only one other camping group was spotted during our stay, so it was like having the whole Sierra Nevada to ourselves. The three of us felt like we were someone between John Muir and Kit Carson.

Another major supporter of the Boy Scouts who often filled in as an assistant Scoutmaster when needed was Mr. Gale Mason. He set a fine example for all of us. One incident still stands out. A new assistant Scoutmaster was introduced to us one evening at our normal weekly meeting in the church basement. He was a family man with four kids, but he was still quite young—I would guess no more than middle twenties. We were senior Scouts at the time and quite taken with him because he was closer to our age. Two or three of my buddies were with me visiting the young assistant Scoutmaster in his home, which was a cheap rental on S. 12th St. He didn't say it, but we could tell he was in financial straits.

The doorbell rang, and it was Mr. Mason with two armloads of paper grocery bags, followed by his wife who also had two armloads of grocery bags. We of course split immediately as it was apparent the new Scoutmaster was surprised, maybe embarrassed. Actually, seeing acts of kindness and generosity painted a very clear picture in our minds.

The 1953 National Boy Scout Jamboree was held at the Irvine Ranch in Orange County, California. All 48 states plus Alaska and Hawaii and 16 other countries were represented by more than 45,000 Boy Scouts. The first national jamboree was in Washington, D.C., in 1937, and the second jamboree was held at Valley Forge in 1950. President Eisenhower sent a supportive message to the Scouts at the Irvine Ranch. A real highlight was seeing Vice President Richard Nixon who not only addressed the group but stayed overnight and then spent the day walking among the tents and signing autographs. There were shows at night that included many Hollywood personalities, but best of all was having Bob Hope as master of ceremonies. It was pretty neat, and I didn't realize until much later what a big deal it was. A huge number of visitors came each day and night for the performances. Think about the number of tents and the number of latrines that had to be dug.

The strongest pull of all that kept my buddies and me in Scouting was the .22 rifle shooting. The Boy Scouts and the NRA shooting programs came together in 1911, so we wore NRA rifle badges on our uniforms that showed our qualifications as marksmen, sharpshooters, and masters. Several people helped us as coaches, but Mr. Albert Marshall was the nucleus. He maintained the rifles, loaned by the office of the Director of Civilian Marksmanship (DCM), and sold us ammunition subsidized by the DCM at 50 cents a box. He also kept our scores and awarded the NRA badges. For those of us who got serious and good enough for higher-quality rifles, he managed to get them at cost. I scraped up enough money, and with his help, I was able to buy a Model 52 Winchester, which was the gold standard. Mr. Marshall was the sub-manager of a citrus packinghouse. He was a very mild-mannered and unassuming gentleman. I don't recall ever hearing him raise his voice to any of the kids. But we all knew he was the boss and respected him. Our shooting range was on the Teague McKevitt ranch just outside the city limits. Mr. Marshall drove a 1939 Cadillac LaSalle four-door sedan. It was old but there weren't many Cadillacs around, so it was neat for us to ride in a luxury car. He coached my little brother Bob and was still coaching kids years later. When I was a lieutenant, home on leave, I teamed up with my friend and high-school classmate Byron Edde, and we took Mr. Marshall to lunch at a nice restaurant in Moorpark. Of course, he deserved much more. He worked for years and years helping kids learn safety, marksmanship, and about accepting responsibility.

Being in the Boy Scouts and wearing a uniform gave us all a feeling of being a little above the pack, and we all followed the Boy Scout rules. When I was assigned at Mather Air Force Base in Sacramento, I became an assistant Scoutmaster. I owe the Boy Scouts, and my financial support to them continues. They were a big part of my early life.

Jobs

Being born to Depression-era parents was both a privilege and a curse. It was an overwhelming benefit to my upbringing and life. I was privileged to have many jobs growing up leading to my Air Force career. Most all of them taught me something and, for sure, gave me great experiences in life. Some of those jobs are listed below. We will discuss the grief later.

Of course, I always had jobs at home helping my mom and dad such as running the vacuum, washing dishes, working in the yard, house painting, mowing the grass, and any other outside maintenance.

When my father accumulated enough savings to buy a couple of rentals, we seemed to always be painting or putting hot tar on roofs. My father did not pay me, and it never even entered my mind that he should. I don't recall my father ever thanking me or even saying I did a good job. It was just expected. My mother gave me a small weekly allowance, only coins, in grade school, but when I moved up to a bicycle paper route I no longer needed or expected an allowance.

My first real paying job was carrying the *Santa Paula Chronicle* newspaper on the downtown city route (really just Main Street) of Santa Paula. That was when I started the fourth grade. I was too young and small for the paper to give me a bicycle route. It was a very short route, just the 800 and 900 blocks of Main Street, which was the middle of town and where most retail stores were located. Some businesses I recall included the Bank of America, Church's Drug Store, Hack's Shop for Men, Chapek's Hardware, the Flower Shop, Fogota's studio, the Toggery, House of Hutchins, Watkins Hardware, Citizens State Bank, Woods Jewelry, and Irene's Dress Shop. Sadly, they are all gone today. Box stores and big shopping malls in Ventura and Oxnard wiped them out. Main Street was a very short walking route- seems like it was around 15 businesses that took the paper. Pay was five cents a day. In addition to the weekly pay of a quarter, I was given extra papers to sell for five cents on the street, and for every one sold, I got an extra penny. Not bad money in those days for a fourth-grader. Remember, you could buy a Coke for five cents. I also collected the monthly payment of one dollar from each of the subscribing customers, so I was very careful to handle the money on collection day. It could be as much as $15 for the group total which was more than a laborer was paid for an entire day. That was carrying big money in my world. A couple of years later, the *Santa Paula Chronicle* gave me a bicycle route. Those early jobs taught, or maybe, trained me in responsibility—never missing work, being on time, always finishing the job and doing the best I could. Of course, my parents taught me that without saying a word.

In between job number one and job number two, I got to work on Friday and Saturday night dispatching taxis. My father owned the taxi company and drove one of the cars during the day. He hired drivers for the night duty and usually extra drivers for Friday and Saturday night. During the day, the drivers waited for a call or walk-up customers. The office was on Mill Street just around the corner from Main Street. Friday and Saturday nights were a different matter because people were out and about— mostly at bars. The cabs were busy, and no one was left in the small office to take calls. The phone number was 55, and I was in the sixth grade so plenty capable of taking orders for cars. It was fun getting to stay up late and to be part of the excitement between midnight and 2:00 a.m., at which time the bars closed. The calls could be fast and furious, and the drivers would complete their run and come rolling back by the office for the next call. I would often stand at the curb and holler out the next location: the Carmelita Café, Van's, the Pastime, or any location that had called in an order for a cab. The drivers would then speed off.

By 2:30 a.m. action was over, and one of the drivers would take me home. You could not get away with that today, but times were different in 1949 and 50. The town cops would come by and say hi; they knew my mom and dad. My dad actually paid me for the dispatching job— a buck a night. It was the only work he ever paid me for. I don't know why he paid me. I think it may have been because he considered it a part of business. I certainly didn't expect to be paid, and it was a surprise but made me feel important. I don't count it as a real job because it was working for my dad.

My second paying job came when I was in the eighth grade. It was with the J.C. Penney Company. Mr. Mason was a manager of the J. C. Penney store on Main Street in Santa Paula. He was a big supporter of Boy Scout Troop 301 and was always a volunteer when needed to drive kids to events out of town or to drop us off at Boy Scout camp. He knew me from Boy Scouts, so I asked for a job. He hired me to work after school. My job was putting price tags on each item of clothing. Trucks would deliver the merchandise in large boxes that had to be unloaded, and then each item was marked with a sticker showing the price. I did this after school each weekday until closing time, which was 6 o'clock. Saturday was the biggest shopping day, and I got to be a salesman, which was really a big deal for an eighth-grader. It was a coat and tie job and I had one suit, but it lasted me all year—only used on Saturday and sometimes Sunday for church with my mother and dad.

Understand, nobody was going to buy a suit from an eighth-grader even though I was ready for the task and hoping it might happen. It never did. But I was plenty busy, mostly taking care of the Mexican braceros. These were small sales, maybe a T-shirt for 79 cents, socks for 35 cents, shorts, and sometimes pants and shirts. It was nearly impossible to screw up. We put the sales price and description of the item on a sales slip, collected the money, and put both in a small container that was then shot up on the electric line to a cashier upstairs. The cashier checked the amounts and sent the change back by the same method. It was not really a challenging task as it was simple arithmetic. For the most part, there really was no salesmanship. I was just handy extra help to take care of customers buying the lowest-priced items. Still, it was pretty neat to have that kind of a job in the eighth grade when no one in my school had a permanent paying job other than bicycle routes.

I said growing up as a child of Depression-era parents was a blessing and a curse. The blessing was learning the value of money, learning to work hard, and accepting responsibility. The curse was the feeling that everyone had to have a meaningful job and work hard at it. I should make it clear my folks bought all my clothes and paid for nearly everything, so I did not need to work at an early age. Money was certainly a part of work for them when I was a kid as my folks were still working their way up from a lower economic level to the great American middle class.

In any case, I wanted to play junior varsity football as I entered high school as a freshman. I was stronger and tougher than about anyone in my class. My Uncle Max came by to see me at work and let me know how important it was to have a job. He said, "Boys play, men work." That settled the question of junior varsity football. I found out many years later that my mother was afraid I would get hurt in football, and she sent my uncle with the message. No real complaints from me as work never hurt me, but it was a shame to miss high school sports. Still, I got to do all the Boy Scout camping and competitive shooting events. I will also add that my mother worked at a paying job until she was 87 years old. It was not about the money, but about being useful. She did, however, love to get a check. When she no longer worked for money, she became a nearly fulltime volunteer for the next six years, working at the Santa Paula Chamber of Commerce.

The ladies in Santa Paula and the wives of surrounding ranches enjoyed an active social life with teas, card games, lunches, etc. Because of the narrow lanes and driveways leading to many of the ranch homes, visiting cars had to be parked on the equally narrow county roads with little space and often deep ditches on both sides used for irrigation or heavy rain runoff. In one case, the road ran perilously close to a barranca that was 30-feet deep. This difficult parking situation gave some of us high-school boys an occasional job. The guest ladies would drive to the house, and we would drive the cars back to the main road or down the lane for parking and then hotfoot it back to the house to pick up another car. We were small-time parking attendants before I even heard about parking attendants. The hostess paid us, and we were often given a tip by the visiting ladies. But that was not what we were after; we would have done it without pay.

The real attraction was driving the cars—it was a chance to drive new cars, sometimes real fancy ones. While many were Fords, Chevys, and Plymouths, there were always a few of the high-end jobs: Cadillac, Lincoln, Hudson, and Packard. Then there were a few in the middle class: Pontiacs, Buicks, Dodges, Oldsmobiles, and DeSotos. As young high-school boys, we wanted to drive any make or model. Remember, in the early 1950s, there weren't that many new cars. Most of our parents didn't drive a new car, and certainly none were found in a high-school parking lot. In those days, if you wanted a car you got a job, saved your money, and bought one yourself. If the girls had a car it was a hand-me-down from their parents. Getting to drive all those cars—often brand-new ones—was a genuine treat. We didn't abuse the cars and drove/parked them very carefully, so none were in dangerous spots. I don't remember ever having one dinged, but we did drive perhaps a little fast, particularly when the ranch house was in the middle of an orchard and the owners couldn't see what was going on. Many of these socials were held at ranches bordering Foothill Road or Middle Road. Foothill Road was curvy so we couldn't drive at high speed, but Middle Road was straight and normally without traffic so we could blow out some muffler soot.

I did learn a few things from these ladies. One lady informed me when I said I would bring her Cadillac up to the house, that she was driving a Fleetwood, not a Cadillac. That was before the Cadillac Biarritz, and a Fleetwood was the most expensive and largest Cadillac at the time. I guess other than being a little snooty, that lady gave me a valuable lesson in recognizing and giving credit or praise to what people have—she was proud to own that Fleetwood. The same would go with owning a fine painting or having a good education or, for that matter, doing a good job at work, showing good sportsmanship, etc. It's always good to recognize people, their valued possessions, and their achievements.

My birthday is in April, so I got my driver's license and was able to join the parking brigade when I was still a high-school freshman and continued driving those nice new cars throughout my sophomore year. It was just great fun—and they paid us!

In high school, I had many odd jobs whenever the opportunity occurred, mostly cleaning up ranches, planting citrus and avocado trees, working on truck farms, and of course, helping my father. At that time the going rate for farm labor was 85 cents an hour. You had to get in a lot of hours. Additionally, jobs were available for high-school boys at night when the temperature got below freezing in the citrus groves. The temperature could get down to 30 or even 29 for a short period of time without much damage to the fruit or tree, but if it got any lower it could be quite costly to the ranchers. Not only could they lose fruit, but if the temperature got too low it would even damage the trees. Some ranches had wind machines which helped, but for the most part smudge pots were used. These were like a small round stove about the size of a bushel basket with a two- or three-foot smokestack. They were filled with diesel oil which would be fired up to heat the trees. Normally, the temperature would fall early in the morning, but the kids would be called out usually before midnight, depending on the forecast. The ranchers really didn't need extra help to light the smudge pots, but they all had to be filled the next morning. The pay was two to three bucks a night if they didn't light up the smudge pots. If they did, the pots needed filling and a five-dollar bill was often in the offing. Getting to school late with smudge on your clothes and face was acceptable. Maybe even a badge of honor in some cases.

During high school I mowed yards and made some good money. My first car was really an old Ford truck—a 1937 model. It was quite rough and looked terrible with a sign painted on the doors advertising TV repair. The cost was $200, and I could have had a better-looking Ford or Chevy coupe for half the price. But the truck was needed to carry my lawn mower. It was hardly dashing, but I could borrow my father's car if I had a date or for special events. Still, I hated to park the truck in the school parking lot. Bad as my truck was, some kids did not have anything to park. It was long before kids got cars from their folks. My friend Don Williams was a class behind me, and he was the only kid who ever got a new car in our high school. His dad was a successful row crop farmer and citrus rancher. George Dabney, a classmate and friend who went on to Ventura College and Fresno State with me, got a new Ford, but that was upon his graduation. Manny Vanegas, who was a high-school friend and a fellow student at Ventura Junior College, joined me in a grass-mowing business. By that time, I had a new truck—a white Custom Cab, V8 Ford. (It would go 90 in second-gear overdrive). Manny had a new, "Write me a ticket" cherry red Chevrolet—not as fast as my Ford. Neither one looked like grass-mowing trucks, which was fine with us. We only needed one truck for our jobs, so we alternated each week. It was a hard, all-day Saturday job. We took the jobs by contract (verbal) and figured them so we each made two bucks an hour and that was super good money in 1956. Our business continued until we went to Fresno State together in 1958.

    Wayne Bailey was a high-school friend and in the Future Farmers of America (FFA) with me. Mr. Woods was our agriculture teacher and one of my favorites. I had no place to keep animals for an FFA-required project, so Mr. Woods suggested I raise avocado trees. Wayne joined me in this project, and we did it for the next two years. We couldn't afford a real hothouse, but we made a short one in my dad's side yard. We constructed it with a wood frame and covered the frame in plastic. The sides were only about four feet high. The roof was also just a skeleton frame but covered in plastic. We made the roof in a couple of sections. When we needed to work on our potted seedlings, we merely removed the roof and stepped over the walls. When the seedlings, which are grown from an avocado seed that comes from good rootstock, get to be about the circumference of a pencil, they are cut off, and the buds of a good eating avocado are grafted to the strong rootstock. When it grows to about two feet, it is ready to be transplanted in an orchard or yard. We found customers and planted the trees for them. It was a good project and made us a few bucks both years.

My last two high-school summers were spent working for agricultural departments for Ventura County or the state of California. The job was inspecting fields for damage caused by the Mexican bean beetle. It was outside work five days a week, so it suited me well; it also left Saturdays open for my lawn business. We worked in crews of five and would appear at the agricultural office with our lunches at eight o'clock in the morning. Once you were assigned to a crew you stayed with that crew for the rest of the summer. Each crew of five was assigned a government sedan. The oldest guy was appointed as the driver and was more or less the boss. I had just turned 17 and was assigned to a crew of older guys in their twenties. Many of these guys were Korean veterans and college students. They were a wild bunch, to say the least, and were always playing pranks on each other and other crews. I don't recall ever seeing a supervisor in the field. I guess you would have to say it wasn't very well supervised. The crew chief often wasn't sure exactly where we were or what field we were supposed to inspect.

Nevertheless, we always trudged on, five abreast separated by six or eight rows of beans. Most of the bean fields were on the Oxnard plain, and in the 1950s you could count on fog nearly every morning. I can remember forgetting a jacket on a couple of occasions and paying the price from cold morning winds off the ocean. Sometimes the leader would call for a break, and he would do so by simply saying down. On that command we would simply plop down in our row and disappear, escaping from any unwanted eyes. I surmised these breaks, which were really naps, were probably not officially sanctioned. From discussions in the car, it seemed the breaks were more abundant after members of the crew admitted or bragged about long nights or overly enthusiastic celebrations—most always including alcohol. We reported very little Mexican bean beetle damage. I wouldn't exactly describe my crewmates as excellent role models, and I can't report any good lessons learned. In fact, I was a little ashamed about the breaks, but I was a young high-school boy, and these guys were college students and a couple of Korean veterans. I will admit they were darn sure fun to be around and made the job much less boring. The big boss was Mr. Allee.

On one summer college break from Fresno, I worked with the state again. This time it was looking for and recording the quick decline disease in citrus trees throughout Ventura Country. The big crews were gone along with all the fun guys. I now worked with a fulltime state employee who was a real professional. Just the two of us, no more breaktime naps or crazy happenings. I learned a lot about the citrus industry from planting trees to orchard husbandry, harvesting, packing houses, and sales. He knew it all and happily educated me.

When I graduated from high school in 1956, I went to work with the U.S. Forest Service. It was kind of a neat deal and sounded impressive for a kid, but the truth is we were simply summer hires to help with forest fires. My station assignment was Piru Ranger Station. It was named after the little town, which was really a dinky little place—gas station, country store, feed store, and a few homes. This was long before the Piru Dam was constructed. Piru is on the eastern edge of Ventura County just off Highway 126. The station chief was Mr. Lynn Freed, and he was a real forest ranger. We were a part of the Los Padres National Forest. Our little crew consisted of Forrest, Billy, Jessie, and me. We lived in a barracks- type building like the barracks used a few years later in my officer training class at Lackland Air Force Base. Only this one was smaller. The bottom floor consisted of a day room, living room/dining room combined, and a separate kitchen. The top floor was bedrooms that were really tiny—you could hardly get a suitcase stored in your room. I guess you could say we were at the low end of the economic scale, purely blue collar.

Forrest was the oldest, around 40, and sort of the unofficial boss. He had three young kids and a wife. Other than me, he had the only car, and it was a junker. Forrest went home most nights. I doubt he finished high school. He was having a tough time paying rent and taking care of his family. He did not buy groceries with us, so he skipped lunch most of the time. Once in a while, he would eat a sandwich when we claimed to have made too many but even then, he was reluctant. Forrest just did not want something for nothing. He left us in midsummer, and I hope he got a better paying job than temporary fire-season employee.

Billy was in his middle 30s, a little guy around 5'2," likable and outgoing. He had very small hands and loved to play poker. He was our cook, but there wasn't much cooking. Mostly it was just opening cans and warming up food. There was no microwave in those days, so everything had to go on the stove or in the oven. Sometimes we just made sandwiches. Billy tried the best he could, but other than hamburgers and chicken he did not have much to work with—we sure weren't buying steaks or pork chops. Billy finished the seventh grade, but that was it for his school education. He was always upbeat and lively. He read people well.

Jessie looked my age but was in his mid-20s. He had a Mexican background and was a Korean War veteran. We could all see he was badly shell-shocked long before people knew about PTSD. He had a sadness about him and often seemed rather lost. A quiet guy, an introvert but very polite. Jessie had some formal education beyond high school, and when we could get him to talk, he was quite interesting. He was just a nice guy.

I became close to Billy and Jessie as they stayed the whole summer, and we were always together at night. No one had any money, so on Saturday we would drive down to the little grocery store in Piru to buy groceries. The store let us put our food on the tab. Then every two weeks on payday, our first stop was to pay off the grocery bill. Old-fashioned, but it worked. Try that today and see how far you get charging groceries.

Partway through the summer we had a couple of college kids join us. I thought it would be neat to have them; they were educated and sophisticated. It turned out the opposite. It became clear to me they were silver-spoon, spoiled kids. They found Jessie would jump if they slammed the door, which they did frequently, and then pretended it was an accident. That was simply BS. I don't think either of them ever worked before, and they certainly didn't want to work with us. They did not last, but I believe it was only a lark for them anyway. They just wanted to pretend they were doing something during their college summer vacation—wiseacres and jerks. There was no TV, record player, or any type of entertainment except for a radio. I think they just got bored. In fairness, I guess at our level we weren't very good company for them, but we sure weren't jerks. They got up one morning, packed their fancy car, and departed. I don't think they even picked up their checks. We were happy when they left.

The big event for my Forest Service career was the famous Chuchupati Fire near Frazier Park, which was a part of the Los Padres National Forest and is located just off the highway between Castaic and Bakersfield. In those days, that highway was known as the Grapevine. The fire was a big one, and all the stations were called in to assist in the fight. We were around 50 miles away and only had one fire truck, which was an old Dodge power wagon with a top speed of about 40 miles per hour downhill. All three of us had test driven the firetruck on a steep hill. It was the first time I ever drove a four-wheel-drive vehicle, and I think I overdid the speed a bit, thinking if I let up on the gas, we might get stuck.

In any case, for this mad rush to fight fire, Billy was assigned as a driver—no fair! That really crushed me; I was a good driver and drove all the time. Billy didn't even have a car and was so short he could barely reach the gas or brake pedal. Nevertheless, we took off with Billy driving, dashing to the fire. Think of us racing full bore with red lights—going at a top speed of 40 miles an hour downhill. The grapevine (Hwy 99, which is now IH 5) is steep and I expect our speed was closer to 35 miles an hour going uphill. No doubt, we looked like the Keystone Cops with our red lights going and every car on the road passing us. It must've been hysterical for onlookers. We got to the fire in time to use our Polaskis. It was mostly just working on hotspots, embers, and sparks that were still smoldering. The truth is we weren't good firefighters, not because we were unwilling, but really never had any firefighting training. Both Billy and I jumped right at it, madly attacking the hotspots. We were exhausted within 30 minutes and embarrassed to realize we were just cleaning up already burned areas and expected to work for a full day. Fortunately, I was wearing a long- sleeved shirt, and I quickly understood why the professionals did this to help keep the heat off their skin. Billy wore a short-sleeved shirt and really suffered, but he didn't give up.

It was a good summer job, and a great experience. While the conversations were hardly intellectual, I did miss our little group. I never saw Billy again. Jessie somehow saved enough money to buy a 1941 Ford and drove over to Santa Paula to see me and have a beer—not so easy as I was not even close to being 21. Jessie had a slight build and did not look his age, so we were both suspect. But we had a bar in town at the corner of Harvard and 12th Street named Van's, after the man who owned the joint and ran it. Van didn't look too hard at anybody who appeared just for a beer, so Jessie and I had a good time talking about being important government employees in the U.S. Forest Service. Jessie came to see me a couple more times, and I remember the smell of cigarette smoke and the mohair seat covers as we talked and drank beer in his old Ford during the rain.

That job, and living with my workmates, really woke me up to people barely making ends meet. Maybe you could say it was an early lesson in empathy and gave me a wider vision and social awareness. Billy and Jessie are no doubt gone, but it would be fun to see them again. By the way, Mr. Freed was a good guy and a good boss to have. He was polite and professional, but everything had to be done right, plus he really looked the part, always sharply dressed. He took me with him a couple of times to the Ranger headquarters in Ojai, California, and twice packing in the backcountry with his horses. I always enjoyed being with him. Sadly, he was killed in an airplane crash fighting a forest fire when I was in Vietnam. I regret not being able to tell him how much I appreciated that summer job working for him.

When my Forest Service job ended, I enrolled in Ventura Junior College and at the same time got a part-time job with the U.S. Postal Service.

Mr. C. Lamb had been appointed postmaster by President Franklin Roosevelt, and he was still postmaster in 1957. It was good, steady work, and as I recall, pay was something like $1.60 an hour. The job started at 5:00 a.m. when I helped unload incoming mail delivered by truck. It came in canvas bags, and the first-class letter and card mail was tied together with string in bundles. We cut the strings and started sorting the mail for the carriers who arrived at seven. I quit at 7:30 a.m. and joined my buddies in a carpool for school in Ventura. On Tuesdays and Thursdays, when my classes were finished by noon, I went back to the post office and carried the mail on a bicycle route. Sounds crazy, but that's what it was—you rode a bike and put mail in boxes like you see on country roads. Only this was not on a country road, it was down Harvard Boulevard. The key was to sort the mail for the next box while riding the bike and then opening the mailbox, putting in the mail, and closing the lid without stopping the bike. It can be done, but you had to practice, and it was tricky with magazines. Good thing in those days we didn't have so much junk mail. I got Saturdays off but then had to work on Sundays.

Sunday was more or less on my time picking up letters from mailboxes throughout town and getting them to the post office. The mail truck arrived at 2:00 p.m. on Sunday, and I had to be there at that time to help unload. The good thing was it left Saturdays free for my lawn-mowing business, which took 12 hours. I had the post office job for two years and along with my lawn mowing business and other odd jobs, I managed to get 30 to 35 hours a week. That was the good part. The bad part was I had no time left to study. I paid dearly for that when I moved on to Fresno State for a BA and then graduate work. Probably another bad thing I learned was to never miss work. Not a good thing for those you're working with if you are sick. I can only remember three times being too sick to show up: once at the post office (alcohol poisoning), once at Lackland with the flu, and once at the Pentagon with the flu. I'm not counting a couple of nights' stay at the Eighth Field Hospital in Vietnam for kidney stones.

Roy Moore, uncle to my high-school friend Butch Moore, was an influential businessman who was friendly and well-liked. He was a member of the Masonic Lodge and someone I wanted to emulate. Roy hired me to help him in his furniture store on a part-time basis during the summer vacation from Fresno State College. I also had a full-time job working for the state, inspecting orange orchards for quick-decline disease. Roy let me work whenever I could fit it in. I mostly worked on Saturdays or sometimes late afternoons when he needed more muscle to move furniture.

Roy was mostly seen in coat and tie. He was a hard worker himself and had a small street sweeper he drove in the early morning hours, sweeping private lots while the town was still sleeping. Much of my work was laying carpet, which turned out to be quite dirty work particularly when we tore out carpet. Dust, soil, and other dirt in the farm fields never bothered me much, but I hated tearing out the old carpet—a different kind of dirt. Roy pushed hard and expected people to earn their pay. He wanted the work to be right and always to the customer's satisfaction. If not, the job was done over. But he was fair and always pleasant; he was a good role model.

My first job out of college was teaching the eighth grade at Hamilton Junior High School in Fresno, California. It was a wonderful experience, but I'm not sure I taught the kids more than they taught me—that's another story and is better covered in my story, "You're in the Army Now."

Three Friends

Jim Gofourth, John Randall, and I were hankering to get out on some adventure with our newly acquired driver's licenses. The plan was a hunting expedition to the Rose Valley off Highway 33 north of Ojai where our quarry would be wily brush rabbits *(Sylvilagus bachmani)*, which are in the cottontail family, and while smaller, are very good eating. Question was: How do we get there? None of the older guys we knew were available or, more likely, did not want to bother with us.

After much postulation about finding a car, by some miracle, we got hold of Jim's father's brand-new 1954 green station wagon. It was as spectacular to us as any new car was in those days. In those times, if you wanted a car you had to get a job and save money to buy your own. We loaded our battery of expedition firearms, two .22-caliber rifles for the shooters with John Randall's .38-caliber Smith & Wesson revolver, and away we went. We reckoned the revolver might come in handy for any number of emergencies, but probably not a charging brush bunny. It was called a lemon squeezer because it had a safety in the grip much like a 1911 Colt pistol. It was rather rinky-dink for a revolver, but that was what he had.

The Rose Valley was open country in those days, and no one paid much attention to .22 rifle fire. After spending a couple hours with a total bag of only three bunnies, we came upon the idea of covering more ground by using the car as a shooting platform—that is a moving platform. This would get us to more rabbits quickly, not legally, of course, but we were on gravel roads and tiny dirt trails, so no one paid attention to us. All went well until a beautiful, large king snake was spotted.

None of us worked very hard in school but we had a wonderful biology/zoology teacher, Mr. Ricards, who gave us extra credit if we brought salamanders, snakes, or other interesting animals/reptiles to class. John was quite afraid of snakes, but we were pretty much bankrupt in that class, so our interests rapidly turned from bunny hunting to snake chasing, with John as a standoff accomplice, his lemon squeezer at the ready. We were victorious and soon had the beauty in hand. But now what to do? We had no containers or bags to secure a live snake. The dilemma was brilliantly solved by shoving the snake into the glove compartment. With our prize secured, the rabbit safari continued with the driver in the front seat and the shooters in the backseat, one at each side window. All went well for a while with John driving and Jim and me shooting. All of a sudden, no one was driving. John had simply vanished, and we were just rolling along, gliding driverless in the brand-new Chevrolet down a rocky dirt road with towering boulders on both sides.

Jim and I were both mortified when we heard scraping sounds. The car kept floating forward until it hit a sandy spot, and travel ended as we bumped into a rock. To our great and everlasting relief, all the scraping was underneath, and no damage showed. What about John? He was back down the road leaping up and all around like frog legs dropped in a hot skillet. What was it? The king snake had escaped from the glove compartment, came behind the dashboard, slid down the brake pedal, and dropped into the top of his boot. This caused him to depart the moving car, more or less doing a barrel roll, without being noticed by the two hunters plinking away at our quarry—a chancy maneuver with rifle fire over his head. His ballet performance of kicks and stomps rendered our great catch lifeless. So much for the extra credit we needed.

Upon examining the corpse and hearing of this misadventure, Mr. Ricards allowed no extra credit. However, to our great discomfort, he did award us honorable mention in front of the entire class. We still loved him.

The Flying Stetson

In the early 1950s, somewhere between my middle and high school years, I witnessed the flying Stetson. Well, most Stetsons really don't fly, but this one did a good imitation. The location was the Santa Paula Rifle Club Range in my hometown of Santa Paula, California. This was a high-power rifle range from 200 to 600 yards, located on the Teague McKevitt citrus ranch just outside the city limits of Santa Paula. It was a small range with only two points of fire—which means two targets, so two shooters could shoot at the same time.

John Randall was a school chum and fellow Boy Scout. More importantly, John shot with me on the junior NRA rifle team sponsored by our Boy Scout Troop 301. He and I were working the pits. For those not familiar with high-power rifle shooting, the pits are where the targets are marked for scoring. The shooter fires his rifle at the target, which is then lowered below ground level. It is marked with a spotter over the bullet hole, and then run back up for scoring by those watching from the firing line and readied for the next shot. It was a great job for a kid.

We were paid five bucks for the day, which was really good money, and we got lunch, which was almost as good. Lunch consisted of a salad with avocado, pinto beans, grilled toasted garlic bread, and a two-inch thick sirloin steak cooked on the grill over oak wood and served on World War II metal trays. It was just marvelous. Those steaks were something I had never experienced. It's hard to believe, but even avocados were a first for me.

California was really the hotbed of both rifle and pistol target shooting in the 1950s and early 1960s, with several high-power rifle ranges throughout the state. The Marine Corps rifle range at Camp Matthews was adjacent to Camp Pendleton. The Army/National Guard Range at Fort Ord was also used as were the Marine Ranges at 29 Palms.

Santa Paula was one of the smaller ranges, but their monthly shoots were well attended by top competitors, including a couple of state and U.S. champions. Several of the local shooters were World War I veterans, and I heard first-hand stories of Château Thierry and the battle of Belleau Wood, the Argonne, and the lost battalion. I learned of Captain Lloyd Williams' "Retreat, like hell! We just got here!" answer to the French when he was advised to retreat. And, what many people think was said by General Patton, "Come on, you sons of bitches—do you want to live forever?" was actually voiced by Marine Sergeant Major Dan Daly in the First World War. And, of course, Alvin York of the 32nd Inf, 82nd Div. I was eager to hear all these stories of adventure, and I was all ears. It was a real education. I held those veterans in awe.

Many of the club members had been in the California home guard or militia, a step below the National Guard, during World War II. Their commander had been Major Stewart. He no longer shot rifles, but sometimes came for lunch. When it was announced that Major Stewart was coming, you could just see shooters straighten up a bit, checking their gig lines and such. It was an early lesson for me of demonstrated respect. Major Stewart was older than most of the members and wore a big hat (not the flyer). When he arrived in his large Chrysler sedan, the whole atmosphere changed.

We also had a few World War II veterans, but most of them were still working and did not have time for recreational shooting. Harry Blaisdell, a World War II Navy vet from Ojai, California, was one of the older World War II guys. He helped me considerably in my eventual climb to be a top contender at high-power rifle shooting. Mr. Marshall, who taught our Scouts in Boy Scout Troop 301 small-bore (.22-caliber) shooting, was also a member who gave hundreds of hours of his time teaching and coaching kids to target shoot.

The second Sunday of each month, the Santa Paula Club held a match. Those competitions attracted a colorful group of shooters, and many were my role models. Of course, at that age I did not yet recognize their significance.

Tom Sancomb was an older shooter, maybe around 60 years old, from Oxnard, but he was still a frequent winner in the smaller matches. Tom was rather a curmudgeon, but I got along well with him when I started shooting high power. He lived on the beach and taught me surf fishing. Martin Hull was from the Los Angeles area and had won the U.S. Championship at Camp Perry with the service rifle—M1 Garand.

The M1 Garand was the best combat rifle in World War II. It followed the Springfield aught-six which was really a copy of the German model 98 Mauser. It was so close that the U.S. government ended up paying Germany for patent rights. Lt Col Theodore Roosevelt was responsible for creating the Springfield when he realized the Spanish Mausers used against us in Cuba vastly outperformed our rifles. And, for rifle shooters, the venerable Winchester Model 70 evolved from the Springfield.

Martin Hull was a younger guy, probably in his mid-30s. He worked for Sierra, which was one of the top target bullet-makers at that time. He wore a beautiful white Stetson hat blocked the same as John Wayne's in the classic movie *Stagecoach*.

The shooters took a lunch break halfway through the match. After lunch, Tom was plinking with his 1911 Colt pistol. Martin made some smart aleck remark about Tom not being able to hit anything with a pistol. Tom said, "I can hit your hat." Bets were made. A crowd appeared and up went the Stetson, flying high. All eyes were locked on that white Stetson, and everyone had their fingers in their ears. The hat floated gently down and softly landed front forward as if it were looking at us. Then BOOM! An absolutely perfect center shot directly through the middle of the crown. For a moment it looked like Martin was going to slug Tom, but it passed.

While some got a chuckle out of the episode, everyone was pissed. Half were mad because Tom had tricked Martin and ruined a very fine, expensive hat, and the other half because they had taken their fingers out of their ears when the hat landed and now their ears were ringing from the tardy blast. John Randall and I could hardly believe our eyes, which were no doubt as big as saucers. Tom was shooting military ball ammunition that punched a hole through the hat rather than cutting a hole. Martin repaired the wounded hat by stitching the shot hole shut. He was still wearing the flying Stetson the last time I shot with him on the California state team at Camp Perry in 1962.

The lesson is to know the parameters clearly when making a wager, or maybe, don't bet against a curmudgeon. Or be careful of a smart aleck's remark. You don't see a flying Stetson every day.

Riding Shotgun with the Sheriff

This event took place in 1957 when I was still living in Santa Paula, California, and going to school at Ventura Junior College. Several of my older friends, successful professional and businessmen, were heavy into pistol shooting. Bob Simmons was a TV salesman and repairman with his own business. Joe Taylor was a rancher but had an oil well. Lawrence Outland was a big-time rancher in citrus, row crops, and flower seeds. He was quite colorful from an old-time Santa Paula family. Bob Simmons was really a mentor in many ways. I knew rifle shooting well, but he taught me the basics for pistol competition. We went to local matches in California and the state .22-caliber championship at the Presidio in San Francisco. We even went to the United States Championship at Camp Perry Ohio together. One of the best ranges in California was the Los Angeles Police Academy where top target shooters in the nation competed.

One of the better shooters at the time was Reid Hunt, who was a captain in the Ventura County Sheriff's Department. Actually, Captain Hunt was kind of a bigshot. As I recall, there were only four captains in the department, and they reported to the civil service undersheriff who reported to the elected county sheriff. Captain Hunt was a big man—a polite way to describe him would be to say he was heavy. He wore suits or a sport coat. I never saw him in uniform, probably because he was too fat. Part of his "civilian uniform" was a large-frame revolver often carried in a cross-draw holster. His coat was never buttoned so the big gun was visible. What wasn't visible was a Chief's Special in his right-hand coat pocket. I'm told when he did not want undue attention in a situation, his hand was always in his coat pocket. That also went for interviews and interrogations.

We met at a pistol match, and he was friendly towards me, probably because I was friends with Joe Taylor and Lawrence Outland. I think both of them were reserve sheriff's deputies, which meant that each got a badge and could carry a concealed firearm. They had ridden on patrol with Captain Hunt, so I wanted to do the same. Captain Hunt lived in Fillmore, which is between Santa Paula and Piru about 20 miles inland on Highway 126 from Ventura. He picked me up one night, and we drove in his unmarked black Chrysler sedan with only a red spotlight on each side of the car. Not long after picking me up, he got a hot call—a big fight was taking place in Saticoy. Saticoy is between Santa Paula and Ventura, which in those days was little more than a gas station, convenience store, and a few farm implement repair shops. We turned on the two red lights and the siren and headed for Saticoy. When we pulled up, the highway patrol had just arrived and also a second sheriff's car. An ambulance was just pulling in. Lots of people, a cacophony of shouting, cursing, screams, and plenty of confusion. Several people had been cut or stabbed so there was plenty of blood. Captain Hunt got out of the car, and there was no question of who was in charge. He immediately started barking orders even to the California Highway Patrol. Additional sheriff cars began to arrive, and Captain Hunt started pointing out people and telling which officer to apprehend which individual and to get them out of there immediately to the county courthouse. Pandemonium quieted quickly, but there were still some loud cursing and threats. Those people were rapidly handcuffed, and we took one in our car. Off we went to the courthouse. About halfway there I happened to put my arm up on the top of the seat. Captain Hunt just reached over, without saying anything, and pushed it down. That was before all the fancy cars with cages separating the front and rear seat. The young man in the back was handcuffed, and I think Captain Hunt thought he might lean forward and bite me.

When we got to the courthouse, the prisoners, plus the one we brought in, were all seated in separate areas (sort of little low cubicles) where they could see each other. Obscenities were still being hurled around, including comments directed at the sheriffs. Captain Hunt pulled out a short billy club. Today you might say baton or nightstick.

This one was short, probably no more than 15 inches, but thick. The Captain walked down the aisle in front of the row of cubicles with that billy club, slapping it against the palm of his hand. And it did make a loud slap. Things got quiet very quickly. It was an education for me. His quick action directed at the perpetrators probably prevented a full-blown riot in Saticoy. Additionally, he quieted all those in handcuffs down very quickly without touching or hurting any of them. It was just his presence, and of course, the demonstrated threat, slapping his hand with the billy club. One probably couldn't do that today, but it sure worked.

My friends who rode with him in delivering prisoners from the county jail to the state penitentiary told of his normal advice to prisoners making the trip. It was very polite, professional and to the point. Something like, "I have delivered many prisoners in my career without losing one. I take no joy in this task, and I want you to know it is nothing personal. But understand, I'm too fat to chase you if you run. Be assured I will not do that, but I will for certain kill you if you run. I've never lost a prisoner, and I'm not going to lose you. Dead or alive you will be delivered. But nothing personal." I never heard of him losing a prisoner, but I'm sure he meant 100 percent of what he said. The whole experience was a good lesson of seeing how he accomplished his duty without violence in what was potentially a violent and volatile situation.

I had another very interesting situation while riding with the United States Marshal for the Western District of Texas. Captain Jack Dean was a Texas Ranger for 30 years and a captain for the last 15 years of his career. He was rather renowned for preventing or settling many tough situations. We began hunting together in 1983, and I'm pleased to say we became personal friends. Jack is my age and retired from the Texas Rangers in 1993, the same year I retired. He was then appointed by President Bill Clinton as the U.S. Marshal for the Western District of Texas.

We had been hunting in West Texas as guests of Rich Atwell, a mutual friend who owns Coastal Trucking. While returning from that weekend hunt, we were just past Kerrville on Interstate 10 when we saw a strange white sedan with sheriff markings parked in the median. Thinking it out of place, I mentioned it to Jack, and he agreed. Five minutes later, the red lights came on behind us. Jack was driving and pulled over. The driver of the sheriff's car jumped out and came up rather quickly to our car. Jack exited our car so he could reach the backseat to retrieve his driver's license from his briefcase. The sheriff was too quick for us and got right up to the car. He was a nice-looking young kid, obviously in good shape. It was a little strange as he was wearing military fatigue pants and a tight-fitting black T-shirt with Sheriff in large lettering, both front and back. First thing he said in a rather rude tone was, "Let me see your license." Normally our state and usually county and city police are more polite.

Anyway, Jack paid no attention to his tone of voice. Jack said, "My license is in the briefcase there in the backseat. I'll open it and get my license out, but don't be alarmed, there is also a pistol in the briefcase." That startled the kid, and he backed up a foot or two, looking at Jack and said, "What do you do?"

I thought the question was out of order, but Jack answered, "I'm the United States Marshal." There was a second officer in the sheriff's car, and I noted, by looking in the rearview side mirror, he was now standing with the door open with him behind it, and he looked to be holding a pistol. He obviously heard what Jack said and immediately called out, "Hello, Captain Dean."

It seemed he was a young deputy sheriff, had met Captain Dean, and knew Captain Dean's son Kyle, who was the Texas Ranger for the Kerrville area. As you might imagine, Mr. America in the black T-shirt quickly got very polite. He mumbled and fumbled a bit before saying he thought we might have been going a little fast. Captain Dean didn't blink or mention any rudeness. We merely got back in the car and went on our way home. It turned out Mr. America had come to Kerrville from Fort Worth as part of a hotshot drug enforcement team to work temporarily in the area and a local deputy sheriff was riding with him. I expect the visiting law got his comeuppance from the local boys, laughing at hearing about the big-time hotshot cop getting caught up a bit short. Hopefully, he became more courteous.

Long Shots — Early Days

A longtime, very close friend, Brig Gen J.B. Davis, related an interesting story involving Captain Dean when he was still a Ranger. As background, Mohammad Reza Shah was the last of the Pahlavi dynasty that began in 1920 and was toppled in 1979. He was dying of cancer and taking treatments at Wilford Hall Hospital on Lackland Air Force Base. The Air Force can protect people on base but cannot protect private citizens downtown. The Lackland Hospital ultimately came under the commander of Air Training Command, four-star General Bennie Davis. He was in a bind because Mrs. Shah announced she was going shopping downtown Saturday. There was considerable threat to the Shah and his family. General Davis was not taking any chances on her safety. This was a Friday. He first went to the local Secret Service and was told they only handled heads of state. He then went to the State Department contact and was told they would have to run it up the flagpole. He then tried the FBI senior agent in charge and was advised they would have to get permission from Washington. Finally, he called the Texas Rangers. My friend was in the office with General Davis and relates the short call, which went something like this, "Hello, I'm General Bennie Davis. We need your assistance, and I wonder if you would call the governor." Captain Dean's response was, "I don't call anyone. What do you need?" End of story. Captain Dean was a bodyguard on Saturday. That might be a good lesson in federal bureaucracy versus action by a Texas Ranger captain.

On an interesting note, in 1980 Texas Governor Clements brought in James Adams, who had retired as assistant director of the FBI, to be head of the Texas Department of Public Safety (DPS)—boss of the state police and Texas Rangers. You can imagine what many people thought, "Horrors—a Washington bureaucrat running the show." As it turns out, Colonel Adams proved to be an excellent choice. I met him on a Texas Ranger dove hunt, and it was evident the Rangers held him in high regard. He is quoted as saying, "A Ranger captain made more decisions in a month than an FBI senior agent in charge in a year."

Automobiles

A 1937 Packard! You might say who would care about a 1937 Packard in 1955, but I saw it one night when a couple of high school buddies and I were just driving around town. It was parked at the curb on Virginia Terrace, a rather ritzy part of town, with a For Sale sign on the windshield. It was a neat looking four-door sedan, a John-Dillinger-looking car. I inquired about the price and was told for a $20 bill we could tow it off.

The car had one flat tire, and the battery was dead, but the body was in perfect shape—no dents or dings, and even the paint was fairly good. It had the old mohair cloth upholstery that was naturally spotted and worn, but no tears or cuts, so it looked pretty good. One back door window was sort of milky about halfway up. And if you looked in through the back window, you could see the cotton starting to poke out under the mohair on the backseat, which was probably caused by sitting in the sun. The engine was a straight eight. If it had been a 12-cylinder, it would have been a collectible classic. Anyway, we thought it would be fun to drag Main in a John Dillinger car, so the four of us got together and chipped in five bucks each to buy the car. It was a bit chancy; we were not sure the car would even run. One of the partners, John Randall, was somewhat of a mechanic. We pumped the tire up, charged the battery, and lo and behold, everything worked—even the radio. It had one of those old-time radios. You'd turn the knob, and the different station numbers would come into view.

Dragging Main at night was a major pastime of kids in those days. The real Main Street was only about three blocks long, and then it went into some service stations and a couple of used car lots until it finally ended up on 12th Street at a Ford dealership. Just beyond that was a small hamburger joint owned by George Gonzales' (another classmate) mother. So, we had about eight blocks to drive, and sometimes the kids would just park at one end and watch what was coming and going. Not very exciting, but something to do in a small town. Trouble was, we hadn't thought about insurance. I had done some odd jobs for the State Farm Insurance rep in town, so we got the required liability policy for $47 to cover six months. The Packard was fun to drive around, although it was heavy and certainly not a speedster—a neat car for dragging Main, but not one to take on a date. One other problem was the city curfew of 10:30 for school kids Monday through Thursday. That car was easy to spot and catch.

Somehow, it always seemed to be low on or out of gas, so we had to shell out for gas if we took it out. We renewed the insurance a couple of times, but then the novelty wore off, and we parked it behind my father's house. The car lived there for a couple of years but was seldom driven. My dad finally got tired of it, so I took it down the lane and left it parked on Ojai Road with a For Sale sign. The same day, a guy came by and told me he wanted to drive the car to Mexico, so he got the car and I got our 20 bucks back. It would be interesting to know where the car finally ended up.

The 1957 Lincoln Premier Coupe was 18 feet and 7 inches long (slightly longer than a 2019 Chevrolet Suburban). I believe it was Lincoln's answer to the Cadillac Biarritz, which was the most expensive American car at the time and is a collector's car today. The Lincoln price tag was $5,150, at a time when the average U.S. household income was $4,550. Obviously, the car did not belong to me. It was a beautiful coupe, pink on the bottom with a white top and all-white leather interior. Pretty fancy, and the only one in town. In fact, I never saw another Lincoln Premier Coupe anywhere. With that color scheme they would probably only be found in Southern California or Florida. The car was owned by Mrs. Hernandez. We did not have a Cadillac Biarritz in our town, but strange as it seems, Mrs. Hernandez's friend from Santa Barbara had one, and they were often parked together at her house—a rather impressive pair indeed. Her son Manny Vanegas was a high-school friend and a partner in a little grass mowing business we did together on Saturdays. We had both just graduated Ventura Junior College, where the history professor inspired and encouraged me to continue my travel and learn more of the world.

My best friend in high school, Doug Udall, who also graduated from Ventura College, was interested in seeing Europe, so we hatched a plan. This was in 1958, and the most common and cheapest way to travel across the pond was by boat. Air travel was still pretty much restricted to rich folks. Doug and I both had wheels—Doug had a Chevy coupe and a Triumph motorcycle, and I had a pickup truck and a BSA motorcycle. Neither one of us had been able to save much money, but by selling our rolling stock we had enough for three months in Europe and our travel by ship. I must admit, it was a pretty low-level ship, which took nine days sailing from Montréal to Europe. Most everyone was sick by the third day—me included. But that is another story. Now the problem was how to get from Santa Paula, California, to Montréal. To make it more fun and to get us to Montréal, I enlisted Manny and two other friends to travel with us on a road trip. Don't confuse our road trip with those currently depicted in the movies as a glorious, drunken escapade of bored folks with too much money. We were five high school and junior college buddies with no money and not yet old enough to sign a legal document. But we were all adventuresome, and somewhat free from the responsibilities of full adulthood, at least momentarily.

My other two friends on the trip were Randall Best and Richard Hyde. Our plan was to drive a 1941 four-door Chevy sedan that we were borrowing from Wayne Bailey, another good friend and classmate. The car was no beauty, but it was in good shape and roadworthy. Two days before our trip departure, Manny's mom, Mrs. Hernandez, presented her beautiful car as our chariot! It was a real dream, like someone handing you a magic flying carpet. We were riding in style! Now understand that style was limited to the car we were driving. We all had sleeping bags and spent most of our travel nights in cemeteries. There weren't many good motels in those days, and we sure didn't have money for hotels. Cemeteries are quiet, dark, and with nice grass for sleeping bags. We were headed to Iowa for a week of visiting, sleeping, and eating off my grandparents, uncles, and aunts. It was before many freeways and most highway speed limits were 55 mph, so it took us a few days and cemeteries to reach Iowa.

Our first Iowa stop was in Pocahontas where my Great Aunt Irma and Great Uncle Louie Elbert lived. They owned farms but lived in town and owned the town paper, the *Pocahontas Register Democrat*.

They had combined the Republican newspaper, *The Register*, and the Democrat paper into one. Uncle Louis and Aunt Irma had traveled the world and were quite cultured. My great-grandmother, Irma Consuella Sykes, lived with them. They had an extra bedroom and a den with couches, so we were quite comfortable our first night away from cemeteries. They weren't used to five extra guys, and we just about ate them out of house and home. We were semi-starved because we did not want to waste gas money (it was 24 cents per gallon) on trip food. They were most gracious to my friends and me and kept buying more food.

Our second stop was with my Uncle Elmer and Aunt Irma Wagner on their farm near Webster City. They had just built a new house next to their old farmhouse but had not yet moved in. The new house had no furniture, but it did have wall-to-wall carpeting (not common at the time), so it was perfect for us with our sleeping bags. My two boy cousins, Dale and Larry, were there, and we had a grand time with horses and all manner of things on the farm. One of my cousins had a new motorcycle, and I nearly killed myself racing him—me on his motorcycle and him in his father's new Buick—on a gravel county road. We were going hell-bent for leather, and I forgot those roads often dead-ended or came to 90° angle corners that were not curved. I barely got that big Harley stopped in time, and the Buick came close to running over me. It was one of those "hold-my-beer-and-watch-this" episodes.

Our next layover was on my grandparents' farm near Blairsburg, Iowa. I had spent a lot of time with them on the farm as a child as well as a couple of summers there when I was in middle school. They had moved off the farm when my Uncle Joe took it over. It was a great place for us to hang out.

Mrs. Hernandez, who owned the Lincoln, was very classy and a beautiful lady. Manny had more Mestizo looks. His father was killed in World War II at the Battle of the Bulge. There were no Mexicans or Negroes in the central Iowa farmland at that time. One of my Uncle Joe's buddies had recently married. A common practice was for friends of a new couple to show up at the newlyweds' farm unannounced and uninvited for what was called the charivari. They all came with picnic baskets and plenty of booze, plus tables and chairs for an outdoor lawn party. Joe invited us to come along on the charivari. Imagine five California boys in that splendid Lincoln Premier pulling up with Manny driving. It caused quite a stir for sure. Everybody wanted to inspect the Lincoln and look Manny over. The girls wanted to talk with the "fast guys" from Southern California.

    We went on and stopped in Detroit to visit relatives of Randall Best and then on to Montréal where Doug and I left our friends and the Lincoln. It had been a really fun time together, and we all remembered that trip fondly. Sad to say, Richard and I are the only ones still alive. Richard still claims it was the best trip of his life. The Cadillac Biarritz is a collectible car today and one of my favorites, but the Lincoln Premier will always have a special place in my memory.

Wanderlust

Early travel

My father must share some of the blame for infecting me with this travel disease. Of course, he never knew what a monster of wanderlust he had created. He liked people and just enjoyed the open road and seeing things. On our many trips between California and Iowa he always took us on side trips—to see the Painted Desert, The Grand Canyon, Boulder Dam, the Petrified Forest, and all manner of things on or close to that famous Route 66 from Chicago, Illinois to Santa Monica, California. We saw it all. In addition, we made trips all over California and saw the sights from the San Diego Zoo to the Golden Gate Bridge with camping trips to Sequoia and Yosemite National Parks. Mom and Dad were brought up on farms in Iowa and came to California to find jobs. One of my first recollections on travel was going through Las Vegas in 1940 (I was three years old) and seeing that huge neon sign with the cowboy tipping his hat at the Pioneer Club that was on the main street in Vegas. That was long before there was much of a Las Vegas Strip. We also went to see Boulder Dam which is now called Hoover Dam.

Long Shots — Early Days

The next trip I took to Iowa was sometime early during World War II when I made the trip by train back to my grandfather's farm in Iowa with my Aunt Jeanette, who was still a teenager. My suspicion now is that, with both my parents working and no one to take care of a four or five-year-old, they decided to ship me back to the farm. I can remember Jeanette putting all our money in her shoes for safekeeping. And it was just coins! We only had half dollars, quarters, and a few dimes and nickels—probably not more than three or four dollars, if that much. The train was packed full of soldiers and sailors. It is doubtful there were any sleeping cars on that train, but they would not have been on our menu in any case. We were in seats the whole trip. I do remember Jeanette and a sailor kissing, and, of course, I spilled the beans as soon as we got to Grandpa's. That did not go over well, especially with Jeanette. She would have been 16 or 17 at the time.

My family made several trips back to see family and friends, and Dad bought a little teardrop trailer for these trips. It was a very small trailer shaped like a drop of water with room for only a mattress and not high enough for me to stand up. You just had to open the door, back in your rear-end, and then pull in your legs. The back end opened much like some of the modern crossover cars, and it served us with some storage and a small sink. We kept food and a small Coleman gas stove stored there for meals. It really was just a homemade plywood copy of the commercial models and did not even have fenders, but it worked well for us. Mom and Dad slept in the trailer with my little brother Bob, and I slept in the car. Later, my brother joined me in the car. When we moved to Santa Paula in 1947 that trailer became my bedroom for the next three years.

My first travel alone was in 1948 when I was eleven. It was a trip by bus from Santa Paula, California, to my grandfather's farm close to the small town of Blairsburg, Iowa (near Webster City). My mother was not overly thrilled about me going alone, but my fifth-grade teacher, Mr. Belasco, stood up for me and said I would be fine. The bus ride was three days and two nights with stops for passengers, bathroom breaks, and cafés. Otherwise, it was straight through driving night and day. Remember, it was long before any interstates, and the speed limit was 55 miles an hour. Transfers were made in Los Angeles, California,

St. Louis, Missouri, and Des Moines, Iowa. Blairsburg did not have a bus stop, but a filling station just out of town on the highway to Webster City served as a bus stop.

On the trip to Iowa, I had enough money to buy hamburgers and Cokes, but on the return trip, my grandmother gave me enough fried chicken wishbones (she saved them up for me all summer) to last three days. I carried these in a brown paper bag with some bread and was as happy as a little prince could be. Being on the farm with three sets of cousins living close by, Iowa was a big draw, and I made this trip again the following two years by myself—after all, I was a "seasoned traveler." By the eighth grade, I became too involved with my buddies and my job at JC Penney to leave Santa Paula for the whole summer. My father took my brother and me on another trip to Iowa during my second year in high school, and that was my last visit with my cousins until 1958 on my way to Europe.

In 1957, I bought a motorcycle. It was a 1956 English bike—a BSA. A couple of my buddies also bought motorcycles at the same time— both Triumphs. That purchase very nearly got me kicked out of the house. A lot of kids wanted to get away from home, but I was working and going to Ventura College and certainly didn't want to waste money renting a room or anapartment. My mother was livid and wanted me to get rid of the bike. Many years later, my mother told me that Dad got rid of his motorcycles because of me. He rode a big Indian motorcycle much like a Harley-Davidson from our home in San Fernando to Santa Paula, where he had purchased a taxi company. We only had one car, and my mother kept that. Later, he rode an English bike in Santa Paula. He told my mom they were too dangerous, and he did not want me to start liking them. I could tell he wasn't overjoyed when I brought the BSA home, but he didn't suggest I get rid of it. Still, I was teetering on the fence with keeping the bike. I guess it would be better described as my mother was teetering on the fence whether to throw me out or let me stay. I was walking on pins and needles and knew it. After a couple weeks, things kind of blew over, and the bike was great fun. I have to admit that often I rode it like a fool just straight down the white line that divided lanes. Dumb for sure, and it was before the days of helmets. There were a few around, but no real bike rider would be caught wearing a helmet. Twice I fell off the bike, both times in the dirt. And I would neither admit nor deny alcohol was involved both times—the legal drinking age was 21 and I didn't yet meet the minimum.

My high-school friend John Randall had one of the Triumphs, and we made a marvelous tour in 1957 of the San Joaquin Valley and the Sierra Nevada Mountains, which included Sequoia and Yosemite. We rode over the Golden Gate Bridge and rode the hills in San Francisco. Then down California Highway One through Pebble Beach, Carmel, on to Santa Barbara, then Ventura and finally ten miles more to Santa Paula. We took bedrolls and mostly slept out at nights except for Napa, where I visited my Uncle Arlo and Aunt Irma as well as my six cousins. I had already been to all these places with my folks, but doing it on a bike was really a fun little adventure. My best high school buddy, Doug Udall, also bought a Triumph, but in the end, it brought him pain and grief. Late one night, we were both riding our bikes on Harvard Street going west toward Fillmore. A car was coming fast from the other direction toward us as we approached the Quinceletres Mexican restaurant to make a left-hand turn going north on 10th St. I slowed down to let the coming car pass, but Doug sped up, got past the turn, then hit some gravel, jumped the curb, and smashed into the building and a large plate glass window. It was a mess with the bike on the ground and Doug lying flat on the sidewalk, glass everywhere. His face was cut from the top left end of his forehead straight across to his right jaw, exposing his teeth. Things did not look good, but we were less than one block from the Santa Paula Police Department, and miraculously a cop showed up almost immediately and called the ambulance.

Booker Ambulance, the single ambulance in town, showed up quickly and we were off to the hospital in Ventura. In those days, the ambulance was more like a hearse or station wagon. Booker drove but was not medically qualified for much, and no doctor or medical attendant came with the ambulance. The cop and I rode in the back hunched over with Doug. The bleeding on his face had mostly stopped, but he complained of his leg feeling hot. We never even thought to look at or take off his pants. Just after arriving at the hospital, Dr. Carlson, our family doctor from Santa Paula, arrived, and I was there as they cut off Doug's Levis. His leg muscle was cut in half, somehow missing the artery. What dumb heads we were. If the artery had been cut Doug could have very well bled out before we knew it. You may wonder why this history of Doug and motorcycles appears in accounts of wanderlust—a year later, we both sold our motorcycles and cars (in my case a truck) to finance a backpacking and hitchhiking trip through Western Europe, which really opened my horizons, and the die was cast.

I have since been privileged to visit all 50 states as well as 70 countries. It has been a marvelous education and given me many friends—a real array of eclectic personalities, some with panache and sophistication, others not. Regardless, all were friends and held in my highest esteem. Travel has shown me how alive the world is and how most people strive for the same things—family, security, and a better life for their kids. It has been a profound impact on my life and provided unlimited joy. Several more countries and destinations remain on my bucket list. The Texas historian J. Frank Dobie wrote, "If during a decade a man does not change his mind on some things and develop new points of view, it is a pretty good sign that his mind is petrified and that he need no longer be counted among the living."

One could say I'm mixing apples with oranges, but I believe it also applies to travel, as travel is an education and hopefully enlarges one's picture and understanding of the world. You may not be able to visit foreign countries, but even traveling to different parts of our country can be illuminating. My Greek secretary in Korea told me of a Greek saying: "Those who travel smell—those who stay home stink."

Hitchhiking through Europe in 1958

The idea of seeing Europe was no doubt conceived by listening to my great uncle and aunt Elbert who were world travelers. They owned a small newspaper in Pocahontas, Iowa, but came to California for visits with my grandmother and all their nieces. I loved to have them come to our house as they had interesting stories from all over the world. Often, we would have a mini family reunion when they came and all my mother's sisters with their families would be together. Along with my great aunt and uncle, my high school history teacher, Mr. Jennings, who had fought in World War II, and of course, the history and geography teachers at Ventura College galvanized my interest in seeing the world.

Although school was out for the summer, that didn't mean you could just play around. I had a job every summer, which was expected. Still, taking a summer off was tantalizing. I decided to visit Europe as a gift to myself for graduation from Ventura Junior College. My best friend from high school, Doug Udall, agreed to join me on a hitchhiking adventure.

The cheapest way to reach Europe was by ship so we purchased passage on a ship departing from Montréal, Canada. Our tickets were at the lowest level and placed us with other students and young people, which suited us fine. The price round-trip was $300, and that suited us even better. We had a marvelous cross-country trip by car from Southern California to Montréal, with three other buddies from high school and junior college.

The ship we boarded was not a luxury liner. We sailed from Montréal via the Saint Lawrence Seaway, and it took us two days to reach the Atlantic Ocean. Those first days were fine. Although the weather was cloudy it was still comfortable on deck with a good coat. Things changed when we got into the real Atlantic. First, the weather got colder, the wind got stronger, and it was no longer fun to be on deck. Then the seas got rough, and most everyone on the ship got seasick, including me. The meals were not particularly good anyway, but now climbing the stairs to get to the dining room was even less fun as people were up-chucking their dinner all over the stairs and everywhere else. Many could not even get out of their beds.

There wasn't much to see crossing the Atlantic, although I did see one iceberg. Then again at our level, we didn't even have a porthole, and no one really had proper clothes to be on deck in the cold weather of the North Atlantic. There were no shows or banquets like on today's vacation cruises. We did have a small indoor pool, but I never saw anyone use it. Our first sighting of land was Ireland, and we anchored off Cork. Some kind of an exchange took place, but no passengers were allowed to disembark. I was weak from being seasick but managed to stay on deck for short periods the last couple of days. It was still cold and not a fun trip.

For some reason, the ship sailed to Le Havre, France, first and then on to Southampton, England, which was the port used by the British liner RMS Titanic to set sail on its ill-fated maiden voyage in 1912. What a joy it was to get back on solid ground. We took the train to London and spent several days prowling around seeing the sights. By sheer coincidence we ran into our Ventura College history teacher and his wife on a London street. The weather was absolutely perfect, sunshine every day and warm for London. Young people, mostly foreign students including us, were taking off their shirts in London parks. The Brits didn't much care for disrobing in their beautiful city parks or for traveling students. We were not dishonest but were considered rascals who didn't adhere well to protocol. I suppose we could best be described as adventurous vagabonds with our backpacks and mostly dirty clothes, often broadcasting strong body odor. We stayed at youth hostels pretty much throughout our European journey—many of which did not have showers. But the cost was right, normally two or three bucks, which sometimes included a very basic evening meal.

Crossing back across the channel, we first visited Holland then were on to Belgium. Brussels was hosting a World's Fair so there was much to see. Venturing into a gun store we discovered that a Browning Superposed shotgun could be purchased for just over $300, less than 1/3 of the price in the United States. It was too good to pass up and a deal was made with arrangements to have it shipped to California. I could picture myself as a dashing sportsman at home shooting a gun that cost over $1,000 when the average U.S. yearly income was just over $3,600. I might even be seen in newsreels like Gary Cooper and Ernest Hemingway—well, one can dream. We traveled through Luxembourg into Germany. Hitchhiking was not easy in those days for two guys both carrying very large backpacks. Most of the cars in our initial hitchhiking through Holland, Belgium, Luxembourg, and Germany were small, German Volkswagens and little French Citroen 2VCs. Their nicknames in German were Kaefer (beetle) for the Volkswagen and Ente (duck) for the little Citroen. The Renault or small Italian Fiat also presented a challenge with our large backpacks. There were a few Mercedes, Peugeots, or other large cars.

Buddy Foster, our high-school classmate and my friend from Richmond Road days, had joined the Army and was stationed in Heidelberg. He married Joan Fulton, who was a class sweetheart—and still is. So, we made a visit to say hello to them and then went on wandering around Germany. We were in Wiesbaden and lost, looking for a youth hostel. We had an address but could not find it. An older man, probably in his late sixties, apparently recognized the bewildered look on our faces and came over to help. He couldn't speak English, and we couldn't speak German so giving or understanding directions was pretty much a lost cause. Apparently, we were not even on the right side of the river; he finally gestured for us to follow him, and he took us on an hour walk across town to the youth hostel. It was quite a nice gesture on his part, and I must say throughout Europe and in all the countries we visited Americans were welcomed and we were treated very well. There was still a great deal of rubble and obvious war damage in London, Belgium, Germany, and Italy, but the European Recovery Program also known as the Marshall Plan was taking hold. Franklin D. Roosevelt appointed General George C. Marshall as the senior general directing World War II from Washington. That position would later become Chairman of the Joint Chiefs of Staff. It was President Harry Truman who labeled him as the "architect of victory" in World War II. It's rather ironic that our senior military leader in war would also develop and direct America's economic recovery efforts for Western Europe, including our previous enemies of Germany, Italy, and the Vichy French government of Marshal Petain. Of course, it was also in our best interest to abut the influence and threat from the Soviet Union. General Marshall was awarded the Nobel Peace Prize in 1953 for his role in developing the recovery program.

It was at the hostel in Wiesbaden where we met Brian. We were far from polished whereas Brian was a college graduate and had been around a bit. He had a car, a black Ford Prefect, an Anglia model two-door coupe. It was Britain's lowest-priced car, vintage of about 1947 to 1949. Brian was lonely or tired of traveling alone or maybe both, so he invited us to join him. He did not appear to be on any kind of a budget plan, and he was good company, as well as being more educated and wiser to the ways of the world. Jumping from hitchhiking to a car was a huge step up. We were now seeing Europe from a touring car. Well, maybe not a real touring car, but we could move faster along any route we pleased. Brian had no set plans, so Doug and I pretty well set the course. We went from Germany to Austria and met up with Kurt Meissner, our high-school senior class exchange student. His family lived in a large home in the city of Wels. Kurt's dad was a hunter and put on a much-appreciated dinner for us. Kirk was a little embarrassed because it was a sausage dinner with sauerkraut and potatoes, and he didn't want us to think it was like hotdogs in the states. We couldn't care less and were just delighted to be guests. Kurt told us of his family visiting Rome earlier that year when his father realized opening day of hunting for some species of animal was nearly upon them. They packed up immediately and left for home, cutting off some of their planned visit. I thought that rather strange until years later when I began hunting with Germans and Austrians. They are dedicated and serious about their hunting.

We went on to visit Vienna and rode the famous Ferris wheel shown in the movie, *The Third Man*, starring Joseph Cotton and Orson Welles. It's an interesting Ferris wheel, with large compartments containing benches to accommodate six or eight people. The wheel makes one complete turn, but it can take quite a while because it was only moved each time someone bought tickets for the next compartment. We were informed at our youth hostel it was a perfect place for young lovers to meet at night where they were likely to have unlighted privacy for 30 minutes. None of the gentler species were found to accompany us, but it was a beautiful platform for viewing the city. After World War II, Austria was occupied by the four major powers: the Soviet Union, the United States, the United Kingdom, and France. Vienna was in the Russian sector, but it was collectively administered by the same four nations until Austria gained independence in 1955. A hunting and gun store in Vienna offered me a Simpson side-by-side shotgun for three hundred bucks. I had never heard of Simpson before, but it was a beautiful 12-gauge gun. I knew it was made in Germany, but it wasn't until later that I found out it was made in Suhl, communist

East Germany. Suhl was, and still is, a center for making fine hunting guns. Other famous makers in Suhl were Krieghoff, Merkel, Heym, and Sauer. All top-quality guns but with names that were unfamiliar to me. I had much to learn. The Simpson, which was very similar to a Merkel, became a gift for my father.

From Austria we were off to the tiny country of Liechtenstein and then over the Italian Alps and down to Florence to see Michelangelo's David. The first David we saw was in a plaza square where we had viewed one of the three magnificent sets of bronze doors in Florence. A pigeon dumped on me as we were admiring the doors, soiling my only clean shirt. That put a damper on my day as I tried to wash it off in the fountain. Then we found out we had not seen the original David. It was in the Accademia Gallery, so we marched there to see the original David. Seeing the original perked me back up. We walked across the famous Ponte Vecchio Bridge with its high-dollar jewelry and art shops. Interesting to see but we weren't buying. Our next destination was Rome to see the Coliseum, the Roman forum, and the Vatican's treasures. Basically, we saw anything that we could see for free. If a fee was required we simply passed it up.

One of the youth hostels we used in Italy had been a barracks or training area for the military or police. It was built in a square with a plaza in the middle. An arched entry was at one end, and the opposite end was for administration and the dining hall.

Each side was made up of a three-story barracks with a large flowing fountain in the plaza. The boys were housed on one side and the girls on the other. The second floor on our side contained a large, open shower with 20 to 25 showerheads. Water was intermittent and only lukewarm at best. One late afternoon, several of us were trying to grab a shower before dinner and were soaped up when the water simply stopped flowing. As often happens with late teens and early twenty-somethings, stupid stepped in quickly. Someone suggested we rinse off in the fountain located in the plaza. What a marvelous idea! We all marched down the stairs, crossed the plaza, and hopped in the fountain—bare-ass naked with no one attempting to cover up with towels. Windows on the girls' dormitory were soon full of faces, which, of course, we welcomed anyway. We pretended not to notice, showing off our hardware or, in this case, our software. Before long, some of the guys began waving to the girls, urging them to come join us in the fountain. Enthusiasm for water games was not forthcoming from their building. I thought some of the Swedish girls might be daring enough, but it was not to be. It wasn't long until an official appeared in a quasi-uniform wearing a billed cap like a policeman or maybe postman. He was a large man and less than amused at a dozen naked young guys in his fountain. He was speaking Italian and gesturing for us to get out. We couldn't understand Italian, but we knew what he wanted although we pretended not to understand. Finally, red-faced and clearly frustrated, he pointed his finger at us and shouted, "Mussolini, a bang, a bang, a bang." That brought a roaring chorus of laughter. However, thinking there might be a price to pay for our bravado, we felt our post was no longer worth defending and reluctantly retreated from the fountain to our building thoroughly rinsed off and pleased with our stupid selves.

In Rome, I was tempted once more in a gun shop and purchased a Beretta case-hardened, two triggered, over-and-under shotgun—another $300 gone. It was tight-choked and was probably made for pigeon shooting, but I knew nothing about pigeon shooting at the time. That was the gun that Clark Gable said must have a tight choke after l obliterated a clay pigeon on the skeet field. A small Beretta pistol was also too good to pass up. Why I took possession on the spot now escapes me, but the pistol and shotgun ended up in our little black touring car for the rest of the trip. Then it was up the coast of Italy to Pisa for the obligatory photo holding up the leaning Tower of Pisa with one hand. In those days you could still climb the tower, which we all did.

From Pisa it was back north through the Alps into Switzerland. We were mostly on very small roads in those days, and it was just a magnificent drive. We were in search of the Matterhorn and took the train to the town Zermatt (cars were not allowed in the village). The Matterhorn overlooks it on the Swiss side. It is a striking and beautiful mountain with a pyramid peak. But it is also one of the deadliest peaks in the world for mountain climbers. The first successful climb was in 1865, and even then on the descent four of the seven climbers fell to their deaths. Several hundred climbers have lost their lives on the Matterhorn. Beauty can often be deadly. It was interesting to see houses built high up the sides of mountains with no roads leading to them. In some areas, people simply parked their cars below and hiked up to their houses. The glades, hillsides, and valleys were all colored green from the grass with cows brought to the higher areas for summer grazing.

It was getting late in summer, and once we left the Alps we headed straight for Paris. Brian's car was giving us trouble, but we found the subway worked well in Paris. We wandered all around Paris and went to see the Mona Lisa in the Louvre Art Museum. I will probably not be selected as an art critic, as I felt the Mona Lisa was overrated. Nevertheless, the museum held many beautiful paintings and was certainly well worth seeing. Paris was in a bit of turmoil with protests against General de Gaulle and the end of French rule in Algeria. Many Frenchmen and other Europeans, some born in Algeria, with farms and property in Algeria wanted to keep it under French control. Most Algerians wanted independence from France. The Algerian war for independence began in 1954. The struggle was often deadly with some estimates of two million killed. Algeria did gain independence in 1962. While we were in Paris, a bomb was set off in the section of the subway we used. It was blamed on the Algerian National Liberation Front. Time was running short for us anyway, and the bombing was just a reminder to move on. We packed our backpacks and loaded everything into our little touring car. By now, the Prefect was making a considerable banging noise, and then it simply stopped. We were in front of the Paris Opera House. What to do? It was not our car, but Doug and I felt a moral obligation to Brian. We were just about out of money, including Brian. What would it cost just to tow it to a garage? Brian made the decision: "Pull off the license plates and let's go." License plates were hurriedly stuffed into backpacks, and we skedaddled hurriedly to the nearest subway. Brian thought no one could trace the car to him until he was long gone. That car may still be parked in front of the opera for all I know. We later rationalized that the city sold the car for more than the towing fee. Surprising how not doing the right thing can be rationalized away. Not a very honorable thing on our part.

We made it to another youth hostel in France, but it was really difficult for the three of us, with three large backpacks, to hitchhike. With small cars being prevalent we had to split up. Brian was ready to go back to Germany, Doug wanted to see Spain, and I needed be back in the U.S. for college. Four of us, all high-school friends, were transferring together from Ventura Junior College to Fresno State. I hitchhiked to the coast, caught a boat to England and then a train to London. Brian and Doug went their separate ways. It turned out the return trip by ship would not work out in time for me to start school, so I flew home. Best I recall it was on a TWA aircraft, my first-ever flight on a commercial plane. It was a time when people traveled by plane in coat and tie. I had no tie but a pretty good coat and managed to pass muster. It was long before credit cards, and I had just enough money to buy the plane ticket but since I was out of cash I hadn't eaten much of anything in the three days waiting for the flight. I was famished. Somehow, the stewardesses picked up on my plight and continued to bring me sandwiches after serving the regular meal. I must've eaten six or eight. We landed in New York, and I thought, Wow I'm home! I was happy to be back but also a little melancholy knowing the trip had ended. We saw and did about everything that could be done with little money and living plainly in youth hostels and on low-priced food. None of that really mattered. It had been a marvelous time, enjoyable and certainly educational, meeting so many different people. I would not trade that experience for any fancy trip. We saw the famous cities, buildings, statues, and museums, but some of the best times for me were the drives through the Italian, Swiss, German, Austrian, and French Alps, never knowing what you would see around the next bend.

In New York, I went through immigration and then to customs. Remember that Italian shotgun and pistol purchased in Rome? They were in my suitcase and the customs officer asked what was in the suitcase. There was no x-raying of luggage or even screening of passengers for flights in those days. I told him truthfully about the pistol and a shotgun I had purchased overseas. That got his attention, and he informed me I would be arrested as soon as I stepped out of the airport into New York, and he waved me through. You can bet I hustled with my luggage to a connecting flight. But the hook was set hard, and my wanderlust ways continue to this day: over 79 countries, 64 years later. By the way, the Simpson and Browning shotguns arrived by post. If you noticed, all three shotguns cost about the same, around $300 each. They made an impressive battery of shotguns for a young guy. The stock on the Beretta broke at the pistol grip. I sent a letter and picture of the break to the gun shop in Rome, showing a flaw in the wood. Lo and behold, they sent me a new stock. The nice wood on the broken stock was not wasted and can still be seen as grips on a favorite .38 Smith & Wesson Chiefs Special.

Going to College

In high school I was more interested in farms and orchards than college prep courses although I did particularly enjoy history classes. I more or less centered my school interest in agriculture. I have always liked being outside and I worked on ranches, farms, and orchards. Additionally, I worked after school from the fourth grade on and didn't participate in school athletics, clubs, or the many extracurricular activities. The Boy Scouts and the junior rifle team were my major activities in all four years of high school. Between that and working several different jobs, I simply didn't have time for extra school club activities. Because of my fine teacher Mr. Woods, who was the advisor, I was active in the Future Farmers of America, and I was also a member of the science club but only because another of my favorite teachers, Mr. Ricards, taught science and was the club advisor. Our high school career counselor, Mr. Ely, convinced my mother and me that I should go on to college. Many of my friends went on to prestigious universities: Robert Uffen, Byron Edde, and Lou Grivetti all went to the University of California at Berkeley; my girlfriend Charla Leavens went to Stanford. To put it in polite terms, those of us less academically qualified or those without funds were left with the junior college option. Even then, I nearly missed it as I was known as a good hard worker, and I'd worked for many of the local rancher; I knew I could get a good job anywhere. However, many of my good buddies: Manny Vanegas, Wayne Bailey, Doug Udall, Coy Thomas, George Dabney, and others were going to Ventura Junior College and that helped tip the scales; I joined them.

Ventura Junior College was only 10 miles from Santa Paula, but several of us carpooled. My father let me borrow his car every fifth or sixth week when it was my turn to drive. In my stories titled "Jobs," I tell of working during Ventura College days at the U.S. Post Office before and after school during the week.

Work at the post office started at 5:00 a.m., and that allowed me to get in two and a half hours every morning before heading to school. Wayne Bailey was studying agriculture, and he also had an afternoon job, so we always hustled to get back to Santa Paula. Mr. Aspinwall was our professor in agriculture, and he was good, but it became increasingly evident that owning a citrus or avocado orchard was a bridge too far, at least in the foreseeable future. Nevertheless, in 1958 I graduated from Ventura Junior College with an AA degree in agriculture. My mother, grandmother, and a couple of aunts came to my graduation. When I transferred to Fresno in 1958, I changed my major to social studies. While I didn't recognize it at the time, Ventura College was really a major milestone in my life. If Ventura had not been there, I would have most likely not gone to college and therefore would have missed the many great opportunities that opened up because I had a college degree. Community or junior colleges rank high for me.

Two guys I became friends with were also just out of high school—Mike Bodle and David Scholle. They were already fast friends, and we were in the same agriculture courses. Mike was a handsome dude and attracted the ladies. Of course, having a new Ford coupe didn't hurt his attraction. We palled around a bit and would often meet to go bowling with David in Oxnard. Mike's mother was a McGrath.

The McGrath family was a dynasty, a prominent and very powerful family in Ventura County. They had vast farming properties in the Ventura, Oxnard, and the Camarillo area. I had lunch once with Mike in their huge family home, three or four stories high, that stuck out like a castle in the middle of their Oxnard farm fields. Mike never said it, but it appeared to me that his mother and father were separated. He lived with his mother, who took care of her elderly father. I was at lunch one time with Mike, his mother, and his grandfather, who was frail and could hardly speak. He was assisted by a nurse who sat at the table and fed him. Mike did not have to get his hands dirty in his farming. David, on the other hand, worked out in the field with his dad, and it showed in the stained creases of his hands. But they were prominent also, and I think owned more than a section of prime farming soil for vegetables and fruit. Like Mike, David was driving a new car when I met them, and they weren't making car payments. I liked them both, and we made several trips together to Las Vegas. They never acted like they had money, and I don't think they really had a lot of cash. It was just that their families were worth a ton of money.

On our Vegas trips, we would chip in to have a total of five dollars stashed in the car ashtray to ensure we would have enough money to get home. I was never going to go down to less than five dollars in my own pocket, but they were both gamblers and weren't worried about a flare-out. Gas was only 25 cents a gallon at the time. The Vegas Strip wasn't fully developed, just a few casinos: the Tropicana, the Sands, and maybe the Riviera, but nothing like it is today. The Flamingo was operating, and although Bugsy Siegel had been murdered In 1947, the bouncers made me think the Mafia was still in charge. They wore civilian suits or sport coats. The legal age for drinking was 21, and we were not of age. Coat and tie were the expected dress of the day so we would dutifully walk into the casino wearing coat and tie. The bouncers were quite recognizable even in their civilian dress—they were gorillas. They would look at us and give us a little nod, basically saying, "We know you're not 21, and you know that we know you're not. Don't even think about giving us any trouble." It was plain, and we nodded back subserviently. Both Mike and Dave liked to gamble but really it was mostly just poker and blackjack as they never had a lot of money. I was far too tight to risk my hard-earned cash and just casually fooled around with slot machines or watched them at the blackjack table. The real draw for me was the lounge (bar) shows that were free. All you had to do was buy a drink and nobody bothered you even if you nursed it along through the whole show. My favorite, hands down, was Louis Prima and Keely Smith, one of his five wives. They put on a super show. Sometimes you could pick up a free drink even playing the slots, and I mostly just had a beer, but both Mike and David liked mixed drinks. We didn't stay in the casino hotels because they were too expensive. We stayed at one of the motels close to the big hotels and casinos. Breakfast was free in many of the casinos in those days, and often there was enough free food at night that we didn't have to waste money on chow. All Vegas stories needn't be told, but we had great times on those little sojourns— drinking openly at the casinos while we were still considered juveniles and not allowed to frequent bars in California. It was just great fun. Mike is gone now, but David is still farming near Camarillo.

Going to college at Fresno State (now called University of California at Fresno) was next. The four of us, Manny Vanegas, George Dabney, Coy Thomas, and I had all gone to high school and Ventura Junior College together. We rented an old house at 516 South 5th Street in the small town of Clovis. It was just off Main Street and only 15 minutes from the college. The place was a two-bedroom, one bath house of tongue-and-groove construction without insulation and no heating or A/C. One bedroom was very small, and George took that one while Manny and I shared the second bedroom. It had a back porch, and Coy used that for his bedroom. The owner, Mrs. Dallas, was a sweet, elderly, widowed woman who had lived in the house for many years. She had recently moved in with her daughter and we did not see her much, but she liked us, and we liked her. Also, we paid the rent on time and fixed anything that needed fixing without bothering her. Trying to attract some girls, we decided to have a party at our house. That required some decorations, which ended up being rather crude signs on the front porch and over the front door, inviting people inside. The neighbors squealed, and Mrs. Dallas thought we were opening a real bar or a dance hall in her home. She appeared with her daughter and a town cop. Not only did she disapprove of drinking, but dancing was also in question. I believe her church group convinced her debauchery was imminent. Of course, that is exactly what we had in mind. After a lengthy conversation, explanations, and pleading, Mrs. Dallas finally agreed to let us have a party. However, all signs had to be removed, even the less offensive "come in for a cold beer, wet T-shirt candidates welcome," and "no picking your nose while dancing." Also, the party had to end at midnight, and all the girls had to leave. The party ended at midnight—at least the formal party.

Manny borrowed my car on another Saturday night. It was a 1950 gray four-door Dodge sedan, hardly a chick magnet but all I could afford after my hitchhiking trip through Europe. I bought the car from a high school buddy, Alex Villa, for two hundred bucks. Manny was not normally a heavy drinker, but when he did drink heavily, he kept everyone in the house up with his walrus-strong snoring. I tried turning him over with his face down a couple times, but then worried he would suffocate. We all suffered. Sunday morning after he had borrowed the car, we slept in. Manny finally quit snoring, but he was dead in the water, so to speak. George went out of the house but quickly returned to tell me my car had been wrecked. The back light on the driver's side had been busted in, and the chrome rim was missing. We all (except Manny) went out to look and discovered the front light on the same side had also been bashed and the chrome dented. The paint around the light and front fender was badly scratched but fortunately not dented. How do you break out the back light and the front light? Manny was clueless as to what happened. He could not remember anything, not where he had been or even who he was with. Minor dings on my car were not a great catastrophe, but we were all worried what amount of damage Manny may have caused. It was agreed the prudent maneuver would be to deploy the wounded Dodge to the rear of the house for a rest and to keep it from unfriendly prying eyes. There it sat in quarantine for three weeks. Manny didn't have a car and Coy didn't even have a driver's license much less a car, so George had to haul all three of us around. He got tired of that rather quickly, and we made the trip to a junkyard and managed to pick up chrome rims and lights. Once that was done, we went to Earl Scheib for a paint job. They offered a cheap special for $49.95, but that only included masking (covering parts that were not to be painted with tape) the windows. The deluxe job for $99.95 included all the masking of door handles and chrome trim, hood ornament, etc. Manny was paying half, so we took the deluxe job, and the old drab gray-colored Dodge turned into a rich brown color. Unfortunately, it was still a rather dull 1950 four-door sedan even with new paint. The Air Force cadets call the ugly, black-rimmed issue eyeglasses, which look like they've come out of a Walmart sales bin, birth-control specs as no self-respecting girl would come close to anyone wearing them. My Dodge proved to fit in the same category.

We didn't live in a modern dorm, had no maid, cafeteria, or laundry service, and didn't belong to a fraternity. We had no rules or any particular need for extracurricular activities. I think we all rather enjoyed our circumstances, and we did whatever we wanted whenever we wanted. We went to social and sporting functions as we saw fit without any membership or obligation dragging us along. Of course, we started as juniors and were past the freshman level of trying to belong. We just wanted to get through college and maybe learn something. Coy was the best student, but we all worked at being good students. The courses I enjoyed most were in the social sciences, behavioral science, history, criminology, and geography. The criminology professor had been a street cop, a detective, and a deputy chief. He was sort of a "been there—done that" kind of guy, not just an academic. His classes were quite entertaining with some of his stories. He carried a concealed pistol, and when he found out I had a California concealed-carry permit I became one of his guys. One of his classes actually included pistol shooting, and naturally I got an A grade in that class. One of the few, I must admit.

Neither Manny, Coy, nor I had a parent visit us in college. George's folks on the other hand visited several times, and we loved it because his dad always took us all to dinner at one of the fancy restaurants that offered a big all-you-can-eat salad bar and then both fish and steaks. His dad was a Texan and a large man with a solid presence. I liked him better than I liked George, and I liked George. He had worked for Humble Oil before the war and helped open the King Ranch to oil exploration. He bought George a new 1957 Ford

Long Shots — Early Days

as a high-school graduation present; George was the only one in our class to receive such a grand gift. That car was a pretty good girl catcher. We all went home for the holidays, and after getting used to the dry hot Fresno climate, Santa Paula with its cool ocean breezes felt cold for the first day or so. Driving on Highway 126 from Castaic just after crossing over the Los Angeles County line, one can often catch the beautiful perfume of citrus tree blossoms in Ventura County.

All of us had help from our parents for those last two years of college. We were able to get along with $100 each per month. That included rent, food, tuition, books, and gas. For sure, we didn't eat steaks, and the old house was a wreck, but we graduated in our fourth year of college.

My father gave me $900 each of the last two years to cover the nine months of my living and school cost. It was about time I started paying my own way, so I went to the Citizens State Bank in Santa Paula and applied for a loan of $1,000. Mr. Shively was the bank president and knew me and my father, so the loan was quickly approved. The interest was low, and the payback time allowed was long. Whatever it was, I had paid off in half the time, but that loan really helped me propel my life to a higher level, and I was hired to teach in a wealthy district of the Fresno City Schools. Just from my own experience, I remain much in favor of student loans, provided the recipients pay the loan off as we all should.

By the way, Mr. Shively, the bank president, is Douglas Shively, the well-known landscape painter from Santa Paula. Most of his paintings are of areas around Ventura County and are easily recognized, often depicting the local foothills and eucalyptus trees. He was a contemporary and close friend of Jessie Arms Botke also of Santa Paula who became quite a celebrated California artist known for beautiful paintings of birds, particularly parrots and peacocks. I purchased a couple of small paintings from Mrs. Botke when I was an Air Force lieutenant. Sadly, they have since slipped away.

Later, I earned a master's degree in international relations from Troy University by going to school at night and on weekends in the late 1970s. College didn't make me any smarter, but it certainly enhanced my knowledge and opened avenues and opportunities that enriched my life beyond measure.

Dad and Mom circa 1940

Mom—bottom right in the light colored blouse as a Rosie Riveter working at Lockheed during WW II

Dad with one of his taxis - note the tie and cap in 1947

My brother Bob and I next to the teardrop camper – my private bedroom at home but used on trips by my parents. My brother and I slept in the car

Our family in front of my grandmother's house dressed for church

The 1957 pink Lincoln Premiere loaned to five high school buddies for a cross country trip. L-R Manny Vanegas, Randal Best, Doug Udall, Richard Hyde

Five California boys on my Uncle Elmer Wagner's farm in Iowa. L-R Doug Udall, Randall Best, DDB, Richard Hyde, Manny Vanegas

Our wedding in February of 1967. I am proudly wearing my new Captain's bars

My father with his little brother and sister, Arlo and Neta —circa 1912

My mother with Bob and me—1945

A two gun dangerous man - 1946

II

MILITARY

In the Army Now

As the song goes: "You're in the Army now; you're not behind the plow; you'll never get rich digging a ditch, you're in the Army now."

While it would be nice to say I joined the military as the act of a patriot doing his duty, alas, that was not the case. I am a patriot but there was no war on, or a driving need to join the military at that time. It was a beautiful spring day in Fresno in 1962. I was teaching at Hamilton Junior High School and had grown quite comfortable with my eighth-grade students, the school staff and Mr. Lehr, the principal. It started out a little rough as I had hoped to teach high school but ended up with younger kids. In fact, my first week at Hamilton I asked myself, "What am I doing here?" The cacophony was unbelievable in the hallways between classes and at recess. Within the classroom the kids were good, and I have to admit I really became attached to my students. I still have my wooden desk nameplate signed by all the kids on my last day at school.

Fresno was an excellent school district and paid teachers well. My yearly salary was $5,500—good pay for a teacher in 1962. In those days men wore coat and tie to school, and the kids were well behaved and receptive to learning. The students addressed teachers as Mr., Mrs., or Miss. One of my duties included working with the school's junior rifle program, which was part of the California Cadet Corps—sort of a junior ROTC. We practiced shooting .22-caliber rifles, using reduced targets and bullet traps on the stage of our school auditorium.

Of course, this was great fun for me, and I'm proud to say we won the state championship in Sacramento that year. What a super

99

bunch of kids I had. The rifle program also got me into an Army uniform and commissioned as a second lieutenant in the California Cadet Corps, with relative rank in the California Army National Guard.

And then, BOOM! Here comes a flying missile from the draft board telling me I have been drafted into the United States Army and to report in July. Really quite an unexpected surprise as it was before our heavy commitments in Vietnam. Not really bad news or even shocking, just a surprise. While I enjoyed Hamilton, the principal, the fine staff (who were very helpful to me), and all my kids, I was getting restless and ready for a little more excitement. Mr. William Lehr, our excellent principal, wanted me to stay and offered me the opportunity to teach science or math. At that time deferments from the draft were offered to teachers in those fields. My California General Teaching Credential allowed me to teach any subject for any grade from 6 through 14 so I could actually teach at a junior college. Still, it was time to move on and leave my comfortable environment. There was no way I was going to take any kind of deferment although there was not much of a stigma or shame at that time. Vietnam was a distant country not yet on the radar screen.

Earlier in the spring I had earned a spot on the California State High-Power Rifle Team. This team would represent California at the United States National Championship Matches, which have been held at Camp Perry, (named in honor of the hero of Lake Erie) Ohio, since 1907. This was really a big deal—each state sends a team to this match and the members are paid transportation costs. That amounted to $250, a considerable amount when my teacher salary was not much more than $600 a month. Now I had a dilemma. The national high-power rifle championship was held in August, and my reporting date for the selective service was in July. What to do? I decided to go in person and appeal to the draft board.

Ventura County, was my legal residence, so I got an appointment to visit the local draft board at the county seat. Turned out the board was three old guys—at the time I thought they were anyway, probably in their 50s and 60s. I had a letter from the California Rifle and Pistol Association on gorgeous letterhead with a beautiful California Golden Bear verifying I had made the state team and requesting an adjustment

Long Shots — Military

of my reporting so I could represent the state of California. Of course, I had no idea what to expect from this powerful group, but to my great relief the meeting turned out to be informal and relaxed. To me it was a very important matter as I had shot my way onto the team and really wanted to represent my state. The California Team was always one of the top teams in the nation, and I wanted to be a part of that team. After laying out my case and presenting the letter from the California Rifle and Pistol Association, I explained my desire to join the military after Camp Perry, which would be held the middle of August. The board became congenial, and one board member said his brother had shot at Camp Perry on the Navy team. They all started nodding and agreed to delay my reporting date. One member suggested that my reporting date be changed to the end of September. (That decision comes into play later).

So, there I was, free for Camp Perry followed by entry into the U.S. Army. Or, as it turned out, maybe not. The Marines came marching into the picture. In July 1962, the Marine Corps hosted an NRA regional rifle match combined with a Director of Civilian Marksmanship (DCM) competition that capped off the final day. This event was held at Camp Matthews, adjacent to Camp Pendleton near San Diego. The Marines were a huge influence in Southern California target shooting with many of their top shooters stationed at Camp Pendleton or the 29 Palms Marine Corps base. Besides being top riflemen, they looked and acted like someone I wanted to be. One could not help being impressed. Marines had taught marksmanship at a couple of Boy Scout camps where our Troop 301 attended. They held my highest respect.

The military M1 Garand was "my rifle," and I was shooting it well. It was the service rifle for the national matches in those days and was the required rifle for the excellence in competition match (often referred to as a leg match). The leg match was the prestige event, and winners were awarded a badge that was worn on the service uniform. This was the same for all services including the Coast Guard. Even some police departments made it a part of their uniform. Civilians are also eligible for this badge. "Every man a rifleman" is a Marine Corps creed so you can imagine the importance and the competition

101

to be able to wear this very special badge. These leg medals are also a steppingstone to the coveted solid gold Distinguished Badge. As best I can recall, we had a couple of hundred shooters competing in that match. It was shot at 200, 300 and 600 yards, and, of course, the M1 has iron sights (no scope).

Guess who won the match. I was pleasantly surprised, but the Marines were shocked. As good sportsmen, they were generous with many handshakes and pats on the back. I suspect deep down they wanted to kill me. Remember we were on a Marine Corps base with Marines competing, and a Marine general would be making the presentation to a stupid civilian, an unknown, hardly old enough to be a butter bar (2d Lt). Being quite chuffed with myself would be an understatement. Then I learned later one of the Marines, a warrant officer, who congratulated me had won an Olympic medal. That brought me back down to earth. Most of my medals have been given to the National Firearms Museum in Washington, D.C., the California Rifle and Pistol Association, or the Texas Rifle and Pistol Association. But that first gold leg medal with silver crossed M1s is still in my living room.

On to Camp Perry and the national matches in August. This is really the Mecca of competitive high-power shooting in the United States. The California team was a standout, and the best part for me was being a member of that super team. The Herrick Trophy Match is one of the major long-range team events.

It dates from 1907 and is named after a former governor of Ohio. The rules allow any rifle and any sight so naturally we were shooting heavy rifles with scopes—Winchester Model 70s with Unertl target scopes. This was the same scope and rifle Carlos Hathcock, the famous Marine Corps sniper, used in Vietnam on his first deployment. It is a four-man team match shot at 1,000 yards, and the rules allow for an outside coach. We used a Marine volunteer from Camp Pendleton, and he was good. The match is conducted with two team members shooting side by side in turn. One shooter fires his rifle, and the target is lowered in the pits for scoring and then run back up for the second shooter to fire. We used the same two rifles with the second pair of shooters taking over from the first pair. This was done so the second shooters would shoot rifles that were already zeroed in and be less

Long Shots — Military

likely to screw up the team score with their first shot. One of our rifles was a .30-338, and the other was a .35 Whelen.

I was put on this four-man team because I could squeeze the trigger and call my shots—absolutely essential in a team match as the coach has to make the decision on sight adjustments after each man fires and calls his shot. Calling your shot is telling the coach where you think the bullet hit the target. The coach makes adjustments for the next shooter based on the previous shooter's call and estimated wind conditions. You and your shooting partner have to depend on each other's call for the coach to give proper sight adjustment instruction.

Problem was, I had never really used this type of scope or any scope, for that matter. These old Unertl scopes were mounted on the barrel by a rail, and the scope slid forward after the recoil of the fired shot, so it had to be manually pulled back into battery after every shot. Not long into the match I shot a four rather than a bull's-eye five, costing the team one point. Then I followed with another four. I was struggling to see through the center of the scope and had lifted my head off the proper position on the stock. The shots looked good to me, but were either high or low, so it was not the coach making bad calls on the wind. Team time was ticking away, and it looked like I could not hit my tail. Well, not that bad, but it seemed like it to me. The Marine coach realized what was happening and reached down and tapped me, rather sternly, on my pointed head and told me to pull the scope back after each shot. Happily, I can report keeping the remaining shots in the black for a score of 98, which was acceptable but hardly anything to brag about. Surprising as it was, we were the high civilian team and were awarded the Port Clinton Trophy. One of the Marine Corps teams won the match, but our score of 596-81 V's was second and set a new civilian 1000-yard record. All the other service teams were shocked to have a civilian team beating them.

News moved quickly down the line of this new record, and we were hanging around, kind of basking in the sun over our accomplishment. Coming down the line toward us was a small group in uniform attracting lots of attention. Clearly, they were important, as people were standing up and some coming to attention as they grew closer. It turned out they were coming to congratulate

103

us! It was Lt Gen Edward W. Snedeker and several Marine Corps colonels. No one does PR better than the Marine Corps – they are masters. Gen Snedeker congratulated our team and our Marine Corps coach. Winning the match with a new record score was a considerable accomplishment. And he bragged on us as only the Marines can do. We were, of course, on cloud nine when one of the team members said, "Behrens is going in the Army." Gen Snedeker looked at me and said, "He looks like a Marine to me." Then he told me if I could speak a foreign language, he would give me a direct commission. I told the general that I did not speak a foreign language, and he repeated I should be in the Marine Corps anyway. Quite flattering, to say the least. Gen Snedeker was a 1926 graduate of the Naval Academy. He was awarded the Navy Cross for his valor as commander of the Seventh Marine Regiment in 1945 during the battle of Okinawa. For those not familiar with military decorations, only the Medal of Honor ranks higher than the Navy Cross.

It took about a week to drive home from Ohio to Santa Paula, California, in those days. Remember, the interstate highway system wasn't complete and the speed limit in many places was still 55 miles per hour. When I got home my mother told me she had received several calls from a captain in Los Angeles. I shot target pistol many times at the Los Angeles Police Academy, so she thought it was a policeman calling about pistol shooting. The caller said it was rather important and urgent that he speak to me. It turned out the caller was a Marine Corps recruiting officer, and he had been ordered to come see me in person.

About the same time Air Force First Lieutenant Gene Taft, the cousin by marriage of my high-school friend John Brock, was visiting Santa Paula. Gene was a handsome dude with a Robin Olds mustache, and he was an F4 fighter pilot. Turns out he was on leave, and I think couldn't find any of his buddies to play with during the work week, so he asked me if I'd like to go with him to Oxnard Air Force Base. He wanted to check the promotion list he thought might have been published while he was on leave. Gene was driving an Oldsmobile 88, and it was hot. We took off, and as soon as we cleared town we were going 90 miles an hour. The speed limit was 55. We were flying,

Long Shots — Military

and Gene seemed to care less about speed limits or possible cops—he just flew down the road. Sure enough, he was selected and was on the promotion list to captain, so we started flying home in his Olds 88. Only we didn't go home. I mentioned my dilemma about the Army or the Marine Corps, asking which would be best. Keep in mind, my interest was to shoot rifle competitively with the top shooters; I had no intention of making military service a career.

Gene said, "No, no, no" (in stronger terms) to both the Army and the Marine Corps. He wanted me to see an Air Force recruiter, so he detoured and headed to Ventura. The recruiter was a born salesman armed with a good story and finally ended with a very good question. "What are you going to do when you get out of the Army or the Marine Corps? What skills will you have learned?" Putting my thinking cap on, I began to realize it might be prudent to think about the future. I had not contacted anyone in the Army about getting on their rifle team so did not know where I might end up. The recruiter offered several different career fields that would be guaranteed if I enlisted in the Air Force, and that was enticing. The deed was done, and papers were signed. Remember, my Army reporting date was the end of September. I reported for duty at Lackland Air Force Base on 24 September 1962. The Army may still be looking for me. The Marine recruiting officer in Los Angeles was not happy when I told him it was too late.

Captain-select Gene Taft could very well have saved my life. *Quien sabe?* Fast forward a few years and I was in Vietnam—shot at by small arms (which is quite personal), under rocket and mortar attacks, and a satchel bomb, with several close calls. I served during Tet in 1968. Everyone was in danger—but my danger was minuscule compared to the grunts and leathernecks who slugged it out in the field. They were the heroes, and we lost more than 58,200 of our best in Vietnam. Luckily, I was not a Marine or Army trooper at that time.

The rest of the story of my march to join the military concerns the Marine Lieutenant General. After finding that I had joined the Air Force he sent me a letter. That letter has slipped away over the years, but it was another complimentary note on our team winning the Herrick Trophy at Camp Perry. But it was so much more; the

105

last line was "Congratulations, you have joined a fine service and I wish you fair winds." Think about it—I had already been sworn in by the Air Force and no chance left to join the Marines. But here was a Marine Lieutenant General (a very considerable big shot), taking the time to wish a young nobody fair winds. A thoughtful gesture from a fine gentleman. I will never forget Lt Gen Snedeker. A good lesson in leadership and remembering everyone is somebody. By the way, my pay went from $611 per month as a teacher to $222, plus a food allowance of $47 per month as a second lieutenant.

Air Force

The Air Force really made me who I am. I had good parents and a fine upbringing in Southern California and on the farms of Iowa, with Boy Scouts, Future Farmers of America, and an excellent high school. I had teachers, aunts, cousins, grandparents, uncles, and many good role models contributing to wonderful experiences growing up with lifelong friends. But, with the Air Force, I became bigger by belonging to something much bigger than myself. I hear people looking for a meaning in life—I was much too busy working to worry about such things. On a more philosophical note, maybe my destiny was to serve our country in the military—a group that has a clear purpose. There was no epiphany in this; it just happened or perhaps evolved. The Air Force fit me and I fit the Air Force. I'm immensely proud of being in the Air Force and eternally grateful for the opportunities it offered me.

  The Air Force allowed me to travel the world to live in different countries to learn from them and appreciate different customs, religions, and life experiences. It also whet my appetite to travel beyond my military requirements. I was able to see and do things far beyond my wildest dreams. My first assignments were in the field, or as we say, the trenches. My later years were served in senior headquarters. I guess you could say I moved through assignment levels and enjoyed it all. It was my great privilege to work with the finest people on the planet. Most all the officers I worked for were of strong moral character and I naturally wanted to emulate them. The enlisted men who worked for me or with me were top of the line. The people were always the best part of the Air Force, the other U.S. military services, NATO and foreign services I worked with. I still miss it—the sense of mission, the excitement, and especially the great young guys who kept me young and never disappointed me. More will be said about them later in this text. The real value was the deep respect I gained for the Air Force—the customs, history, and the character it builds. It is like a family with the highest moral values. Duty and mission trump all else no matter how painful or personally hurtful it may be. Do the right thing every single time. That takes courage. I owe the Air Force one especially great debt—I met my wife over 60 years ago in the Air Force.

  Volumes would be required to cover my experiences in the Air Force. Some of those will be covered elsewhere but for now I'm submitting a letter I wrote to the Chief of Staff of the Air Force, General Merrill A. McPeak, when I retired. It may sound like I'm bragging and maybe that's true, but I wanted to tell the Chief what a grand time I had, other than strictly normal duties. On my last day of active duty, on 31 December 1992 with over 30 years' service, I stopped in to pay respects and say goodbye to the Chief. We had served together when he was a colonel at Ramstein AFB, Germany. I reiterated what a wonderful career it had been and professed it to be the best career of anyone in the Air Force. He tapped the four stars on his shoulder, and I said that was true, but he certainly did not have the fun I had. Gen McPeak laughed and said that was indisputable.

OFFICE OF THE UNITED STATES REPRESENTATIVE
MILITARY COMMITTEE
NORTH ATLANTIC TREATY ORGANIZATION
WASHINGTON, D.C. 20310

16 November 1992

General Merrill A. McPeak
Chief of Staff
United States Air Force

Dear General McPeak:

December will be my last month in the Air Force and I have long thought that at the time of my retirement I should write to our Chief of Staff and tell him what rewarding service I have enjoyed in my career. It is especially gratifying for me to be able to tell that to you, someone I know, had the honor of working with, and respect.

My career has been challenging and satisfying. I have had five overseas tours and have been in eight different MAJCOMS/separate operating agencies: ATC; PACAF (Vietnam); HQCMD (4th ATAF); USAFE; MPC; PACOM (8th Army, Korea); USAFE (AAFCE and 4th ATAF); OJCS; ESC; and JCS (NATO). These assignments have given me the opportunity to see many different sides of our Air Force and have introduced me to the other U.S. Services, members of NATO, and varied allied forces. Hopefully, I have been able to make a contribution to the Air Force and our country in these diverse assignments.

Being in the Air Force has allowed me to travel all over the world and to see and do things that even millionaires and celebrities do not have the opportunity to see and do--things that simply cannot be purchased. Being an officer has enabled me to do things that I never dreamed of as a young man. The status of being an officer provided me the opportunities to shoot and hunt with the lords and ladies of Europe, senior civic leaders, industrialists, and others who were far above my economic class. Many friendships were developed and continue to this day.

The people I have worked for and with have brought my highest reward. In my present assignment I have been privileged to be the executive assistant to five different four-star general/flag officers, and I consider that to have been a real honor (also a test of survival). Several general officers have helped me in promoting MWR and shooting programs. Among them were Generals Huyser, Bellis, White, and Teagarden in Europe during the seventies, and more recently, Generals Oaks and Davis. Generals Peek, Pickett, Beckel, and Nelson also were very helpful to me and our teams. All provided fine examples of interest in morale and welfare programs for service personnel. Many very fine officers worked for me over my 30 years service and certainly some of the best NCOs in the world.

In addition to all this, I have had the extra bonus of being on the Air Force Shooting Team and have been able to continue that throughout my career. This allowed me to remain in contact with our young Air Force members and has been a continuing source of satisfaction as I saw them progress. Additionally, I am pleased to have had some considerable shooting success personally. I was the team captain and high scorer on the *first* and *only* Air Force team ever to win the most prestigious of all high power rifle events, the National Rifle Team Trophy. I was Air Force High Power Champion in the days when we had many competitors and all the commands had strong teams. Twice I won the General White Trophy at the U.S. Championships, the *only* officer ever to do so. Additionally, I won the 1000 yard service rifle title at the Interservice Championship, setting a new record. And, the following year I won the Navy Cup. I am a member of the President's Hundred and hold the Distinguished Rifleman Badge.

Even more rewarding to me have been the many accomplishments of those I coached or for whom I acted as team captain. Two people I worked with were selected for the U.S. Olympic Trap Team--one earned the Gold Medal. One of my team members, SSgt Bobby Smith, was the *first* and *only* Air Force shooter to win the National Individual High Power Rifle Trophy. Another of my shooters, SSgt David Thompson, was the *first* and *only* Air Force shooter ever to win the highly coveted President's Hundred Award. He received a personal letter from the President of the United States for that accomplishment. Additionally, this year one of my shooters won the Silver Medal in Olympic trap at the Interservice Championship, beating out full time shooters on the Army and the Marine Corps Teams, and nearly-full-time shooters in the Reserves and National Guard. Many others I worked with have had great success. These people all had enormous talent and would have, no doubt, achieved high laurels without my help; however, I do believe that I was of assistance to them.

Among special privileges I enjoyed was being team captain for the U.S. Hunters Team at the German National Championship five times and at the International Hunters Championship three times. Another highlight was coaching cadets from the Air Force Academy and the Naval Academy. In September of this year I was honored to be selected as Mission Chief to take the United States team to the first World Military Championship (Modern Pentathlon) sponsored by Russia. Our team set the standard and I was gratified when the Russians told me the U.S. team was clearly the most military and disciplined of all contestants.

It has truly been a tremendous career with unlimited satisfaction and endless rewards. It will be very difficult for me to leave. I intend to maintain my contacts in the shooting and sports world and hope to continue helping in some capacity with our programs. I have felt great pride in serving in the Air Force and would not trade my career for anything--except, maybe, a set of gold bars and the chance to do it all over again.

I thank you as our leader for our wonderful Air Force and I thank our Air Force for giving me the enormous opportunity of being part of the best military service the world has ever seen.

Very Respectfully,

D.D. BEHRENS
Colonel, USAF
Executive Assistant

Long Shots — Military

A brief outline of assignments might be in order for military or prior military readers. Some of my most enjoyable or most satisfying will be covered separately. The Army Air Force came from the Army Air Corp. The United States Air Force was born when President Harry Truman signed the national security act establishing an independent service on 26 July 1947 while on board the Sacred Cow, an AC 54 aircraft inherited from President Franklin Roosevelt. I entered the Air Force in September 1962 after receiving a draft notice, turning down a deferment for teaching, which at that time would not have been dishonorable as we were not at war, and Vietnam was still a distant shadow. I actually received a notice to report for Army duty. But I was interested in the Air Force or the Marine Corps shooting team and finally decided on the Air Force. Had I chosen the Marines, which is a great sister service, I expect I would either be dead or a general.

In any case, the Air Force turned out great. By some miracle I managed to finish officer training school (OTS) as a distinguished graduate in the class of 63 D with a final parade and commissioning on 21 December 1962. We had 739 graduates in our class at Lackland Air Force Base. The largest portion of our class was housed at Medina which is an Air Force installation adjacent to Lackland. Medina had up-to-date buildings and new quarters. I was on the Lackland side and we were billeted in what were temporary World War II barracks. I can tell you it can be darn cold in San Antonio and the wind went right through those old barracks. All the crazy stuff that goes on in training went on with us, sometimes fun and sometimes extra stupid. I recall one time we were scheduled for inspection and the tiny bit of grass we had around our barracks looked worse than unkempt—maybe a goat yard. There were no lawnmowers available. We were desperate to get our first weekend off and to look better we all lined up with whatever scissors could be mustered and cut and trimmed the grass. It worked, but that first weekend, actually only Saturday afternoon and night plus Sunday morning, my roommate and I got a motel room and slept the whole time. We were simply exhausted.

Lights out in the barracks was 10:00 p.m., and you couldn't finish studies by then so we had to go to flashlights. We were getting up at 4:30 a.m., but as underclassmen no one had time to make his bed inspection ready in the morning so most underclassmen slept on the floor to keep our beds inspection-ready and to keep from acquiring gigs (demerits) for not-perfect bed corners tucked tight enough to bounce quarters on the bed. Crazy, you think? That doesn't fit the brilliant 2014 commencement address at the University of Texas by Admiral William H. McRaven, but it was what it was.

Upperclassmen officers could give demerits and they were worse than training officers in that regard. Too many demerits could bar you from getting off on the weekend. To my surprise, many of my classmates were far ahead of me in Air Force terminology and knowledge—they knew flights from squadrons, and groups from wings, etc. I had a lot of catching up to do but I did it and was made an OTS captain by the time we were upperclassmen. OTS was really a walk in the park and while not always fun, most of us enjoyed it. Interestingly, while we were in training, the last Air Force officer candidate school (OCS) was being conducted at Lackland. OTS was jokingly said to make officers and gentlemen from college boys in 90 days. The OCS guys were candidates without college degrees (mostly prior enlisted) with a more rigorous and longer program than us 90-day wonders. I looked in on one OCS group in the chow hall and they were eating square meals. Try it sometime, lifting your fork or spoon straight up from your plate then straight level to your mouth, more or less half a square movement while sitting at attention. The military academies used to practice this with underclassmen.

We did have a little excitement in October during the Cuban missile crisis. Nikita Khrushchev and Fidel Castro had agreed to place Soviet nuclear missiles in Cuba. Construction of missile launch facilities had begun and some missiles had been delivered. President John F. Kennedy ordered a naval blockade to prevent additional missiles reaching Cuba. It was a very tense time and we were told war was imminent. Fortunately for the whole world, an agreement was reached and the Soviets removed their missiles. Secretly the U.S. was required to dismantle our missiles deployed in Turkey. Officer training went back to normal.

Long Shots — Military

My career has been challenging and satisfying. I've had five overseas tours (assignments) and have served in eight different major air commands (MAJCOM)/separate operating agencies. I began at Air Training Command at Lackland Air Force Base in Texas for OTS and then Mather Air Force Base in California. Following California, it was back to Lackland Air Force Base and assignment in the Air Force Marksmanship School.

Following was Pacific Air Force (PACAF), Nha Trang Air Base, Republic of Vietnam. Then Headquarters Command (4th Allied Air Force), Ramstein, Germany; U.S. Air Force Europe (Rhein Main AFB) Germany; the Military Personnel Center at Randolph Air Force Base, Texas; Headquarters United Nations/U.S. Air Forces Korea/Eighth Army Command at Youngsan, Korea; again at U.S. Air Force Europe, Ramstein Air Force Base, Germany; Office of the Joint Chiefs of Staff in the Pentagon; Electronic Security Command at Kelly Air Force Base in Texas; and my last assignment was back to the Pentagon.

These assignments have given me the opportunity to see many different sides of our Air Force and introduce me to the other U.S. services, members of NATO, and varied allied forces. Hopefully, I have been able to make a contribution to the Air Force in our country in these diverse assignments. I was able to see and do things that even multimillionaires and celebrities do not have the opportunity to see and do—experiences that simply cannot be purchased. Being an officer enabled me to do things that I never dreamed of as a young man. The status of being an officer provided me the opportunities to shoot and hunt with the lords and ladies of Europe, senior civic leaders, industrialists, leaders in business and finance, and others who were far above my economic class.

Many friendships were developed and continue to this day. My Air Force bosses were good role models and leaders. They rightly deserve to be credited in anything I may have achieved, as I gained something from each one of them. In most cases those named were my direct supervisor, or in a couple of cases, the person most directly influential in my chain of command at a particular assignment.

As one might expect, my first Air Force assignment was a real education. Somehow, I managed to be a distinguished graduate

113

(DG) out of officer training school at Lackland Air Force Base. Two good things came from being a DG, one being, I was offered a regular commission as opposed to starting with a reserve commission, which at the time was not very important to me, but it was rather prestigious. The value came later. The real immediate benefit was that DGs were allowed to select their first assignment from a list of available Air Force bases. Being from California and having gone to school at Fresno, I knew there were lots of competitive rifle matches in central California. Mather Air Force Base in Sacramento had a personnel officer opening so that settled the question. I went to work in the consolidated base personnel office (CBPO) in the Assignments Division.

My boss was Major Van, who had been in both World War II and the Korean War. Major Van had been an enlisted man and was on his last assignment prior to retirement. A good no-nonsense officer who didn't waste time on small talk, he really taught me a lot and gave me a good, solid footing in the personnel business.

Quarters on base at that time were pretty limited, and I was stuck in an ancient World War II wooden barracks with private rooms but sharing a bathroom. The rooms were really austere—one light hanging down from the middle of the room, one chair, one single bed, one floor lamp, a small table, and four metal lockers, the kind commonly used in gyms. The floors were linoleum covered with no insulation. The place was just plain cold in January. I was on the second floor and could hear those metal lockers being slammed shut from one end of the building to the other and even on the floor below. A couple of weeks of that living, and I was desperately looking for better quarters.

The students in navigator training at Mather were quartered in three-bedroom, two-bath houses. That would be a huge step up, and fortunately one spot became available when a young lieutenant failed the navigator course. I was quick to jump on the vacancy and became very close to my navigator roommates.

Now back to the job. I had six master sergeants working divisions under my authority. The truth is they more or less did their jobs without any "brilliant" leadership from me. Mather AF Base was known as the home of the navigators because that's where most of them trained, mostly in B-52 bombers. Believe it or not, the U.S. Air

Force is still using the B-52 after many upgrades, and it is the only U.S. bomber that can launch nuclear cruise missiles. We had second and first lieutenant students all over the place with classes graduating every month. Major Van watched that I didn't screw things up too bad and let the sergeants educate me. The one thing Major Van stressed was to never ever give out assignment locations to the graduating navigating officers. Those were to be given only to Lt Col squadron commanders who would pass them out according to class standing. I knew the rules, but remember I became very close to my new roommates who were graduating shortly. You can guess what happened. It was supposed to be a deep dark secret just between us, but, of course, the locations leaked out.

My roommate, who spilled the beans, had to stand "in front of the man," a Lt Col Squadron Commander who read him the riot act and stated he would have me dismissed from the Air Force. Of course, this scared the living bejeezus out of my roommate who had betrayed me, and he now hastened to warn me of the coming storm.

So, there it was, my first Air Force job under a great boss, and I screwed it up. Nothing to do but face the music, which was as dreadful as I anticipated it would be. It was gut wrenching, not the decision to tell the boss but realizing I had let him down. That had never happened to me before, and I was absolutely sick. I went to warn Major Van before the irate Lt Col could call, but he was busy and I had to wait, as they say, "longer than any clock could measure."

When he got free, I laid it on the line, and alerted Major Van that he was likely to get a call from a very irate Lt Col. Naturally, I was very much ashamed of myself for not following orders and letting my boss down. There was simply no excuse. Major Van to his credit, growled, but to my unbounding relief did not boil over. My transgression was deemed a misdemeanor—he was not worried about any mad Lt Col. I believe he could see, or sense how disgraced I felt—the matter was closed, and he never mentioned it again.

"Get on with your work." A very good lesson—don't allow friends or roommates to lead you off the path. And it was a fine example of leadership by Major Willis F. Van, who certainly had license to pound me hard. You can bet your bottom dollar it never happened again in my 30 Air Force years. He was my first boss in the Air Force.

I first went to the Air Force Marksmanship School and the AF Rifle Team in a temporary duty status. It was located at Lackland Air Force Base in Texas where Col George H. Van Deusen was the commander. He was a first-class gentleman and easy to be around: World War II P-51 fighter pilot, comfortable in his skin, strong but well liked and easy on the troops. No doubt it was his influence that brought me back for permanent duty with the Air Force rifle team, which had such a major impact on me and was an important factor in my decision to make the Air Force a career.

Colonel Thomas C. Kelly was my second commander at the Marksmanship School and certainly the most influential in Air Force shooting. Lieutenant Colonel J.D. Farris, chief of the consolidated personnel office (CBPO), was my boss in Vietnam where we were assigned to the 14th Combat Support Group, Nha Trang Air Base. Colonel Farris was tough to work for, demanding and quick-tempered, but he wanted it right. A couple of times he flew off the handle with me or my section (maybe for good cause), but later he would come around and hand me a cigar and we would smoke and talk casually for 10 or 15 minutes. It was just his way to reduce the sting a little. After Vietnam we became good friends—we hunted dove together, had dinners with our wives together, and I even bought properties from his real estate firm.

Lt Col William M. Coleman was my first boss at Ramstein Air Force Base in Germany. He was commander of Detachment 15, 1131 Special Activities Squadron. A good-natured guy, he knew his business and took care of his troops. It was a pleasure working for him. My next assignment was to the 322 Combat Support Group CBPO at Rhein Main Airbase, Germany. Lt Col John H.V. Lorch was the CBPO chief, and I was one of his many section chiefs. He was a real personnel professional and moved all of us around to different sections, which really broadened our knowledge of personnel functions. He interacted well with all of his section chiefs, who were all captains. Brig Gen Thomas M. Sadler was the wing commander, maybe flamboyant, but he got things done. In those days all our bases had football teams, and the competition was fierce. We had a scheduled game against

Long Shots — Military

Sembach Air Force Base. Gen Sadler arrived by helicopter just before the game, landing on the football field. The troops loved him. It was an enjoyable assignment. One Sunday I was pulling duty as officer of the day, pretty much wasting my day off in the headquarters building. One of the duties for the officer of the day was to meet all incoming VIPs— that would be colonels and above. An alert came in that Gen David C. Jones, Commander in Chief of Air Forces Europe, would soon arrive from the states. That was far beyond my pay grade. I advised Col Sadler (he had not yet been promoted to Brig Gen), and he hustled down to meet me on the flight line where we welcomed Gen Jones. The group moved into the headquarters conference room for coffee and friendly discussion before Gen Jones moved on to his headquarters in Weisbaden. He asked Col Sadler how things were going. Col Sadler answered something like, "Not worth a damn, we're short of this, we need more of that, we can't get this fixed, etc." I was shocked, more used to hearing things like we are doing fine. It was a good lesson for me to see a colonel telling a four-star general how things really were. Maybe not as they say these days, "truth to power," but the importance of laying out the truth.

The next move was from Germany to Randolph Air Force Base in Texas, home of the Air Force Personnel Center (MPC). It was the Mecca for personnel and, maybe appropriately, the base had a large tower nicknamed the Taj Mahal. My first boss there was Col John J. McHugh, who was chief of the support officer (non-flying) branch. Another first-class gentleman, he took care of his young officers. If you had a problem, he would get right down into the muck of things to help. If you were called to brief a higher-level officer, and he thought it could be difficult he would be right there with you. My second assignment at the Personnel Center was executive officer to the chief of officer personnel, who was Col Albert D. Audette, Jr. His deputy was Col Johnson, and he had a half dozen full colonels reporting to him with a significant number of lieutenant colonels, majors, and captains working for them. He was always enthusiastic and positive but somewhat erratic in his work schedule. He was a hard worker and might appear for work at 5:00 a.m. and sometimes stayed till 9:00 or 10:00 p.m. We had an assistant Senior Master Sergeant in the office so I had him come in at 5:00 a.m., and he could leave any time after 3:00 p.m. I came in at 7:00 a.m. and stayed till the Colonel departed. This was a busy time period after Vietnam when Congress reduced our manpower levels, forcing us to put many officers out of service, a very distasteful duty. Col Audette was colorful and fun to work for. He should have been promoted to Brig Gen. His wife died after he retired, and he asked me if he should get a couple of 25-year-old beauties and move to the Bahamas or become a Catholic priest. I suggested the first option, but he did become a priest and wanted to work only in the worst poverty areas. He had five kids, and I took one of them hunting a couple of times. He was really one of my favorite bosses.

From Texas, I moved to Korea and was executive officer to the assistant chief of staff, J-1 (personnel). It was a joint command involving those countries that fought as allies with the United States. It was also the headquarters for the U.S. Eighth Army, often referred to as the Eighth Imperial Army. Col Louis E. Herrick, USAF, was the boss, and his deputy was Army Col Longmore. Col Herrick was good to work for, absolutely rock solid. He used to joke that the only two good things about the Army were his two sons, both Army captains. I probably had more interface in that job with Army Col Longmore who really conducted the bulk of our personnel business, leaving Col Herrick to handle the three- and four-star general concerns. Col Longmore was unshakable and didn't get bothered with the small stuff. We were able to do some bird shooting together. Both were good bosses, and it turned out to be a terrific assignment.

From Korea I was sent back to Ramstein in Germany to essentially the same unit I served in on my first assignment to Germany. Only this time I was to be the commander. The unit name had changed to Detachment 6, 1141 Special Activities Squadron (USAFE). Additionally, it was now in support of not only 4th Allied Tactical Air Force (4 ATAF) but also Allied Air Forces Central Europe (AAFCE)—two NATO commands.

My actual reporting official and squadron commander was Col Robert O. McCartan, stationed in Stuttgart, Germany. He was an old-time colonel who let you, and expected you, to do your job without his intervention. But he was always there if you needed him. My real bosses on Ramstein were Col Richard E. Skelton and Major General Robert M. White. They were the senior U.S. Air Force representatives to 4 ATAF and AAFCE. It was a pleasure and honor to work for both of them.

When it was time to leave our wonderful tour in Germany, we said Auf Wiedersehen and headed off most unhappily to the Pentagon where I was selected to be Chief of the Personnel Division for the Office of the Joint Chiefs of Staff (OJCS) and later to become the deputy director of the directorate of support services, OJCS. My boss for most of that assignment was Col Wayne M. Duncan, U.S. Army; he was solid, comfortable, and a straight-shooting officer. Much of my work was with Army Maj Gen Charles W. Dyke, who was the vice director of the joint staff, and with Air Force Lt Gen James E. Dalton, who was the Director of the Joint Staff.

From there it was back to Texas and the Electronic Security Command (ESC) at Kelly Air Force Base in San Antonio, where I was assigned as Assistant Deputy Chief of Staff for Personnel. You may have guessed it, but ESC is the Air Force arm of the National Security Agency. Personnel problems remained the same as with other units, but the command mission was new and exciting for me. It exposed me to a new world of intelligence and was quite an education. Maj Gen Marks was the commander. He gave me some good advice on taking command of a unit. It was, always evolution and never revolution. By that he meant don't come in firing people and making changes until you fully understand the unit, its mission, and its personnel. His point was that the wrong people are often fired, and the changes are often wrong. A new charging commander often causes damage to the unit and mission that requires years to recover.

The most influential officer for me in the command was Brig Gen Regis F.A. Urschler, the vice commander. He did not grow up in the signals intelligence business and was somewhat of an outsider in ESC. I traveled with him throughout the world visiting our units and taking care of the personnel challenges while he handled the operational and political questions. Gen Urschler was a real people person, and Reggie, as he was called in the civilian world, was known throughout the Air Force. In his off-duty time, he flew a World War II

P-51 fighter aircraft named the Gunfighter for fun and at airshows. He was still doing that even after I retired. I was with him one time on an inspection and personnel visit to our unit at Misawa Air Force Base in northern Japan. It was during the winter, and after work a group of the enlisted guys wanted to take us to a Japanese bath. It was in town but close to the base so we walked to the bath and back to the base. Since it was cold and snowing, we were issued heavy coats with fur-lined hoods—trudging along in the snow with our hoods we resembled a group of monks. On the walk back, shortly before reaching the gate, General Urschler threw a snowball at some of the guys behind us. The game was on, and the two of us were the targets for eight or ten enlisted guys—we looked like the abominable snowman. About that time the Air Force security police guard at the front gate called out loudly in quite crude language—cut it out and get your behinds in here. We got in line to show our IDs for base entry. Gen Urschler never said a word, he just got in line. When he showed his ID to the foul-mouthed security policeman, the poor guy actually dropped the ID while trying to salute; he could not believe a general would let a bunch of young, enlisted guys cover him up with snowballs. That was Gen Reggie Urschler. Then it was back to the Pentagon and my final assignment, which is covered separately in Pentagon assignments.

Some things you always remember—my enlisted service number in OTS was AF 19749754. Upon graduation and commissioning, my first officer number was AO 3135440, which was a reserve officer number. The majority of officers serving full time as a lifelong career held reserve commissions. Being an honor graduate from OTS I was offered a regular commission and soon received the regular commission designation 75341A—rather prestigious. Air Force Academy graduates received regular commissions, so I was quite chuffed to use and give my Air Force number as 75341A on the many times it was required. Such wonderful memories.

I could never repay the United States Air Force for the opportunity it gave me. It was such a marvelous experience to work with such fine people and a singular honor to serve my country. I will remain forever grateful.

Long Shots — Military

Vietnam Background

Vietnam was complicated and arguments persist as to whether we should have been involved at all. Many question the huge cost to our country and the horrible loss of American lives. After World War II, Vietnam reverted to French colonial governance. The Viet Minh—Vietnamese communists and nationalists —objected to the French and conducted guerrilla war, known as the Indochina War, for freedom from French colonial rule. Ho Chi Minh was the political leader while General Vo Nguyen Giap was a leader of the Viet Minh communist military forces. They fought the French from 1946 until 7 May 1954 when the famous battle of Dien Bien Phu ended with the surrender of French forces. I was in high school at that time and I can remember wondering how France could possibly be defeated by a small Southeast Asian country. I found out later that the French had completely underestimated their enemy.

Dien Bien Phu was a small town located in a valley surrounded by steep mountains. It was heavily garrisoned and guarded by French artillery; additionally, the French had built a runway for resupply by aircraft. The battle was meant to draw in the Viet Minh so the French, with superior firepower, could annihilate them. Nothing could have suited General Giap better. No one thought the Viet Minh could possibly drag artillery up the steep mountains. The French military were confident their own artillery and air force could easily defend their position. Even after the battle started and the French found themselves under artillery bombardment from the mountains, they compounded their losses by dropping more French and French Foreign Legion troops by parachute into the battle zone.

Eventually, the French forces numbered 14,000 with the Viet Minh at around 50,000. The French losses were 3,000 dead and over 8,000 wounded. Gen. Giap lost approximately 8,000 dead and another 12,000 wounded. But the French troops were forced to surrender. Interestingly, the U.S. supported the French in this conflict with supplies and air transport. Under the Geneva Accords in 1954 the French withdrew, but Ho Chi Minh (communist) was denied complete

121

victory as Vietnam was divided at the 17th parallel with the North being communist and the South becoming the Republic of Vietnam.

The communists controlled the north, and the south went to the nationalists where Ngo Dinh Diem eventually became the leader. Fast forward to 1961 and President John F. Kennedy. Nikita Khrushchev was encouraging and supporting communist insurrections worldwide. President Kennedy felt we needed to stop the spread of communism. Not wanting to lose South Vietnam to the communists, the president and his senior advisors decided to support South Vietnam with limited ground and air forces against the Viet Cong (communist guerrillas).

U.S. involvement in Vietnam began immediately after the Geneva Accords as an element of the Cold War. Our support was initially limited to providing assistance in training and military advisors. In 1962, the number of U.S. military for all services was 500. By 1965, that number had climbed to 23,000 U.S. troops.

After winning the National Trophy at the U.S. Championship in August of 1965, my commander, Col Tom Kelly, called me to his office and in his less-than-subtle manner said, "Lieutenant, you've done all you can do here and you can't top your performance so if you want to make the Air Force a career, get your ass in gear and move out of the marksmanship school." Good advice. Vietnam was starting to warm up, and I wanted to "get in the fight." Col Kelly retired, and our new commander was Lt Col Joe Fry.

At that time, Vietnam was almost entirely an Army operation; the Air Force had only 391 personnel assigned in the country. While flying officers were beginning to receive orders for Vietnam or Southeast Asia, commonly referred to as SEA, non-rated (not flying) officers had to be volunteers and have the approval of their commander. My volunteer request letter was rejected, much to my displeasure. Col Fry counseled that he turned down my request because he needed to maintain unit continuity. I certainly didn't think as a lieutenant I could be that important and continued to object. Shortly thereafter, Col James Hunter took command. He promised to turn me loose in 1966. True to his word, he approved my request in September 1966. Of course, by then, Vietnam was on fire and volunteers no longer needed approval by their commander. In fact, by then, the services couldn't care less about volunteers; they needed troops. My orders came through directing me to report for duty in Vietnam after training and attending personnel school.

Arriving in Vietnam

In February of 1967, I found myself in Nha Trang, Republic of Vietnam, on the South China Sea with some of the most beautiful beaches imaginable. Unfortunately, I was not on vacation. It was also the location of the Nha Trang Air Base, RVN, (Pacific) which was my home from February 1967 through early February 1968. Interesting times indeed. It was also the time of Tet offensive which is another story.

My assignment was to the 14th Combat Support Group as a personnel officer. We had several missions, but one of the most important was support of "Puff the Magic Dragon," which was the nickname of C47 gunships. The gunships got that nickname from a great song by Peter, Paul, and Mary. They were also called the "Dragon Ship" because they carried three 7.62-caliber miniguns (a six-barreled Gatling gun). Each gun was capable of firing 6,000 rounds per minute (on full fire), with every fifth round being a tracer bullet, which at night resembled a fire-breathing dragon. "Spooky," another nickname, was because it would drop out of the heavens in the dark of the night and light up the world with flares and tracer ammunition. These gunships were flown by the Fourth Air Commandos and were our countermeasure to enemy night attacks on our ground troops. They saved many grunts and leathernecks who were about to be overrun by the Viet Cong. When the gunships could not handle all the emergency needs, the Fifth Air Commandos were sometimes dispatched. They had no guns but kicked out flares, and the airplane sound was the same as gunships, which often fooled the Vietcong into breaking off an attack.

The base had very little housing so nearly all personnel lived somewhere in the city of Nha Trang. The first house I lived in was at 33 Phan Phou Quac, near downtown with a group of pilots from the Fifth Air Commando Squadron who flew C47s on psychological warfare missions. One, First Lieutenant Lynn Sirovatka, flew the U-10, a single-engine spotter plane. In addition, three other company-grade officers were in our house—Capt Jack C. Swonson, a C47 pilot, 2d Lt Mark Siefert, an intelligence officer, and me. Both Jack and Lynn were Air Force Academy graduates. A couple of other junior officers who came and went were in maintenance or supply.

    Three field-grade officers lived in the house. Lt Col Mansfield was the senior officer, but he was really quite shaky—I believe it was PTSD. The other two were Major Bill Orange and Major Bobby Presley. All three were C47 pilots. The squadron was commanded by Lt Col Trusty Whitehead, but I believe Major Presley pretty much ran the operations of the squadron. Major Presley also ran our house with no questions asked. If we (lieutenants and junior captains) were home listening to music—maybe "Monday, Monday" or "California Dreaming" by the Mamas & The Papas, "We Can Work It Out" by the Beatles, "Light My Fire" by the Doors, or maybe, "Pretty Woman" by Roy Orbison, we would often have the volume at max.

    Major Presley would walk in and simply pull the plug—no words from him, and certainly nothing from us. No one wanted to play catch with him as he burned a hard ball at you like a hot rocket. Major Orange was my roommate. Our beds were separated by a small table pushed up against a screened window. We slept with our heads toward the window to catch any hint of a breeze as it was mostly hot and humid. One night, a noise woke me, and there was a knife blade sawing away only a foot from my eyes, cutting through the screen. I let out a whoop and jumped out of bed, causing considerable excitement. It was a little unsettling, but we figured it was just a thief trying to reach in and grab something without intent to harm anyone. We cleaned off the table and went back to bed.

    Another time, we got home just as a young boy was leaving our yard with our radio under his arm. He took off like a scalded cat, but Jack Swonson, who was 6 foot 2 inches and in track shape, sped after him. It was no contest, more like a good Quarter Horse after a young calf. Jack had him on the ground in winning time, maybe 10 seconds After letting him up, the kid, who was probably four and a half feet tall, knew it was useless to run. He didn't speak any English, but with gestures he was telling us it wasn't fair for Jack to catch him with his long legs. That gave us a chuckle. We gave him a mean-sounding threat along with a couple of little shoves, retrieved our radio, and let him go. I don't think we scared him much.

Transportation to and from the base and the city of Nha Trang, where most of us lived, was whatever you could arrange—bicycle, walking, hitchhiking, three-wheeled taxis, etc. Major Presley had the squadron pickup, the only permanent transport we had. A vehicle was assigned to me for a night every couple of weeks when I was duty officer for casualty reporting. If we took casualties in the night, it was my responsibility to round up the NCOs who were experts in casualty requirements and reporting deaths and get them to the base. Timely reporting of U.S. deaths to Air Force headquarters in Saigon was a serious and grave matter.

We had an officers' club on the base at Nha Trang, but it wasn't much more than a bar and chow hall. One night after dinner, three of us company-grade officers, Lieutenant Lynn C. Sirovatka, Captain Jack Swonson, and I, left the officers' club and got in the bed of the pickup truck (the cab was reserved for field-grade officers) for the ride home. Out came a major from a different squadron who'd had one and maybe five too many beers. He asked for a light, but none of us smoked so he started cussing and hurling insults at us. About then, Lt Col Mansfield and Major Presley walked out of the club and headed in our direction. The major doing the cussing did not see them immediately, but we did. Major Presley simply hit the intruding major so hard that it sent him flying. It looked to me like he was horizontal in the air. I know that's hardly possible, but I sure remember it that way.

The major was out cold, lying in the street. Major Presley walked around to the driver's side of the truck, got in, backed it out and away we went. Not a word was said, and the major was left in the street. Major Presley could be abrupt with us, but no one else could if he was around. We were "his guys," and while we respected him before, we now genuinely liked him. A good lesson in leadership, never mind the fisticuffs. Major Presley eventually retired as a Lieutenant General and had a full second career as a senior executive in USAA.

The great Coca-Cola shrimp swap, a highly classified mission, took place in 1967. The nature of the event was not nefarious, but it was quite unusual, and perhaps exceeded burdensome and excessive nitpicking regulations authored by hapless morons in a different world. Names of the participants remain clouded. Known facts reveal a certain C 47 departed Nha Trang for an undisclosed Army location. Rumors allege it was carrying a full cargo of Coca-Cola and other sodas. The aircraft supposedly returned with a full load of excellent food supplies meant for large Army kitchens.

Barracks gossip, notoriously unreliable, suggested a certain unnamed lieutenant had previously landed at the Army camp and noticed several pallets stacked next to the landing strip. Upon examination, he found pallets were packed with food. As the lieutenant reported, the custodian of these pallets was in a quandary; for whatever reason, there was more food than there should have been. More is normally a good problem to have. However, in this case, an Army inspection was imminent, and the discovery of this huge mix-up in numbers and amounts would produce, at the very least, severe reductions in ranks and grades.

The lieutenant became a messenger from heaven, and after consultation with older and wiser colleagues, a favorable solution was discovered. This was not C rations; it was quality food that would satisfy the palate of the high-brass princes and their courtiers in Saigon headquarters. What do you do with an airplane chock full of food? As often happens, an industrious, enterprising, and more importantly, crafty noncommissioned officer located a storage facility at the reasonable fair trade of sharing the food with his unit—a marriage was made to everyone's benefit.

Found among this cargo were numerous large cans of dehydrated shrimp. Being raised in a family of rather modest means, I had eaten shrimp cocktails but never experienced full shrimp dinners. My roommates quickly corrected that deficiency. You may scoff at dehydrated, but trust me, those shrimp were absolutely delicious.

By happenstance I was involved in the audit and loss of 1,000,000—that was in Vietnamese currency, called piasters. But a million is a million. The going rate per one U.S. dollar was 100 piasters. Normal pay for a maid working for GIs was 30 piasters a day. A million piasters would equal 33,333 days of work. The military was not allowed to use or even possess U.S. currency in Vietnam. A violation of this directive was a serious offense. Military pay was mailed to home addresses or deposited in stateside accounts. Military Payment Certificates, commonly called scrip, was substituted for greenbacks to be used on the base and the economy. This was done to discourage nefarious money changers and curb black market activities.

Upon arriving at my office early to catch up on a pile of work, I settled down at my desk, and word was passed for me to report to the base commander. So much for arriving early to catch up. When reporting in as ordered, I noted a military security policeman was also in the commander's office. "Captain, you are acting under my authority. You are to proceed immediately to the officers' club and audit the cash accounts. Sgt Smith will accompany you." Gad, I'm up to my butt in work, and now I'm being escorted by a security policeman to count scrip and piasters at the greasy spoon called the officers' club. I'm thinking, "Why me, Lord? Let some other nitwit fool do this so I can get to my work."

We marched into the club and headed straight for the back, where I suspected the manager had an office. It was a large room with several GI metal desks and several people milling around. They were quite startled to see us, and I asked to speak to the manager. The assistant manager advised us he had not yet arrived, pointing to the manager's empty desk. I could see the safe, at the side of his desk, was open! In plain view on a shelf in the safe there were several stacks of U.S. dollars. The assistant manager was ordered along with the security policeman to watch me remove the money from the safe and place it on the manager's desk. The assistant manager and staff in the room all feigned complete surprise and claimed no knowledge of ever seeing the greenbacks.

The money was counted out twice, once by me and once by the assistant manager. The amount was just over $10,000. It would not take Hercule Poirot to figure something was rotten in Denmark. A receipt and statement were made out and signed by me, the assistant manager, and the security policeman. The cash was confiscated. We carried it to the base commander's office in two large paper bags. Obviously, the base commander had known something was up, but

127

he didn't offer to share that knowledge with me, and I knew better than to ask. Where the Office of Special Investigation (OSI) was in this deal I have no idea. Maybe we didn't have any OSI agents in Nha Trang. The commander had the cash and statement. All I wanted was to get back to my work. Still, it was kind of a neat experience carrying a fortune in two paper bags—a million is a million.

The Tet Offensive

General Curtis E. Lemay, Chief of Staff of the United States Air Force, did not agree with limited forces being sent to South Vietnam and advocated direct and major actions against North Vietnam. Sadly, his advice was ignored. Secretary of Defense Robert S. McNamara counseled a more limited approach and diplomatic pressure. The war was not handled well by our most senior leaders, both military and civilian. Many failed to realize it was partly a civil war and fought in guerrilla fashion not suited to World War II or Korean scenarios. We failed in many cases to protect and gain the full support of the South Vietnamese. We simply never won the goodwill of the people.

Crazy as it sounds, President Johnson wanted to select specific bombing targets. Some would even say it was willful disregard of negative information by our leadership. When General Giap came into the picture as a minister of defense for North Vietnam, he orchestrated what was called the Tet Offensive. Tet is a Vietnamese holiday for the Lunar New Year. General Giap planned for massive attacks by the Viet Cong and North Vietnamese Army (NVA) on all the major cities and government sites in South Vietnam. By doing this, he expected a popular uprising throughout the South. Our intelligence and leaders did not see this major attack coming, which was an egregious failure. The nationwide attack was set for January 31, 1968, but because of some mistakes Nha Trang and a few other cities were hit after midnight on January 30, 1968. I was in Nha Trang that night.

My roommates were 2d Lt John Sherwood, Capt Chester, and Capt Roy Gurd. Not long after midnight we woke up to the sound of what we originally thought was fireworks as an early start to Tet. Shortly after that, our maid, Chi Hi, came to the house we rented and said, "Beaucoup VC, beaucoup VC," very excitedly and then quickly disappeared as it became evident the entire city was under attack. Being especially vulnerable (courtesy of Gen Momyer, commander of Seventh Air Force and his ban on weapons), we secured our quarters, shut off the lights, and hunkered down on the second floor. Several people were killed on our street including our next-door neighbor, and three bodies lay dead the next morning in front of our house. Roy Gurd was on base that night so our Army Jeep, which had recently been liberated from some hapless Army troop, was not parked in front of our house. That was good luck and may have saved our lives. Having it parked in front of our house would have given away our presence and identified us as U.S. military.

The front of our house was closed in by a steel folding accordion- style gate much like those seen protecting shops and stores in blighted areas of U.S. cities. The gate would certainly not stop determined entry, but the NVA/VC did not know we were inside. I suspect they thought the house was empty as many Vietnamese in cities had returned to villages and hamlets to celebrate Tet with their families. The real meaning of feeling naked was brought to light. My previous assignment prior to Vietnam had been training and shooting combat rifles, and here I was under attack without a firearm in a combat area, which was double stupid. It was a harrowing night, and the next morning fighting continued on the street and houses next to ours. Making matters worse for us was not being able to see much of what was going on. Our house at 16 Phan Chu Trinh was a two-story cement structure, but our back wall had no windows as it was built directly against the back of another house that faced the next street over. It was the same situation with the house on our left—that wall was shared with our neighbor who was killed during the attack. We could only peek out the front window onto the street and the right window that viewed the side of our neighbor's house on the right.

The Vietcong took over the intersection three houses down the street from us and kept the firing going. It wasn't until the next afternoon that things quieted down, and we dared to use the toilet that was located on our roof. That was after a patrol of five or six Army soldiers carefully worked their way down our street, staying on the sides close to houses. I got downstairs and was careful not to startle them. They were surprised to see me but were not willing to pass me a weapon—those pricks. Not long after that, a Jeep full of "white mice" (national police wearing white shirts) and South Vietnamese soldiers (ARVN) flew down the street. Believe me, we kept a very low profile during all the shooting and certainly did not want to be seen. Lt John Sherwood made a tape recording of the cacophony of machine-gun, small arms, and bombs that came too close. Somehow, that tape recording survived from January 1968 until I found it in 2016 and had it converted to a CD.

Late that afternoon, our roommate Roy Gurd, who had been stuck on the base, rolled up heroically in our stolen Army Jeep with an M-60 machine-gun to rescue us. The danger had passed. Roy was somewhat of a romantic philosopher; he co-authored Invader Stuff, a superb little book of poems. The copy he gave me when I visited him in Madrid after Vietnam was inscribed: "Dennis—To a short time of unreality at #16 Phan Chu Trinh—To a long time of wondering where the unreality is." Roy was also a bit of a rebel and was passed over for promotion to major— really cashiered out. It was a mistake on the Air Force's part, for sure. An organization needs some rebels—especially the military. He later joined the Army Reserve. Ironically, Roy was killed while jogging in San Diego by a drunk driver. We lost a good man.

John Sherwood was a devoted Catholic boy from San Antonio. He came to Nha Trang as a young, inexperienced, naïve second lieutenant and received a worldwide view in Asia. He left the Air Force after a couple more assignments—a fine, honest, and loyal troop. He was an excellent roommate.

Even after the premature attack on Nha Trang, senior leadership failed to grasp the situation. Most South Vietnamese (ARVN) and U.S. forces were caught by complete surprise on January 31, 1968. In a strictly military sense, the Tet Offensive was a major win for the South Vietnamese and U.S. forces. It was really an excellent opportunity for our troops to engage large enemy concentrations willing to fight and not dissolve back elusively into the jungles and general population in normal guerrilla fashion. Nearly 3,000 U.S. and ARVN troops were killed, with the VC and NVA losses estimated at over 30,000 with another 6,000 captured. South Vietnamese and U.S. forces dislodged the NVA/VC and took back all their gains in quick order.

Only Hue and the Cholon section of Saigon required more time to secure. Hue, the former imperial capital, was a 25-day, hand-to-hand, house-to-house battle. The VC were decimated, and the NVA in South Vietnam were severely damaged.

One of the easiest ways I can think of to get knocked off is to appear on your enemies' ground without the ability to fight or even the means to protect yourself. That's exactly the situation Air Force personnel found themselves in during Tet. Just a couple of months earlier than that offensive, an edict came down from on high from the Headquarters Seventh Air Force. The order stipulated that Air Force personnel would turn in all government and private weapons in their possession to base armories. No weapons, government or private, could be carried on your person or stored in your quarters. Our Nha Trang base commander announced that the directive was to be followed to the letter and anyone found in noncompliance would be court-martialed. Who in the world ever heard of a more stupid order than having your troops turn in all their weapons in a combat area? And in a place where the enemy was known to have infiltrated the local communities and could not even be identified. Most Air Force personnel at Nha Trang Air Force Base lived in the city of Nha Trang. It was simply unreal. Just imagine yourself walking around with a big target on your back and no way to protect yourself. Every Army grunt, Marine leatherneck, Air America pilot or crew member, U.S. Naval personnel, South Korean military (South Korea had a large contingent at Nha Trang), contractors from the States, U.S. government officials with special missions, Vietnamese national and local police, and South Vietnamese military were all carrying firearms. And of course, the enemy VC had firearms. Only the Air Force was naked.

This situation was exactly what Gen LeMay was trying to correct when he started the Red Hat program and emphasized marksmanship training. His feeling was everyone needed to be able

131

to protect themselves and engage in the fight. Supposedly, someone in the higher echelons of Seventh Air Force thought Air Force personnel might gain a false sense of security if they had weapons. This notion was especially stupid as it was so vividly exposed during Tet in January 1968. It is unknown what brain trust came up with this brilliant idea, but Lt Gen William W. Momyer was commander of Seventh Air Force in 1967 when the order was given. He was promoted to general in December 1967. It is surprising that he would allow such a directive; he was a daredevil fighter pilot and an Ace in World War II. I have no statistics but expect that order got Air Force people killed during Tet. After the first hours of Tet, the restrictive weapon order was forgotten.

Unfortunately, I was too dumb to know better and turned in my .38 Smith & Wesson along with my M-16 to the armory as ordered. Of course, I had no choice; the armory had records of me holding those weapons. Bad on me again, I didn't take a personal side arm with me to Vietnam. In his excellent book, *The Battle for Saigon—Tet 1968,* Keith Nolan points out incident after incident of U.S. military personnel of all ranks who were unarmed and ill prepared to face the enemy, much less join in the fight. I quote from page 22: "… like the Army generals, the 10 USAF generals headquartered at Tan Son Nhut were in for a rude awakening."

It was later reported, "Their living quarters were modular units resembling mobile homes, surrounded by a high cyclone fence." When the base command post hit the rocket siren, the generals ducked into the bunker in their small compound. Only a captain serving as aide to one of the generals had a weapon: a .38-caliber pistol. With all due respect, one would have to ask what kind of generals did we have?

After all, we weren't in a chess match. I like the Marine Corps' slogan, "Every man a rifleman." After that, you are a cook, baker, pilot, mechanic, computer expert, or whatever. But first, you're a fighting man able to protect yourself and engage the enemy under any conditions. I was too inexperienced and junior to have any effect on the infamous gun program in Vietnam, but after returning to the States, I did write a report to Maj Floyd Smith, who was stationed in the Pentagon and the only person I knew remaining in the shooting program. That letter is in the appendix of this book.

Rick Atkinson, in his book, *The Army at Dawn*, tells how in the battle of Kasbah, a 16th century Portuguese citadel on the site of the 6th century Carthaginian trading post, Brig Gen Lucian Truscott used cooks, clerks, and drivers in his successful assault. Former Secretary of Defense Gen James Mattis shared that as a lieutenant colonel in the 1991 Operation Desert Storm he got too far in front of his logistic elements in Kuwait and was ambushed. He says cooks, drivers, engineers, clerks, and mechanics, who were all trained to fight in his rear echelon, picked up the slack and drove the enemy back.

No matter what your specialty is, you must first be a fighting man and maintain that mentality and be able to defend yourself. Sadly, on April 27, 2011, nine unarmed Air Force members were shot to death by one Afghan pilot with two pistols at the Kabul airport. Why they were in a combat zone unarmed is a mystery to me. I suspect you will find more golf courses on our Air Force bases than you will find small arms training ranges. Combat zones are dangerous for everyone, and we all need to be trained and prepared.

A general uprising in the South did not happen, and North Vietnam leadership realized their Tet plans had been a complete defeat and major disaster. Nevertheless, Tet was a major shock to the public back home in the United States and, I believe, the beginning of the end as the American public lost confidence. The news media portrayed the Tet Offensive as a complete uprising by the South Vietnamese supporting communism, which was the exact opposite of the truth but contributed to the loss of confidence. Chairman of the Joint Chiefs of Staff, Gen Earle G. Wheeler, and Gen William Westmoreland, Army commander in Vietnam, requested 200,000 more troops after Tet, but President Johnson declined these requests. Public opinion forced him to declare he would not run for reelection. There is no doubt in my mind that the continued casualties of dead and maimed, without producing significant positive results, would have eventually eroded U.S. support of the war. Continued demonstrations at universities, government buildings, and in Washington, D.C., the My Lai massacre, and other reports of atrocities, as well as the Pentagon papers, the Kent

State shooting, a hostile U.S. media, steady U.S. casualties, and even returning disillusioned veterans ushered in more opposition to the war and forced a rapid conclusion.

A cease-fire was orchestrated by Dr. Henry Kissinger and President Richard Nixon to go into effect on January 29, 1973. It was the end of fighting for the United States and produced the return of 591 American prisoners from North Vietnam, including one of my personal heroes, Navy Lieutenant John McCain. President Nixon gave his absolute assurance to the South Vietnamese that the United States would step back in if the North violated the cease-fire. The North only slowed down for a short period. South Vietnamese forces could not hold out without our help—they were doomed to defeat. The United States ambassador and the last of the U.S. forces vacated Saigon on April 30, 1975, as it fell to the communists. It was finished. We gave up 58,200 of our best in Vietnam with nearly 300,000 severely wounded physically and no doubt many more thousands wounded mentally who are not even counted. Other thousands who fought the communists—the Vietnamese military, Montagnards, Vietnam police forces, our allies, the Australians, Kiwis, and South Koreans were lost. Thousands of loyal Vietnamese civilians who supported our troops were abandoned to their catastrophic fate. Many ask, what was gained?

Long Shots — Military

THE YOUNG DEAD SOLDIERS DO NOT SPEAK
by Archibald MacLeish

Nevertheless, they are heard in the still houses: who has not heard them?

They have a silence that speaks for them at night and when the clock counts.

They say, We were young. We have died. Remember us.

They say, We have done what we could but until it is finished it is not done.

They say, We have given our lives but until it is finished no one can know what our lives gave.

They say, Our deaths are not ours: they are yours: they will mean what you make them.

They say, Whether our lives and our deaths were for peace and a new hope or for nothing we cannot say: it is you who must say this.

They say, We leave you our deaths: give them their meaning: give them an end to the war and a true peace: give them a victory that ends the war and a peace afterwards: give them their meaning.

We were young, they say. We have died. Remember us.

My tour in Vietnam started in February 1967, three days after Loretta and I were married. The tour ended in February 1968, shortly after Tet. One could say that I was there in interesting times. For sure it was exciting times, and I guess you might call it crazy times. Coming from Travis Air Force Base near San Francisco and getting off the plane on arrival at Cam Ranh Bay, I was met with an unexpected blast of heat and humidity. From there a helicopter carried me to Nha Trang Air Base, my new home. The country stretches from beaches or lowlands to the middle of the country and then to the highland border of Cambodia and Laos. The people were friendly in Nha Trang; however, one certainly had to get used to the overpowering and unremitting odor of nuoc mam, a favorite sauce made from layers from dried fish and salt left in the sun to stew. Noise and congestion in towns: motorbikes, buses, trucks, cars, bicycles, three-wheel vehicles, horse-drawn wagons, and bicycle rickshaws made Saigon traffic insane. I thought it was the most chaotic in the world, but I found much the same in Hong Kong and Bangkok. The Air Base was just outside the city of Nha Trang, which is on the South China Sea where the beaches are beautiful.

One picture that stays in my mind is how happy all the kids seemed to be. I took a photo of one group of maybe 20 middle school-age boys climbing a large tree. They wore white shirts and were all laughing and having fun. I often wonder what happened to those boys. The women were thin and really beautiful in their long traditional (ao dai) dresses, showing a slit up one side. They looked elegant with their wide domed straw hats in their ao dais.

My job in Vietnam was primarily manning personnel, both flying and maintenance, of C47, A1, U10, and other propeller aircraft. That required me to fly and visit nearly all our bases in Vietnam from Tan Son Nhut to Bien Hoa, Da Nang, Binh Thuy and Pleiku. One time, we took some fire and were forced to land at Nakhon Phanom in Thailand, a long way from Vietnam. We were where we should not have been, and I will say no more on that. I saw lots of beautiful country from the air. It was really gorgeous to watch the sunrise on the South China Sea through the palm trees on the beach at Nha Trang.

A favorite spot was Pleiku, the airbase, not the city. Situated in the highlands, it was cool and actually cold at night. It was enjoyable for me to watch the Montagnards (mountain tribes and strong supporters of our special forces). They sold bows and arrows and primitive spears as souvenirs. Vietnamese entrepreneurs turned the brass casings from fired 105 MM artillery rounds into beautiful lamps. Two can be found in my living room.

There were no barracks on the base, so personnel had to find quarters in downtown Nha Trang. I had several roommates and moved quarters a couple of times. Some of those I served with were met again in subsequent assignments. Bobby Throldahl was a personnel officer who served with me in Ramstein, Germany, and again at Randolph Air Force Base. Bobby retired as a lieutenant colonel. Second Lieutenant John Sherwood was one of the few Air Force second lieutenants in Vietnam. Normally such junior grades were not assigned to combat areas. He was with me the night and following two days we were trapped during Tet. We met up again in Berlin, where he was stationed, and later at Los Angeles Air Force Station. John was a good guy and had empathy for the Vietnamese civilians. He left the Air Force and returned to San Antonio, where he is a counselor and therapist. I expect he is a good one. John Nersesian was from Fresno. He left the Air Force after Vietnam, and we later visited him in La Jolla, California.

Mark Seifert was another anomaly; he was a second lieutenant intelligence officer and one of my first roommates. Mark was later assigned at Wiesbaden Air Force Base when we were at Ramstein Air Force Base. Our relationship continued, but this time with both our wives. He and his lovely bride Lynne have become good friends. They have visited us in San Antonio and have often hosted my wife Loretta for skiing in Vail, where they own a home. Mark retired as a full colonel and then went on to a second successful career with Lockheed Martin.

Taking personal firearms home from Vietnam was forbidden by regulation unless a bill of sale could be provided to prove ownership. That rule was even crazier when you understand it was against regulations to bring a personal firearm to Vietnam in the first place. There were, as one might expect, many firearms floating around.

Some were U.S. manufactured: Smith & Wesson and Colt revolvers and a couple of Ruger 44s. But I also saw some German Lugers, and one Broom Handled Mauser. Another favorite was the Browning high-power pistol because of its high-capacity 16-round magazine. I felt it was absurd and not fair to tell a young airman in a combat zone he couldn't take his personal firearm home. Understand, I'm talking about only handguns and those that were not government-issued. After proof of ownership was established, the information had to be recorded on permanent change of station (PCS) orders to make it legal and to give the holder clear passage through the military police and U.S. Customs. Guess who was in charge of preparing and publishing PCS orders? Troopers would come to me with a firearm and were disappointed to find a bill of sale was required. However, after some discussion, upon learning that the bill of sale could be handwritten on any piece of paper and that I had no need to keep the receipt, the airman's second trip to my desk was much more satisfying. Okay, I admit to violating my own rules of integrity and could even be charged with teaching others it was all right to fudge. No excuses, I leave it to the reader to judge.

Close Calls

Several close calls came my way in Vietnam, but, of course, nothing compared to what our real warriors, the grunts and leathernecks in the trenches, faced. Capt Bobby Throldohl, a friend and work colleague, and I went on a picnic with a group of Vietnamese to celebrate on his secretary's birthday. We had taken a landing craft to an island just off Nha Trang with about 60 South Vietnamese civilians and military. They maneuvered into a small lagoon, and just as we landed, one of the Vietnamese military threw a grenade overboard. That was fine, but nobody told Bobby or me, and neither of us saw him throw the grenade, so the unexpected explosion startled and scared the dickens out of both of us. They gathered up some stunned fish, and that started the picnic with lots of food and noisy fun.

Long Shots — Military

Later, I was exploring the beach away from the main birthday party, making a pit stop, probably 90 degrees from the party in a deserted area, when someone took a rifle shot at me. The shot was quite close and cracked over my head just like those shots when I pulled targets as a kid for the Santa Paula Rifle Club, or later, when I pulled targets at military ranges. Rockets and mortars are one thing and can certainly scare the bejesus out of you, but a single rifle shot, which you know was directed exactly at you, becomes very personal. That shot scared the living poop out of me, and I wasn't about to give the shooter another chance—I did not have a firearm (stupid), and retreat was the better part of valor—you can imagine I made tracks to get out of there mighty fast. I take a cue from Winston Churchill, if memory serves, "Nothing quite so exhilarating as being shot at and missed."

Another time, I was working in my office around 10 p.m. We were on the second floor of a temporary wooden structure with no glass in the windows. Instead, we had screens of chain-link fencing across the window frames that prevented grenades being thrown through a window. It was also a good safety precaution by eliminating flying glass from rocket or mortar attacks. We also needed the ventilation as there was no air conditioning. In any case, my office lights were on as I was signing orders and had a young airman helping me. We had a tremendous workload and put in long hours.

No doubt the Vietcong zeroed in on my burning light on the second floor as it was the only light turned on in the building. They sailed in several unfriendly mortars. It certainly got everyone's attention; we cleared the building fast and made for a close bunker as did everyone else in the area. The bunker was pitch black and someone said, "Anyone seen Behrens?" I replied, "I'm right here, boys." Our building did not take a direct hit, but it got a good splattering.

People were on their own getting to and from the base. You had to hitchhike, catch a mini cab or a three-wheeled buggy, which was always a chancy undertaking. We lived close to the center of the city in what was called the Villa— actually, it was more like a two-story cement garage.

My last address was 16 Phan Chu Trinh. We did have a toilet and running water with an outdoor shower on the roof. Unfortunately,

139

we had no warm water and contrary to what one might think, it can get cool in Vietnam. I don't take cold showers anymore. Still rather whiny when compared to the troops in the field who had no showers at all. Any complaining is unworthy considering 58,200 U.S. troops who did not come back. One night, we hitched a ride home in an Air Force van. The Vietcong (VC) set off a bomb just ahead of us in front of the Neptune club, which was a noncommissioned officer and Air America crew hangout near the beach. We heard the first bomb go off, but inside the van I thought it must have been an Army 105 artillery round many of which were fired intermittently protecting our base to keep the VC off balance. However, the second bomb went off shortly thereafter, and we were very close. It was real pandemonium as people were dead and dying all over the street. One man just ahead of us had both legs blown off but was still crawling on his elbows. It appeared the VC had waited a few minutes from the first until the second bomb to gather a bigger crowd.

 It was nearly dark, and Bobby and I jumped behind a little cement wall as we suspected a third bomb might go off. A Korean officer (Korea had thousands of troops in Vietnam supporting us) came along about that time. Bobby and I stood up to evaluate the situation. It startled the Korean, and he pointed his submachine gun directly at me at nearly point-blank range. It was just a reflex reaction because everyone was scared, and he quickly turned away. Still, it got my attention. For some reason I was wearing 1505s, a light tan khaki uniform, which identified me quickly. No telling what could have happened if I'd been wearing my normal green fatigues in that fading light.

 In desperation to get more airmen assigned to Nha Trang, I was dispatched to Seventh Air Force Headquarters in Saigon, basically lobbying for additional aircraft maintenance personnel. We were short reciprocating engine mechanics for our C-47 gunships, and they were hard to come by. As best I recall, the Air Force specialty code was 431X1A. Of course, sending a junior captain on this type of mission was akin to putting a blind kitten into a pit bull ring. Nevertheless, I was pleading with an Air Force major who oversaw incoming assignments to send more mechanics our way. He happened to have a broken arm and was leaning back in his chair with both feet on his desk listening

Long Shots — Military

with a rather bored expression to my case for more mechanics when a rocket came crashing down. It hit about a half block away on the Post Exchange (PX). Fortunately, it was Sunday morning before the PX opened, and it only killed two Vietnamese employees. However, it blew glass out where we were.

I'll never forget the major. He had a cigar in his mouth, and his broken arm was in a cast. Picture him trying to get under his desk with both feet kicking up in the air. He looked like someone doing the old Air Force exercise called "fish out of water." It was really a ludicrous sight, even in those circumstances.

We mostly ate meals on base because it was convenient, relatively clean, and fast. Sometimes, we cooked or ate C rations at home, and occasionally when time permitted, we ventured downtown to one of the many restaurants that served mostly rice and fish. There was a French restaurant named Fourgout's on the beach, right on the edge of town. They served what they called lobster, but it was nothing like a Maine lobster, more like crawdads. But they did have wonderful French onion soup. I had never even heard of French baked onion soup but quickly fell in love with it. They also had nice French bread and butter, so my meal was French bread and butter with baked French onion soup. On special occasions, we tried to go to Fourgout's, but it wasn't often. One time, I wanted to go and get some French baked onion soup, but the rest of the guys were just beat and too tired to go out. I didn't want to eat by myself so decided to stay home. At Fourgout's, we usually sat outside next to the seawall. That night a VC walked by and placed a satchel charge on the seawall without being noticed. A few minutes later, they set it off killing two patrons and wounding many others. I was just plain lucky to dodge that bullet. Some say brave men don't admit courage, but a coward doesn't admit fear. I don't know about courage, but I must not be a coward as I would have to confess to a few moments that gave me a considerable fright. That French baked onion soup set a standard that has never been matched. Talking recently to my Vietnam roommate, Lynn Sirovatka, he revealed using that same standard with identical results. We both order French baked onion soup whenever it is on the menu. None have ever measured up, and I guess none ever will.

A Dangerous Mistake

February 1968 marked the end of my 12-month assignment in Vietnam and I was supposed to rotate out of Cam Ranh Bay along with all other military personnel assigned in II Corps. However, returning passenger aircraft from Cam Ranh Bay flew to Seattle. I was from California and wanted to meet my wife in San Francisco to show her the town: Top of the Mark, streetcars on the hills, Fisherman's Wharf, etc. We had only a three-day honeymoon before Vietnam, and I was intent on doing something special for my bride. The only way I could get to San Francisco was to fly out of Saigon which was in III Corps. While not 100% kosher, orders were arranged for me to fly out of Saigon. Certainly not within regulations or maybe even good sense, I got my roommate, 1st Lt Lynn Sirovatka, to fly me from Nha Trang to Tan Son Nhut Air Base, Saigon, in his observation U-10 aircraft. It was early February and residual fighting from Tet was still going on in Saigon and around the airbase.

We landed at Tan Son Nhut Air Base on the military side of the Saigon airport and my roommate made haste to hightail it back to Nha Trang. He was worried about getting his plane shot up in a place he had no business or authorization to be. I was worried he might get in trouble. Strange now, neither one of us thought about getting hurt. I guess we were just too dumb to realize we were not bulletproof. I hustled to billeting for quarters that night. The attack continued after dark, and it was quite spectacular to watch C 47 gunships in action–certainly a real live Fourth of July show. Every fifth shot from each of the three mini guns was a tracer round and on full fire the three guns combined could fire 1,800 rounds per minute. It looked something like the Jolly Green Giant in the sky, peeing red and yellow on the earth.

Later that night, a senior officer came by the billets, and we were ordered to sleep on the floor under the metal beds with mattresses left on top of the bed in case a rocket hit the building. The fight was still going on and we could hear distant fighting but nothing close. So, as soon as he left, we slept on our beds, disobeying yet another order.

Long Shots — Military

The billet on the military side of the airport was quite a distance from the international terminal, which was actually across the flight line. I called the motor pool that night requesting a car in the morning for transport to the international terminal. When the car arrived, a major and his crew from a 130 aircraft commandeered it. It was my car, the driver knew it, the major knew it, and I knew it. It was simply a matter of our RHIP (Rank Has Its Privilege), and since I was going home the major couldn't care less—he took the car in the opposite direction to the military terminal. I came very close to punching him, but they were three, and I was without help in a brawl. Now I'm in a bind. It's five in the morning, and because the VC attack was ongoing, people had to drive with lights out and it was a long way to the terminal. It was unrealistic to walk on the flight line carrying a B-4 bag. Additionally, I risked being shot by our own security police.

I finally got a ride in the back of an Army deuce-and-a-half that I was lucky enough to wave down. What they were doing there, I have no idea. The cab was full, so I threw my B-4 bag in the back and then jumped in myself. By then, it was getting quite late for my flight, which would certainly take off on time, and it was becoming daylight. Mortars and gun fire could still be heard as we drove up to the international terminal, but I noticed people streaming out of the building. We could only get within about 80 yards of the terminal in the Army truck because of heavy cement barriers. Troops were pouring out because the terminal had taken a direct hit shortly before our arrival. Only three GIs were killed, but many were wounded. The Russian 122 rocket had blown a big hole in the roof, and, of course, shattered all the windows. It also blew the entire plywood paneling off the walls. It was a real mess. Ambulances arrived just after us, and medics were busy.

To restore order, those of us who were ambulatory were directed to stand in formation while a full colonel inspected each man. Anyone bleeding was pulled out of line and not allowed to board the commercial Braniff ready for takeoff. For a moment it looked like we might have a mutiny from those pulled aside. They were bitching about only having a flesh wound or barely bleeding, and it was not fair to pull them off the flight home. I felt they were right, but the Braniff flight waited for no man, and I was just grateful to get on myself. We

143

went back to the States only about half full. It was a marvelous flight with real-life stewardesses and the works. I remember they fed us hotdogs. Did the major who pulled rank and took my car actually save me from harm? One never knows how things will turn out.

The Vietnamese in Nha Trang were friendly, and I felt no resentment from anyone. To me they appeared to be industrious and hard-working people, striving for improvement and success by hard work as farmers, fisherman, laborers, merchants, maids, and all manner of entrepreneurial ventures. They wanted a better life for themselves, their children, and their families. Not much different from what would be found back in the States. In many farm areas of guerrilla fighting there was considerable bellicosity toward the U.S. military. Of course, that is understandable, with the destruction of crops, burning of hooches and entire villages, and the collateral loss of civilian lives either directed or caused by our troops.

Vietnam was certainly a major experience in my life. I felt a great deal of concern for the Vietnamese people and sadness for the loss of life for us and for them. More than once I witnessed large stacks of filled body bags at the end of our runway near the Eighth Field Hospital. I lost some good acquaintances, but none of my close personal friends were killed in Vietnam. Overall, the Vietnamese welcomed and appreciated our help. It was heart-wrenching to witness the inglorious evacuation of our personnel on 30 April 1975, leaving our Vietnamese friends to such a dreadful future. The death count for the Vietnam War was 3.4 million.

Coming home from overseas even from a pleasant posting is always uplifting, maybe tribal—you are back in your place with your people. Coming home from Vietnam was extra special. I was not just getting back home but meeting my wife to start on our married life together. I will admit my first couple of weeks back in the States felt a little strange, sort of surreal. I was not traumatized or anything like PTSD, but it took a bit of adjusting.

Nevertheless, it was a magical time. We started my 30-day leave in San Francisco and just soaked in that experience from the Golden Gate Bridge on. Our next escapade was a wonderful gift from my high-school friend Doug Udall; it was a one-night stay at the famed and majestic Ahwahnee Lodge in Yosemite National Park. We were living high. Then we moved on to Santa Paula to visit with my family and friends. San Antonio was our next destination, and we stayed at the deluxe St. Anthony Hotel. It was good to visit with my former rifle team members and my previous commander, Col Tom Kelly. From there, we moved on to East Texas to be with Loretta's family. Maybe not a very romantic or classic honeymoon, but it was pure ecstasy to be together.

My next assignment was to Germany, so fortunately I missed the utterly shabby and disgraceful treatment suffered by many Vietnam veterans returning to the states. I quote from Frederick Downs' telling book *The Killing Zone*:

> "In the fall of 1968, as I stopped at a traffic light on my walk to class across the campus of the University of Denver, a man stepped up to me and said, 'Hi.'
> "Without waiting for my reply to his greeting, he pointed to the hook sticking out of my left sleeve. 'Get that in Vietnam?'
> I said, 'Yeah, up near Tam Ky in I Corps.' 'Serves you right.'
> "As the man walked away, I stood rooted, too confused with hurt, shame, and anger to react.
> "Ten years have passed. The hurt, shame, and anger still flood over me with the memory. But of one thing I am certain—none of the men I knew who served in Vietnam deserved to die or be maimed either physically or mentally."

Much of the public seemed to blame veterans for the war and vented their frustrations on them—a shameful and very dark blot on our history. It was heartwarming for me to be with Vietnam veterans from across the nation, and from all the services, who came together in Washington, D.C., in November 1982 for the dedication of the Vietnam Memorial and the march down Constitution Avenue. It was a needed catharsis and brought out numerous flasks of spirits that were passed around, often from old veterans to the young underage privates and corporals in attendance. That did not go unnoticed, but no one cared. There were many leaking eyes that day. Some vets came in uniform and some in civilian clothes and others with a mixture of both. To an outsider, we must have looked like a motley squad. To us, we were just showing who we were and that we were together. Several VFW units came in matching civilian suits. One group I recall came from a steel mill in Pennsylvania wearing matching three-piece pinstripe suits. They looked uncomfortable in those suits but were still sharp and marched proudly in step I felt pride and humbled to be with my Vietnam brothers.

I am immensely proud of my Vietnam service and especially to have served with the outstanding officers and airmen of the 14th Air Commando Wing and those units under its command. Our unit was awarded the Presidential Unit Citation and the Air Force Outstanding Unit Award with V device for valor.

Two in this group earned the Medal of Honor. One was Airman First Class John Levitow, who saved a C47 gun ship and its entire crew by throwing an armed flare out of the plane just before it ignited and exploded. This was after he had been severely wounded and had 40 fragments from a mortar round in his body. At the battle of A Shau, Major Bernard Fisher landed his Skyraider (A1E) on a too short and badly damaged runway during the battle to rescue Major D.W. Myers, who had crash landed. His plane was shot up and full of holes, but they made it out. Both are excellent stories of courage under fire. I met Fisher later when he was a colonel at Bitburg AFB in Germany—a very low-key quiet guy.

Military decorations come with a miniature ribbon lapel pin for wear on a civilian coat. I'm honored to have been awarded several decorations, making a nice set of ribbons on my uniform, but the only lapel pin I have ever worn on civilian clothes represents a service medal which ranks low on the official order of precedence. It is green, red, and mostly yellow: the Vietnam Service Medal. Why do I wear that one when it is not even a decoration? It represents all 2,709,918 Americans who served in Vietnam and the 58,200 who gave their lives. That pin identifies me as being in the fight and bonds me with special brothers. It ranks at the top of my list. *Virtus junxit, mors non separabit.* "Virtue has united, and death shall not separate."

Father Denis Edward O'Brien, a Marine chaplain, said, "It is the soldier, not the reporter, who has given us freedom of the press. It is the soldier, not the poet, who has given us freedom of speech. It is the soldier, not the campus organizer, who has given us freedom to demonstrate. It is the soldier, not the lawyer, who has given us the right to a fair trial. It is the soldier, who salutes the flag, who serves beneath the flag and whose coffin is draped by the flag, who allows the protestor to burn the flag."

The Three-Year Hochzeitsreise (Honeymoon)
Germany 1968-71

My follow-on assignment from Vietnam was a consecutive overseas tour (COT) to Ramstein Air Force Base, Germany. Coming from Vietnam, it was like arriving in Shangri-La. The airbase is adjacent to the village of Ramstein, which is near the city of Kaiserslautern located in the Rhineland Pfalz. I had not explored this part of Germany during my 1958 visit. The area was covered with green pine forests, small farms, and vineyards with their orderly rows of grapevines formed up like military ranks. Autobahns allowed driving as fast as the car could go. Better yet were the small roads winding through the hills and spotless little villages. In nearly every hamlet you could get a hearty meal for little cost at the local gasthaus (tavern). The German mark was valued at four to one dollar and all the local shops and restaurants accepted U.S. coins.

It felt strange being out of Vietnam at first, but the best part of this assignment was being with my bride, whom I had left behind three days after our wedding when I shipped out for Vietnam. Now it seemed like we were really on our honeymoon. To this day, I still feel like our time in Germany was a three-year honeymoon. Loretta was still a civilian. She was an Air Force wife, taking college classes nights and weekends to earn her college degree. She worked on base as a volunteer for the Red Cross in the base thrift shop.

We hardly had two nickels to rub together but fortunately base housing was available. Housing for officers was four, four-story buildings built in a quad, with a large lawn area in the middle. The front of each building butted up to the street. All units were the same: two bedrooms with one bath, a kitchen and a larger room that served as both a dining and living room. One thing I liked about the layout was that I could stand in the spare bedroom and practice shooting my pellet rifle the length of the bedroom through the doorway across the hall and the length of the kitchen, which was 10 meters—the normal distance for pellet rifle competition. I set up my targets in the kitchen with a bullet trap to catch the pellets. Of course, we did not own one piece of furniture, but fortunately the base issued that also. When our furniture was delivered, I was surprised that it appeared to be brand-new or recently reupholstered. It was not expensive but very acceptable for two newlyweds. All units had beautiful hardwood floors which is a good start for any house. Our apartment was clean as a whistle. And no wonder as nearly everyone employed a German putzfrau (maid). Later I learned anyone using government quarters had to pass a clean house inspection by a stringent German inspector before clearing out of the base. Their maintenance was superb. Our first purchase together was a high-quality Persian rug that gave our house a little character. We then added a beautiful wood inlaid coffee table, and those two items are still with us. Quality is always quality—maybe our marriage will last also, who knows? Fifty-six years is a good start.

Lt Col William M. Coleman, my new and very good, boss, was the commander of Detachment 6 of the 1141 Special Activities Squadron. I was the personnel officer. Our job was providing support to U.S. personnel assigned to the Fourth Allied Tactical Air Force (4ATAF), a major element of the NATO Air Force operating in central Europe. Those NATO countries represented in 4ATAF were Germany, Great Britain, Belgium, Canada, the Netherlands, and the U.S. Luxembourg and France were associates. All the countries were integrated and worked together so one might find a German working

Long Shots — Military

for a Belgian who worked for a Canadian who reported to an American. And of course, all mixes were possible.

One of the most enjoyable aspects of being in NATO was meeting and working with Allied officers. In military uniforms they made a colorful group. A big event still sticks in my mind: the change of command of U.S. Air Forces in Europe and 4ATAF from General Maurice A. Preston to General Horace M. Wade. The event was held outside at the front of headquarters building on Ramstein Air Force Base. Bleachers were set up in a semi-circle facing the building filled with senior NATO officers and their wives. There were many four-star generals in fine-looking uniforms. I had never seen so many senior generals. There were so many four-star generals that people were not standing when another one came walking to the bleachers. Finally, they were all seated with Generals Preston and Wade in position. At that point a sedan drove in front of the bleachers, everyone got off their tails and stood at attention as General Lyman Lemnitzer, Supreme Allied Commander of NATO, emerged from the sedan. The change of command is a significant and serious matter; it is the passing of the torch and the acceptance of a huge responsibility. In this case, it was the most senior of NATO officers conducting the ceremony.

Gen Lemnitzer was the longest serving Supreme Commander of NATO from 1963 to 1969. He was a 1920 graduate of West Point. The general served in World War II and Korea, where he earned a Silver Star. He served as chairman of the Joint Chiefs of Staff from 1960 to 1962 and was best noted for his diplomatic skills in World War II, Korea, the joint staff, and NATO. I was delighted to meet him in the Pentagon when he stopped me in the hall to congratulate me on my Distinguished Rifleman Badge. He was retired by that time and wearing a civilian suit, so it took me a couple moments to recognize and realize who he was. He said he had earned a leg medal (credit toward the distinguished badge) during his early 20's tour in the Philippines.

Another perk was enjoying the many NATO holidays that we celebrated in addition to our own. I particularly enjoyed being able to take every Wednesday afternoon off, a 4ATAF practice. We simply closed the doors and took off. We could get to Luxembourg in time for a late lunch, although most Wednesday afternoons were spent in the local area as there was much to see and do. One of our favorites was going to the nearby village of Landstuhl for lunch at the Green Lantern. I suppose it wasn't that exciting, but at the time we thought we were quite sophisticated eating Forelle Blau (trout) with small, boiled potatoes and drinking white wine at lunch. The restaurant owners had a beautiful large black poodle that checked everyone out at their table. Germans often brought their dogs to restaurants.

When I was first reporting in for duty, it happened that a colonel was processing out at the same time. He was giving me pointers on some of the fun things to do in the surrounding area when I mentioned I needed to buy a car and was considering a new Volkswagen Beetle. It turned out he owned a 1966 Beetle with very low mileage and neat as a pin which he offered to me at half the price of a new one. The deed was done, and Loretta and I now owned a slightly used Beetle. It was no fun on the Autobahn but was exactly the right car for driving around the small, windy country roads. We drove the wheels off that little car all around Germany, and visited Luxembourg, Belgium, Holland, France, Austria, Switzerland, and Italy. Not many people drive a Beetle on a three-year honeymoon tour of eight countries. We even took my folks on a tour of Belgium and Holland with all four of us and our luggage in the little Beetle. That car was well-educated, having visited so many countries. Later in life we graduated to Porsches and Mercedes, but I don't think we ever had more fun than we had with our little secondhand Beetle. We used to go out in the evening on the small roads, looking for game, particularly the shy little Reh bucks (Roe deer). Loretta wasn't much good at spotting game to begin with, but by the time we left Germany, she was better than I was.

My friend from rifle shooting days, Army Capt Frank White, told me there was wonderful target shooting (hunter's style) and hunting in Germany. He made it sound enticing, and I must admit it blossomed into magnificent opportunities and endless enjoyment. A big factor was multiple bases, posts, and kaserns — American, Canadian, and English— Army and Air Force, which all had rod and gun clubs (R&G). Another major element was the Status of Forces Agreement in Germany, which reserved wild game hunts for American, French, Canadian, and English forces. Rod and gun clubs offer an excellent venue where officers and enlisted men can meet on a social and more equal level than at the office, field, flight line, or official functions. Military service personnel are not welcome or even allowed at each other's clubs, but at the R&G they could have a beer or dinner together, compete in shooting events, or just hang out in the gun room. The Ramstein R&G was one of the largest with a full bar, large dining room, and a sales room loaded with guns of all types. It was really a going concern and even featured slot machines when I first arrived. Things slowed down a bit when we lost the slot machines, but the shooting and hunting activities continued. We had a rifle range out to 100 yards and a running boar range.

Mr. Pearlie White, a retired NCO, ran the Ramstein R&G gun department. Naturally, we became good friends. I bought several guns from him, and we shot international (bunker) trap together at meets in Germany and Belgium. Pearlie knew all the gun makers in the sister cities of Liege and Herstal, the gun-making towns of Belgium. The major arms manufacturer in that area was Fabrique Nationale (FN) with a prolific production of military arms. The legendary Belgian manufacturer also made Browning firearms, including the famous and desired Browning Superposed over-and-under shotguns. Other fine side-by-side Belgian shotguns were Labeau Courally, and my favorite, Francotte. Pearlie introduced Mr. Andre Jacquemart, a Browning distributor and independent gun dealer, to me and my Ramstein friend, Lt Col Robert (Rip) Sewall. Andre and Rip became close friends, and he invited Rip and me, with our wives, to one of the most elegant and memorable French dinners imaginable in his home. Food in Belgium can absolutely ruin you. His house was rather nondescript with a front door directly off the street. But inside of the house was another matter; it was filled with shooting memorabilia and with fine shotguns but still tasteful and classy with antique furniture and Persian rugs. Every drawer he opened contained a Luger, Mauser, Walther, or another interesting and collectible pistol.

Capt Frank White, who was stationed in Frankfurt with the Army, also introduced me to international bunker shooting. I'm still holding him responsible for my addiction to a most difficult and frustrating sport. Really, I should be thanking him as I'm still shooting international trap 54 years later. It ushered me into so many things. For one, it brought me to the international shooting circuit occupied by many of the lords and ladies of Europe—certainly many of the Ferrari crowd. I would arrive in my Volkswagen Beetle but was accepted because I was an officer and because I could shoot. The Graf (count) and Graefin Elizabeth von Soden were often at the trap matches. Elisabeth had won the ladies world championship. She was a large, stout lady and was always helpful in working on the range, often sweeping up the empty hulls. The Graf von der Muehle was another frequent shooter on the trap range. The Graf von Soden also shot at the international hunters' championships. It also brought me together with René Haillez from Gentbrugge, Belgium, who became a lifelong trap and pheasant shooting friend.

The young Charlie Underberg, whose family made the highly popular Underberg digestive bitters drink, also came to shoot international trap at Ramstein. He rolled up one time in a large, black Mercedes sedan. Charlie jumped out of the driver's seat wearing Levis, and out of the backseat came the chauffeur wearing a beautiful double-breasted gray suit and the chauffeur's cap. That caused people to take a double look. Charlie loved to drive fast.

About being accepted, Frank White explains it better than anyone. He says a playboy has a certain gene that is also found in a hobo. However, with money, that gene allows one to become a playboy, while with no money, one remains a hobo. The one saving grace if you have that gene is to become an officer; you have no money, but you can act like a playboy. I believe he's right.

Capt Don Berry was at Ramstein when I arrived, and we became boon companions in shooting and hunting. He was a good organizer, and between the two of us we really got things rolling on the shooting side of the rod and gun club. Don was an accomplished skeet shooter and tutored me into an almost respectable skeet shooter. Our primary game was international trap, or more often, *Deutscher Jagdschutz-Verband* (DJV—German Hunters Federation) matches—a hunter's match combining rifle and shotgun shooting. DJV matches were shot throughout Germany, and ranges could be found in even the smaller villages so there was ample opportunity for competition.

In the rifle shooting, the competitors had to use a hunting rifle within standard weight. The simulated game targets of reh buck, fox, and uberlaufer (one-year-old boar) were shot at 100 meters. Running boar was shot at 60 meters. The shotgun portion involved both trap and skeet shooting in the international style of low gun. The same shotgun had to be used for both events with no barrel or choke changes. The only change could be in the size of shot used.

A separate DJV event was conducted for pistol shooting. That included slow fire, rapid fire, and QuickDraw. But it wasn't like a Western Quick Draw; in DJV the pistol had to be concealed by a buttoned or zipped-up coat before the draw. It was wild. I used a .22 High Standard pistol with a 4-inch barrel, and my draw was from a shoulder holster under a green sports coat. It worked well enough for me to win the Gold DJV Pin at the regional championship in Bad Kreuznach. These little DJV competitions exposed us to German hunters and their traditions in addition to providing all of us with enjoyment and good solid training for better hunting. They were usually followed by beers or dinner at the local gasthaus or R&G club. I was fortunate enough to attend three international hunters shooting championships, one in Luxembourg, another in Holland, and one in Austria where I was the team captain. It was also my honor to be the U.S. team captain for the German national DJV championship five times.

Because of our large clubhouse size and range capability for both rifle and shotgun shooting, we were able to hold good-sized matches for DJV and international trap. We did not have a bunker trap but substituted two very good ground-level wobble traps. International competitors came to our matches not only because they were well-run but also because of the great steaks, cheap cigars, and one-armed bandits in our R&G club. We had the top trap shooters from Germany, a world champion from France, and another world champion from Belgium. Our regular local German shooters were Herr Pfeifer, Herr Steiger, and Dr. Engle. The regular R&G club trap shooters were Lt Col R. Sewall, Capt D. Berry, TSgt Jungers, Mr. F. Benson, Mr. P. White, me, and the Pan-American pilot, Otto Kiehl.

One of our local German trap shooters, Herr Rubsaamen, was from Bad Durkheim, less than an hour away from Ramstein. It is a center for German white wine, and the city hosts a major wine fest each year— smaller but like Munich's Oktoberfest. He owned a winery tucked away in the mountainside. It was a real treat to be invited to a winetasting inside his cave. It was cold and damp in the cave, so we were all given red wool capes with hoods that made us look like Catholic Cardinals. His tasting room was deep in the cave with a large round table in the middle of the room crowded full of wine glasses. We picked up a clean glass for each wine and were told that if we didn't like the wine to simply dump it in buckets located on the floor. I don't recall anyone dumping wine. Before the wine tour we would have dinner at the Wine Academy Restaurant close by. The chef was from Lebanon, and he prepared the most delicious pommes frites any of us had ever eaten. His best dinner was a superb tenderloin with salad, pommes frites, and deep-fried Camembert cheese served with Preiselbeeren (wild cranberry). It was mouthwatering. We have tried every which way to duplicate the deep-fried Camembert with only minimal success.

Lt Col Rip Sewall joined us in DJV and international trap shoots. He and I also shot trap in Belgium and France. Senior Master Sergeant James McCausland was at Ramstein prior to my arrival and knew the ropes; he was already hunting with Germans. Mac was an accomplished shooter with both rifle and shotgun who made an excellent team member for DJV shooting; he could compete with the best. Mac had won the coveted large gold pin in DJV competition. It can only be won at the German National Championship. Only one other American, Army Col Alexander Marchioli, held that distinction. I'm proud to say I made it three Americans with a score of 331 at the 1972 German Championship held in Liebenau/Weser. A score of 320 was the minimum score required.

Capt Doug Forsythe arrived from Vietnam shortly after me. He was an excellent skeet shooter and started hunting with us. Capt Tommy Brown also arrived from Vietnam to join our hunting and shooting group. We became a tight circle of friends. Tommy Brown recently died, but I'm in touch with each of the others, and I am still shooting/hunting with Don Berry and Doug Forsythe.

We had some crazy but fun shoots. Rip Sewall and I, along with our wives, were invited to a New Year's Eve international trap shoot at Bad Durkheim. It had been snowing all week and was snowing on our drive from Ramstein to Bad Durkheim. The clubhouse and range were at the end of a winding road on the top of a hill. The match was organized by Herr Ruprecht Doppler and Herr Klaus Rubsaamen. It was shot under lights and started after dinner around 10:00 p.m. It was darn cold, so the shooters stayed inside the clubhouse and watched through the large glass windows until it was their turn to shoot. After shooting, they would race back into the clubhouse for a little drink to warm their insides. It is common throughout Europe to have a bar and restaurant on site, and both shooters and spectators drank whenever they felt like it. It was New Year's Eve, and the drinking was heavier than normal. The shooting stopped at midnight for some hooting and hollering along with champagne drinking to welcome the New Year. Then it was back to shooting. The snowing and champagne drinking continued. Finally, the prizes were handed out, and they were all magnums of champagne. By then the snow had piled up on all the cars, as well as on the winding road up to the range. Nothing to do but finish off all the champagne, which we did. I believe the chauffeuring home was done 100% by the wives—after it became light. It was a fun New Year's Eve but not a fun New Year's Day.

To jazz up award ceremonies for our shooting competitions, I invited Brig Gen Charles "Chuck" Yeager to make the award presentations. He was a regular at our R&G club, and I had shot with him a bit, so I made an appointment to ask him to hand out trophies. He agreed but then said; "Do I have to wear my uniform?" Of course, we wanted him in uniform, but what does a young captain say to a general with a question like that? I sort of stuttered and stammered and replied it wasn't necessary but would be nice. We never knew how he might show up; one time it would be in uniform and the next time he would be in Levis wearing those light-colored Red Wing lace-up hunting boots and a plaid shirt. German and other European international shooters would often question me when he showed up in Levis, asking if he was really a general, much less the one who broke the sound barrier. Most of the time he did show up in uniform, and every time he came to one of our dinners, he wore his uniform. I didn't realize until many years later what an imposition it was for him to take the time out of his schedule to come out on Sunday afternoons or Saturday nights to support our R&G efforts. He got along well with the enlisted guys and put them at ease. He went into the Army Air Force at 18, straight out of high school as an aircraft mechanic and had no college education, which I believe made him feel closer to our hard-working enlisted troops. He put on no airs and didn't have to. Much later, I learned his hunting was at a considerable higher social level than ours, but he never mentioned that in our get-togethers at the Ramstein R&G Club. My belief is he just didn't want to upstage any of the club members in our modest escapades. One of Gen Yeager's hunts I am absolutely jealous of was with General LeMay, shooting partridge in Spain as a guest of General Franco. Driven partridge is the sport of kings and certainly one of my favorites. I can just imagine what it must've been like to experience that with Gen Franco. He did tell us of his crazy escapade or maybe better described as a misadventure of trying to transplant golden trout from the California High Sierra to the Rocky Mountains — illegal, of course. They managed to drown a helicopter in a High Sierra Lake in that deal and nearly get a couple of guys killed, including a general. They tell me Gen Yeager could be difficult to work for, but I found him easy to be around and I always enjoyed his company at the R&G club or on the shooting range.

  Later in life, it was my pleasure to meet him several times at the Safari Club International Convention, often at the life member's breakfast, and veterans' event, where we would reminisce about our hunting and shooting days in Germany. He remembered my name, which is amazing considering all the famous people he knew, including four presidents who each decorated him: President Truman, President Eisenhower, President Ford, and President Reagan. He also knew President Johnson. The list of luminaries he knew is extensive. It included world leaders, top military brass, industrialists, scientists, artists, and the Hollywood gang starting with Bob Hope. Gen Yeager didn't just meet these people; he socialized with them and was often a guest at dinner parties with them, courtesy of his mentor Jacqueline Cochran. One time, I was in Santiago, Chile, at the Delta lounge waiting for my connection to Córdoba, Argentina. As I walked over to the coffee machine, I noticed a man wearing Levis with his head down reading a paperback. He closed the book, and I saw it was *Yeager* by Chuck Yeager. Sure enough, it was Gen Yeager with his new wife (his beloved Glennis had died). They were on a fishing trip. I asked him what in the world he was doing reading his own book. He replied he was only trying to remember what he said.

Gen Yeager was the father of the sonic boom, being the first man to fly faster than sound in the Bell X-1, which made him famous. But he was much more than that. Flying a P-51 Mustang fighter in World War II he became an Ace by downing 13 enemy planes, five in one day. He was shot down over France and received a Purple Heart for his injuries. With the help of the French underground (Maquis) he escaped to Spain and then returned to England to complete flying 64 combat missions. He did this when pilots who had been shot down were not supposed to return to their previous combat duties. He actually met with Gen Eisenhower for permission to stay in the fight. No shirker was he.

In 1962, he took command of the USAF Aerospace Research Pilot School at what is now Edwards Air Force Base where he constantly pushed for state-of-the-art training. His book, *Yeager: An Autobiography*, is entertaining, exciting, and inspiring. Much of it is accounts written by his friends and fellow flyers. Especially interesting is how and why he was selected as a very young test pilot, over many jealous educated hotshot test pilots, to push the X-1 past the sound barrier. Col Albert Boyd, who retired as a major gen, was the officer in charge and had the authority and responsibility for the selection. The colonel realized whoever broke the sound barrier would become the face of the Air Force. Capt Yeager had no sophistication and apparently spoke English poorly. Boyd fretted about the Air Force image if its hero didn't know a verb from a noun. He decided that before Chuck would meet the public, he would give him English lessons. History proved the colonel made the right choice. Even with all his test pilot fame and breaking the sound barrier, Gen Yeager said, "For me, combat remains the ultimate flying experience."

We lost a great American at age 97 when Gen Yeager died in 2020. I have his autographed book and recommend it to flyers, historians, or anyone interested in a good read. As an aside, Lt Bob

157

Hoover was Capt Yeager's backup on the X 1. He was shot down - escaping to Holland in a stolen plane. His book, Forever Flying, tells how Yuri Gagarin saved him from Soviet prison. He graciously autographed a copy for me. I met triple ace Brig Gen Tex Hill shooting pigeons. His book, Flying Tigers, is an excellent read.

The hunting in Germany turned out to be even better than my friend Frank White described. We were treated as guests by German forestry officials who cheerfully guided us on individual hunts for red deer, reh deer, fallow deer, mouflon, or chamois. American military personnel were authorized a game quota by the Status of Forces Agreement with Germany, but remember, Germany was their country, and it was their animals. I considered it a special privilege to hunt with them. They have a great abundance of game for such a small country, but it is managed carefully. Both females and fawns are harvested to keep the number of wild animals in proper balance. They also made it easy for us to obtain a German hunting license. The normal study time for a German license, called a Jagdschein, was one year. They learn everything about the game and predatory animals. They really study the flora and fauna and can identify the animals and birds by their tracks and scat. Their program produced real woodsmen. Our program was a couple of times a week for three or four weeks. After receiving my Jagdschein I helped teach the American course.

While I did do some hunting for what was classified as higher game, such as red stag, chamois, and Russian boar, my main interest was Niederwild (small game), which included pheasants, partridge, pigeons, snipe, hares, and rabbits. Reh deer were the only hoofed animal classified as Niederwild. I hunted reh deer on both federal forest land and private property. Nearly all the reh bucks I took were Abschuss (management bucks) that the Revier owner or forester wanted taken out. All the trophies (skull mount) were shown at the local trophy show each year. Good Abschuss trophies were valued as much as top trophies, and the hunters taking them were praised. The same is true with chamois, and I have a couple of old aunties (old barren females) from Austria that rate high. By the way, they get very smart and can be hard to hunt as they are not distracted like bucks during the rut. Bird hunts were done for the most part on private property. Hunting areas are called Reviers. Much of the time, several hunters would go together and purchase the hunting rights of several farms or parts of the forest. They then owned the animals and the rights to hunt, but they were also responsible for managing the animals and paying for any damage caused by animals or hunters. The hunting Revier contract for small game, including reh deer, was for nine years and for big game, which included red stag, chamois, mouflon and fallow deer, was for 11 years. Just another example of long-range proper game management.

German hunting is rich in tradition with many customs. It is also somewhat aristocratic and very social. Much of my hunting was done around the small villages on farms and vineyards near Ramstein. Two very good friends, Johannes Freiherr von Schorlemer and Dr. Heiner Kausch, lived in Saarbrücken, and we had many good driven hunts for hares and pheasants in their revier. John, as you can tell by his title, was a baron. He and Dr. Kausch were leaders in the hunting community, and both were fine gentlemen. John had an elegant apartment in Saarbrücken. Lt Col Sewall and I, along with our wives, were invited to a dinner party celebrating John's birthday. It was one of those dinners one does not forget. In my case it was the first time I had Cherries Jubilee. John's daughters acted as waiters, and I can still see and smell the steaming pot of cherries placed in the middle of the large round dining table. John and his lovely wife Renate remain good friends of ours to this day.

A good friend and hunting partner was Klaus Winter, a pharmacist who owned the Apotheke (pharmacy) in Ramstein and later bought the Schwanen Apotheke in Speyer. He hunted with a fine Kleiner Munsterlander hunting dog that rode on his motorcycle with him. He took me and my friend Capt Doug Forsythe on a memorable pheasant hunt at his uncle's vineyard on the Weinstrasse after the grapes had been harvested. It was memorable on two counts: one, the high number of pheasants, so many that I ran out of shells, which I can tell you doesn't happen often—I carry lots of shells. I can vividly recall Doug Forsythe toward the end happily flaying away at pheasants without offering me any ammo. The second memory was not so happy—recovering from drinking all the new wine that was not yet ready for bottling. Klaus and his wife Doris became good friends. Unfortunately, Klaus was killed by his best friend, a Catholic priest, in a tragic hunting accident, leaving a wife and three young daughters. Just a couple of years back, my German boy Max took me to Speyer to see Doris. She was delighted I came to visit, and I was pleased to learn she and her daughters were all getting along well.

Another good German shooting and hunting friend is Manfred Mack, who was introduced to me by my friend Frank White. Frank and Manfred formed a tight friendship, and Manfred has visited Texas many times. He is a Doctor of Engineering and worked four years in the States for Black & Decker at their global headquarters in Maryland. Manfred is always good company and has a keen sense of humor; it's a pleasure to be with him.

Many of the German hunters carried a small Jagdhorn (hunting bugle) with them, and they played various tunes to honor the different animals taken. Dress was more formal than in the United States; green clothes were required, and wearing a tie while hunting was not unwelcomed. Proper dress would require a loden coat for inclement weather. The hooved animals, such as reh deer, red deer, and chamois are given a letzter Bissen (last bite); a small branch from an evergreen was placed in their mouth. Another branch would be wiped in the blood of the animal and then worn in the hunter's hatband as a trophy. Additionally, after a drive hunt, all the animals taken are laid out in the proper order according to ranks, called a Strecke. Then each species is given the proper Jagdhorn salute as a last tribute. This is often done after dark witnessed by the light of torches. Some boar hunting was done at night— particularly during a full moon and when there was snow on the ground, which reflected more light for rifle scopes. No artificial light was allowed. With their excellent wildlife management and all their different game, one could hunt nearly year-round.

The American Rod and Gun Clubs, Europe, was in Heidelberg along with Headquarters United States Army Europe. Part of their responsibility was allocating game quotas to U.S. forces and coordinating hunts with German organizations and private German hunters. Lt Col Lloyd C. Hall was the Executive Secretary Custodian. We got to know each other at a German DJV shoot. He was good at his job, and I liked him.

German hunters in the Regensburg area in Bavaria organized a pheasant hunt for military VIPs each year. Invitations for this hunt were given out by the Association of American Rod and Gun Clubs, Europe. As it happened, Capt Don Berry and I were somehow included in 1968. Several flag officers, some four- and three-star rank, were in attendance, including an admiral who came up from Naples, Italy. The military had two private trains in Europe, each with a command-and-control car that insured movement and communication for senior officers in fog or inclement weather. I noted both trains were in the German town of Platting, where the hunt social activities were held.

Don and I were shuffled off to hunt with farmers around Altenbuch and Wolferdorf, which were just little villages, called dorfs. These farmers may not have been aristocrats, but they owned their farms and combined them into a large and fine hunting Revier. The farmland was rich and productive much like the country I had known in middle Iowa. They raised corn, other grain crops, and sugar beets. There were many ditches, small, wooded areas, and grown-up fence lines — perfect for pheasants. It was long before the clean farming and insecticides of today. The hunt with those farmers was the beginning of a fine friendship that lasts to this day. Their unofficial leader was Herr Paul Fladausch. He headed up the local co-op bank. Don and I dubbed him the "DO," director of operations, as he was continually giving instructions to ensure the hunt went as planned. My favorite farmers were Albert Krinner, Josef Maier, Paul Thone, and Franz Fischer.

Paul Fladausch never learned English, and my German was less than poor, but we became fast friends and understood each other. He and his wife came to visit us in Washington, D.C., but we also did a side trip to Texas for a little hunting. They came a second time, and I drove them from Montana to the West Coast and then back to Texas to show him our country and to visit with friends who had hunted with him in Germany. He is gone now but Frau Fladausch was still alive six years ago when I visited Altenbuch. Her son Paul Jr. and the hunters listed above arranged a wonderful afternoon reunion dinner and beer bust with me sitting next to Frau Fladausch in her yard. Some of the hunters' children and grandchildren have visited us in Texas.

Those pheasant hunts in Altenbuch were simply amazing. They would start after lunch, and we would all hunt together in a mini driven shoot with the neighborhood kids and farmers who didn't hunt acting as beaters in the cornfields driving the birds out. Then, around 3:00 p.m., we would break and head to different farmhouses for coffee and cake. Frau Fladausch was a superb cook, and she always made three or four cakes for us to try — all quite yummy. Her strong German coffee was topped with homemade whipped cream. After the cake and coffee, we would hunt in pairs with a dog or two in good areas and sometimes just drive around sugar beet fields until we saw pheasants run into the beets. Then we would stop the car, take the dogs, and walk up the pheasants. Many afternoons, I would shoot 25 to 35 roosters. These were not English pen-raised or South Dakota early-release birds; these were all 100% wild with long tail feathers. On the opening day, our little group would often shoot well over 300 roosters. All would be pulled (partially cleaned) and hung with the feathers on in a cool barn. The birds were then sold to a local gasthaus and restaurants in Regensburg or surrounding cities. The funds for these sales were then used to help pay for the Reviers' expenses.

Hunters put out feed for wild game during heavy snow or severe storms. Each hunter on these shoots was normally given two pheasants, but I frequently took a dozen back to Ramstein. They were stored in paper bags in my refrigerator until the next day when I finally got home from work to clean them. Living in a high-rise apartment, I cleaned birds using the bathtub as a catchall for feathers, guts, and pheasant feet. It was not a fun task. During the hunting season, wild game was served in nearly every gasthaus or restaurant. It was always a fun time and most enjoyable to share in the camaraderie of these farmers, all good men, and enjoy the wonderful meals prepared by Frau Fladausch. Loretta became a favorite in their household because she loved Frau Fladausch's cakes and dumplings. We flew back from the States for those hunts, and I made opening day of pheasant season in Bavaria 17 different years. Herr Fladausch and his Altenbuch hunters allowed me to bring friends on the pheasant hunt. Those I took at different times were Frank White, Pearlie White, Doug Forsythe, Rolf Smith, Charlie Weaver, Ron Lumpe, Mark Taishoff, and of course Loretta.

Another hunt that came to Don Berry and me from the American Rod and Gun Clubs, Europe, was an invitation to shoot Rebhuhn (Hungarian partridge). The hunt was sponsored by the German hunters of Bamberg. It was a two-day hunt in early September; we were staying in the Gasthaus Schmidt in Berg, just 4 km south of Bamberg. Loretta was with me. She did not yet hunt, but she liked to come and walk with me and often retrieved the birds, although she didn't like picking up those that were still alive. Don was shooting a 20-gauge Browning automatic, the old humpback model, and when we met with the German hunters, he attracted a little good-natured teasing about shooting a Damen Flinte (ladies' shotgun). Nearly all the Germans shot 12-gauge guns in those days. This was not a high-volume hunt nor was it an English-style driven shoot; instead, we were positioned around brushy areas and had little mini drives. On the very first drive Don drew a spot where most shooters could see him. The first bird went whistling his way, and bang it went down. Then another and bang it went down, followed by a third bang and a bird went down. Then a fourth bird went his way, and the fourth bang brought him another bird. Finally, a fifth partridge came barreling out on his side, and another bang brought him five for five. Most of the hunters witnessed his shooting, and there was no more teasing about his Damen Flinte. We did a partridge hunt not far from Ramstein in a rather hilly area around sugar beets and alfalfa fields. The German hunting friend who had invited us had a wire-haired Dackel (dachshund) as his hunting dog that he used for tracking wounded reh deer and Russian boar. Now we were using his tracking dog as our bird flusher. It was almost comical: a covey of Hungarian partridge had flushed and flown into a sugar beets field, and we went after them. We walked down the rows, but they were holding tight. The short Dackel could not be seen under the sugar beets, but every now and then he would jump straight up and look around to see where we were as he trailed and flushed the partridge. It was quite an education for me, and while the Dackel was certainly not a bird dog, he was useful. I learned they were very popular as trackers for wounded game. My friend Charlie Weaver had a little Dackel male named Dingo that he used in hunting Russian boar and reh deer. That tiny hound managed to bite most of Charlie's hunting friends. It really wasn't Dingo's fault as the biting normally occurred at little beer drinking fests after the hunt when exuberant and inebriated hunters would get down on all fours face-to-face with Dingo and growl. It was a very chancy endeavor. Charlie very rightly refused to pay for any of the stitching-up of lips and noses.

I was guest on a couple of quite interesting and fun kaninchen (cottontail rabbit) hunts in Germany and Belgium using tame ferrets. The hunters kept ferrets all year just for these hunts. They became real pets, and the hunters could hold them in their hands; the ferrets appeared to enjoy being petted. The hunters would surround a rabbit mound, and then put the ferret into one of the rabbit tunnels. Talk about fast shooting! The rabbits would explode out of the rabbit mound from every direction when they detected the ferret. It was pandemonium. The only problem was the ferret would sometimes catch a rabbit, and then maybe take a nap in the rabbit mound. The hunters had to dig the ferret out, which could be dangerous for the ferret. Sometimes they would leave the ferret cage and the hunter's coat out in the hope the ferret would recognize (smell) it and get back in the cage, which they often did. The hunter would then pick them up later. That hunt was near Mannheim where General Patton's Cadillac collided with the U.S. Army truck that caused his death. He was on his way to a pheasant hunt with a bird dog riding in the front seat.

Most of the large hunts for hasen (hares) were done in the hard winter when snow was on the ground. Those hunts were not my favorite, but they offered camaraderie and it was always fun to watch the dogs. Another attraction was Gluhwein (hot spiced wine) served with sausages and a bun at an outside lunch. Those drinking beer often had to heat up frozen beer bottles to make them drinkable—the Germans don't favor ice cold beer. It happened that I had received an invitation for three hunters for a hasen hunt in Bavaria, and of course I invited Don Berry. He suggested we ask Brig Gen Robert Ellis, commander of

Long Shots — Military

the 86th Air Division, who had shot some skeet with us to be our third member. The general accepted.

The hunt was on a Saturday morning, but I had a function Friday night that was pretty much mandatory. The plan was to leave after my function, which would put us at the hunt location around one in the morning. Don's wife needed her car for something over the weekend, so we were taking my Beetle; the general would ride in the front with me, and Berry would get the backseat. Friday afternoon the general called and said he thought it would be better if we took his wife's car. No arguments from us. She had a new white Pontiac coupe with a beautiful white leather interior. We were invited to stay Friday night at the Jagdleiter's (hunt leader) farmhouse. I got loose from my function around 7:30 p.m., but it turned out our calculations on miles and time were off a little and we arrived in the hunter's barnyard around three in the morning. It was late, but a light was on, and our options were: knock on the door or sit in the car the rest of the night. We knocked and it was answered by the owner's son, a large lad of probably 20 years who was quite happy to see us. Many of the German farmers' barns were attached to the house, and he took us to a room with three beds above the cows' stalls. It was freezing outside and not much warmer inside. He fiddled with the stove a bit but could not get it going. He said, "macht nichts" (never mind) and left us. The pillows were so cold you had to warm them up with your hands before putting your face on them. We all pulled the covers up over our heads to keep warm.

Six-thirty in the morning came early; the young enthusiastic owner's son wanted us to shoot ducks before the hasen hunt. We had coffee, good hard German bread, and some sausages before adding on all the extra clothes we had. We went out in the freezing barnyard to collect two dogs, and then we loaded into the general's car, with the dogs held on the floor of the front seat by the young hunter. The general was driving with Don and me tucked in the back. The young German was urging us to go faster as it was getting light, and he wanted to be on a stream across the plowed field that was frozen solid. We were racing along when we must've hit a high frozen ridge, which ripped the muffler off the general's car. I felt bad about the general's car and thought that he would never want to go with us again. We got to the little stream and fired a few useless shots at fleeing ducks.

Then it was time to get back to the barnyard to meet up with the hunters for the hasen shoot. Our boots were muddy, so we were walking back in the snow off the track to clean them off a bit. The dogs were, of course, mud balls from being in the stream and muddy bank. When we got to the general's car, the young hunter opened the door on his side, and in a nanosecond both dogs leapt in on the white front seat, jumped into the back seat, and then jumped back to the front. It was just like Ping Pong—mud covered the whole car interior. Don and I were speechless; the beautiful white inside of the general's car looked like it had been the recovery area of mud wrestlers. What other destruction could we organize for the general's car? To his credit and our immense relief, the general took it well and even joked about getting it cleaned before giving it back to his wife.

We got back to the assembly point at the barnyard as the hunters and drivers arrived. This would be a Kesseltreiben (circle drive). The hunters would start from a central point with one group going right and another group going left in a large arc. As they went, they would drop off a Treiber (driver), and another 20 meters further on drop off a Schutzer (shooter), alternating drivers and shooters until they completed a large circle. Nearly every hunter had a dog on a leash. When the circle was complete, a hunting horn would sound, and the shooters/hunters and drivers would move forward, shooting and driving hasen to the middle of the circle. The drivers were filling gaps in the line between shooters so the hasen would not run out. They also helped carry the hasen that had been shot.

In the early stages of the hunt, shooters would shoot toward inside of the circle and then outside the circle if a hase ran out. Most of the hasen would run into the circle, but invariably, someone's dog would get off its leash and tear after a hase — some would race from the opposite side of the circle. It was quite a sight to watch a fast German shorthair racing after a crafty hase. A hunter would, of course, end the chase if the hase got within range. The shooters could not enter the circle to retrieve their runaway dog so a lot of yelling and cursing would be heard. When the circle got too tight (unsafe) the Jagdleiter would blow his horn, indicating shooting direction was allowed only outside of the circle after the hasen ran out of the circle. Eventually, a bugle would call to halt all shooting, and those hasen still in the middle would remain free.

We finished the hunt about one in the afternoon, having taken several hundred hasen for the market. Each shooter and hunter was presented a hase for participating. The Revier owner (who had invited us) hosted a lunch, and this would not just be bratwurst and bun. It was held in a huge hall for all the hunters and the drivers, which was the normal practice. In this case there must've been close to 200 guests. As custom and tradition dictated, the hunters sat at their tables on one side and the drivers sat at their tables on the other side. It was a noisy and rowdy and muddy affair with all the dogs under the tables with lots of beer and good times.

Hase or Hasenpfeffer was a favorite German meal and could be ordered in nearly any Gasthaus during the season. The general was happy with the hunt and lunch celebration. We went on that afternoon, car growling like a tank, to another small-town hotel for a DJV hunters match on Sunday, where he became the first general officer to earn a coveted DJV shooting qualification pin. The car remained dirty.

Some of the dinners after the hunt with many hunters and beaters could be quite colorful. Hunters were often chastised and fined for violations of protocol, which were often made-up charges. A fine could be buying a round of beer, drinking beer poured through the barrel of the shotgun, and such. It was somewhat like an Air Force officers' dining in, which is for officers only—no wives. It was silliness but enjoyed by many, particularly as the night wore on and the beer flowed freely. Often there would be a dogfight or two as all the hunters brought their dogs in and put them under the dining tables. Sometimes the tables would jump as the dogs struggled with one another.

Those years at Ramstein were arguably the most enjoyable in my career. My job was not overtaxing, and I had little real responsibility. I had a job to do as well as I could, but not many tough decisions or worries. Loretta was still a civilian and traveled with me to most of the shoots and hunts. The target shooting was not very interesting for her so she would often take the car and explore the local area while I shot. She claims to have seen every castle and cathedral in Germany at least twice. It could be true. Still, we had a lot of fun just traveling and seeing the local sights and people on hunting and shooting trips.

Some things stick in your mind, and I recall stopping at a small hotel/restaurant in Italy. We had no reservations and were happy to get a place to stay. No one spoke English and we didn't speak Italian but that was all right; they knew what we wanted. We didn't expect much and were hardly looking for or wanting to pay for luxury. Our room was good sized but nearly bare. There were a couple of wooden chairs, a wooden bed, a small wooden table, and a dresser. The bath was down the hall but there were two glasses and a water pitcher on the table and a larger bowl and second pitcher of water for washing with soap and a towel on the dresser. There was not even a throw rug on the wooden floor and the only thing on the wall was a Christian cross over the bed. However, that room was scrubbed so squeaky clean you felt like you shouldn't walk even barefoot on the floors.

We had traveled to most of the western countries of Europe and visited Istanbul, Turkey; Athens, Greece; and Tehran, Iran. The three-year honeymoon came to an end at Ramstein, and we moved on to our next assignment.

Assignments after Ramstein

After leaving Ramstein AFB in my NATO support job, we stayed in Germany and moved to Rhein-Main AFB, which sat across the runway from the Frankfurt International Airport. The unit of assignment was the 322 Combat Support Group, and my job was in the consolidated base personnel office (CBPO) along with four other captains working under the CBP0 Chief, Major William Sparks. Lt Col John H. V. Lorch, the Director of Personnel for the base, was our big boss and a good one. Rhein Main was a small but important support base as we were the main terminal for passenger travel for all the military services from the States to northern Europe, but we didn't have as many senior officers as were found at Ramstein. Our Wing Commander was a colonel. It was a good assignment for me both professionally and socially. I learned a great deal more about the personnel business and was twice chosen to fill in for the absent deputy combat support group commander, who was a lieutenant colonel. It was pretty heady for a captain, particularly since the Wing Commander selected me. It certainly broadened my perspective. I still don't know why I was chosen, but it made for some jealous captains and majors.

Socially, we had a lot more interface with other captains. Friday nights at the officers' club were a must and always entertaining. We had moved up to a new forest green (proper color for a hunter) Mercedes coupe that made travel easier and more fun, particularly on the Autobahn. The Beetle was still with us as Loretta was racing around to different Air Force bases and Army posts chasing a college degree through extension and night courses. Naturally, we acquired an additional group of friends. Capt Rosalyn Knapp was my favorite from the CBPO. We remained friends and Ros was eventually promoted to full colonel. Capt Melvin Grover was in the police squadron. He was in Vietnam during Tet as I was and earned a Bronze Star during a gun battle on the flight line of Tan Son Nhut Air Base (Saigon). Mel was later promoted to colonel and became the chief cop for the Air Force Training Command. Tom Riffe was another captain we met, and he and his wife Ruthellen became fast friends of ours and still are to this day. One day, I noticed Tom taking a shotgun out of the trunk of his car, and I recognized it as a Browning superposed; he was obviously a man of good taste. Tom left active duty but stayed in the reserve and retired as a full colonel. He introduced me to some great antelope hunts, and he has hunted with me in Argentina. Quarters were not available on base at Rhein Main, but we found a very fine apartment that a countess had recently vacated at #7 Schubertstr in Langen, a small town only 20 minutes from the base. It was a lovely one-bedroom unit with a long, combined living and dining room with a large sun porch at one end. It was actually above the owner's home. An extra most desirable feature was a one-car garage for our new Mercedes coupe. We liked living on the economy and resolved to do it whenever we could; you get much closer and learn the people better.

One memory that still sticks out in my mind was a joint promotion party. Promotion parties were common and expected, but this one was a combined party for all those who were selected for promotion to major, lieutenant colonel, and most of all, brigadier general.

Our Wing Commander, Thomas M. Sadler, had been selected Brigadier General. I was in the mix of those selected for major. Tradition was those being promoted contributed a dollar amount equivalent to the difference in their present pay and their new grade/rank for a promotion party. We all chipped in our designated amounts, and I think Brig Gen (Select) Sadler must have tripled his donation. Every officer on the base was invited along with his wife. Our officers' club was not large enough to hold such an affair, so we ended up on the other side of the runway at the Frankfurt International Airport in a very large room that could handle a big band along with all the officers and wives from the base. It was a memorable affair with food and dancing along with a great deal of drinking. Brig Gen Sadler was colorful, to say the least. He was later promoted to major general and became the head cop of all our security police. He is credited with bringing up sagging morale and revitalizing the security police field. Credit him for having the beret approved for our security police force.

From Rhein Main, I was assigned to the Military Personnel Center (MPC) at Randolph Air Force Base, San Antonio, Texas. MPC is the mecca for those in the personnel career field. It was another eye-opener for me. I started as an assignments officer. It was trying to get the right guy in the right place, first for the needs of the Air Force, second for the individual's career progression, and third, desires of the officer. Matching the resources with the requirements is not an easy task, particularly when it involves people and their careers or personal desires. It was also a rather difficult and emotionally trying period as we were exercising a very significant and rapid reduction in strength as directed by Congress in their budget process. In the very clearest language, we were kicking good officers out of the Air Force, many of whom had served honorably in combat. Sad indeed, actually an atrocity. I ended my MPC tour as executive officer to the Chief, Officer Career Management Division. That was Col Albert Audette. His deputy was a full colonel, and he had several divisions all manned by full colonels, so as a junior major I learned to dance on a very small table.

I mentioned the great MPC bosses in the chapter on the Air Force. I have to add a lieutenant colonel who was an assignments officer in the rated (flying) Manning branch. That was James B. Davis. It happened that we were each invited to a dove hunt where we discovered we had a mutual friend in René Haillez, a Belgian hunter. Lt Col Davis was promoted to colonel while we were both serving at MPC. Bobby Throldahl, who had been assigned with me in Vietnam and at Ramstein, was at MPC as an assignments officer for personnel folks. Jim Delaney was an assignments officer for administrative people. Jim served with me again in the Joint Chiefs of Staff, and as a full colonel became Chief of the Administration for the entire Air Force—a very key position. He was a good leader and made significant improvements in the administration field.

Loretta had joined the Air Force and received an assignment to Korea after serving her first assignment on the flight line at Randolph Air Force Base. I was not keen on returning to the Orient after Vietnam, and I had already seen Japan, Hong Kong, and Thailand. But naturally I wanted to be with my Loretta and applied for a joint assignment to Korea. It turned out to be a marvelous experience, which is covered in my chapter: Land of the Morning Calm.

Never Go Back

Finishing up our tour in Korea in 1976, we were thinking it would be nice to go back to Europe, perhaps Belgium, Holland, Spain, Italy, Norway, or even England, for a different experience and to broaden our knowledge. All these countries had requirements for Air Force officers. We put our request formally in the system on what was commonly referred to as a "dream sheet," which seldom matched up with the actual assignment you were given. The local personnel people called me and told me my new assignment was to Germany. That was okay with me. Then they said it would be at Ramstein Air Force Base, which was even better since we knew people there, and I had good hunting connections. Then I was told the assignment was to Detachment 6, of the 1141 Special Activities Squadron. Gad, I had been assigned to that unit 10 years earlier. There was a saying in the Air Force, "Never go back." First, things are never the same, and second, it looks like you're regressing professionally. The next news was I was to be the commander of the unit. That was a little better, but I was still uneasy about returning to the same unit.

I sent a note to my friend Rip Sewall, who had been promoted to full colonel and was base commander of Zweibrucken Air Force Base, asking him to buy me a car: a Mercedes, BMW, or Porsche so I would have wheels when we arrived in Germany. Loretta didn't care which car we bought as long as it wasn't black. A couple of weeks later, I got a surprise call on Sunday from Colonel Rip Sewall on the red military phone in my civilian off-base quarters. I had the phone because of my position as executive officer to the J1 (Chief of Army Personnel or in this case Joint Personnel). But it was still a surprise to get a personal call from Germany, and it caught me off guard. Rip told me he found a very good used Mercedes, low mileage and clean. It had been chauffeur driven. All of this sounded good, so I told him to please buy it. After he hung up, the light bulb came on, and I thought chauffeur driven sounds like the car could be black. Nothing to do at that stage; sure enough, it was black. One nice thing about the car was it had an aftermarket gooseneck lamp in the backseat, which allowed me to sit back there and do paperwork while Loretta drove when we took off for hunts or vacations on Friday nights. I liked to brag to my friends that I had a uniformed chauffeur who drove my Mercedes. Loretta was not amused. We did find a picturesque home to rent in the little village of Weilerbach, and that added some glamour. The address was Schelmental 1. It was just off a small road on the edge of town. Our backyard was a farmer's field that backed up to a state forest. We had privacy, which is hard to find in a German village and also a great viewing area for wild game behind the house.

Long Shots — Military

Upon arrival at Ramstein Air Force Base, I learned that Det 6, 1141st, commonly referred to as Det 6, was a train wreck, a complete shambles. Morale was lower than whale turds, and people had no unit cohesion. The previous commander and first sergeant had been relieved of duty. That is a very serious thing. It is a grave decision and never done lightly. It is basically the end of an officer's career. Det 6, 1141st had grown from supporting the Fourth Allied Tactical Air Force (4ATAF) to additionally supporting Allied Air Forces Central Europe (AAFCE) and some small units of Allied Forces Central Europe (AFCENT), headquartered in Brunssum, Netherlands. The senior U.S. representative for AFCENT was Maj Gen Whitlatch. A Chief Master Sergeant from AAFCE had been temporarily assigned to hold the unit together until my arrival. I reported in to both the senior U.S. representatives to AAFCE and 4ATAF. Col Skelton was the senior U.S. rep for AAFCE. He represented General Richard H Ellis, Commander in Chief of U.S. Air Forces in Europe (CINC USAFE), who was duel hatted as the Commander of AAFCE. Col Richard E. Skelton was a no-nonsense straight-to-the-point officer. I liked him and we got along well; he welcomed me on board. Maj Gen Robert M. White was the senior U.S. rep for 4ATAF which was commanded by a German officer, Lt Gen Carl-Heinz Greve. Gen White welcomed me and mentioned that his son was named Dennis so he would have no trouble remembering my name. I resolved then and there he would remember me for much more than being named like his son. Neither Col Skelton nor Gen White gave me any instructions or told me to fix this or that or clean up something. It was simply, "Welcome aboard," and that was it. No one told me why the previous commander and first sergeant were fired, and it really didn't make any difference; the unit was mine and I had to move it up and forward.

It gets a little complicated, but while I was responsible for the personnel and held court martial responsibility, the officers and enlisted men reported for work to NATO units where they could very well be working for military members of the NATO countries in 4ATAF or AAFCE. One of my guys could be working for a German whose boss was Belgian, who could be working for a Canadian, and so on. Nevertheless, I owned the dormitory (barracks) and was

173

responsible for the morale and welfare of 380 officers and airmen; 80 were field-grade officers (majors and up -- we had no company-grade officers), and nearly all outranked me in military grade. In addition, I was responsible for dependents numbering nearly 800. I was the daddy rabbit (the authority) for all manner of things. As the commander, I was responsible for keeping order and discipline, so I was the sheriff and sometimes the judge and jury. In addition to all personnel functions, assignments, decorations, efficiency reports, military professional schooling, and other associated personnel matters, I was accountable for all ration cards for each military member and their family. Those cards covered such things as liquor and cigarettes. It wasn't a matter of limited supply; it was an assurance to the German government that U.S. personnel were not funneling high-tax items to their German friends to avoid taxes. I also had supply and budget functions. A major element of my job was morale and welfare. For those who may have been in the military, my job was similar to that of the headquarters' Squadron Commander. To further complicate matters, my boss on paper and the one who wrote my efficiency reports was Col Robert O. McCartan, the commander of the 1141 USAF Special Activities Squadron headquartered in Stuttgart-Vaihingen, Germany. He was another old-time colonel who let me do my job without any interference. I saw him four times in my three-year assignment. I also had to recognize Brig Gen Bennett, who was the 86th Wing Commander and his base commander as we were tenants on their base (Ramstein). I know it sounds quite convoluted, but it actually worked out well. Remember, this was a specialized NATO assignment and not normal Air Force operations.

    The two senior U.S. representatives of 4ATAF and AAFCE wrote letters of evaluation that were attached to my yearly efficiency report—they were the ones who witnessed and could best evaluate my performance. I was responsible to them in every way. Col Skelton was a powerful leader and had several colonels working for him. He answered only to the commander of AAFCE, who at the time was four-star General Richard H. Ellis. One day when I was in the office with Col Skelton, Gen Ellis walked in to ask him a question. I was more than surprised as a four-star general seldom walks to a colonel's office. Col Skelton left AAFCE to be the wing commander (senior officer) for Spangdahlem Air Force Base, which was the main fighter aircraft base in central Europe for NATO. It was a sure step for promotion to Brig Gen. Unfortunately, just as Col Skelton completed landing an F4 fighter aircraft, he had a massive heart attack and was dead when they opened the cockpit. It was a sad day for me when I attended his memorial service in Spangdahlem. His replacement as senior U.S. representative in AAFCE was Col Robert D. Anderson, a highly regarded fighter pilot who had flown as a member of the Thunderbirds and on combat missions in both Korea and Vietnam. He was another excellent boss.

Major General Robert M. White flew P-51s in World War II and jets in the Korean War and Vietnam. He was shot down over Germany on his 52nd combat mission in 1945 and was a prisoner of war in Stalag Luft 3. He left active duty after the war but remained in the reserve. He earned college degrees in business and engineering. Called back to active duty in the Korean War, he flew fighter jets, and he did the same in Vietnam, earning the Air Force Cross for his actions in combat. After the Korean War, he was assigned to Edwards Air Force Base in California at the Experimental Test Pilot School. He flew the rocket-powered X-15 to speed records of Mach 4, and then Mach 5, and finally at six times faster than the speed of sound at 4,093 mph. He then flew the experimental airplane to 59.6 miles above the earth, becoming the first Air Force-rated winged astronaut. Commendable are the civilian-funded flights in June 2021 by Richard Branson's Virgin Galactic that reached 53 miles above the earth, and Jeff Bezos' new Shepherd that reached nearly 66 miles altitude. I noted the rocket spaceflight seat auctioned by Jeff Bezos went for $28 million. I believe Gen White's salary to include flight pay was around $800 when he flew the X-15 into space in 1962 and then flew it down to a successful landing. His flight was not controlled by scientists and engineers; he flew it. The X-15 was really a forerunner to our manned spaceships and a learning process for space suits and protective equipment. One X-15 pilot was killed when his plane came apart as he was descending back to earth. I must admit my ignorance in not knowing any of this when I went to work for Gen White, which confirms my lack of preparation prior to the assignment.

My office was on the bottom floor of our dormitory, which was directly across the street from headquarters 4ATAF where his office was located. He was in my office twice: once just to say hello and another time to celebrate our unit winning the Base Commander's Trophy. I was in his office four times: once when I first reported in for duty, once when he presented me a meritorious medal from my previous assignment in Korea, again when he pinned on my silver Lt Col oak leaves, and then finally when I said adios as I moved to my next assignment. I did see him at two or three social functions, and every now and then I would see and salute him from across the street as he came or went from the headquarters. I called him a couple of times a year and sent him a "how goes it" report on squadron activities, good and bad, every quarter. One of those quarterly reports was passed by Col Anderson, the AAFCE senior rep, to Gen William J. Evans, the Commander of AAFCE, who credited it as "an excellent record." Getting an evaluation like that from a four-star general is pretty high cotton for a major. Gen White did tell me when I reported in that if I had to see the Commander-in-Chief of USAFE to give him a back brief if I thought it was important. Can you imagine that? Today, if you are working for a two-star and are briefing a four-star, the two-star would want to review every note, slide, or comment in your speech or presentation. And probably change every glad to happy and then every happy back to glad. Gen White was comfortable in his own skin; he didn't bother with the small stuff and left me to do my job as I saw fit.

On one occasion, I lost my temper with a colonel who told an airman who worked for him that he, the airman, did not have to obey my instructions about dormitory inspection. By regulation, I was required to inspect the dormitory monthly. We had a four-story cement building. The bottom floor was used for offices, and the next three floors were enlisted men's barracks. Those floors had gang showers and toilets on each floor, 20 men's showers and toilets lined up in perfect rows with no toilet stalls. In other words, there was simply no privacy. And to make matters worse, we needed to fit two men in each room, none of which even contained a sink. Some of our men living in the same room were on different shifts so barracks life was less-than-perfect. We had fixed it up as best we could by adding good wooden furniture, getting rid of all the old metal beds and cabinets, and adding color TVs to the day rooms located at the end of the hall on each floor. Additionally, to make it a little more livable, I let the guys paint and decorate their rooms anyway they wanted and did not bother them except for once a month when the room had to be in inspection order. To make it easier for shift personnel, I did the inspection over a two-day period at different hours, and the occupants could choose which day/time they wanted. Additionally, they did not have to be present. The guys did a remarkable job, often innovative, in how they decorated and arranged their rooms. Bad as the setup was with two men to a room, gang showers and open-room toilets, we still managed to win barracks of the quarter for the base most of the time. I was quite proud of the guys and their rooms so I would often invite NATO officers from the other countries to accompany me on my monthly inspections. One reason was to show off a bit, but the second and more important reason was to show the NATO supervisors how difficult and uncomfortable housing was for U.S. junior-level troops working for them.

  The junior personnel of other NATO countries serving at Ramstein were allowed to live off base and were given a housing allowance to do so. The troop involved in this story was a young aircraft controller, and their aircraft controller directive stated they did not have to pull additional duties. On the day of inspection, I had a NATO officer, a Dutch major who supervised some of our guys, with me. We opened the young airman's room, who at that particular time did not have a roommate, and it looked like a grenade had gone off. The bed wasn't made, and there were clothes on the floor. It was just a scrambled mess. I was shocked but assumed he had just not gotten the word. Still, it was embarrassing for me and the visiting officer. After the inspection, my first sergeant located the young airman. He reported that his U.S. Air Force colonel work boss told him he didn't have to follow my orders. Now I was livid. Making your bed and cleaning up your room is not an additional duty, which I pointed out to the offending officer, who I shall call Col K, but he wanted to argue about it when I confronted him in his office. By then we were getting quite loud and were in a large room with many offices divided by chest-high partitions. Speaking truth to power is one thing, but this was a major arguing aggressively and loudly with a colonel; pure dumb and doing it in a public way makes it double dumb. I lost my temper and told Col K if he wanted to accompany me to see the four-star Commander in Chief, we would see who the (expletive) was right. About that time, my acting first sergeant, Chief Master Sergeant Bays, who was standing behind me started tugging on my shirt. He had little reverence for officers he felt were inferior and didn't mind letting them know it. His tugging on my shirt brought me back to my senses. The colonel and I broke off, and by the time the chief and I got back to my office, I realized how stupid I had been. I embarrassed myself, Col K, and worst of all, could be an embarrassment to Gen White, who I was supposed to represent. I was really sick about possibly embarrassing Gen White. I was supposed to represent him and set the example, not act in an impulsive, explosive, and disrespectful manner. What to do?

I had never called him or bothered him in any Det 6 business. However, I did not want him to get bad news from anyone but me. What do I say? Should I offer to resign? Certainly, I felt he would be justified in firing me. It was particularly painful because he had been so trusting and never questioned my decisions, direction, or leadership. The call had to be made, and I was prepared to pay any price leveled. I rang up his office, and he got on the line immediately. I did not feel it was appropriate to name names so I said I'd had a little confrontation with a colonel and was sorry to say I may have embarrassed him (Gen White) by losing my temper. He asked me what it was about, and I told him it was merely a misunderstanding of unit responsibilities, orders, and authority. His next question was, "Who is the commander of this outfit?" He did not say of Det 6 so I wasn't sure what he meant. Was he talking about the CINC or maybe himself?

That all flashed through my mind before I answered, "I'm the commander."

He then said, "Do I have to remind anyone?"

I answered, "No sir, no sir, not necessary. I believe the problem is settled."

I doubt he ever heard from Col K or any of the people who obviously heard the overly loud argument. However, a couple of days later, Col McClarren, one of the more jovial U.S. officers in 4ATAF, came barging into my office and threw a letter on my desk laughing as he asked me, "What the heck is this about?"

The letter was from Gen White addressed to all U.S. officers in the headquarters. It was short and sweet: There is one commander of this outfit and that is Major Dennis Behrens. If you have any questions, see me. I of course feigned ignorance with Col McClarren, but he was still laughing when he left. Wow, what trust and confidence from Gen White. His strong support strengthened my resolve to make our unit the best on Ramstein AFB. And not to act so stupidly in the future.

I must admit that inheriting a unit that was failing, had lost its identity, and was suffering from low morale was daunting to say the least. Learning the previous commander had been relieved of duty was not happy news, either. However, I decided to look at it in a more positive light and accepted the challenge. Things would hopefully get better, and anything I did would be an improvement. I was fortunate and delighted to have Chief Bays as my acting First Sergeant. As I mentioned earlier, the chief was not enamored with high-grade officers, nor would he put up with any nonsense from NCOs who he considered unworthy. Sure, he was a prima donna, but he was soooo good.

Chief Bays was an old-time admin NCO and could take dictation. He had a master's degree in English and could write circles around me. He was a holdover from World War II and seemed to know every general in the Air Force. He worked for Col Skelton in the senior U.S. representative's office next to the Commander (four-star general) of AAFCE. I don't expect he was overjoyed to be sent down to squadron level to hold the detachment together, but he never complained to me. I liked him, and he had a great sense of humor. We often laughed together at some of the ridiculous rules and regulations that were supposed to improve things. The authorized rank for First Sergeants (often called first shirts) was Master Sergeant, which is two steps down from Chief Master Sgt. Chief Bays was just too valuable, and I knew we couldn't keep him for long. There was no sense crying about it when, after three months, he retreated to the lofty levels in the headquarters building.

All the personnel supported by Det 6 worked in a variety

179

of NATO jobs, and my efforts could not distract from that mission. The very first thing that had to be done was to establish trust between the unit and with me. The officers were all field-graders (majors and up) so I didn't worry much about them. Three quarters of my unit were enlisted men, which was the core of my challenge. I'm pleased to report the "never go back" rule was reversed in this case. Because many of the NCOs knew me from my previous NATO assignment and welcomed me back.

Duty hours for me in the first months were 7:00 a.m. to 7:00 p.m. daily. I had an open-door policy in order to be accessible for airmen and NCOs to come see me without interfering with their NATO duty hours and also to accommodate shift workers from our 24-hour war headquarters in the Kindsbach underground facility and the Boerfink War Bunker. I had a steady stream of NCOs coming in to see me. The majority of those early visitors were NCOs who knew me from my first assignment to Det 6 in 1968-71. Many of the NCOs had married German ladies and stayed in Germany as long as they could, which was known in the Air Force as "homesteading." Others just liked Germany and wanted to return for another tour. I had good rapport with the homesteaders and that helped greatly in establishing trust throughout the unit. I knew without a doubt that there's no way to fool the troops— they will find out your true colors even if it takes some time. I wasn't trying to win any personality contests, establish special friendships, or become best buddies with anyone. But they needed to know I was there to be their leader, which meant to support and help them in any way possible.

We needed to establish a unit identity, and one way to do that was through sports. Sports were a big deal throughout our bases in Europe. Ramstein Air Force Base was home to 27 squadrons, all competing for the Base Commander's Trophy for intramural sports, which was presented to the squadron that won the highest number of combined points in the various sports. We put our sights on that trophy, which included basketball, golf, volleyball, tennis, flag football, bowling, handball, racquetball, softball, and skeet shooting (which I had added). Our bowling team, made up of several old master sergeants, was just about untouchable. We had a few officers who played tennis and competed very successfully. A big boost for our kids in basketball was a couple of majors who had played basketball in college. Some officers began helping our effort in handball and racquetball. Most of our enlisted personnel were middle- or high-grade NCOs so there were not a lot of candidates for our flag football team. But our young team turned out to be the "Energizer Bunny" and fought in every game like it was a life-or-death struggle. They ended up winning their league championship! We were able to get some new sports uniforms for the basketball and softball teams, which jumped up their enthusiasm. We were not Titans in any particular sport with the exception of our bowling team and possibly our skeet shooters. Most of the other squadrons were much larger than Det 6. I think the security police had over 700 cops, mostly young and barely out of high school where many had been top athletes. It's hard to beat youth, but we had huge support for such a small unit. We gathered a good number of fans and spectators in the larger sports, and many of our older guys, officers and enlisted, came out of retirement from sports either to compete or coach. In most sports, we ended up third, fourth, or even fifth place. We were entered in every sport offered, and our guys were out there slugging to earn us points. Sports not only provided additional activities for our members, they also really helped achieve unit identity without conflicting with international job loyalty. And we claimed title to the Base Commander's Trophy. We were the little mouse that roared—the team to beat.

We stressed an attitude of maximum effort by being the very best we could be. That attitude permeated into all areas. We continually exceeded our Combined Federal Campaign goal. In the Air Force Assistance Fund campaign, we consistently reached double the established goal and contributed the largest amount of any base unit. Our personnel were frequent winners of the NCO of the Quarter Award for the entire base. I placed a great deal of emphasis on continuing education, and our unit produced a significant number of distinguished graduates from the USAFE NCO Academy. Our dormitory was frequently judged best in the quarterly base competition. We established a mid-duty-day Christmas party just for Det 6 military members, which was quite a success with over 200 members attending, including the four-star commander of AAFCE. We established a family picnic with kiddie games and even movie cartoons set up in a tent for the little tots. Music and sports provided entertainment for the adults; over 500 people attended, including the Commander of AAFCE and his wife, Gen John W. and Mrs. Pauly.

Another activity that brought the unit together (to my amazement) was our annual PT test. It was a 1.5 mile run that had to be completed in various times according to the runner's age. It wasn't exactly a popular event, so to make it a little more fun I decided to publish the best times run by each grade or rank. Everyone had to participate, so we conducted the runs over several days to allow our folks to pick a schedule that best fit them. I ran the first day to put my score up at the beginning. And then as we went along, I would publish the name of the fastest Col, the fastest Lt Col, Chief Master Sergeant, and on down to the lowest-ranked airman. I updated the list every day as the runners' times dictated. Our fastest colonel was Merrill A. McPeak, who became Air Force Chief of Staff in 1990. I was amazed at all the interest, and even those who could not beat me were delighted in telling me that their friend had beat me. You never know what works.

Of course, the basis for everything was our primary mission of providing the highest quality of administrative and personnel help possible. My orderly room staff deserved all the credit for the outstanding support that gave us the reputation of being the best in people service on the base. If someone came in with a question or problem, they got it taken care of. We made certain that efficiency ratings and reports were submitted on time before promotion boards. We helped supervisors prepare recommendations for awards and decorations that clearly depicted their outstanding people and accomplishments. My personnel guys knew all the tricks of the system and did everything that could be done to obtain desired assignments for our departing personnel. On the administrative side, no one could touch my guys in the speed of processing emergency leaves, assisting with financial matters, and providing information on flights departing for the U.S. from the Ramstein Military Airlift

Long Shots — Military

Command (MAC) terminal on base and also their terminal at Rhein Main AFB. For example, emergency leave is a special category that is given to those with urgent need to return to the States. The military member with emergency leave orders goes to the front of the line on any military aircraft with available seats. Active or retired military, from all the services, may travel by military aircraft anywhere in the world provided there is space available. Grade or rank is not a consideration; it is simply by sign-up date. An Army private or Air Force airman on emergency leave orders outranks a general who may have signed up weeks in advance. Normally, those are personnel returning for deaths of close family members such as parents or siblings. In some cases it can be grandparents who raised them. In any case, it's a very tense and stressful time for the military members. I had to approve all military leaves, and they were supposed to be verified by the Red Cross. Most likely, I could be found guilty of not always getting the Red Cross verification, but time was of the essence, and I don't think I ever had a kid cheating on that. Sometimes the Red Cross would be the first one to notify us, and we would notify the individual, but for the most part, the military member involved would be called by their family, and they would tell us. Regardless of how we were notified, any day of the week and any hour of the day, it was all hands on deck immediately. My guys normally had the emergency orders published before the affected individual could get to our office.

My orderly room staff worked hard and was exceptionally successful in obtaining NCO Academy quotas. During commander's call I made it a point to always recognize our many personal achievers: airmen or NCO of the quarter, distinguished graduates of schools, and those receiving medals for meritorious service. To make some of the awards more tangible, I would add a three-day pass. My friend, Major Doug Forsythe, from my previous tour at Ramstein, was back and now flying 130s to Torrejon, our U.S. airbase in Madrid, Spain. He made sure there was space on his flights for my guys who were on "achievement-earned" three-day passes. Of course, we often had to extend the passes a day or two to coincide with his flights. For those promoted from airmen to sergeant, we made a big deal of having our most senior Chief Master Sergeants on stage with the brand-new

183

promoted sergeant.

I took a legal officer, Capt Kelly Beckley, with me on my visits to our seven microwave sites that were located on tops of mountains anywhere from 100 to 200 miles from Ramstein. This was to allow my folks to make out wills and gain assistance in any personal legal matters. Actions like that, showing that people matter and demonstrating a personal interest, do not go unnoticed. My orderly room was staffed with seven NCOs who provided absolutely top service.

Chief Bays was my initial First Sergeant, and Master Sergeant Ted Spencer was my last First Sergeant. He had been running the personnel portion of the orderly room and impressed me with his calm demeanor. Master Sergeant Spencer was a big man, and while he looked intimidating, the troops soon found out he was quite approachable and helpful. He was practically unflappable; his words were measured and soft. But make no mistake, he was solid as an oak tree. He was able to settle many of the problems of the enlisted force before they ever reached my level; I was very lucky to have him. The many accolades directed to Det 6 must be credited to the First Sergeant and my fine staff in the orderly room. Not everything was peaches and cream; with nearly 400 military personnel and 800 family members there's bound to be a certain number who go astray. We had plenty of counseling sessions, and our share of formal letters of reprimand, but most were for minor violations that did not warrant the establishment of an unfavorable information file. We did have our share of DWIs, and, of course, the offenders lost their driving privileges. Very few Article 15s were issued for a unit of our size. Our civilian dependents caused little trouble, and it was often just teenage girls stealing makeup at the Base Exchange. They had to come in with their fathers for counseling, but I tried to make it a learning experience. I did have to return the dependents of one family to the United States. Sadly, we learned after their return that one of their sons shot his uncle to death.

I was ready to shoot an airman second class. I'll call him Airman X. The First Shirt came into my office and told me the AAFCE commanding general ordered Airman X to be relieved of duty and reassigned immediately! What the heck was that about? What could have happened that would cause a four-star general to order me to fire an airman? It turned out Airman X had been a driver for General John W. Pauly and a visiting German four-star general, from the headquarters building to the flight line; it was only a one-mile drive. Apparently, Airman X needed a haircut and must have embarrassed Gen Pauly in front of the German general. Just after the First Sergeant passed on the general's orders to me, in comes the Dutch captain who was chief of the motor pool to tell me Airman X was the best driver he had, and they needed him. The Dutch captain was rapidly followed by a Canadian major who headed up NATO ground transportation who told me it was all nonsense, and Airman X was wonderful and a perfect soldier. They were followed by a couple of U.S. NCOs singing the same song. This kid had impressed his supervisors. It seemed like everyone was in on this except me. This all happened in a period of 30 minutes. While the incident was hardly earthshaking, I knew it had to be settled quickly considering who issued the order. Understand, personnel working in NATO adhere to the uniform and personal standards of their own countries. Some countries allowed long hair, and the Dutch even issued their troops hairnets to accommodate their hair in helmets. Another challenge was that neither the First Sergeant nor I saw our airmen every day, and often not for a month or two as they were working for NATO personnel in other buildings and in other areas. I don't offer that as an excuse, but only as an explanation. I was the commander, and it was my responsibility. I told the First Shirt to round Airman X up immediately and get him to my office in a Class A uniform. Airman X arrived within 10 minutes in blues (Class A uniform) with a very fresh haircut. He obviously knew what was up. He was a good-looking boy, 20 or 21 years old, fit, and looking smart in his blues. I did notice he had a 4ATAF patch on his left shoulder that was obviously missing some stitching right at the top, but there was no time to worry about that. He admitted he may have been overdue for a haircut but thought he was fine. Now what to do? Airman X had a spotless record and excellent efficiency reports, plus several people practically broke down my door to tell me what a good troop he was and they wanted to keep him. I could easily dump him out of NATO and send him back to the regular Air Force without any blemishes on his record but was that the right thing to do? Arguing about the fate of an airman second class with senior officers who were fighting the Cold War—guarding the Fulda Gap against the evil Empire—is fraught with danger. I was more than irritated at Airman X for putting me on the spot, but I thought, what the heck, the kid's got a good record—so I called Gen Pauly's Chief of Staff, Col Gaylie. His secretary told me to come on up to the headquarters and he would see me.

Gen Pauly had a three-star deputy and several two-star generals working for him, but the Chief of Staff is the chief enforcer to ensure what the commander wants happens. He has to be strong and is as powerful as a colonel gets. Smart staff generals try to stay on track with the Chief of Staff. I took Airman X with me, but I reported in to Col Gaylie alone. He was a powerfully built man and looked like he could have been a linebacker. After exchanging salutes, he very cordially told me to have a seat. He asked me how things were going in my job, and after a few minutes of polite small talk, he asked what he could do for me. He was obviously no dummy. He knew I came for something. I laid out the situation and told him I was embarrassed bothering him with such a small matter. I then explained all the support the kid had from his NATO bosses and his sterling work record. When I told him I had Airman X outside, he said, "Bring him in." After saluting, he told the kid to stand at ease. He talked to the boy without lecturing for a couple of minutes about standards being important, and for our U.S. troops to set the example. Then, just before he dismissed him, he said, "Your 4ATAF patch needs some stitching on the top edge." Holy Toledo, I couldn't believe it, he didn't miss a thing. When the airman was gone, Col Gaylie told me to just sit tight on the order, and if I didn't hear from him in a week to consider the matter closed. Not many colonels would bring up such a trivial matter to a four-star general, but Gaylie was strong, although he was obviously waiting for the right time to speak with the general. Sadly, the old solid colonel chiefs of staff who weren't working to be promoted have been replaced with Brig Gens looking for a second star.

Det 6 members became involved with the Dads Club, the Mexican American Club, the Cub Scouts, AYA, Little League, Rod and Gun Club, Boy Scouts, Peewee League, and various church activities. We were virtually involved in every activity in the community.

Detachment 6, of the 1141 Special Activities Squadron, had clearly established unity and identity. We had a family and had a superb reputation on the base. I suspect you may have picked up how proud I was of Det 6 and all the people who made it such an outstanding unit: my First Sergeant and Orderly Room personnel, and then officers and airmen of AAFCE, and 4ATAF all came together. The largest component of bringing us together was our mid- and senior-level NCOs; many of them knew me from my previous assignment to Det 6 and that was a big help. Perhaps the conventional wisdom of "never go back" should not be considered sacrosanct. My greatest respect and thanks go to the senior representatives of both AAFCE (Colonels Skelton and Anderson) and 4ATAF (Maj Gen White), and my superb boss, the commander of the 1141st Special Activities Squadron at Stuttgart, Col Robert O. McCartan, for their trust and confidence in allowing me to command the Det 6 without their directing, second-guessing, and I must say, even guidance. It was one of the most satisfying assignments in my Air Force career.

Returning to Ramstein in 1976 did present many advantages. One of the best was reuniting with old friends from my first assignment in 1968. The Baron Johannes von Schorlemer was just down the Autobahn at Saarbrucken; Klaus Winter was in nearby Spire; Rubsaamen was in Bad Durkheim; Manfred Mack was in Wiesbaden, and my pheasant shooting friend Paul Fladausch was in Bavaria. René Haillez was still shooting trap and putting on pheasant hunts in Belgium. A new German we became friends with was Adolph Nessel, an avid local hunter. I hunted with him later in Paraguay, and his son Volker came to live with us in Washington, D.C. That's a whole other story. A 1 a.m. call from Adolph announced his son would arrive by plane in Washington, D.C. at 0800 that morning. I didn't ask why, but it didn't matter, a friend needed help and I don't turn down friends.

On the American side, Col Rip Sewall had become base commander at Zweibrucken AFB, less than an hour's drive away, and Pearlie White was still at the Ramstein Rod and Gun Club. Reuniting with all the old friends was a great pleasure. And, as always, we connected with a whole raft of new friends. Bobby Kuhlo is one of the few non-hunters that we still keep in contact with. Lt Col Barbara King became good friends with Loretta. Her husband was a retired colonel and had been a wing commander. Barbara was later promoted to full colonel, which she fully earned. Lt Col Burt Miller was assigned to AAFCE. I knew his father, who was a lieutenant colonel in charge of the Air Force gun shop when I was rifle shooting. I had never met Burt before, but he proved to be just like his father, a real gunman—rifle, pistol, or shotgun. He retired as a full colonel, and I enjoyed many years of hunting quail with him and his Drahthaars in Arizona. Lt Col Ron Lumpe and his wife Marge became friends, and we were able to continue that friendship when they moved to San Antonio. Rolf Smith, who had worked for me as a second lieutenant when I had the Air Force rifle team, came to Ramstein as a lieutenant colonel along with his talented wife, Julie, and I helped him move to AAFCE. He joined me in wonderful German hunting. He has been on 13 African safaris with me and is with me as I write part of this journal in August 2022 on safari in South Africa.

  Then there were the three majors: Charlie Weaver, Barry Borgiet, and Dick Erickson. They were all hard-core hunters and more or less ran together, always trying to outdo each other in shooting the crafty little reh bucks. Lt Col Ron Lumpe often joined them. Barry went with us to Kenya on the Troy State Master's degree trip and later hunted with me in Namibia. Charlie really favored hunting Russian boar, and usually carried Dingo, his nasty little biting wire-haired dackel, with him. We became exceptionally close friends, and he hunted in Africa with me several times. Charlie had earned a Ph.D., and upon retirement he was hired to be an aircraft controller in Saudi Arabia where he climbed to the top. Sadly, he died of cancer. I still miss him and his wonderful sense of humor.

  Two young captains joined our circle. John Odom, an Air Force lawyer, was not stationed at Ramstein, but we became hunting friends, and he has also hunted with me in Texas, Argentina, and Kenya. His wife Gale has a Ph.D. in music and teaches at the University. She also sings opera, and her strong, trained voice can bring roaring lions to attention. After completing his active duty service, John went into the Air Force reserve until his retirement as a full colonel. He became the world's expert on the Service Members Civil Relief Act, and I believe testified before House and Senate committees four times. John has a beautiful and unique Kreighoff shotgun with a set of four barrels for the different gauges and exquisite engravings of his favorite bird dogs.

Kelly Beckley and his bride Connie were still fairly new to the Air Force with Ramstein being only their second assignment and the first one overseas. We took them under our wing and showed them around a bit. Our relationship grew into a strong friendship. Kelly was not a hunter but would sometimes go on what I called a "mystery weekend." It would go something like this: I might call Kelly, telling him to bring French francs and meet us Friday night at six. Then the travel adventure would begin, sometimes in the local areas, sometimes to France or Belgium. He and Connie came with us to Kenya, and they took us on a glorious ski vacation along the border of Austria and Italy. Capt Kelly was an Air Force legal officer and gave a lot of extra service to my unit by helping with wills and accompanying me on my trips to visit mountaintop communication sites. Kelly remained in the reserves after active duty and retired as a full colonel. Most of his reserve duty was in Germany supporting the military legal staff for all of Europe.

Col Robert (Scotty) Cameron was assigned to 4 ATAF and was a serious shooter and hunter. He was a WWII vet and fine officer who set an excellent example. We became friends, and after his retirement we became even closer friends when he walked us through the tangled ropes and showed us all the bright spots of Washington, D.C. I was amazed at his knowledge in many fields. He was a favorite of the shotgun-shooting crowd in D.C. Scotty came hunting with me to Kenya and then Zimbabwe. He was a Master Mason and lived by that code of high duty, integrity, and philanthropy. We remained close friends until his death at age 94. He is buried in Arlington.

Col Claude Teagarden (later promoted to Brig Gen) was the staff judge advocate (senior legal advisor) on the staff of the Commander in Chief, U.S. Air Forces in Europe. We became hunting partners, and he was helpful in Rod and Gun activities. My previous boss from the Air Force Military Personnel Center, Col Albert Audette, had been assigned to Portugal as the defense attaché. He called me from Portugal and asked me to get him a .44 Smith & Wesson Magnum revolver. The bodyguard to the president had tried to get a .44, but people kept sending Smith & Wessons in .357 caliber. This was in the time frame of the Dirty Harry movies when Clint Eastwood made the .44 Smith & Wesson famous but also scarce as production could not keep up with demand. I knew the Kaiserslautern Rod and Gun Club had one and quickly procured it. But now, how do I get it to Portugal? I mentioned the transfer problem to Col Teagarden, and it was determined to be an essential movement of sensitive and important diplomatic value. It flew unhindered quickly in the diplomatic pouch to Lisbon, Portugal. The next call I received from Col Audette was to thank me with loud pistol shots heard in the background. The Col explained they were test-firing the revolver by shooting rounds into his swimming pool, right there in the middle of Lisbon. Loretta and I visited him a year later, and I carried him a Model 1911 Colt pistol along with an ACE .22-caliber conversion kit in my suitcase. Airline travel was different in those days.

Another incident with Col Teagarden was rather humorous. We had been on a hunt together with Lt Gen Benjamin Bellis, Air Forces in Europe vice CINC, and Lt Gen Ernst-Dieter Bernhard, the deputy commander of AAFCE. We were driving home from the hunt in Col Teagarden's Mercedes, which he had recently purchased from a major. The grade insignia on the car had not yet been changed from major to colonel, and we may have approached the base gate a little fast. In any case, the Air Force security policeman motioned us to pull over. We did, and he sauntered up to the car rather nonchalantly. We were all in our hunting clothes, and the guard said rather bluntly to Col Teagarden, "Get out your lD, and you guys in the back do the same." Everyone complied as ordered, and we handed all four over to him. He then quickly realized he was talking to a full colonel and had two three-star generals in the backseat. No one said anything about rank, and it did not matter – he had the authority – but his demeanor changed abruptly. We all had a chuckle as we drove through the gate.

One thing that was especially enjoyable for me was a continuation of involvement in the U.S. Army and Air Force Rod and Gun clubs in Germany. The Association of American Rod and Gun Clubs in Europe was located at U.S. Army headquarters in Heidelberg. Army Lt Col Lloyd C. Hall was the executive secretary of the Association of 80,000 members, the majority of whom were stationed in Germany. It was divided in what are called land councils. I became the Land Council Chairman for the German state of Rheinland-Pfalz, which covered 11 Rod and Gun clubs with over 7,000 members. Lt Col Rolf Smith was drafted as my head of shooting, and Major Charles Weaver became my chairman for hunting. They really got their programs buzzing as we energized all the rod and gun clubs in the Rheinland-Pfalz. Each month we would visit a different club for lunch and work with the managers to see how we could assist them in their programs. Being head of the land council also got me involved once again in the DJV (German Hunters Federation) and particularly the shooting competitions. The Chairman of the Association of American Rod and Gun Clubs in Germany and Land Council was General Robert E. Huyser who was stationed at Stuttgart, Germany. Having the largest land council, I became a sort of quasi-deputy to General Huyser and worked closely with him. It was always a pleasure to attend his board meetings held in his cavernous board room with a table that would certainly accommodate thirty. Our combined land council meetings would normally have three or four staff people from Association Headquarters and about the same number from land councils; we barely covered one quarter of the table. Those from the land councils were all volunteers, and they came from all ranks and grades, as well as U.S. civilians working for the military forces. Sometimes council members would bring up subjects or make motions without having done any staff work as to why it should be done, how it could be done, and what the cost was. I was often just shaking my head, figuratively, of course, but amazed at what was being suggested without any staffing.

Gen Huyser was just a master of handling "stupid" stuff without embarrassing those making the motion or suggestion. Usually, when you could tell there had been no homework done, he would say something like: "That could be a very good idea. Why don't you staff it a bit and come back at our next meeting with what you have found as to the feasibility and cost, etc.?"

The big Association event of the year was the Rod and Gun Club Convention held at Berchtesgaden. It was a combination of trophy show, shooting and fishing instruction, gun show, conservation presentations, and just all-around gathering of rod and gun club members across Europe.

Berchtesgaden is quite a nice little town in the German Alps but with some big hotels that were taken over by the U.S. military after World War II. They provided a perfect place for the convention. One time, Charlie Weaver and I flew up to Berchtesgaden from Munich with Gen Huyser in his helicopter. That was sure flying with the big boys. He had served in World War II, Korea, and Vietnam. When I knew him, he was Deputy Commander-in-Chief, United States European Command, and he later served as Commander of Military Airlift Command. His book, Mission to Tehran, tells firsthand how and why we lost Iran. He was ordered on a secret mission to Tehran to save a democratic system of government and prevent a military coup—that may have been the only thing that could have saved Iran from Khomeini. It's an exciting read of his secret movements around Tehran with a price on his head. He did not agree with the direction, or really the lack of firm directions, and knew some of his Iranian military friends would be killed. He refused to take the mission unless he was ordered to do so from the White House. And we all know what happened to Iran. He wrote me a very nice note of appreciation for my "dedicated service to our great nation …" and he signed it Waidmannsheil (a hunter's salutation) and "God bless." It's quite humbling to receive such a note from a four-star general. I was honored to serve as his escort officer at the change of command of U.S. Air Forces Europe and AAFCE from Gen William J. Evans to Gen John W. Pauly.

As I mentioned earlier in the review of my first assignment in Germany, the change of command of four-star officers is a big deal, indeed; all four-star officers in the theater show up, and it gets even bigger for those serving in NATO as all the senior NATO officers are also in attendance. I was only a Lt Col at the time, but Gen Huyser took me with him to a meeting with just the American four-star generals before the ceremony. Gen Evans was well-liked, and it was apparent from the warm handshaking—it appeared to me the generals showed a genuine friendship for each other.

Gen Alexander M. Haig was the presiding officer and senior in position, but in that room they were all equals. I must tell you one story about Gen Evans. He was holding an informal officers' call for those in AAFCE, really just a come and have a drink together at the Ramstein Officers' Club. The general knew me, but Loretta had just recently been assigned to AAFCE. Our self-imposed rule was I never went to Loretta's office, and she never came to mine. We kept the husband-and-wife life strictly apart from Air Force business. The same held true for this unofficial officers' call. I was standing near the general, and Loretta was on his other side some distance apart. He gestured to me and then Loretta and back to me with a "what's up?" expression on his face. Just for fun, I answered, "She's my sister, sir." He immediately corrected me, smiling as he said, "You mean, your younger sister." No wonder people liked him.

Serving in NATO was a good opportunity to learn how the services of other countries conducted their military affairs and to learn their customs. German Lt Gen Carl-Heinz Greve was the commander of 4ATAF. Five U.S. Air Force officers in 4ATAF were selected for promotion to lieutenant colonel in the same cycle, including me. He invited us to his office; we all dutifully showed up at the proper time and were ushered into his office. Gen Greve was a large man and rather imposing. He had been a fighter pilot in the German Air Force during WWII and often reminded his American contemporaries that he "had them in his sights." As a pilot in the German Luftwaffe in WWII, he was decorated with the Knight's Cross—the highest military award. He gave a nice speech about our earning the promotion, but what really stood out were his comments about our representing the United States and that we followed some of the greatest military men in history. More importantly, he stated that our country was the guardian of democracy and of the entire free world. His secretary then brought in six crystal cognac glasses already loaded on a silver tray. The general toasted us and the United States of America. Real class.

"Never" and "always" are two words that should be used with care; in this case the never, in "never go back," to my earlier assignment proved to be very wrong.

The Pentagon

"**N**o! There's been a mistake; I don't want to go." That was my immediate, forceful response to the orders assigning me to the Pentagon. I'd heard too many horror stories about the long hours, cramped office space, high cost of living, traffic, and long commutes. Not to mention the frustrating work with constant short time suspense that required late night hours, which were only to be discarded the next morning. It was dubbed the "puzzle palace," with haughty perfidious mandarins and scarlet-plumed princes roaming the halls. How could this happen to me? I had just worked my tail off by taking a failing unit from the bottom to the top, turning it arguably into the best squadron on Ramstein Air Force Base. And this was my reward? "Not fair!" I wanted to yell. Out of sheer frustration and disappointment I called Col McCartan, my boss in Stuttgart, to protest, or maybe just vent, as I knew the outcome was preordained. He sympathized, but the message was clear: "Get going."

The Pentagon is an imposing five-story building made up of five sides with five rings of descending size to an open center court lawn area in the middle, often referred to as Ground Zero as it was suspected to be the aiming point for missiles from our enemies in the "Evil Empire." The regular assigned personnel total nearly 26,000. Those visiting daily on official business add another 10,000, making the daily population around 36,000. It is indeed a busy place. The design of the building with five sides and five stories allows a person to reach the furthest office in 10 minutes. Perhaps the assignments officers who reviewed my records saw joint service with the Army in Korea, as well as my experience with officers in NATO, but for whatever reason, I was assigned to the joint staff. Looking back, I can hardly believe my good luck. I was assigned as Chief, Personnel Division, Office of the Joint Chiefs of Staff (OJCS) with an office one floor below and outside of the main joint staff area. Even more amazing, I had a large private office. Full colonels in the joint staff area often worked in small rooms crammed in with four or five desks all pushed together. Maybe I was a plumed prince; I felt like I must be in my spacious office.

My fields of responsibility were military personnel, civilian personnel, manpower, and budget, which included an office to handle all official travel. Mr. Robert (Bob) Jones was my deputy. He was a GS 14 at the highest pay step. Bob was an excellent deputy; he had been in the Pentagon since 1945 when he came home from WW II. Counting his military time, he already had 40 years of government service. Bob knew every mouse in the Pentagon and where all the skeletons were buried. The Pentagon is really in many ways a small city with its own little bureaucracy to keep the wheels turning, so his knowledge and experience were invaluable. There is a constant struggle between the services, Department of Defense, and the Joint Chiefs of Staff (JCS) over who gets what and how much in resources, including money and office space. The most vicious and bloodied battles are normally over space. Even though I was only a lieutenant colonel, all my section chiefs were lieutenant colonels or GS 14s (approximately an equal civilian grade to lieutenant colonel). They were all talented and pretty much conducted their business without outside interference or guidance. I only got involved if it looked like trouble. Things were running well when I arrived, so I only had to make a few small tweaks. A couple of the senior NCOs had managed to have their duty hours set from 5:00 a.m. to 1:00 p.m. to supposedly get more done. I came in at 5:00 a.m. only to find those hard workers reading the morning papers. Come to find out one of them was running a full-time business in the afternoons. I love an entrepreneur but not if it detracts from his day job. He wasn't with us long. Another idea that was floating about was to close for lunch. We had a little "come to Jesus" meeting to review our responsibility of providing good and timely service; we had no customers at 5:00 a.m., but we had many over the lunch hour. Everyone got in step, and that's the only time I had to remind folks that our business was providing service.

    The section chiefs worked together well. I don't ever recall a conflict between them. It was a pleasant work environment, and I intended to keep it that way. The work could be hard and sometimes frustrating, but we all maintained a positive and friendly attitude. I branded them the "Fabulous Five." They satisfied any requests and conquered all problems or nearly so. Mr. Bob Jones was my deputy; manpower was handled by Air Force Lt Col Young; Mr. White was chief for civilian personnel; Army Lt Col Roush managed military personnel; and Mrs. Brooks was chief of budget and travel.

My immediate boss, Col Wayne M Duncan, was the Director of Administrative Services (DAS). He reported to the Director of the Joint Chiefs of Staff. Most people think the Chairman of the Joint Chiefs of Staff runs the joint staff, but that is not true. He is the boss and meets with the director daily, but his primary function is to advise the President, the Secretary of Defense, and the National Security Council on national defense matters. Of course, he conducts meetings of all the service chiefs of the Army, Air Force, Navy, and Marine Corps. During my time in the Pentagon, I served under four JCS Chairmen: Air Force Gen David C. Jones, Army Gen John W. Vessey, Navy Admiral William J. Crowe, and Army Gen Colin L. Powell. And I got to interface with all four. Although I was never in his office, I conducted officer orientation programs for General Jones and had met him twice previously when he was a three- and then a four-star general in Germany. When you were with General Vessey it was something like being with a patron. He treated you like you were his family. Adm Crowe had a wonderful sense of humor and always seemed to be enjoying himself. Gen Powell was absolutely first-class in every way. Additionally, I met Army Gen Lyman Lemnitzer, who was Chairman of the JCS 1960 to 1963, long after he had retired (he wore the Army uniform for 53 years), and I took my Military Games Pentathlon Champions to meet Air Force Gen Richard B. Myers when he was Chairman after I retired. Working for or meeting six Chairmen of the Joint Chiefs of Staff is a bit of a record.

The Director of the Joint Staff during my time as JCS Personnel Chief was Air Force Lt Gen James E. Dalton. He basically ran herd over the OJCS divisions and offices headed by other Lt Gen's: J-3 director of operations, J-4 director of logistics, J-5 director of plans, J-6 director of communications, and so on. Most of the personnel work requiring my involvement came down from Gen Dalton or his deputy, Army Maj Gen Charles W. Dyke. Of course, any of the three-star flag officers who headed the JCS directorates needing personnel assistance or a request came quickly to my attention. The DAS, Col Duncan, was my boss on paper, but in practical terms I worked for the JCS Director and his Deputy. Their inquiries or requirements came directly to me, and I responded directly to them. The DAS was fine with this, and I kept him informed of any situation that might come to his attention. Col Duncan was a perfect boss. Gen Dalton was a peach to work for probably because he was smarter than the rest of us. At least that was my impression. During discussions, presentations, or answering his questions, he got the picture early without requiring a lot of explanation. He would call me directly, often saying, "Send your expert up to see me" in whatever field he had an interest. I think he did that for two reasons: one to cut down on wasted time, and second to keep from embarrassing someone who was not qualified or prepared to fully answer his second or third questions. I would grab the right expert and hightail it up to his office in those cases. He was always cordial and put people at ease, particularly enlisted personnel who were not used to briefing a three-star general. We had a budget of only $52 million, but it was somewhat complicated. It always amazed me to see how fast and thoroughly he could navigate through it. Of course, I always took my trusty chief of budget, Mrs. Brooks, with me to those meetings. Gen Dalton was promoted with a fourth star after leaving the JCS.

  Gen Dyke was my most frequent contact with the director's office. He was a no-nonsense, get-it-done officer. If you were working on a problem and took him alternatives, he would ask your opinion, and then make a decision, without any handwringing—just simply, do this one and press on. He did not vacillate. I never saw him rude or nasty to anyone. However, after a briefing or presentation, if the officer making the presentation looked overweight, he might ask, "Now what are we going to do about your belt?" Junior Army officers treaded lightly around him, and he could be tough, but I liked him, and we got along well.

  One time when I went to see him, I rounded the corner and there he was standing toe-to-toe with two three-star Army generals who apparently wanted him to do something, and he was saying, "No, sir." One of the three-star generals blurted out, "God damn you, Bill." But Gen Dyke kept up, "No, sir, we are not going to do that." He wasn't backing down. I retreated rapidly in order to escape any misdirected flak, so the nature of the discussion and outcome remains a mystery. He was not warm and fuzzy, and while he went right to the point without small talk, he treated me like his personal staff and was generous with handwritten notes of thanks for various projects or duties we performed for him. I could work for him any day. He was later promoted to Lt Gen.

Sometimes, it's the unexpected things that result in a pat on the back or maybe makes a person known. I was working long hours doing my best to provide outstanding service and make things happen as they should. I would not describe it as worked to death, but I certainly didn't have time for tomfoolery or peripheral activities. One day, an order came down making me the Combined Federal Campaign Chairman for the entire OJCS. Why me, Lord, what have I done to deserve this? Now I had to give up time that I should have been devoting to my job for this extra project. Of course, each of the major directorates appointed an officer to help with their internal fundraising, but I was the "stuckee," and it was my responsibility to make it work. We held a kickoff meeting with a two-star general (not Gen Dyke) who made a glorious and completely worthless speech saying he didn't care how much money was collected as long as we had 100% participation. I was flabbergasted but could hardly correct him in front of all the action officers.

What planet he came from, I don't know, but he was sending exactly the wrong message. The Combined Federal Campaign is intended to collect money, not participation percentages. Lord love a duck, what was he thinking, and now I'm stuck with trying to correct a major general's message from participation to dollars. Another meeting wouldn't work. I was frustrated and disgusted with the general's preposterous remarks sabotaging my mission. There were two main entrances to the OJCS; each one was guarded by police to keep those who did not have a JCS badge from entering. This naturally caused a little bottleneck that slowed people down. It's far from an original idea, but I had 6 x 6-foot charts made up and put on pedestals, so they were eye level at each entrance. The charts listed each major office or directorate and showed clearly how much they were contributing, using the old thermometer-style gauge. They were updated daily so each three-star or head of a major OJCS component entering and exiting the

OJCS area would see how his directorate was doing. Having put the wheels in motion there was really nothing more I could do. Fate would either carry or drop the ball. I left for Germany to hunt pheasants with my friends in Bavaria.

When I returned home, I found General Vessey had contributed $500, which was more than twice the suggested amount for a general. That helped jump his personal office to over 100% almost immediately. Nobody wants to be left behind when the record is up for the world to see every day as they arrived and departed the Pentagon. We, the OJCS, were the first major agency in the National Capital Region to reach 100% of our goal! Talk about unexpected, it was a shock but a good one. When I left for Germany, I was in a bit of a funk, concerned about this additional duty and how it would turn out. I felt more relieved than joy over the great success. I was invited to join the Chairman and the Director of the Joint Staff for a picture with Secretary of Defense (Sec Def) Caspar Weinberger. Most officers in the OJCS never see the Chairman, much less have an office call or even a one-on-one discussion with him, and to be praised by the Sec Def is beyond the scope for anyone below three-star level. And here it was for me, a mere lieutenant colonel, for doing an extra-duty job that I would have given any amount of money to escape from. Sometimes the world turns in strange ways. I felt a little guilty about meeting for a thanks and photo op with the Sec Def when thinking of all the good hard-working troops in the trenches, working overtime, usually without any thanks. Nevertheless, it was a positive experience to be around Secretary Weinberger; he instilled a profound level of confidence not only in DOD but in relations with the CIA, the National Security Council, the Congress, and the President. We were lucky to have him as Secretary of Defense.

Fighting, or at least dreading, the Pentagon assignment with all the foreboding rumors and even some testimonials proved to be a mistake, at least for me. Of course, we could afford to live inside the Beltway, and we didn't have to worry about long commutes, or getting kids in good schools. I can understand pilots not wanting to be in the Pentagon because they lose out on flying. Some senior officers prefer being on a small base or environment where they can command the unit, and maybe just to be more important and have a big office. But it is a shame to pass up the opportunity for a front-row seat where the most vital decisions for our military and country are made. It was an educational and enjoyable experience for me, and I'm sorry for those who have passed up or were just never offered that opportunity.

An experience that is etched in my mind took place at Ground Zero, the open area in the middle of the Pentagon. President Ronald Reagan presented the Medal of Honor to Army Master Sergeant Raul (Roy) Benavidez, who served with the 5th Special Forces in Vietnam. His exploits would put Rambo to shame. He was wounded with bullets, bayonets, and shrapnel 37 times and is credited with saving the life of at least eight fellow soldiers. It was a very moving experience, and I still get a lump in my throat when I visualize the ceremony. There was President Reagan standing on the outside stair landing at the second-floor level, reading the award citation himself, adding his personal comments of praise, commending MSgt Benavidez. It was like Moses reading the 10 Commandments. Ground Zero was packed, and if the President had said after the ceremony, "I want you to all to go out and lay on the tracks to stop the next Metro train," I believe it would have happened. He was held in the highest esteem by the military, both enlisted and officers. Another moving experience with President Reagan was when the hostages were returned from Iran. Many of us from the Pentagon were invited to the White House lawn to witness their historic return.

One Christmas, I was racking my brain to come up with a nice gift for Loretta. It happened that our friend Laura Revitz knew of an exclusive jewelry show hosted by her sister-in-law and offered to help me pick out a nice piece of jewelry. In those days, you could drive up to the Pentagon entrance. She came to pick me up in her V-12 Jaguar coupe. Laura got out and moved to the passenger seat so I could drive. She was wearing a full-length mink coat. I made the purchase of a "surprise" Christmas gift and drove back to the Pentagon. Once again, we had to trade places as she moved from the passenger side to the driver side. I proceeded to my office, and just as I sat down my secretary told me Loretta was on the line. Loretta never called me at work; this was an exception as she asked if Laura and I had been out for a quickie over the lunch hour or what. How she found out that fast is beyond me, but it was the end of a Christmas "surprise."

The social scene and entertainment offered in Washington, D.C., and the surrounding area were an unexpected but delightful benefit, particularly for those of us who lived inside the Beltway, making it convenient to attend functions in D.C. When I finally resigned myself to being assigned to the Pentagon, Loretta got on her horse, so to speak, and flew to Washington to find us a place to live. She selected a condominium at the Watergate at Landmark in Alexandria, Virginia, which is a 34-acre, high-fenced campus with four 18-story buildings of condominiums, housing nearly 5,000 occupants. It was an excellent choice, on a main bus line, and close enough that driving to the Pentagon was easily doable. The complex had one entrance/exit that was manned by armed guards 24 hours a day. It had indoor and outdoor pools and a fully equipped gym with both sauna and steam rooms. Additionally, we had our own mail room. We had a jogging track around the enclosure that was lighted at night to accommodate shift workers. Many of the people living at Watergate were high-level U.S. federal employees in the FBI, CIA, and other intelligence communities. Congressman Wayne Grisham lived across the hall on our floor.

Convenience, along with good security, and lack of outside yard and house maintenance made it "easy living." I even entered politics a bit by running for the Board of Directors. It was kind of a big deal, and the election was run by the League of Women Voters. We had a huge fiduciary responsibility and had money invested mostly in very solid bonds or money market accounts that were drawing as much as 20% interest in 1979 and 1980. It was always a struggle to keep the condo fee at a reasonable rate but still high enough to give us a good cushion cover not only for emergencies, but long-term maintenance without having to make an extra assessment to the owners. Being on the board of a condominium with 5,000 inhabitants is not recommended by me; some people wanted the condo fee lowered and others wanted it higher. Complaints included: the toilets made too much noise for some, others wanted faster elevators, and still others wanted a hotter sauna.

The list went on and on, but as board members we needed to listen patiently to all suggestions and complaints. My advice is to avoid that duty if possible. One of our longtime friends, Herb Treger, still lives there and has served on the board at least twice. Herb served with us at the Military Personnel Center in San Antonio, and we met him one time in Kenya when the lucky dog had snared an assignment as a liaison officer with the Kenyan Air Force. Herb retired from the Air Force as a major and completed a second distinguished career as a high-level Department of State official. He is a train aficionado and has traveled on all the important and famous railroads in the world.

Washington, D.C., abounds in wonderful museums crowned by the Smithsonian Museums on the mall. Historic homes dot the entire area, including Mount Vernon, the Custis Lee Mansion, Lighthorse Harry Lee's home, and many others. Numerous battlefield sites from both the Revolutionary War and Civil War are in close vicinity. During the summer months, the military bands of each service put on performances, taking turns at our national monuments and the Capitol steps. The Marine Corps band played on Monday nights at the Iwo Jima Memorial. You might see the Air Force at the Lincoln Memorial on Tuesday, and the Army at the Washington Monument on Wednesday, and the Navy at the Jefferson Memorial on Thursday. They always put on fine performances. The king of all military performances was unquestionably the United States Marine Barracks Parade held on the grounds of the original Marine barracks, dating from 1801, each Friday night. Their performance not only included great John Philip Sousa music but also entertainment by the U.S. Marine Drum and Bugle Corps, a parade, and fine performance by the silent drill team. Another event not to be missed was the United States Air Force Band in concert at the DAR Constitution Hall.

The John F. Kennedy Center offered world-class talent in the performing arts. We enjoyed several plays at the Kennedy Center, but especially appreciated the National Symphony. At one performance in honor of the 84th birthday of Dr. Armand Hammer, the conductor, Mstislav Rostropovich, invited Dr. Hammer to the stage to acknowledge his gift of $150,000. He then handed the baton to Dr. Hammer and proceeded to move Dr. Hammer's hand as if he were conducting as the orchestra played the 1812 Overture with big booms for the cannon fire. At the conclusion, Dr. Hammer took the

Long Shots — Military

microphone and announced his contribution would be increased to a quarter million dollars. It was a great performance and uplifting to see the contribution increased. Was it planned by Rostropovich or was it spontaneous? I love the violin, and we were privileged to see performances by Itzhak Perlman and Isaac Stern.

All kinds of music are available in the Washington area. We saw Willie Nelson perform at the Capitol Center in 1983—it was a smash hit, no warm-up acts, just Willie Nelson in his prime, from start to finish. The Air Force Rifle Team members had exposed me to country/western music, and I had heard bluegrass, but I became a real fan after attending a bluegrass concert at the Warner Theatre in D.C. That piqued my interest, and we became frequent patrons at the Birchmere in Alexandria, Virginia, where the Seldom Scene—John Starling, Eldridge, and Duffy—often played. Doc Watson was another favorite. And later, Ricky Skaggs put on a concert at the Filene Center. That hooked me on bluegrass. Many years later, I was able to talk with Ricky Skaggs backstage after a performance at the Grand National Quail Club. It was really a pleasure visiting with such a talented performer who was humble and down to earth. Although I was congratulating and praising him for his music, he treated me like I was someone special. No wonder he's so popular with his many fans.

The great shows, theater, and marching bands aside, the most important of all were the many new people we met and the longtime friendships that developed from people in and around the D.C. area. As one might expect, these new friendships revolved around shooting and hunting. And by the way, there was great goose hunting on and around the Eastern Shore of Maryland in those days. Additionally, shooting sea ducks from a boat in rough water on the Chesapeake Bay can be quite challenging. Farms in northern Virginia and southeastern Maryland offered many opportunities for dove shooting. George Revitz was one of the first of our new friends. I actually met him in 1979 at Fort Benning, Georgia, when I was there for a bunker trap competition, and one of the Army troops told me George was from Alexandria, Virginia.

I met Roger Bain and Bob Harding during a bunker trap shoot at Quantico Marine Corps base. They were shooting bunker trap, but we soon found we also had a common interest in hunting and hunting-style shooting, now called sporting clays, which was just starting up around D.C. and particularly on the Eastern Shore of Maryland. Both were accomplished shotgun shooters, and Roger was also an excellent rifle shot. We became close friends. Jimmy Owings, an avid bird hunter befriended me, which was my good luck.

Al Clark, a retired Army Lt Col, and I met at what is now the Prince Georges shooting range. Al liked to shoot all the shotgun events, and we hit it off immediately. He was a great fly fisherman and spent time in Alaska nearly every summer. Mark Silverman, a tax attorney who became a senior partner at Steptoe and Johnson, joined our group. John Kern and Bill Blackstone also became part of our group; later Jon Swindle joined us. Tom Held made all the shoots and often brought his three stout sons. Tom has been with me in Africa and many trips to Argentina. He is excellent company. Then Les and Barbara Norman, who were both shooters, joined us. Another husband and wife who were both shooters, Kinsey and Mona Robinson, came aboard. Paris Fisher, an attorney and lobbyist, and Army Col Jack Wood added to our group. My friend Col Scotty Cameron had retired in Alexandria, and he naturally became a part of the group. He was a gentlemen's gentleman and someone I tried but couldn't hope to emulate. John Allgood and Mark Taishoff returned from England and Germany respectively to join our circle. Col Bob Fechner and Maj Gen Cameron were assigned at Walter Reed Army Hospital and were both avid shooters. We pretty much shot sporting clays every weekend—weather permitting. Another hunter and fine shotgun aficionado was Tom Holland. He and his wife Lael joined me on trips to Africa and Argentina along with their kids Josh and Amanda.

One weekend, a couple of us were shooting sporting clays on the Eastern Shore and tried the Chesapeake Gun Club, a beautiful three-story clubhouse with a commercial kitchen, large dining room, and a combination sitting and reception room on the bottom floor along with the business office. Floors two and three held nine bedrooms. Their sporting clay course was superb; each station offered targets from four to six different machines, giving the shooter a great variation of targets. The shooting was so good a group of my friends decided to try it the next weekend with me. Then it morphed into coming with the wives every quarter. We would arrive Saturday afternoon and shoot clays while the ladies shopped. The club would simply close at 6:00 p.m., leave us the keys, and depart. The ladies would return and decorate the tables beautifully according to the time of the year. Dinners were coat and tie except for January, which was black-tie. Bob Harding was an excellent cook and acted as chef. Les Norman had owned a couple of restaurants, so we had two chefs when he joined our group. I was the chief waiter and bottle washer. The hors d'oeuvres were elaborate: fresh poached salmon and Whitetail deer backstrap were my favorites. It was worth coming just for the hors d'oeuvres. The meals were delicious, really gourmet, along with fine wines. Of course, the best was the excellent company. We acquired the moniker "Best Guns," and the group continues today under the leadership of Col Jack Wood at Pinehurst, North Carolina. Those quarterly get-togethers were a real happening, and we all eagerly looked forward to them. When my tour of duty at the Pentagon was up, we reluctantly left our many good friends in D.C. The Pentagon had been proven to be a very rewarding assignment both professionally and socially.

My next assignment was to the Air Force Electronic Security Command (ESC) located adjacent to Lackland Air Force Base in San Antonio, Texas. It is the Air Force arm of the National Security Agency. Knowing little about the intelligence world, it was an education, and traveling to our units and sites around the world broadened my perspective considerably. However, as Assistant Deputy Chief of Staff for Personnel, most of the work challenges remained familiar. The rest of my ESC assignment remains classified.

Not Again
or
The Five 4-star Flag Officers

Colonels were expected to move every two years in those days, and that time for me was nearly complete. My hope was to be assigned as a

Director of Personnel (DP) of a major command or operating agency. If those options were not available, my next choice would be as a chief of one of the directorates at the Military Personnel Center located on Randolph Air Force Base near San Antonio. The Colonel's Group, the unit in charge of making assignments for full colonels, sent orders for me for travel to Brussels, Belgium, where I was to interview to become the Executive Assistant to the United States Military Representative to the NATO Military Committee (MIL REP), liaison officer for a four-star Army general, with a permanent duty station in the Pentagon. NOT AGAIN. Bummer indeed! What happened to my assignment wish list of being a DP? I had just come from the Pentagon two years prior, and while it had been an outstanding assignment, it was far from my preferred location. Then I found out the Army was sending a colonel and the Navy was sending a captain to interview for the same job, so the assignment was not firm. Maybe I could still escape.

    I wasn't enthusiastic, but the Air Force said go interview so that's what I did. I arrived at NATO headquarters in Brussels on the date and time designated. As you might expect, people are not assigned to a four-star general's personal staff – he selects them. I reported in to Army General Roscoe Robinson Jr. It was a very cordial meeting. He obviously had already reviewed my records, so it was mostly just small talk and a couple inquiries about some NATO experiences as we drank coffee. Then, to my surprise, he said he would be delighted to have me on his staff. What happened to the Army and Navy officers who were interviewing for the job? I have no idea. Did I win or lose? Only time could tell. The only thing to do was say thank you and tell him I would do the best job possible. Then he said, "If your schedule permits, it would be good if you could come and see us every quarter."

    My schedule? I'm thinking, What? I don't have a schedule. My job was to support him and make his job easier in any way I could. Gen Robinson was a first-class gentleman and rather than say, "I want you to come and see us every quarter," he made it sound like more of an invitation than an order. His wife was a grand lady and just as polite.

    A little background on General Robinson. He was a 1951 West Point graduate who was awarded a Bronze Star for outstanding valor in the Korean War battle for Pork Chop Hill in 1952. He was also decorated with the Distinguished Flying Cross, earned 11 Air Medals and two Silver Stars in combat during Vietnam. He later served as the commanding officer of the 82nd Airborne Division. As an historical record, in 1982 he became the first African-American four-star general in the Army. Daniel (Chappie) James was the first Air Force African-American promoted to four-star general. General Robinson is listed as one of the 100 veterans in the last 100 years in the November 2018 publication of the Military Officers Association of America. I was fortunate to know nine of the 100. His retirement was held at Fort Meyer, adjacent to Arlington National Cemetery, with Army Chief of Staff John A. Wickham presiding. The actual ceremony was held inside a large gym with a formation and mini-parade prior to the retirement orders and retirement decoration. After remarks by General Wickham, who was also a paratrooper and had commanded the 101st Airborne Division, Gen Robinson moved to the podium. He was wearing a Class A uniform wheel hat with all the scrambled eggs on the bill. He looked to the audience and then to Gen Wickham and said, "With your permission." He then reached under the podium, pulled out his 82nd Airborne beret and exchanged his headgear. The room simply exploded with a tremendous roar from the paratroopers. What a show of respect and camaraderie. It was an honor to know and work for Gen Robinson.

Gen Jack N. Merritt replaced Gen Robinson as Mil Rep on October 1, 1985. He was also a decorated Vietnam veteran, having earned the Distinguished Flying Cross, two Bronze Star medals with the V device, and Air medals. Gen Merritt was born in Oklahoma. He graduated from the University of Nebraska and earned his commission through the Army officers candidate school (OCS). His early service was primarily in artillery and as assistant division commander of the First Cavalry Division. Eventually, he was designated as commanding general of the U.S. Army Field Artillery Center. Just prior to becoming the Mil Rep he had been the Director of the Joint Staff for OJCS, considered by many to be the senior three-star general position in the military service. I must say he was a live wire, and when he came to town we had our hands full. The bad part was he always scheduled more than he could handle. The meetings, whether in our office or elsewhere, always ran over time, and there was nothing I could do to stop it. Consequently, we were most always late. His style was more direct than Gen Robinson, so no one had any trouble figuring out what he needed or wanted. One morning, an older retired general who had been a previous Mil Rep and obviously a mentor to Gen Merritt was scheduled for a 0800 meeting in our office. I bought some croissants and, of course, we always had coffee for early morning visitors. The retired general arrived at 0750 and took a seat in one of the leather couches in our outer office. I offered coffee and croissants, which he politely but firmly turned down. The minutes ticked on, and then the clock struck 0800. No Gen Merritt in sight. Now the minutes were dragging, and the visiting general was obviously not interested in discussion. At 0810 Gen Merritt came flying in the door. Our visiting general stood up and blasted him with, "Goddamn you, Jack, you be on time." Of course, we all hit the deck, diving under desks, which is always advisable when Titans collide. Gen Merritt quickly ushered his visitor into his private office. We all had a smile after the fact, but Gen Merritt continued to overload his schedule.

It was during Gen Merritt's time that my two-year tour (assignment time) was coming to an end, and I was again looking forward to a possible DP job. The Colonel's Group, which was responsible for making assignments for colonels, was making no such offers but told me to be ready to move. Loretta had been selected for Air Command and Staff College at Maxwell Air Force Base in Alabama. She had no idea where she would be assigned upon completion of her one-year course, so I was in no hurry to jump into an assignment that would not be compatible with where she might be assigned. The Colonel's Group continued to drag their feet, insisting I had to go but not knowing where, or what. They were suggesting a possible base commander or an atomic safety position. Neither interested me much and seemed a little boring compared to meetings with the most senior military and civilian members in the Department of Defense and the many powerful players on Capitol Hill. Gen Merritt asked where I was being assigned, and I told him it hadn't been decided. He asked me if I would stay on with him. I relayed that request to the Colonel's Group, which they abruptly denied. I figured that was that until Gen Merritt asked me what I had decided, and I reported the Colonel's group would not allow me to stay in place. We were in his office, and I could actually see his face turning red; that picture remains in my mind's eye. He said thank you, more or less dismissing me, and as I was walking out, he said to the secretary, "Get me the Chief of Staff of the Air Force," and he closed the door. The language got rough, and the volume was high; we could hear him shouting, "God damn it." Was he talking to the Chief or who? It didn't matter. I thought that the Air Force was going to skin me alive. I worried. Without question my next assignment will be to Shemya, a very small Air Force base on a very small island in the Aleutian Chain—if I survive long enough. What happened? Nothing. The Colonel's Group never called back. And I mean never.

Having been director of the joint staff, Gen Merritt was not receptive to anyone telling him no. However, he was double smart for certain, and he would listen—sometimes. He was assigned to the NATO position from a staff job where he was not authorized an aide de camp. When he came on board, I suggested it would be a good idea to select a top Air Force major who knew the flying business as his aide de camp. One advantage was having someone on his staff who could arrange military air for his trips to and from Washington, D.C., or other NATO countries. Having someone who could speak the right language (pilot to pilot) is often helpful. A converted KC 135, (a four-jet engine plane) call sign SPAR 60, stationed at Ramstein Air Force Base, was dedicated for use by only four-star generals or admirals in the European theater. His answer to my suggestion of an Air Force pilot was good: "Get one." I interviewed three and picked a young fighter pilot major who worked out well. When he moved on, the general challenged me to pick another one that good. Not much of a challenge really; an easy task. The Air Force was offering many top officers for such a plum job, and I'm good at recognizing talent. I'm pleased to say both majors made below the zone (early) promotions to lieutenant colonel, and the last I knew of them they were full colonels. Their efficiency reports were signed by a four-star general, but who wrote the reports remains confidential.

On a trip from Washington to Brussels, I was on official business and sitting in the front of a SPAR 60 with Gen and Mrs.

Merritt. A partition separated a section in the back of the plane for additional passengers or space-available personnel. Loretta and I had planned to take a few days leave in Europe after my official duties were finished if she could get on the flight as a space-available passenger. I did not feel it appropriate that I bother General and Mrs. Merritt about my wife, who was waiting in the terminal to hopefully get on our flight. We were in an official car and drove directly to the plane, so I did not know if she was able to get on the plane or not. If she did get on, we would take a short vacation in Europe. If she didn't get on, I would simply go home. We were sitting at a table having coffee when the steward noticed my name tag and asked, "Is that your wife in the back?" Feeling relatively sure it was, I answered, "Yes." Mrs. Merritt turned to the general and said in an annoyed tone, "Jack, why didn't you tell me Loretta was on this plane?" The general was looking at me, and now I was red-faced trying to explain it was my fault and that I didn't want to bother them. And I wasn't sure Loretta would get on in space-available status anyway. They had been to dinner at our home, so Mrs. Merritt (Rosemary) knew Loretta.

They were hosting a dinner the following evening, and we were made the guests of honor. That is not a small thing, and it is not necessarily announced. But it is very obvious at the dinner table. Loretta was seated to the right of the general (host), and I was seated to the right of Mrs. Merritt (hostess); that establishes the protocol. Four Stars do not have dinners for colonels, but this one did. The next day while I was working, Loretta was being toured around Brussels in the general's white armored Mercedes. United States' rules would not allow that, but NATO rules applied in this case. Working for General Merritt could be taxing but it was never boring. Upon retirement from the Army, he became president of the Association of the United States Army—a very powerful organization. When I retired, he wrote me quite a nice note that said in part, "Just think you have kept five Mil Reps out of trouble!" It was a generous remark but appreciated.

Admiral Powell F. Carter Jr. had been director of the OJCS staff just prior to assuming duties of the MIL Rep, and he asked me to stay on as his executive assistant. I did not call the Colonel's Group and just simply continued my duties. Adm Carter was from

Long Shots — Military

California and had attended UCLA and Cal Tech before being appointed to the United States Naval Military Academy. He was selected early in his career by Adm Hyman Rickover to enter the naval nuclear power program. Adm Rickover was an engineer and developed the world's first atomic-powered submarine. He was said to be the hardest taskmaster in the Navy. Commander Carter (captain of the ship) had the distinction of being commander of the submarine U.S.S. Hammerhead, which in June 1970 became the first nuclear submarine to surface through the ice in the winter at the North Pole. He commanded submarines at squadron and group level and held key positions in the U.S. Atomic Energy Commission. Like Gen Merritt, he had been Director of the Joint Staff and knew how it operated but his style was the exact opposite of General Merritt's. When he visited Washington, he took two or three meetings in the morning, followed by a nap after lunch and then one or two in the afternoon. He was punctual, and his meetings never ran over the designated time. He was more of an introvert, which made for a much quieter office. One might think an atomic engineer could have a limited scope, but he was interested in history, art, and linguistics. He had knowledge of French, but his qualifications in Spanish and Russian were at the translator level. Years later when I retired, he sent me a congratulatory letter. He said, "It is hard to imagine the U.S. Mil Rep's office in the Pentagon without Col Dennis Behrens defending the fort. You have earned a special place in the memory of all of us you serve so well."

Adm William J. Crowe, who later served as U.S. ambassador to the Court of St. James, was Chairman of the Joint Chiefs at the time, and when he and Adm Carter put their heads together in a close and quiet conversation, I was amazed how much they looked alike. I mean in size and both of them baldheaded, slightly hunched over in the conversation. From his duty as Mil Rep to NATO he moved on to become CINC United States Atlantic Fleet, headquartered at Norfolk, Virginia. I visited him there and found how small and tight officers' sleeping quarters are on a guided missile cruiser ship.

Admiral James R. Hogg followed Adm Carter as the NATO Mil Rep and he asked me to stay on his staff and continue to run the Pentagon office. And again, I did not call the Colonel's Group and just continued. Adm Hogg was a graduate of the Naval Academy in Annapolis. His father was also a graduate of the Naval Academy and retired as a Rear Admiral. Adm Hogg was a surface warfare officer for ships that float on top of the water, not submarines. He was commander of squadrons and groups and eventually Commander of the Seventh Fleet, which covered the Western Pacific and Indian Ocean. Even after military retirement, he served our country as Director of the Strategic Studies Group and is credited in the development of the electromagnetic railgun. He was an extrovert, and I always enjoyed his company and his two youngest sons Robert and William. He was married to an English lady, Ann-Margret Cheeseman. Adm Hogg had an original Ford Mustang that he had purchased in 1965. It was candy-apple red, and I can tell you, it would draw a crowd. The car was stored in a warehouse at the Navy Yard. He never asked me, and it was certainly not in my job description, but when I knew he was coming back to D.C., I would go over and pick it up and drive it over to Bolling Air Force Base to get it washed. The security police (mostly young kids) at the Air Force entry gate would swamp me to look the car over and sometimes take pictures.

My final four-star boss was Admiral William D. Smith, who also asked me to stay on as his representative in Washington, D.C. He was a graduate of the Naval Academy 1955 class. His first command was of the USS Henry L. Stimson, and he later commanded both squadrons and groups. He served in many key staff positions in the Navy including a tour on the Nuclear Propulsion Exam Board and later as Director of Nuclear Power Personnel. After retirement, he continued to serve as a Capstone Fellow at the National Defense University. Capstone is the program that takes newly promoted one-star generals and admirals from all the services and gives them an introduction to becoming a general or admiral. He also became an advisor, board member, or chairman of many Navy and defense boards and academies. But most important, he was known as a gentlemen's gentleman, and I will attest to that firsthand. He was simply first rate in every category. We all worked extra hard for him. He was very low-key and never wanted to be in the spotlight. When he visited the Pentagon, we would often walk to the offices of three-star generals and admirals

Long Shots — Military

rather than have them come to his office for appointments. His feeling was they had tight schedules, and he wanted to be the least disruptive as possible. Of all the five four-stars I worked for he was the only one who ever gave me any specific direction. What was it? He said, "Please be sure I am never somewhere I shouldn't be."

Some execs and aides de camp push their bosses to the front or have them seated in lead cars. Adm Smith was quite modest and didn't want or need any ego pumping. He retired after I had moved to San Antonio, but I thought enough of him that I flew back to Washington, D.C., for his retirement ceremony. It was he who told me why the Navy admirals all asked me to stay on during their assignment. He said it was because General Merritt recommended it, saying, "Behrens can get tickets to the opera when there ain't no opera." Not true of course but quite flattering in any case. Adm Smith died last year, and I would've attended his funeral had I known of it. We, my staff and I, accumulated accolades galore, and obviously the flag officers (generals and admirals) were well pleased.

You have to ask yourself, "How bad does a four-star admiral need an Air Force colonel? He could have any captain in the Navy." In fact, I had several Navy captains come by to ask me when I was going to retire. Much of the credit for our success and the reason for the bosses asking me to stay was my superb staff. They were the "two-man band" that could do any and everything. Linda Davis was just a prime secretary. She could take dictation and straighten up my messes. She ran the schedule and kept everyone straight. I assisted only when she ran into stubborn resistance to our requirements. She was steady and unflappable.

Army Sergeant First Class Roy Eberhart was a perfect fit for the job. Roy was intelligent and should have been an officer. I counted on him much as I would any junior officer. He preferred to wear civilian clothes, which was fine with me, so his duty uniform became suits and sport coats but always with a tie. I believe he felt he was more effective in civilian threads. Roy was low key but enterprising; he would find a way to make it work, whatever the task. He worked well with the many support people we needed when our boss visited from Brussels. He handled all the transportation and housing requirements, and anything else that had to be done. Understand, our boss, the general or admiral, had a large staff in Brussels: a Brig Gen deputy, a full colonel executive officer, secretaries and Navy writers, drivers, bodyguards, aides, and several full colonels on staff. When he came to the Pentagon, we had to make everything work and we were only three.

What did I really do as the Executive Assistant? The job description is long and says in part: "Acts as point of contact between the U.S. Mil Rep and offices of JCS, OSD, DIA, military departments, and other government agencies." And I was designated as the personal representative of the Mil Rep in Washington. We did those things, but the truth was I saw my job as simply making my bosses' life easier and saving him time in any way I could. And that goes far out of the official job descriptions. We did everything possible to enhance his effectiveness by maximizing scheduling and time used in his visits to Washington or at his headquarters in Brussels. The less he had to fool with, the more time and effort he could devote to major issues. Heck, I would've shined his shoes if it would've helped.

We had a couple of senior generals every month visiting us or coming through a NATO orientation program that I developed, depending on where they were being assigned. Military dependent schools are managed by the Department of Defense, specifically, the Dependence Education Council made up of general and flag officer commanders of major services, combat, and unified commands. The Council is chaired by the Assistant Secretary of Defense for Manpower and Reserve Affairs. I sat on that council in their biannual meeting as the representative of the United States Mil Rep to NATO. It was always an enjoyable and interesting sidetrack from normal military matters to the challenges of providing the best education possible for our nearly 90,000 military dependent kids worldwide. An additional duty all my bosses felt was of vital importance was escorting the Chairman of the NATO Military Committee in his visits to Washington, D.C. That responsibility would normally demand a more senior officer. I think probably one of the reasons I had the duty was neither the JCS nor any of the services wanted to be too closely tied to the NATO Chairman's visits since he was essentially lobbying the Congress for stronger support and assignment of more U.S. troops to Europe.

Long Shots — Military

I was assigned to NATO and not the JCS so it could be said that the Chairman's visit was strictly a NATO initiative. That was interesting duty. We visited the Congress, the State Department, and the White House. One chairman was Wolfgang Altenburg, a German general who had fought in WW II as a 15-year-old. He had what I would call elegant manners and spoke perfect English. I always enjoyed his company. He did cause me some minor extra problems as he brought along two of his bodyguards. Bodyguards were my responsibility, and I used the Naval Investigative Service (NIS) for that duty. The NIS agents were civilians, and their dress was straight out of GQ. Much like the FBI, they wore earphones for communication with each other. They were especially helpful in bringing the Chairman who traveled with a black diplomatic passport through Dulles Airport bypassing customs and the normal pressure points. Their cars were black Buick sedans with the red and blue emergency lights mounted unobtrusively in the front grill. Their chase car was the same, but I got a third car for the general's bodyguards. He really brought them more for a vacation in the States.

A later NATO Chairman was Norwegian Army General Vigleik Eide. He would bring his wife, and they were both very pleasant. About the bodyguards: there was a considerable threat in Europe and although there was little threat in the United States, you can imagine what a prize target the chairman of the NATO military committee would be to any terrorist group. No way could we allow anything bad to happen. We also assisted the American Ambassador to NATO just as a courtesy. He claimed we took better care of him than the State Department. The Mil Rep normally made 8 to 10 trips a year back to Washington. They were mostly short-notice or emergency trips and were usually only two or three days in duration. It was always a challenge to get them in to see the officials they needed to visit. The list normally included the OJCS Chairman but could include the Secretary of Defense and maybe Secretary of the Navy or Chief of Staff of any of the services, plus various planners in the OJCS. Those were all in the building, and you might think it would be easy, but Pentagon schedules are established weeks in advance.

My requests for meetings always, and I mean always,

interrupted schedules of the most senior people in the building. Believe it or not, most schedules are handled by high-level civilian secretaries. In my earlier four-year Pentagon tour, I became acquainted with several secretaries. Gen Dyke's secretary Lil had moved up to become secretary of the Chief of Staff of the Army. Topsy Taylor, Loretta's friend from our assignment in Ramstein, had become secretary to the Chief of Staff of the Air Force. Just knowing people was a big help. The secretaries knew I was honest and would not fudge on our availability, but I was asking favors to have them cancel people so we could get on the schedule. If they insisted they could not change or get us on the normal day schedule I would suggest lunch, or breakfast, or riding home with whomever we had to meet. I was persistent, and we got it done one way or another.

The secretaries would tell me this was the last time they were canceling people on short notice to get my boss in, but it never was. Remember also, those who we wanted to meet with did not always have full control of their own schedules; the Chairman could be called away by the Secretary of Defense, the National Security Adviser, or the President. Our meetings were not just in the Pentagon; they might be at Langley to visit with the Central Intelligence Agency, they could include embassies and with members of the House and Senate including the ranking members of both Armed Services committees and Defense Appropriations Committees. Congressman John P. Murtha was a powerful Congressman and ranking member of the Armed Services and Defense Appropriation Committees. He was always hard to schedule, and we ended up twice having breakfast with him in the Capital. I loved it; he paid. I was simply a note-taker, escorting a four-star general, but on those breakfast occasions he said, "Colonel, come sit next to me." He was a Marine Corps Vietnam combat veteran, earning a Bronze Star and receiving two Purple Hearts. He was the first Vietnam veteran elected to Congress and was still in the Marine Corps Reserves serving as a colonel. He eventually served 36 years in the House of Representatives.

Senator John W. Warner had been Secretary of the Navy and was a favorite of mine. He was always a gentleman, and it was fun to be in his office. I was not inclined to speak first or even speak at all, but he teased me by saying, "Isn't that right, Colonel?" knowing full well there was no way I was going to be quoted as saying anything, which would have been a sure way to be decapitated. I had no authority to make any remarks. He had been married to Elizabeth Taylor, so he probably needed to do some teasing. He was a strong supporter of the military.

When General Merritt was the Mil Rep, we would meet with Senator David Boren, who was Chairman of the Senate Select Committee on Intelligence. They were both from Oklahoma as was Admiral Crowe, Chairman of the Joint Chiefs of Staff, so they were empowered to tell Okie jokes. My favorite was, "Oklahoma matching luggage: two paper grocery bags." They both loved Oklahoma, and Gen Merritt elected to have his retirement ceremony at Fort Sill, Oklahoma.

Senator Stevens had a massive map of the United States covering one wall of his office with the map of Alaska, including the Aleutian chain, overlaying the United States. I had caught a king salmon bigger than the one pictured on his desk, and he remembered that. We also met with Senator Sam Nunn of Georgia.

One meeting I was worried about was with Congresswoman Patricia Schroeder from Colorado. She was the first woman to serve on the House Armed Services Committee and was an outspoken feminist. I was escorting General Wolfgang Altenburg, the Chairman of the NATO Military Committee and the senior general in NATO. He was basically lobbying Congress to keep over 100,000 troops in Germany. It became a very genteel meeting, and I must say Congresswoman Schroeder turned out to be a first-class lady. I always stood back and looked for a chair in the rear unless invited to come forward. She recognized me and said, "Come sit with us," and had an extra chair brought forward. Unfortunately, her staff had not properly briefed her, and she didn't realize the position or importance of this visiting German general. At one point they were discussing numbers, and she said, "Great Britain would never agree," and General Altenburg answered, "I was with Margaret last week and her position is ..." Only then did she realize he was someone who spoke with heads of state.

On that same visit I escorted Gen Altenburg to an insightful meeting with Secretary of Defense Dick Cheney. More interesting

217

was a meeting with the Joint Chiefs of Staff. Gen Powell was gone on TDY that week, so the Vice Chairman Gen Robert T. Herres chaired the meeting. All the Chiefs (heads of military services) were present; Gen Alfred M. Gray, Commandant of the Marine Corps; Adm Carlisle A. Trost, Chief of Naval Operations; Gen Carl E. Vuono, Chief of Staff of the Army; and Gen Larry D. Welch, Chief of Staff of the Air Force. Gen Altenburg was briefing, more like giving a tutorial, to the Chiefs. His subject was turmoil in the Soviet Union after the death of Leonid Brezhnev. He named several senior Russian officials but said the Russians needed someone with charisma who could reach the Western markets before their country imploded. While musical chairs were still going on in Moscow, he said the new General Secretary would be Mikhail Gorbachev. It was the first time I'd ever heard the name. I wondered who else, if anyone, in the room knew it would be Gorbachev. The Chiefs were stone-faced; it reminded me of a poker table—interesting times for sure.

My favorite of all was Senator John McCain. He was simply a class act all the way around. He pushed for democratic governments across the globe and was a world humanitarian. On my second visit, he could recall my name, and Behrens is not that easy. I suspect he had a very good administrative assistant who made sure he knew the names of everyone on his schedule. Don't forget I was only an escort officer, not the main player. Think of all the world leaders and famous people he dealt with. When we left his office, he would always say to me, "Thanks for coming, Colonel." He was truly an American hero and had my highest respect. His "The Most Wondrous Land" remarks at the Liberty Medal ceremony in 2017 are in the appendix. They are inspirational and ideals we should all strive to achieve.

I had been to the Capitol twice as lieutenant when I was passing through Washington. The first time was to visit my Congressman Charles Teague, who let us Boy Scouts swim in his pool and was from my hometown Santa Paula, California, and later with 2d Lt Sammy Rhodes, one of my rifle team shooters, to meet Senator Ralph Yarborough from Texas. But those were purely shake-hands-and-take-picture meetings. Escorting the four-star officers gave me insight on our congressional representatives' firsthand working issues in their offices, far away from campaigns and the media, which was a real treat and an education.

The previous executive assistant worked in part as an action officer between the Mil Rep's action officers in Brussels and the European division in the JCS Plans Directorate (J-5). He went to the European division staff meeting every morning at 0730. I saw that as a waste of time and of little value. Often, one would only become a third wheel and manage to delay and confuse issues. The action officer in Brussels wanted to talk to the expert in the JCS and vice versa. There was no way I could become the expert in tanks, submarines, tactical, or supply aircraft. The action officers needed to talk or work directly with their counterparts; I got out of their way and simply stopped trying to do action officer business or going to JCS European division staff meetings. That made staff officers on both sides of the ocean happy as no one was meddling in their affairs. I did go down to JCS staff meetings now and then to find out what might be interesting at the four-star level. The European division action officers were Colonels Dick Knob, Tom Hennessey, Dick Edward, Dave Bice, Jim Riley, Bob Gill, and Vernon Pike. They were a good bunch but had their hands full most of the time. My schedule was my own, and I could do whatever I wanted as I worked in complete autonomy. That allowed me to do the important things and free up time for other activities, one of which was to promote Air Force target shooting and work with young guys as a team captain for the Air Force International Trap Team.

Being an administrative assistant or exec officer to five four-star generals or admirals for eight years has to be a world record. Most execs make it for one year. Of course, my position was unique in that my four-star boss was stationed in Brussels, and I didn't get so badly beat up with working long difficult hours although my normal hours after Loretta left were 7:00 a.m. to 7:00 p.m. No one asked me to stay that late but every now and then the boss would call after returning from a late-night dinner or formal event. And I was in no particular hurry to mingle with the Washington rush-hour traffic. With the time difference, Brussels was normally shut down by 1:00 p.m. Washington, D.C., time. Many officers would be horrified with the idea of such a job, but it worked perfectly for me. There could be downtimes, but it could also become exciting and hectic in keeping all the Washington, D.C., balls in the air when one of the four-stars was in town. Even preparation for their visits required a lot of legwork to make it smooth. And it was intriguing to watch the big wheels in action.

Loretta had been selected for Air Command and Staff College at Maxwell Air Force Base in Alabama, which is a one-year program, and we didn't know where she would be assigned upon graduation. She was already a major and looking to become a lieutenant colonel soon. It made no sense for me to move until we found out what her next assignment would be. It had also more or less been decided that it was her turn to look for the best jobs after following me for 20 years. And, as I said earlier, the Colonel's Group was suggesting possible jobs that sounded boring, and quite frankly I liked my job and did it well. I would also have to admit it was quite flattering to have a four-star general or admiral ask me to stay on with them when they could have nearly anyone in the Armed Forces. It made sense for me to remain in Washington.

When we were assigned back to the Pentagon we moved once again into Watergate, this time into the penthouse on the 18th floor. We had a three-bedroom, two full-bath unit that Loretta had completely redone with the help of a couple of interior decorators; it was truly a showplace, kind of an equivalent to a New York Fifth Avenue apartment. After Loretta left for the Air Command and Staff College, I sold the unit and moved to Bethesda, Maryland, and later Arlington, Virginia. The good thing was that I had civilian friends all around the area from my previous Pentagon tour, and it was like old home week being back with them. We played and shot sporting clays and bunker trap.

My friend John Allgood had retired from the Air Force but stayed in the area and always furnished us with dove hunts. A good spot for shooting dove in Maryland was a Naval Academy dairy and farm. It was open to active duty and retired military. I helped the Naval Academy shotgun team with bunker trap shooting, and it was a treat when they showed up at the dairy to hunt doves. When I shot a bird, they wouldn't let me go pick it up, they would race out and get it for me, just a really fine group of young guys: Midshipmen Johnson,

Dave Springer, Jay Schnelle, Kevin Ellzey, and Fillipi. Air Force Capt Mark Taishoff joined us for sporting clays and hunting geese on Kent Island with John Allgood. Paul Facchina entered our shooting clays circle. George Revitz was still shooting and always happy to join me for bunker trap. Local trap shooters included Lou Ritchie, Col Gary Mahon, Kevin McCormack, Ray Yeong and later lieutenants John Linn and Dominic Grazioli, who were on the Air Force team. Other favorites joining us from Pennsylvania and New Jersey were Shelley Gitman, Whitey Bristow, Art Goodman, Mir Khan, and Carol Gephardt. Steve Holtzclaw was a college student and became a consistent bunker trap shooting partner who often traveled with me and the Air Force team to competitions around the country.

Brig Gen Ted Giddings had recently retired. He had been the Commander of the Air Force District of Washington, D.C., and had joined us as a member of our Kent Island goose hunters when I was assigned to my first tour in the Pentagon. He had two tours in Southeast Asia, one as a forward air controller assigned to the first U.S. Air Cavalry Division in 1966 and later as a fighter pilot. He flew 205 combat missions. Loretta had worked for Gen Giddings and credits him as a prime mentor. I count him as a friend and am embarrassed at the number of meals I had at his house after Loretta left for the year-long command and staff course. The number was really shameful, but Gen Giddings' wife Jane is nothing less than a professional-class cook. She was from the Midwest and made the best pot roast dinner in the world, and I am from Iowa pot roast country. Her superb tenderloin would make a French Chateaubriand chef envious. Their home really became a second home for me when Loretta was in Alabama and then in San Antonio. I was always welcome and enjoyed their good company. We hunted and shot sporting clays together and even fished some in the Chesapeake. Beyond the Pentagon days we traveled to Missoula, Montana, to fish with my friend Rob Braach. The General fell in love with Montana and particularly Rock Creek, which is a blue-ribbon trout stream. His fly casting would put any maestro to shame. He can put a fly exactly where it needs to be. He and Jane live the better part of the year in a beautiful custom-made log cabin on Rock Creek. They are wonderful hosts, but you better be prepared to gain some weight because Jane is constantly preparing very nice things that even the strongest constitution can't resist. I had the Air Force team shooting a match in Missoula, and for a little treat I arranged an afternoon float trip on Rock Creek. 1st Lt John Linn and SrA Mike Herman were surprised to learn their guide, who would be rowing the raft, was retired Brig Gen Giddings. They caught fish. We hunted together in Maryland, Virginia, Texas, Oregon, and Montana. I visit them every year, and we keep tabs on each other.

There was always an abundance of official functions in D.C. One that was a highlight for me was a reception given by the Commandant of the Marine Corps, General Gray, in honor of the Chairman, Joint Chiefs of Staff and Mrs. Powell. It was on a beautiful midsummer's night and held outside on the spacious and immaculate lawn of the Commandant's House, which dates back to 1806. The British burned the U.S. Capitol in 1814, but the Commandant's house was spared. Legend reports it was in respect for the Marines who had impressed the British in battle. The house is decorated in accordance with each Commandant's style, but tradition dictates the Commandant leave a house gift for the incoming Commandant. It contains fine American antique furniture, exquisite China and crystal, and superb Persian rugs. It is worth seeing. I brought some friends along as my guests and introduced them to both Gen Gray and Gen Powell. I knew Gen Gray from shooting at Quantico and of course I knew Gen Powell from meetings with my boss. One of my guests was Mrs. Laura Revitz, who had just won the world championship of live pigeon shooting. Both generals were interested and seemed pleased to talk to a lady shooter, particularly a charming world champion. It was a delightful reception followed by the spectacular Friday night Marine Parade. Another fun social event—free food and champagne—was the State Department's annual reception for major donors and supporters. Laura Revitz invited me as her escort twice. It was held in a large room with the receiving line next to the entry and food and booze at the far end. Guests went through the receiving line before they got to the food and drink. It was a formal line with an officer announcing your name as he introduced you to the Secretary. Each time when shaking hands with Secretary Baker I would ask him about quail hunting in South

Texas: how did he do, what did the quail population look like, etc. That always slowed the line as Secretary Baker would not let go of my hand. Most likely he needed a break from just, "How do you do and nice to have you with us." I always enjoyed our brief little conversation, but I noticed a number of scowls from those who wanted to advance quickly to the food or, more likely, the booze at the far end of the room.

The Air Force version of Toys for Tots was running its annual campaign for toys as Christmas gifts for disadvantaged children in 1987 when I decided to collect a few toys by turning it into a sporting clays match with a few of my friends. Everyone brought a toy or Christmas gift, and we had a fun team match with the winning team buying beer for the losers. Yes, the winners bought the beer for the sorry losers. After the second year in 1988, I realized we were not doing much good by donating teddy bears or toys. There was much more need than just a toy. Col Jack Woods' wife Judi was a schoolteacher in Northern Virginia and alerted us to kids who badly needed clothes. That changed our direction, and she furnished us with a list of kids and what clothing they needed with the sizes required. Many of them were immigrants. I remember one case where two kids lived in a car with their parents, so even though Northern Virginia had a wealthy school system, many of the kids needed help the school could not provide.

That program grew into a nice event of friends coming together on the second Saturday in December to celebrate Christmas with a sporting clay competition and gifts of clothes with additional books, toys, and candies, for grade and middle school kids in Alexandria. We changed the name from Toys for Tots to Secret Santa so as not to be confused with the fine Marine Toys for Tots program. All the gifts were Christmas-wrapped and tagged with either a kid's name or appropriate size/age of the intended recipient. The program has grown in numbers, and we normally have more than 30 shooting friends join us. We collect enough gifts for a hundred kids. It is such a big help to the school kids that even the principal has come to meet us. We cater a lunch of lasagna with salad, and the shooters bring wine. It's a simple lunch but has become a must-attend event. I'm pleased to report even with the pandemic of December 2020 and the restricted gun club attendance our program continued, and the kids got their gifts. Thanks particularly to John Kern, Bill Blackstone, Jon Swindle, John Allgood, Paris Fisher, and his daughter Caroline for carrying the load in that difficult time. On 11 December 2021 we completed our 35th consecutive year. And a very special thank-you to our teachers Beth Reidy and Lily Del Campo from Mount Eagle Fairfax County Elementary School in Alexandria who for the last 29 years have faithfully identified the kids needing help, provided us with lists of what was needed, and come to our event to pick up and then distribute the Christmas gifts each year. John Allgood and Jon Swindle are the on-site organizers—keeping count of those attending, coordinating with the gun club on the shooting course and lunches. During the last few years my trip to Washington for this event has been greatly facilitated (and I must add happily) by staying with my friends Kinsey & Mona Robinson. Additionally, Erik Search has most generously picked me up at the airport at all hours of the night and chauffeured me throughout my stay, which also includes a shooting match in West Virginia with John Allgood and members of the Royal Order of the La Paloma. His help has simply been valuable beyond estimation. Erik has been shooting with "my boys" in the States and Argentina. Neil Walther has dutifully shared in these support tasks. They are both faithful and loyal friends who also fit under my tent.

My first reaction to an assignment back to the Pentagon was, "Not again." It should have been, "Thank you very much" to the Colonel's Group. They got it right, and under the circumstances, the assignment proved to be a perfect fit for me. I was once again able to run my show, small as it was, without interference. While it was not a particularly challenging job, it was interesting and often exciting. It certainly allowed me to witness decisions by military and civilians at the highest levels.

During my Pentagon assignments I had the honor to serve under three Commanders in Chief, all men of honor and character: Presidents James E. Carter, Ronald W. Reagan, and George H.W. Bush. Most of my time in the puzzle palace was battling the Evil Empire during the Cold War. Other hostile events included the hostage taking of our embassy personnel by Iranians and our failed rescue attempt. I was on the White House lawn when they were returned. The dustup between Margaret Thatcher and Argentine President Gen Leopoldo Galtieri over the Falkland Islands or the Islas Malvinas caused us concern. The islands had been contested since 1833, but it turned to war in 1982. The successful effort to depose the de facto Panamanian leader, Gen. Manuel Noriega required our troops. The Persian Gulf War to drive Saddam Hussein out of Kuwait was our first full-scale war after Vietnam. It was excellently planned and conducted with Gen Powell in the Pentagon and Gen Schwarzkopf in the field. Not hostile but a big event was the fall of the Berlin Wall in 1989. Those were interesting times. I lucked out with excellent bosses and a fine staff that kept me looking good. I gave the military the best I could, and it gave me opportunity, satisfaction, and magnificent experiences in return. Who could ask for more?

Air Force Retirement and Coming Home to Old and New Friends

I was happy in the Air Force, doing an important job that I enjoyed. However, Title 10 of the U.S. Code limits full colonel line officers to a maximum of 30 years' commissioned service, and that milestone was fast approaching. I didn't want any kind of a retirement ceremony, but my boss, Adm William Smith, who was stationed in Brussels, suggested I come there for a small retirement ceremony followed by a reception and dinner at his house. He also invited me to bring along any family or friends I wished. Of course, Loretta joined me. Scott Coby and Albert Menefee flew over from the States as did Olli Weaver (Charlie Weaver's wife). Capt Taishoff was assigned in Germany, and he came, along with my Belgium hunting and trap-shooting friend René Haillez. We made a small, intimate group. As an added surprise, and to our great pleasure, my friend Gen J.B. Davis, who was stationed at Shape Headquarters Allied Powers of Europe, (SHAPE) in Mons, Belgium, crashed the retirement ceremony. Those reading this account who are not military, you should understand that four-star admirals or generals do not give dinners for colonels. That doesn't mean they don't like or respect them, it's just not possible; otherwise, they would be giving dinners every night. Adm Smith was the epitome of a gentleman. I was honored indeed.

Making my retirement even more enjoyable, Gen Davis and his super bride Carol had a dinner for me and my friends in their home in Mons. It was a very classy affair with a three-piece combo playing for the reception and dinner. The dinner was over the top as would be expected; Carol is simply a superb hostess. Loretta and the guests at the dinner in Brussels were with me again. And small world that it is, Gen Davis knew and had hunted with my Belgian hunting friend René Haillez many years earlier when he had been aide-de-camp to Gen Horace M. Wade. While it was a very high-end affair, Carol and General Davis were laid back and put everyone at ease. Another very comfortable and enjoyable evening. How do you get a better friend than that?

We went on to Ramstein Air Force Base in Germany where my hunting friend Gen Robert C. Oakes was commander-in-chief of U.S. Air Forces in Europe. We had hunted together in Texas, and he had hunted with some of my German friends. Gen Oakes suggested celebrating my retirement with him hosting a dinner to include my German hunting friends. That list grew to over 20 quickly so the dinner was moved to the officers' club. His protocol staff were a little concerned and asked me who all these people were. Of course, I confirmed it was a very influential group with high-level social and political standing. Although, I neglected to report, a couple of them had to finish milking before they could make the dinner. It was a very fun affair with singing and the recounting of hunting adventures and misadventures.

It was then back to the Pentagon to finish up my duties, tying up the loose ends and processing out. My last duty day was December 31, 1992. I went into the Pentagon to finish my last day and say goodbye to my staff. I was having a second cup of coffee when my secretary said the Chairman of the Joint Chiefs of Staff's exec was on the phone. I picked it up, and he said the chairman would like to see me if I was available at 9:00 a.m. If I'm available? Right. What could

Long Shots — Military

this be about? The Chairman had been out the first part of the week and was back in just for this day of New Year's Eve. When I got to his outer office, the exec motioned me to go right on in; the door was open. I went in and saluted. Gen Colin Powell returned my salute, got up, walked around his desk, and shook my hand. He motioned me to a chair and couch to the side of his office. He congratulated me on completing 30 years and thanked me for my service. We chatted for upwards of 30 minutes. He told me about a shotgun the Russians had given him. He had to reimburse the value to the U.S. Treasury to keep the gift. And we talked a little bit about days in Vietnam. He had obviously seen my record. Then he had a photographer come in and take our picture. I must say, I was a little embarrassed. After all, there were 200 colonels on the JCS staff, many of whom had never met him, and I didn't even work for him.

Think about it, a man of his importance and overwhelming schedule taking his precious time to wish me well, a guy who was walking out the door forever. I had seen him in action and was impressed by his demeanor. But this was far and above duty. How many men do you find like that? I was honored beyond belief. I have a collection of "I love me photos" with generals who were friends, but few people have ever seen that precious book. You won't see much military memorabilia in my house apart from some pictures of my kids or teams. But you will see one of Gen Powell.

Loretta retired in 2000 and we returned home to San Antonio from the Pentagon where I had been the most worthless military dependent in the world. I had already come home from the Pentagon in 1993 upon my Air Force retirement. Loretta was assigned to the Inspector General's Pentagon office in 1996 so we moved to Alexandria and took an apartment a pistol shot's distance from the Braddock subway station. The restaurants on King Street were nearby, and we were only one stop away from National Airport. Loretta was busy at work, and I was left to play with my friends in the Washington area, shooting sporting clays and bunker trap as well as taking hunting trips to Africa and Argentina.

While it's always difficult to leave your friends, we had the very good fortune to return to many friends in San Antonio. Dr. Larry

Trick was still practicing and teaching medicine but was always up for sporting clays or a hunt. He is a member of the Bunker Club. Capt Jack Dean was now the U.S. Marshal for the Western District of Texas, Tom Krcmar was still repairing guns, and David Thompson, who coached the champion Air Force Rifle Team, had turned into a superb cabinetmaker with a shop in Helotes. Henry Evans, Emmett Adkins, Barney Bernard, Chuck Hathaway, Paul Stapper, and others from my Air Force rifle team were still alive and had retired in San Antonio. Col Steve Richards had retired and became the director of the prestigious Dominion Country Club. P.D. Parker returned to San Antonio shortly after us and became the manager of the San Antonio Gun Club. Retired Army Major Maxey Brantley, my hunting and bunker shooting friend, soon appeared on the scene re-invented as a civil servant working for the Air Force. Col Rolf Smith had moved from Houston to Fredericksburg, and Dr. Gene Bishop and Leslie moved to Fredericksburg from San Angelo. There were many friends in San Antonio or close by, and we were delighted to get reacquainted with them.

    Some new friendships were established: Jeff Julig, who had shot on the Air Force shotgun team after I left, came to town from Washington and retired as a Chief Master Sergeant. He married one of Loretta's friends, Ashley. They have become good friends, and Jeff is now a vice president and chief of cybersecurity for Southwest Business Corporation. Ashley puts on lovely parties in her home and arranges other enjoyable get-togethers. We became acquainted with Art and Roberta Aiken through the San Antonio Gun Club. We have enjoyed their good company on clay target fields, on dove hunts, and breaking bread together. Dr. Ken Krueger and his wife Pat have become friends, and we hope to do more things together. He is a dental surgeon and loves to shoot birds. They have been with us for shooting in Spain. Dr. Danny Valdez and his wife Patricia, who is also a medical doctor, came to us through Larry Trick. Danny and Patricia are a lovely couple, quiet but interesting. They are always super to travel with --smooth and easy. They are members of the Bunker Club. They have been hunting with us in Argentina, Spain, and Hungary, always good company.

    We met Mike Molak and his wife Janet. Mike is the boss of the five Plains Capital Bank branches in San Antonio. He and Janet are very active in San Antonio social life, and they always seem to have something fun going. We love to attend dinners and activities at their house. They always make it nice and congenial—easy for people to relax. Mike has joined me as a California Indian and a member of the Grand National Quail Club. He's also a member of the Bunker Club. He is a very competitive skeet shooter but also loves to hunt. We both enjoy their company.

Loretta and Shara Ward became acquainted through shooting with the ladies' skeet league. That brought her husband Doug and me together. Shara bought Doug a trip with me to Argentina for dove hunting for his 50th birthday, and that started a string of hunting trips to Cordoba, Patagonia, Spain, Hungary, and the Czech Republic. Shara grew up in the military, and her dad retired as an Army major general. She sets a beautiful table, which no doubt comes from her mother's experiences when social life was more dominant in the military. Shara makes the most beautiful hand-painted birthday cards you can imagine. They are members of the Bunker Club. Doug is a CPA and was a vice president at USAA. He is a good sporting clay competitor, and I love to go out and shoot the 28-gauge guns at clays with him. Doug is a member of the Grand National Quail Club. He and Shara have also traveled to Scotland with me. We get in quite a bit of hunting and shooting together and have become quite close to them and their family. Nothing beats having fun playmates.

Becoming a California Indian in 2007 brought a whole new group of friends. Steve Jeffress, Bob Herold, David Tucker, and their lovely wives—Gail, Jeri, and Ann—sponsored Loretta and me and ushered us in as members. Both Tucker and Jeffress had headed up the Indians as the High Chief. After their tenure they became Ex High Chiefs. The California Indians Club dates to 1919 and remains much the same. Many members have belonged for more than 40 years, and dozens count over 25 years' membership. The Club bases its ritual on American Indian culture and tradition. At the yearly Pow Wow, a formal ceremony is conducted to honor Indian lore and tradition, with the Chief and previous Chiefs dressed in authentic Indian dress. It is a social club, and its medium is shooting shotguns in competition. At least, it starts that way. I have found it becomes so much more. The shotgun events continue and are very competitive, but it becomes more of a time to engage and enjoy friendships.

The Indians hold two major events each year, a Potlatch and a Pow Wow. The Pow Wow is the crowning event. We shoot trap and skeet for five days, but the social events start Sunday night and go through Saturday morning. Cocktails and hors d'oeuvres are standard each night. Two nights are coat-and-tie dinners, and Friday night is a celebration banquet in black tie. The non-shooting ladies have a full social activity calendar each day. The Pow Wow is a busy time and not to be missed. The California Indians is a volunteer club. The members do the organizing, making hotel, shooting range, catering, and all matter of arrangements. A new High Chief heads up the Indians each year. They make their way up to Chief through their work over many years making the Potlatch and Pow Wow and other activities such a success. Ex High Chief Robert Falaschi is chairman of the Ex High Chiefs, and it is a well-run organization—with nearly military precision.

In addition to our three original sponsors, Loretta and I have become close friends with Mike and Karen Melarkey, Steve and Gail Jeffress, Bob Herald, Mike and Tana Gallagher, Carolyn and Doug Jensen, Berry and Rosemarie Bauer, Dr. Peter and Rosemary Wittlinger and Roger Leone. Some Ex High Chiefs are Robert Enzenberger, Roger Evans, Carl Reynolds, Don Priest, Robert Falaschi and Richard McElvany. It would take pages to list all the members of the California Indians. They and their wives are exceptionally fine people, and it is a distinct honor for me to be counted as a fellow Indian.

*December 1962 Officer Training School Graduating Class 63D.
OTS Capt DDB front row, second from right*

*Mather Air Force Base, California. First Assignment
2d Lt Behrens and his six master sergeants*

The AAFCE vice commander's front office staff with the junior executive, Loretta, being promoted to Captain.
Her boss, German Lt Gen Ernst-Dieter Bernhard on her right, the executive officer English Group Capt Bryant (colonel) on her left.

Brig Gen Chuck Yeager at the Ramstein Rod and Gun Club relaxing after making presentations to a group of German and American hunters.
L-R Gen Yeager, Capt DDB, SMSgt James McCausland, and SSgt Fuchs

2d Lt Loretta Behrens in Korea with General Richard G. Stillwell, Commander in Chief of the United Nations Command in South Korea and Commander of US Forces.

1st Lt Loretta Behrens discussing the Reforger Exercise with Herr Fingerhut, German MOD Secretary (Secretary of Defense) in 1977

2d Lt John Sherwood one of my roommates in Vietnam—1967/68

Capt. Roy Gurd in the liberated Army Jeep in front of our rented house. Note the folding metal gate that may have saved our lives

1st Lt Lynn C. Siravatka with his O-1 Bird Dog in which he flew me to Saigon in my nearly fatal departure from Vietnam.

Gen White accepting the Ramstein Base Commander's Trophy. L-R Maj Gen White my 4 ATAF boss, DDB, Colonel Anderson my AAFCE boss, and Col McCartan my 1141st boss and reporting official from Stuttgart. It was the only time Col McCartan visited me in my three year tour. A great boss!

Another Commander's Trophy with some of my star athletes

My fight to the death flag football team. They had no team uniforms and wore their scruffy clothes as a badge of honor when attacking bigger squadrons in sports uniforms.

Maj Gen White promoting me to Lt Col with Loretta as witness

Brig Gen Ted Giddings honoring Loretta at her Change of Command

The "magnificent five"—my section chiefs in the Pentagon. Mr Bob Jones seated with me. L-R Lt Col Young, Mr White, Mrs Brooks, Lt Col Roush. They made me look good.

JCS first in Combined Federal Campaign. R-L DoD Sec Casper Weinberger, Chairman of the JCS Gen John W. Vessey, Director of the Joint Staff Lt Gen James D. Dalton, a deputy secretary, and DDB

Retired Colonels Rolf C. Smith and DDB celebrating Armed Forces Day

General Robert C. Oaks, Commander USAF Europe and Allied Air Forces Europe

*General James B. Davis,
Chief of Staff,
Supreme Headquarters
Allied Powers Europe*

*General John W. Vessey,
Chairman of the Joint Chiefs
of Staff*

Lt General Benjamin N. Bellis, Vice Commander USAF Europe

Gen Jack N. Merritt, US Mil Rep—1986

General Roscoe Robinson, U.S. Military Representative to the NATO Military Committee (US Mil Rep) 1985

Admiral Powell F. Carter Jr, US Mil Rep—1987

*Admiral James R. Hogg,
US Mil Rep—1989*

*Admiral William D. Smith,
US Mil Rep—1991*

Norwegian General Vigleik Eide, Chairman of the NATO Military Committee—visiting Wash DC in 1992

Gen Colin L. Powell, Chairman of the Joint Chiefs, honoring me on my last duty day-1992

The Body Guard for my boss in Brussels

Russian General Georay Schyurievich —Director of the 1992 Modern Pentathlon World Championship. In hopeful times for democracy under Boris Yeltsin—the first president of Russia

Col D. D. Behrens invited back to USAF duty in 1993-2003

Retirement gift from my friend Akio Mitamura—a 20 gauge Belgian Browning pigeon grade shotgun

Flying as guests in Admiral Smith's plane –L-R Capt Grazioli, Col Behrens, Adm Smith, Capt Linn, A1C Herman

Flying courtesy of my friend Gen J. B. Davis

Taking tank driving lessons from young, gung-ho Swedish officers

III

Hunting

I Am a Hunter

I seek no accolades but neither do I petition for parole or for absolution. Some might think I had a bad gene or perhaps reverted to a Neanderthal. I would have to plead guilty on all counts but with no remorse. The truth is, I am what I am and cannot change nor would I want to. The following quote was written by Finn Aagaard, a Kenyan professional hunter, rifle and ballistics authority, acclaimed author, and good friend: "The kill is the satisfying, indeed essential, conclusion to a successful hunt. But I take no pleasure in the act itself. One does not hunt in order to kill, but kills in order to have hunted. Then why do I hunt? I hunt for the same reason my well-fed cat hunts—because I must, because it is in the blood, because I am a descendent of a thousand generations of hunters. I hunt because I am a hunter."

Finn was not bloodthirsty. Nothing could be further from the truth. I hunted with him in Kenya and in the States, and I know he always enjoyed the animals and the outdoors, but never the killing. I've seen him pass up trophy-quality animals to let them breed or leave them for another hunter while he took a lesser quality animal. It is a dichotomy, but the vast majority of hunters I know love animals. In my own case I will not deny exultation when an animal is taken fair and square (hopefully a one-shot clean kill) on a free-range hunt. But I will also admit sadness over a dead beautiful animal, and that even extends to picking up a beautiful California valley quail.

You may notice I refuse to use the term "harvesting." We are killing animals and need to own up to that fact. Harvesting could be appropriate if you're taking animals from your farm or from a high-fenced operation where animals are raised and bred for hunting, but if you're taking trophy animals in the wild it seems like harvesting is used as an excuse or an apology.

Do not think hunting is merely killing. It is a total experience, a journey, the process and skill of stalking, spotting, selecting, shooting involve planning, equipment, physical conditioning, and all manner of things to become successful. The hunter and famous author Robert Ruark said, "Nothing is any good unless you work for it, and if the work is hard enough, you don't have to possess the trophy to own it."

One of the best hunting experiences in my life was a full day in 1984 chasing an immense herd of Cape buffalo in Zimbabwe. My wife and I were merely observers, trailing behind Lt Mark Taishoff and his professional hunter, Lou Hallamore. We were behind the herd, in front of the herd, on both sides of the herd, and in the middle of the herd. It was an exciting, hypertensive, grueling hard day of stalking. Every time a good bull was spotted, a cow or another bull would step in front or behind the bull we wanted, nixing a clear, safe shot. Twice, the whole herd stampeded in complete pandemonium. Finally, at the end of the day, we had once again moved to the front of the herd with the wind right as they came down a hill to a large watering hole. We were undetected, but they were too far for a sure shot. The sun was to our back and produced a beautiful sunset picture of the herd as they moved to water that remains in my mind to this day—I own that picture. The true sportsman strives to do everything right—a fair chase hunt and one-shot kill. President Grover Cleveland was a hunter, and his advice on ethics was, "It is better to go home with nothing killed than to feel the weight of a mean unsportsmanlike act."

In my humble opinion, most hunters enjoy the sport more than the prize. Don't get me wrong, we always want to be successful. However, the hunt can generate success through solace of the wilderness, watching magnificent bird dogs, or through the simple camaraderie with hunting companions. In reading the biography of the Duke of Wellington, I found, "Foxhunting—he hunted to ride – not one who rode to hunt—and enjoyed watching the hounds."

Speaking of dogs, let me tell you about some of my close hunting friends who are dog people. Joe Kelly, a retired military friend, lives in Boise and has superb German Drahthaars. He takes more pride in his dogs properly working the birds than he does in any shooting. He spends much of the year working with and training his dogs to perfection. In fact, he is a judge in the schooling and training certification process for the Drahthaar Association. Doug Forsythe, a retired Air Force Colonel friend of over 50 years, has trained two Portuguese water dogs to become magnificent bird finders and retrievers. By the way, his dog Caeli took a ribbon at the Westminster Kennel Club Dog show. His wife, Joanne, gets to show the dog through August, but then he takes over hunting with the dog in September—same dog, two duties. Doug wrote a beautiful tribute to his friend:

"She's gone. Fifteen years of active partnership, friendship, companionship, and love. All gone now. Beamer was put down today. It was time. I hurt, but I'm not going to mourn. I am going to remember the good things:

- The first upland bird she flushed followed by at least 2,000 more.
- The ruffed, sharp tail and sage grouse, the Hungarian partridge, the bobwhite, California, scaled, Gambel's and Mearn's quail, and all the pheasants she flushed. The occasional mallard and green-winged teal she retrieved.

    The covers she hunted in Montana, Washington, North Dakota, South Dakota, Nebraska, Iowa, and Arizona.

- Showing up with a Montana sharp tail 20 minutes after we had given up looking and not noticing she hadn't. The pheasant hidden up and under a water runoff bank thick with weeds and cattails that she wouldn't let me leave.
- The thousand hours riding as my copilot to the next hunt, the next cover, the next bird, the next thing.
- The hundreds of nights on my motel bed after our special time together, removing hard-earned burrs.
- Her first boat-plane ride followed by her first fishing experience and her jump from the boat to escape a vicious and thrashing 42-inch Manitoba Northern Pike.

- Our first time fishing a river when I thought she was exploring its edge and didn't notice she was swimming against the water current to stay at my side for over 30 minutes.
- Her passing the AKC Canine Good Citizen Test without ever practicing because I didn't know about it.
- The over 3,000 times she carried my morning newspaper up the driveway to her waiting biscuit.
- The 5,472 days of providing me joy.

"Rest in peace, Beamer. You earned it."

My hunting companion Doug Ward has trained an English Cocker to be the best retrieving dog you can imagine. She sees doves before he shoots, and even if they don't drop, she will follow those that appear wounded. Watching Doug, it's apparent to me that he gets as much enjoyment seeing his dog work as he does from shooting. My good friend Al Clark, a retired Army Lt Col who hunted with me and for many years was my sporting clays partner in Maryland, wrote the following poem before he died:

"When I die, don't say, "He passed away." Merely say, "He went to find his dog Paco."

And then, maybe one day, you'll look up in the sky, And think you see a man and his dog go by.

Believe in what you think you see,

Perchance it may really be my bird dog Paco and me."

Each of these friends were or are hunters, but it is clear their satisfaction or enjoyment comes from more than just shooting birds. Deryl McKinnerney who owns and operates the 4R Ranch for preserve bird hunting must have a kennel of over 30 dogs: Pointers and English Cockers. He loves them all and treats them as personal pets. They pay him back with superb performance in the field, which gives him joy and pride. I've seen him pick up and carry hard-working cockers just to give them a break.

My Montana bird-hunting friend, Tom Curtis, keeps five English Pointers as pets in the house. English Pointers are not normally known as loving pets, but his are both superb pointers and pets. He hunts and likes to shoot birds, but his real satisfaction comes from the fine dog work. His pointers are hunters, but he sometimes takes them to field trials where they often win a ribbon. Beating professional handlers and dogs tickles him pink. Don't tell me these guys are animal killers just because they hunt.

Some people object to hunting, but before criticizing too much, I would ask them to examine who pays for and preserves our wildlife. The Pittman-Robertson Act signed by President Franklin D. Roosevelt on September 2, 1937, established an excise tax on firearms ammunition and hunting equipment. Those funds go to the Secretary of the Interior and then to the states for management of wildlife and habitat. For the year 2017, the income was over $629 million. Since its inception, the act has produced over $11 billion for conservation. Hunting license fees add significantly to states and their fishing and game departments.

Ducks Unlimited was formed in 1927 from the Boone and Crockett Club. In 2017, they raised $86 million for restoring grassland and wetlands on private property with projects throughout the United States and in Canada and Mexico. They partner with the federal agencies, including the Department of Agriculture and the National Fish and Wildlife Foundation. They have conserved 14 million acres of waterfowl habitat. Pheasants and Quail Unlimited work on habitat expansion and enhancement. Grouse, sheep, elk, and many other hunting groups help in preserving wildlife. For the non-hunters, I would ask, what have you done for wildlife? Safari Club International and the Dallas Safari Club both contribute enormous amounts of money for anti-poaching and to support hunting in Africa.

If hunting in Africa is stopped, wild animals will no longer have a value, and once that happens, they'll become extinct. Dr. J. Cudd Brown was a professor at Troy State University, conducting graduate classes in Germany. He had been the United States Consul in Mombasa from 1948 to 1950. I did a master's thesis under his guidance on Kenya, and more specifically, on wildlife issues with an emphasis on the loss of elephants. In addition to extensive research, I traveled to Kenya with Dr. Brown in 1977 for interviews with people on the ground floor and prior game department officials, conservationists, ranchers, farmers, and safari outfitters. Evidence clearly revealed a huge loss of wild animals in the bush when hunting was banned. Hunting is much more beneficial than non-hunters and many conservationists realize.

My father was not a hunter, although I do remember him returning home in San Fernando from shooting jackrabbits in the Mojave Desert. He had a .22 rifle and taught me to shoot it when I was five or six years old, but he never took me hunting. How it started remains an enigma, but my buddies and I bought shotguns about the time we got our drivers licenses. Mine was a brand-new Stevens 12-gauge side-by-side with modified and full chokes and 30-inch barrels. The cost from Sears was $53.50. It was hardly a beauty, but it was mine, and in my mind, it was the image of the classic bird guns I'd read about. Our quarry were California Valley quail or dove, so an open-choke 20-gauge would have worked better, but none of us were knowledgeable enough to know that. We all thought a real man had to shoot 12-gauge guns. My best friend Doug Udall bought a Sears and Roebuck 12-gauge pump gun with the cutts compensator choke. We chased quail up and down the hills with lots of blasting but very little success. Dove hunting along the Santa Clara riverbed, nearly dry in September, produced slightly better results mainly because there were more targets. I did buy a well-used LeFever side by side 12 gauge a couple of years later. We were all good shots with a rifle from our experience in the Boy Scouts and had all been trained in safe gun-handling, but none of us had any instruction or training in shotgun shooting. For those who don't know, there is a world of difference.

Most of my close high-school buddies were gun enthusiasts, and we all read about fine hunting guns, but higher-grade shotguns were out of our reach. It wouldn't be inaccurate to say just behind girls and cars in the lust lineup would be a Browning Superposed or Winchester Model 21 shotgun. During a backpacking trip through Europe in 1958, I purchased three quality shotguns: a Browning Superposed in Brussels, a Beretta over-and-under in Rome, and a Simpson side-by-side in Vienna. The three guns cost nearly the same amount, all around $300. They were more than double that amount in the States. I carried the Beretta home in my luggage on the airplane, and the others arrived by mail shortly after I got home. We now had a battery of quality guns, not at the highest order or fancy level, but quite respectable. For my money, the Browning Superposed (American-designed but manufactured in Belgium) stands up well even measured against top-dollar European guns. I'm now fortunate enough to have the "best guns" from England, Belgium, Germany, and Italy, but my "go-to gun" for all-around bird hunting is still a Browning Superposed. It's like a Winchester Model 70 rifle; you can pay more, but you can't buy better. I gave the Simpson to my father.

My friends could use my guns anytime they wanted. We didn't have any formal shotgun ranges in the Santa Paula area but heard of one called Agua Sierra in Santa Monica. We piled in one of their cars (I sold mine to pay for the Europe trip), including my dad, and drove down to the Agua Sierra Gun Club. It was a first-rate club with a nice clubhouse and both trap and skeet ranges. They also had a Hightower, which I had never heard of although almost all sporting clay ranges have them today. A couple of us had shot trap on a ranch with a makeshift range, but none of us had ever seen a skeet range except in books. Surprisingly, they didn't give us any instruction, so we were on our own to figure out what birds to shoot on skeet. But we were safe and enjoyed ourselves. I hit one bird far out hard, shooting the Beretta, which had a full choke, and it completely disintegrated. The shooter walking by said, "That's a tight choke."

The shooter was Clark Gable. Many of the movie stars in that era were shooters and hunters, and we learned later that they shot at the Agua Sierra Club. Clark Gable was driving a beautiful Mercedes roadster and had a gorgeous lady with him. I think she was his wife, but she didn't come out on the range. I went in the clubhouse to look at Mr. Gable's gun. He was shooting a Browning Superposed with four different barrels of the gauges used in skeet-12, 20, 28, and 410 (410 is really not a gauge but we won't get technical). Since then, I've owned a couple of those four-barrel sets, but at the time it was all new to me and nice of him to show me the gun neatly cased up with the four barrels. We had good guns, but his was another step up. It was quite a good day: shooting the new guns with my father and friends, meeting a movie star who had flown combat missions in World War II, admiring his Mercedes and his wife, and examining his Browning four-barrel set.

I'm a very lucky boy and have been able to hunt in 26 of our beautiful United States, including both Alaska and Hawaii. Believe it or not, Hawaii has some good wild-bird hunting on the Big Island. In addition to Canada and Mexico, I've been able to hunt and fish in Central America, South America, Europe, Asia, Africa, and New Zealand. I've talked about pheasant and quail hunting in other sections of this text, so I'll report on a couple of other bird shoots, an Alaskan bear hunt, and a misadventure that taught me about hypothermia.

In Texas, many dove hunts are as much a social event as a hunt. In fact, sometimes they're more a social event. The "Almost Annual Dove Hunt" was instituted and orchestrated by my friend Ranger Capt Jack Dean, who was the commander of Company D of the Texas Rangers. It was one of those don't-miss affairs held every year on the Circle T Ranch between Carrizo Springs and Crystal City in South Texas. Captain was the highest rank in the Rangers at that time, and nearly all the captains (I believe it was eight) in the state would be in attendance. An invitation was not only to shoot dove but included dinner and a dance with a small band playing under the massive oak trees. It was a family affair with a picnic area next to a tank (pond) so the kids could fish. Many of the sheriffs in South Texas would attend.

One year, Col James Adams, Department of Public Safety Director who also oversaw the Texas Rangers, joined us. The senior FBI agent in San Antonio, along with the chief Border Patrol officer in South Texas, were in attendance. It was a great reunion each year for the Rangers, and a real treat for us and other invited guests. Most of the official attendees came only to socialize and reminisce with fellow law-enforcement officers. Some were skilled at barbecuing, including the popular Dimmit County Sheriff Ben "Doc" Murray. Sadly, he was later murdered in his home by a couple of no-goods.

Texas Rangers had a storied history in the late 1800s and early 1900s. However, the Rangers I got to know in Company D were all hard-working, good men who upheld the law. Some of my favorites besides Capt Dean were Doyle (Dolly) Holdridge, who collected 1911 Colt .45s, Bob Steele, who was from New York (but that's another story involving the Mafia), and, of course, the always entertaining Joaquin Jackson. Ray Martinez was the Austin cop who climbed the University of Texas Tower in 1966 and took out the shooter, Charles Whitman. Bruce Casteel and C.J. Havrda were in Company D, and both were later promoted to Ranger Captain. Five or six Rangers who worked for Capt Dean were eventually promoted to Ranger Captain, quite a compliment to Jack's leadership.

Loretta and I were on a quail hunt with Joaquin Jackson, the Texas Ranger stationed in Uvalde. We were riding in his official car so he would have all necessary communication, and his trunk was, as always, full of guns for any emergency. A large rattlesnake was killed on this hunt, and Joaquin skinned the snake so we could take the meat home. A couple of months after the hunt, a package arrived from Joaquin: a nice rattlesnake belt for Loretta. The Rangers were a tight-knit group, but I enjoyed them and admired their dedication. It was Capt Dean who put the finger on Charles Harrelson for the murder of United States District Judge John H. Wood in San Antonio. Killing a federal judge brought attention from the President, the Attorney General, the Governor, senators, and "every color of politicians," according to Captain Jack. The FBI was at a loss in their investigation of the crime, but Jack had known Charles Harrelson (father of the actor Woody Harrelson) from his days in the Valley and suspected him of being a hitman. Charles was convicted of the murder. Capt Jack was a fine role model, and his Rangers followed his stellar conduct. After he retired from the Texas Rangers, President Bill Clinton appointed him as United States Marshal for the Western District of Texas. He retired with 43 years of law-enforcement service. I am immensely proud to be an honorary member of Company D, Texas Rangers.

The social side of Texas dove hunting comes in many forms, even a wedding. It was a shotgun wedding—but not the kind commonly referred to. Here is how it happened: My wife and I were at a dove shoot on a Saturday in southern Texas as guests of Loretta's friend Priscilla "Pris" McClaugherty. Pris was an accomplished live pigeon shooter having won several international events, including world cups. She was also a first-class lady. She and her husband Lynn had been ranching and farming on their small place near Tilden. It was too small and poor to make much of a living, but a recent oil well on the property changed all that, and they were now both shooting Purdeys. Pris did not forget her roots and remained the same fine lady. She enjoyed inviting her same old friends to hunts on the ranch. Our friend Laura Revitz, herself a fine shot and a ladies' world champion in live pigeon competition, was with us along with my friend Capt Mark Taishoff.

There were three or four other couples shooting with us. Don Bice and Susan were in the mix. They had been going together but were not married. Susan let it slip that they had gotten a marriage license but hadn't gotten around to a wedding. It was December, the second half of the dove season, and the birds were plentiful. All the ladies had their shotguns and were shooting. Nothing would silence the ladies, but that Don and Susan should be married the very next day. Don realized he was outmaneuvered and outgunned. He acquiesced to their demands and accepted fate. It was decided a judge would be brought out to the ranch. and the wedding would be conducted on Sunday at noon. Some shooters were staying overnight, but we raced back to San Antonio to purchase champagne and a cake before closing time. Pris did not have champagne glasses, so we packed up our crystal and headed back to the ranch Sunday morning. Dove shooting continued until noon. The judge arrived on time, but the marriage was held up as it was discovered no ring had been procured. No problem, the brass from a 12-gauge shotgun shell was the solution and soon pounded into a ring. The wedding went on. After the cake was devoured and the champagne bottles emptied, it was all hands back to the hunt, including the new bride and groom. It only happens in Texas.

Many businesses, law firms, and banks hold elaborate dove shoots for their customers and colleagues. My friend Mike Molak, Region Chairman for the Plains Capital Bank, sponsors a superior dove shoot every September. It is a major social gathering with a delicious steak dinner, including all the trimmings. Of course, it's accompanied with beer, wine, drinks, and dessert. Mike gifts T-shirts and caps to commemorate each year's hunt. All the shooters are given raffle tickets for various prizes given out during a lively dinner. Mike and his super wife Janet are very active in the community. They are a gregarious couple, and Janet is probably more of the hunt host than Mike. It is always a splendid outing, and one we look forward to.

 A hunt I seldom miss in October is with my Behrens cousins, sons of my Uncle Arlo. All five brothers grew up hunting and eating game, particularly the coastal black-tailed deer found in the hills around their home in Napa, California. I do have to add that Allen has three mule deer mounts on his wall with trophies that all measure 36 inches or better. For those not familiar with mule deer measurements, it is the distance between the antlers; a 30-inch is considered good. Sometimes all five brothers would show up in October, but the regulars always there for sure are: Earl, Allen, and Clifford. Allen started it all and encouraged me to come for my first time in 1984. The hunt is for wild chukar partridges. It is a physically demanding, dusty, dirty, and frustrating hunt. Chukars run faster than scaled quail, and they only run uphill and only fly downhill. They prefer steep terrain with rock ledges and cliffs. Chasing them requires perseverance, physical strength, and agility—falls are not uncommon. It is a rough hunt without the niceties of a lodge and staff. We do it all ourselves out of camping trailers and tents. It is not a hunt for the timid or the weak in discipline. Many have questioned my judgment as I return to this punishing hunt year after year. These last few years I tell myself at the end of the hunt, it is my very last time. But then I guess dementia takes its course, and I find myself again the following year in the rugged Lake Owyhee area of Eastern Oregon with my cousins. All the brothers have dogs, none of which has been to a formal training school, and they are often unruly, but they find birds. Allen had a wonderful but strange pair: Gypsy was a small female Brittany, and her buddy Ty-Ty was a large female German Doberman. Gypsy had an uncanny ability to find birds and an excellent nose. Ty-Ty was a champion in retrieving any runners. She was a real racehorse in that field. If she saw 'em, she got 'em for sure. Weird, I know, but true. Of course, it is not just a hunt, it's a family reunion with my cousins, and I treasure the time we have together, birds or no birds.

 Joe Kelly and his wife Cristianne have very generously hosted me for a number of years either before or after my cousins' Oregon chukar hunt. Joe lives in Boise and knows Idaho chukar country. Of course, we hunt with his very well-trained German Drahthaars, which is always a treat. Cristianne is a dedicated educator working with families and schools to help those with learning deficiencies. She is a serious Italian cook and has developed a small boutique business making beautifully packaged and fragrant soaps. Additionally, she has written a lovely little preschool children's book—a lady of many talents. After hunting we retreat to their house for a home-cooked meal and wine. Patching up our wounded, sore feet and having a nice bed after a shower greatly lessen the pain of the hunt. Often, October finds me in Wyoming visiting my friends Bart and Gay Byrd. They are accomplished hunters and have both been with me on African safaris. Gay's father owns the large Allemand cattle and sheep ranch, which she and Bart manage. Gay grew up on the ranch and is a true cowgirl. Bart was a professional bull rider in his younger days and rode over a thousand bulls—you don't have to ask how tough he is. They are not gentlemen ranchers. They get out there and do the work every day. We've had some marvelous times chasing antelope on their place. For several years I took 20 friends there for hunts, and we'd set up a regular camp. Each day at noon we would hold a different shooting match: rifle, pistol, or shotgun. It was great fun, and the Byrds would join us at the campfire every night. It was always successful. Those large hunts have ended, but Gay and Bart are both very generous and I'm still invited to come and bring a friend anytime.

The end of October normally finds me with my friend Lee Seemann on his farm near Omaha, Nebraska. He invites eight to ten out-of-town hunters to be his guests for pheasant hunting and sporting clays. Some local friends as well as his farming partner and budding chef, Tim Markel, join in the fun. Lee is a most generous and gracious host. He puts us up in his excellent lodge guest quarters and feeds us well. It is more of a reunion of friends than a hunt. Often, my longtime friend Gen J.B. Davis joins us. The camaraderie is well worth the travel and is always something I look forward to. Lee has become a very good friend, and he has been a great help by promoting young target shooters in their quest to become Olympians.

Long Shots — Hunting

Another "don't-miss hunt" is the annual Grand National Quail Hunt held during mid-November in Enid, Oklahoma. I mentioned that hunt in my accounts of bobwhite hunting, but I need to say more about this hunt, which I have been lucky to attend for the last 23 years. The city of Enid goes all out in making the hunt a real premier event. I think half the town must be involved. Businesses of all kinds, large and small, are sponsors as are many of the surrounding ranches and farms. I don't think you could find a more hard-working and dedicated group than Grand National Quail Club Members in Enid. They do all the heavy lifting year after year for the new shooting members and us past shooters to experience good shooting and even better camaraderie. They have a whole army of volunteers who repeat year after year. Some of those who served as president in my years and who are still volunteering are David Henneke, Jim Wright, Terry Lix, John Estill, Jason Turnbow, Mark Pettus, and Mel Phillips. Other stalwarts are Mike McCormick, our faithful photographer, the Dillingham and Evans brothers, Bill Sutherland and Dan Sommer.

In 2017, I was honored and humbled to be inducted into the Grand National Quail Club Hall of Fame. Normally, the president of the club makes the presentation, but I was doubly honored when my friend John Groendyke read the citation. The list of famous attendees is long and impressive, including movie stars and TV personalities, professional athletes, gold-medal Olympians, governors, senior federal government and cabinet officials, generals, admirals, ambassadors, U.S. Senators and Congressmen, a Medal of Honor recipient, major corporation CEOs, company presidents, and all manner of luminaries. It's a great place to meet people and rub elbows with the high and mighty. But the one thing they have in common is a love of bird hunting. It's always an interesting group. Astronaut Charlie Duke was inducted in 2018. How many get to shake hands with a man who at 36 walked on the moon?

One year we arrived early. Two good friends, General J.B. Davis and Captain Jack Dean and I were having breakfast with our mutual friend John Groendyke when a couple of Texas law men appeared. They were invited to sit down with us, and it turns out they were SWAT team members—an advanced security detail for Texas Governor Rick Perry.

Capt Dean and Rick Perry had been hunting friends for years, and he was invited as a special guest. The breakfast discussion got around to where we would be having the dinner events, two of which were held at the Groendyke Lodge. John was asked if he thought any of the participants or guests might be carrying a handgun to the dinners. John replied some could very well be armed. Both members of the security team visibly stiffened up. One of them said it would be necessary to set up a screening at the Lodge. John calmly replied, "No screening will be allowed at my lodge." It looked to be a standoff, but Capt Dean stepped in and said, "Don't you boys worry a bit, I'll be standing right next to the governor." No Texas state trooper in his right mind is going to argue with a Texas Rangers captain, retired or not.

The Governor of Kansas, also a guest for the hunt, arrived with only a driver so it was a little embarrassing when Governor Perry arrived by jet with two assistants and four more bodyguards. Gov. Perry shot with our group and took a terrific and un-ending beating from Gen Davis and Capt Dean. Every time he missed a bird, they would scatter negative remarks in his direction. Gen Davis, a fighter pilot, prefaced most of his remarks with, "You trash haulers," the governor being a prior C-130 pilot. Capt Dean was no more generous in his remarks about politicians who couldn't hit their tail. The words were perhaps a little more colorful than I am revealing. Nevertheless, I have to say Gov. Perry was an excellent sport and took it all with good grace.

Broken Bow, Nebraska, is another town that goes all out for a hunting event. They host the annual "Nebraska One Box Pheasant Hunt." Again, the whole town and surrounding community come together in making their event special. The Nebraska Governor welcomes the hunters, and Broken Bow townspeople host hunters in their homes for socials before the evening banquets. It's a fun hunt with five-member teams given only one box of shells for the hunt. When the 25 cartridges are fired, the hunt ends. Lee Seemann and Tim McGill, both from Nebraska, formed up a team that included friends, Gen J.B. Davis, Glen Haley, and me. We ran out of shells after hitting our 14th bird and were concerned about another team coming in with the full limit of 15.

Fortunately, our score held up, and we were declared winners. The competition is tightly run with each team given two guides, a bird dog handler, and a scorekeeper, all selected by random drawing with everyone watching. Only seven teams are allowed in the competition each year. Once you've been on a team you are no longer eligible for the team event and must come as an individual shooter. At the opening banquet, the teams are sold much like a live pigeon match with a regular auctioneer handling the bidding. The Calcutta tournament jackpot can be rather large, hence the random drawings for guides and scorekeepers.

Bill Zutavern was a local cattle rancher and big supporter of the "One Box." Bill had hunted with me in Bolivia and was good friends with Lee and Tim. He was also a Nebraska State Commissioner of Fish and Game. Bill wanted to have some active-duty military at the match and asked me if I would bring some of my boys. The only way you can be on a team a second time is to become a team captain and bring a full team. The entrance fee was something around $800 per person and I explained to Bill it was a little steep for active-duty military guys, but Lee and Tim stepped in immediately and said, "It's paid for." The die was cast, and I rounded up a team: Air Force Capt Mike Herman, Army SFC Lance Dement, Air Force SSgt Mike Agee, and Army Sgt Mark Weeks. Herman was a super international trap shooter, and Weeks was an international skeet shooter. Both had won World Cups. Agee was from Nebraska and was an up-and-coming trap shooter. Dement was not a shotgun shooter, but he was a good gun pointer, a distinguished rifleman and one of the best marksmen the Army ever produced. We had a solid team for shooting, but Weeks and Agee had little hunting experience and wild pheasants are not easy.

We had a little warm-up before the competition when Bill Zutavern invited us to hunt on his ranch for pheasant, sharp tail, and prairie chicken. I did not do a good job of instructing the guys about the importance of not using up our 25 cartridges in the team event as my mind was more on just showing them a good time and having them represent the military well to the community. The Broken Bow folks showered us with Middle America hospitality. The first night, one of our hosts had a large cocktail party at his home in our honor before the banquet. The guys were in their uniforms and were a handsome bunch. The Governor of Nebraska spoke at the opening banquet and was given enthusiastic applause. Each team captain was then invited to introduce his team, and they did so with little more than polite applause. When I introduced my team, the guys came up in their uniforms and received a standing ovation. Bill Zutavern was pleased, but I'm not sure what the governor thought about being upstaged as nobody stood up after he spoke. Still, it makes you proud to be an American when military boys are embraced like that.

After the teams were introduced, the auction commenced with rapid bidding. Most of the teams were sold for under $2,500. Two teams were clearly the favorites: a team of local Nebraska men and my guys. The bidding went significantly higher, but I didn't like it because my friends were putting money in the pot betting we would win. We had a team meeting that night, and I made it very clear that our mission had changed somewhat from just making a good impression. We were now duty-bound to win the match. After all, my friends had paid the entry fees and were expecting us to win. We were on a military mission. At breakfast, we were introduced to our scorekeeper, the county district attorney. So, for a little fun, I asked if he had been an attorney before he became the DA. When he confirmed that was true, I slowly pushed a folded $100 bill across the breakfast table toward him. My guys' eyes were all bugging out, not realizing it was a joke. The district attorney announced, "Boys, the thought's right, but the money's wrong." He turned out to be a really fine guy, and while his duty was only to keep score, he was often in the middle of the cattails trying to flush a bird out for us.

The first two birds out were killed by Mark Weeks; he was a very fast skeet shooter, but in both cases, it was bang, bang and one pheasant fell. Then a bird got up between Mike Agee and me but more on Mike's side. He didn't shoot and the bird was nearly out of range when I fired. But as I fired, he fired. In fact, it sounded like one shot. Our scorekeeper was just over a rise out of sight, and he yelled, "Who fired the shot?" so he could record it on the scorecard. I had to report it was actually two shots. Now we stopped and you might say that we had a strong come-to-Jesus meeting where I explained we had three birds dead, but with six shells gone? At 50% shooting we were not going to end up with the limit of 15 birds. It was time to get down to business, and they did. When we reached 15 birds, we had three shells remaining. Now, I was still a little worried about the local Nebraska team: how good were they shooting, and were they getting into enough wild pheasants? The rules allowed shooting of quail, but I forbade my guys to shoot any as it used up our ammo and quail scores were of a lower value than pheasants.

Anyway, I had not seen any the year before. Quail was now our quest, and we broke up into two parties looking for quail. Mark Weeks was with me, and we walked into a spread-out covey. I didn't have a safe shot, but Mark did. He knocked down a bird but then opened his over-and- under to reload when the second part of the covey exploded while his gun was open. He did not have the experience to hold ready for the possibility of more birds getting up. I beat him up a little bit, but not too much as it's happened to me more than once.

To Mark's credit, we chased that covey around until he had two more shots and connected with both, bringing us to 15 pheasants and three quail. The local team was the highest of the other six teams with 13 pheasants and no quail. It's always nice to win! After the hunt, my friend Lee Seemann most generously hosted us for two days at his lovely lodge near Waterloo, Nebraska. In addition to shooting, we had great meals and plenty of booze.

Lee invited some of his friends to the dinners to meet us and give my guys a chance to meet some Omaha leaders. It was a fun time for me and a great experience for my guys. I can't thank Bill Zutavern and Lee Seemann enough for their kindness in making it all happen.

Rob Braach, a native Montana boy who was about 30 years old and has taken about the same number of elk, called the Pentagon one day to invite me for a day's fishing. He would be guide and operate the oars using his new commercial sturdy raft on Rock Creek, which is a premium blue ribbon trout stream. Naturally, I jumped at the chance even though the rules are fly fishing only, and Rock Creek is basically a catch-and-release stream. I knew there wouldn't be much releasing because my skills as a fly fisherman are about zero. Nevertheless, it would be a fun day, and Rob is always great company.

The day of the trip turned out to be quite cold. It was May 30, and all Montana streams were running at record levels due to snow runoff and heavy rains. While Rock Creek was running too high and swift for fishing, we decided to make the trip anyway since we were already there and would have the fun of seeing the country and game even if we didn't catch fish.

I took the front of the raft on a swivel seat with my legs hanging over the front. My hunting and fishing partner, Capt Mark Taishoff, took the back of the raft, sitting on the raft with his feet safely inside. Mark and Rob both had on neoprene waders while I had on hip boots, which would allow us to beach the raft and fish from various sand bars, etc. In retrospect, it wasn't very smart since the river was high and running so fast. It was simply impractical to do any wading. The outside temperature in Missoula was 51 degrees, and Rock Creek is considerably higher in elevation – so colder. Dry flies were out of the question in these conditions, so we were using wet flies—wooly buggers were the best, and I managed to hook a couple of trout, one nice cutthroat. These were released, and I noted the water was quite cold, probably around 45 degrees—it seemed colder on my hands.

The new seat on Rob's raft tilted slightly forward so whenever it looked like we were in rough water I would hang on to the back of the seat or turn around and put both of my feet in the raft. Rob had selected a run of about 16 miles, and we were having quite a good time fishing and seeing the country. At one point, a moose crossed the creek in front of us, and we also saw a nice young mule deer buck. While we had an occasional sprinkle and it was cool, we had on extra clothes and were wearing wool watch caps, so it was not too uncomfortable. We beached the raft after about a five-mile float and had a nice lunch with hot coffee courtesy of Rob's wife Dawn. After lunch, we were on a fairly smooth portion of the creek but headed toward a log sticking out from the bank. The last I recall was Rob saying, "We will be all right" and then I was in the water, and it was cold! I wasn't scared, but I could not get to the bank. I kept going under and, no doubt, bumped my head on every rock for at least 50 yards downstream. In the process, I nearly broke my nose, pretty well bruised up my face, and took some skin off my forehead. Finally, I made the bank about 50 meters downstream from where I went in.

Miraculously, as I climbed out, I still had a death grip on the fly rod. Good thing, as it was a nice Fenwick borrowed from Capt Taishoff, who had moved up to an expensive Sage rod. Had it been lost, I probably would have been executed. Mark and Rob managed to get the raft to the bank about 100 yards farther downstream from where I got out. They came running back, and apparently both had really been scared as they watched me flailing in the water, frantically trying to keep my head above water while being dragged downstream with two hip boots full of water. Guess I looked a little bit rough as I was bleeding pretty good, and they were both very concerned. The cold water had really got to me, but I hadn't realized it until I tried to unbutton my pants. My fingers simply would not work. Rob and Mark had to undress me—rather embarrassing when you can't even get your own pants off. In any case, Rob had a big beach towel and some dry clothes in his waterproof kit, so in 15 minutes we were back on Rock Creek after more fish. I even got a few nice trout. Not much else we could do since we still had 10 miles to go, but I had warm clothes and felt fine. This time I was fishing from the back, and Mark fished from the front. However, chicken that he is, he took no chances and kept at least one leg in the raft for the rest of the trip—good move. By now, Mark was howling with laughter, telling the world what a great swimming-with-hip-boots demonstration I had put on while frequently diving to bust rocks with my head and continuing to make my usual sorry casts with his fly rod the whole time.

All in all, we had a really great day—caught some trout on flies, saw some game, and had a little extra excitement. Also, I managed to catch more fish than Mark, and that never happens. He claims he had to spend most of his time keeping my line straight and dodging wild casts, which is partly true. Lost my glasses and wool watch cap in the cold-water swim, but that was a small price for a good lesson. We all learned a thing or two, and I developed a very healthy respect for cold, fast water. Lifejackets are now a must on fast water or when wearing hip boots in a boat.

A Black Bear Hunt
Lake Veleska, Alaska Range

My hunting partner, Captain Mark Taishoff, and I departed base camp mid-morning after a large breakfast of flapjacks cooked up by Mr. George Howard. We had fully loaded backpacks, including a two-man tent. Our destination was Bear Valley, as Senior Master Sergeant Terry Howard reported seeing a couple of big black bears there two days earlier. A black bear has to be over five feet to be considered big in Alaska. The previous day we had a very hard and difficult ten-hour hunt. After a perfect approach up a steep and treacherous mountain, I missed a full curl Dall ram by a bad overestimate on the range. It had been a super day and a clean miss, so the hunt was not marred, but we had higher aspirations for this day's hunt.

The first couple of miles hiking was relatively easy around Lake Veleska, but the next two or three miles were tough going through muskeg (a marshy/soft terrain—tundra-like landscape, but heavily wooded). Travel in muskeg is quite fatiguing, even without packs. The last one-third of the hike was crisscrossing Bear Creek and climbing the valley slopes.

Around 3:00 p.m., we found an acceptable camp site on a canyon slope with good viewing of both sides of the valley and some distant ridges, just in case any Dall sheep showed themselves. Both of us were thoroughly soaked from the waist down due to creek crossings and wet vegetation—boots no longer waterproof and socks soaked. Unfortunately, it began to rain before the tent could be set up. Everything was wet, save the sleeping bags, which were rolled inside plastic garbage bags. A couple of extra tarps were used to cover the tent and make an awning for cooking, which really saved our tails. We were exhausted. Cloud cover was quite low, which obscured vision and prevented any hope of seeing game.

Cooked soup around 5:00 p.m.—heavy rain—couldn't see 50 yards—slept two hours—cooked more soup—still heavy rain. Collected rainwater from the tent runoff for our cooking and drinking.

Still had rain. Went to bed at 9:00 p.m.—rain persisted—cool temperatures—a stygian night indeed. The tent was far too small for comfort. Even sleeping we were breathing in each other's faces.

Woke up early the next morning to heavy rain and thick cloud cover—vision obscured—stayed in tent all morning, except an occasional foray after blueberries—rain continued. Established 2:00 p.m. as deadline to break camp to get off mountain and back to base camp.

The deadline arrived—still raining. Started to decamp, but quietly—no talking. Clouds began to break, offering some sunlight, which presently produced a bright rainbow. At 2:30 p.m., Mark grabbed me by the head and pushed my face in a puddle of water. He whispered loudly, "There's a bear—don't move."

Who could move? He had his arm locked at the elbow with all his weight pushing on my head. I thought I might drown. Mark described what was happening: "Don't move—he's looking right at us." Of course, I couldn't see with my face underwater.

Mark continued, "Now he's sitting down on his rear end—now he's rolling on his back—now he's on his back with his paws in the air, just like your cats. Now he's looking around. Now he's eating berries."

Finally, Mark released his death grip on me. I was able to breathe and peered over the bushes to see the bear. Our rifles were ten meters away, lying in the wet blueberry bushes. Mark crawled over and retrieved them. He removed the sopping wet leather scope cover—scope completely fogged and cleared scope. We both take aim at the bear about 200 meters up the hill and approximately at a 30-degree angle. BANG!

The bear did a 180-degree turn and raced full gallop into the alders. We gave him 10 minutes and then started up the hill. No blood or indication of the bear being hit. We went into the alders and started our search, looking for any signs of blood. There were several game trails in the alders, and we followed likely routes. After about 15 minutes, Mark found bear scat. Black bear at this time of year has a heavy diet of blueberries. The scat contains a lot of undigested berries, and the droppings somewhat resemble a cow patty. This scat was about

20-inches high on grass and bushes, spread out in about a two-foot line—not common. Therefore, the search intensified. Still no bear or positive spoor. Mark and I then worked different trails.

After about 30 more minutes, and no sure sign the bear was hit, we were about to give up. Still in the alders, I started down a steep trail but decided to first check a trail going to my right, as I didn't expect to come back up the hill. Peered down the track and saw the bear—dead as a skunk. I called the good news to Mark. The bear was shot through the front leg at the first joint, which broke his leg and completely destroyed his heart. Yet he still managed to run more than 100 meters. He was taken with a 165-grain Nosler from a .30-06 Model 70 Winchester. Mark mistakenly thinks it was a 165-grain Nosler from his .300 Winchester. In any case, an exceptionally large bear in perfect shape with a nice coat and no rub marks was taken.

Now the work really began. Neither of us had ever skinned a bear—no small job. We started before 4:00 p.m. and finished around 7:00 p.m.. The bear was on quite a steep hill, which did not help, and he was simply too heavy to move. I did the skinning, and Mark did the holding. There was lots of grunting, pulling, and attempted manhandling—quite a hard task for a couple of chechaquos, but a pretty good job was done, if I do say so. We certainly dulled two Puma knives.

We loaded the bear on packs along with all our other gear. The packs were very heavy, and Mark fell on his first attempt to get up. He carried the hide and the head, and I carried the hind quarters and the guns. Getting back to our main base camp was difficult as Bear Creek was running full bore after 27 hours of steady rain.

We left our temporary site before 8:00 PM and didn't stop walking until we reached the main camp close to midnight. George Howard cooked us a huge meal of Dall sheep meat and fried potatoes, along with a generous portion of Yukon Jack—quite good Yukon Jack.

The bear measured out to six feet. Happy, and feeling lucky, we broke camp on August 13, 1987. That bear can still be seen in the guest bedroom at our house.

Long Shots — Hunting

Pheasants in England

To some this heading would bring thoughts of tweed, plus fours, Land Rovers, Purdey shotguns and fine dinners in a castle. This experience was just a little different. It happened because the Air Force C5 airplane I was on was diverted to Mildenhall Air Force, England. We were flying from Dover Delaware with the destination of Ramstein, Germany, my duty station. I was in a space A category (allowed on only if there was room and with no guarantee of where you might end up), trying to get back to my German home. My valuable leave time was slipping away, so I was not very happy when the plane was diverted. Thinking about it a bit, I remembered my friend Leon Linscott was assigned at Mildenhall. He had worked for me when he was a master sergeant as the noncommissioned officer in charge (NCOIC) of our Air Force High-Power Rifle Team. He was a member of the eight-man team that won the U.S. National Championship (National Trophy) at Camp Perry in 1965. We had become very close when he was my NCOIC, about as close as an officer and enlisted man can be and still stay within the parameters of military custom and courtesies. And, by the way, he was an excellent NCOIC. He managed to keep me somewhat under control. I liked and respected him and was delighted that he went on up in the promotion line to Chief Master Sergeant. There are fewer Chiefs in the Air Force than there are colonels. I called the Chief just after landing. He and his wife Velma insisted I come over and stay with them. We had a grand time reminiscing about record-setting and when we beat the Army and the Marine Corps at their business of combat rifle shooting. The Chief was not an avid hunter, but he knew I was and suggested we might want to try out the Mildenhall morale and welfare program offer of shooting some planted birds.

That jolted my memory of my previous commander and mentor, Col Thomas Kelly, from rifle shooting days. Col Kelly had been the commander at Mildenhall AFB. He was also an amateur archaeologist and had even published a couple of pamphlets on his digs in England. One of his colleagues in digging was a gentleman named Mr. Pooley who had farms around Mildenhall where he and Col

273

Kelly had hunted. So, our search was on to find Mr. Pooley. It wasn't too hard as he was well known. After finding the address, we put on our uniforms and quickly scooted over to his farm. We turned off the road onto his lane, which was quite impressive. It was 200 yards long and lined with towering old trees. Even more impressive were rooster pheasants strutting around on both sides of the lane. Much enthused, we drove on toward the house and noticed there was a man working in some pig pens attached to a couple of farm buildings. Thinking it might be a good idea to talk with the worker before approaching the main house, we pulled over and got out. The man inside the pen was mucking it out. He had on rubber boots. However, as we got closer, we could see he was wearing a suit and tie. When we got to the fence he stopped, looked up, and moved in our direction. After saying hello, I told him we were looking for Mr. Pooley and wondered where we might find him. His answer was, "You're talking to him."

So now what do we do? I couldn't just say we came to murder your pheasants, so I stuttered and stammered a little bit and said we knew Col Kelly. He very abruptly answered, "I recognize the badges." Both the chief and I were wearing our Distinguished Rifle Badges, which I guess really established our bona fides to Mr. Pooley. I suspect he knew what we were after anyway, so I said, "Col Kelly had mentioned he did some pheasant hunting with you."

Mr. Pooley allowed, yes, they had done some pheasant shooting, and he could provide us some shooting as well. He said he was too busy to be with us but would arrange something for the following day. We were instructed to park across the street from the White Swan Inn at 1:00 p.m. to meet his friend Mr. Morley. We did not discourage this plan, so we were off to the Air Force morale and welfare facility to borrow guns. The best they could come up with was 30-inch full-choke Model 5 Browning automatics, often referred to as the "humpback." As an aside, Remington made a few of the same guns and called them the Remington Model 11. Savage also produced the same gun for a short period. They were not the ideal guns for our purposes, but they worked. The chief didn't have hunting clothes and all I had was uniforms, but he managed to borrow enough to get us semi-attired as hunters. I'm sure we looked more like field hands than

Long Shots — Hunting

hunters to any Brit who might be watching. We arrived at the White Swan at 12:30 to be sure we were on time. The minutes ticked away as we waited and waited—then it was 1:00, but no Mr. Morley. Then 1:10, then 1:20, then 1:30. Still no Mr. Morley. We knew we were in the right area just across from the White Swan, and Mr. Pooley told us he owned the field. So, taking the situation in hand, we loaded up the humpbacks and started down the rows of sugar beets. Pretty soon a hen jumped up. We kept going and another hen, then finally a rooster. Bam! The rooster was down. Then another hen and then another rooster. Bam! The second rooster was down. Then a hen and bam! She was down. We had to think about that for a while. In the States we normally only shoot roosters, but I had seen pictures of the Brits shooting hens, and I knew in some places on hunts in Germany the owner allowed hens to be shot.

In any case, we decided we might as well make it a day, so on we went. Hens got up and roosters got up and we shot both. We continued clear to the end of that field, and at the end it exploded with everything. Using those humpbacks without plugs we were knocking down pheasants right and left. I mean we could hardly carry them back; our game bags were running over, and our hands were full. Out of ammo, we turned around and started back to the White Swan. As we neared the end of the field, a black sedan pulled up next to our parked car. What do we do now? We had more than a dozen each, and probably half were hens. Nothing to do but continue on. It was Mr. Morley, and he said he was happy to see us. Still, we were worried about all the hens we had stuffed in our game bags. I rather timidly told Mr. Morley we really had not had instructions on what we were allowed to shoot. At that stage we weren't sure whether he would order us to leave or what. Mr. Morley answered that Mr. Pooley's instructions were that we should shoot all the roosters we could shoot, and all the hens we could shoot, and all the partridge we could shoot, and all the hares we could shoot, and all the rabbits we could shoot. Wow, what a great relief. He then popped open his trunk, and out jumped two dogs. Neither one could be said to resemble a bird dog. One looked something like a shepherd, and the other looked more like a large sheepdog. Mr. Morley allowed as how we had better get going, and we moved to an adjoining field. He announced that he'd walk in the middle and scare birds out to us on the sides while his dogs would work back and forth. Fine with us, we just wanted to shoot.

Mr. Morley was shooting a side-by-side Army/Navy 12 gauge, and he managed to shoot at every single bird that got up—in front, on the right or on the left, it made no difference. The good thing was he had a break-action gun that could not be loaded quickly, and we were shooting autos that were not plugged, so everybody got in lots of shooting. The dogs didn't point, but they did work close enough, and both flushed and retrieved birds. Hunting was not new to them. Mostly they carried the birds back to Mr. Morley, I mean, all the birds, so we had to stop several times to take some of his load. When he finally left us, he had a trunk full of pheasants and threw in those two dogs. With pheasants and dogs together in the trunk, he waved goodbye. Quite a jolly guy, but I've yet to know anyone who could steal so many shots from his fellow hunters. Hardly a classic English pheasant shoot, but we had a great day thanks to Col Kelly, Mr. Pooley, and Mr. Morley.

The Purdey and castles came later—much later. While the later hunts were and still are wonderful, it's hard to beat the first. I ask for no pardon, but for the reader who might think this was just a slaughter, maybe it was, but you should know that all the birds were used. Some are given away (considered a fine gift), but most are sold to pubs and fine restaurants. In both England and Germany the sale of game from hunting is used to pay for the hunts and conservation of the animals and birds in the areas.

Pheasant in Belgium

This account might better be titled, "Eating Pheasants in Belgium." The story starts in Germany, moves to Italy, and finally arrives in Belgium. We were shooting a little bunker trap match I had organized in Wiesbaden, Germany's International Trap Range, where the 1966 World Championship was held. It happened that a Winchester ammunition rep showed up and was looking for Americans to attend a Winchester-sponsored match in Italy, all-expenses-paid—are you kidding me?! All-expenses-paid for the shoot in Italy was immediately added as a prize for the top four shooters at our match. They turned out to be Mr. Chuck DeCastro, Mr. Frank Benson, Mr. Jimmy James, and me.

What a deal it was, truly. First, the plane to Milano, Italy, then a train to the beach city of Rimini, then a bus trip up the mountain to San Marino, which is an enclosed microstate surrounded by Italy. Founded in 1600, it is the oldest sovereign state and constitutional Republic in the world. The most fun on the trip was a train ride that stopped at several stations en route. These stops were for loading and unloading passengers and also gave us a chance to buy coffee, pastries, and lunches that were being sold by vendors on stands just outside our windows. The trains were old, but still in fair shape, and they were organized in compartments with a long aisle down the right-hand side of the train. We had our own compartment just by right of possession, but our tickets did not guarantee seats. That was in the days when you could carry a firearm on the airplane with you, so naturally, to protect my shotgun and make sure it made the trip, I carried it on board. It was in the normal takedown case for an over-and-under shotgun. They look like something that a trombone would be carried in. When we landed in Milano, we were directed through a clearing area to baggage collection. I was stopped on the way by a policeman and told to open my bag. When I opened the Browning case, the cop literally jumped in the air backwards a couple of feet. I think he was more or less bored when he stopped me, but the shotgun woke him up. He looked a little embarrassed from his surprise jump, and he then got quite cranky. He couldn't speak English, and I couldn't speak Italian, so we had a little standoff while he called a higher official. After producing a letter of invitation, I was free to go on my way.

The match was really a high-end deal as most are in Europe—shooters dressed well as did many of the guests—especially the ladies, who were dressed to the nines. A restaurant and bar overlooked the range. The Winchester rep was a young Italian who was happy to have us, and we were even happier than he was. As he told us, everything was covered— transportation, hotel, dinners, ammo, and entry fees. Only one dinner was left out. That's where the real story starts.

The one night that dinner wasn't included, my wife and I chose a rooftop restaurant with a great view. We were looking over the menu when I noticed a gentleman I had seen at the range, sitting by himself. Loretta agreed we should ask him to join us, so that's what I did. René Haillez joined us, and we had a most enjoyable evening together. We continued to socialize for the next couple of days, and he seemed like a nice guy, so I invited him to join us for one of my monthly trap matches held at Ramstein Air Force Base, Germany.

A few months later, he came to our match. I was happy to see him. He shot with us, and I took him to the base officers' club for dinner. He ventured that he had taken Americans hunting and especially General Wade who was a four-star general. Gen Wade had gone from Germany to Belgium. I'd seen the general, but of course captains normally don't get very close to four-star generals, so I had never met him. The connection with Gen Wade will come up again with my friend Lt Col J.B. Davis (later a four-star general). René then invited me to come and hunt with him in Belgium. I didn't think it would be much of a hunt, but I wanted to see more of Belgium, so I took him up on his offer and traveled to his home in Gentbrugge. Boy, was I wrong again! Belgium was full of pheasants, hares, partridge, ducks, and pigeons, and we hunted them all. It was usually a very mixed bag; one was never sure what might jump up. Mostly, we shot pheasants. We also chased hares, shot partridge, now and then, a duck or pigeon just as targets of opportunity, and even some rabbits. Rabbit hunting in the snow with ferrets can literally cause rabbits to fly out of their dens. Some of the hunts would be a combination of mixed bag shoots, walking behind dogs combined with short driven pheasant drives, not as organized as in England but with large numbers of wild birds.

It was great fun shooting with René and his friends. We normally had lunch at one of the taverns in the small towns near where we hunted. Those places never looked like much from the outside, but the food was always outstanding. I think the Belgians beat the French at cooking. René always had me stay in his home, and several times I brought a friend. He had a number of very fine Belgium Browning Superposed (over/under) shotguns, much higher-grade guns than are sold in the States. All the Belgian-made superposed guns were actually made by Fabrique Nationale in Herstal, Belgium. Three guns that he kept just for loaners were D5 G grade. I think the cost today for a new D5 G from the factory is around $40,000. Remember, these were just as loaners to friends.

René would cook the Saturday night dinner, and it was always the same: pheasants, small croquet potatoes, *Preiselbeeren* sauce (similar to cranberry) and applesauce, both served warm. The pheasant was the best I have ever eaten. René cooked it in sort of a heavy, large, but not too wide pot. I watched him, but to this day, I can't duplicate the outcome. The bird would go into the pot neck first with the legs pointing to the pot lid, with at least a pound of butter and then a few other ingredients with some seasoning. René would then cook the bird until it was nearly done under a tight lid so no moisture escaped. At the right moment he would take off the lid and add a cup of cognac, which he then lit. I guess you would call it flambé pheasant. After the cognac, he would strip the meat off the bird and lay it on warm dinner plates. It wasn't pretty like pheasant under glass, but it was delicious. He served lemonade before the dinner; his lemonade was outstanding French champagne. We never switched to wine, so it was always a night of pheasants and champagne. Those dinners were so good I would start salivating halfway on my drive from Ramstein, Germany, to Gentbrugge. I hunted and shot bunker trap with René off and on from 1970 until the early 1990s. He was a great friend and certainly a wonderful chef for pheasants. I still miss him.

The Browning factory held a VIP pheasant hunt on St. Hubertus Day. Loretta and I were invited twice to this along with our friends Col Rip Sewall and Josie, his charming French wife. The hunt started off in a small chapel with prayers honoring St. Hubertus, the patron saint of hunting, along with a considerable quantity of early-morning schnapps. The ladies were not invited to shoot, but they accompanied the gentlemen shooters. I noted a lot of these gentlemen seemed to be in their mid-60s, accompanied by ladies who appeared to be in their mid-20s—often introduced as their nieces.

This hunt was completely driven birds where the hunters would circle an area that was mostly forest, and the beaters would drive out the pheasants. No loaders were provided, so it was a one-gun shoot with the wives along just to watch and show off their fine hunting attire, beautiful loden capes, and often hats with feathers. Different from English driven hunts, but still elegant. Before each shoot we had a small group with white pants, high black boots, and tailed black coats who blew their horns, which announced it was time to load up and be ready.

The dinners were spectacular. I remember one dinner at a small country restaurant that looked dilapidated. The urinal was off to the side outdoors but wide-open in view. It was basically a rock slab on the ground for standing, and a vertical slab six or seven feet high (to pee against) set five inches from the slab on the ground. These two rock slabs were probably 10 feet long so they could easily accommodate four or five guys at a time. Only the backs of the gentleman using the facility could be observed, but it was plain what their business was. There was no running water. Maybe the breezy outside facilities were not the best visual advertisement, but remember this was in the land of Manneken Pis. That small distraction was completely discarded once the food came around.

This particular night, rabbit was served as the main dish. People talk about meat falling off the bone, but this really was the case. They were cooked, smothered in prunes, and I have never had anything more delicious. Sounds crazy, but my record that night, never to be beaten, was eight rabbits. Remember, these were little guys similar to our cottontails, and I was a big eater in those days. We will never admit to the volume of wine consumed. A marvelous evening to be remembered.

Land of the Morning Calm

Korea is the Land of the morning calm. In 1910, Korea was taken over by the Japanese and remained under their brutal control until August 1945, when World War II ended in the Pacific. The United States and the Soviet Union agreed to divide Korea at the 38th parallel with the

Soviet Union administering North Korea above the 38th parallel and the United States administering South Korea below the 38th parallel. U.S. President Harry Truman persuaded the United Nations to assume responsibility for South Korea in 1947. The U.S. military remained for stability, and the Republic of Korea was formed in 1948. In June 1950, South Korea was invaded by North Korean troops. The United Nations called for the invasion to halt, and the Security Council called for member states to provide military assistance. The countries that joined the Republic of Korea and U.S. forces were: United Kingdom, Turkey, Canada, Australia, France, Colombia, Thailand, Ethiopia, Netherlands, Belgium, Philippines, South Africa, Japan, New Zealand, Norway, Luxembourg, and India.

Following South Korea, the United States provided by far the bulk of troops. China and the Soviet Union joined the North Koreans. Several Soviet satellite countries joined North Korea, providing medical support. Fighting ended in July 1953 with the Korean Armistice Agreement. The border was again set at the 38th parallel with a Demilitarized Zone established between the North and South. We lost nearly 37,000 American troops in the Korean War. By the time I was assigned to Korea in 1975, we still had approximately 48,000 American military troops in South Korea.

Loretta, a lieutenant at the time, had been assigned to the Hermit Kingdom. I was not very excited about the assignment. We had only been back from Germany for two years, and I had seen plenty of the Orient in 1967 and 1968 during my Vietnam assignment. Plus, I didn't think there would be much hunting available. Still, I was anxious to join Loretta. My assignment was three months later, so I was left to sell our house in San Antonio, put our furniture in storage, sell the cars, and select goods to ship overseas. We were on an unaccompanied tour, which meant we could only send 400 pounds each. I packaged up silver, china, crystal, and the one Persian rug that we owned.

Additionally, I packed a 12-gauge Broadway Browning 32-inch shotgun and 12-gauge 28-inch Browning shotgun with an English stock. The Broadway ribbed gun was as a result of my good friend Frank White introducing me to international (bunker) trap. I'd heard there was an international trap shooting range in Seoul. There was, and I joined. I became a very popular life member, mainly because I always brought a bottle of Johnny Walker Red Label Scotch with me. They liked Johnny better than me for certain. I could buy Johnny on the base for seven dollars, and the same bottle on the economy cost $75. The lighter gun was just in case there was some hunting available. Insurance is always good, and remember, I was a Boy Scout, so I was looking and ready for the opportunity to hunt. Koreans in 1975 were still very pleased to have American troops in their country, and we were treated very well. In fact, an American officer could just about do no wrong.

However, Seoul was still under curfew from midnight to 0600. Sirens went off throughout the city, and no one but the police could be left on the street, and that had to be obeyed by all. When I arrived, a brand-new flat became available for rent, so we snapped it up. It was the upper floor on a two-story building, which also gave us a roof patio. It was quite a nice place with a kitchen, combo living room, and dining room, two bedrooms with two baths, and even a small garage. Our address was number 7-8 2Ka Yongsan-Don Yosan-Ku, Seoul. It was near the Itaewon district, which was a sort of sin-city area. You might imagine with a large number of single GIs, 19 or 20 years old, it could be a wild area. But, it was walking distance to the base. The best part was yet to come—officers could afford full-time maids and cooks. Boy, was that nice. We almost had to get a divorce when we came back to the States and found that we no longer had a cook and a maid. Holding nice dinners is so easy with a cook and a maid. Remember, we could not ship furniture, and the Korean rentals were not furnished. I went out and purchased a stove and refrigerator, so that took care of the kitchen. The living room was furnished more or less with patio stuff. The bedroom had a small cabinet, and futons (heavy mats like bed rolls) were on the floor as our beds, which was pretty much standard with the Korean people. We used folding card tables for the dinners and just added extra tables as the crowds got larger. And we had some wonderful dinner parties. Of course, there were many inconveniences—all the vegetables had to be washed in chlorine, and electricity often went off for an hour or so and every once in a while, for a day or two. Some people complained about not having all the conveniences and voiced hardships. Nonsense, of course. Loretta and I considered it practically palatial living.

Our house person was Ms. Choe Pill Soon. I say house person because she was the cook and senior maid. She was an older lady with grown children. Ms. Choe had a lot of experience working for senior American Army officers. There was no question about who ruled the house. She was efficient and unshakable. I could call her at 5:00 p.m. and say 10 people for dinner at 6:00 p.m. and it would happen. Most often, she would also add flowers to the table. I think she also paid off local cops who kept our street clean from vagabonds and begging children. Loretta and I were using our annual leave for a trip to visit Southeast Asia—Taipei, Hong Kong, Manila, Kuala Lumpur, Penang, Bangkok, and Singapore. We would be gone nearly three weeks. A bachelor friend, Maj Larry Weeldreyer, who lived in the barracks on base asked if he could use our flat while we were gone. Understand, in those days women could not be in the same barracks as men and vise-versa. Getting a place where he could entertain would be a nice break from the barracks. Ms. Choe knew Larry and some of the other single men who came around for dinners. In fact, Larry, who liked to cook, often joined in preparing meals with her at our house. It seemed like a good plan to me, and I told Ms. Choe our friends would be using the house. She stiffened up and said, "No, no. They bring girls and girls steal." We had a considerable confrontation, close to a knock-down, drag-out fight during which I explained I was boss of the house, not her. The question was settled in my mind, and I told Larry to go ahead with his plans. Good luck with that.

Larry appeared with one of his male friends to cook and stay overnight, and they hadn't even brought ladies. Miss Choe did not leave before the curfew, so she had to stay with them overnight. Then she claimed she was sick and couldn't leave the house, more or less barricading herself in our bedroom with, as Larry described it, ever peering eyes. She never left the house for three weeks. Larry's plans were thwarted, and I accepted defeat as house boss. We had a fine set of English china, and a 12-place sterling silver set. Maybe we needed Ms. Choe as house boss.

Felix, Loretta's black cat from Germany, came with us. I came home one day from work and found the maid sitting in a chair with Felix asleep on her lap. She was afraid to get up. Sounds crazy, but she was afraid of the cat, and for good reason, as she had never seen one and never had one on her lap. Apparently, Felix had jumped up on her when she was already in the chair. In our year in Korea, I only saw one other cat and that was a Siamese in the very upscale home of a world-renowned Korean opera singer who hosted us at an American/Korean friendship dinner. We were assigned to Yongsan Base, which is next to Seoul. Yongsan translates to Dragon Mountain. Supposedly, the area had been used by many armies since ancient times, even as far back as the Mongols in the 13th century. Now it was headquarters for the United Nations and U.S. Forces Korea command. Four-star General Richard Stillwell was the Commander of the United Nations Command and Eighth Army. Lt Gen James Hollingsworth was subordinate to General Stillwell and was commander of our main fighting troops stationed in Uijeongbu. He was reported to be the third most decorated serviceman in United States history.

There were over 48,000 U.S. military in Korea at this time. It was really the Eighth United States Army (affectionately called Eighth Imperial Army) with two Air Force Bases and a smattering of other U.S. forces and a small number of honor guards from other nations that served in the Korean War. South Korean forces were integrated throughout the headquarters at Yongsan.

It was my good fortune to meet Andy Moore early after I arrived. Andy was the field director for the American National Red Cross in Korea. He was a retired Air Force major and served as a field director for the Red Cross in Germany where he did considerable hunting. He was also a contributor to Rod and Gun, a publication of the rod and gun clubs in Europe. He was a good writer, and I enjoyed his stories, so it was a treat to meet him in person. He explained to me that hunting was illegal, but really just gun control. True or not, according to Andy, someone tried to knock off President Park Chung Hee. He missed him but killed his wife.

The farmers were anxious to kill pheasants as they were considered pests because they continually ate seeds during rice planting time. Andy assured me Americans could hunt with impunity. Turned out he was right, and we hunted all over. Andy was serving without his wife and family who remained in the States. He did not have a car. I bought a used Japanese sedan, pretty much a junker, so we could get around with our guns and hunting gear. Andy had a contact who led us to General Lee, a Korean general on the DMZ who controlled a long section of no-man's land. It was said to contain bushels of pheasants. We traveled up one Saturday to meet the general in his headquarters. It was sparse—a Quonset hut that served as both his office and his quarters. I can tell you, it's hard to heat a Quonset hut. He had a stove that burned hot when you were close, but if you got more than four or five feet away, you couldn't feel it at all. General Lee spoke fair English, and we sat down to have tea with him in our hunting gear. It was obvious what we wanted. Nevertheless, we spoke not of hunting but just other niceties and drank tea. Then he said, "Oh, perhaps you would like to do some hunting?" Our response was, "What a marvelous idea."

Gen Lee then assigned each of us a Jeep with a corporal driver and either a Lt Col or a major military policeman. Away we went, and shoot we did. There were no rules and no limits. The corporals were not only our drivers, but also our bird dogs and retrievers. I found out later they would actually fight over who would get this duty. Not because they liked us or cared about hunting, but because they knew we would take them to lunch off post. I have to tell you, the lunches were pretty poor—some places still had floors of hard-packed earth. While the food was sorry, it was hot and met our needs on those cold hunting days. More than once, I was sure ptomaine poison would be the true and unhappy result of lunch. We shot pheasants and more pheasants without hesitation under the observation of both South Koreans and the North Koreans—both watched us from gun emplacements. Things were pretty tense in those days, and we'd recently had an Army major at Panmunjom who took a karate chop to his throat. It nearly killed him and destroyed all of his vocal cords. We lost a lieutenant commander who was blown up by a booby-trap while inspecting a tunnel dug by the North Koreans. Those hunts always started the same way: first, tea with General Lee and small talk until he suggested hunting. We would pretend to be surprised. I still have a brass ashtray presented as a gift from General Lee.

The U.S. forces had a small Rod and Gun club with a trap and skeet range. Neither skeet nor American trap are my game, but it was a place to shoot, so once in a while I would drop by just to shoot a round or two. One afternoon, I was shooting trap and I could tell one of the other shooters really had no idea what he was doing. He was safe, but he did not know how to move from station to station and then come around from station five to one. He was a small man, about my size, and he was just lost. I showed him how to shoot American trap. Afterwards, he approached me in the clubhouse, thanked me for my help, and gave me his card. Then he invited me to come by and have a drink with him sometime. I thanked him and said, "perhaps," but really didn't pay much attention until I got home and read his card. In standard print was his name, John DeSilva, and then in very small print at the bottom it read: Ambassador.

That didn't mean too much to me at the time, but I later found out how nice it was to be an ambassador. He represented Malaysia. Previously, he'd been ambassador to Vietnam during the war and seemed to know everybody in the U.S. military as well as high-level U.S. civilians. As I said earlier, the commander of the United Nations Command and Eighth Army was General Richard G. Stillwell, and subordinate to him in command of U.S. and Korean forces was Lt Gen James Hollingsworth. John had known them both from Vietnam when Stillwell was a lieutenant general, and Hollingsworth was a major general. We hit it off for some reason and started hunting together using his black Mercedes sedan. He would run the flags up on the fenders of his sedan, and nobody stopped us anywhere. Often, an Englishman, Mr. H.H. Liller, who was the president of the Charter Bank, would join us. We would just drive until we saw pheasants and then get out and hunt. Sometimes, we would see what looked to be a good spot for pheasants, and we'd simply stop the car and start hunting, leaving his chauffeur in the Mercedes. Normally, we'd shoot six or eight pheasants in a Saturday morning hunt. John was a real scamp, and it was fun to have him tell me what was going on in the high levels of Eighth Army or the

Long Shots — Hunting

U.N. Command. Sometimes at receptions or cocktail parties, he would slip up next to senior officials and even General Stillwell to make some comment just for fun. Then he'd disappear in the crowd, having uttered comments like, "I know it isn't true what they say," or maybe something like, "Don't worry, we will support you." No doubt, many conspiracy theories were hatched because of his shenanigans. On one of our Saturday morning hunts, John told me he was hosting a dinner for a large number of diplomats and wanted to serve pheasants.

Our Saturday morning hunts would not produce the number of birds necessary. We figured the only way we could get the 70 birds necessary was to hunt on Cheju Island, which is claimed by South Korea. It is located where the Korean Strait and Yellow Sea meet, more or less between the mainland of South Korea and Japan. Just as a little history reminder, after the Sino-Japanese War, Japan started controlling Korea. The Russo-Japanese war of 1904-05 ended when the Japanese crushed the Russian Navy, and Korea came completely under the influence of the Japanese. Theodore Roosevelt was sent to negotiate a peace settlement between czarist Russia and Imperial Japan. In 1910, Japan annexed Korea and dominated the country with brutal suppression and harsh policies, reminiscent of how the Japanese army in World War II used Korean women as "comfort women" for their troops. Not a lot of love here. Cheju was the one place in Korea it was legal to hunt. I still have my license from JeJu Province.

My own belief is hunting on Cheju Island was really Korean revenge. Most of the hunters on Cheju were from Japan. The Koreans had a couple of high-rise hotels, and they charged the Japanese high rates. This allowed them to take from the Japanese without allowing Japanese on the Korean mainland. In any case, it was a great area to hunt as there were no natural enemies for pheasants. There was a strict limit, which I recall as being something like six or eight pheasants per day. That number could be exceeded in some instances, but it cost a pretty penny—and the Japanese paid.

Earlier, I mentioned my lack of knowledge (complete ignorance) about the value of being an ambassador. I found out on this trip. In the first place, when traveling on an airline in Korea at that time (the mid-'70s) every passenger was patted down, and luggage searched—no exception. This was before x-ray machines were in use. I thought there were no exceptions until we boarded the airplane, and John pulled out his credentials.

No one touched him or looked at his luggage. It was strictly, "Your Excellency this," and, "Your Excellency that." I was impressed that ambassadors were addressed as Your Excellency. I was searched. We hunted a day and a half and shot 79 pheasants. I don't know how his Excellency worked a deal as we paid for one limit each. Now we had a little problem: we had no coolers. How were we to get 79 pheasants back to Seoul? We enlisted the hotel staff and put those pheasants, feathers, guts, and all, in three large cardboard boxes tied with string and tape. We carried the whole mess to the airport with some boxes already leaking a bit. His Excellency had no trouble checking his unopened bags and boxes back to Seoul. And yes, I was patted down and had my luggage searched.

Hunting on Cheju was fun. I went back a second time, but it was not as much fun without the mischievous antics of His Excellency.

Quail

Bobwhite quail *(Colinus Virginianus)* are often referred to as "Gentleman Bob." While not a clear trail, and with no empirical evidence, I suspect the term originated in the East and South when wealthy hunters were shooting side-by-side shotguns—Parkers, A. H. Foxes, L.C. Smiths, Lefevers (my first good gun was an old and mean-used 12-gauge Lefever with a Prince of Wales style stock/grip and twist steel barrels), and later the Winchester 21. This was originally a gentleman's shoot with relatively easy walking but sometimes on horseback or in wagons drawn by mules. Bobwhite quail hold tighter for the pointing dogs than their western cousins, and the moniker "Gentleman Bob" was born. The coveys were handled carefully by the shooters and not overshot. Some gentlemen limited the birds taken from each covey to only two or three. Those were the days when small farms with fence rows, weed patches, spilled grain, and just good habitat for wild quail were prevalent before modern "clean farms." Sadly, those days in the 1920s, '30s, '40s, and '50s are gone. Still, there are several outstanding commercial lodges that replicate those fine hunting experiences, even down to horses and mule-drawn wagons. Alas, the birds are now pen-raised, but properly handled they can still offer a good sport.

My introduction to shooting bobwhite was when I was first assigned to the Air Force shooting team at Lackland Air Force Base in 1963. Airman First Class (AIC) Bob Dickens had a place to hunt south of San Antonio, and when he heard I liked shooting birds, he invited me and some of the other team members to come on a quail hunt with him on Sunday. None of us, including AIC Dickens, had proper hunting attire. In fact, none of us even had a quail gun. So, what to do? We all checked out 20-gauge Remington Model 1100s. Team members were allowed to become familiar with firearms and courses of fire of the other teams. We took off in a couple of cars, headed for the hunt. We must have looked like a motley crowd with some in fatigues, some in Levis, and one or two with a hunting vest. All of us did have licenses, but we did not have dogs.

We parked along the gravel county road and crossed a barbed-wire fence as directed by A1C Bob Dickens. It was typical South Texas country—mostly flat, and the field we lined up in looked as if it had once been farmed and then reverted to grazing. There was plenty of mesquite and cactus, but it was open enough for good shooting. It was one of those banner years when the quail had several hatches. The hunt started as soon as we crossed the fence, and people began shooting. It was simply an explosion of birds. I could hardly believe it. I'd shoot a bird, and when I went to retrieve it, another covey would explode. A bird knocked down would fall into another covey. It was just complete pandemonium, birds flying in all directions. It was simply amazing, and I doubt could happen anywhere other than South Texas—at least not in those numbers.

After scarfing up a number of birds we started back to the cars to dump birds and get more ammo. As we were just crossing the barbed-wire fence, a black Buick sedan with the tallest antenna I had ever seen pulled up—out stepped a sheriff. He didn't look at guns, birds, or license. It was merely a command," Get in your cars and follow me." Dickens was talking fast about how it was an honest mistake, etc. I was still fairly new to the unit but was the officer in charge (OIC) of the Air Force Rifle Team, and here I was, an officer likely to be arrested for trespassing, carrying a firearm on private property, shooting too close to a road, and possibly other offenses (along with my subordinates). Additionally, we all had government firearms that might very well be confiscated by the law. A good question could have been asked: Where was the adult supervision? I thought second lieutenant might be the highest grade I would ever achieve when the commander heard about this.

We followed the sheriff a mile or so before he turned into a dirt lane that led to an old farmhouse which looked fairly rundown. The sheriff got out of his car and motioned us to follow him up the walk to the house. It was a small wood-framed house that looked 100 years old, maybe an old Sears catalog house, with an unkempt yard under some giant oak trees. In we went, and there sat an elderly gentleman in a wheelchair with his wife sitting next to him in a straight-backed kitchen chair. It was rather dingy inside, and even though it was in the middle of the day, light was poor with what looked like lace curtains over the small windows. I was quiet as a mouse as Airman Dickens was once more double-talking fast and furious about being down here hunting before, etc., etc. The old man seemed to acknowledge that but said before was before and now was now, and we did not have permission to hunt and had not even come to the house and asked for permission. It was a standoff. The sheriff asked the old gentleman what he wanted to do and offered that he could take us all into the jail and call out the county judge. That really got my attention. I was frantically trying to figure how I could help in this mess when the old man told the sheriff it wouldn't be necessary to bother his friend, (I don't recall the name) the judge, on a Sunday. The old man allowed we could go but admonished us to always ask permission first. We walked out with the sheriff, who told us the old guy owned lots of land, and he didn't want to see us on this property or any property in HIS county ever again. Believe me, I was thinking the same thing. I thanked my lucky stars we were headed out of HIS county.

Long Shots — Hunting

Good thing I didn't have a pistol or Airman Dickens might have met his maker. I was embarrassed and highly pissed off. Airman Dickens was a big guy, built like an NFL lineman, and he certainly was a wonderful shooter, particularly in the National Infantry Trophy match—better known as the "Rattle Battle" match at Camp Perry. He could put 48 rounds in the black (20-inch circle) at 500 yards, in 60 seconds shooting the M1 Garand rifle. That means starting with one eight-round clip loaded in the rifle, firing that, loading, and firing five additional eight-round clips. He was a swing shooter, which meant he had to put half his rounds on one target, and the other half on a second target. That took a slight but time-consuming moment or two, as he had to reposition his elbows and body for firing at the second target. It was something to see him hitting the bull's-eye 48 times in one minute. I am happy to report he eventually retired as a Master Sgt.

Col Tom Kelly, who had been my commander when I was the officer in charge of the Air Force High-Power Rifle Team, brought me to my next bobwhite experience. After he retired, we became hunting friends and eventually good personal friends. Upon returning to San Antonio from assignment in Germany in 1973, I was anxious to start hunting and called Col Kelly. He had a tip about a man on the south side of town who had quail hunting, and it was a good year for birds.

Telephone contact was made, and we drove down to see Mr. Brazil, who invited us in for a cup of coffee. The house was an old wooden structure that looked to be tongue-and-groove construction. It was plainly furnished with linoleum floors but clean as a pin. I thought he was quite old, but looking back now I expect maybe only 70 or thereabouts. We must've looked okay as he invited us to come back and shoot with him the next week.

The invitation was to come to his house for breakfast, and then he would guide us in hunts on his properties. We showed up at the appointed hour, and his wife served us bacon and eggs along with coffee. We may have had toast, but we certainly didn't have hash brown potatoes or grits. It was simply bacon, two eggs, and coffee—meager, but we were most appreciative of his hospitality especially since he hardly knew us. It turned out to be a marvelous hunting day, and we took three limits of birds—45 quail. They were mostly bobwhites. We did get a few scaled quail, which was a first for me. They are also called blues and sometimes cotton tops.

It seemed that Mr. Brazil had no end of properties in South Texas—mostly small plots of 10 acres, 20 acres, and such, often corner properties. He didn't shoot much, but he carried a single-shot 12 gauge with a hammer. I think it was an Iver Johnson. He did get a bird every once in a while, but I suspect they were taken on the ground. He loved taking us hunting or maybe just being with us, but for sure we loved hunting with him. One of his properties was very close to town, and I don't believe it was over 20 or 30 acres. We were there one afternoon with Mr. Brazil and took the usual three limits of birds. We cleaned birds in the field and always made sure Mr. Brazil got 15 cleaned birds. We were relaxing with a beer after the hunt, which Mr. Brazil also appreciated, when a young man, my guess would be somewhere between 19 and 22, drove onto the property. Mr. Brazil introduced him as the lease-holder of the property. He was young but dressed well in Levis and a dress shirt. The kid looked sharp. He was driving a shiny red pickup, so he didn't appear much like a ranch hand. Turned out he really was a cowboy and leased several small properties where he ran cattle. I guess he must have been driving his Sunday truck.

Mr. Brazil retained the right to hunt personally and with friends on any of these properties. With the kid standing there, Col Kelly asked Mr. Brazil if we could lease the hunting rights on the property we had just hunted on. Mr. Brazil allowed that would have to be up to the kid as he had the property leased. It was pretty evident the kid wasn't overjoyed about more people tramping across the lease and pushing his cows around. But here's where I learned the difference between five 20s and a hundred-dollar bill. Col Kelly mentioned one hundred dollars. The kid looked less than enthusiastic. However, Col Kelly pulled out a $100 bill and held it out—that cinched the deal. To this day I'm convinced it was the $100 bill that got us the lease. Even Mr. Brazil said he was surprised the kid let us in as he was quite particular with his cows and other people on the property. Of course, today lots of folk have a $100 bill in their wallet, but that was not so common in 1973—even carrying around 100 bucks in twenties was a lot of cash for me.

The lease turned out to be super. It was in Bexar County not far out of the San Antonio City limits. Col Kelly and I shot it many times and always took three limits—one for Mr. Brazil. Readers will no doubt question me or at least hold me suspect on what I'm about to say, but more than once we collected every bird shot. That's not an easy thing, particularly without a dog. When we shot a bird, the shooter and the non-shooter both marked the bird. The non-shooter would keep his eye on the mark as the shooter walked forward and picked up the bird. It was a boom year for quail, so we could take our time and diligently search for each downed bird without worry of not finding more coveys. Many would think it's a fib, but we did it. At that time, I was shooting a 12 gauge over-and-under Browning Superposed, and Col Kelly was shooting a Browning 12 gauge named the Double Automatic. Sounds a little weird to call a shotgun an automatic that has a two-shot limit, but that's what it was. One selling point for this gun was speed loading via a port on the left side of the receiver. Not my cup of tea, but it worked well for him. The main selling point for this gun was that it was light, weighing only six pounds, and consequently smooth handling and easy to carry in the field. The receivers were made of an aluminum alloy and came in many colors. Best I can recall, Col Kelly's was either green or brown—whatever the color, it never looked right to me.

Accompanying Col Kelly could often become an adventure. Having been shot at both on the ground and in airplanes desensitized the colonel, and he was indifferent to normal pedestrian fears. Not much scared him with the exception of the dangerous and deadly Texas Galiipadiller. There was only one antidote to this dangerous critter—Scotch or bourbon. And, it was best taken as a prophylactic before sighting the Galiipadiller as they were rumored to be able to kill with eyesight alone. They, like rattlesnakes, were often encountered around cattle guards and fence gates. A dutiful swig of preventive medicine was administered at each gate and cattle guard encountered. I luckily never saw a Galiipadiller.

Herman Mashburn was a retired Air Force Chief Master Sergeant and had been a part of the initial cadre to set up the Air Force Marksmanship School. He became the coach and team leader for the Air Force trap and skeet shooting teams. I first met him when I was shooting rifle for the Air Force, but I didn't really get to know him well because we traveled in different circles—the rifle team going one way and the shotgun team going another. Additionally, he was a Chief Master Sergeant and far above my level as Lieutenant, both in knowledge and experience. Quite frankly, I don't think he wanted to fool with me or any other lowly lieutenant. The full-time shooting teams for the Air Force closed in 1968/1969 but competitive shooting continued in a more modest way through the Air Force Morale and Welfare and Recreation programs (MWR).

I was invited to return from Germany for temporary duty in 1971 to join Air Force trap shooters for the Pan-American team selection. Chief Mashburn, who was retired by this time, was selected to be the coach. Other team members were Second Lieutenant James DeFilippi and three young airmen first class (A1C) Wally Zobell, Bob Green, and Phil Wright. Wally represented the United States when he shot on our Olympic team in 1984. We traveled together for a couple of months training before the tryouts and got to know each other. The Chief had a wealth of knowledge and was willing to share—and I was pleased to receive it. He had bird dogs and bird guns so made excellent company. One never knows where the road will lead. In this case it led to Mr. Travis Richardson when the Chief took me on a hunt where we were both guests.

Chief Mashburn came as a close friend of Travis, with me as a sort of a tagalong. The hunt was simply spectacular—the dogs found the birds, and the birds held for the guns. It is beautiful to see good pointers working and finding a covey of birds—tails high, eyes focused, with nose nearly touching the quail, often so intense they would be quivering, sometimes with several other dogs backing the point. I'm excited and nearly quivering myself when moving up to the dogs, anticipating the covey flush—quail with rapid wing beats blasting out in all directions. Birds going in all directions like little rockets makes the covey rise exciting and challenging as birds may go straight away from you, to the right, to the left, or maybe straight back at you.

The dogs holding at the shot until told to retrieve the downed birds was a new experience for me, and it was total fun. I had hunted Valley Quail as a middle- and high-school kid but without dogs (Valley

Quail don't hold for dogs nearly as well as bobwhites) which makes all the difference in a good quail hunt. The Fuller brothers from Floresville worked their dogs for Travis. Charlie ran a feed store, and Bert was a retired state policeman. What they really liked was to breed and train bird dogs. They had superb English Pointers and would often bring 10 dogs each, so for weekend hunt we would have 20 dogs staked out at night. Usually, English Pointers are not pets, and many don't seem to care if they are petted or not. They want to hunt, and that is all they want. The Fullers' English Pointers did it all: They found the birds, pointed, held them till the hunters walked up, flushed and shot the birds. Then the pointers would retrieve the birds. That's not an easy thing to teach the pointers because they want to hunt and not spend time retrieving dead birds. Many commercial outfitters today use pointers to find and point the birds and then have retrieving dogs, mostly labs, and today quite a number have English Cockers retrieve the dead birds. That's much easier than training the English Pointers to do it all. The Fuller brothers and Travis would have none of that—they wanted their dogs to handle the whole show. As I said, most English Pointers didn't care much about being petted, and normally they do not make the best pets, but my friend Tom Curtis who lives in Livingston, Montana, has super English Pointers. I have seen them in the field with one pointing and four backing—a lovely sight. All five of his dogs can also be seen in his house and even on laps of dog-friendly visitors. Strange but true.

Travis managed several cattle ranches for the prominent San Antonio Moorman family (nice folks and fun to hunt with). He was the unquestioned boss in cattle and quail hunting matters. Quail hunting in Texas is often a very social affair, and the Moorman family entertained the top echelon of Texans, including Governor John Connally, the Bass family, and many other luminaries. As an aside, Gov. Connally graduated from Floresville High School; Charlie and Bert Fuller, the great bird dog men, were also from Floresville. They knew the governor well, and he gave them his dog Trailer. Travis managed the hunt, and the Fuller brothers ran the dogs.

We hit it off well. For some reason, Travis took a liking to me and Loretta. His wife Dorothy was a great lady and a good cook, so we always enjoyed being at their home, which could be called cozy. It was small with a kitchen, a living room/dining room combination on the bottom floor, and bedrooms upstairs. It was sparsely but tastefully decorated. He did have a leopard skin on the floor and the tusks of a 100+ pound elephant on each side of the fireplace, which belonged to Tommy Moorman. If the weather was cold or even cool Travis would have the fireplace going, always burning live oak logs. We soon found ourselves hunting with Travis on some of the best quail country in Texas and with the finest bird dogs that could be found, thanks to Burt and Charlie Fuller. It was pretty heady indeed.

Travis was a no-nonsense kind of guy and a man of few words. Reticent comes to mind. He never talked much, but when he did, you'd better pay attention. He was a Texas A&M graduate from before World War II and still had his A&M Corps boots. He did not laugh at A&M jokes. He was also a cowboy who could ride and rope. I never saw him wearing anything but cowboy boots.

We were hunting on his birthday one year, and the Fuller brothers brought him an English Pointer puppy as a gift along with a nice new collar. We went out after Mr. Bob with trained pointers and the puppy following along. The puppy did not perform up to Travis' standards. Nothing was said but he quietly reached down and took the collar off the puppy and put it in his game pouch, and that was that, without anyone saying a word. He knew South Texas, its country, and its people. His uncle was the sheriff in Jim Wells County (very much involved in politics) at the time of the infamous precinct Box 13 in Alice with 202 voters who all signed up in alphabetical order, and all signed with the same handwriting. That, along with George Parr (the Duke of Duvall), and other mischief the 202 votes were strangely reported several days after the election—200 for Johnson and 2 for his opponent Coke Stevenson. Those events in South Texas allowed LBJ to win by 87 votes out of a million and began his Senate climb in politics. Travis walked with a bad limp, and it got worse as the day went on. I was told his limp came from an accidental shooting. The story was a little murky but involved a .357 revolver and a pesky neighbor who may have needed shooting. It was apparent Travis' limp was painful, but he never said a word and just gritted it out. He gave me a peek at paradise quail hunting. I'm grateful he shared his hunting and bird dog days with me. I miss him.

Other great bobwhite quail hunts have come my way, and one that appears annually is the Grand National Quail Club in Enid, Oklahoma, of which I'm honored to be a member. John Groendyke's father was one of the founding members, and John hosts me every year for a day shooting on one of his ranches with guides and his superb bird dogs. We normally hunt, riding four-wheel mules with dog boxes on the rear containing multiple pointing dogs. It's normal to have two dogs working the field looking for quail. When they find a covey, they point the birds, the hunters then dismount and walk to the pointing dogs. It doesn't get any better than that, and I have been pleased to be his guest at the Grand and on occasions other than the Grand National Quail Club Hunt.

Mr. Brian Huntley has taken me after bobwhites in areas around Abilene. I was with him on some hunts during the latest boom years of quail population explosions. We hunted from a four-wheel gator and had a super young lab named Goose. It was simply fantastic shooting. You almost had to see it to believe it. Wild quail were just everywhere. When a covey was scared up, we would park the four runner and go after them without pointers but with his superb lab. Goose was just over a year old, but you could tell when he was on a bird. I don't think we lost a dead or wounded quail that day. Additionally, Goose would kennel up without any argument and just curled up on the floor in the Suburban, going and coming from the hunt.

Another enjoyable quail hunt we do every year is at the Last Buffalo in the Texas Panhandle. It's a commercial operation run by two brothers, Josh and Jared Robertson, and their lifelong friend Jordan Shearer. All these boys are right around 30 years old, and I am quite fond of all three. I first started hunting at the Last Buffalo with the brother's grandfather, J.R. Robertson, who happens to be a superb dog man with a kennel of somewhere between 35 and 40 dogs. Wade Robertson, his son, took over after J.R., and we had many fun days together. As an aside, Wade is a tough Columbaire (pigeon thrower) in a live bird competition. The Columbaire stands a few meters in front of the shooter, whose shotgun is pointed over Columbaire's head. When ready the shooter says "Listo," the Columbaire goes into a wild turning motion much like a shot putter and hurls the bird in the air in any direction he chooses. It's a kind of hairy and dangerous situation with the person shooting a shotgun over his head. Not for the faint of heart for sure.

    I happened to win a small match in West Virginia, much to my surprise. Several of my friends whooped and hollered about challenging the match because I knew Wade. I can assure you that Wade is a professional and would throw me out in a minute, as his job is to beat the shooter. My friends knew that but were just having fun. After Wade moved away from quail hunting, his two sons and Jordan took over the operation. They do an outstanding job, run a fine lodge, and know how to take care of people. It's just a real pleasure to be with them. It's all wild quail with them, and the pointers also do the retrieving. They don't have the big boom years for quail in the Panhandle like areas in South Texas, and some might suspect the hunting is just sort of an excuse to visit with them each year. I enjoy their good company.

    Scaled Quail *(Callipepla Squamata)* are also called blues or cotton tops because of the distinct little Mohawks they wear. They are hard to hunt. I was warned to have on my best tennis shoes while chasing the little rascals because they wore Nikes. It is true. I think they are the worst runners of all quail. They are dryland or desert quail usually found in rough, rugged country without good cover. They can see you coming and usually get a good start on you. Dogs have a very hard time holding them because of the sparse terrain. It doesn't give much cover or places where they can stop and feel secure. Many people say you just can't hunt scaled quail with pointing dogs. After a few foot races with these little demons, I was pretty well convinced they were right about it being impossible to use a pointing dog. In fact, I began to think you needed a fast four-wheel-drive pickup to catch up to them. Most of my early forays were more or less incidental to other hunting, and getting three or four birds was the norm.

    Cal Sugg has a ranch in West Texas, and I was invited to hunt with him. The connection came from my good friend Frank White. I want to tell you about Cal and his wife Donna. They are genuine, lovely people; Loretta and I were fortunate to become good friends with them.

We hunted on their ranch and often stayed in their beautiful home. We also traveled a bit with them in the States and a couple of times to Argentina. They are generous, low-key, and easy to be with. Cal is the antithesis of the archetypal Texan. I have never seen him wear cowboy boots or a cowboy hat. There is no braggadocio about him—more quiet and laid back—no pretense would be an accurate description. Cal held a hunting camp each year with around 25 invited guests. It was always a fun, interesting, and eclectic group. The parking area told the story well. You might see the newest, biggest, and costliest Mercedes, while next to it would be a cheap Ford or maybe a sad-looking pickup. Some people were bankers and lawyers while others worked in the oil patch as pumpers. Cal has friends in all levels of life, and he treats everyone like a special guest.

His annual hunt drew mainly deer hunters, but turkey and hogs were on the menu as was quail, chased by just a few of us. Cal had no rules; you could hunt anything you wanted. We never used dogs on the quail hunt and seldom shot more than four or five birds. But one year stands out as an all-time high. It was the very first time I shot a limit of 15 scaled quail. Conditions, mostly weather, must have been perfect, producing enough grass and seeds for cover and food (also insects for the chicks at just the right times). Six of us hunted with Cal that day. It was overcast and cool, with only slight wind—excellent bird shooting weather. Each of us took the limit of 15 birds, so we had a total of 90, which was a ranch record. We took all the birds fair and square, shooting them flying. Some people shoot blues on the ground as they are such bad runners, but it is sort of a shame. Most sportsmen would agree shooting birds on the ground is less than honorable.

For the next 15 years I thought limits of blues taken in the air would probably not be repeated. Then I found Steve Brugman in New Mexico, who hunts with pointing dogs for blues. Some people will tell you scaled quail can't be hunted with dogs.

What I can happily report is, those people are wrong. Steve has very good dogs, not show dogs, and they may not be perfect pointers, but they find birds and hold birds and retrieve birds. I take some of my "kids" out there every year, which makes a large shooting party for quail hunting with dogs, so we divide up—three with Steve and the others with his assistant guide. The kids are Col John Linn, Max Jungk, Zane Kuenzler, and Commander Derek Hotchkiss. I started them all at an early age. John was 14 or 15, Max and Zane were both 16, and I believe Derek was 19. Doug Ward has joined us, but he was married with children in college and very successful as a vice president for USAA when we met. He has amalgamated into the group—they like him, and he likes them. They have all been successful in their own endeavors and make an outstanding squad to be with. I would put them up against any group, and I'm proud to be with them. So far, we have ended each day with the total limit of 15 birds each, and that is really saying something. It's not easy because of all the walking on rough terrain not suited to four runners, but it is becoming one of my favorite hunts. My friend and partner, Gordie White, and I make a hunt with Steve every year as a sort of annual retreat. And I'm not telling you where Steve lives.

Callipepla Gambelii are called Gambel's Quail. They are first cousins to the California Valley Quail and look very similar except they wear a rust-colored skullcap on the back of their heads. They act and sound much like the California Valley Quail, but they seem to prefer flatter ground, and in my experience, they don't seem to congregate in such large coveys. The greatest concentration that I have seen of the Gambel's has been in Arizona and northern Mexico, just across the California and Arizona borders (not Baja California). They are also found in New Mexico and West Texas. I had the great fortune of being introduced to these little beauties by Col Burton T. Miller, who lived in Tucson, Arizona. We had served together in Germany in the late 1970s and became good hunting and shooting friends. I actually knew his father, who was a Lieutenant Colonel, running the Air Force master gun shop when I was a second lieutenant and shooting on the Air Force High-Power Rifle Team. Burt was a West Point graduate and a highly decorated Air Force pilot with two tours in Vietnam, earning two Silver Stars. He was an Air Force brat, meaning he grew up in an Air Force family. His father and Gen Curtis Lemay were friends and hunted together. Gen Lemay was also Burt's godfather, and upon graduation from West Point presented him with a very fine German drilling shotgun/rifle. I can attest that it was quite handy and shot well.

Long Shots — Hunting

Burt was a real gun guy. He had good guns: rifles, pistols, and shotguns. They all shot well, or he didn't keep them. In civilian life, I don't think I ever saw him when he wasn't carrying a handgun, usually in a shoulder holster. He hunted all over the world, but his greatest pleasure was hunting quail with his German Drahthaar hunting dogs. He had several good ones, but the very best was a large male named Ace who could smell out the birds no matter what the weather. Burt invited me to Tucson each February to meet the Gambel's along with a smattering of blues. Gambel's will hold for dogs if you can catch them in heavy cover and especially after a flush when the birds are scattered. Ace was perfect at finding the singles and was an outstanding retrieving dog. We seldom lost a downed bird. The hunts were at the end of the season, and we seldom got limits, but we always had a grand time, especially after the hunt, reminiscing about our fun times in the Air Force and especially shooting the DJV matches (hunters style competition) and hunting in Germany. Often, we were fortified with what some might suggest was a rather copious supply of wine.

Cyrtonyx Montezumae are called Montezuma Quail in some parts of the country; in other parts they are called Mearns Quail. Sometimes they are referred to as Harlequin Quail. This dandy little game bird was also introduced to me by Burt. They are found mostly at higher elevation than desert quail. A good population is found in the area around Patagonia, Arizona, which is pretty grass country dotted with oak trees. Huntable populations are also found in New Mexico. These dressy little dudes are a real joy to hunt as they hold for dogs even better than Gentlemen Bobs. Sometimes you can walk into the middle of a covey before they blast out with a cacophony of wing beats that will startle even the most seasoned hunter. Their coveys are generally small, so it's important not to take more than a couple from each covey. The males are the most stylishly dressed of all the quail--wings with black spots on brown, a waistcoat of bright white spots, a dark brown underbelly, a brown cape with white stripes, a large mostly white head, black and white face with a tan-colored fedora perched jovially on the back of its head. Hence, the moniker Harlequin. On our first trip out to hunt them near Fort Huachuca, I only bagged one bird, which I quickly grabbed up before the dogs could retrieve it and slipped it into a section of a ladies' nylon hose to best protect its feathers. Burt was charged with giving it to a good taxidermist. Several months later, I inquired as to the progress and what I owed for the work. Burt reported the taxidermist advised the bird was young and too small for the standard quail mold so the work could not be done. I had been anxiously looking forward to receiving this little trophy and was disappointed at the news. A couple of months later a package arrived with my mounted Montezuma Quail as a gift. That was Burt Miller.

Mountain Quail *(Oreortyx Pictus)* is the largest of the quail family, and I have found them in the coastal range from Baja California through Oregon. It is my understanding they have now spread through Washington and even up to Vancouver. They are not nearly as common as the California Valley Quail, and their habitat seems to be at the higher elevations, usually above 3,000 feet. They seem to shy away from human habitation, and I've never found them around farms or structures. I must admit my earliest successful encounter with these birds was using a .22 revolver.

They were taken before I really understood what a sin it was to shoot birds with a pistol or on the ground. I don't ask for clemency, but I was an inexperienced minor, and the early birds were taken on camping trips when we hiked into the back country of the Los Padres National Forest and Sespe Wildlife Area (now designated as the Condor Sanctuary). To add sin on sin, I have to admit they were mostly taken out of season.

Four of us high-school freshmen, Doug Udall, John Randall, Jim Gofourth, and I purchased a burro named Rosie to help carry our camping gear and supplies on a nine-day trip into the National Forest and the Sespe Wildlife Area. We got a pack saddle and a set of panniers for Rosie but knew little about what we were doing. In fact, on our very first outing we started up in the Maricopa off Highway 33 at the Piedra Blanco Campground with our destination being Fillmore. We unloaded the horse trailer borrowed from the forest service office in Santa Paula and packed most of our goods and gear on Rosie. The trailhead started just on the other side of Piedra Blanco Creek, which was only about knee deep. Rosie made it halfway across when she decided her load was too big, and she simply sat down in the middle

Long Shots — Hunting

of the creek, not exactly a decorous start. We attempted to get her up with poking, prodding, pushing, and pulling, all to no avail; Rosie was having no part of it. We unloaded everything from the panniers in the middle of the creek and repacked some of the heavy stuff in our backpacks, which lightened Rosie's load considerably. She never gave us any trouble from there to Fillmore, still a week away, or on any of the many subsequent trips. In fact, none of our burros were ever snarky. Later, we acquired another burro named Blackjack along with one named Grey so we could come into the Los Padres National Forest from different directions and rendezvous at the Sespe Hot Springs.

A favorite trip was for one group to come in from the Maricopa at Piedra Blanco on the Sespe River Trail, and another from Mr. Graff's Ferndale Ranch (now Thomas Aquinas College) on Santa Paula Creek, following the Last Chance Trail, and still another from the Sisar Creek in in the Upper Ojai, on the Red Reef Trail, crossing over Hines Peak at 6,716 feet, and dropping down to the trail from Piedra Blanco to our favorite camp site, Coltrell Flat near the Sespe Hot Springs. From there we would follow the Ader Creek Trail out to Fillmore or on to Piru on the Buckshot Trail. All of this was in the Topatopa Mountain Range. I'm told the trails were mostly cut by the Civilian Conservation Corps during the Great Depression years but were little used in the late 1940s and early 1950s. We seldom saw other hikers or campers during our trips. Most of the trails were not even marked, and some were in bad repair. On one occasion, my buddy John Brock and I were hiking from Cross Camp near the headwaters of Santa Paula Creek on the Last Chance Trail that led to the Sespe Hot Springs, when we came upon two high-school acquaintances who had shot and killed a pair of very young black bears. We didn't mind shooting a few rabbits and an occasional quail that we ate, but this was beyond our tolerance. It was springtime, so of course they were taken out of season, probably really cubs. The shooters had no preparations for handling dead bears. We had our burro Blackjack, so we helped them carry out the bears, but we were not happy about it.

All of us were young teenagers. These trips into the backcountry were great mini-adventures with no adults and, for the most part, in very rugged country not accessible by vehicles. We were on our own

303

for everything—planning, supplying, and making the trek. There was no communication with the outside world, long before satellite or cell phones. Heck, we didn't even have satellites in 1952. We had to make everything work, but we had good training in the Boy Scouts and with the junior rifle club. You might wonder why parents would let young teenagers go in the backcountry without an adult, where it would take at least two days to walk out if we had an emergency? It was just different times. Those mini-adventures were lots of fun and a good education in growing up. Each of us carried a pistol or revolver of one kind or another and scarfed up on all the rabbits and quail to supplement our food supply. At the higher elevations it was mostly Mountain Quail. We could all shoot well, but we didn't hurt their population much. They are a handsome bird nearly half again the size of other quail with a long head plume extending to the rear of their head as opposed to Gambel's and Valley Quail with a top notch leaning forward. They are colored gray blue on their back, and they sport a lovely white striped waistcoat on their breast.

I became a little more sophisticated and began using a shotgun when specifically hunting Mountain Quail, but I must admit with little success. They are hard birds to hunt, and in my experience live in small coveys of 8 to 12 birds. They rarely venture out of the heavy cover and easily escape under the chaparral found in the Southern California coastal mountain range. I do recall one hunt somewhere between Castaic Junction and Gorman where I took a right and a left with my Lefever shotgun, which shocked even me. It never happened again. The Lefever was the first quality shotgun I owned. Unfortunately, its proud body had more than a few scuffs, and it displayed much honest use. I shot only low base shells in the Damascus barrels, and I doubt it could pass a proof test. But I was proud of it and shot it reasonably well.

Callipepla Californica is the California Valley Quail. Some had been taken by me with a pistol on camping trips, and they were the first of the quail I hunted with a shotgun, really the first of all my bird hunting. I love hunting all species of quail, but how can one not have a special place in the heart for the very first of anything? In my opinion, they are the quail that are easiest to hunt without a bird dog. They call frequently and can often be seen running or moving about feeding, so sight and sound give them away. They are runners, but not as bad as scale quail. When I say easiest, I'm talking about easiest in the sense of finding them, but they are normally in rough and steep terrain, and one has to be in good physical shape to chase them. They can't be successfully hunted from four-wheelers. Of course, one can always do better with a good bird dog. Nevertheless, I trudged all around Santa Paula and the foothills of both South and North Mountain chasing quail. Results were less than spectacular—two to three bagged birds would be counted as success without a bird dog. The limit was eight, which I don't recall ever achieving in those days. Jim Gofourth was the first of my friends to get bird dogs. His lab Shadow, smart as the dickens and a good retriever, came first. When I returned from Vietnam, he treated me to a fine pheasant hunt with his English pointers Tex and Rex from the King Ranch.

Once I could drive, my range of hunting extended from Ventura to Piru. My high-school buddies Doug Udall and Jim Gofourth were often with me. The Valley Quail is a very pretty little guy—very close in looks to his first cousin, the Gambel's Quail. He has a top knot that leans forward on his head. They are a very gregarious bird—I think more than any of the other quail. Sometimes several coveys come together at a feeding or watering area. Doubtful you could see it today, but I believe that I've seen a covey of 500 quail. I know that sounds unreal, but Gen Chuck Yeager told me he once flew over what he thought was a group of at least 1000 quail in the California foothills. Of course, he is 15 years older than me, so his sighting had to be in the 1940s. Gen Yeager is not one who blows smoke. I only witnessed those size groups twice, and if you found them, that would be the only covey in the area. I suspect it was several coveys that just happened to rendezvous together. Most of the coveys were 30 to 40 birds, and I find that to still be an average size today in the Western United States. I have hunted them in Baja Mexico, California, Oregon, and Idaho. I've also seen them in Nevada, so they are pretty widespread.

The best Valley Quail shooting I know today is in Patagonia, Argentina. The story is they were imported from California to Chile in 1954 when a Chilean decided he wanted to raise them in pens. That didn't work out well, so he turned them loose. They migrated over or around the Andes, even without green cards, to the Argentine side of Patagonia where they are now solidly established and appreciated immigrants. On a red stag hunt at Tipiliuke Ranch, near San Martin de los Andes in Patagonia, my horse nearly stepped on a covey that burst out like a bomb, scaring the horse and me. I barely stayed on the spooked mount, and it was not by skilled horsemanship. I'm not ashamed to say I grabbed the saddle horn. Of course, I recognized quail, and we saw and heard others during the stag hunt. It appeared to me there were significant numbers to support hunting, and I suggested including quail as a way to add an additional venue to the ranch program.

Kevin and Maria José, the superb team who manage the Tipiliuke tourist adventures, took hold of the idea, and it is now a significant part of their program—fishing, stag and boar hunting, and quail shooting. Several good friends accompanied me on stag hunts at Tipiliuke, and several came just for quail and trout. Rob and his father Dave Braach, Col John Linn and Dr. Paul Googe were frequent quail shooters. All wild birds fluctuate in cycles, but it seems to me the California Valley Quail fluctuate less in Patagonia. Not being an animal biologist, my guess is that because they have a constant and continued water supply that doesn't change much from year to year. After hunting at Tipiliuke for a dozen years, we moved further south in Patagonia to an area close to the city of Esquel where two Montana boys, Travis Smith and Rance Rathie, own and manage Patagonia River Guides. Their main business is fishing, but they do some stag and quail hunting. This is near the area where Butch Cassidy and the Sundance Kid raised cattle and sheep after being chased out of the United States and before their deaths in Bolivia.

The Patagonia River Guides operation is professional and run right, down to the smallest details. I give them an A-plus rating, and I'm not an easy grader. Quail hunting has been superb the last six years. Three shooters hunt with two superb guides. We normally hunt for six straight days using only one dog each day but trading out dogs every day. It is hard, rugged hunting, but the success rate has been phenomenal. Fifteen quail per shooter is the limit, giving us a total of 45 birds per day. We have seldom missed bringing in a full bag. Some very close friends and hunting partners have accompanied me on these hunts. The list includes Max Jungk, Isaias Miciu, Dr Paul Googe, Col John Linn, Joe Kelly, Derek Hotchkiss, and Doug Ward. Erik Search, Zane Kuenzler, were with me on this hunt of May 2022. It is certainly one of my favorite hunts, and I'm most pleased to still be able to physically make this hunt. The young guys don't say anything, but I notice they always go wide or high when one of us needs to, leaving me the easier trail. They are not fooling me, but I thank them.

Hunting in Italy

The dogs were racing around, more like flushers than pointers, noses sniffing the ground like Deutsch Drahthaars (German wirehaired pointers) after a wounded stag. Suddenly, one screeched to a halt, nearly flipping over, but holding a hard point. What did he have? I wondered.

We were on a mission with Dave Senter to help him coach some athletes in Bunker Trap in preparation for the world collegiate championship which was soon to be held in Moscow, Russia. Luciano Rossi was Executive Secretary of the Italian Shooting Federation and had just completed an event center for Olympic trap competitors that had five bunkers (international trap ranges) in a row. It also included a hotel, restaurant, and a swimming pool. It was the ideal setup for training, being situated away from any distractions. Rossi's sons met us in Rome and drove us there where we were received like dignitaries. The event center was in a farming region between Rome and Florence known as the "Green Zone" because of all the green crops. It was just beautiful and reminded me of Bavaria.

After the training session was completed, we were going to stay to compete in the Green Cup Challenge to mark the official opening of this new range. Colonel John Linn was with me, and Dave's friend Pat Laux was with him. Our mutual good friend Ron Hill was also along. It was apparent that Rossi was well connected, which we appreciated. He ruled the area like an Italian prince. Some dignitaries arrived for the match later in the week, Sheik Al Maktoum from the UAE, and my friend Colonel Rajyavardhan Singh Rathore (Chilly), a member of the Indian Parliament, arrived. Several top shooters, including Richard Falls, an Olympic gold medal holder, attended the match.

On one of our training days, Luciano Rossi came by to talk with me. A young man in rough dress who looked to be about 20 years old appeared during our conversation. He stood there quietly, but it was obvious he wanted to speak with Russo. Based on his attire, I took him to be a groundskeeper. He had a brown paper bag that he held out to us—it was bearing "gifts," Rossi told me. The contents were black and ugly looking. To my surprise, the gift was truffles! I had never eaten or even seen truffles before. The young man had gathered them that morning.

That night we were invited to have dinner with Rossi, which consisted of pasta with truffles. The pasta was good, but I could barely taste the truffles that were lightly sprinkled over the pasta. I thought it was kind of a waste and much overrated.

Rossi explained to us over dinner that one of the most efficient ways to harvest truffles was with the help of good scenting dogs. Pigs were once used for the same purpose, but apparently they quickly scarfed down much of the bounty. Rossi told us that there was a very successful truffle hunter in the area who would take us out. John and I were on for that and arranged for a hunt the following afternoon.

The hunter and dog handler picked us up at the hotel. It turned out the hunter was really a huntress. When we arrived at the hunt area, the huntress's husband and daughter met up with us, and we learned they would assist in the excursion. They each had neat-looking mini spades with wood staffs, which appeared to be custom-made and were lightweight for carrying. Their five dogs were the most mixed breeds imaginable, and each one was different. None were English Pointers, for sure.

When the dogs were released, it was pandemonium. They took off in all directions, right and left, up and down the hills. There was no dog discipline that I could see. They just went their own ways back and forth but had to be watched carefully. When they started to dig, we would hustle up to them and dig ourselves or, in some cases, grab the truffles out of their mouths. We would get the truffles, and the dogs would get a little treat that was about the size of a large pill. The dogs liked those pills more than the truffles, so it was a fair deal. However, if you were too slow and the truffle was small, the dog might have gulped it down already.

Many of the truffles, particularly the small ones, were above ground so the dogs could snatch them up quickly. It was a fun bit of entertainment, and I tell my bird shooting friends if they haven't hunted truffles with dogs, they haven't hunted. Of course, that was just joshing. After the hunt, all of us and the dogs piled into the two small Fiats. Then we headed back to our hunter's farm and home.

When we arrived at the farm, I thought the outing was finished, but the huntress asked if we would like a glass of water while she put the dogs up. It was a beautiful summer evening, and we sat on the shaded porch, drank our water, and enjoyed a view of the Italian countryside. Suddenly, our hostess appeared with two trays of toasted bruschetta floating in olive oil and heaped with truffles. Now I could really taste the truffles. They were strong and earthy, but very good. Our hostess then asked if we would like some wine, a silly question in our case. I thought perhaps a glass would be offered, but she came back with a very large plastic pitcher and motioned for John to come with her to get the wine. It came straight out of the barrel! We finished that pitcher, and it's a good thing we didn't have our car. I don't recall leaving, but I do know our host and driver had to wake both of us when she got us back to the hotel. Hunt truffles if you get the chance. If you eat truffles, you might want to forget that a hound may have had them in his jaws.

Driven Bird Shoots

As the name implies, birds are driven (chased) by people referred to as beaters. The beaters use noisemakers and flags to drive the birds toward a line of shooters, sometimes called a team. This requires a considerable number of people: beaters to drive the birds, loaders to assist the shooters, and in Spain, a secretary who is also assisting the shooter. A Spanish line of eight shooters would then require 16 loaders *(cargadors)* and secretaries *(secretarios)*, plus two or three others to manage the line. Add to that the five or six vehicle drivers needed to move the team from lodging to the shooting field and sometimes from one field to another. The beaters might number 60. Dogs are used to assist in recovery of downed birds, which require dog handlers. Some waiters would be necessary to serve drinks and food at a mid-shoot break called a *tapa* in Spain or elevenses in England. The number required to conduct a proper shoot could be 100, which does not include the number of managers, butlers, waiters, maids, and chefs required at the finca (estate), castle, or fine Spanish home where shooters are hosted. Added to the above is the cost of birds, which are raised or cared for all year by gamekeepers. The value of the shooting areas and the *finca* or castle must be considered as another cost element.

They say it is the sport of kings, and some say you must be a king to afford it. I believe both are correct.

In 1984, I was the Assistant Chief of Staff for Personnel in the Air Force Electronic Security Command (ESC). It is no secret that ESC was the Air Force electronic leg for the National Security Agency (NSA). The deputy commander of ESC, Brig Gen Regis Urschler, was making an assistance visit to our units in England and asked me to accompany him to handle the personnel requirements. Our command chaplain learned of the trip and told me to be sure to contact SSgt John Allgood, who was a hunter. That was the beginning of a 46-year friendship. SSgt Allgood was not only a hunter, but he was also the RAF Chicksands Air Base gamekeeper. Some would say "fox in the hen house," and I would not argue. Being the gamekeeper, John bought and raised pheasants. That brought him in contact with all the local gamekeepers, and he was readily accepted in their circles. Of course, John married a sweet English lady, Janet, and that did not hurt his standing. Shooting driven birds is a high-society affair. I say "shooting" because the word "hunting" in England describes foxhunting on horseback and with foxhounds.

Commanding officers at RAF Chicksands Air Base were often invited by the local gentry to these driven shoots. John was the resident expert. He helped fit out the commander with correct shooting clothes and advised him of proper etiquette. As often happens, the commander would be occupied with government business, and John was always ready and qualified to fill in as the commander's representative. As such, he got to know the Lords and the Ladies of the Manor.

When I first met John, he took me to meet his friend Mr. C.H. (Charlie) Bone, the owner of Barhams Sporting Goods in the village of Hitchin. After introductions and some chatter, Charlie asked me what gun I was shooting. When he learned I did not bring a shotgun and was borrowing from John, he insisted on loaning me his personal gun. It was arguably the best Spanish sidelock, a Garbi. Charlie said, "Take the gun and kill some birds." I did as directed. What a wonderful and generous gesture to a visitor he had just met. Of course, I suspect it was more for John than me. Charlie and I still correspond to this day. Later that day, John and I went on a bang—a small bird shoot for doves and pigeons. After shooting, we went around and met several of his gamekeeper friends: Brian Mann, who was gamekeeper at Hexton Estate, Alan Fletcher, who was gamekeeper of Parish Farms with Steve Deere as underkeeper.

It was on a subsequent trip that John Introduced me to another gamekeeper friend, George Oliver. He was gamekeeper for Home Farm Wrest Park, owned by Tony Burton. George was quite a character, straight out of Central Casting. He claimed he only had two jobs in his whole life— one was the army, and the other was gamekeeper. Obviously, it worked for him as Queen Elizabeth II presented him with his 50 Years Gamekeeper Service Award at England's 1989 Game Fair. George loved to have us come by and chat in the evenings, and he always offered up a bit of scotch. The problem was he gave it to you in a water glass that was filled to the top—generous, but too much for me. Much as I enjoyed listening to George, I struggled getting through those evenings and usually paid a price the next morning.

Estates normally had a last shoot of the season (that was long before all the syndicate and commercial shoots) called the Keepers Day Shoot. The gamekeeper still ran the show, but he also invited the guests, who were normally other gamekeepers, beaters, or pickers-up. It was a time to shoot all the remaining pheasants and partridge that had been raised and put out early in the year to strengthen up and become good flyers for the scheduled estate shoots. That meant cleaning up a lot of the hens in addition to the cocks, which made for plenty of shooting. George honored me by inviting me to his Gamekeepers' Shoot. It was quite an affair with the gamekeepers all dressed to the nines. In fact, on most of the driven shoots, the best properly dressed person is the gamekeeper. The poorest dressed is often the owner. It was a marvelous shoot, and I met the owner, Tony Burton, who invited me to come back on one of his shoots the following year. You can bet I did that. Home Farm-Wrest Park had once been shooting grounds for the famous Lord Ripon. He was considered the best shot in the great shooting parties during the reigns of Queen Victoria, King Edward VII, and King George V when shooting was a major part of high society. He lived from 1852 to 1923. It is reported he died at the end of a hunt after he killed a snipe on his last shot. Not a bad time to die.

I was visiting John one year when a farmer asked him to come over and give the wood pigeons a go that were harassing his field of brussels sprouts. Pigeons are not good for brussels sprouts. They stand on one, eating on another one, while defecating on a third one. We put up a blind and put out some decoys in the early morning of a very cold icy day. Ice was actually on top of the snow. After freezing our tails off for a couple of hours, we decided to call it quits and head for a pub to warm up. England is full of public footpaths with rights of way that date back centuries. These footpaths cut between farms, and lots and are often bordered by a hedge or stone wall. We gathered up all our decoys, gear, the few pigeons we had knocked off, and our shotguns before starting a hike back on the public trail that led to the paved street, slipping on ice all the way. When we reached the road, we put the gear and pigeons down and set two shotguns against the rock wall while we recovered the car. It was freezing with a cold wind as we loaded our decoys, blind, ammo, and the dead pigeons. We packed quickly and jumped into the car. The heater was going full bore as we headed for a pub to get some lifesaving hot soup and normal room-temperature English beer.

The sun had come out and the wind decreased. It was quite comfortable in the pub, where we were warm and content looking out the window at the beautiful countryside, when suddenly, the light bulb came on. "You did put the guns in the car, didn't you?" Neither one of us could remember doing that. We rushed out to the car, but no guns were found. We dashed down the road as fast as John's little car could go, squealing tires on every curve until we reached the public trail. There they were: two shotguns leaning against the rock wall on the footpath that crossed a public road. How many cars had passed that spot, or did someone strolling along the footpath in the sunlight pass by? We'll never know.

By the way, John did have an Air Force job. He was a Morse code expert, keeping tabs on the Evil Empire. His claim to fame was that he was one of the first to detect the Russian invasion of Afghanistan. After ten years in England, John had the bad manners of returning to the States in 1985, which cut off my shooting in England. Seemed like a poor way to treat a friend—maybe he owes me a hunt or two.

Many years later, in 2014, Scott Coby the younger, the eldest son of my friend Scott Coby, invited me to join him along with his family and friends on a driven red grouse shoot. Scott the elder had joined me in Germany when he was a new second lieutenant. He and his new bride Francine had come to one of my trap shoots at Ramstein Air Force Base. Both were shooters, but Scott was a superb shot and could beat me most any time with the shotgun. He was a strong competitor and an excellent team member. We partnered up on many hunter-style shooting competitions. And we won them. When Scott completed his military obligation, he returned to the corporate and finance world. Loretta and I visited him at his home in Greenwich, Connecticut, in 1976 and he introduced me to the Campfire Club. In earlier days, it was Teddy Roosevelt's hangout. Scott also introduced me to pigeon shooting at the Philadelphia Gun Club. True or not, members claim it to be the oldest, continuously operating gun club in United States. They only shoot pigeons.

Scott and Francine have a farm in upstate New York at Keene, near Lake Placid. They held a magnificent get-together each year over the Columbus Day weekend for hunting grouse and woodcock, as well as shooting rifle and shotgun matches. It was mostly a couples gathering, and everyone shot in the shotgun match whether they were an accomplished shooter or not. Scott assigned handicaps to the part-time or beginning shooters, which made it a very fun but still competitive event. I often won the rifle portion that was called the Adirondack World Championship—just for fun, of course. Rifles had to be patented before 1900 until Scott bought a 1903 Springfield, and suddenly the rules changed to rifles patented on or before 1903. It was always an enjoyable weekend. Sometimes we got a grouse or two and maybe a timberdoodle. Scott's kids were there a couple of times, but they were still in middle school, and I didn't pay much attention to them. They must have listened to our stories because a few years later, I got a call out of the blue from Scott the younger who was working in London. He wanted to go on a trip with me and asked if he could bring a couple of his English buddies. I said "sure," and they signed on to join my group in Argentina. They arrived at midnight, a day and a half late, having been in travel mode for three days, missing planes in Spain and Argentina. My driver picked them up at the airport for delivery to the hunting lodge. He had loaded a cooler of beer for a group coming the next day. I will not say my guys arrived drunk, but they were feeling no pain when I ushered them to bed. I had to pay the driver extra for the beer that disappeared from his now-empty cooler. They turned out to be great troopers, fully accepted by my group, and we all had a marvelous time together.

Fast-forward another six or eight years and again I get a call from London. It was Scott the younger putting together a driven grouse shoot, and he invited me to join them (his team) and stay with him and his beautiful wife Anne-Laure at their home. I flew over the pond, and we had a wonderful time in London. We even went to the theater to see the production War Horse. We also visited a sporting range for simulated red grouse shooting.

Scott's father-in-law, Maurice de Preux, came from Switzerland to join the hunt. He had been a private banker and after retirement was elected president of the Bank of Switzerland, even after announcing he did not want the job. Now he was retired again, and the two of us had a most enjoyable afternoon visiting pubs and settling the world's problems. The others who joined Scott's team were his younger brother, Laird, who was also working in London and his father, Scott the elder, who also flew in from the States. And then, the two young guys who had joined Scott in his first trip to Argentina showed up, Hugh Crossley and Andrew Bessemer Clark. It was a fine group for certain.

We flew to heather country in the north of England. When I say the north, I mean nearly on the border of Scotland. I walked on Hadrian's Wall. Our destination was the Knarsdale Estate west of Newcastle. We stayed in Knarsdale Hall, an elegant manor house. It was in September but already quite cool. The morning started out brisk, with a damp heavy fog over the heather. Our heavy coats were quite comfortable. Soon the fog cleared, and the action commenced. The shooters are located in butts, (pits in the ground or rocked enclosures) which are shoulder-deep, keeping shooters at a low profile from the incoming birds. They come high, low, left, or right. Some hug the terrain and come at eye level. Shooting is fast and challenging. The shooter can take birds in front, behind, and safe shots on the right or left. I like it in part because of the many different angles and elevations that grouse present. Pheasant shooting can be fun, and it is not my intent to "break anyone's rice bowl," but here is how one person described the difference. I quote from the May 2017 National Geographic: "Unlike a pheasant, which flies straight and high and presents a fat complacent target, the red grouse—*Lagopus lagopus*—flies fast and low. Like a feathered dart on an erratic trajectory." It is just more exciting for me. It is pure fun, I must admit. The field lunch, served in an attractive modern cabin with a large landing, started with champagne and oysters on the half shell followed by all manner of exquisite gastronomical delights.

It was outdone only by the magnificent dinner served that evening in a dining room under a beautiful chandelier. Grouse are my favorite—a sport for kings.

We had another fine shooting experience in Ireland where I took a team of eight guns and their wives to shoot at the renowned Humewood Castle, owned by Renata Coleman and operated by her able partner, Alex Brant, possibly the world's most widely experienced bird hunter. They specialized in flighted ducks and driven pheasants. The pheasants were more to my liking, but they were famous for the ducks. The castle was run flawlessly with two butlers and a full staff. They had a French chef who prepared the best soup I have ever enjoyed. It was so good one hardly needed the rest of his magnificent dinners. We had dinner each night in a different dining room in the castle, and all were spectacular. One dining room had a fireplace so large a man could actually have walked into it if it had not been ablaze. The table, when set with four or five cut Waterford crystal glasses at each plate, combined with the huge crystal chandelier, made the whole room sparkle. This was to be a black-tie dinner each evening. Horror of horrors—when unpacking my suitcase on arrival no tuxedo was to be found. I had everything else: the tie, the shirt, the cufflinks, but no tux. I could hardly believe it. I am a careful and meticulous packer. How could I have missed my tuxedo? I could still see it hanging on the doorknob in our spare bedroom. And that's where it stayed. Now what to do?

  I was the trip leader and needed to be as correct as in Downton Abbey. I called the butler and asked him to rent me a tuxedo very discreetly and have it to me by that evening. Someone found out and spilled the beans, so the guys had the butler bring me pants with leg lengths that would fit a giant or someone on stilts. It was a job, but I finally got them tucked up enough underneath and pinned all the way around to make them work. Of course, the crowd showed no grace and burst out laughing as Loretta and I walked down the stairs to join them for cocktails. What friends.

  Those on the trip with us were Dr. Paul and Cindy Googe, John and Pam Kern, Dr. Larry and Judy Trick, Mr. and Mrs. Harold Snyder, Kinsey and Mona Robinson, Laura Revitz, and Bob and Barbara Ziegler. The ladies were just gorgeous in their gowns, but it requires a lot more luggage for different gowns each night. Nowadays we stick with just coat and tie. Life is easier.

  Red-legged partridge are also at the top of my list for driven shoots. Red-legged partridge fly much like a red grouse, sometimes close, sometimes at mid-level, sometimes at eye-level, offering shots at different angles, making for a great variety and often very tricky shots. Additionally, like red grouse, the shooter shoots grouse in front, behind, and safe shots right or left. Groups of birds barreling at high speed directly at you creates considerable excitement. Two of the best shoots in Spain are Las Golondrinas, owned by Fernando Bustamante and operated by his son Jacobo, and the other is Pinos Altos where Fernando Saiz and Beltran Cotoner orchestrate the event. They are real productions with good shooting, wonderful lunches, mid-shoot tapas breaks, and memorable dinners with gorgeous china and delicious food. The best paella in the world has been served at both places for lunch. They have a high percentage of wild birds, supplemented by release birds put out months in advance of the shoot to mix in with wild birds and become strong flyers. Releasing birds directly from the crates just before a shoot is not allowed in their operations.

The list of luminaries at these shoots is impressive, but it is considered poor form to release the names of clients. Nevertheless, after the second or third shoot, I saw pictures of King Juan Carlos shooting at both Pinos Altos and Las Golondrinas. I also know that General Norman Schwarzkopf shot at Pinos Altos. My first encounter with Gen Schwarzkopf was when he was still a three-star general visiting the Interservice Rifle Matches at Quantico, but I knew him later from Safari Club conventions. He was an inspirational speaker and often spoke at the Veterans Breakfast.

I always went up and congratulated him after his presentation, and he received me enthusiastically, talking about past military experiences. He was also a member of the Grand National Quail Club. It would make you proud to be an American if you read President George H.W. Bush's letter thanking Fernando Saiz and his wife Koki for their wonderful hospitality during his visit to their shoot and historical home. I won't quote the whole letter, but here is the last sentence, "I am not sure I will make it to the next Safari convention, but the best reason for my going would be to give you both a warm abrazo." A fine letter from the fine gentlemen. It says a lot about his character. It has been most enjoyable to introduce many of my best friends to both these shoots.

Other good shoots and hunts are found in South America. In my estimation, wild pigeon shooting is best in Paraguay with Erik von Sneidern, and mixed bag hunting being best in Uruguay with Mercedes and Bernardo Barron, owners of the Uruguay Lodge.

They have beautiful English Setters. Dove shooting is found in nearly guaranteed large volumes in Bolivia and Argentina.

We booked Bolivia in 2004 with Erland von Sneidern, who was considered the best outfitter, and it was good, but sadly, he had passed away before our trip. His charming wife, Liliana, continued until the government of Evo Morales made it too hard to conduct business. A short history of the von Sneidern family influence is merited. Kjell von Sneidern Johansson emigrated from Norway. He was an ornithologist and a university professor. He brought people to Colombia for duck hunting and to collect bird specimens for museums in the 1950s. His son Erland started sponsoring Colombian dove hunts around 1975 and is credited with being first in bringing dove hunters to South America. He moved his dove operation to Bolivia in 1998.

Our group numbered 12 and was mostly Lee Seemann's gang from Omaha and Minnesota: Bill Zutavern, Glen Haley, and Chuck Van Heel, Tim McGill, and a couple of others. My friends Gen J. B. Davis and Major Don Berry rounded out the group. Upon arriving in Santa Cruz, we were directed to a small bus for transport to the Lodge. The passenger door on the bus was about a quarter of the way back from the front. Our gang piled in and moved toward the rear where the beer was located. A young man was sitting toward the front behind the driver, and I had heard him say something in English when he was loading the luggage. I moved up to the front and asked where he learned English. His answer was he went to the American school in Colombia. Then I asked if he was still in school, and his answer was yes, he was in college, so I asked where. He answered in the United States, and his answer to my next question of where in the United States, was Texas. Of course, I asked where in Texas and he said San Antonio. The last question was, "What school?" He puffed out his chest a bit and answered, "Trinity."

It happens that my home is only two blocks from Trinity. A very small world indeed. It turned out he was the son of Erland von Sneidern. He had finished his freshman year, and his father had just recently died. Trinity requires all students to live on campus for the first three years, so I made it a point to take him out to dinner at least once every quarter. He is a clay pigeon shooter and has a wicked sense of humor. His name is Kjell, named after his grandfather. I became quite fond of him. Kjell is now in Colombia, but we correspond regularly. He recently married and is planning is to bring his new bride to meet us in the spring.

For my money, nothing touches Argentina in the dove arena. Not just because of the consistent good shooting, but because of the numerous outstanding lodges with the best steaks and Italian food in the world, along with fine wines. How can you do better than that? The Argentine people receive us well, and the money exchange rate makes visiting quite affordable. Buenos Aires is chock full of good hotels, entertaining tango shows, and outstanding restaurants.

Combining shooting with a side trip to the Mendoza wine country, Patagonia, or the world's greatest waterfalls of Iguazu can make a very enjoyable holiday. I will talk more about their hunts in my chapter on Argentina.

Women Shooters and Hunters

I've had the great pleasure of shooting and hunting with a number of fine ladies. I've talked about Kim Rhode in my recollections of rifle shooting. She is the most famous of Olympic shooting ladies whose record of medaling in six Olympics is unlikely to be broken.

Air Force Lieutenant Gail Liberty was on the Air Force pistol team and dominated women's pistol shooting. She competed in matches across the country from coast-to-coast and became well-known. She was the one to beat, and not only did she beat all the ladies, but she also often gave the men a good run for their money. When she won the U.S. Championship at Camp Perry, Ohio, her picture was on the cover of the NRA's *American Rifleman Magazine.* She was an excellent representative of the Air Force, always perfectly dressed, and with a pleasing personality. She was a winner and a champion. But what is the rest of the story? We were shooting in different worlds of rifle and pistol competition in the mid-1960s and did not have a lot of contact, but I got to know her much better later when she was a retired colonel helping with Modern Pentathlon in San Antonio.

In 1991, during a world championship here in San Antonio, three young athletes on the Bulgarian Olympic Pentathlon Team defected. Their chief of mission and coach had to return to Bulgaria empty-handed. The defectors, Velizar Iliev, Dimitar Chinin, and Jerrar Levonian, were invited to hide out at Gail's house. The FBI knew where they were but did not interfere or help. The Bulgarian government, coaches, fellow athletes, and family all pleaded for them to come home. Velizar was a superb athlete and a top pentathlete. Bulgarians were putting their hopes in him to bring their country a gold medal from the 1992 Olympics in Barcelona, and he very well may have. The defectors would not yield to any pressure and gave up their dreams of becoming Olympians. They stayed with Gail for three months, and she helped them learn about our country and how to fit in. Gail jokingly told me she used to buy one loaf of bread a week; then the boys ate one loaf of bread every day. Velizar says she was like a mother to him and the others. She continued to help them in their early days. After Velizar became a U.S. citizen and was eligible to compete for the U.S., he brought home two gold medals from World Cups and a bronze from another World Cup, plus a gold from the Pan-American Games. Representing the U.S. in the 2000 Sydney Olympics, he was the oldest contestant at 39 to compete in modern pentathlon. He may have been past his prime, but he still carried our flag proudly. He became a businessman and valued citizen of San Antonio, where he still devotes time teaching fencing. Gail passed before she could witness the success of her young defectors, but they would've made her proud. And I am proud of her for helping three good young men in distress and cut off from all support. She was a leader and a fine lady.

Joetta Dement came to a trap match in Missoula, Montana, in 1990 with her mother and father. My Air Force team shooters were with me, but I noticed this young redheaded high-school girl not only concentrating on her shooting, but also smart enough to watch the top competitors. Her mother and father were nice folks, and I encouraged them to keep her in shooting. Fast forward 10 years and Joetta had turned into a very competitive trap shooter. She joined the Army in 1993 so she could continue her trap shooting as a member of their trap team. She married a good young Army rifle shooter, Lance Dement, who was arguably the Army's Number One rifle shooter for many years. He not only shot on teams, winning the National Trophy, he also won the Wimbledon Cup. Joetta maneuvered her way well through a pretty much all-male environment. For several years I took young shooters who represented USA Shooting (Olympic) to the Grand National Quail Club (GNQC) for their annual event. This was mainly to show off our Olympic hopefuls, with them putting on some demonstration shooting and coaching with clay target shooting between days of quail hunting. The GNQC is an all- male organization. Ladies are not invited for the hunting, so I was a little apprehensive when I first took her. She won them over and became an absolute favorite. She and Lance came with me several times.

Terry Dewitt (Wetzel) followed her father, Charles Wetzel, into trap shooting. Charlie still runs trap matches at the Fairfield Sportsmen's Association in Cincinnati, Ohio. Terry joined the Army to further her shooting career, and she certainly succeeded. She medaled in three World Cups and represented the United States in the Atlanta Olympics. Today, Terry works for the nationwide Scholastic Shooting Sports Foundation as the coach for international trap. She, like Joetta, managed to work her way successfully through a male-dominated organization to become a top competitor while remaining a first-class lady.

Mona Robinson, wife of my longtime friend Kinsey, is one of my favorite people to have on safari. She is a nurse and, unlike my doctor friends, is sympathetic to my aches and pains. She actually offers me help while most of my doctor friends simply say, "You'll be fine." But she is also a killer and attacks hunting with passion. I shouldn't say killer because she is actually a fine huntress and only takes the proper animal she is after in a fair chase hunt. Her collection of big game and dangerous game species now numbers 46. She recently completed a safari where she collected a monster Cape Buffalo. She has hunted Africa 14 times; Europe 6 times; Argentina 28 times; Paraguay and Nicaragua twice; and New Zealand, Canada, and Alaska 12 times. She doesn't just do the easy, comfortable hunts. She shot King Eiders out of a 14-foot zodiac on the swells of the Bering Sea during the frozen winter. She's been charged by leopard in Zambia and holds the Number Two cape kudu taken by a woman. She has also collected many species of ducks, eiders, and geese in addition to many upland game birds. Mona is dedicated. She is always up, and I have hunted with her in Europe, South America, Africa, and New Zealand. Our next trip together is scheduled for shooting wild red-legged partridge in the Atlas Mountains of Morocco. Mona is always fun to be with.

Laura Revitz was the wife of my good friend and bunker shooter George Revitz. Laura is a good clay target shooter, particularly in skeet, but that is not her choice in shooting. She is a passionate live pigeon shooter, and in addition to shooting in the States, she has competed in Spain, Argentina, Brazil, Italy, Morocco, Mexico, Portugal, and Egypt. She has won many matches to include two World Cups and the European Championship. In 1992, she called me in the Pentagon from Egypt to tell me she had just won the World Championship. I asked what her score was, and she said, "I don't know. I have five more to go, but I have won!" She is in the American Pigeon Shooters Hall of Fame. Laura and George introduced me to live pigeon shooting in Pennsylvania in 1979 at the famous Higgins shoot, and I became a mini-addict, but the European tour takes time and money of which I had neither. George was not a hunter, so Laura and I became hunting companions. Laura is a good hunter and doesn't complain about rough conditions. We had some mighty cold days shooting in the snow. She has shot red-legged partridge with me in Spain several times. On one shoot, we were on the shooting line at our pegs when a hard rain blew in. All the other shooters rushed for the cars for cover. Game was already flushing in front of the drivers and heading our way. The two of us shot through that rainstorm alone. Although soaking wet, we had a marvelous shoot and stuck our tongues out at the wimps peering through the windows and windshield of their retreat vehicles.

Laura has a large array of friends and also shooting acquaintances in Spain. While visiting Madrid en route to a partridge hunt, Laura suggested the two of us go for dinner at Tiro Somontes, the most prestigious live pigeon shooting club in the world. Like most top European gun clubs, they have a full bar and fine kitchen. Lunch and dinner are served on white tablecloths with fine china and silver and, of course, ties are the norm even when shooting. King Juan Carlos is a member as is Laura. She hadn't been there for a while, and the staff didn't recognize her until she mentioned Rambo, her miniature long-haired dachshund and they immediately knew who she was. That lovable little dog traveled with her everywhere and made many friends. The club members invited us to a small shoot before dinner. We had to borrow guns, but everything was arranged quickly, and we jumped into the match. Unexpectedly, I wound up in a two-way shoot-off for the top spot. Unfortunately, the Spaniard won, but my second place paid for drinks, our entry fee, ammo, and dinner. We still hunt together, and my wife is often with us in the dove field. Laura has introduced me to many interesting people. We have known her for over 40 years and count her as one of our dearest friends. She is a classy lady.

Another lady shooter who must be included in this group is Francis Strodtman-Royer. She grew up in Montana with shooters—her father Dale and her brother Wally Zobell. Wally was on our 1984 Olympic Trap Team. Francis represented the US in Cyprus at the 1995 World Shooting Championship. I was honored to be Chief of Mission for the United States at that event.

Expectations for our team by other nations was not high. Francis paid no attention to that, put her head down and went to work. And, she won! We had other successes but the best was her winning the Women's World Championship. Quite a feat. Many consider it harder to win than an Olympic medal because so many more shooters enter the competition. It was always a pleasure to shoot with Frances and Wally whether in competitions or on their home range in Montana. Her son Dale is also a trap shooter -- a shooting family.

No Good Deed Shall Go Unpunished

No good deed shall go unpunished is a phrase often passed around by cynics, but unfortunately, sometimes it is true. On my last tour in the Pentagon, my duties revolved around the European theater and particularly NATO. Every now and then I would visit the JCS European Divisions staff meetings to check on what was hot news or maybe advise them when my boss visited from NATO. Army Col

Dick Knob was chief of the division, and he had six full colonels meet with him every morning.

One morning, when I was visiting his staff meeting, he asked me if I could help them out just for an hour. Dick was a good guy, and I told him sure, whatever he needed. I ran my own schedule and could do whatever I wanted, so it would be easy for me. He explained he was up to his ears in scheduled briefings and deadlines. The next morning, he was to be visited by a German Lt Col, for what reason he hadn't a clue.

I thought it strange that a Lt Col could get an audience with anyone in JCS, but I gathered up some croissants and figured we'd have a nice coffee hour talking about NATO. The Lt Col showed up looking sharp in his German army uniform and seemed to enjoy the croissants. I think the previous morning he'd been loaded with sugar doughnuts. We went through the niceties, and I told him I'd had wonderful assignments in Germany. At some point in the conversation, I mentioned German hunters had treated me well. That sat him nearly upright in his chair. Then he told me what his mission was about. Apparently, General Klaus Naumann, the Chief of Staff of the German Army, was concerned that U.S. senior general officers' main contacts with Germans seemed to be at Mercedes, BMW, or VW dealerships. He wanted them to meet and associate with more prominent Germans.

This was no ordinary Lt Col I was talking with. His name was Alois Loewenstein, and I found out he was only a reserve Lt Col. His day job was Managing Director for the Bank of Liechtenstein. Later I learned he was Alois-Konstantin, 9th Prince of Loewenstein-Wertheim-Rosenberg. He was looking to connect with some senior American generals who were hunters, and by wild chance ended up in my office. Talk about luck: how'd that happen? He wanted to invite an American general to a drive hunt for Russian boar on his estate. He asked if I could help with that. You bet your bottom dollar I could bring him a four-star. We parted on a happy note, he had completed his mission, and I had won the lotto—again.

Two four-star general friends who I had hunted with were stationed in Europe. It was a no-brainer, and Prince Loewenstein set up the hunt. Gen J.B. Davis was stationed in Belgium and could

Long Shots — Hunting

not arrange his schedule to attend the hunt, but Gen Robert C. Oaks, Commander of U.S. Air Forces in Europe, headquartered at Ramstein Air Force Base, was pleased with the invitation. He had a German hunting license and had already hunted with my friend, the Baron Johannes von Schorlemer. One of my boys, Capt Taishoff, was stationed at Sembach Air Force Base close to Ramstein, and I asked Prince Loewenstein if I could bring a captain along as an observer. He said the general's aide was certainly welcome. I'm not sure he fully understood the captain was not the general's aide, but I saw no need to complicate the issue.

The invitation was for us to arrive Friday for a banquet and an overnight at the Prince's castle about an hour east of Frankfurt. Gen Oakes could not clear his schedule for Friday night, so unfortunately we missed the early camaraderie. We drove up early Saturday morning. Gen Oakes met me and Capt Taishoff at Sembach in his armored Mercedes. He kicked his driver back to the chase car and put Mark and me in the backseat of the Mercedes while he drove. It was raining, but that didn't seem to bother the general. He was a fighter pilot, and we were driving on the autobahn. As you can imagine, the horses weren't spared.

Members of his bodyguard had already surveyed the hunting area and met us upon arrival. They were all in camouflage uniforms, driving a Ford Bronco and weren't hiding their hardware, which was a little embarrassing. Nevertheless, they faded into the background. Guests were being introduced to each other, and a couple of late arrivals were busy getting their rifles ready as were we. Several forest officials, quite senior, obvious from the badges of rank they wore on the shoulders of their loden green overcoats, were also assembling.

The Prince called the group together, and he introduced each hunter by their full title. Five were introduced as prince, and of course we were introduced as general and colonel. That made it six princes and two military for our shooting party of eight. The Prince then gave us the charge or instructions for the hunt. They had had some disease that took out many of the breeding stock, so we were instructed to let the *Keilers* and *Baches* (large males and females) pass as on parole and shoot only *Frischling* and *Überlaufers* (small and medium size). Each

325

forester was assigned to a hunter. My forester spoke little English, but it really wasn't necessary as we both knew what to do. Capt Taishoff came with me but without a rifle so there were three of us that occupied our first shooting station (blind), which was just a few logs stacked up. The forester easily showed me, by pointing, where my field of fire was, which, of course, is vital on the drive hunt, so the hunters don't end up shooting the drivers, dogs, or another hunter. The drivers came through the woods banging their walking sticks against trees and making noises. In this case they also had small brown terrier-looking dogs along with them, yapping. The rain continued but detracted little from the excitement of hearing the hunting horns and the anticipation of seeing Russian boars running through the woods. On the first drive, I shot a *Frischling*, about the size of what you see in the movies being served on a king's dining table. On the second drive, I took a nice *Überlaufer* around 90 pounds in weight.

Lunch was taken in a small field in the middle of the forest with chairs and benches made from rough logs that surrounded a large fire pit that belched high flames even in the mist. Several of the ladies showed up all dressed to the nines in beautiful green hunting clothes, their hunting hats adorned with decorative feathers. No one seemed to mind the heavy mist as we munched on sausages and drank hot *Glühwein* passed around by waiters.

The third and last drive followed lunch, and it was only fair that I turned the rifle, a 30.06 Model 70 Winchester, over to Capt Taishoff. Our shooting station was at the bottom of a fairly steep hill. The constant mist had turned into rain. Even with our heavy coats, we were uncomfortable.

We were sort of hunkered down with coats buttoned to the top and our hats pulled low. It was getting late with visibility fading. We could just faintly hear the dogs yapping in the far distance, and it was evident they were not chasing boars our way. It was quiet, and I figured the hunt was over, but then we heard some movement and saw a single boar coming down the hill to our left. He was about 100 meters out and looked to me as big as a Volkswagen. Mark had his rifle trained on the boar, which I was certain was much too large for our prey. I was watching it through binoculars when the rifle boomed. It startled me, but the forester had given Mark a nod and that was that. The boar went down dead in its tracks. Mark kept the rifle trained on the boar for a couple of minutes just to make sure it didn't get up. We waited in the blind until a hunting horn announced the end of the drive and the hunt. Then we went forward to the now dead-as-a-stump boar.

Hunters often suffer what is known as ground shrinkage, that is, shooting an animal that you think is larger, but upon close examination find it has shrunk considerably. This was not our situation. When we got to the boar, it was apparent it was a real trophy and exactly what the Prince had told us not to shoot. Remember, it was rainy and cold. The forester took out his handkerchief and wiped his forehead. It was not wet from the rain; he was sweating. I was sweating a little myself. How are we going to explain that the captain, who had no invitation to shoot, managed to kill an animal we were charged to protect? Like the Laurel and Hardy movies, "Now you've done it, Stanley." Rather than face the music, I'm thinking maybe we could just get dropped off at a guesthouse and have the bodyguards pick us up. Americans screwing things up at a hunt was not a good thing. A large truck with a covered back and seating benches for the hunters came around to pick us up, and we went on picking up all the hunters. Our forester went another way. When we arrived back at the castle, the Prince met us all as we dismounted from the truck. As I started to apologize and admit we had shot the wrong animal, he said, "No, the forester has already given me his mea culpas for making a wrong call." What a relief.

All the dead Russian boars, 34 in number, were laid out in order of size, called a *Strecke,* on green pine limbs in the courtyard. I noted Mark's was fourth in size. That made me feel a little better. The largest was taken by the Prince himself but only because it had been previously wounded. The drivers, foresters, and hunters assembled in their groups as the hunting bugles sounded the appropriate tune to recognize and respect the game taken. It was a formal ceremony in honor of their Saint Hubertus tradition, an impressive affair with bugles announcing the end of the hunt in a magnificent courtyard with only torches giving light and forming shadows. After the formalities, Prince Alois added a little humor by knighting those who had killed their first boar. That was me. I had hunted Russian boar previously but was never successful. The ceremony consisted of the hunter lying across the boar, and having the Prince swat you across your tail with a sword. Everyone got a big laugh, even the swattee. This was followed with drinks and snacks before departure.

      Gen Oakes is a Mormon and does not drink alcohol, so as a superb host, the Prince immediately offered him tea. When he told the General he drove to work and back every day in Frankfurt an hour away, Gen Oakes wondered if that wasn't quite a drag. Prince Loewenstein answered, "Ah, what can I do? My family has lived here for over 500 years." That told it all. When the Berlin Wall fell, Gen Oakes was invited to a celebration ceremony in Berlin. Among the passengers on his plane flying to the event were Prince Alois Loewenstein and Baron Johannes von Schorlemer. Mission accomplished on all fronts. Not all good deeds are punished.

Argentina

Argentina deserves special notice as it is truly a paradise for bird hunters. I know of no other country that can provide the variety and number of birds found in Argentina, including ducks, doves, pigeons, perdiz, and California Valley Quail. They have some type of bird hunting every month of the year. Like many of us in those days, I simply overlooked the great bird shooting opportunities in South America, and particularly what Argentina had to offer. In the early 1980s, Colombia was a real hotspot for high-volume dove shooting. While shooting box pigeons at the Philadelphia Gun Club in 1981, I was invited to join their group going to Colombia. It was a pretty highfalutin' crowd, good guys, and I wasn't sure I could afford to keep up with them. As they say, "If you have to ask the price, you probably can't afford it." Bad mistake. I missed out on some wonderful shooting that won't be repeated. Bandits and revolutionaries chased out the outfitters and landowners, and the area never recovered from it. Another example of "Do everything you can while you can—you may not have another chance."

Long Shots — Hunting

Argentina came up on my radar just by chance. George Cowden was an attorney from Austin. We met at a corporate sporting clays shoot put on by the law firm where his son, also named George, worked as an attorney. I like them both. The senior George and I shot together a few more times and hit it off well. We were the "old guys" but could hold our own in sporting clays matches. George called me one day and invited me to join him, his best friend, and his three sons for a dove hunt in Argentina. Being ignorant about the excellent bird shooting in Argentina, I turned him down. When I thought it over, I recognized it was quite a compliment for him to invite me on a hunt with his three sons. Turnabout was quickly completed, and the rest is history. Twenty-eight years and more than 100 Argentine shoots and hunts later, I'm still going to Argentina. I was privileged to introduce many of my friends to the joys of shooting, hunting, and fishing in Argentina. Often, I'd have several groups, one after another, and I would stay in Argentina for a month or two at a time. Some friends who brought several groups were: John Allgood, Paul Facchima, Capt Carl Kilhoffer, John Groendyke, Kyle Miller, John Odom, Dr. Donald Posner, Lee Seeman, and Mike Larkin along with A. W. Smith and Jacques Pare. The California Indians came twice with 24 strong shooters. That's a serious group of hunters. We started with Luis Sier in what was supposed to be a dove shoot, which turned out to be a perdiz hunt. Luis hosted my friends and me in those early days.

There are good lodges throughout Argentina catering to bird hunters. Some lodges in the north combine dove and duck shooting and some add fishing for Golden Dorado, which I might add is great fun with a fly rod. Two good guys, Diego Guerineau and Felipe Crespo, ran a very successful combination duck and dove operation in the north near Santiago del Estero. We would often bag five or six different duck species on our morning shoots. They also did successful dove hunts at the Lodge San Pedro Viejo. They have both stayed with us in San Antonio many times, and I always enjoy their company. Carlos Sanchez does a superb job combining doves, ducks, and perdiz at his lodge Ombues. He has excellent English Pointers, and I have used them for quail in Patagonia.

Quail hunting can be combined with trout fishing in the beautiful clear rivers and lakes of Patagonia. Our favorite Patagonia location is Tipiliuke near San Martin de Los Andes, managed by Kevin Tiemersma and Maria José Gahan-Tiemersma. They have become close personal friends. They keep Loretta's preferred horse and employ her favorite fishing guides, Adrian Cataldi and Lucas Buxton, both of whom have been our guests in San Antonio. Kevin has a Dutch ancestry. Maria José is from an Italian background. She is lively, and always fun to be around. Kevin is a superb fly caster. He has tutored me for 20 years and is continually disappointed in my lack of talent. I think he's given up, so I will remain at about the C-minus grade level in fly casting. Their three fine sons, Ian, Matthew, and Benji, are all in college or in business. Our favorite quail guide at Tipiliuke, who has stayed in our home, is Adrian Cataldi. He always produces.

Another excellent quail and trout operation is Patagonia River Guides run by Travis Smith and Rance Rathie near Esquel. They and their excellent staff do a superb job. The lodge is top-notch along with the meals and service. They have provided my friends and me the very best California Valley Quail hunting I have ever seen. Trusted and favorite guides are Adolpho Alonso and Alejandro Jones. Adolpho Alonso is the world expert at finding birds. Alejandro also plays guitar and sings.

The big attraction for most Americans is the high-volume dove shooting—*Zenaida Auriculata,* commonly called the Eared Dove. There is no closed season and no limits for dove. They are hunted year-round. The main shooting area is around Córdoba with its preponderance of grain crops produced by its rich soil. The dove population in this area is estimated to be somewhere between 35 and 55 million. The mild weather allows for five or six hatches per year, and unlike our migrating doves in North America, the doves in Argentina stick close to their groceries. They do not migrate. They are considered pests. According to farmers, they cause huge crop decimation, estimated to be as high as 30% of some grain crops.

On one occasion—after several groups of my friends following one after the other and each group shooting high numbers of birds—I had the opportunity to visit with an Argentine wildlife official.

The volume of birds was staggering with my friends shooting from two to four cases of ammo (a case holds 500 shells) per day. We discussed the large number of birds taken, and I asked how he thought it would impact the dove population. His opinion was that it had very little impact, and he was pleased we were there because if we weren't shooting doves, the farmers would be poisoning them. That would then kill the songbirds, ducks, and very possibly the raptors and foxes that either drank the poisoned water or ate the poisoned birds. Were we doing good or doing harm to the dove population? For sure, we were helping the farmers, who should have been paying us for our assistance. As for the doves, I'll leave others to ponder that question.

Two very good lodges in the Córdoba area, Posta del Norte and La Aguada, were owned and operated by Manuel Lainez and Dr. Octavio Crespo. We used their lodges almost exclusively for nearly 10 years when Felipe Crespo and Leonardo Foresti were managers. I still keep in touch with Felipe. His birthday is the same as mine although he is many years younger. He has stayed with us in San Antonio, and we enjoy his company. Manuel was always interesting company at the dinner table. He had been a highly ranked polo player and spent considerable time in England playing polo. He is one of the bluebloods from Buenos Aires and laughingly complains about being the first one in his family ever to have to work. He claimed his family gave all their money away to sorry politicians. Manuel spoke perfect English, and I thought he might have picked it up in England. He told me no, that he learned it from his nanny. Apparently, it was the custom when he grew up for wealthy families to have a nanny from England.

Octavio Crespo is a doctor of law but is too busy farming to practice law. He is also the chairman of the Córdoba Hunters Association. One time, I flew to Atlanta to meet with Octavio and the Governor of Córdoba to discuss the future of bird hunting in Córdoba. It was a productive meeting, and the governor invited me to visit him on my next trip to Argentina. Otavio has become a favorite and is always fun to be around. He and his beautiful wife Carolina have visited us in San Antonio. His grandfather was a senator representing Cordoba province, and his family dates back to the early 1700s in Argentina. He can be quite humorous, and

331

you can be sure to hear how it rains all around his farm but never on his farm. Singing the blues about his farm and cattle reminds me of my Iowa farming family. Octavio lives in Córdoba but built a private country residence for his family that he has converted into a delightful hunting lodge called Rio de Piedras. His son Manuel is an accomplished young man just finishing law school.

Another good lodge was Los Chanares owned by David Perez, a young American from Miami. He had sunflowers and dove blinds within walking distance of the Lodge. Tomas Frontera and his jewel of a wife, Clarita, who is a dynamo at organizing and scheduling, own the La Zenaida Lodge for dove shooting. They also operate other lodges including the Veracruz Lodge for ducks in the northeast near Santa Fe. We've had some excellent duck shooting there and even did a little combo for ducks, perdiz, and doves. We have also shot wild pigeons with Tomas at the Montaraz Lodge. He and his wife are hard workers, and I value their friendship. They have stayed in our home and are welcome anytime.

The David Denies Company owns several good lodges in Argentina and Uruguay. Horacio oversees their lodges in the Córdoba area. Two we have used for dove are Pico Zuro and La Dormida. Joaquin manages the Dormida Lodge and is fun to shoot with. I wish I had his hand-eye coordination. They also book Montaraz for pigeons. Zeke and Alex Hayes (H&H) own and operate several lodges, but the flagship of them all is Guayascate. It is truly over the top. You think you're at the Park Hyatt. It is first class all the way. They have a dozen large bedrooms with huge showers, a dining room that will easily seat 20 guests, and a smaller intimate dining room for eight. Naturally, they have excellent wines and gourmet dinners. After the first day, the bartender knows your drink before you ask for it. They have a beautiful swimming pool, and their indoor Jacuzzi, which is as large as some backyard swimming pools, has piped-in music ranging all the way from classical to Western. The Jacuzzi cooler is chock-full of wine, beers, and even champagne along with stemmed plastic glasses. The shooting is good, and their bird boys, or shooting assistants, are the best of any lodge I have ever used. Many of my friends are repeat customers there every year. H & H also operate the La Portenita Lodge that I like near Jesus Maria. It is smaller with the same H & H quality, managed well by Daniela Borgogno.

Estancia de Charme El Colibri is a hotel for polo players with two polo grounds and nearly 200 horses. It is my preferred lodge for couples and is absolutely elegant. There is a difference between first-class and elegant, I assure you. They have 11 very large bedrooms with couches and overstuffed chairs. Each room has a fireplace. And they all have extra-large bathrooms, each with a massive bathtub and a separate glassed-in shower. The toilets are in a separate room. The 12th room has a full living room, double king-size bedroom, separate dressing room, and an enormous bathroom. The Colibri formal living room, bar, and dining room are all decorated with elegant crystal chandeliers. A less formal dining room is on the beautifully tiled veranda with an outside fireplace for cooler evenings. Their wine cellar is special, and it is a treat to be invited there for tasting fine wine along with superb cheese, prosciutto, and other Argentine delicacies.

I'm told Madonna stayed at El Colibri, arriving by helicopter when she put on a concert in the Córdoba city. Off-duty federal police officers cover their gate and security. The owner is Raul Fenestraz, a Frenchman who lives in both Buenos Aires and France. In addition to polo, he loves to drive racecars and owns other luxury destinations in Europe. Some claim he is difficult to work for, but I suspect he just demands perfection. For some reason we get along very well.

Jackson Owings sent a delightful letter describing dove hunts in Argentina. It is as follows:

Dear Colonel Behrens:

You don't know me, so let me introduce myself. I'm Jackson Owings, Jim's black lab. Other than the obvious, there is one major difference between Jim and me. I love to retrieve, and he loves to shoot. We go together like salt and pepper, Mutt & Jeff, horse & carriage—a perfect fit. Which brings me to the purpose of my letter. Are you horning in on our relationship? If not, who is? I mean, Jim and I love doing marshes together. He shoots, trips, falls, and gets stuck in the mud. I gracefully run and swim to retrieve whatever falls: ducks, marsh hens, or snipe. We do Jamaica Point together—ponds or river, no matter. I'll swim to the far shore to retrieve his crippled birds if necessary or run from the pond clear across the field and then swim the river. Then there's the September dove fields. Man, it is hot, but we go anyhow.

It's the best.

Jim shoots, I retrieve, Jim shoots, I retrieve. Over and again, until I just cannot go anymore. Well, maybe just one more.

Through all of this, what is my reward? Making Jim happy and riding to and from the hunts with my head pressed tightly on his left shoulder. At night I lie at his feet, listening to him brag about me to his friends. In the backyard, we work on tricks—double and triple retrieves, blind retrieves, all those wonderful things.

But now what? He's gone for one lousy week. Gone to some unknown field called Argentina. Dove hunting? Dove hunting in February? Col Behrens, what have you done? All he can talk about is Argentina. The food, better than cookouts in Pollesville? Yes, better than that—filet mignon, beef tenderloin, dove paella, fresh ensalada. Service? The best. You had service on a dove hunt? They served vino blanco, vino rojo, cerveza. What is he talking about? Isn't that just good old beer and wine? What's so great about that?

Forget all those minor things. What he really talks about is millions and millions of doves. He never stops, millions of doves, he shot 200 here, 400 there, 800 this day, over 1,000 another day, almost 3,400 in 4 days. Is that true? He usually doesn't lie. Over and over, he tells his friends about the trip. How you had everything perfectly arranged. No trouble with customs; great connections; Luis, the best outfitter; courteous people; good transportation; nice accommodations; magnificent weather (as if you had anything to do with that) and wonderful fellow hunters.

But Colonel, there's one thing that doesn't make sense. He says there were no other dogs on the trip, but I overheard him talking about the retrievers. He was dove hunting, he had a retriever with him, but there wasn't another dog? Now, I may be a big blockhead, but what kind of fool does he think I am? Retrievers with clickers, retrievers carrying cases of shells, retrievers picking up hundreds of birds. I can't do that, what kind of dog can? His only regret seems to be that he couldn't stay for the night in Buenos Aires. What's that? A Seeing Eye Dog camp?

Jim's already talking about the next trip. Does this mean there is a new dog in his life? I'm desperate, Colonel, maybe pictures would help. Yeah, that's it. At least I'll see what his "retriever" (probably a bitch) looks like. Could you send me some pictures, especially of you know who? I get the paper and check the mail every day.

So, if you'll just drop a dog biscuit in the envelope, I'll get to it first. Just pretend you're sending the pictures to remind Jim of the most perfect trip he has ever been on. He's still so excited, he'll never catch on.

Thanks for everything.

Jim's jealous friend,
Jackson

Before leaving Argentina, I must recognize some of the other people who have made our trips so successful. David Singermann was our first transportation adjunct in Buenos Aires. He was followed by the young Sergio Pizzagalli, the owner of Alchemy, a company specializing in assisting tourists. They meet and greet our folks upon arrival. They also handle hotel reservations, dinners, and internal flights. Additionally, they set up in-countryside trips along with travel to other South American locations. We depend on them 100%, and they do an excellent job. Sergio is a businessman, and he has become a dear and trusted friend.

Laura Bonelli is another vital agent for our needs in Córdoba. Her company is Scouting Sur. We depend on her heavily. Laura speaks five languages and personally escorts our non-shooting ladies on local tours. Laura is in her own category and is irreplaceable and precious. One of her sons, Pedro, has just started in the tourist industry. He has the same crazy gene I have, which causes wanderlust. He left home alone at 19 to travel the world. I like him.

Pedro did return after two years of living, working, and traveling in New Zealand and Australia. His travels took him to Thailand, the Philippines, Vietnam, Singapore, and six other south Asian countries. In addition, he has visited the cities of Paris and Barcelona in Europe. He has also worked in Jackson Hole and Miami. He is working hard to improve his station in life—my kind of guy. Now at 24, he has just completed his first gig as a tour guide. Borrowing his mother's car for transportation, he chauffeured two white-haired gentlemen for a week to explore the country and visit the interesting sites in North Central Argentina. It was a fun trip, and he did an excellent job. His two clients were myself and my friend Col Doug Forsythe.

Two others who have always come to lodges when I have asked them are Marcos Furer and José Cozzani. Marcos is a world-class photographer who has furnished us with beautiful pictures to remember our adventures. He has won prizes for his work and has also published a fine book of photos. José is an excellent silversmith and has assuredly assisted my male friends in making repeated trips by furnishing them beautiful one-of-a- kind silver jewelry to carry home to their wives. José's wife Gabie has also taken photos of our groups. José, his oldest daughter Mariel, and his son Jeremy have all been our house guests and we enjoy their good company. Mariel married one of my favorite boys from Argentina, Isaias Miciu. He is an accomplished wildlife and outdoor photographer. Emiliano Celiz is an acclaimed silversmith from San Martin de los Andes in Patagonia. People from around the world have commissioned his beautiful silver masterpieces. He made beautiful things for me and those in my groups, and we have become personal friends. He has also stayed in my home.

Over the years, I befriended and encouraged three young men from Argentina. Luciano Fontana is a fine young man who first came to my attention as a hotel porter carrying luggage when we stayed at the famous Alvear Palace Hotel in Buenos Aires. He was going to school at nights when he worked days, and days when he worked nights. I was impressed and encouraged him. He earned a BS and later went on to earn a master's degree in Spain. It was gratifying to watch him climb the hotel ladder from porter to front desk to assistant manager. Luciano's first crack at being the overall boss was of a new ultramodern boutique hotel in Buenos Aires, located in the high-end Recoleta district just a couple of blocks from the swanky Alvear Palace Hotel. It was a small hotel, and I remember it as only 25 rooms or so but all very top end. I thought a really fine suit would be in order and told him I wanted to gift him one. The Argentine Peso had recently been devalued and 500 U.S. dollars would buy Ralph Lauren or Prada quality suite in the two-to-three-thousand-dollar range. He was reluctant, again not wanting something for nothing. His hotel was up for evaluation to be listed as one of the best in the boutique world. Of course, evaluators would not only grade the hotel but also the manager. I am pleased to say this hotel made it into their best listing. Luciano is tall and thin and could model for any top-end men's firm. The very rewarding news to me was that he wore the high-quality suit he was gifted during the committee's investigation and interview.

I was invited to visit him in Rio de Janeiro when he was managing the largest hotel on Ipanema Beach. His next move was to become the general manager of the palace-like Sofitel in Montevideo. He treated my shooting group to a marvelous wine tasting on our last trip to Uruguay. His family is growing with a wife and two boys. I am delighted to report he is now the general manager of the Sofitel Dubai—The Obelisk. It is the second largest Sofitel in the world.

Loretta was fishing with a young guide who had great patience and helped her catch fish bigger than those I was catching. Lucas Buxton was a good tennis player who had attended college in the U.S. on the East Coast and then Montana. That is where he fell in love with fly fishing. He's a fishing guide now and very good at what he does. Lucas is mild-mannered, skilled, and able to transfer his knowledge and skill to his fishing clients. We became friends. Married now with two sons, Lucas is making a go of it in Patagonia. We fished with him on an afternoon in May 2022 on the Rio Chimehuin. As normal, Loretta landed four very good trout, all larger than the two I caught, proving once again the guides are all against me.

One evening, I was by myself at the Tipiliuke Lodge in Patagonia. The guides and clients were all out fishing or hunting red stags, and the staff were taking siestas. Two young guys wearing berets showed up, Isaias Miciu and his brother. Isaias was 19 or 20 at the time. They were there to hang a picture, but I had no idea where it was supposed to go. We got to talking and I told them about a fine photographer I knew, Marcos Furer, from the Córdoba area. Isaias's eyes lit up—it seems he'd been with Marcos the week before. He has a keen perception and a wicked sense of humor. I liked him, and we became good friends. He was not college educated but traveled across

Russia and through Europe. As a little adventure, he had sailed from Portugal to Central America in a very small craft. Isaias was already a highly skilled outdoor photographer. It occurred to me that I might help him by taking him on a trip to Kenya for the Serengeti migration to enlarge his portfolio. We did that with six couples; either the man or the wife were good photographers. By the time the safari was finished they all wanted copies of his photos. I don't think he needed my help much. He was picked to do the Beretta clothes catalog. They could have picked anybody in Italy, or Europe, or the world. It is akin to an artist being selected to do our Duck Stamp. Later he was selected to join Shackleton descendants on the hundredth anniversary of that Antarctic adventure. Those photos are spectacular.

He and his wife Mariel now have three children. One of his photographs, taken on our safari together, resides in my living room. Isaias published a beautiful book of photos with his brother Eliseo that illustrates the scenic town of San Martin de los Andes in all four seasons. It reminds me of an Austrian village. I told Isaias if he ever needed help to let me know. Three or four years went by before I got a call from him. He asked if I really meant it when I offered to help. Of course, the answer was yes. I had tried to help him earlier by starting an account for his two boys. It was to be a gift and not a loan. He wasn't receptive so I quit pushing. Now teaming up with the distinguished biologist Javier Urbanski they built a book draft that combined stunning photographs with scientific descriptions and dialogue about trout in their lifecycle.

Unfortunately, they did not have the funds to have it published. It got published and it is a brilliant book entitled *Wild Trout*. I chalked it up as simply a good deed. When I next visited Patagonia he surprised me with a spectacular enlarged photo of a cheetah and her cub taken when he was on safari with me. He also handed me an envelope that contained a check, but not for the amount I had sent him—he added an additional thousand dollars. That's Isaias, insisting on paying his way and wanting nothing for free. Lucas and Isaias have stayed with us in San Antonio, and all three of these young men are married now with children. But they are included in "my guys." I'm proud of them and their accomplishments.

I suppose it is apparent that I have made friends with many of our Argentine outfitters, guides, and agents. In many cases, Loretta and I have become close to their families. One could cynically say it is good for business, and that would be true. But our friendships far transcend business. We are welcome in their homes as they are in ours. My friends in Argentina make me feel as comfortable and safe as I am with friends at home in San Antonio. I treasure them.

African Adventures

People People say they have hunted in Africa, and I wonder what they mean. Africa is the second largest continent, covering 11.6 million square miles with a population of 1.3 billion people. The total size of all the countries in North America is 9.5 million square miles, holding a population of nearly 500 million people. I have been fortunate to have hunted in Kenya, Tanzania, Zimbabwe, Mozambique, South Africa, and Namibia. We have tracked the mountain gorillas in Rwanda, followed the footprints of John Hanning Speke in Uganda searching for the source of the Nile, and taken the Rovos Rail through Botswana. We have visited Cairo in the north and Cape Town 7,210 miles to the south, but there's a whole lot in between. I certainly make no claim to know Africa.

The reader should also understand my many safaris do not qualify me as an expert. Tourist hunters like me can have many safaris and experiences that allow them to tell tales and write books, but they can seldom measure up with the seasoned professional hunter (PH) in understanding the local people, knowing the flora and fauna, perception of animal habits, setting up the blinds, clearing shooting lanes, and dragging the baits properly. The PH does not just hunt. He secures the food, directs the staff, is often the chief mechanic, supervises the camping and preparation of trophies, and maybe he even functions as a psychologist. He takes care of the billion details to make the hunt successful and to give his clients the best safari possible. It takes years of being on the ground and experience in a myriad of situations to become a top PH. Gordon White, my friend and business partner in Expedition Adventures, spent four years on safaris in Zimbabwe, doing everything from entertaining clients at dinner to butchering Cape buffalo and baiting leopards. He has hunted the smallest duiker to buffalo, elephants, lion, and leopards. Yet I have never heard him masquerade as an expert even though I feel he has license to do so.

The safari hunts I have been on have all been appreciated and enjoyable. If the reader reviews my safari listings in the appendix it will be noted that many of my safaris have been in Kenya. There is a reason for this. It was my first, and while others stand out, none can ever compare with my first. It was in the golden age of safaris before permanent camps. The PH would simply reserve a hunting block, often more than 500 square miles in size, and then we simply went out searching for a nice area to camp and put up our tents. Only one outfitter and one local Kenyan were allowed to hunt each block at the same time. I never saw another hunter in any of the blocks we hunted. Sadly, those golden days ended when Kenya outlawed hunting in 1977. A time lost and never to return.

Permanent concessions and fancy camps today have greatly reduced the adventure of safaris in my opinion. Elephants are, of course, the exception, but I do believe the majority of trophies taken today are better than in my early safari days. Concessions allow the PHs to acquire a much more thorough and in-depth knowledge of their hunting areas, as well as the amount and quality of trophy animals. They can better advise their clients on when to take an animal or to wait with the chance of taking a better trophy later in the safari. In my earliest hunts, we took any reasonable trophy we saw. I'm still good with that and have no need to win gold medals. If you've had a fine hunt with a good stalk, taking a good representative trophy should be enough of a reward. Nothing wrong with winning medals, but if that's only what you are there for, I think you have missed the whole point of hunting. Carrying a tape measure in the field would ruin a hunt for me. An inch or so will soon be forgotten, but the memory of a good hunt should last forever.

Going on an African safari was not a longtime goal. I thought of it more the purview of the rich and famous, far out of my price range.

But maybe the thought lingered in the back of my mind. In the 1950s and '60s many popular Hollywood stars were shown in movies and in newsreels on glamorous safaris. Frank Coleman was one of the Air Force premium rifle gunsmiths when I was shooting on the Air Force Rifle Team. He did private work in his home gun shop and made a rifle for Elgin Gates, who was considered to be the leading global hunter in the world. He gave Frank a striking photo of a magnificent kudu bull with him holding the trophy horns. That photo has always remained in my mind's eye. I met Mr. Gates when his kid was shooting on the Army shotgun team. He was low-key for such a celebrated big-game hunter. Coming back from Vietnam, I told myself I was going to experience everything I wanted that I could possibly do. I'd saved a small amount of money in Vietnam and figured maybe a safari could be worked out. My high-school friend Jim Gofourth was a hunter with more experience than I. He had hunted in Alaska. I enlisted Jim as an accomplice, and we plotted a plan of hunting together with one PH, shooting in turns and splitting the cost.

To make it work, we bought a cheap tourist package trip for three weeks on the beach in Malindi, a city just north of Mombasa. It included airfare, hotel, and meals. The entire package cost was considerably less than a normal airline ticket. The flight originated in Switzerland, so Jim flew over and met me where I was stationed in Germany. That gave Jim the opportunity to do some shooting and become familiar with handling my .375-caliber Winchester before the safari and I got familiar with his .30-338 Mauser. We set off for safari in February 1971. On arrival in Kenya, we quickly ditched the tour group after explaining we would show up at the beach hotel in 17 days. I felt the safari cost was rather outrageous at the time. Our outfitter Bateleur Safaris was charging us $110 a day—for two hunters. That was $55 each, and I thought they must have gold-plated toilet seats for that price. How little I knew. The general hunting license, which included numerous plains animals, zebra, and buffalo, was $300. An elephant license cost another $300. Cats were also on special license as was black rhino. There were still over 20,000 black rhinos in Kenya during the early 70s. I had no interest in rhino and it required a 21-day safari which was out of our reach.

We really hit the jackpot with Bateleur Safaris. It was a young company started in 1967, owned and operated by three partners: Joe Cheffings, Peter Davey, and Finn Aagaard. The nucleus was really Finn; he had grown up on a farm in Kenya and was a hunter from his boyhood days. Finn had all the bona fides: hunting experience, knew guns and ammunition, graduated from Egerton Agricultural College, served in the Kenya police reserve during the Mau Mau uprising, and later served in the Kenya Regiment, shooting on the regiment rifle team. Joe and Peter were both from England and became friends while they were working on coffee plantations. Their experience was much more limited. Peter was dating Grete Aagaard which brought the three soon-to-be partners together. The partnership was formed, and Peter married Grete. Peter had come to Kenya for work and maybe for some adventure. He became quite well-known as a wildlife photographer. Some of his photos appeared in top U.S. magazines including a series of six photos of lions taking a buffalo down that appeared in the 1972 August-September issue of *Life* magazine. He smoked a pipe, so his nickname was Kiko, which means pipe in Swahili. I liked Peter but was never on safari with him. More's the pity as he loved to shoot birds and I'm told was a keen fly fisherman. I think we would've hit it off well. With Joe, it was a different story. He told me of going to the basement of their house in England with his mother when sirens sounded announcing a night bombing raid by the Germans. They came up the next morning to find the house was destroyed. He had dreamed of Kenya and wildlife, maybe becoming a game warden. His mother wrote to Colonel Mervyn Cowie, the director of parks in Kenya. He was the founder of Kenya's national parks. She told Col Cowie her 16-year-old son was interested in wildlife and wondered if he could work in one of the Kenya national parks. Col Cowie wrote back that he did not have a vacancy, but if Joe came to Kenya, he would find him a farm job. How many would go to that trouble today? Joe sailed through the Suez Canal looking for adventure in Kenya. He found it.

Being licensed as a professional hunter was not an easy thing in Kenya. The British had instituted a rigorous program of classroom and practical field experiences and even apprenticeships to be credentialed. The apprentices were called "stooges" (learner-hunter). That system continued even after independence in 1962 and was still the norm when I hunted Kenya. Most of the PHs and many game wardens were holdovers from British rule. Shooting from cars was strictly forbidden, and, in fact, one had to be at least 200 yards from a vehicle to fire at game. They had a sense of fairness and high standards and rigidly followed the rules of ethical hunting. It was a pleasure to hunt with them.

They say hunters often fall in love with their first PH, and that's what happened with me. Joe and his wife Simonne were a perfect pair to run safaris. Simonne handled much of the administration and logistics, planned the menus, and secured the food. Additionally, Simonne was active for many years in conservation and worked with the Masai of Koyaki group ranch which borders the Masai Mara National Reserve. Joe and I became fast friends and had many enjoyable days in the bush together.

That first trip to Kenya was in 1971. It was really a different time. Idi Amin had just overthrown the elected government of Uganda on the Kenyan western border. It is estimated more than 300,000 of his countrymen were killed under his regime. He was known as the Butcher of Uganda. He evicted all the Asians (Indians) who were the merchant class, and without trained replacements, the economy collapsed. Refugees streamed into Kenya. The Palestinians gained his assistance in their hijacking of a French airliner, which brought the Israeli commandos to action in Operation Thunderbolt. The commandos led by Lt Col Yonatan Netanyahu, the older brother of Benjamin Netanyahu, carried out what is known as the Entebbe Raid to rescue the airplane hostages. The raid was successful, but Lt Col Netanyahu was killed. After a disastrous war with Tanzania in 1979, Idi Amin fled Uganda. Emperor Haile Selassie, known as the Lion of Judah, was ruling Ethiopia on Kenya's northern border. His dynasty is supposedly traced back to the 13th century, and he was said to be a direct descendant of King David and the Queen of Sheba. He had been Regent since 1916 but became Emperor in 1930 and ruled until 1974. He is credited with abolishing slavery and modernizing Ethiopia and was a Christian of the Ethiopian Orthodox Church. Kenya had a population of about 11 million in 1971; today it is over 50 million. A different time, indeed.

How do you describe the first safari? The proliferation of animals, the sights, the sounds, the smells penetrate your senses. The lions roaring at night, or maybe grunting outside your tent, the crescendo of hyenas on a kill, or maybe the cough of a leopard after he was drinking from the hand-washing bowl on your tent porch are all a part of the magnetism. Even hearing the Muezzin call to prayer in Nairobi from a minaret adds to the awe of East Africa. All these things are intoxicating and define that first safari. You don't invade Kenya, it invades you.

I believe ours was one of Joe's earliest hunting safaris. He was well read and a student of history, particularly East African and World War II, making him excellent company. Our safari was really bare bones by today's standards. We had one Toyota pickup, and three of us, Joe, Jim, and I, rode in the cab, a little tight and awkward since it was a stick shift. The three-person native staff, our cook, a camp helper, and the famous tracker and gun bearer, Kinuno, rode in the pickup bed on a wooden bench with our provisions. We pulled a small trailer with all our other gear—tents, tarps, salt for hides, etc. Our camps consisted of two small tents, one for Joe and one for Jim and me. The staff used canvas to make their shelter. Joe's tent had a large front overhang that served as our dining area. Everything, including bread, was cooked on the coals. We used the truck primarily to move from one area or camp to another. I loved it all.

Jim and I hunted all the plains game, buffalo, and elephant, saw all kinds of game, had thrilling encounters including our own rapid fleeing from a cantankerous rhino, met interesting people, and saw beautiful country. Mbogo (buffalo) were the most stimulating for me, and my first buffalo was the only one that sure enough charged us.

Having shot competitive high-power rifle, including rapid-fire events, I was pretty good with the Model .70 Winchester, a bolt-action rifle, the same as I was now carrying. We had chased buffalo all day and came close twice to getting a shot at a good bull. It was my turn to shoot, and Kinuno, our tracker, had put up the shooting cross sticks twice, but both times the buffalo thundered off before I could

Long Shots — Hunting

get a sure shot. We were discouraged, hot, hungry, and worn out, hiking back toward our camp walking single file, not really hunting but walking quietly when Kinuno suddenly stopped and held out his hand, pointing to the left. We all froze in place, but looking left we could see some black in the brush. It was three buffalo, two standing with the other one in the middle lying down. No words were spoken, but we all crouched down. Joe motioned for me to follow him, and the two of us along with the tracker made a sneak on the buffalo. There wasn't much cover, but Joe and I got within 50 yards behind some low brush. We both had .458s. Joe studied the bulls and then showed me with his three fingers the one in the middle was the one to shoot. Then by pantomime he motioned to stand up and hammer the middle bull, which I promptly did. Immediately after my shot the bull jumped up and Joe fired. The other two bulls disappeared, but the wounded buffalo came charging like a freight train straight for us. I got off two more shots, and Joe got off another shot. For some reason the bull turned slightly to the right, which allowed Kinuno and Jim Gofourth to each get off one shot with .375s. Mbogo was down and out at powder-burn closeness. That's seven shots with big guns, and all but one .375 were well placed. Tell me those buffalo aren't tough critters. It happened too fast to be scared, but afterwards, I felt like it might be nice to sit down and have a cigarette (I didn't even smoke) or a beer.

We were all shooting solids (bullets). That's what was used for buffalo and elephant in those times. Today there are much better bullets for buffalo hunting. Jack Carter's Trophy Bonded and the Barnes X are hybrids and more efficient killers. For those who may not understand what all the shooting was about on this buffalo, Joe explained the rule on taking dangerous game, any of the big five—elephant, lion, buffalo, rhino, and leopard: the PH would follow up the client after the first shot if the animal was not down. It's a good rule for several reasons: first, the safety of the hunters should the animal charge them; second, safety of the PH should he have to follow up a dangerous wounded animal; third is the safety of unsuspecting natives who might encounter the wounded animal, and fourth, the need to put any wounded animal out of misery. Bateleur and most of the top PHs stuck to that rule. If a client's ego was too big to allow the rule, you probably didn't want him with you anyway.

After the safari we went back and joined our tour group in Malindi where I went out for sailfish. Mr. Hans Lindstrom, father of PH Soren Lindstrom, was an older gentleman with a white goatee. He was the fisherman, and we launched from the beach through the surf in a small rough-looking little boat hardly bigger than a normal rowboat. We went out about a mile, and to my utter surprise I actually hooked a sailfish that made two or three beautiful jumps, which ran my fun meter up before I lost it. Still, it counted as a success in my book, and I was pleased for the experience. That first trip was magnificent, and who knew it foretold the events of so many safaris to follow. The report on that first safari was recorded in the following *Rod and Gun* article.

Rod and Gun Magazine
Volume 19 Number 7 July 1971
Kenya Safari
By CPT Dennis Behrens

I have just returned from a very successful and enjoyable Big Game Safari and felt perhaps I could pass encouragement and some of my advice (learned the hard way) to other members of the military community in Europe.

My safari was in Kenya, East Africa, and covered a period of 21 days, 15 of actual hunting. In addition to a general license for the normal plains game and birds, I had a license for two of the big five: elephant and buffalo.

J.A. Gofourth, a longtime friend from California, was my hunting partner. We took the following: sand grouse, Thompson's gazelle, impala, zebra, hartebeest, elephant, buffalo, waterbuck, bushbuck, warthog, gerenuk, eland, and oryx. Any number of most species could have been taken, as it seemed they were unlimited. We limited ourselves on zebra, because they have been very badly poached lately (stores in Nairobi are piled high with zebra skins.) On others, we decided one good specimen each should be the limit. However, game was more plentiful than I had ever imagined.

Getting the right professional hunter and outfitter is the most important aspect of a safari. Costs range from $60 to $200 per day or up, depending on the client's desires. For me, the cost had to be moderate but at no expense to the hunting. This meant I did not care for all the frills but wanted to ensure the outfitter had good equipment. A broken-down scout car can cost you valuable time and money that cannot be made up. This becomes even more important if one is on your package tour vacation for transportation. Be sure that whichever hunter you choose has top-notch equipment. I went with Bateleur Safaris and could not have been more pleased. They have me booked again in December. They are recommended without reservation and I just cannot say enough about their operation. Three young men are partners in this operation. Two specialize in hunting safaris and one is an expert in photo-camping safaris. I have met all three and they are real professionals. Further, they are partial to U.S. military personnel and will even give preference to GIs. It seems they have had a number of good military clients. They are convinced we are in better physical condition and shoot better than our civilian counterparts.

Our first morning was quite an experience. After tea at first light, we started out along the river in the scout car, hoping to come across buffalo tracks, which we could start to follow. From the left, we noticed a large object moving fast—buffalo! After stopping the car, we loaded our rifles—all .458s and .375s, as we were only after big stuff—and started off on foot. After moving cautiously for 10 minutes, we came around a bend in the trail and up over a small rise. There, not 50 yards away from us, were five of the largest elephants I will ever remember. Upon close examination, none appeared to have heavy tusks, and we backed down the trail. Now we made a large half circle around the elephants and again moved in the direction we had seen buffalo. After another 15 minutes of stalking, we heard buffalo—quite a large group of 50 or more—but had not yet seen them, as cover was quite thick. From our left came three huge gray mounds (elephants) leisurely passing between the buffalo and us. Tactfully, we withdrew again. When the gray mounds passed, we again moved into position and continued our stalk very slowly, as buffalo were close at hand. The tracker who was leading suddenly froze. Directly in front of us, approximately 30 yards distant, was a rhino and a big one. Tactful withdrawal would be a great exaggeration. It was more like a Keystone Cops riot! Our white hunter, Joe Cheffings, had already briefed us on the rhino situation in the area and had explained that he had previously had to shoot two rhinos when charged without warning. Since both were shot without licenses. Joe had to do lots of explaining to the Game Department. He certainly wanted to avoid another rhino shootout, and we were in 100% agreement. We had no rhino licenses either. Moving in another wide half circle, we picked up the buffalo spoor. The stalking and taking of buffalo ranks highest in my book. I will save the details for those really interested. In big game hunting, however, we did take one that morning and it certainly gave us a quick moment or two. This was our first morning out and as far as I was concerned, the cost of the trip had been repaid to me that morning.

    Here are some of my recommendations on clothes and equipment. Jim and I both wore khaki shirts and green Levi pants. Neither of us bought any "Hollywood" safari clothes; didn't need them. At times I wished I had a pair of short pants. Jim wore a wide brim Texas-style hat, and I used a fatigue cap. Neither of us would trade, but the tops of my ears suffered from the sun. For boots I recommend very lightweight ankle or short lace-up type. Heavy German-type hunting shoes would certainly be a mistake. A sweater or light coat may be necessary in the mornings (we used four blankets each for sleeping during part of the safari). Two changes of clothes and three sets of underwear are plenty, since the camp boys wash daily. I took an expensive pair of Leitz field glasses and used

Long Shots — Hunting

them only for sightseeing. The white hunter and the tracker could tell game even without their glasses better than I could using mine. Additionally, I had enough trouble trying to be a super sleuth while tracking without carrying glasses that inevitably clanged loudly against some rock, my rifle, or my head. We did a very limited amount of help with the skinning, so each of us carried an adequate skinning knife, but it is not necessary. Joe Cheffings carried none.

Guns: most hunters will agree that they have an obligation to take game by the quickest, most efficient, and most humane method. Therefore, one should go adequately gunned for the animals hunted. Being over-gunned at times makes more sense than being under-gunned at any time. Jim carried a .30-.338 (very similar ballistics to the 300 Winchester Magnum), his pet for many years. We used this rifle very successfully on almost all the plains game, using 180-grain Nosler bullets and a 4-power Bushnell scope. I took a Winchester Model .70, .375 H&H with a 2X7 Red Field scope and used 300-grain Norma bullets, both solids and soft nose. The rifle, scope, and ammo performed well. Jim and I took most of our game by shooting turnabout and generally swapped rifles as the situation demanded. We each carried ammunition for both rifles while we were hunting, but this can be dangerous if the wrong ammo is loaded in a rifle. Most of our game was taken with one shot—not all. I have read authors that claim African game is tougher than American game and considerably harder to kill. Others claim this is nonsense. My hunting partner has hunted all manner of game in North America and feels that African game is very tough indeed. Not being qualified, I will not enter the debate, but I did see animals that did not drop with one shot that I felt certainly would, and we were not under-gunned.

In addition to the two rifles we took with us, I took a 12-gauge Browning over-under which we used only once to shoot 24 sand grouse in about thirty minutes. We had two .458s furnished by Bateleur. They had peep sights and suited both Jim and me well, as we both done considerable target shooting. The apertures were quite large, which enable quick pointing. We sighted in all the rifles before ever firing a shot at game. I took both elephant and buffalo with the .458. Jim took his buffalo with my .375, but afterward we both agreed it was just a little light for that work. We took one buffalo that dropped 20 yards from us after receiving seven shots, .458 and .375, all but one in the chest cavity and shoulders. If I had not seen it, I would have not believed it. Buffalo can be taken with a single well-placed shot, but don't count on it. The value of a big gun and heavy bullets cannot be overstressed; however, it should be noted that much of the plains game can be taken adequately with a .270 or a .30-06. Don't worry about the recoil of the big ones. My .375 weighs more but actually kicks less than my lightweight .308. My partner's .30-338 is much more vicious on recoil than my .375—I will gladly show you color slides of my shoulder attesting to its recoil effects after a day's shooting.

My costs were $300 for round-trip transportation. This included full meals and board at a beach resort near Malindi, and I did use it for five days—quite nice. The 15-day safari (including elephant license) cost $1,500. Shooting of only plains game would be considerably cheaper. Additionally, 7-day safaris are available for plains game and while not as desirable as 15 days, it would certainly be sufficient to see Kenya and get a good selection of game—eight or nine species. Bateleur can arrange this type of safari for two shooters at approximately $500 each. Hunting the big stuff takes lots of time and I recommend sticking with plains game unless 10 days or more are available.

My safari must certainly be considered as one of the experiences of my life. It cost me about the price of a Volkswagen Beetle, and I would not trade the experience for 300 Mercedes. I am taking my wife on the next one, a combination photo and hunting trip in December 1971. If you have the chance to go, don't pass it up.

Long Shots — Hunting

They say if you want to come back to a place before you leave, it's a good sign. Before leaving, I arranged with Joe to bring my wife six months later when I figured I could save enough money for another safari. We did that second safari as a short plains hunt with a longer photo visit. That may have infected Loretta as she has been on many more safaris with me and has led photo safaris on her own. Joe became quite well known and took Marlin Perkins, the producer of *Wild Kingdom,* a documentary show of wild animals in their natural habitats. It was quite a popular TV program for many years. He also took the news commentator Walter Cronkite at a time when he was considered the third most powerful/influential person in the world. The Cincinnati Zoo Society chose Bateleur for their frequent Kenya visits.

I cherish the memories of many Kenya safaris and was exalted by being made an Honorary Associate Member of the East African Professional Hunters Association. John Sutton, managing director of Ker and Downey, along with my friend Joe Cheffings, presented the handsome bronze medallion to me. It now resides proudly in my living room. John Sutton was trained as a PH by Harry Selby (made famous by the author Robert Ruark), who was trained by Philip Percival, who had worked with Frederick Courteney Selous and hunted with President Theodore Roosevelt on his celebrated 1909-10 East African Safari. President Theodore Roosevelt's primary professional hunter was R.J. Cuninghame, but Selous provided the inspiration and was with him along with Percival. So John Sutton traces back to Harry Selby, who traces back to Philip Percival, who traces back to Frederick Selous and President Theodore Roosevelt. Pretty neat history, I would say. John Sutton was a tough character himself. He was badly mauled following up a client's wounded leopard. By the time I knew John he was the chairman of Ker and Downey safaris. The East African Professional Hunters Association (EAPHA) was organized in 1934 at the Norfolk Hotel in Nairobi where I stayed on some of my safaris. In 1977, when hunting was outlawed in Kenya, the East African Professional Hunters Association disbanded. Where did John and Joe come up with the beautiful honorary medallion that they presented me 20 years later? Who knows? It may not be prestigious to become an honorary member

351

of a club that disbanded years previously. Still it was a special honor to receive the award from both my first professional hunter and another PH who can trace his history back to President Roosevelt's safari.

Frederick Courteney Selous started exploring Africa in 1872 when he was just 19. He dreamed of being an African hunter, and he certainly accomplished that by exploring lands that no European had ever traveled. He wrote several books on his adventures and sent African animal species to museums around the world. He hunted in the United States, Alaska, and European countries. An adventurer, for sure. He was killed by a sniper in 1917, fighting the Germans in Tanganyika during World War I at the age of 65. The great game reserve in Tanzania is named in his honor. President Roosevelt said, "He closed his life exactly as such a life ought to be closed, by dying in the battle for his country while rendering her valiant and effective service. Who could wish a better life or a better death, or desire to leave a more honorable heritage to his family and his nation?"

Philip Percival had been inspired by Selous. He hunted with President Roosevelt and later with Ernest Hemingway in 1933, who proclaimed him to be "the best man I ever knew." Philip Percival took English royalty and Hollywood personalities including Gary Cooper on safari. Philip had a sterling reputation and was well respected throughout the professional hunters' community and was especially well known for training other professional hunters. That not only included Harry Selby, but much earlier he trained Syd Downey, who claimed, "Phil Percival was the greatest white hunter of all time." Downey said whenever he got in a tight situation, he asked himself what Phil would do. A pretty good endorsement, I would say.

It was my pleasure, and I was lucky to meet some of Kenya's old-time professional hunters. Brian Nicholson was known for tracking man-eating lions and was at one time the game warden for the Selous Game Reserve. We met in the Amboseli area where I was shooting birds with Joe Cheffings. I didn't know the famous Bill Woodley, who had been a PH and the game warden for Mount Kenya, but I did meet his son Bongo Woodley on Mount Kenya when he was the warden. It was either Finn or Joe who introduced me to their hunting companion Soren Lindstrom before any of them became PHs. I'm told Lindstrom is still hunting in Botswana. John Lawrence had been a Kenya national park warden and later became a co-director of White Hunters Ltd, a premier safari company, with Tony Dyer and Dave Lunan. He was retired but still in Nairobi when I met him in 1994. I used his shotgun on a bird hunt that year. We hunted twice in Danny McCollum's Tanzania camps, and I had the privilege to stay with Danny and his talented wife Joanna at their home in Arusha with a beautiful view of Kilimanjaro. Danny's sister Iris, following Beryl Markham's lead, was a bush pilot. I flew with her, and she admired my cowboy hat, so it quickly became a present. I admired her spunk and skill. Terry Matthews and Robin Hurt were also Kenya professional hunters. Terry lost an eye to a shotgun pellet fired by a client, which ended his professional hunting. He moved on to become a very successful bronze artist in Nairobi. It was always fun to visit his workshop and showroom. Robin Hurt was trained by Ker and Downey and became one of the most successful of modern-day professional hunters, but I have only met him casually at safari club conventions. One I hated to miss was Douglas Tatham Collins. He was still alive when I first went to Kenya and had worked for Bateleur on a couple of safaris. Apparently he was very hard on equipment and people he didn't approve of. His books *A Tear for Somalia* and *Another Tear for Africa* tell of his exciting life. He was godfather to Richard Moller, one of my favorite guides with Bateleur Safaris. Alas, he died before I could meet him. Richard now works for the Tsavo Trust flying a light airplane across the vast Tsavo area to protect wildlife and especially the elephants. He flew in to meet me when I last visited Tsavo West in 2017. Another one I'm sorely disappointed to have missed was Colonel Wilfred Patrick Thesiger, who was living with the Samburu when I was first hunting in Kenya. Educated at Oxford, he came from wealth and privilege. He attended the coronation of Haile Selassie as Emperor of Ethiopia. His book *The Life of My Choice* is a spellbinding record of amazing travel, danger, hardship, accomplishments, and always adventure.

In my earlier safari days, Kenya seemed to be loaded with interesting and accomplished military, hunters, and explorers. One I will tell you about was Ray Mayer. He looked straight out of central casting in his voluminous khaki shorts, knee-length stockings, large

Australian hat, and booming voice. Ray and his wife Helen lived on a hill one mile off the main road between Mombasa and Nairobi. Their farm, which was more of a ranch as they ran cattle, covered over 100,000 acres. From their front porch one had a magnificent view of West Tsavo with elephants and buffalo herds. Joe took me to meet Ray on my first safari, and he lent Jim and me shotguns to shoot sand grouse on his place. When we arrived at his house there was a large puff adder, void of life on their front porch, an uninvited guest. In our case and apparently with almost everyone else, we were invited. They wanted guests to stay a week and were disappointed if they did not—seriously. Ray was actually from Australia, but he had served as a District Commissioner during World War II in Somalia. He had a large painting in his living room of a man wearing a military dress uniform with a Sam Browne belt and riding boots. He told me it was one of his bodyguards in Somalia who had saved his life. In one skirmish on horseback in either Somalia or Abyssinia in World War II they apparently had the upper hand when they heard an Italian light tank or tracked armored car coming, and they knew they had to skedaddle. An Italian officer wearing beautiful boots had been killed. One of Ray's native staff wanted the boots but couldn't pull them off, so he simply took his sword and whacked both legs off at the knee, tied the boots quickly around his neck and retreated at full speed on his horse with the boots leaking blood and flapping as they dashed away. In Douglas Collins' book, *A Tear for Somalia*, he tells of serving as an officer in the Somali Gendarmerie under the able command of District Commissioner Ray Mayer, known as Indo Adde (white eyes). Ray was a mentor and friend to Dougie. Another time, I took my wife to meet Ray and Helen. As soon as we arrived, he said, "Jump in the truck, jump in the truck quickly! The elephants are breaking my concrete water tanks with their drinking and playing in the water." Apparently, they were also trying to put their mtotos (babies) in the tanks. He raced his truck madly down the road, and upon reaching the tanks, he jumped out and began shooting the elephants with his shotgun. Of course, it didn't hurt the elephants, but it scared them off the tanks. His house had no doors, which was a little more than odd considering all the wild animals about. The kitchen was a separate enclosure. In the week before our arrival, a rhino got stuck in the doorway trying to get in the kitchen. I was told he got free after causing some considerable damage to the wall. Later Helen was bitten by a cobra. She survived, and Ray was reported announcing to the world, in the long bar at the New Stanley Hotel, that a cobra had bitten Helen and the cobra died. He had many stories and was fun to be around. I always took him a bottle of cognac as a little visitor's gift, which he seemed to enjoy.

Before leaving remembrances of Kenya, I must speak of the Masai. Joe Cheffings introduced me to a group of Masai who were relatively untouched by civilization, tribesmen who still followed traditional ways and were unspoiled and free. Their history is cloudy, but legend has it that they came from the North following the Great Rift Valley. Their skin is light brown, and they are built lean with a Grecian nose and thin lips, obviously related to the Hamites. From pictures, it appears they are tall, but it is because their physical build is so thin. Men's dress was a single red or purple calico cloth robe tied to one shoulder, and they almost always carry a long-bladed spear and a short sword the size of a machete but sharp on all edges like a Roman stabbing sword. The women wear more colorful robes with bracelets around their wrists and ankles and large flat necklaces made of brightly colored beads. Both men and women stretch their earlobes with ornaments. They project a dignity and pride, nearly aloof, and move with an athlete's grace. Historically, they were warriors who raided and killed their enemies. They believe God gave them cattle, so they can take them back from anyone else. Cattle represent their wealth. The Masai moved to lion hunting with spears when raiding and killing was stopped. Honors on the lion hunt went to the man who threw the spear and the man who grabbed the lion's tail. Their courage and pride were then stolen by laws and so-called civilization when they were barred from lion hunting. How long can they last? Joe treated them with respect, which gave him trust, which in turn allowed me and my friends to visit their village and enter their little rounded huts made of cow dung and clay. Their little villages are called *manyatas* and are encircled by a thorn-bush fence that is enclosed each night after the cattle have been brought in. Because of Joe and because I hunted in the area for over 35 years I was accepted or maybe better described as tolerated. Their *manyata* was located on the site of a large rock outcropping where we often took sundowners. We nearly always took them school supplies with pencils, pads of paper, and soccer balls for the kids. I was allowed to visit a secret camp of boys waiting to be circumcised. Another time I was allowed to attend a wedding. Two Masai that I became close to were Kisham and Anyika. I knew them when they were still kids or *ilamala* (candidates) for circumcision, which is normally performed in mid-teenage years. The mother prepares the boys, who could show no fear or pain during the ceremony. They were circumcision brothers and became my assistants in my many Kenya bird hunts. I watched them as *moran* (warriors) when they were covered with red ochre and fierce face makeup. Finally, I knew them as *ilmoruak* (elders) with wives and children. They remained friends, and a few years back when I was with a group that would not visit this area, Anyika heard where I was and walked 20 miles overnight to be sure and see me. Masai are herders and warriors not known to be good workers, but I found them to the honest, trustworthy, and faithful. It enriched my life to know them.

Who can explain why so many interesting and famous people were in Kenya? Lieutenant Colonel Edward James Corbett's riveting book, *Man-Eaters of Kumaon,* tells his story of hunting man-eating tigers in India, which will keep you nailed to your seat. The Chow garb man-eating tigress had taken 64 human lives before she trapped Col Corbett. I will not give that suspenseful story away here, but it is worth reading.

My high-power rifle friend and mentor, John Harness, was President of the California Rifle and Pistol Association. He was the only person I know who hunted tigers. John mailed me a photo of his huge tiger in 1967 when I was serving in Vietnam. But there is a world of difference between hunting tigers and tracking down man-eaters. Ironically John's note on the back of the photo said, "I sure sleep better since I heard you were in Vietnam. Hurry up and get it over with. I miss you and my dollars." It was six more years before the troops came home. John was on target more than I realized.

Lord Robert Baden-Powell was a highly decorated Lieutenant General, but also the founder of the Boy Scouts. He served in the

Long Shots — Hunting

British Army from 1876 to 1910 and survived some horrific battles in the Second Matabele war of 1896 and the Boer war. It was an American, Russell Burnham, a military scout doing reconnaissance missions, who taught Baden-Powell scouting and woodcraft. Burnham had served in the American West as a military scout. Why are Lt Col Corbett and Lt Gen. Baden-Powell both buried in the cemetery at the little town of Nyeri in the Kenya Highlands? Why and how did they get there? Sadly, an enclosure close to theirs contains the headstones of four young British soldiers killed at the time of the Mau Mau insurgency.

In the early 1970s Loretta and I took the train from Mombasa to Nairobi. Mombasa is the largest seaport of East Africa. The city's most important landmark is Fort Jesus. The fort was built by the Portuguese in 1593 to guard the harbor. It changed hands a few times, but the Portuguese had possession again when the Omani Arabs took control after a 33-month siege and a final battle massacring all the inhabitants in 1698. It is reported that more than 6000 lives were lost in that battle. After that battle the Arabs pretty much retained control of the East Africa coast until the arrival of the British.

The British began building a railroad in 1896 from Mombasa to Port Florence (now Kisumu) on Lake Victoria's shore. It was named the Victoria–Uganda Railway. Nairobi (meaning the place of cold water) was merely a water stop for the train. One of the reasons given for building the railroad was to reduce slavery and increase commerce. The real reason was to expand British influence. Winston Churchill named Uganda as the Pearl of Africa on an earlier visit. Many in the House of Lords objected to the high cost of this endeavor and dubbed it the lunatic express, coming from nowhere, going to nowhere. Of course, it was a major undertaking with the multiple challenging construction problems along with diseases such as sleeping sickness and malaria. The British had already built many railroads in India so Indian coolies were brought in as the labor force. What had not been anticipated were major problems with wildlife. Lieutenant Colonel John Henry Patterson was an engineer, had been raised in India, and knew the language. He was the perfect man to build a needed bridge at the Tsavo River. He arrived just as the lions, later known as the man-eaters of Tsavo, had begun to munch on the Indian workers. It

357

wasn't long before the coolies were terrorized. The lions would often crunch the bones of the victims within hearing distance of the coolies. Col Patterson's repeated efforts to kill the lions were unsuccessful, and the workers began to think of the lions as demons. His book, *The Man-Eaters of Tsavo,* published in 1907 recounts his daring and brave attempts to kill the lions along with the frustration of not being able to protect his workers and the loss of coolies night after night and week after week. It's a a fascinating tale. The foreword of his book was written by none other than Frederick Courteney Selous.

Loretta and I navigated through the hustle and bustle of Mombasa streets with noise from the crowds of people: native Kenyans from different tribes, Indian merchants, Arabs in their long white djellabahs, seamen from Middle and East Asian countries, and Europeans. Businessmen and merchants of many languages came together by speaking Swahili, which combines the indigenous Bantu with Arabic words. We made our way to the train station with guns, ammo, and suitcases. It would be an overnight trip to Nairobi. The train was ancient and reminded me of the photograph of President Theodore Roosevelt and Frederick Courteney Selous sitting on a train engine cattle guard in 1909. That photo can be found in Bartle Bull's excellent chronicle of African adventure titled *Safari.* From the looks of our train, it may have been the same one. It was clean but hard used. We were in first class, which was mostly used by whites; second class was filled with Indians, and most native Kenyans were in third class. Not long after the train left the station, I heard, "ding-dong, ding-dong, ding-dong, ding." Stepping out of our compartment into the aisle, I was confronted by a steward dressed in white uniform with a high-collared coat secured with large brass buttons. He was using a xylophone to announce dinner would be served at three different seatings. He asked us which seating we desired. I answered we would prefer the first seating. His response was no, there were too many children at the first seating. I said, okay, we would take the third seating. He responded that the tables were too messy by then. It was settled. We would take the second seating. Dinner was in a dining car that was beautifully wood paneled with lace curtains and lighted by sconces, a view of past elegance. The tables had a small wooden ridge border around them to keep dishes from sliding off. We found that was necessary as there was nothing smooth about our ride. It was still a grand experience. While having breakfast the next morning, we crossed the Athi Plains, which was nothing less than spectacular, with game teeming in every direction. It made me wonder what it would've been like to cross our prairies on the transcontinental railroad when construction was finished in 1869. Loretta and I later hunted at Javens Ranch on the Athi Plains. Michael Cheffings flew his Gyro copter over the Athi and reported that it still had an abundance of plains game in 2021.

Two other professional hunters who were not from Kenya who I particularly enjoyed were Peter Hathaway Capstick and Tony Sanchez-Arino. Peter was an American who hunted mostly in central Africa. He told stories of his hunts but mostly related the hunts and adventures of many famous persons. Ernest Hemingway was the first in our modern time to successfully market African hunting tales. Following Hemingway would be Robert Ruark. I would put Capstick next in line. Some professional hunters don't give him the credit he deserves, but I think it was mostly jealousy. As Peter told me, he turned ink into gold. I miss those little visits we had at the Safari Club. Tony Sanchez was the key speaker at a gathering of fancy hunters where I was a guest. What a magical and exciting life he led. Tony was from a wealthy and educated high-society family in Spain. He was given an African hunting trip as a school graduation present, and he never went back. His talk was mostly about his early wild hunts before concessions and permanent camps were the mode. I doubt anyone in the audience understood the difference. I had a most enjoyable afternoon visit with him.

We had many trips in Kenya–all with Bateleur Safaris. Why Kenya and why Bateleur? Kenya simply had the most to offer, in my humble experience. Mount Kilimanjaro at 19,341 feet is in Tanzania but just over the border from Kenya, and obviously it sticks out. You are in its shadow when visiting the area around Amboseli. Mount Kenya with its double canopy forest and snowcapped peaks reaches 17,057 feet. The Serengeti migration is best seen at the Masai Mara.

Numerous national parks and game reserves are found throughout the country, with the largest number of animals I have ever seen anywhere. There are beautiful lakes with flamingos and Nile perch in Lake Victoria, gorgeous beaches at Malindi and all along the coast, the Chalbi desert in the north, where I have witnessed nearly biblical scenes of caravans exceeding 200 camels, the Great Rift Valley and the Aberdare forest, and the many large plains areas. Add to that the colorful Masai, their close cousins the Samburu, the Turkana, and a multitude of other different tribes and people. Kenya has it all, and I know of no country that compares to it. In 50 years of traveling around Kenya I always find something new.

    The Bateleur tradition and legacy are carried on by Joe and Simonne's two sons, Michael and Anthony. Being born in Kenya and growing up among all the wildlife, they respect nature in all its forms. Michael was educated in England, and Anthony took his higher learning in Canada, earning a bachelor's degree. They are both naturalists, know and understand the game, and are excellent birders. And they are accomplished photographers. They even tolerate snakes, which is rather amazing considering Anthony's reptile club school friend Emanuel died after his captured puff adder struck him. His mother, Kuki Gallman, authored the best-selling book, *I Dreamed of Africa*. They each have their own company. Michael, the oldest, inherited the Bateleur name, and Anthony chose *On Safari* for his company moniker. One clue to recognize a good outfit is how long they keep their staff. Kinuno, the head tracker, was so good I dubbed him the man who could track wingtips through Manhattan. He stayed on for more than 25 years as a game spotter and all-around camp helper after the big game hunting ended. Musyoka, the head waiter, and Nzioka, the cook, were also employed for over 25 years. In many cases the staff's sons followed their fathers. Muia was the headman for 35 years. That would tell you something about trust and loyalty between employees and employer. Joe told me that when he needed help he simply let the staff find someone who would work well with them. That kept everything in harmony. Most of the staff was from the Kamba tribe. Michael and Anthony are top-notch and do a wonderful job leading photo safaris in Kenya, Tanzania, Rwanda, and Uganda. Their safaris are done in the old-fashioned way of putting up real tents. Until the recent closure of bird shooting in Kenya, Michael led me and my friends on many bird shooting expeditions combined with photo safaris. Both Michael and Anthony are passionate about their work, and you can be assured of a memorable experience with them.

It may surprise the reader to learn that photo safaris are probably my most fun. They are full of surprises and excitement; you never know what you might see. You can get fairly close to cheetahs, and once in a while, a leopard. Lions and elephants are often quite entertaining when their young are playing. You just don't see that when hunting. Michael and Anthony keep their trips as traditional as conditions allow. It has been my privilege to take friends on safari with Bateleur Safari and On Safari. Those safaris range from early days when we concentrated on elephant and buffalo hunting through the days of bird shooting safaris and now to strictly photo. In all those safaris, I've never had a friend voice disappointment. In fact, many have told me it was the best trip of their lives. A couple of ladies even cried when they left. What more can be said?

Some of my friends have enjoyed and appreciated the Kenya trip so much that they made a second trip, taking their children and grandchildren. It is much more than just seeing animals. It is a significant life experience, often leaving a profound effect on the traveler. In that regard, I'm submitting the following essay written by Alexis Hibbs, the granddaughter of my friends Robert and Jeri Herold. I think you will find it quite insightful. She was a high-school freshman at the time.

Alexis Hibbs
English 2/1st hour
Schaeffer
Personal Narrative Essay

Learning a Lesson While on Summer Break

It was early Monday morning in late July. Our large group of 22 had just arrived in Nairobi, Kenya, from a long overnight flight from Amsterdam. The airport was dark, depressing, and scary. Military guards were everywhere carrying their weapons. I was tired, nauseous, and frightened seeing the men and their guns. I stayed close to my parents and followed their directions. I was hoping to leave the airport quickly, but the line at customs was very long and it took two hours to clear.

I began to feel better when we got out of the airport and into the fresh air. There were still military men with guns, but I wasn't as concerned anymore. Our journey was about to begin, and the excitement took over. We met our guides, and they took us to their lorries. They would be our vehicles for the next nine days during our incredible safari.

We headed south from Nairobi toward the Amboseli National Park. I didn't know what to expect, but quickly realized this was nothing like my home. I'd never really thought about what a third world country was like. I'd never had to. I've seen pictures on TV, but honestly didn't give it much thought. I never knew what it was like until I was there. We passed through several small villages where beat-up shacks were also used as businesses. Some homes, if you could call them that, didn't have doors or roofs. People, goats, dogs, trash—everywhere. It was dirty, dusty, depressing.

As we neared the National Park, the scenery changed, and I got more excited. Gone were the villages, replaced by miles and miles of plains of interesting terrain. It didn't take long until we began to see the animals. We first saw giraffes. They were reaching to the top of nearby trees for a snack.

They were adorable. So cute, I named one Molly after a friend. I couldn't wait to tell her. I bet she'll laugh! Animals as far as the eye could see. Elephants, zebra, cheetah, ostrich, lion, leopard —so many animals I was shocked. I'm not sure I'll ever look at the zoo the same way. The trip really was the experience of a lifetime.

But it was a visit to a Masai school during the middle of my trip that left the most lasting impression. It was a Wednesday morning. The sun began rising high in the sky and it started to get warm. We made our way through the wide-open plains with dust devils spinning up all around us. A look off in the horizon showed water, but it was only a mirage. I'd never seen that before; it was really cool. It felt like we were surrounded by water. Far off in the distance I saw a lone tree. And as we approached I realized under that tree was actually a classroom!

We were greeted by three teachers and at least 50 kids ages 3-8. They were lined up sitting on wooden benches. And they were all wearing blue. That was very noticeable, but so were the smiles on their faces. They have very few visitors to their school. You could tell this was a special day—for them and for us. They had prepared several songs for us in English. No matter the age, no matter the size, each child took turns singing loudly and enthusiastically.

Then they turned the tables on us! They asked our group to sing them songs. We happily agreed and sang "I'm a little Teapot" and the "Itsy Bitsy Spider." I've got to admit, we were not as good as the kids. We were off-key and not singing together. But they still clapped and cheered for us.

After that, we headed to a big, dirty, dusty field bordered by rocks placed in the shape of a rectangle. It was where they had recess. We played several games including duck-duck-goose.

That's when it dawned on me—the kids were always smiling and laughing. Not only the kids, but so were the Masai warriors who joined in the fun. We brought school supplies and soccer balls for our visit. The school supplies could wait, the soccer balls were an immediate hit. There was chaos. Five soccer balls flying through the air, off every body part you could imagine.

The smiles, the laughs, the fun! The funniest part was when the warriors played soccer while wearing their machetes.

The kids were infatuated with us and I felt the same way. I wondered why they were so happy when they had so little.

They were fun-loving and carefree. I have much more than they do, yet I'm not always happy. Maybe I could take a lesson from the kids. Maybe we all could take a lesson from them!

We spent nearly two hours at the school and then it was time to leave. Time to resume our safari and eventually head back to the states. I have many wonderful memories, souvenirs, and pictures from our trip. But it was the visit to the school that I'll remember the most. I returned home to my nice home with televisions, refrigerators, cell phones and computers, yet I often think about the kids in Kenya. They have nothing, but they're always so happy. Why is that? I guess they don't know any better. I now try to be more like them. I rely on my friends and family to make life enjoyable. I try not to get wrapped up in technology. I try to find good in everything. It's not always easy, but with a little more practice I may be as good as the Masai kids one day.

My most recent Kenya safari was in 2017 with Anthony in his tented camps in both Tsavo and the Masai Mara. Here is my account from that safari:

"The assassin moved quickly and had cleared 40 yards before the victim knew what was up. The target sprang into action, but alas, it was too late. In less than a minute, his throat was in an iron vise grip. He was doomed the moment he turned his back on the killer. Witnesses, on holiday at a famous location, mostly Europeans but from several nations, had observed the dangerous pair, the killer and most certainly, his brother, lounging in the shade. But it was midday and beginning to warm up, so avoiding the "Mad Dogs and Englishmen in the Noon Day Sun," they had abandoned their howdah for cooler and more accommodating respite.

"We remained watchful as it was clear that these two, although young, were intent on their violent, deadly mission. The attack had been sudden. One moment, the victim was enjoying a leisurely lunch, munching on succulent greens, and then instant terror. It was a like a Corvette—0-60 in three seconds—almost over before it began.

"Saint-Tropez or Copacabana? No, the Masai Mara."

Long Shots — Hunting

Thomson's gazelles (Eudoras Thomsonii) have a wide degree of vision, so with Tommie's back turned straight away, the cheetah launched his deadly attack. Cheetahs are the fastest land animal and reportedly can reach a speed of 70 miles per hour. Top speed for a Tommie is 55. Life on the Mara is beautiful but also deadly. The wheel of life turns once more.

I've had some thrilling times on safari with buffalo and twice following up wounded leopards. Following up wounded big game in Africa is a dangerous business, indeed. It demands more than casual caution. If a PH invites a client to join him in such a task it is not only a sign of accepted competence but also of trust. I'll tell you about two leopards and one memorable buffalo encounter. In 1984 Lt Col Tommy Brown and I were hunting in Zimbabwe along with our wives and my young friend Lieutenant Mark Taishoff. Our PHs were Trevor Landrey and Lou Hallamore. Trevor was in his early 20s but experienced far beyond his age. His father, Don Landrey, was a longtime PH and owned the successful Denda Safari Company. I was told Trevor saw action serving as a teenager with the Selous Scouts, but he never spoke of it. Lou had retired from the Rhodesian Army as a 20-year combat-decorated Regimental Sergeant Major. He had plenty of hunting experience and was a master storyteller. He can keep any camp in stitches. Zimbabwe gained independence in 1980, and, needless to say, neither one of them would be invited to tea by the new government. Lou wrote an excellent book, In the Salt, about his life and giving good practical advice on hunting Africa. We hunted on the Diamond T Ranch in the Matetsi area and stayed in the old ranch house that had been pretty well shot up with bullet holes and damage to all of the farm buildings. The game animals were simply prolific in numbers. Beautiful sable, kudu, and other plains game were abundant along with buffalo. My main quarry was cats.

One day after a very hearty lunch Trevor suggested we try for a cat because a leopard had been sampling one of his beckoning baits. I was shooting a .375 caliber Winchester with a dot reticle scope. Leopards often feed in the late evening when fading light is poor, so I traded my rifle with Lou Hallamore, who was also shooting a .375 but with a heavy crosshair reticle scope. We headed out on a warm, bright sunlit day. I expected a well-concealed blind and was surprised to find our shooting station was behind a log with a few spindly bushes and a couple of dead limbs placed in front of the log. From all I had read about leopard blinds this appeared to be a halfhearted effort. Nevertheless, we set up, and I lay the rifle on the log with the barrel pointed down the shooting lane toward the bait, which was tied to a tree limb 79 yards from our blind. There were three of us: Trevor, his tracker Tapera, and me, behind the log in this abbreviated blind. I was tired from the hard day before, and after the big lunch with the day warming up, I became a bit sleepy. I suspect Trevor was getting little sleep since his vivacious girlfriend Kelly Keill was staying with him. She was a camp favorite and took the ladies on excursion every day. They later married. Trevor and I both laid back and were soon snoozing. Suddenly, I felt Trevor's hand. Then I heard elephants coming our way, which had woken up Tapera, who woke up Trevor, who was now urging me to get up as he started to run back away from the log. I quickly joined him as the elephants started trumpeting. After going 20 or 30 yards the light bulb came on, and I realized I had not grabbed the rifle. Too late now, I kept running, but thinking Lou would kill me or, at a minimum, judge me as a complete incompetent for leaving his rifle. Leonidas would certainly have kicked me out of the 300. We stopped behind some brush about 100 yards out. Apparently, the elephants smelled the leopard or the bait or maybe something else that put them in an uproar. Perhaps they had newborn babies. For whatever reason, they moved on, and 15 minutes later we were back behind the log. To my great relief the rifle was still there.

    With all the commotion I was certain the hunt was finished. It had grown even warmer with the sun still high, so Trevor and I once again stretched out and were soon back to our napping. Suddenly Trevor touched me again, and I knew it had to be the leopard. I rose to the sitting position, and almost immediately the scope's crosshairs found their mark and I squeezed off the shot. Lou had restocked the rifle with very heavy wood, reducing the recoil greatly and I actually saw the leopard take the hit and fall or jump from the tree limb, but he was not upside down; his tail was still on top. Upon hearing the shot our driver brought Trevor's pickup to us. We waited 10 or 15 minutes while Trevor and his tracker searched the area under and around the baited tree with their binoculars. Trevor then told me to get in the back of the pickup with him, and we would drive to the killing zone ready to shoot. Once dangerous game is wounded, all rules of fair chase are out the window. The mission then is to kill the dangerous animal as quickly as possible without anyone being hurt. We drove slowly to the baited tree, which had been cleaned of all underbrush. It was still clean, no sign of the leopard with just a couple specks of blood. Not good. Trevor ordered his tracker to get the shotguns out. They were over and under (O/U) 12-gauge guns. He gave me one, and he took the other. Autos would have been better, but all he had was the two O/U guns. I noticed the tracker putting on more cloths, and both he and Trevor wrapping oil and other car rags around their wrists and throats. Trevor put on a heavy Air Force flight jacket, the kind that were green colored on one side but could be reversed to an orange color on the opposite side for easy spotting in a rescue operation. Trevor also retrieved a Marine Ka-Bar knife from the truck, pulled it out of its sheath, and stuck it loose in his jacket pocket. What I found out later was that both had wounded leopards on them the year before. Trevor told me we would not have time to aim and would have to act instantly and shoot if the leopard came. Certainly, it was pucker time as we set off one slow step at a time following the leopard spoor. There were a lot of tense and suspenseful moments making that follow-up. We were both sweating. The Ruanda and Kivu proverb applies; *Nta wukina n'ingwe* (nobody plays games with a leopard).

  The leopard had made a horseshoe track from the bait to nearly back to the bait before he ran out of gas. My shot had been a little far back and high, missing the heart but taking out both lungs. We were not disappointed with the anticlimax of our stalk. Was the leopard coming back to meet his tormentors? He was a beauty, 7 feet and 1 inch from nose to tail, with not a scratch on his hide. He now rests permanently on my dining room wall. Talk about luck, it was 5 p.m. when we found the leopard dead, still good sunlight and not normal for a leopard to be out hunting. This was the first time I had ever sat for leopard. I'd heard from earlier safaris in Kenya that the normal was about seven safaris before one connected with a leopard. Of course, that was before leopards were shot under lights in some other countries.

The other leopard was wounded by my good friend Paul Facchina, who prides himself on one-shot kills. On four safaris with me for lion, buffalo, hippo, crocodile, elephant, and all manner of plains game, his steady well-directed first shots were true. This leopard was an exception. It happens even to the best of hunters. We were in Zimbabwe on an elephant hunt with PH Dudley Rogers, owner of Tshabezi Safaris. A leopard had been causing trouble near a small village. Paul set out with Dudley probably too late in the afternoon, and the leopard was spotted as the light was fading. In any case, Paul's shot was not fatal.

Tracking leopards can very well be fatal to the pursuers, and tracking at night would be quixotically foolish. We started tracking the next morning after a local native arrived with what he described the night before as leopard dogs. I was hoping for a pack of hounds but was sorely disappointed. His dogs were the typical sorry-looking underfed mongrels found throughout Africa. However, they were not fools as it was apparent early on they realized what was up. Did they smell blood or the leopard's spoor? Who knows what dogs are thinking? They were not about to enter any heavy brush or get far from us humans. We were moving slowly and carefully, keeping in line so no one would get shot in a leopard charge. You might be surprised at the number of PHs who are shot by their clients in a dustup with dangerous game, or even worse, they end up shooting another client. In his book *Another Tear for Africa,* Douglas Collins tells of a horrible shootout in a sudden unsuspected buffalo attack. It is a sad read. In the attack, he shot and killed his beloved brother, who had come from England to see Kenya. Paul and Dudley were carrying Benelli 12-gauge automatics with buckshot loads for the follow-up. That would've been my choice, but the only thing left for me was a .500 Jeffery Mauser that must've weighed 15 pounds. I was worn out carrying that rifle at port arms to be ready for a quick shot. Several times we thought we had the cat located with monkeys squealing or birds chattering, but all were false alarms. We were exhausted after just two hours of intense mental alertness. It was clear the trackers with us had given up, and the dogs now walked in the footprints of their masters.

Dudley said he wanted to try one more area, on the top of a small hill, which meant we could not walk abreast of each other and had to walk one behind the other on the narrow trail leading up the hill. We got to a fairly flat area at the crest of the hill when Dudley abruptly stopped. He was staring ahead and slightly to the left. I was the third man in line, so I stepped to the left for a clear shot if needed. As we went over the scenario later, Dudley revealed that he thought he saw the tip of the leopard's tail in the short grass 50 yards out and started to say so. Either his voice or my stepping to the left provoked the leopard to charge. My sincerest hope is to never see that again. The leopard covered 50 yards before Dudley or Paul could get shotguns to their shoulders. They both fired from the hip. I distinctly saw the front sight of my rifle and leopard come together. And while I don't recall shouldering the rifle, I don't think I could have taken the recoil just in my hands. I suspect Paul and Dudley hit the leopard, but it was a 500-grain bullet from the Jeffery that stopped the show. The leopard was so close that I could touch his dead body with the barrel of my rifle. It happened too fast to be frightening, and we were working only on reflexes. Trust me, you don't want to have that experience. Afterwards, we were a bit shaky but initially elated that no one was hurt, and we had finished off a dangerous wounded animal. Leopards bite and scratch everyone in an attack, and both the bite and scratches from the claws are septic. As we recovered our composure, there was a feeling of sadness in knowing this beautiful animal suffered during the night and had the courage in the end to charge his antagonists.

Paul Facchina is a well-known and respected major construction contractor in the D.C., Maryland, and Virginia triangle. One of his major contracts was repairing and upgrading the Pentagon. When the terrorists attacked on 9/11, Paul had just finished the section they hit. It had not yet been fully occupied because another contractor, charged with conduits and venting, had not completed his tasks. That turned out to be a lifesaver as few people were in the newly upgraded section when the attack occurred. Both President George W. Bush and Secretary of Defense Donald Rumsfeld had met with Paul and charged him to do the demolition of the destruction and rebuild that portion of the Pentagon before September 11 of 2002. Paul initiated the Phoenix Project, named after the mythological Arabian bird that rose from the ashes. His crews of over 1,000 men worked 24-hour days six days a week. Their mantra was, "Let's roll." Paul and his guys were real patriots. They wanted the job done as much as the President wanted it done. The trust of the President and Secretary of Defense was rewarded. Work was completed three weeks ahead of schedule, under time and under budget. It sent a signal to the world and was a strong symbol for the American public. Paul was selected and recorded in the Congressional Record as Contractor of the Year. He was saluted by his arch political enemy Congressman Steny Hoyer. Paul is a delight to have on safari. He accepts hardship and difficulty as they come and never complains.

On the subject of animal charges, it is certainly nothing to be proud of. What it means for the most part is that the hunter has done a poor job in placing his shot and making the desired one-shot kill that true hunters strive for. The famous elephant hunter Capt James Sutherland said, "After all, we are all in the business to kill elephants and the more efficiently and humanely we do it the better—common humanity demands that if we are to kill, we at least do so with maximum dispatch." There are exceptions, and even the best hunter sometimes makes a poor shot, but it's to be hoped that these are few and far between. There are so-called hunters who feel standing up in a charge shows their mettle. That is not what hunting is about. If you want to prove your courage, join our combat troops.

Anyone can tell the story of a perfect hunt—creeping through the mosquito- and tsetse fly infested jungle, noiselessly approaching the dangerous prey at close range, undetected, with the wind just right. Anticipation and tension are high, your clothes are soaked with sweat, and with gnats in your nose and ears (maybe even ants crawling up your legs), the sweaty salt stinging your eyes with the light fast fading. At the last possible moment, (possibly after you have dodged a cobra) using your favorite (one-of-a-kind) custom-made rifle and superb ammo designed especially for the dangerous and vicious beast you have tracked, you aim through dense cover and make a superb one-shot kill. Sundowners are in order. Boring…right?

Well, it doesn't always happen that way anyway—I mean the one-shot kill that all good hunters try for. The first story below was supplied by my friend and PH Finn Aagaard, which is given the reader as an introduction to Cape buffalo. It appeared in *Petersen's Hunting Magazine* in April 1981. The second story was written by his adventurous wife Berit and is from her book *Aagaard's African Adventures,* published by Safari Press. She asked me to write an introduction to her book on Finn's adventures, but at the time I was up to my ears in a project and my typing is just with two fingers. So, I suggested she come by and tape a hunt experience with Finn that I would give orally. She did just that. I'm especially proud that after my account she smiled and said, "Yes, exactly." She then passed me Finn's diary and there it was, laid bare. For all you story-writing hunters out there—be careful what you say—it may be in someone's diary. No one likes to report when things go to pot or attach one's name to a misadventure, but it is what it is and more interesting than making the perfect shot. I thought it would be better for Berit's book. Excuses are for wimps, but I will say this incident happened in 1973 before all the good ammunition we have today—long before Jack Carter's Trophy Bonded or Barns X bullets were introduced. We were strictly shooting solids. By the way, 20 years plus later Finn helped Jack Carter develop his superb Trophy Bonded Bear Claw bullet which is now Federal's Premium Safari Ammunition. I was invited to sit with Finn and Jack at the SHOT Show luncheon when Federal announced they had purchased Jack's superb bullet.

Cape Buffalo—Only a Sort of a Cow
Petersen's Hunting Magazine in April 1981
By Finn Aagaard

Why do you chaps make such a big thing about how dangerous it is to hunt buffalo? I saw hundreds of them in the Mara Park, all they did was stare at us and grunt stupidly as we drove up. Surely, hunting them is about as exciting as shooting a cow in the field?

Ken, a game-control officer in the Kenya Forest Department, looked at his guest quizzically, then grinned and said: "Tell you what, I had to shoot up a herd on one of our plantations last night, and have a runner that I must go and follow up, so why don't you come along and see for yourself?"

An hour later, they were following the blood trail through a cool, damp Mount Kenya forest with chest-high stinging nettles and patches of even thicker young bamboo—hundreds of places for a sick and angry buffalo to hide. There was no encouraging pink, frothy lung blood, just a few dark, dirty-looking splashes and the occasional ominous glob of half-digested grass.

Ken had taken the lead now, the tracker at his heels, the guest close behind. Tension gripped them, a tight band of fear around their chests. They had followed him through dozens of lovely thick ambush spots, they had to come upon him soon. Adrenaline flooded their bloodstream, shocking them with an extraordinary intensity. In the total, timeless concentration, seconds passed like hours. A few slow steps...then stop, look, and listen. A movement caught out of the corner of an eye. The flick of an ear? No, just a bird. Two more slow, careful steps—and then it came. An angry grunt, a bush heaving and swelling, branches shaking violently. Out bursts a huge black shape, wet nose aimed like the muzzle of a double 4-gauge.

The animal is close, too close to get off more than one shot, so make it good. Let him come, wait for exactly the right moment, wait. Finally, split seconds before impact, the bull dropped his nose to present the heavy battering ram of his boss. This was the instant that Ken, who had been through this scores of times, was waiting for. He drove the 500-grain solid bullet straight down between the massive horn bosses and into the brain. As he fired, the buffalo's head hit the muzzle of the .458 and threw it over the man's shoulder, and the falling body knocked Ken off his feet. As he picked himself up and looked around for the rifle, a shaken voice from fifty yards behind stuttered, "K-K-K-Ken, is it always like this?"

Well, of course it is not always like that, not even very often. But the fact that it can be is the reason we hunt buffalo. One does not hunt him for his beautiful trophy—a mounted buffalo head is downright ugly, nor for his impressive size; an old bull eland is just as big. One hunts buffalo for the pure challenge of hunting them, for the quiet satisfaction of proving that one can face fear and not go to pieces, that one can function and do what is necessary when meeting the moment of truth. That is what buffalo hunting is all about; that is why the man who shoots a buffalo from the safety of a hunting car is cheating—he is cheating HIMSELF out of one of the greatest experiences hunting has to offer. I hasten to add that it is not necessary to get yourself charged. Old *nyati* will generally provide all the excitement a sane man could ask for without that.

Aagaard's African Adventures
By Berit Aagaard

Finn's diaries are full of buffalo hunts, even some that were not successful, but in each one the reader nonetheless senses tension and excitement. There are clients who, 30 years later, still relive their memorable pursuits of the Cape buffalo with Finn with an almost quivering voice. Recently I met with Col Dennis Behrens, USAF Retired, of San Antonio, who happily and enthusiastically told about a particular buffalo hunt with Finn. Dennis had been on two previous safaris and taken both elephant and buffalo, so he was not new to the African bush, yet this particular hunt stands chiseled in his mind.

Dennis came with his good buddy, Mac McCausland, then a USAF senior master sergeant; this was Mac's first African experience. Mac brought two pre-'64 Model 70 rifles, a .300 and a .375 H&H. Dennis, a highly experienced competitive shooter and instructor of U.S. military shooting teams and Olympic hopefuls, described Mac as one of the best all-around shots he had ever known—an expert at trap, skeet, offhand rifle, and running boar.

His hunt with Finn took place during the golden age of safaris, Dennis told me. Kenya was divided into hunting blocks controlled by the game department, vast tracts of land sometimes 500 square miles in extent; in each, only one professional and one local party would be allowed at the same time. You brought all your supplies with you; there were no permanent camps. A basic camp was moved and set up according to the hunting area chosen. There were no frills such as noisy generators to disturb the night sounds. There was romance in waking up and seeing the snow of Kilimanjaro floating in the predawn light with a steaming cup of early morning tea while the staff readied breakfast. You drove out from camp shivering both from the cold and from the thrill of anticipation, knowing that you were with one of the most famous professional hunters in the business, one who not only understood hunting and game, but also had a solid knowledge of firearms. This was not common among Kenya professional hunters, and both Dennis and Mac felt this experience was a real bonus.

They hunted buffalo in Northern Kenya in Block 5, west of the Meru area, in dry, semi-desert surroundings. Finn writes in his diary: "We hunted buffalo hard, spent many hours each day tracking them in the heat. The one time it looked good, we were spotted by a herd of giraffe that bolted and took the buffalo with them."

One crisp, cool morning they found tracks of two bulls coming up from the local river and followed them carefully inland on foot on an elephant path. Suddenly, rounding a corner, Finn saw a bull on the trail about 70 yards ahead of them. He stood facing the men, but with his head down, grazing. This was to be Mac's buffalo. As Kinuno the tracker put up the shooting sticks, the buff must have seen or heard or smelled the men; he lifted his head briefly and stared at them. "He'll do, let's take him," mouthed Finn, whereupon Mac's rifle roared! At the shot, the buffalo bucked and disappeared into the bush on their left. The blast had come so instantly it startled both Finn and Dennis. Mac was confident about his shot placement, being a seasoned shooter, but Finn was not convinced. Nobody had time to use their binoculars; it had all happened so quickly.

Now uncertainty gripped the men and they moved hurriedly up to where the buffalo had been to look for blood. Standing quietly, they thought they could hear his labored breathing not

Long Shots — Hunting

far away, when Kinuno became aware of elephant noises close by to their right. They retreated to a tall tree, from where Kinuno reported that a herd of elephants was feeding around the tree about 50 yards from the path. They advanced cautiously again and had just reached the buffalo tracks when, 10 yards in front of them, a tiny calf stepped out onto the path. Finn wrote dryly: "We again advanced rapidly—to the rear!" Dennis recalls the urgency in Finn's voice as he commanded the group to get out of there, and then hearing the elephant screech and trumpet behind them. Encountering a calf, with the mother no doubt close, is about as dangerous a situation as you can ask for, and this, complete with a wounded buffalo close by, would cause legitimate excitement for even the most seasoned hunter.

Eventually, the elephants settled down and moved slowly away, so the men were able to continue the rather sticky prospect of following a wounded buffalo through thick bush. Most clients want to go with the PH after dangerous game they have wounded, but not all are "invited" to come along by the professional. Sometimes rapid shots must be fired at fleeing targets—a situation in which people can get hurt—or shots are not fired quickly enough during a charge. Finn had seen both Dennis and Mac shoot earlier and was confident they could handle their weapons in an emergency and not lose their heads. There was obvious pride in Dennis's voice when he told about being allowed to accompany the professional, along with Mac and Kinuno, and the local tracker they had hired. Everybody wanted to be in on the action!

Step by wary step, they moved forward, searching for evidence of the buffalo, watching out for each other. They found him about 100 yards away, looking very sick and standing in dense bush, not 30 yards ahead of them. Finn was able to put a quick .458 into the bull as he melted into the bush. He later found that the bullet had hit the middle of the ribs angling forward, but it was going sideways when it hit and thus produced a perfect "keyhole" in the hide. Mac and Dennis fired at the rapidly departing backside, then all three guns blasted at the moving bush as the hulking creature disappeared. Again, the men crept forward, all senses alert. They could smell the quarry and hear his heavy breathing close by, but he remained hidden from view. The day was getting hot and sweat trickled down their faces, obscuring their vision; they could smell each other as well. The thought crossed their minds that if they could smell each other, surely the buffalo could smell them too and figure out where they were. But this buffalo did not choose to charge, he just slipped away as the men gingerly approached him, preventing a good shot. They had to get closer, not only to put him out of his misery, but also to make sure he did not get away and later charge some innocent fellow walking through the bush. Adrenaline was surging and a mixture of fear and frustration gripped their chests as the men inched forward, fingers off the triggers.

In his diary Finn comments, "He only went about 50 yards, and we could hear him groaning. We moved up very cautiously and finally saw his tail. He was lying down, and Mac and I moved around till we could see his forequarters, but just as we were about to fire, he got up and went off. This time he only went about 20 yards and I got a good broadside shot at his shoulder. He took just one step forward and stopped, then all of us pounded two or three more shots into him as fast as we could work the bolt, and he went down."

When it was all over and everyone could utter a sigh of relief, Finn did his usual autopsy. Mac's first bullet had gone a little too far to the right of center and had most likely gotten only one lung; this was probably why the buff had stayed on his feet for so long. They consequently found nine holes in his left side and quite a few in his rear end, and they figured they had put a total of 15 or 16 shots into him, which was nothing to be proud of. Dennis, who has since been on 20 or 30 Cape buffalo kills, stressed that to him the important thing was that all three hunters were seasoned shooters who knew how to handle firearms quickly, without hesitation in an emergency. He remembers the tension and excitement of not knowing what would happen next, the almost impermeable bush that made it difficult to locate the beast, and the act of working the bolt quickly to reload as more and more cartridges were used up. The buff would have eventually died from the first shot, but it would have been messy and cruel, not to mention downright dangerous not to finish him off as quickly as they were able.

There was joy around the campfire that evening, and Mac, looking back, remembering being suitably impressed; he had been saying that he could not believe the buffalo's reputation for toughness. Mac was not the one who said they were only a cow, but now he was fully convinced their reputation was well deserved.

Professional Hunters and Friends

In East Africa, we stuck with Bateleur Safaris for all our Kenya trips, starting with Joe Cheffings and Finn Aagaard for big-game hunting. When the big-game hunting ended, we went back to Joe for bird shooting and photo safaris, and then we went with Joe's sons, Michael and Anthony, on photo safaris. They, of course, were the main guides but brought on many other guides to assist in our safaris. Some of our favorites were: Richard Moller, Chris Brennan, Alex Rostercil, Chris Trent, Phil West, and John Clark. Brennan worked on the excellent BBC documentary series called Big Cats. John's father, Ken Clark, a well-respected PH, was killed in a gunfight with marauding Shifta, a Somali gang whose members were poaching rhinos. Phil was attacked by a crocodile in Shaba while swimming in the Ewaso Ngior River at a spot we often visited. It was where a pool formed at the bottom of the rock cascade, not quite a miniature falls. We never even considered swimming in that pool; it was just a nice place with a sandy beach. I can't imagine what he was thinking, but there were some young ladies with him, so who knows? He escaped the deadly jaws when a fellow PH jumped on the croc. Phil suffered irreparable nerve damage to his arm and shoulder.

My initial trip to Tanzania was with Tanzania Trophy Expeditions in the Selous. Phil Lozano was the owner and a professional hunter. We were searching for buffalo with two elderly German hunters in the tall grass that was seven or eight feet high. Very tough hunting, for sure. One day, a native from a nearby village came to us for help with a large python they had wounded when it was trying to take one of their baby goats. Normally, pythons should be left alone, but this one was now up in a tree in their village, and it was clear from the wound that it would not survive. The snake was dispatched and brought back to our camp for skinning. It took three men to carry it from the truck bed to the skinning shed. People tell me they don't get that big, but I recall the measurement at 17 feet.

We had another good safari in the Selous with Isemonger Safaris. We camped on the Ruaha, and I never saw so many crocodiles in my life. It was hard to sleep with all the hippo grunting and burping. They walked through our camp on several nights. On one memorable occasion, while creeping up on a buffalo herd, we looked to our right only to discover we were not the only ones creeping up on the herd; several lions were making a stalk. We changed our course abruptly. Bill Isemonger was our PH. The second PH, who was bringing two more tents, failed to appear at the appointed time. I was there before my three friends' arrival, so it was left to Bill and me to construct sleeping quarters, using the tall grasses as building material. You do what you have to do—it worked. The staff managed to kill a large cobra that was found inspecting our pantry. That encouraged a thorough search of our sleeping quarters each night.

The following incident took place on that hunt in the Selous:

Once upon a time, there was a hunting safari into the great wild Selous area of Tanzania by two colonels, a major, and one civilian. All were world travelers, hunters, and expert gun men.

One colonel ventured ahead to set up a proper camp for the group to enjoy (no permanent camps are allowed in the Selous). The only reasonable and convenient travel to the Selous from Dar es Salaam was by air or train. The train skirted close to the appropriate area, and that mode of transportation was elected. Colonel Number One left Dar es Salaam three days early by train, after making proper arrangements for the group to follow (a private compartment with plenty of beer and ice) and leaving explicit instructions and a map for the other three hunters to have the train stop at a specific location.

Long Shots — Hunting

Colonel Number Two, the major, and their civilian friend were all quite fond of an occasional social drink. In order not to scare the natives or the train crew, and to ensure some alertness, the beer in the private compartment was limited to three cases (it was a 12-hour trip).

Later investigation revealed some good soul traveling on the second train, and wanting only to be neighborly, supplemented the rations extensively with a fine African homemade brew. This was consumed, according to the hunters, only in friendliness to keep from offending the donor. Colonel Number One set up hunting cars along the track at the appointed time and place to meet the train. The Selous is not famous for good roads, or any road, in most cases. It is not an easy area to travel. It was a two-hour trip, requiring four-wheeled vehicles from camp to the train tracks. After several hours of waiting, the train finally appeared and was flagged down. It was then near dark, and no hunters appeared. After much confusion, it was surmised the hunters had disembarked (or been dispatched by the conductor, more likely) earlier, possibly kidnapped by marauders. Remember, this was before cell phones. It was pitch black by now with only train tracks to follow. Marauders and poachers were known to be in this area. Colonel Number One was perplexed and worried. A search and rescue party was rapidly assembled.

Six hours later, the threesome was found up the track happily sitting on top of their luggage with their guns, and six empty cases of beer bottles. Just waiting for dinner and, of course, a little before-dinner scotch. Which proved to Colonel Number One that no good deed shall go unpunished. Those on the hunt were: Colonel Dennis Behrens, Colonel Rolf Smith, Major Charles Weaver, and Mr. James Gofourth. Which colonel was Number Two?

Danny McCallum Safaris was tops for Tanzania. Danny was from Kenya and maintained the high standards of his earlier days. His hunting concession was vast, covering more than 2,800 square miles. After the second day of hunting out of his camp, my neck was swelled to double size from tsetse fly bites, but the hunting was excellent—all wild and no fences. We were on a 14-day safari, and the only non-staff we encountered were three native Africans gathering honey. They were quite frightened of us and disappeared as quickly as lesser kudu. Honey gatherers hollow out logs about three feet long to make hives that attract African honeybees. They hang these logs in trees, and after they see enough bee activity, they lower them down, smoke the bees into a sleepy state, and dig out the honeycombs. A few days after our first encounter, we came upon these three honey gatherers again. This time our native trackers assured them we were not dangerous and wanted to trade meat for honey. A deal was made, and the next morning, we had African bee honey on our toast.

Our favorite PHs were Chris Trent and Tom Dames. They were young guys from Kenya, too young to have experienced the Golden Days of big-game hunting, but they kept to the same high standards. Chris had been a guide on one of our bird shooting safaris in Kenya with Bateleur Safaris. He was a keen leopard hunter, and we took a fine lion along with good buffalo while hunting with him in Tanzania. Tom Dames led us on another very successful safari to collect the unique antelopes in northern Tanzania. On my first hunt with Danny McCallum, I was viciously attacked. That incident is related as follows in my letter to close friends:

Incident in Tanzania

28 July, In the Year of Our Lord 2002
For the Committee (All seeing, All-knowing)

Mr. Robert Harding   Mr. Kinsey Robinson
Col. Jack Wood   Mr. Mark Silverman, *Esq*
Mr. John Allgood   Mr. Thomas Holland, *Esq*
Mr. Roger Bain, *Esq*   Mr. Thomas Held

Most dear and honored friends,

Near where the Pite River and the Rungwa River converge, on a flood plain with intermittent woodland, about 120 miles east of the Congo and 150 miles north of Zaire, Mr. Paul Facchina, the then-friend of Colonel Dennis Behrens, claimed to be suffering from severe effects of mefloquine (Lariam), his malaria preventive. Seeing his then-friends so distraught at not being able to face the day's challenging tasks of hanging lion baits, (Mr. Facchina was most desirous of hunting the lion, and hanging of baits was essential to his success), Col B volunteered to handle the hazardous and quite distasteful task (the bait was aging hippo meat covered with flies with a quite gamey aroma). This duty was taken on without reservation and in the most Christian spirit of friendship for his then-friend, Mr. Facchina.

A fine site was selected in the woodland close to water, and after selecting an appropriate tree, the work began—hoisting the bait—200 pounds plus of meat into the tree. After securing it at a proper level above Fisi (hyena) height, and then covering the bait with branches so the vultures would not discover the free lunch, work on a proper blind could commence. In the process of hoisting the bait, while standing in the tall grass slapping with one hand the formations of dastardly tsetse flies stabbing with deadly razor-sharp proboscis and swatting at squadrons of other tsetse flies on the attack (twirling arms much resembling an Italian traffic cop), Col B unknowingly stepped on an army of safari ants of which a corps-size group commenced to silently move to higher elevation—up his pants—both in and out. About the time they reached mid-level, which coincided with the time the tsetse flies reached mid-level, the ants joined in the attack. The jungle was no longer silent as Col B reached the top of the safari truck in three long strides. At that point, his pants came off faster than a 17-year-old in the heat of passion can shuck his Levis. The PH, the tracker, the skinner, the driver, the turn boy, and all others stood wide-eyed and gawking as the white belly who was buck ass naked did a wild fast tango on top of the truck that reportedly would have won any audition in Buenos Aires. Needless to say, the pain was severe, but nothing compared to the humiliation of the performance presented to a rather vast African audience. Col B, upon returning to camp that afternoon—in great pain and shame found his then-friend Mr. Facchina fully recovered, sipping tea. As he scarfed down the last biscuit in camp, he grunted only the very slightest of acknowledgements for the truly Herculean efforts on his behalf by Col Behrens, proving once again that no good deed shall go unpunished. Needless to say, redress must be obtained. Col Behrens has agreed, due to the scarce supply and difficulty of obtaining good dueling pistols, to more lenient terms. The Honorable Counsel, Mr. R. Bain Esq., acting as second, is entertaining the acceptance of a fishing trip to Alaska or Belize to ease the pain so the injured party can recover enough to settle on the major issue of humiliation. This trip would include, in addition to Col Behrens, Mr. Bain and one other member of the committee. Mr. Facchina, the then-friend, could, of course, accompany the group. Speedy action is essential as the fishing season is rapidly coming to an end.

After the pain and suffering is reduced—it is only appropriate and honorable that Col Behrens be compensated for the horrible humiliation. Taking into consideration that Mr. Facchina is a fellow member of the "Bunker Club" supporting the U.S. Olympic Team along with Col Behrens and other members of the "committee," it is suggested his fine be set at the lowest level, ten cases of shotgun ammo, to be immediately delivered to Mr. Bain as the acting second. Col Behrens has already (his Christian heart in full view again) agreed to this small compensation, but with the firmest stipulation that the compensation delivered to Mr. Bain be "only" 28 gauge. Mr. Bain is an avid shooter and owns many shotguns of all the gauges except 28. While Mr. Bain is quite reliable much of the time, it is felt best not to put temptation in the path of someone who has been known to lose his way. After all, he is a lawyer.

Of course, the scars of humiliation, the naked dance being a horrendous blow, will never completely heal, but Col B feels a forgiving soul is always rewarded. The gravity of the incident clearly demands swift justice. Full and complete confidence in the actions of the committee is confirmed.

The matter now rests in your most noble and honorable hands.

Your most obedient servant, The Colonel

Long Shots — Hunting

Our Our first big-game hunt after Kenya and before Tanzania was in Zimbabwe with Denda Safaris. Trevor Landrey and Lou Hallamore were the PHs. It was nothing less than brilliant. Three of us took everything we were after: all manner of plains game, including kudu and sable. Each of the kudu horns were over 52 inches and the sable were 42 and 43 inches, really quite nice trophies. Lion and leopard were also on the menu and successfully hunted as were buffalo.

Following the hunt with Denda, we went back to Zimbabwe and hunted with Tshabezi Safaris, owned by Dudley Rogers. Our favorite PH after Dudley was the young Kirk Mason. On one particularly successful safari with Dudley, I took five hunters with the main quarry being buffalo. They ended up with five good buffalo with horns averaging 41 inches and all the assorted plains game, plus a leopard. Needless to say, the safari was a brilliant success, which led to additional trips with Dudley. On a later hunt, my friend Paul Facchina took a trophy elephant with tusks of 82 and 83 pounds. I believe it was the largest elephant taken in Zimbabwe that year. We also took a fine leopard.

The most recent safari for buffalo was in Zimbabwe in 2018 with Lou Hallamore (my first PH in Zimbabwe 34 years earlier) and his PH son Clive. We had two shooters, Dan Himmerich, who was by now an old hand, and a first-time African hunter, Bobby Dobson. Col Rolf Smith was along as an observer. The hunters were after buffalo, and both connected with fine bulls having trophy horns of over 40 inches with solid bosses. Dan had taken a buffalo before. In fact, I was with him, and we were almost run over by a confused bull in the aftermath of a shootout. I don't believe he was charging us, but he was stampeding directly at us clearing ground rapidly. My safety came off and I nearly always shoot when that happens. It was a close one but he turned away just in time. Dan joined me again in 2022 along with Rolf Smith for a plains game hunt in the eastern cape of South Africa. We went with Crusader Safari, owned and brilliantly operated by Andrew Pringle on family property dating back to 1820.

My friend Dr. Steve Wilhite earned a position on the U.S. team to compete in the FITASC (an international form of sporting clays) world championship to be held in Sun City, South Africa. I was invited to be the honorary team captain. Being in South Africa demanded a bird hunt, so we hooked up with professional hunter David Fowler, owner of Wild Wings Safaris. David had excellent dogs, and he introduced us to Coqui, and Orange River francolin, and Swainson's spurfowl. We also took some guinea fowl, pigeons, and yellow-billed ducks. The day before the world championship, Steve arranged a dove hunt. He and I would shoot with three U.S. sporting clays national and international champions: Bobby Fowler, Andy Duffy, and Scott Robertson. I knew Andy and Scott previously and met Bobby on the way in from the airport. There were plenty of doves, and it got to be a competition of who could shoot doves at the longest range. I must say, those guys could shoot. Several years later, we did another enjoyable bird hunt with Mark Haldane's outfit, Bird Hunters Africa.

Since 1968, my longtime German friend Dr. Manfred Mack hunted and shot trap with me. Manfred lives in Wiesbaden, and he introduced me to a fellow German hunter who owned a ranch for hunting in Namibia. That hunter was Dr. Peter von Seck. Okunduka Seibe was his ranch, and it was indeed a beautiful place with a mixture of plains, hills, and a couple of dry riverbeds, making colorful rocky canyons. He is a medical doctor with a large and very successful practice in Wiesbaden. Fortunately, there was a direct flight from Frankfurt, Germany, to Windhoek, Namibia, which allowed him to enjoy his ranch frequently. Dr. Peter is the most non-German German I know. You can't imagine how much fun he was, even more so after a half-dozen glasses of white wine. He was always doing crazy things. I stayed with him in Wiesbaden a couple of times, and he was just as crazy there.

On one occasion when I was visiting, we went to lunch with some of his friends. He was dressed in a green sports coat, but not hunter green–it was a brilliant Tropicana green. He matched that with a pair of orange pants and a polka-dot shirt. He is a big guy who stands out naturally, and in that outfit, he looked like a ringmaster under the big tent. Picture us on the sidewalk in the middle of the old town, walking to the restaurant with Dr. Peter, holding a huge basket containing zebra meat and mushrooms in one arm while dragging along an undisciplined Norwich Terrier on a leash that appeared to be an old bathrobe belt. Wiesbaden is a very conservative city, prim and proper, with people dressed accordingly in the downtown area. Dogs are common in restaurants, but they are well-behaved and have proper dog leashes and collars. The zebra and mushrooms were to be used in a lunch prepared by the restaurant. We met his friends at their normal reserved table, and I sat next to Dr. Peter, where I observed the tablecloth was pretty much in shreds from the top of the table to the floor, the signature of his Norwich Terrier, which seemed right at home chomping on it again. This group met nearly every day for lunch together.

Dr. Peter was past taking things too seriously. He accepted things as they are. He did not mind telling self-deprecating stories. One related to me tells how crazy he could be. It seems one night he was up very late and ready to go to bed when he realized he hadn't put the garbage out for the morning collection. Living in a high-rise with the garbage chutes close to his door, he stepped out in the hall to dump his garbage. His door closed and locked behind him, and now he was in the hall bare-ass naked.

The old people in his building were not about to open their doors at 1:00 in the morning. Even if they did, his spare key was with his mother in another high-rise. All he could do was get to her, but it was in the middle of winter with snow on the ground. He left his building barefoot and freezing to death. There was some trash on the street, and he recovered a plastic bag to be used as a covering. He tried to hail a taxi, but who would stop for a naked man in the middle of the night standing barefoot in the snow? Finally, he made it to his mother's apartment. He was shivering uncontrollably as he pounded on the door. His mother opened the door, looked at him, and announced, "You can't come in here with those filthy feet." That's Dr. Peter.

His ranch held an abundance of plains game and was an excellent place to start new African hunters. He didn't have buffalo, but Dan Himmerich did take a nice leopard on the ranch. Our favorite PHs there were Dr. Peter, Christoph, and Dirk Rohmann. Dirk's gorgeous wife Rita kept a wonderful kitchen that was always beautifully decorated for our dinners. I was able to take many of my best friends there, and we made ten safaris to Okunduka. Dr. Peter was more or less forced by the government to sell his ranch to the locals. We all miss him. Namibia had heavy German influence and is the cleanest African country I have visited. Before leaving Dr Peter von Seck I want to give you his take on the U.S. occupation in Wiesbaden after WWII. He said the GIs brought jazz music, chewing gum, big cars, and they were happy and always smiling, exactly what the Germans needed.

Mark Haldane is a longtime professional South African hunter. He owns Zambezi Delta Safaris. His hunting area in Mozambique is a huge playpen of wild animals — no fences anywhere. He flew me over the massive swamp area where he hunts, and I witnessed vast numbers of buffalo, more than I have ever seen anywhere. He has large numbers of sable and many of the other smaller antelope. One of his PHs I particularly liked was Craigh Hammon. All our safaris with Haldane have been quite successful.

Many of my closest friends have been with me on African safaris. I value all of them highly. The list is extensive with several going at least twice. Those who have been with me on three or more safaris are listed in alphabetical order. Hopefully I have not missed anyone. Roger Bain was with me in Kenya, Zimbabwe, and Namibia. Roger had grown up shooting a .22 rifle in competitions and was an excellent rifle shot. He was also very good with a shotgun and frequent winner of sporting clay matches. Roger retired from practicing law and became a gun dealer of high-quality shotguns. He was a pleasure to hunt birds with. Roger killed a fine buffalo at the longest range I have ever seen, somewhere between 180 and 190 yards. I paced it off. Most hunters would be shocked to read this. I was surprised the PH allowed it but learned afterward that the PH had suggested he take the shot. It happened after Roger had taken kudu, sable, and other plains game at long ranges with perfect shots. We had been chasing buffalo all day, looking for a good bull but failing to get properly positioned for a shot.

The sun was sagging, and we were headed back toward camp in the hunting car when a big herd was spotted on the opposite side of a large clearing. Roger and the professional hunter Kirk Mason got out and started a stalk. From the top of the truck, I had a bird's-eye view of the whole scene—hunters and buffalo. They crept up behind a large ant hill but there was no more cover between them and the distant herd. Roger was shooting a .458 caliber Winchester Model 70 with a good scope. It was a tack driver. A 500-grain bullet is normally used in a .458, but Roger had loaded some 400-grain bullets and sighted them in for 150 yards. They were not intended for buffalo but were to be used for shy zebra, kudu, or sable. I figured the buffalo were simply too far but could see Roger and Kirk moving around the anthill strangely—sort of like monkeys on a football. Even with my binoculars, I couldn't tell what they were doing, but it turned out Roger was trying to find a comfortable position to ensure a good shot. Then boom! The shot startled me, but the buffalo was hard hit. The herd did not recognize what was happening and milled around the wounded bull, which appeared to be anchored but not down. Roger kept the sights on the bull and when the opportunity for a clear shot came, he was ready and added the killing shot. That long shot was an anomaly, and I do not recommend it.

The rule on buffalo is to get as close as you can and then get 10 yards closer. The PHs I have hunted with like to get within 50 yards, and I think that's a good rule. I have enjoyed long-range shooting and got pretty competent at 1000 yards. But I'm absolutely against excessively long-range shooting at animals. Some sheep hunting requires long-range marksmanship, but for the most part, other game can and should be approached by a stealthy stalk. There is just too much room for error and the chance of wounding rather than a one-shot humane killing. Those people who want to play sniper should go to Camp Perry and try to win the Wimbledon Cup or sign up with the Marine Corps Weapons Battalion.

Dr. Gene Bishop has been on four Kenya safaris—bird shooting and photo. His lovely wife Leslie and daughter Jordan have also been with us. Gene is a medical doctor who is a good hunting and traveling partner. I've also enjoyed his company in Texas and Argentina. He appreciates fine shotguns and owns a few. He is a highly skilled photographer. I think he could switch from being a doctor to a professional photographer quite easily. The 8x10 photos in his leather-bound books could compete favorably with any *National Geographic* photos.

Barry Borgiet has been with me in Kenya and Namibia. Barry is a retired Air Force major and was in my unit at Ramstein Air Force

Base in Germany. He learned to hunt in Germany and knows how to do it right. Plus, he can shoot. Barry married Frau Helene Dessaur, who was the hunting and fishing clerk for the Rhineland Pfalz. She was the liaison between the U.S. military and German Forestry. Her job was helping all of us Americans to schedule hunts with federal foresters. She allotted quotas to the hunters and did a super job helping Americans become acquainted with the customs of German hunting.

Paul Facchina is a contractor and major force in Maryland. He hunted with me in Namibia, Tanzania, Zimbabwe, and then again in Tanzania. Paul lives at Mount Air, a large historical property on the Potomac River. He has plenty of room for target shooting. Paul is one of those guys who is just a lucky hunter. He seems to be in the right place at the right time and has collected some fine trophies. He trains enough with his rifles and ammo to be 100% ready when the time comes. Paul's trophy collection is quite impressive. I like hunting with him.

Dan Himmerich has been on safari with me seven times in Zimbabwe, Namibia, South Africa, and Mozambique. Dan runs business development for Kyndryl Strategic Markets and is stationed in Singapore. He started out as nearly a novice on a Namibian safari, bringing two rifles on his first trip, thinking one was a medium and the other heavy. They were actually light rifles with nearly the same performance capability. He is a quick study, for sure, and the next thing I knew he was shooting a .375 Model 70 Winchester almost exclusively. We were hunting in 2018 for plains game and buffalo in Zimbabwe, but Dan was there only for buffalo, and it had to be bigger than the one he already had. He was there for the hunt and not the killing. St. Hubertus would love him. It was the last day of our hunt when Dan connected with a fine dugga boy, over 40 inches with a good solid boss.

Carl Kilhoffer is a retired businessman from Maryland. More importantly, he is a retired captain from the Navy Reserve. He trained in underwater demolition and was a Navy Beach Jumper. His Vietnam service included incursions into Cambodia. We served in Vietnam during the same period, which included Tet. Carl is an excellent traveling companion and good roommate. He has been with me in Kenya, South Africa, Namibia, Mozambique, Argentina and Paraguay.

Kinsey and Mona Robinson have hunted with me in Kenya and Namibia, and I hunted with them in New Zealand. Kinsey is the union president of the Roofers and Water Proofers of America. Mona is a nurse. They are my favorite hunting couple and are also close friends. I don't know who is the more dedicated hunter, Mona or Kinsey, but I'll put my money on Mona. They have hunted all over and have a beautifully displayed collection of trophies. It's always a pleasure to be with them. Also, I like having a nurse with me.

Rolf Smith is a retired Air Force Colonel. He has hunted with me in Africa many times—in Kenya, Zimbabwe, Tanzania, South Africa, Namibia, and Mozambique. His twelfth safari was in 2018, but he was really just there to immerse himself one more time in another South African safari. Rolf worked for me in 1965 as team adjutant of the first and only Air Force Rifle Team to win the coveted National Trophy. I was a first lieutenant, and he was a second lieutenant. Rolf set some 600-yard and rapid-fire records. Needless to say, he is an excellent shot. We also hunted together in the States, Europe, and Argentina. He is always optimistic and enthusiastic, a real pleasure to travel with. I rate him the consummate *Jaeger*.

Dr. Larry Trick and his beautiful bride Judy are the king and queen of Kenya bird-shooting safaris. They are wonderful travelers and have been with me several times in Kenya. Larry is a retired orthopedic surgeon, and Judy is a retired nurse. Larry also retired from the Air Force reserve as a colonel. He loves to shoot birds—that is his main hunting activity. He's good at it and keeps his hand/eye coordination sharp by shooting sporting clays in the off-season. It's always good to have him and Judy with me.

Shooting African animals ended for me in 1984, with the exception of shooting the backup shot on dangerous game. That continued until I sold my .458 to Kinsey Robinson. Now I go armed with a pair of binoculars but am careful not to get in the way of the dangerous big stuff. Even in the beginning, I always hunted with friends, which gave me double enjoyment—getting my quarry and watching my friends successfully get theirs. Hunting by myself or only with a PH just doesn't interest me. If someone offered me a trip and I would be the sole hunter, it would be a no-go. After 1984, I hunted for pronghorn, mule deer, Russian boar, and red stags, but always with friends. These days I'm sticking to bird hunting but again only with friends.

My good friend and mentor, Colonel Scotty Cameron, wrote the following epilogue after our 1997 safari in Zimbabwe:

> *"For those who have shared the experience, there is no greater pleasure than sitting around a campfire after a tiring day afield, watching the moonrise through the trees—whether in Wyoming or Zimbabwe. Sated by a meal from the day's harvest, enjoying a drink with old friends, exchanging tales of stalks and shots—listening intently, and adding a few of your own. This is the stuff of memories, and memories are food for the soul."*

Hunting has made my life so much fuller. It has brought me untold joy and introduced me to a whole community of excellent people. I am grateful for all the bounty they have brought me.

Expedition Adventures, Inc.

Taking people on fun trips has always been one of my favorite activities. Mostly, they're hunting and fishing trips, but some are sightseeing just to see new or interesting and different things such as the Upsala Glacier near Calafate, the Inca ruins at Machu Picchu, the Sphinx in Egypt, the Iguazu and Victoria Falls, the Great Wall of China, Petra in Jordan, Persepolis in Iran, the Potala Palace in Tibet, and the Taj Mahal in India. And besides these, there is the thrill of visiting major cities of the world with the many treasures they guard. The best part is meeting people, eating different foods, and learning different cultures. Touring our own 50 states is a magnificent kaleidoscope by itself.

The genesis for Expedition Adventures was my many trips to Africa and Argentina. Originally, it was just a few trips where everyone paid their own way, including me. I collected the money for the outfitters and was just using my personal account, but since

I wasn't charging extra, I didn't think much about it. While flying back from a Kenya trip with my friend Col Rolf Smith, he suggested I start a hunting business. Incorporating and making the real business sounded like too much trouble and didn't interest me much.

Oftentimes, I would make deposits in my bank of $40,000 or $50,000 and then send funds overseas to outfitters and agents wherever we were going. My accountant, Gene Brehm, said the IRS would probably look at me as a mule for the cartels or maybe a hitman or perhaps someone just laundering money with my frequent trips to Europe, Africa, and especially South America. Also, mixing other people's money in my account wasn't a good practice and could certainly look suspicious.

Gene also suggested I set up a business. To be honest, organizing the trips was becoming a great deal of work and took a horrendous amount of time to get things done right. Rolf, who started his own company, chimed in again for me to do the same, so in 1994, Expedition Adventures, Inc. was established. We still priced the trips as reasonably as possible and never added extra fees above the outfitters' price. I wanted the trips to be good value and, I hoped, cherished in the memories of my friends. It was a special business and not advertised as I wasn't interested in taking strangers on trips. It was for my friends and me. It's an important point because I went on all the early trips myself as the group leader.

If one studies the history of my travels it would reveal that I always had friends with me from the very first safari in 1971, even on dangerous big game hunts. I got satisfaction and enjoyment myself, but also shared the enjoyment from my shooting and hunting partners. I considered it double value, and having said that, the leader might discover I get little pleasure from hunting by myself. In fact, if offered a hunt at no cost but for only me, I would turn it down without a second thought.

So, what is Expedition Adventures? It's a small-volume company that specializes in arranging personalized hunting and fishing adventures, with a few interesting tourist trips thrown in now and again. We book these adventures with the best outfitters we can find. Perhaps we could be described as "boutique" in the world of booking companies. Our aim is to give excellent service to our friends, always remembering some have been saving and planning for this experience for years. We treat each trip as something special and not just another booking. Every outfitter, lodge, castle, or camp has been vetted personally by me before we take or send our friends. In the few instances when we sent people or groups to areas we had not previously previewed, either my partner or I accompanied the group. We no longer purchase the airline tickets, Instead, we explore the best routes and recommend a credible airline agent for ticket purchasing. Our airline agents will track down wayward luggage and unsnarl messes created when flights are canceled, changed, or delayed. It may sound easy but getting the right lodges with the right outfitter and the right program that best fits the clients (our friends) requires good knowledge of the areas, a firm understanding of what our friends want, and knowing what the outfitter/guides can produce. All of this is best done by having personal relationships with those we work with. We strive to build strong relationships and keep in constant contact with the outfitters and all the support people we work with.

Eventually, the company got too busy for me to go on all the trips, and it was taking all my time just to keep up with booking trips. My wife and I were both involved heavily with nonprofit organizations and wanted to keep a strong hand in supporting those activities. About that time, along came Gordie White. I first met Gordie in 1995 when we were hunting buffalo in Zimbabwe. There were five hunters with me, so we had a party of six with four professional hunters (PHs) for my five shooters. It was a busy camp with the hunters bringing in a good many animals. Gordie was managing the skinning and butchering of the animals taken by my friends along with baiting for leopards. He was on the go constantly, and I could tell he was a good worker, but we really didn't have time to visit. One night, we were all sitting at the dinner table, six of us with four PHs and Gordie. He had seen my letterhead that listed a board of advisors, one of whom was Finn Aagaard, a noted PH from Kenya. Finn had become a highly respected author of hunting and shooting articles. Gordie piped up from out of the blue at the end of the table, "I've read everything Finn Aagaard has written, and I have his new book. Could you get it autographed for me?"

It took me by surprise, but after watching him for several days I knew he was my kind of guy. My answer was "No!" The table fell silent; you could've heard a pin drop. Gordie was turning red when I said, "But if you would like to come visit me in Texas, I'll take you to meet Finn, and you can have him autograph your book." That started a friendship, and Gordie showed up that Christmas. We visited Finn, got the autograph, and expanded the friendship to the three of us. The next year he came again and brought his younger brother Mike, who like Gordie, was a top-notch young man. I liked him immediately. They could come and live with me anytime, although they both have their own families now.

I was invited, along with my friend Col Tommy Brown, to visit them at Mike's deer camp in Alberta. We hunted ruffed grouse and ducks, and I met his parents, who had come from Montréal for a visit. Mike could skin out a trophy head, splitting the ears and even saving the eyelashes, but he had never boned out a deer or an elk. Carcasses from his hunts were simply dropped off at a butchering center and ended up mostly made into sausages. His father shot an elk while we were there so Tommy and I boned it out and packaged the meat for them to freeze and serve up to their clients.

Gordie grew up in Canada and was a licensed hunter in Alberta and British Columbia. He spent four years in Zimbabwe, running camps, culling game, guiding, and learning the safari business. He has taken lion, elephant, and about every trophy animal in Zimbabwe. Gordie can shoot and knows guns and ballistics. He married an American and moved to the States to help manage the well-known Burnt Pine Plantation in Georgia. From there, he went to Texas to manage the Herradura Ranch, followed by the Rancho Estrella. Both were high-end hunting operations. He was looking to do something different, and I was looking for someone to work with me who had the knowledge, experience, and the right temperament to take care of my friends. I am picky in that regard and is not easy to find someone with those qualifications. It was a marriage made in heaven. Gordie was a perfect fit, and in 2008 we formed a partnership.

He has simply done a magnificent job and won over my friends right away. He is extra conscientious, never loses his temper, and tries to make everything perfect. When we have friends in the field, Gordie is often communicating with the outfitter to check on how things are going. His congenial personality makes him a perfect companion on trips. He takes care of business and has been an excellent partner; we have never had a cross word about anything. His efforts have turned the business into a professional operation, and he does a much better job than I. He is the boss now and runs the show.

Gordie is a prolific reader. He keeps up with current affairs and continues to read history. In fact, he's written a very nice book of short stories on hunting, *Field Notes from Wild Places,* that tell much more than the chase. In addition, he works with the local school PTA and helps in counseling with a group working with those in difficult family situations. And he is the doting father of a teenaged daughter. Few people know it, but Gordie is a closet gourmet and excellent cook.

We do at least one trip every year together without other friends, just the two of us. The last few years we've been doing our private hunt in New Mexico, bunking in a doublewide and making our own meals. Or, I should say, with Gordie doing the cooking. It's a highlight for me and tops off a fine day of hunting. The lure of big game hunting has passed for him, and like me, his passion is now shooting birds. It's a pleasure to hunt with him. We watch the dogs reacting, know where and how to move, and know how to get ready to shoot. The idea is to have a good day's experience, not just to fill a limit or game bag. Competition is fine on a clay target range but has no place in the hunting world. Gordie doesn't hog shots or try to outmaneuver his hunting companion.

It's my good luck and a pleasure to have him as a partner for hunting and in business—in both he will be right every time. More importantly, he is a fine friend who can always be counted on.

Kenya—1973 James McCausland and his elephant. PH Finn Aagaard

Kenya—A very nice Grants Gazelle in 1971

Kenya – Lesser Kudu – a fine trophy

Zimbabwe 1984 – Lt Mark Taishoff with a hard to kill Buffalo

German pheasant hunt in Altenbuch. Kneeling - DDB and Paul Fladausch. Herr Fladausch standing on left. Circa 1968

Lt Taishoff and DDB hanging birds after an Altenbuch pheasant hunt —1982

US Team at the German National DJV Championship.
L-R SMSgt James McCausland, DDB, Lt Col Rip Sewall, Col W. J. March, Capt Frank White, 2d Lt Scott Coby. Circa 1970

Goose hunting on Kent Island—1983
L-R Brig Gen Ted Giddings, DDB, John Goodman

Chasing chukars with my Behrens cousins at Lake Owyhee. L-R Earl, Allen, DDB, Clifford

Joe Kelly and Steve Hyams after chukars and huns in Idaho with fine German Drahthaars

Hunt on the Allemand Ranch in Wyoming. L-R Mark Taishoff, DDB, Bart Byrd

Argentina Pigeon Shoot L-R Roger Bain, DDB, John Allgood

Red Stag free range hunt in Patagonia. L-R Guide, Kinsey Robinson, DDB

High volume dove shoot in Argentina. DDB with Carlos, a superb loader.

Korea pheasant hunt on the DMZ.
L-R A Korean Lt Col as security, DDB, Andy Moore. Bottom is a Korean corporal, our driver and bird retriever.

Cheffings family. L-R Michael, Simonne, Joe, Anthony

Joe Cheffings and DDB bird hunting near Amboseli, Kenya

Studying bullets and ballistics with Finn Aagaard

My faithful Masai bird guides L-R Kisham, DDB, Anyika, David

Zimbabwe 1984. Old lion (kicked out of the pride). DDB and Mark Taishoff

My Masai body guard

A brave leopard that nearly got us. Note Facchina has a shotgun and I have a heavy rifle – not a good sign.

Paul Facchina's elephant 82 lb tusks. Circa 2004

Zimbabwe in 2018. Dan Himmerich with a fine buffalo, taken on the last day.

In Namibia with two fine friends – Rolf Smith & Dan Himmerich.

Grand National Quail Club (GNQC).
L-R Gen Davis, Lindy Baker, Capt Dean, Jim Wright, DDB. Lindy and Jim were presidents of the GNQC

Two Olympians, Dominic Grazioli and Josh Lakatos, with Oklahoma Governor Frank Keating at the GNQC

Team winners at the GNQC
L-R DDB, Gen Davis, John Groendyke, Scott Coby, and Walt Broich

Laura Revitz dove shooting in Argentina

My best nurse, Mona Robinson, with her fine Strumberg Ram

DDB shooting a pair of guns in Spain

Dr Paul Googe and Willard Dow with me on a partridge shoot in Spain

Grand National Quail Club Hall of Fame induction

Chasing scaled quail in New Mexico—photo by Gordie White

Pheasant hunting in Belgium with René Haillez

Chasing chukars at Lake Owyhee with Max Jungk

Col Rolf Smith with a fine kudu taken in Namibia

IV

Teams

Air Force Rifle Team

I hit the lotto in 1964. History reveals the lives of most lotto winners spiral down. The experience often ruins them either socially, morally, or financially, or even all three. For me it was a huge boost not only professionally, but also to my own personal fulfillment. We are not talking about money; this was something far greater than money. It was an opportunity to become a member of a military high-power rifle team where I would pit myself, along with my teammates, against the best military riflemen in the world.

I was already a known civilian shooter on the West Coast and at Camp Perry, but this was moving in with the big boys, for sure. When I received orders to report for permanent duty with the United States Air Force Marksmanship School at Lackland Air Force Base in San Antonio, Texas, my feet did not touch the ground for two weeks. I was in seventh heaven. Not many people get this chance. The previous summer of 1963, I had been assigned temporary duty (TDY) for three months at the Marksmanship School to shoot with the Air Force High-Power Rifle Team. I traveled with them to the U.S. National High-Power Shooting Championship held at Camp Perry, Ohio. My duty as a TDY team "add-on" was only to shoot. I had no official authority, or any say so regarding the team.

The team was a first-class mess. The previous officer in charge had been fired, leaving a long-in-the-tooth Master Sergeant, who had been promoted far beyond his capabilities, temporarily in charge. He was a good guy but could not organize or lead. Additionally, he brought his wife and six of his kids with him to matches. Lt Col Palmer was an elderly retired Army officer who had come to the Marksmanship

School to help organize competitive rifle shooting. He had competed at Camp Perry in the 1940s. Although unofficial, he more or less guided the team, and they liked him. Nevertheless, discipline and team spirit were nowhere to be seen. The team was successful shooting match rifles (bolt-action target rifles) against civilian teams, but Army, Marine Corps, National Guard, and military reserve teams all outshot the Air Force, using M1 Garand service rifles. I believe their highest service rifle team finish for the National Trophy was seventh place, not very impressive for full-time shooters.

Colonel George Van Deusen commanded the Marksmanship School and was a first-class gentleman. He had been a P-51 fighter pilot during World War II and was a Distinguished Pistol shooter. His badge number is 113. After coming back to Lackland from my TDY with the team at Camp Perry, the Colonel asked me to give him an out brief before returning to my permanent assignment at Mather Air Force Base in California. I gave him my candid views and recommendations. He said, "Thanks, we need some changes, and you can help with that when we get you back here permanently." Boy, did that sound good to me.

He worked with the "gods of assignments," and in January of 1964, I was headed back to San Antonio. It got even better as I learned I was to be the team officer in charge (OIC). Wow! I was a second lieutenant in charge of the Air Force's High-Power Rifle Team. It was ridiculous, absolutely unheard of, and in defiance of convention. Lt Col Harry J. Copsey was the OIC of trap, Lt Col Rowden was OIC of skeet, and Lt Col R.F. Perkins was OIC of smallbore and international rifle shooting. The commander, a full colonel, oversaw the pistol team, but I believe a couple of excellent senior NCOs really managed the team. Two officers who were very good shots were on the pistol team, but they just concentrated on their individual shooting.

While being OIC was daunting and a huge amount of responsibility, it also gave me authority. Not only did I have to worry about my shooting, but I also now had to develop a winning team. In my first Air Force assignment at Mather AFB, I was the supervisor and boss, on paper, of six master sergeants. Each had a full staff reporting to him, but I didn't set programs or make major decisions. Now, however, I was the guy who had to make the decisions, develop the strategy, select

Long Shots — Teams

coaches, set the goals, and work out the training. I also had to recruit shooters and secure the budget, equipment, and personnel to complete our mission. Sure, I had some good noncommissioned officers (NCOs) to help, but I was "holding the pickle" and there would be no passing the buck. Somebody had to pick the point man and that responsibility would now be mine. Apparently, the team's last OIC had been a martinet, and upon my arrival a couple of shooters supposedly said, "Here we go again," and simply quit. I don't think we lost much, and I refused to comment or criticize previous leadership. We still needed to be military, so bearing and behavior could not be compromised. But I cut out excessive trivia and reduced saluting to just one salute as a good morning before we started training, and then no more saluting on the firing line. What I needed to do was prove I would be a good, effective OIC and build a winning team. I resolved to be the best leader to ever guide the team and worked hard at it every single day.

I was boss because of my rank, but I needed to prove myself to the men as only the team members could make me their leader. We did not have the luxury of time as the two most important matches, the Interservice Championship at Quantico, Virginia, and the National Championship at Camp Perry, Ohio, were conducted in August. Having shot with some of the team members at Camp Perry the previous summer, I knew there was talent—it just needed to be harnessed to a team wagon.

The first thing that had to be done was to gain trust and establish consistency with no surprises. There could be no jumbled directions. I not only let the team members know what I expected of them, but also that I would be right with them in the fight. Some young officers make the mistake of trying to be friends with their subordinates and call them by their first names, which normally ends up with hard feelings all the way around. I made sure to address all the team members by their military title to show them the respect they deserved. Of course, it helped also that I didn't have to learn 25 names immediately—all I had to say was "sergeant" or "airman" without adding a last name.

The coaches were charged with setting up training schedules and were responsible for selecting teams. Their decisions on the firing line were to be followed by all, including me. That established proper authority regardless of rank. Everyone reported to me, and I wrote all the efficiency reports, so the coaches did not have to worry about calling out someone more senior in rank. The one thing I did ask the coaches to do on team record training days, and in matches, was to let me fire the first shot at 600 or 1,000 yards. There are no sighter shots in team matches so the first shooter takes the chance on the wind call (estimating wind direction and velocity for sight adjustments). This is important because if the wind call is wrong, his shot will not be centered, and his personal shooting average will suffer. Shooting averages were crucial as they were a major factor in selecting who would shoot in the team matches. My taking the risky shot did not go unnoticed.

Setting rules and extra requirements for a team is almost worthless. When a team comes together, they set their own rules, or maybe it's better described as they set their own standards. I don't like a bunch of "chicken rules." Too often, they only distract from the main mission. My only requirement was to be in bed by midnight before a team match because that match reflected on all of us. If they wanted to ruin their individual average that was their business, but of course they all wanted to shoot well every day, and I was stressing working as a team. One thing I forbade was taking wives and kids on our road trips to competitions. That caused a minor dustup, and I was quite unpopular with some wives. My position was that we were on official duty, taxpayers were paying us and anything that detracted from the mission needed to be eliminated. Some guys were spending more time buying groceries and taking care of kids than doing their job. I emphasized that no matter how well I shot or any of us shot, we needed everyone working together to make us winners. And winners we would be.

A critical element in the success of any team, office, or any organization is to ensure all parties understand the goal or mission. Our mission was to win shooting matches against military and civilian teams, shooting the national match course (NMC) of slow and rapid fire at 200, 300, and 600 yards. We competed with the M1 Garand service rifle, designated as the U.S. military combat rifle. Our mission was to defeat the U.S. Army and U.S. Marine Corps teams in the National Trophy Team (NTT) match at Camp Perry. The NMC was used in most military and civilian- sponsored competitions, which included the national championship at Camp Perry, Ohio. A secondary goal was to win 1,000-yard matches with both service and match rifles. Match rifles were bolt-action precision firearms for competitive target shooting. Model 70 Winchesters were the favorites.

Some of our guys were experts and were shooting well with match rifles, winning in NMC competitions. That was fun, but it was not our mission, and it was mainly just beating up poor civilian teams. My order to turn in all match rifles except for those specially configured for 1,000-yard shooting was not well received by a couple of diehard match rifle shooters who subsequently left the team. Why this had not been done earlier was beyond me, but everyone now fully understood the mission. And, of course, a third mission, sort of an umbrella over everything, was to represent the U.S. Air Force well in or out of competition. That encompassed not only the military but also the civilian community. Adjacent duties included putting on shooting demonstrations for VIPs and conducting shooting clinics for the entire Air Force. We often did clinics at civilian competitions that were well received and much appreciated. I'm certain some civilians secretly wanted to see us come to their competitions so they could police up our fired brass for their reloading. We also coached and trained cadets at the Air Force Academy and had them train with us in San Antonio.

We went through a gestation period, and like most young officers, I charged too fast and pushed too hard. And I was certainly irascible at times. But, with the patient and good, honest guidance of some excellent team NCOs, my leadership ripened. I managed to gain the team's respect. Goals were set, routines established, training and areas of responsibility were made clear. Individual and team scores were published weekly so everyone knew where they stood. There were no secrets or mysteries as to who would shoot on the top shooting teams in competition—the blue team, silver team or the red team. We made it hard to get on our team, but very easy to get off. Low scores and not looking or acting right (in a manner that would discredit the Air Force or our team) brought swift removal.

Lest the reader think everything was peaches and cream, I have to admit to making many mistakes, mostly from moving too fast and being harsh. The following comments are taken from an account of team reflections written by Gene Reinartz in 2001:

> "Leadership on the team seems to always be in turmoil—we would get one officer and he would last a short time—each coming into the job riding a "white horse," thinking, "I'll be the one to straighten this motley crew out." I admit, as an NCO, we, as a group, were difficult to deal with. Shooters are high-strung, Individualistic, rather self-centered, which caused much of our grief. As you know, Wayne D. Owens gave us fits day in and day out. Every one of my teammates knew Dennis Behrens and I did not get along. However, he was always commissioned, and I enlisted. Let me say here and now, I did not like 2d Lt Dennis Behrens and for years I have been vindictive toward him. But the years seem to mellow a GI and I am one of those. He may not know it, but I buried the hatchet last year at Emmitt's. I accept 75% of this problem, for as a senior NCO I should have been a better soldier than I was. Dennis, I apologize for my actions and for sure recognize that you did bring the team together like no other officer did, and as such, won the National Trophy Team Match. My hat goes off to you, sir, both as an officer and shooter. I must also say my teammates wanted me to do this years ago, but this square-headed German did not respond and here I let them down. Sorry, guys."

Gene Reinartz was a Technical Sergeant when we met in 1964. The crazy thing is he misinterpreted something I said. It was meant to be in levity, which he didn't recognize, and I did not realize how badly the team had been beaten up by previous officers. The whole thing was a mistake: it was my fault, and I told him so after he wrote the above. Of course, that was 37 years too late. The good thing is he moved to the Air Force Academy and made Chief Master Sergeant, the highest enlisted rank in the Air Force (In the Army or the Marine Corps he would be a sergeant major). There are actually fewer chief master sergeants in the Air Force than colonels. His promotion would not have been possible if he had stayed in the competitive shooting business as enlisted promotions were notoriously stingy. We actually became closer in later life. At one of our retired team reunions, I commented on the fine-looking lapel pin he was wearing. It was a miniature distinguished badge. A week later one arrived in my mailbox. I will also give him extra credit for raising a grandson who turned out to be a fine young man, serving as a paratrooper in Iraq and Afghanistan.

At the time I did not recognize how badly the team had been neglected, but it becomes very obvious when reviewing those officers who had been assigned as officer in charge (OIC)—no one higher than the grade of captain while the OICs of the other teams, skeet, trap, and international smallbore were lieutenant colonels. The Commanders of the USAF Marksmanship School were pistol shooters and traveled with that team. Less visible and maybe only subconsciously, I suspect part of the equation was a feeling that the high-power rifle team could never compete on an equal level with the big Army and Marine Corps teams, so were more or less the stepchildren. In fairness, I will admit the high-power team attracted fewer officers as competitors. After all, pistol shooting was shot under a cover, with less gear to drag around, and the shooters wore nice uniforms. Shotgun shooting was an outside sport but again with less gear and snappy uniforms—no fatigues for these guys; they weren't getting down into the dirt. It must be pointed out that there were more pistol and shotgun ranges on Air Force bases than high-power rifle ranges out to 600 and 1,000 yards, which probably attracted more officers to those sports. Both shotgun and pistol shooting were considered more elite by many although high-power rifle guys referred to their shooting as the manly sport. I'm only pointing out the facts here and not complaining. I was treated very well and given full support to do about anything I wanted in leading the high-power team.

We trained hard and in all weather conditions—wind, rain, cold, and steamy hot days. It's like the rule of needing 10,000 hours to become an expert in your specialty—just keep after it until it becomes second nature. The guys pretty much had the mechanics down before ever joining the team. It was now just a matter of fine tuning and minor adjustments to techniques. What was more important was developing an attitude of "We will win." Each team member had to establish in his own mind that he was a winner. And that meant whether it was in good or horrible shooting conditions, they still had to believe, "We will win." Easy to say, but it takes time to build that confidence. Yogi Berra said, "Baseball is 90% mental, and the other half is physical." You gotta love the guy. I think he was not far from wrong on the 90%.

It's hard to shoot in strong winds, especially offhand (standing). Cold and rain limit visibility and make your actions standing, sitting, or prone disagreeably more difficult. Extreme heat and humidity drain your strength. But all these conditions are found in competitions and must be overcome. As I said before, we trained in all weather, no matter what. To make training more significant, we added "match days" that were conducted with the same rules as a regular competition, no alibis, or excuses. It also made training days more serious. Those match day scores were added in with equal weight of regular matches to compute a shooter's average. When the wind came up on nonduty days or after duty hours, I would take my M1 and stopwatch out to my backyard and dry fire (practice without live ammunition) offhand, fighting the wind to get off 10 shots in 10 minutes. In a heavy wind of 25 miles per hour and up it is a struggle and requires hard concentration. Squeezing or pressure on the trigger, normally stressed, won't work. You have to do what I call directing or muscling the trigger. You must hold the rifle tighter with more strength, keeping trigger pressure just on the breaking point, but then force it a bit at the right moment. It's a tricky maneuver and exhausting both physically and mentally. When you're fighting the wind and your time is running out there is a dangerous tendency to jerk the trigger.

Of course, that won't work. This was some of the extra training I did when not on the rifle range, and with all the guys doing something similar, it paid off. Everyone was working for improvement to advance the team.

The team won a few matches and began to grow with pride. We bloused our boots to look sharper on the range. No one wanted to screw up, and they policed each other good-naturedly, but any infraction was called out. A real chemistry developed, and the men saw themselves as valued members of the Air Force Rifle Team—bigger than they were before. One of the shooters, I think it was TSgt Kenneth Horst, came up with the idea of team blazers. Next thing you know, we all had matching blue blazers with gray slacks and silver ties. A nice team crest in blue and silver thread was made for the left pocket. Remember, military pay was quite stingy in the early 1960s, and each man had to pay for the outfit out of his own pocket. I don't know that it could be called a brotherhood, but a certain bonding took place. It became prestigious to be a team member. A team was born. Team members were now loyal to the team, to me, and each other. Loyalty begets loyalty. I guarded them fiercely. They were now my team, and I was their lieutenant. It wasn't verbalized but neither one would let the other down. General Dwight Eisenhower defined leadership as "the art of getting someone else to do something that you want done because he wants to do it." This team now wanted to do it. I still can't fully say how or why it happened, but as you read on, you will find THEY wanted to do it.

There were instructors, trainers, and shooters throughout Air Force bases worldwide working hard on the task of preparing officer and airmen personnel for combat, which required small arms, a large and vital mission. However, the competitive teams, a tiny spur of the overall Marksmanship School mission, got all the glory. The world is not fair, for certain. Yes, we had the spotlight, and in our own very small little world we were mini rock stars. But it was not all fun and games. Our mission was deadly serious.

The shooting competitions were nothing like intramural sports meant for fun and relaxation. Success was expected and, in fact, demanded. There was immense pressure to succeed, and those who could not cut the mustard had to be relieved from duty, which is never a happy task. Being dropped from the team also cut their income. Prizes of monetary value were seldom awarded. There were no wampum belts passed out, although once in a while a rifle could be won. We were not getting any special duty pay, but we were collecting TDY travel money at 7 cents a mile for the driver and 5 cents a mile for any rider. Two guys riding together collected 12 cents per mile when gas was selling for 25 cents per gallon. Additionally, we were paid for meals and motels on the road. If the guys skimped a little on meals and doubled or tripled up in motels, they could save a couple of bucks to take home to momma. That wasn't much for sure, but military pay was very poor in the 1960s, so it helped out quite a bit.

A brief history of the United States Air Force Marksmanship School is in order to give the reader a background and better understanding. We are not talking about fun shooting sports. This was serious and an important war and lifesaving business.

The Marksmanship School was the brainchild of General Curtis LeMay. He had directed much of the World War II Army Air Force bombing in Europe. His concept of box flights by our bombers saved the lives of many crewmembers. His firebombing of Tokyo and other parts of Japan were highly effective. As commander of the Strategic Air Command from 1948 to 1957, he built and directed our bomber and missile force as the world's counterweight to the Soviet Union. He was a proven warrior and well respected and some say even feared by our own Congress. His words carried weight. His book, *Mission with LeMay*, is an excellent history reminder.

The Air Force became a separate service in 1947. By the time of the Korean War in 1950 we were sorely unprepared for the ground defense of our aircraft. Our air base in Korea was overrun by communist troops. The base was retaken, but General LeMay was said to be horrified and shocked, finding bodies of airmen trying to load the wrong ammunition into their weapons. It was scandalous, and he was disgusted to learn of their lack of training. He knew it had to be fixed to save lives and our airplanes, and he resolved to fix it.

The opportunity came when he became Vice Chief of Staff under General Thomas D. White, who was the fourth Chief of Staff of the Air Force. They were hunting and fishing partners. I was told that the idea of a marksmanship school was pitched to the Chief in a duck blind on a cold and wet morning on the eastern shore of Maryland. This was no small thing. The concept included training throughout the Air Force and would require the support and cooperation of all the Air Force Commands. The Chief gave General LeMay the green light, so the program was on.

No matter how noble or valuable an idea, it must be implemented and properly managed to bear fruit. The main emphasis was to train all Air Force personnel to become proficient with small arms as well as to keep officers and airmen proficient by providing skilled small-arms instructors throughout the Air Force. This required a new Air Force specialty code (AFSC) that identified Combat Arms Instructors, who we now call Red Hats. But to begin with they had to establish who trains the trainers. Questions included: Where do we get the syllabus and training manuals? Where do we get the necessary gunsmiths? Where can we build shooting ranges? Where should the marksmanship school be located? Who is going to orchestrate and ramrod this new Air Force-wide program?

Colonel Thomas C. Kelly, holder of Distinguished Pistol Badge Number 1, was the keynote speaker at the 30th anniversary of the combat arms Air Force Specialty Code at the Wyndham Hotel in the fall of 1993. He gave me a copy of the speech, and here is what he said:

> "Picture a happy base commander of Holloman Air Force Base back in November 1957 who just succeeded in opening up the White Sands guided missile range for mule deer hunting after it had been closed to hunting since 1942. Routine message on Wednesday suggested he report to the Vice Chief of Staff, with no date specified. The hunt opened on Friday, and on Sunday an H–19 helicopter located him atop a mountain in the San Andreas with curt instructions from 'Curt' LeMay saying, 'Report immediately.'" Some shaking in boots, night flight in a T–33 and in a brace before Gen LeMay at 0800 hundred Monday. No preliminaries. Just, "Tom, (I had never even seen him before, being an old fighter jock) the Air Force can't shoot anything with small arms but each other and holes through the B-52s they're supposed to guard. Our terrible performance when airfields were overrun in Korea cost us unnecessary lives and aircraft. The Russians have been winning the Olympics and all international shooting competitions, and we are supposed to be a nation of shooters. The carbines and Garands I've looked at are in sorry condition, and very few people can hit anything with the .45s. I want you to sit down with whatever help you need and have me a program ready

by next weekend to correct this sorry situation Air Force wide. Any questions?"

Naturally, there were none.

Col Kelly called in a long-time acquaintance, Colonel Pete Agnell, a successful survivor of several Pentagon assignments. He knew how to make the wheels turn in those high-altitude, rarefied air halls. The two of them, along with the commanding general of Air Training Command (ATC), carried a 40-page document with a 12-million-dollar budget to Gen LeMay. Col Kelly relates that the Air Training Command (ATC) commander was told to, "Take care of Kelly." And then he told Col Kelly, "You find a place in ATC and get going. End of conversation." That's when Col Kelly's work really began. He got help from the Army, the Marine Corps, the NRA, the Director of Civilian Marksmanship, Smith & Wesson, Colt, Winchester, and ammunition companies. A headquarters had to be established and staffed, ranges and test tunnels had to be built. Supply people, gunsmiths, and shooters were rounded up. Specialists from other services were borrowed. It was a Herculean task.

Gen LeMay became Air Force Chief of Staff on June 30, 1961. The major commands (four-star generals) were on board in supporting his program of small-arms training for all personnel and building strong security police forces proficient in combat arms. That was the primary purpose and foundation for the Air Force Marksmanship School. Competitive shooting was a sidebar, but it was the showcase. That's where the Air Force high-power rifle team comes into play. Gen LeMay wanted the U.S., and particularly the Air Force, to win Olympic medals, but he also wanted to beat the Army and Marine Corps at their own game—high-power rifle marksmanship with their combat rifle. That would be winning the most coveted prize: The National Trophy at Camp Perry, Ohio.

The National Trophy belongs to the United States Government. It is a beautiful, recessed bronze, depicting a naked Greek warrior holding the reins on four bloodhounds. It dates from 1903, Teddy Roosevelt's time. The trophy inscription starts with

"Presented by the Congress of the United States." Names of the winning teams are engraved on the border edge of the trophy, which is often referred to as the "Dogs of War." In early years, National Guard teams from several states were contenders. Later, it was pretty much a competition between the Army and the Marine Corps. Sometimes, the Army would win five or six years in a row, and then the Marine Corps would take over and win a number in a row. They traded back and forth with few interlopers of the National Guard or Army Reserve Teams, and, if memory serves, one or two civilian state teams along with the Navy.

Our strongest competition would obviously come from the Army and the Marine Corps. The all-Army team was stationed at Fort Benning, Georgia, with field teams found at First, Second, Third, Fourth, Fifth, and Sixth Armies across the country. Additionally, Seventh Army in Europe and Eighth Army in Korea would send top shooters each year to Fort Benning for training and possible add-on to the all-Army team for the Interservice Camp Perry matches. The Marine Corps' master team was stationed at Quantico, Virginia, but very strong teams were found at the first Marine Division stationed at Camp Pendleton and the 2nd Marine Division from Camp Lejeune. Additionally, many bases and stations had strong teams, particularly 29 Palms Marine Corps Base, and Cherry Point.

The idea of an Air Force team winning the National Trophy was considered ludicrous. People said it simply could not be done. How could the Air Force find eight men, six shooters plus a captain and coach, who could even load the M1 Garand service rifle? Impossible! What were these guys in blue thinking? Let 'em go play with their airplanes. Infantry combat troops will handle the rifles. The gamblers in Vegas sure weren't making positive bets on the Air Force.

Authority for the National Trophy and coveted Distinguished Rifleman Badge dates from the Department of War Appropriation Bill passed by the Congress in 1903. Elihu Root was Secretary of War and supported marksmanship training as did President Theodore Roosevelt. The Boer War brought interest in long-range shooting as did the poor performance of unprepared U.S. soldiers in the Spanish American War. This act established the National Board for Promotion of Rifle Practice (NBPRP) to promote marksmanship, training, and national competition, which included developing civilian marksmen in case they were called to war. The Assistant Secretary of the Army serves as president of the NBPRP. When I earned a position on the California State Team in 1962, my travel cost to attend the national matches was provided by Uncle Sam, basically under the congressional acts passed in the early part of the 1900s. It was my honor in the late 1980s to serve on the NBPRP with retired Marine Corps General (four-star) Walt. I had last seen him in 1964 when he was a brigadier general (one-star) presenting the Interservice Gold Medal to me for winning the 1,000-yard match with the M1 rifle. You never know who you will meet again in later life.

During my days of shooting, the National Rifle Association was still primarily concerned and associated with rifle and pistol marksmanship. They had a marvelous program for juniors in teaching marksmanship and gun safety. The NRA sponsored competitions across the United States, zones, regionals, etc., at local clubs, and military installations. The NBPRP authorizes matches (service rifle only) at some of the NRA competitions that allows competitors to earn credits (legs) for the Distinguished Badge. So many matches were a combination of NRA and DCM competitions. The Director on Civilian Marksmanship (DCM) was the operating arm of the NBPRP for civilian marksmanship.

Earning Bragging Rights

Be ready to hear lots of trumpets playing, but I can't help it. This Air Force team in 1964 was beyond outstanding. No service rifle team before had even come close to matching their success. There were good earlier individual shooters and successful match rifle teams, for certain, and many helped lay the groundwork for our success, but I'm talking about a powerhouse of individual and team wins with the service combat weapon against the Army, Marine Corps, other services, and the civilian world. There were far too many wins, both individual and team, to list them all. I'll cover the most important team accomplishments along with some heartbreaking losses and highlight just a few of the most significant individual wins.

Before discussing the team accolades, I need to give credit to two elements often left out of the limelight that are critical to success. First, the Range Branch (Red Hats) were the guys who made sure areas were set up and ready to go when we arrived for training. They ran our practice sessions as the match officials would in a major competition. These guys were pros in their support, and day in and day out, they arrived before us and left after us. When we insisted on shooting in the cold and wind, they worked in the cold and wind. When the team shot in the rain and mud, they got wet and muddy the same as we did.

The second group often overlooked were the superb craftsmen in our gun shop. I'll include our ammunition reloading experts and our R&D specialists with the gunsmiths as they worked hand in hand. They were simply at the top skill level. Technically, they got far ahead of the Army and Marine Corps, who had originally given the Air Force advice and help in our infant days. The other services were now coming to us to learn and improve. The gun shop started doing special work for other government agencies, including making the silencers for .22 pistols required by some government entities. We had the very best competitive firearms available anywhere. One gunsmith must be recognized: SSgt Alvin Estes. He traveled with us to the big matches and must be credited with everything we achieved. Alvin was often found in the wee morning hours at a match still smoothing triggers to perfection. Maybe I'm biased, but I would rate him Number One in the world as an M1 rifle specialist. Combine his skill with his dedication to the team and you get an unparalleled paragon.

As an aside, while still on the subject of the gun shop, I would also like to mention Tom Krcmar. Tom first came to my attention as a shooter, and he was in the top ranks with both pistol and shotgun—disciplines that seldom go together. He was a Technical Sergeant at that time but went on to make Master Sergeant before retirement. Tom was skilled in machine metalwork and came back to the Marksmanship School to work in the gun shop as a civilian. He mastered all aspects of gunsmithing and advanced to the top of the gun shop. He designed and built the first miniaturized (cut down) model of the revered but deadly 1911 Colt .45. The big full- time shooting teams were gone by 1969, but there were still plenty of challenges throughout the small arms community in the Air Force and other government agencies worldwide. He was selected as gunsmith for the 1988 Olympics in Korea, the 1992 Olympics in Barcelona, and the 1996 Olympics in Atlanta. Tom also represented the Air Force as a member of the prestigious Joint Service Small Arms Committee. This group is made up of representatives from all the services including the Coast Guard. They study the technology of proposed small arms weapons and decide which are most useful and can best be adapted. Some of the technology is classified and includes lasers and all manner of space-age thinking. He worked and guided the gun shop for over 25 years, which is quite a record. When combined with 22 years active military duty he completed 47 years of government service—a treasure for sure.

Only four shooters from the 1963 National Matches at Camp Perry remained on board after my first month of being OIC. They, however, were on their first or second year of shooting with the team. A few experienced shooters who had missed Camp Perry in 1963 came back to the team. We were mostly a very young team with high-level experience. Establishing a team required building confidence and an attitude of winning. The guys wanted to win and had talent. They needed guidance and coaching. Previously, some shooters thought they could read wind and shoot better than the coaches and, in some cases, they could. Of course, if the coaches were giving sight adjustments in rapidly changing wind conditions and a shooter and his partner were making their own contradicting adjustments, it wouldn't be long until no one knew where they were. That situation produced disastrous effects in short order. Winning team matches requires good shooters, but also a solid coach who is highly competent and respected in his trade.

Two young top shooting staff sergeants took up the tasks of lead coaches: SSgt Barney Bernard and SSgt David Thompson. Coaches don't just read the shifting wind and give sighting instructions, they pair up team-shooting partners who are compatible, decide in which

Long Shots — Teams

order pairs will shoot, and find who is the best anchorman and who is best leadoff. They learn their shooters, pick up vibes, and recognize team moods. Building interpersonal trust to ensure strong mutual respect is essential. You could say they have skills akin to psychiatrists or psychologists. Some shooters don't want to talk prior to shooting, others want to chat with the coach, some will tell jokes and laugh, and others prefer quiet. The coaches must learn each shooter and figure out how to make the mix work best. Master Sergeant Leon Linscott, Technical Sergeant Ken Horst, and Staff Sergeants Henry Evans and Paul Stapper were also excellent coaches. It seems the best coaches are those who get along well with people. I mentioned Sergeants Bernard and Thompson first because they coached the winning teams at Interservice and Camp Perry.

Shooting rifles and pistols is much different from most sports. Rah-rah and cheering do not work well. The shooter must concentrate on what he or she is doing as in any sport, but a steady hold and careful trigger control can best be maintained at a resting pulse rate. He doesn't throw the ball harder, run faster, or jump higher. He must control his emotions, slow down his heart rate, and steady the sight on his target as he applies increasing pressure on the trigger. Plenty of whoops and hollers are invited after a rifle match but not while shooting.

During January and February of 1964, we trained on Air Force shooting ranges at Camp Bullis, an Army installation just west of San Antonio. This was a time of getting to know each other. They needed to know me, and I needed to know them. We also needed to shoot training matches and record scores, so we knew what we had on our team. Coaches shot with us in training for two reasons: First, I wanted to see how well they could shoot. Second, to show team members their coaches' competence. Having coaches shoot with us turned out to be good policy, and I extended the policy to individual matches at competitions. They won more than their fair share, which boosted their morale, kept their shooters on their toes, and delighted me with Air Force wins.

The coaches worked through the scores and personalities to line up the teams. The top four shooters were designated as the blue team; the second four were the silver team, and the next four were the red team. Our shooters knew they better make one of those teams or they might be looking for new jobs. To make things transparent and visible every day, we lined up on the range for training according to scores. The rifleman with highest score shot on station one. The next high scoring man was to his right on station two, and so on down the line. Scores were tabulated and posted each week so shooters could change positions if they outshot the shooter on their left. Of course, the opposite could happen. Nevertheless, everyone could see on paper, and on the range, exactly where they stood. They all worked to move left on the firing line.

In March, we started out with our new teams shooting in the Southwest Region of the U.S. We needed to build confidence, and we did that by winning the team event in the San Antonio Big Bore Tournament, the Boulder City Open in Nevada, the Phoenix Regional in Arizona, and the Southwestern Regional back in Texas. These matches were not just against the top Army or Marine Corps teams, but they were fought against the U.S. 4th Army, U.S. Marine Station teams, Army Reserves, National Guard, and some darn good civilian teams. We weren't the biggest boys yet, but we had been in the fight and won, and team mettle was building. The "We will win" attitude was coming about smartly.

At one of our early competitions, we met up and defeated shooters from the First Marine Division team stationed at Camp Pendleton. They were a good strong team, and any time you beat a Marine Corps rifle team you've accomplished something. Their motto, "Every man a rifleman," means something to them, and you'd better take notice. When we got back to Lackland, I was sort of bubbling over with pride in my guys and happened to see Col Kelly, our commander, in the headquarters hallway. Of course, I should've known better—lieutenants were not invited to initiate conversations with full colonels—but I blurted out we had beaten the Camp Pendleton Marines. He looked at me and said, "We don't take candy from babies," turned, and walked away. Wow, it was like a cannonball straight through my gut. I was crushed but got his point. We had not beaten the big Marine team at Quantico. Maybe not the best example of leadership, but it was before the lovey-dovey days of making everybody happy. The WWII colonels were more, "Don't expect a pat on the back for doing your job." I never relayed that encounter to the team or anyone else.

Pride in being a member of the team became evident; maybe it was character or virtue. In any case, the shooters seemed to lose any jealousy. They were happy and celebrated wins by any team member. Perhaps you could say we had crossed the Rubicon from individuals to a team. As John Marshall, Chief Justice of the United States Supreme Court for 35 years, immortalized, "United we stand: divided we fall." This was now a team I wanted.

Our next major competition was at Fort Benning, Georgia. Fort Benning is called The Home of the Infantryman. It is also the home of the Army Marksmanship Unit (AMU) with all their attending schools, which include sniper training and competitive marksmanship. The Army High-Power Rifle Team is forceful and imposing. Their record is stellar, and they don't have to prove anything to anybody. We were well received, and some of the shooters on both teams knew each other. This was the Carrot Match, held once each year as a challenge competition between the Army and the Air Force. It is shot in the same format as competition for the U.S. National Trophy at Camp Perry. The eight-man team consists of six shooters, team coach, and team captain. It is often referred to as NTT, abbreviated for "National Trophy Team." To be clear on team sizes, most civilian competitions were conducted with teams of four shooters, while military team matches normally called for six shooters. The course of fire remains the same for six or four men and it is designated as the National Match Course (NMC).

To give the reader some background, I will explain how the NMC match is scored and the sequence of the shooting at different distances. For the first phase, each shooter fires 10 shots offhand (standing) at 200 yards from the target. Each shot in the black, a circle that is 12-inches in diameter, about the size of a dinner plate, counts as five points. The scoring rings outside the black go to 24-inch diameter for four points and 36-inch for three points. A perfect score with 10 shots in the black would be a total of 50. A smaller circle, four-inch in diameter inside the black is called the V ring and is used to break ties.

In the offhand phase shooters fire as pairs at the same target, the first shooter fires, and after his shot is scored, the second shooter fires and so on as they trade back and forth. Each pair is given 20 minutes for their total of 20 shots.

The second course is rapid fire, shooting from the sitting position with a 50-second time limit. The target distance and target size are the same as offhand—12-inch black circle at 200 yards. The shooter starts in the standing position with his rifle locked and loaded. Targets are hidden from view, but as they are raised into view, the shooter drops into the sitting position, takes aim, and fires two rounds. He then loads a full clip, firing the eight rounds. If all 10 are in the black, it would give him another 50 points.

The next course is 10 shots rapid fire in the prone position shooting at the same target with a 12-inch bull's-eye from 300 yards. Again, the shooter starts from standing position. When the target is raised, the shooter drops down into the prone position and fires two rounds, reloads with a full clip, and fires the last eight rounds. This must be done in 60 seconds. If all 10 shots are in the black, he gains another 50 points. Obviously, the rapid-fire courses are fired by one team member at a time.

The last course is 20 shots per shooter, slow fire at a 20-inch bull's-eye from 600 yards with shooters shooting in pairs, trading off shots. The coach really goes to work now, reading wind and calling sight changes to the shooters. This becomes a true team effort, and each shooter must be able to call his shot, which means telling the coach where he pictured the shot when he fired his rifle. The coach makes changes, if any are required, for the next shooter based on the first shooter's call and any wind changes. Shooters must have complete confidence in each other to get this right. A shooter who can't accurately call his shots costs everybody points. Hitting the black 20 times gives each shooter 100 points. A perfect individual score for the total NMC is 250, but that doesn't happen often with the service rifle. I have had fewer than 10 in my entire shooting career, and I was a top contender. They are rare indeed.

Now, back to Fort Benning and the Carrot Match. Each side for the Army and Air Force shooters designated one team (six shooters, coach, and captain) to represent their service for this competition. Ours was named the Blue Team and, of course, our best shooters were on the team. Their team was called Army Red. We were hyped up for the match, not overexcited but ready to take on the best. The offhand shooting at 200 yards went well, and the scores were solid. I knew we were in the running. Matches are often won or lost in the offhand stage, and that is where shooters are most nervous and prone to jerk the trigger, causing a miss. The Army team was rather nonchalant and confident that they would give us a good shellacking—not expecting much of a challenge. After all, they crushed the Air Force every time at Fort Benning, so why should this be different?

We held our own in the 200-yard rapid fire, and when the teams moved back to 300 yards for the prone rapid-fire stage, one of the Army shooters said something like, "You guys are hot and good luck." This is a tactic that is sometimes used by poor sportsmen trying to make their opponent nervous and disturb their mental and emotional stability. I don't believe in this case that was the intent at all. We did not know what the Army score was and quite frankly did not care. Top competitors don't look at scoreboards or worry about their opponent's scores because that only adds unwanted pressure. The top guys just concentrate on each shot. We needed to stay the course and shoot our best. But of course, word was spreading, and we had more people watching us when we moved back to 600 yards. I was concentrating on my own shooting so wasn't sure what the total team score was. We had a good run at 600 yards, and our team captain reported the Blue Team score as 1486. The Army Red team came in with a score of 1491. They had won, but it wasn't a smashing victory and we made them sweat a bit. Lt Col Bill Pullum was the officer in charge of the Army team. Being the gentleman that he was, he came over and gave me a hearty congratulation on a fine team score. They had beaten our six shooters by just five points, less than one point per man. Our team average was 247.7 and theirs was 248.5. Nobody was happy about losing, but the team gained strength and resolve. We got our revenge by beating the Army in the annual team-eating contest at Pletcher's all-you-can-eat catfish diner in Columbus, Georgia.

The most significant matches for service rifle shooting are the Interservice Championship held at Quantico Virginia, and, of course, National Matches held at Camp Perry, Ohio. Truth to tell, the Interservice Championship is the toughest competition to win credits/points toward the coveted Distinguished Marksman Badge. Although classified as a badge, it is a handsome solid gold medal authorized for wear on Class A uniforms of all the services. Credits (called Legs) to earn this badge are given only to the top 10% of specified competitions. Civilians also compete for the Distinguished Marksman Badge, but not at the Interservice Championship. Legs were awarded as bronze, silver, or gold, depending on one's placement in the top 10% of the match. In my day, the shooter had to earn three legs to qualify for the badge, but at least one had to be precious metal, either silver or gold. The shooter could shoot for years winning bronze medals by being in the top 10%, but he had to reach to the top of the 10% for silver or gold medals to qualify for the Distinguished Rifleman Badge. You can imagine how the military guys would fight for these medals. They look good on a uniform but also said something about your skills, particularly for the Marines and infantry troops. A leg was much easier to win in competition with lots of civilians. The badge is awarded by military orders, and it is most always presented at a ceremony. The winner's name, and grade if in the military, is engraved on the back of the medal along with a number according to those awarded in each service. Mine is number 78. There are no replacements, and you can't buy one of these badges, so they are guarded closely.

Our team traveled to the Interservice Championship in early August. Competition at Quantico is the toughest you could find anywhere with over 700 expert marksmen from all military services. We held our own in the individual service rifle matches and remained competitive, but not at the top. We had some success with SSgt Thompson winning the long-range open aggregate, a combination of 20 shots at 600 yards and 20 shots at 1,000 yards. He shot a superb score of 200 with 38 Vs—meaning out of 40 shots fired he kept 38 in the 12-inch center (V ring) at 600 yards and the 20-inch center (V ring) at 1,000. That match allowed bolt action (match) rifles with scopes. Most shooters used Winchester Model 70s. Our concentration was with the service rifle,

Long Shots — Teams

but we didn't mind taking a few awards away from the snipers. I had a particularly good day on August 9, 1964, and managed to win the 1,000-yard service rifle, M1 or M14 event. That was our only individual gold with the service rifle, but it was a good one. The weather was good with wind eight to 10 mph from 11 o'clock, temperature around 80°, and the skies were clear. There was not much wind fluctuation, so all you had to do was "hold um and squeeze um." My score of 100 with 14 Vs tied the all-time record. And I think the two of us still hold the record. The truth is the targets were changed a couple of years later to a larger size but different scoring system. The target used in our 20-shot event was scored five points for each shot in a 36-inch black circle. The V ring inside the circle was 20 inches. I can't speak for GYSGT Leroy F. Cross, USMC, the record co-holder, but the young guys are shooting such terrific scores today that I doubt our record would have held up for long. Several of our shooters placed in the top 10 of various individual matches at Quantico, and while there were only two individual gold medal wins, we kept nipping at their heels, so the Army and Marine Corps knew we were there.

The celebration at the completion of the Interservice Championship is a sit-down dinner in class A uniforms (coat and tie). The gold medals are presented by flag (generals and admirals) officers. Brig Gen Lewis W. Walt presented my gold medal for placing first at a thousand yards with the service rifle.

The biggest single prize for a Marine is winning the individual service rifle event. Tradition dictates that the Commandant award a meritorious promotion to the Marine. That is a match hard fought for by all the services, so it is not always won by a Marine. I was pleased to be there when a Marine won the match in 1964. The Commandant's comments when presenting the award start with: "Be it known to all men" and of course the whole room explodes with cheers.

A Marine somewhere out there owes me for his promotion. While serving in the Pentagon in 1990, I was asked to bring a general officer to the Interservice Rifle Championship banquet at Quantico to represent the Air Force. My clay target shooting friend, Maj Gen Keithe E. Nelson, who was the Judge Advocate General of the Air Force, agreed to go with me, and we drove down in my car.

I had had met General Alfred M. Gray, the Commandant, a couple of times, so during the drive I briefed Gen Nelson on what I knew about the program and told him of the Marine tradition of a meritorious promotion if a Marine won the match. Gen Nelson sat on the dais next to the Commandant. He read the program during dinner and saw that a Marine corporal had won the individual competition. The Commandant was caught by surprise when Gen Nelson mentioned what a great tradition the meritorious promotion was—it was clear no one had briefed him. I could see something was happening as a couple of lieutenant colonels were obviously summoned by the Commandant during the dinner. Gen Nelson told me on the way home what had happened. A Lt Col had been dispatched to get a set of sergeant stripes. It was still a roaring event as the Commandant announced the meritorious promotion.

We can't leave Quantico without introducing you to the Commander of the Weapons Training Battalion, Colonel Walter R. Walsh, truly a legend in his own time. The Marine Corps rifle team came under his authority. He was strict but revered. Young Marine company-grade officers told me how they dreaded facing his cold, steely gray eyes. He was built small, maybe 5'6," and while he was a man of few words, his presence alone captured attention. I did not know what to expect for quarters at Quantico and was concerned where my small team of 16 shooters would be billeted. Some of the barracks were quite large and would hold well over 100 beds. Remember, there were over 700 military shooters at this competition, and most of them needed quarters on base. Can you imagine trying to sleep in an open bay (no walls) barracks on bunkbeds with 50 guys snoring? When reporting in with my team to receive billeting instructions, I was told we would be using camping trailers in a recreation area on one of the base lakes. The trailers were old and well-used, but what a super set up for us. I had my whole team together with me, comfortable and away from the snoring crowd. I don't know why we were singled out for this privileged treatment. I never asked and Colonel Walsh never spoke of it. Did Col Kelly call him? They knew each other before the war from pistol competitions. Maybe Col Walsh was just looking out for a young lieutenant with a big responsibility. Guess I will never know.

Long Shots — Teams

Col Walsh was shooting competitively before I was born. He attended the national matches in 1928, shooting rifle, pistol, and smallbore as a member of the New Jersey National Guard. He won about everything one could win, setting many new records. At Camp Perry, he was once recognized as the best all-around shooter. This was before World War II, after which he came back to competitive shooting and continued to win throughout the 1950s, becoming Marine Corps champion in both service rifle and service pistol. He was a shooting member of the 1948 Olympic team and won world championships. His shooting record is lengthy and impressive. I have only covered some highlights, but he was still shooting in the 1990s as a civilian.

He joined the Marine Corps reserve in 1939 and came on active duty in 1942. His original duties were marksmanship training and especially snipers. He requested combat duty and was sent to the Pacific. During the battle of Okinawa, it is reported an enemy sniper had his group pinned down, and he took that enemy out at 90 yards with his 1911 pistol. I would've liked to have heard the full story on that one. The Marines lost 3,443 men in the battle, with the Army losing 4,718, and Navy KIA was 4,022 in the 82-day battle. Japanese military losses were estimated to be 90,000. Unfortunately, it is thought that as many as 80,000 civilians committed suicide.

I'll share a story Colonel Walsh told me himself. Previously I said he was a man of few words—at least that was my impression. Technically, he told the story to my boss Col Hunter, who had replaced Col Kelly and was at Quantico to watch us shoot. Here's how it happened. Col Kelly, who had been acquainted with Col Walsh before the war had given me part of the story. I related that to Col Hunter, and he asked Col Walsh about his FBI days, so he told us the story. I've seen it written up several times.

In 1934, the FBI was just beginning to allow agents to carry guns. Mr. Walsh was known to be a shooter and signed up. It was an era of gangsters: Baby Face Nelson, John Dillinger, Bonnie and Clyde, and others. The Brady Gang had been on a crime spree for a couple of years, causing many deaths and giving J. Edgar Hoover ulcers. They had the distinction of being classified as Public Enemy Number One. The FBI was given a tip in 1937 that someone in Bangor, Maine, was trying to buy a magazine for a Thompson submachine gun. Fully automatic firearms had been tightly restricted by federal law in 1934, but parts and accessories were still around. A trap was organized with Mr. Walsh being the set piece, posing as a bank teller. As he told me, he had a Colt 1911 in his right hand and the new .357 Magnum Smith & Wesson that had just come out that year in his left hand. Things didn't go as planned, and either Alfred Brady or Clarence Schaffer got off the first shots with the Thompson hitting Mr. Walsh in his shoulder and right arm, knocking him down. Guess what? He's left-handed, and Schaffer was killed with the .357. The stories I've read report that Mr. Walsh chased after Brady, who was being shot at by FBI agents outside, and put an extra .357 bullet in him. Mr. Walsh told me he grabbed up the Thompson that Schaffer dropped and killed Brady with that gun as he was trying to get away. I've also read that he met the outlaws at the front door. Mr. Walsh told us he was standing behind a counter when the shooting started. Since he told me the story himself, I'll stick with that. Dalhover, the other gang member, was seized and disarmed. It was the end of the Brady Gang.

He told us of some other encounters. I think he permanently eliminated a dozen bad guys. One telling story was capturing Doc Baker, who was wanted for murder, kidnapping, and robbing banks with his famous outlaw mother, Ma Baker. Mr. Walsh had tracked him down and had the drop on him with a pistol to Doc's head, warning him that if he moved, he would kill him. Asking him where his heater was, Doc said he made a mistake leaving it in the hotel. Mr. Walsh's reply was something like, "You're lucky, Doc. I would've killed you."

Col Walsh retired from the Marine Corps in 1970, and he stayed in Northern Virginia. On my first tour in the Pentagon (1979/84), I would see him at gun shows or various events. For sure, he would show up at the George Mason University yearly gun show. He moved through the crowd unnoticed, just a quiet elderly gentleman. He still had cold steely gray eyes, but now I was more comfortable talking with him and he seemed to enjoy talking about Quantico days. You had to wonder what people walking past him, paying him no mind, would've thought if they knew his story. It's a mystery to me that no one has written a book about him and his exploits. His story would make a good adventure movie. He died in April 2014 at the age of 106. What a life, a real jewel for our country.

Camp Perry is the absolute Mecca for competitive shooting and particularly for high-power rifle shooting. There are certainly other fine and prestigious rifle matches, including, of course, the Interservice Championship at Quantico, but the apex of glory can only come at Camp Perry. The National Matches are held at Perry traditionally one week after the Interservice Championship in August. Camp Perry is on the southwest shore of Lake Erie, adjacent to the city of Port Clinton, Ohio. It is owned by the Ohio National Guard but was leased each year by the Department of Army, the Director of Civilian Marksmanship (DCM), and the National Rifle Association to conduct the National Rifle Matches that have been held at Camp Perry since 1907. The range is named after Commodore Oliver Hazard Perry, the hero of Lake Erie in the war of 1812. As a reminder, the National Board for the Promotion of Rifle Practice (NBPRP) was authorized 1903. That legislation also established the National Matches and support for civilian marksmanship training. The executive arm of the NBPRP was the Director of Civilian Marksmanship (DCM). In 1996, those functions and responsibilities were transferred to the Civilian Marksmanship Program. Pistol, and smallbore rifle (.22 caliber) championships are held before the high-power rifle championship. As a civilian, I competed in all three: pistol, smallbore rifle, and high-power rifle in 1960. But my love was high-power rifle (sometimes called Big Bore) shooting, and I competed in those matches again in 1961 and 1962 as a civilian, and then from 1963 through 1966 as an Air Force lieutenant.

For those not familiar with competitive shooting or firearms, smallbore shooting is done with a .22-caliber rifle that is often used for plinking or hunting small game such as squirrels and rabbits. Smallbore competitions are often held indoors or at least under covered shooting positions. High-power rifles are more powerful and recognized as a firearm for hunting larger animals like deer and for combat. High-power shooters claim theirs is the more manly sport. I suppose that attitude comes from the infantry and Marines. They like to make the point they shoot outdoors in the sun, wind, rain, and

443

lying in the mud, without shooting mats or covered positions. The smallbore shooters are quick to point out they quit playing in the mud after their second birthday.

A major and very important difference between high-power rifle shooting and pistol, shotgun, or international competitions is in the team event. In the other disciplines the team event is merely an aggregate of individual scores. In high-power team events, the competitors shoot in pairs during the slow fire portions, alternating shots. In the offhand phase, often a word of encouragement from a shooter or the coach can calm or strengthen a shooting partner. But the real test is in the long-range phase where partners can make or break each other. They must be able to accurately call their shots so the next one firing can be confident his shot will be true. The coach also becomes an active team participant by calling sight corrections. The team test is how well the partners and the coach can work together, and not just adding up individual scores. Air Force Chief of Staff General J.P. McConnell put it best, "While individual excellence in competition is always commendable, the real test of unit capability is in team competition."

Equipment and training can be different for the various shooting sports, but skills, determination to win, and mental toughness are the same. My friends and fellow USA Shooting board members, Lones Wigger and Gary Anderson, are legends and were standouts for the free world against communist-backed teams. Gary shot smallbore and international high-power events but under covered ranges. Gary's win in Cairo, Egypt, in October of 1962 was the first significant pushback on the Russians since WWII. They are both world champions and hold gold medals for more than one Olympics. Lones Wigger fired competitively from 1964 to 1987. He is an icon in international smallbore shooting. More recently, Matt Emmons has carried our flag internationally in smallbore shooting. He is a handsome young guy, friendly, and personable with many international medals, like Lones and Gary, including Olympic golds.

I like Matt, but what made me proudest was seeing him shoot a wild shot in the Beijing Olympics. It was torture, and here is why. My wife and I were in the audience in the specially built arena for this event. It was the final shoot-off for the Olympic medal with only eight or 10 finalist competitors. A large screen was set up above the shooters that showed their target and each shot fired. All competitors except Matt had finished firing, and he was on his last shot. The scores were up, and he was well ahead of his closest rival, a Chinese team member. One more shot and another Olympic gold would be his. He could win with eight or even a seven, which he had never been known to shoot in an international match. All the shooters in this final shootoff were firing 10s with a scant nine or two. Half of the audience was international, and the other half was Chinese. The arena was deathly silent waiting for the last shot of the match. Matt fired his shot, and on the massive screen it showed a four! The entire crowd gasped. A second of silence followed and then a huge bellow as the Chinese realized their native son had won. We were stunned, completely shocked, and in disbelief.

Television cameras and reporters swarmed Matt immediately. I was sick, so I could just imagine how he felt. He handled it like the champion he is. It was the same as the military: "Yes, sir," and, "No, sir," or, "No excuse, sir." There are no other answers. No one wants to hear excuses and he gave none. His wife, also a top shooter, was there as a reporter for her country, the Czech Republic. She stood with him through the gaggle of reporters, bright lights and microphones pushed in his face as TV cameras from around the world zeroed in on them. The Chinese media made a great but positive story out of it, in sort of a Romeo and Juliet mode. We watched it on Chinese TV as it was replayed for several nights. Matt lost the gold, but he won the Chinese and the international community. There is a major difference between a winner and a champion.

Kim Rhode is a legend in shotgun competition. She has dominated that world and is the only woman to win individual medals in six consecutive Olympics. As a young high-school girl, she was on two U.S. Teams to World Cups where I was the Chief of Mission: Cyprus in 1994 and Lima, Peru, in 1995. While she was not yet a big winner, it was apparent she would be. No one can match her record.

One more I must add is Virginia Thrasher, a 19-year-old University of West Virginia freshman. Ginny, as she is called, was a good collegiate air rifle shooter, but she had never traveled or competed overseas. She was not yet selected for the USA shooting (Olympic) team, so had no financial support. A fine group I am associated with called the Bunker Club provided funds for her to attend a competition in Munich, Germany. She won one of the medals, which jumped up her confidence level, and came back to the States to earn a position on our Olympic team. The rest is history: she went on to win on the first gold medal of the Rio Olympic Games in the women's air rifle event.

Vincent Hancock is a fine young man and a superb skeet shooter. It was my pleasure to watch him in the suspenseful shoot-off in Beijing to win the Gold Olympic Medal. He went on to win the Gold again in the London and the Tokyo Olympics. He just won his fourth Gold Medal in Paris. He is the first shooter and one of only six Olympians to win gold in the same event. He is an excellent spokesman for USA Shooting and a fine role model for younger shooters. We shot quail together, and he let me get a few so you know he's a good guy. I have the highest regard for all our international shooters. They represent our country well.

International high-power rifle shooting and American high-power rifle are as different as baseball and basketball even though they are similar in skills needed. However, one thing in common is the drive to win and the mental toughness required. Why do I like the high-power shooting? Is it the roar of the guns, the smell of powder, the rapid fire and reloading, the team event, or maybe the recoil of the rifle? It remains an enigma to me still. But I suspect it is the people, the order, and ties to the military. No, I don't like lying in the mud to shoot, but it's part of the game. Camp Perry is operated with military precision. The cannon is fired at 0600 hours, announcing reveille, and the Stars & Stripes are raised. A trumpet sounds retreat, and the National Anthem is played as the flag is retired at 1800 hours. Often the Army band would march to the flag ceremony and afterward put on a musical program for the crowd sitting on the grass. It was most enjoyable. A French World War I railroad car rested at the flagpole. It was called 40 and eight as it held 40 men or eight horses. France gifted it as a thank-you to Americans for our help in liberating their country during World War II.

Long Shots — Teams

There were 2,721 high-power rifle competitors in 1964, military and civilians shooting in events for both service and match rifles. It is a week of intense competition. A Small Arms Firing School originally authorized in 1918 is conducted by the U.S. Army Infantry School from Fort Benning before the competition. Expert instructors from all the services assist in this training. It is an excellent and professional school well received by the civilian community. It's interesting to note that Lt Gen Arthur MacArthur, father of General Douglas MacArthur, suggested establishing a special school to train shooting instructors for the Army in 1907. He had been awarded the Medal of Honor for valor in 1863 during the Battle of Missionary Ridge. No doubt, his foresight led to the Small Arms Firing School. Counting the competitors (in pistol, smallbore, and high-power), instructors, students, match officials, security, support personnel, and spectators, the Camp Perry population would rise to well over 7,000 during the championships.

Our Air Force Team moved into quarters at Camp Perry in August 1964 with a total strength of 16 shooters. Many of them had not yet earned the Distinguished Rifleman Badge. Rather puny compared to Army and Marine Corps numbers. Some state teams were nearly as large as we were. While I was jogging around the grounds, a voice called out, "Lieutenant!" It was Colonel Joseph J. Peot, the commander of the Army Marksmanship School and Commander (big boss) over the Army team. Colonel Peot said, "Come over here and shoot some arrows with me." He was known as a good guy, but colonels are known to bite hard, and I was a little nervous. Additionally, Colonel Peot was a decorated combat veteran of World War II, which can certainly cause an untested lieutenant some anxiety. He had an extra bow, and we stood out in the grass shooting arrows for distance. He was built heavy through the arms and shoulders. I was sorely mistaken in thinking I could keep up with him. His arrows flew high and far, while mine were wimpy. I'm thinking, How can this be happening, an old guy beating me? We were talking casually, and I soon felt at ease with him. That would end shortly. After shooting a dozen arrows each, we went down range to recover our missiles. His could be located as the feathered ends guided us to them, the shafts sticking up nearly perpendicular. My sorry shots hit the ground at a much lower angle and were nearly horizontal, concealing the shaft and feathered ends in the grass. It was quite embarrassing to be sure, particularly when the Col said, rather emphatically, "Those arrows are expensive! They cost a buck each!" Then he said, "Take off your shoes and socks," as he did the same. There we were, an Army full colonel and a stupid Air Force lieutenant cruising around in the grass barefoot with our toes searching for errant arrows. I think we found all but one, which he referred to as collateral battle damage.

He started competitive shooting at the University of Wisconsin in 1930, was commissioned in the Army reserves in 1934, and went on active duty in 1940. As I recall, he had two Bronze Stars from WWII. He commanded the AMU from 1963 to 1967. The more I got to know him, the more I liked him. He always came by to check on me and see that we had everything we needed whenever he was at a match we attended. Col Peot later made me an honorary member of the Army Marksmanship Unit. Quite an honor, and I keep the pin set with the AMU Seal in Lucite on my desk.

Several individual and team matches, sponsored by both the NRA and DCM, were conducted at Camp Perry during the National championship. Our guys were doing well and being noticed. Some bright spots in individual matches were SSgt Barney Bernard, winning the Slow Fire Preliminary; SSgt Aldo Frascoia, winning the Nevada trophy; and SSgt Ray Lewis, winning the Marine Corps Cup. None had ever been won by an Air Force shooter before. Several team members, including me, made the President's Hundred. It's a highly competitive match and particularly prestigious for Army shooters as they wear shoulder patches on Class A uniforms designating their prowess. The President's Hundred designation and authorization is published by Army orders and is filed in the recipient's permanent military record. One of our team members, coach and shooter SSgt David Thompson, won the President's Hundred in 1996. A special honor comes with winning the President's—a letter from the White House. How many have a congratulatory letter from the President? The first letter of congratulations for winning this event went out from the White House in 1904 signed by Theodore Roosevelt.

SSgt Thompson was a super coach and shooter. We were all mighty proud of him.

The DCM competition follows the NRA-sponsored matches and is where the military really bears down. This is when only service rifles are permitted and Legs (credits) can be won, leading to the coveted Distinguished Rifleman Badge for both civilians and military shooters. The last and most important event is the competition for the National Trophy Team (NTT). Before that team event, an individual match titled the National Trophy Individual (NTI) is fired to select the highest scoring individual shooting the service rifle. That is a really big deal with the military community because the winner normally receives a meritorious promotion or a military commendation. Our team member, SSgt Bobby Smith, shot a perfect score of 250 to win the match and the award of the Daniel Boone trophy in 1964. He was the first and is still the only Air Force member to win the NTI award.

As you might expect, we were elated. The whole team practically exploded with jubilation and pride. The Army and Marine Corps shooters and their leadership were shocked. This was not supposed to happen. The Marine Corps was particularly out of sorts, not so much that the Air Force won but because SSgt Smith had been a Marine and transferred to the Air Force when he wasn't picked up as a shooter for the Marine Corps team. SSgt Smith accomplished the impossible, and we all walked a little taller. In my opinion, SSgt Smith was the first shooter to bring real stature to the Air Force at Camp Perry. He did it with the combat service weapon against all comers. Winning smallbore and pistol are nice, and I take nothing away from excellent shooters, but they are not firing the major combat trooper's weapon.

For the National Trophy Team Match, our band was small, but we were punching far above our weight. There would be 150 teams competing in this match. Our firing team was made up of Technical Sergeants Horst and Tossas and Staff Sergeants Patrick, Smith, and Evans. I made up the sixth shooting member. MSgt Linscott was team captain, and SSgt Bernard was the coach. None of us had ever represented the Air Force in this match previously, with the possible exception of TSgt Tossas. We were green but carried the Air Force

449

Flag to our shooting station with confidence. The weather was perfect for shooting: clear and calm.

We started out a little shaky on the first course of fire, 200-yard offhand (standing), which is shot in pairs. One of our pairs was nervous and excited, and both shooters shot a three, which is not in the black. Heck, we were all nervous and excited. A three is hard to overcome, but they both managed to get through it. Our second pair of shooters shot 48s, and my shooting partner Sgt Horst and I both managed to keep all our shots in the black for scoring 50 each. That kept us in the running with six points down. No one was paying any attention to the Air Force team. After all, it was ludicrous to think we could be competitive in the National Trophy Team (NTT) match. All of us shot well in the 200-yard rapid fire, losing only one point, so we moved back to 300 yards in reasonable shape score-wise, just seven points down. Crowds were beginning to gather behind the high-scoring Army and Marine Corps teams. Once again, we all shot well at 300 yards, losing only one point. That left our team score eight points down. Our flag had been carried back to the 600-yard line, the last course of fire. As we moved back, one of the guys noticed a crowd gathering behind our flag. We didn't know what other teams were shooting and had long ago learned not to chase scores of other competitors: keep your head down and concentrate on your own shooting.

I learned later, after the match, that we had passed the top Army teams in points after the 300-yard line and were neck-and-neck with the leading Marines. My experience is that most matches are often won by scores in the 200-yard offhand stage but often lost on the 600-yard line. Now, at 600 yards, much depended on the coach and his correct reading of the wind and recognizing changes rapidly. Sgt Bernard was up to the task and did a great job calling the wind and calmly coaxing us all to "hold um and squeeze um" for each shot. I lost my 18th shot to a four just out of the black and 2 o'clock. That could be on the shooter or coach, but I called it slightly right and felt it was me, not our super coach.

As in *A Tale of Two Cities*, "It was the best of times, it was the worst of times …" Our score was 1,486. We had two shooters with scores of 246 each, two shooters with scores of 248 each, and two shooters with a scores of 249 each. We had beaten all the Army teams, but we were tied with the Marine Corps top team. They were declared the winner by having more Vs (center shots). My partner and I both fired 249s, one point less than perfect, but I had more Vs, so was awarded the General Thomas White Trophy. That did not lessen the sting of the team defeat, and I would gladly have traded my trophy for one more point in our team score. GySgt M. Pietroforte scored a perfect 250 for the Marine Corps Team, and Lt Dave Willis had a 247. You will hear more of Lt Willis as you read on. They beat us fair and square. *The American Rifleman Magazine* of October 1964 describes the Marine and Air Force teams shooting it out at 600 yards as interesting. I felt a little like I let the team down with my score of 249. After all, I was the boss and the leader. Of course, I knew better. It's a total team score, but it was a huge disappointment to be so close and lose the match. I think everyone on the team was sick about losing and in a state of depression.

To quote a great man and President of the United States, "The credit belongs to the man who is actually in the arena, whose face is marred by dust and sweat and blood; who strives valiantly; errs, and comes short again and again, because there is no effort without error and shortcoming; but who does actually strive to do the deeds; who knows the great enthusiasms, the great devotions; who spends himself in a worthy cause; who at the best knows in the end the triumph of high achievement, and who at the worst, if he fails, at least fails while daring greatly, so that his place shall never be with those cold and timid souls who know neither victory nor defeat." All of us were feeling the agony of defeat. However, it could not show. We didn't have to be good losers, but we did have to be sportsmen and gentlemen to our fellow competitors.

Because of the tie score, which never happened before in anyone's memory, both our teams, the Marine Corps and Air Force, were called to the presentation stage together. Wearing our false smiles, we were presented with silver second-place medals and excused from the stage. As we departed down the stairs, someone in the audience said loud enough for those of us departing to hear, "What the hell? It'll be the Coast Guard next." The Coast Guard is a great sister service that performs a dangerous and vital mission. I have high respect for them, but they do not have winning rifle teams. The comment was supposed to be a joke, but it implied we were an aberration or a mistake. It hurt my heart to have the team hear that stinging remark, but none of them ever said anything. Nevertheless, it torqued my jaw to the point it hurt my teeth and I could bite through nails. We were bloodied but had run a good race, and I suppose most thought it would be incredible for this little Air Force team to think we could do it in the first place, much less do it again. After all, lightning does not strike the same place twice, and you can't capture it in a bottle. Right? Betting on NEVER or ALWAYS is a dangerous game indeed.

A Shocking Win

The team had a watershed year in 1965. Many individual matches were won by our team members but again I'll concentrate on the team competition. We started out like gangbusters in early February, winning the first match of the year at Edwards Air Force Base in California. Then we moved to Nellis Air Force Base in Nevada where we won the Sahara Open and another match competing against all comers, but particularly the Marine team from Camp Pendleton and the Marines based at 29 Palms. Californian civilians could always put up some top shooters, but it was harder for them to put a winning team together. We moved back to Texas in early March for the Southwest Invitational held at Camp Bullis and won the six-man team match, setting a new range record of 1491 with 149 Vs. That's an average of 248.5 out of a possible 250 per shooter, which is mighty fine shooting. It was back to California on 26 March for the Masters Hi-Desert Invitational held at the Marine Corps base 29 Palms, and we won both first and second place in the team event. Marine Brig Gen William K. Jones presented the winning trophy to us and sent a congratulatory letter to Maj Gen Mooney, our home base commander at Lackland. Our next win was in April at the Desert State Regional held at Nellis Air Force Base, Nevada. Then it was on to the South Pacific Regional held in Phoenix, Arizona, for another win with our second team in second place. Because most of these matches were registered NRA Regional competitions, team events were made up of only four shooters, plus a coach. We were building strength and depth. It was quite visible when we entered two teams: we didn't know which one would win. That was a good sign when you're building a strong six-man team that also needs some alternates.

We moved back to the East Coast for the Southwest Regional held at Fort Benning, Georgia, in May. This would be a real trial. It was a registered NRA Regional, which meant a four-man team event with our best four shooters against the best four shooters in the United States Army. From start to finish, 200 yards through 600 it was touch and go by every man—neither team could pull ahead. It ended in a tie with both teams shooting the excellent score of 991 out of the possible total of 1,000. That is an average individual score of nearly 248 per shooter. Ties were not common in team events, and this was only the second one I'd ever seen. The Vs (center shots) had to be counted. Our score was 991 with 95 Vs; their score was 991 with 99 Vs. A good run, but no cigar for us. Then it was back to Texas for the Southwest Regional held at Camp Bullis in June, and we had another team win.

We were at our headquarters on Lackland Air Force Base, and it was time to strategize our campaign to win at Interservice and Camp Perry matches. Our budget limited the number of competitors who could attend, considering the travel cost to the competitions and return to San Antonio. The team needed competitions in different locations and conditions to keep sharp. Our home training range at Camp Bullis was too familiar, with the temperature above 95 in full sun almost every day. What to do? The Army team traveled to Fort Niagara in New York each July to train in weather conditions similar to those at Quantico and Camp Perry. All service teams would assemble at Quantico, Virginia, in August for the Interservice Championship and travel from there to Camp Perry.

I'm not certain who came up with the idea, but I believe it may have been Airman First Class Bob Dickens. You never know who will come up with a good idea, even the most junior troop, so be sure to listen. The plan was to take all our gear—extra guns, scopes, and enough ammo— to make a grand swing, shooting in competitions

453

around the East Coast and ending up at Quantico for the Interservice Championship. And then it would be on to Camp Perry with the hope of winning the big prize, the National Team Trophy. Illusory hope is not a plan. Each one of our team shooters had an extra duty in supporting the team, and they worked in units called flights. Some worked on the budget, some worked on travel and hotel arrangements, coaches did the scheduling for training and matches. One flight handled statistics and administration; another flight handled all our ammo requirements. We didn't have enough money to cover hotels so where would we stay? Lots of questions had to be worked out. All of the flights worked on their portion of the puzzle—money, logistics, training schedules, hotels, and quarters. They determined how many cars we would need, who would drive and who would ride along. Every little detail, including securing gunsmith support, was considered. SSgt Henry Evans, who was chief of our admin flight, fitted most of the puzzle pieces. The plan that came together meant we would have to leave July 1 and would not return until the first week in September. Nobody in the headquarters or chain of command bothered me or gave me any direction as long as I stayed within budget, so I OK'd the plan and had the travel orders published. Col Kelly was advised of the long trip and told me to find an officer as a traveling companion. I selected Second Lieutenant Rolf C. Smith, who was yanked out of Strategic Air Command (SAC) and assigned to the Air Force Rifle Team. He had organized the Keesler and SAC teams. He was an excellent choice and made a perfect team adjutant. We remain boon companions to this day.

Our first stop was in Oak Ridge, Tennessee, to compete in the Southern States Long Range match. It was a small competition of mostly civilian shooters and was really just practice for us. Of course, we won all the service rifle matches. The civilian shooters didn't mind and were quite happy to have a service team shoot on their range. From there, we traveled to Quantico where we could get government quarters. The morale and welfare trailers on the lake were ours again. The Atlantic Regional Match was being hosted by the Marines at Quantico.

Now we had some real competition. A six-man, thousand-yard team match with the service rifle was up first. We won that match to the utter amazement of the Army and the Marines. Some said it was

Long Shots — Teams

rather traumatic for them. This was an NRA-sponsored competition, so we would be shooting the NMC team of four shooters, plus a coach. Weather on the team match day was overcast, damp with a slight drizzle, which caused poor visibility. Nevertheless, things were clicking, and all four of us fired perfect scores of 50 offhand at 200 yards. We did a repeat on the 200-yard rapid-fire phase, and all scored a 50. That's a pretty good start, and word went around the range that the Air Force had cleaned the 200- yard line with all four competitors shooting a perfect score. By the time we moved back to 300 yards, several people were watching us from farther back. The 300-yard event can be tricky. It's rapid fire from the prone position while shooting a 12-inch plate-size target. All four of us cleaned the target with 50 each. Now a big crowd was gathering behind the 600-yard line. Lt Col Bill Pullum, the officer in charge of the Army team, and his boss Colonel J.J. Peot, the Commander of the Army Marksmanship Unit, showed up in the crowd.

Shooting 600 yards with an iron peep sight is never easy, but it becomes much more difficult in poor light. First off, your front sight looks much larger than the bull's eye at 600 yards. The front sight must be kept in sharp focus, which means the 20-inch target at 600 yards appears fuzzy and is even fuzzier in gray light. Remember, shooting is in pairs during the slow fire portions of the team match—one shooter fires, the target is lowered into the pits, scored, and run back up for the second man to fire. They continue until each has fired 20 shots. My partner for this match was SSgt Degerlund. I don't recall which shot it was, and I really prefer to forget it, but I was the first shooter to score a four—a one- point loss for the team. The guys all loved to make a big deal out of me losing a point in the team match, but it was always goodhearted and only after the competition. They had fun with those antics, and I didn't mind; they knew how much I wanted the team to win. I don't recall who shot what scores except for my partner SSgt Degerlund, who fired a perfect 250 with 21 Vs, which was just remarkable in that poor light. The team ended up with a score of 995, with 85 Vs, out of a possible 1,000, which set a new national record. That is nearly a 249 average. The Army and the Marine Corps teams took notice and were now watching us. We were building a solid reputation.

455

The match at Quantico was over on July 11, and the Interservice competition would not start until 6 August 1965. We were a team of 22 men with no money for hotels. Of course, we knew this before starting on our journey and made a request for billeting with the Army at Fort Meade, Maryland, with authority to train on their rifle range. Our request was granted, and we were given a private barracks. I had my guys all together, but it was pretty primitive. I think the barracks was built in the very early days of World War II. There was one large room with metal beds and wooden footlockers with each bed, and two small rooms at the front designed as offices. We turned those into rooms for the master sergeants. The construction was wood flats with no insulation. Naturally, there was no air-conditioning, nor were there any fans and the weather was darn hot. Even worse, the flush toilets were lined up 25 in a row, and there was only a gang (all open) shower. The military is not used to modesty, but stalled toilets and showers are nice. It gets worse. Hot water was not to be discovered, so cold showers and shaving were the order of the day, every day.

Army mess halls are not in the same league as Air Force dining halls. It's not only the lower quality food. They were still eating off metal trays. Between the barracks and the mess hall there was much to complain about, but the guys knew it could not be helped. They handled it more like a joke, labeling it as our bivouac with the Army. The training area was excellent, and we had a range dedicated just for us. We had to manage the range and pull our own targets, but that was expected, and we trained hard.

Training was fine, but we still needed to be in competition. Fort Dix, New Jersey, was hosting the Northwest Regional from July 15-19. That was on our agenda for two reasons: first, we could use government housing, and second, we would be shooting against part of the Marine Corps team. Civilians and reservists were running the match, not only the administration but the scorekeepers and even the tower. I got lucky and won the service rifle portion of the match with a score of 495 with 36 Vs, which was shooting the NMC twice. But it was painful. We were shooting from morning till dark with inexperienced volunteers, mostly Army and Navy reservists. They were competitors but were also pulling targets in the pits and trying to run the firing line.

Long Shots — Teams

The "leg match" (the competition where credit toward the Distinguished Badge is earned) was scheduled for the last day. A train wreck was in the making for certain. My guys didn't need to be in the leg match, so I volunteered to run the match. The competition and management were relieved and immediately accepted our offer. I put SSgt Ward, who had a commanding voice, in the tower. The tower orchestrates the match, calling the competitors to the firing line, directing the shooting, and making the line safe after firing. The tower operator is like a circus ringmaster. The rest of our team became line and block officers. The volunteers still pulled targets, but we took over as pit masters and had guys making sure everything was according to Hoyle in the scorekeeping. I was given the match director duty. Our team did an absolutely superb job. All I had to do was watch them conduct a first-class professional competition. They made me proud. Needless to say, match officials and particularly the shooting competitors were most grateful. In fact, the New Jersey state secretary sent quite a nice letter to the Lackland Air Force Base Commanding General commending our service. Chalk up some public relations for the Air Force.

I didn't mention the team match in New Jersey. I could say we won it, but the truth is it was given to us by the Marine Corps. If you know the Marine Corps you know they will not give any competition away, you have to fight for it. Sadly, there was no fight, which was a disappointment for us but much worse for them. Here's what happened: the operation of the tournament was slow and disorganized; they got behind quickly and were forced to make several and frequent schedule and program changes. Somehow, the Marine Corps did not get the word on one change and missed their appointed time to shoot. That eliminated them from posting even a poor score. Capt Dave Willis, a top shooter and I believe a superb officer, was acting as their officer in charge for this small competition. He was sick and I was sick for him. Understand, this was not a game for the Marine Corps or for us, it was business. I was commiserating with him, and he told me flat out, he would rather be shot than face the cold steely gray eyes of Col Walsh— not for losing the match but for failing in his duties as an officer. He was miserable. I am pleased to report 20 years later, Capt Willis was a Colonel, and the Marine Corps Weapons Battalion (shooting team) had another fine leader.

We retreated from Fort Dix back to Fort Meade and our spa accommodations for a week's training before traveling to Albany, New York, for the Forbes Long-Range Match. It was all individual long-range shooting, combining both 600 and 1,000-yard matches. We won all the matches in both the match rifle and service rifle categories as there was no serious competition, but we needed the 1,000-yard training. The Albany Rifle Club was delighted to have a service team at the match and made us promise to come back. We put on a little clinic and also coached a number of their members. The weather was nice, and they had a beautiful range surrounded by pine trees. Another advantage was we stayed in a motel and got hot showers. Once again, we retreated, this time from Albany back to Fort Meade for a week of training and cold showers before the Interservice Matches at Quantico.

Our guys were shooting well at Quantico and placing high in the individual competition, but SSgt Callahan winning the rapid-fire at 300 yards with a score of score of 100 - 12 Vs, was our only individual first place. Our eyes were on the Commandant Marine Corps Schools Team Match. The course of fire for this match was 10 shots at 200 yards, slow fire, offhand (standing); 10 shots at 300 yards, rapid fire, prone; and 10 shots at 600 yards, slow fire, prone. Total points available would be 900 with perfect scores by each man. My shooting partner SSgt Kurt Degerlund and I fired on the first relay offhand and cleaned the targets. We finished all three courses of fire 200 yards, 300 yards, and 600 yards with perfect scores of 150 each. The rest of the team followed with good scores. Other members of this six-man team were Technical Sgts Dean and Tossas, SSgt Bobby Smith, and Airman First Class Aldo Frascoia. Team captain was Master Sgt Carter, and the coach was SSgt Thompson. Our team total score was 889 - 79 Vs, out of a possible score of 900, beating the other 47 teams representing United States Army, United States Navy, United State Marine Corps, United States Coast Guard, National Guard and Reserves.

August 9, 1965, was a good day for the Air Force. It was the first and only time the Air Force captured this coveted Interservice Trophy. It was presented to us by General Wallace M. Green Jr.,

Commandant of the Marine Corps. We received the trophy in his office, and he presented each member of the team with an engraved pewter mug commemorating our win. It is interesting to note, second place was U.S. Army Eastern with a score of 886, third place was U.S. Army Europe with 885, fourth place was U.S. Army Western 885, fifth place was U.S. Army Pacific with 885, sixth place was U.S. Marine Corps Smith with a score of 884. The year before, Marine Corps team Zham set a new record with a score of 891. Other Marine teams were in seventh, eighth, tenth, twelfth, and fourteenth places. This was a major upset for the Marines, falling to sixth place, and the Army, losing to the Air Force. I've listed the scores and places of the top teams to point out the challenge of our little Air Force team competing against the Marine Corps, Navy, National Guard, Army and Army Reserves, with such large numbers and deep breadth of experienced shooters.

Somehow, the news got back to San Antonio, and an officer brought a naval message to me on the firing line. I'd been told that a captain was looking for me but had no idea why. He showed up and told me he had a message for me from a general officer, and therefore an officer was required to deliver it. Naval message YM 469/10/2309Z/Aug65 is as follows:

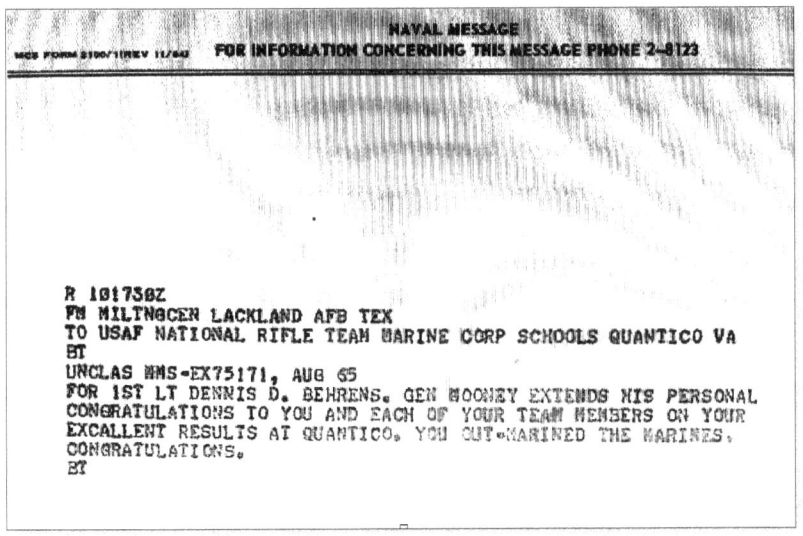

Our team arrived at Camp Perry on August 13, 1965, in an exuberant mood. That optimism was not uncalled for considering the preparation, persistent hard training, and mental toughness of the team. Our little band of 22, counting our gunsmith and adjutant, was vastly outnumbered with shooters and experience, but we were determined not just to count and be recognized, but to win the National Team Trophy. Some still thought our near win in 1964 was an aberration and considered the idea of us winning audacious. A cursory review and the idiotic idea of pulling lightning out of a bottle a second year was incredulous to the point of being funny to some. A broader analysis might have given the naysayers pause. We were back "in the ropes "and not laughing—maybe even showing a little insolence. In his book, *Facts and Fears,* Lt Gen James Clapper talked about the will to fight or not fight as an "unpredictable imponderable." Our guys were going to fight. They knew the mission: beat the Army and Marine Corps using their primary small arms combat weapon, the M1 Garand rifle.

I suppose one could say we were there to prove that we were the little mouse that roared. Our guys shot well, but we claimed no individual or team gold medals in matches prior to the National Trophy Match. TSgt Kenneth Horst did win the silver medal in the individual service rifle aggregate. Airman Aldo Frascoia won the Vandenberg Cup, but that was as the highest Air Force shooter in the President's Hundred, not the match winner. We did put three people in the Wimbledon 1000-yard shoot-off. That's the most famous 1,000-yard competition with the match rifle and scope. The Wimbledon trophy, a beautiful silver tankard, was presented as a gift to the United States in 1875 by Princess Louise at the Wimbledon rifle range, which was opened by Queen Victoria in 1860. The Wimbledon match was won in 1965 by LCpl Carlos N. Hathcock, the legendary Marine Corps sniper. His biography entitled *Marine Sniper* is a telling account of combat in Vietnam. Lots of military are trained in long-range shooting, but a real sniper has stealth, concealment ability, iron determination, and cunning. There is a difference. By the way, in 1966, Carlos Hancock, then promoted to Sergeant, used the same Model 70 Winchester topped with a Unertl 8X in Vietnam for his effective and deadly duty on his first deployment.

Long Shots — Teams

At Camp Perry, shooters compete in 1,000-yard preliminary qualifying matches to earn one of the 10 positions for the Wimbledon sudden-death shoot-off. In addition to those competing for the Wimbledon, using match rifles with scopes, another 10 shooters, who had earned positions with the service rifle, would fire at the same time, hoping to capture the Farr Trophy, which was named after a famous shooter in the 1920s. The firing line then consisted of 20 shooters. Ten lined up with match rifles, and 10 lined up with the service rifle. Sudden-death competition means each shooter fires only one shot at a time. This must be done in one and a half minutes in 1,000-yard competitions. Once the time limit is up, all targets are lowered and scored in the pits. There is some suspense as the range director in the tower calls for targets to be raised and disked (marked). That means the target is pushed up from the pits and a long-handled stick with a round marking disk on the end is held over the target to signify the score. That tower director first calls for misses, then for treys, then fours, each in turn. As those shooting the lower scores are identified, he announces in a booming voice, "You are excused," and the recipient of his order must pick up his rifle, shooting mat, ammo, and spotting scope, and unceremoniously leave the firing line. Finally, he calls, "Raise and disk all fives" (shots in the 36-inch black circle). Those shooters are allowed to fire another shot. This goes on until one is declared the winner. I was "excused" in the Farr Trophy, and it was a little humiliating to slink off the firing line in front of a thousand spectators in the bleachers.

Another 1,000-yard competition sometimes overlooked is the Leech Cup, a beautiful silver trophy gifted to the United States by Major Arthur B. Leech. He was on the Irish team visiting us in 1874, a year before the Wimbledon. SSgt Paul Stapper is the only Air Force member to win this cup.

The National Trophy Team match (NTT) was the last to be fired. We woke up to a rainy, cold, and windy day. This was in August and should not have happened. A storm had come in off of Lake Erie with 25- to 30-mile-an-hour winds, just the worst possible conditions for high-power rifle shooting. Mats are not allowed in the NTT, so we had to shoot sitting and lying in wet grass, hoping to miss the mud.

That's the small problem. It's a major challenge in the first course of fire, shooting offhand, keeping your sights aligned on a 12-inch bull's-eye (plate size) at 200 yards, and getting off a good shot while squeezing the trigger in hard winds. All the teams hate shooting in those conditions as good scores are seldom found.

There was nothing for us to do but carry our Air Force flag out to the range and get on with business. Rain, poor visibility, cold, and heavy winds presented every chance for failure, but we were all in the same boat. Our team was heavily outnumbered by Army and Marine Corps teams, not to mention the National Guard, Navy, and Reserve teams. Remember, our training program meant shooting no matter what weather condition occurred. We would now test our training to its limits. I admit it was disconcerting that we had not won any of the 21 individual or team completions at Camp Perry leading up to the NTT match, but we had not given up and were ready for battle. As Gen Dwight Eisenhower said, "What counts is not necessarily the size of the dog in the fight—it's the size of the fight in the dog." Some individuals and teams give up before they start because they think conditions are too rough for them to win. We were small but mighty. It would take dogged perseverance and an indomitable drive to win. This was not just a rifle match; it was a match of wills between my team and every other team on the firing line. My partner SSgt Degerlund and I led off as the first pair.

The offhand stage of fire allows each pair of shooters 20 minutes to fire their 20 rounds. In wind it is hard to get a good shot off so a shooter sometimes has to take the rifle down (off his shoulder) for a break and then start again, but time is running so one can't dillydally around. By some miracle, I came off with a 49 out of a possible 50. It was the best score of anyone shooting on any team that morning and there were more than 150 civilian and military teams (six men shooting on each team) competing. I must admit it could have been a score of 30 with wind howling as it was. None of my shots looked that good, and I was close to the edge of jerking the trigger more than once. My partner came off with a 47. We moved off the line so the second team pair could shoot. Word came to me that the first pair of the Army's strongest team was jubilant to come off the line with a 45 and 44. We were not chasing scores by others but were seven points ahead with our first pair, which was a good omen. It was a huge relief to me when we finished the offhand phase in super shape for the conditions. Now we just needed to put our heads down and follow our training. The next three courses of fire would be sitting or prone, and if we hung tight, I knew we could win.

I was the first shooter for rapid fire from the sitting position but made the mistake of looking back to the 300-yard line, and there was Col Kelly with his boss Maj Gen Mooney, commander of Lackland Air Force Base. Visiting firemen, a complete surprise, and just what I didn't want. I needed to concentrate not only on my shooting but the rest of the team without entertaining spectators. The target came up; I lowered myself into the sitting position, fired two rounds, reloaded a full clip, and fired the remaining eight rounds. It was over in 50 seconds. My score was 48, that's two shots NOT in the black. Nobody shoots a 49 offhand, the most difficult position, and then shoots a 48 in the 200-yard sitting position, felt to be the easiest. I considered it a complete failure of mental discipline on my part—what a dumb head. No doubt it shocked the team, but no one said anything as our doctrine prevented criticism or discussion of poor shooting until after the match was completed. It was disheartening to me to have allowed the sudden appearance of Col Kelly and Maj Gen Mooney to distract me from my duty.

My other teammates shot respectable scores. We gathered up our gear and moved our flag to the 300-yard line where we met Col Kelly and Maj Gen Mooney. I saluted the general, and he said, "What the hell happened to you, Lieutenant?" No excuses, I just screwed it up. Nothing to do but cowboy up and soldier on. I was the team leader and needed to get back to leading. All the top teams shot about the same total scores in the 200-yard rapid fire event, so we still maintained a lead going into the 300-yard prone position rapid fire event. I managed to clean the target for score 50, and my teammates followed again with good scores. Now we would move back to the last course of fire, which is 20 shots by each team member but shooting in pairs: one man fires, the target is scored, and then the second man fires.

At this stage I did not know scores from other teams, but I could see five or six groups of spectators gathering up behind the 600-yard firing line, and one group had gathered behind our firing position, so I knew we were in the running. Now our coach, SSgt David Thompson, would be put to the test of not only reading the wind but also coaxing us into good scores. It is vital at this stage for the shooters to be able to call their shots (tell the coach what it looked like when they fired their round). The coach sits behind the shooters with a large spotting scope, reading the wind velocity and direction while also figuring in where the shooter called his shot. If the shooter calls his shot to the right, and the target comes up showing his shot went to the left, the coach has to decide whether or not to call for a sight change, tell the next shooter to favor one side or the other, or tell the shooter, "down the middle," meaning shoot with no change. Typically, the coach is talking and giving directions to the shooters through earphones. If no change is required between shots he would, in a very calm manner, tell the shooter, "knock it down, knock it down, knock it down," until the shot is fired. If he sees a sudden wind change, he would simply say, "hold up," in a calm voice, and the shooter would immediately stop pressing or squeezing the trigger. Shooters would not talk to the coach unless the coach asked him how it looked. The coach is watching the shooters, looking at the wind flags for direction and velocity while also watching the mirage and changing light. He is a busy guy, computing all of this in this in his mind while still calmly communicating with the shooters.

At 600 yards I was once again the leadoff shooter. Sgt Thompson called the wind right, and my first shot was in the black—a 20-inch circle. SSgt Degerlund and I were firing our alternating shots as fast as we could but still maintaining precision, sight alignment, and trigger squeeze. The shorter the time you're on the firing line, the fewer wind changes. Target service was excellent. Personnel in the pits were rapidly pulling our target down, marking the score, and running the target up for the next shot. As soon as I fired, SSgt Degerlund would load up his rifle and be ready when the target came out of the pits, and I did the same when he fired. The time allotted for slow fire at 600 yards is one minute per shot. No one could recall our time, but I suspect we finished firing 20 rounds each in less than 15 minutes. We shot well, and with the excellent coaching, I cleaned the course—all in the black for a score of 100. Our other two pairs shot equally good scores.

Our teammates who were not firing in this event were keeping track of the top four or five teams and told me after the match that we were trading off shot for shot on the 600-yard course of fire. That meant we might be ahead by one point, and the next shot might put us one point behind. Of course, our team shooting didn't know or want to know this while we were shooting, because it only adds pressure when you're trying to be calm and keep a slow heartbeat and pulse rate. The best guys know they have to beat themselves, and they don't waste energy romancing scoring boards. The top teams shot similar scores in the 200 and 300 rapid fire stages and again at 600 yards. But remember how well we started on a 200-yard offhand stage? Our score was 1,455—31 points below our score and also the U.S. Marine Corps winning score of 1,486 in 1964. That clearly verifies the poor weather conditions, but I knew we were in the win, place, or show arena. Word came down the line that we had won the match. How sweet victory can be, particularly after the heartbreaking tie score and loss to the Marines by V count the year before. In the early morning rain, someone told one of our support staff that we didn't stand a snowball's chance of winning the NTT since we hadn't won even one of the preceding matches. We were vindicated. There was joy, but I wouldn't say we were ecstatic. Everyone was just simply exhausted. I would say we were pleasurably content. Our teammates, not shooting in this match, were jubilant for us. The reader might be surprised how much extreme concentration and tension can drain one's strength. It's even worse when fighting a heavy wind all day.

Of course, jubilation came later after we had rested up and put on clean uniforms for the awards presentation and pictures. I won the General White Trophy again, by being the high scorer on the Air Force Team. In fact, there were only two of us, out of all people shooting on the 150 plus teams, who shot 247s. That confirms the horrible weather conditions. The General White Trophy was nice, and I believe I am the only officer to ever win that trophy twice, but it paled compared to winning the National Trophy—not even in the same league. As you can imagine, I was proud as a peacock for my team, not just the NTT match shooters and the coach but also team captain MSgt Linscott, our gunsmith SSgt Estes, 2d Lt Rolf Smith, a shooter but also our adjutant, and all the other teammates who were with us on our journey. They had done the impossible. All odds were against us, and knowledgeable, experienced people said it could not be done, but they were wrong. The Army and Marine Corps teams were apoplectic and in disbelief. This should never have happened, but it did. Talk about a long shot!

The team celebration party was off the charts, at least on the drinking side. How we got booze on a Sunday in Ohio remains a mystery, but all liquid refreshment was exhausted, as were all the attendees, by the time it was consumed. The team adjutant's report stated, "SSgt Estes introduced the two officers on the team to two fine fellows, a Mr. Jack Daniels and Mr. Jim Beam from Tennessee, both wearing brown paper bags and little else." Accolades came from all directions—match officials, state shooting associations, civilians, NRA, DCM, and NBPRP officials. But most impressive and important for us were congratulations by the highest-ranking officers of the military: General Wallace M. Greene, Commandant of the Marine Corps, General Harold K. Johnson, Chief of Staff, United States Army, and General J.P. McConnell, Chief of Staff, United States Air Force. Pretty heady for a lieutenant and a group of mostly junior NCOs.

It got even better. When the team was back home in San Antonio, I was ordered to assemble them, in Class A uniform, and meet Col Kelly and Maj Gen Mooney in the early morning hours on the flight line at Kelly Air Force Base. Col Kelly told me a very important VIP was flying in to meet with the team. The VIP turned out to be General John P. McConnell, Air Force Chief of Staff. He had followed General LeMay as Chief and had the same enthusiasm for small arms combat training and marksmanship.

As the plane landed, we marched in formation to the disembark area. We stood at attention while the Chief was greeted by Col Kelly and Maj Gen Mooney. He then came to us and decorated each team member with the Air Force Commendation Medal. Some people today might scoff and say, "only the Commendation Medal," but it was a big deal and the first decoration several team members, including me, had ever been awarded. That was before the proliferation of awards by the new addition of the Air Force Achievement Medal and Meritorious Service Medals. In those days, some NCOs retired at 20 years without ever receiving a personal decoration. There were only two noncombat decorations for outstanding service at the time, the Commendation Medal and the Legion of Merit. The Legion of Merit was pretty well reserved for generals and colonels. The general then put everyone at ease and told us how pleased he was with our team win over the Army and Marine Corps. Once again, we were on cloud nine with a decoration to wear on our uniforms, in addition to fancy bragging rights. Not many get to shake hands with the Chief of Staff of the Air Force.

Gen LeMay's vision had been achieved. Air Force marksmanship training was ongoing, and a strong, competent Air Force security police force was complete. In the Tokyo Olympics of 1964, the United States took 7 of the 18 shooting medals with the Air Force shooters contributing. The Russians won only two. And the cherry on top was the Air Force rifle team beating the Army and the Marine Corps, shooting their combat service rifle at Camp Perry and winning the National Trophy. I'm told by good sources that General McConnell took the miniature trophy plaque of the National Trophy to a meeting of the Joint Chiefs of Staff and said in a friendly way, "Now, you sons of bitches, how about taking me on in strategic bombing?" obviously pointing out he could beat them at their game. Would they like to try his game? All in fun, I'm certain.

The Longhorn and the Carrot

No, this is not about feeding treats to cattle. It's about two rifle matches held each year between the big Army High-Power Rifle Team and the Air Force High-Power Rifle Team, shooting the service rifle, .30-caliber U.S. M1 Garand. The Air Force trophy was a magnificent set of longhorns from a Texas longhorn—a beautiful trophy. The Army trophy was an ugly dirty-looking carrot mounted on a plaque—hardly becoming. Most of the time both trophies resided in Texas. That sounds good, but alas, it was bad news. The winner of the trophy was the team with the lowest score. That's right, the loser got the trophy. The longhorns were meant to prod the lowest scoring team to shoot better. The carrot was more or less like a bribe to get the low shooters to shoot better. Of course, the Army described it as an incentive to shoot better. These matches were bitter struggles and hard-fought. But the camaraderie was very strong, and many tight friendships were formed among the combatants on both sides.

The Carrot Match was held at Fort Benning, which is adjacent to Columbus, Georgia. We always stayed at the Magnolia Motel, which by today's standards would be considered rather low end. But it served us well and even had a swimming pool. Best I can recall, the cost per unit was less than 20 bucks, so if we put four guys in a unit it was less than five dollars a person, which was fine with us. The upstairs held two bedrooms and a bath, and downstairs had a small kitchen, dining room, and living room combined. That small kitchen is where I was introduced to fried snapping turtles. I must say, they were quite delicious. Many of the Army guys fished, as did many of our guys. Trotlines and night fishing were going on the entire time.

In addition to fried fish and snapping turtles, the Army guys introduced me to moonshine liquor, commonly referred to as white lightning. It came in a Mason jar just like in the movies. The colorless liquid was clear. I must question my sanity for trying it, and I was much relieved when I didn't go blind, although it did make me quite pie-eyed. I can certainly attest it was alcohol, and I paid the price the next morning. This was before Green Beret time, but the majority of the Army team were either paratroopers (they got extra pay of $50 per month) or early Special Forces types. Remember, the Magnolia Motel had a swimming pool, so we often had beer drinking socials at the pool after shooting with the Army team.

One time, one of the Special Forces types brought his scuba gear, which included a couple of large tanks attached to a backpack. I tried it out, and they dropped me into the deep end of the pool where I quickly found out the mask didn't fit me tight enough, and I couldn't get the tanks to work. Thus, I was floundering around like a wounded manatee, thinking I would drown for sure before they hauled me out. Of course, all the NCOs had a great laugh, and I heard about it on the rifle range for several days.

A separate but equally competitive event was held in conjunction with the Carrot Match. It was "The Catfish Massacre." In this competition, each team, Army and Air Force, would select their top six members to represent their service. All would form up at Pletcher's Catfish House, an all-you-can-eat restaurant, serving catfish with hushpuppies, coleslaw, and iced tea for $1.95 per person. The winning team forfeited all trophies for the highly prestigious bragging rights for the following year. The catfish were fried whole, and it was always a close thing—kind of like the battle of Waterloo where victory was not clear immediately—the fish skeletons, not dead princes, had to be counted. Because I was a good eater in those days you can imagine my disappointment at not being chosen as a team member. I felt sort of like a little kid always picked last for a kick-the-can game. Even worse, I was not even considered, thought of as being a lightweight in this big-boy competition.

This was a prestige match, and rank had no privilege. Our guys were smaller but determined—and hard fighters, particularly at the trough. Although we held the dubious honor of possessing both the Longhorn and the Carrot trophies more than the Army team, we mostly accounted for the greatest body counts (skeletons) at the catfish massacre. Pletcher's served catfish about the size of a bull head (small catfish). Body counts per contestant could be well over thirty. As you might imagine, no contestant ate the hushpuppies or coleslaw. Those of us not in competition cheered the teams on from noncompetition tables as we munched on catfish. We did eat the hushpuppies and coleslaw.

The Longhorn Match was scheduled, as usual, to be shot in Texas at Camp Bullis Army Rifle Range, adjacent to San Antonio. It was our training range and was also used by Fourth Army. Lt Col Bill Pullum was the officer in charge of the Army High Power Team, but he was skipping this match and sending Capt Willie Powell to run the team. Capt Powell was a prior enlisted man and a veteran of the Korean War. He was rather a colorful guy who always carried an undercover pistol in an ankle holster. We got along well, and I liked him. I don't recall which one of our teams won the match, but I suspect the Army won, leaving us holders of the Longhorns.

In any case, while we were arch enemies on the field, we were good friends off the field, and we wanted to show the Army a good time while they were in town. At that time, I rented a house in Valley High close to Lackland Air Force Base that had a large backyard. Many of the Army shooters and our guys were musicians who loved to play the guitar and sing Western music. It was decided to have a barbecue in my backyard and include the local Fourth Army team. Because there was a visiting team in town, I thought I better tell our commanding officer Col Tom Kelly just as a courtesy. I called to advise him that the Army team was in town and invited him to join us. There was no field grade officer visiting, so I fully expected him to decline. For sure, I didn't want him to come to our party. And certainly, none of the NCOs wanted him to join us. It wasn't that anyone disliked him, it was just a matter of being a full colonel. Everyone thought it would cramp our style somewhat and did not want to be bothered with the senior officer. To my shock and horror, Col Kelly said, "Yes, I'll come, and I'd like to bring a guest."

I said, "Well, we'd love to have you, sir, and we're starting at 6 p.m." The Army team showed up on time, and my guys were already there with chairs and electric cords set up for the little band of guitar players and singers from both teams to perform. The match was over, so the beer started flowing pretty rapidly as bragging about shooting skills, hunting prowess, and all manner of things was getting pretty loud. The barbecue and beans were ready, so people were scarfing down the chow. In walks Col Kelly with a six-foot, six-inch-tall man in uniform, which included a badge and a Sam Browne belt with holster. It was Bill Jordan, assistant chief patrol inspector of the U.S. border patrol. He had been a Marine officer in World War II and Korea and was famous as a deadly Pistolero on the Texas/Mexico border. He was also a participant in some historic gun battles along the border and in the El Paso area. The crowd went quiet.

Col Kelly brought out a quart of whiskey and passed it around. To begin with, no one was comfortable with the colonel, but as the bottle went around, they soon began to enjoy his stories and were delighted to meet Bill Jordan, who had a full library of experiences that he shared. He had just published a book entitled *No Second Place Winner* with accolades from Elmer Keith, Maj George Nonte, and Col Charles Askins, who were the pistoleros of the day. His book is a thesis on mortal combat shooting with the handgun, and as it states, there is no second-place winner in a gunfight. Mr. Jordan had just picked up the skin of rattlesnake that had recently been mounted on a strip of felt. It was rolled up, and as he unrolled it for our viewing, he told us the snake story. The party, which had threatened to be a bust, finally cleared out in the wee hours of the morning, having been a great success in large part because of our unwelcome but subsequently embraced guests.

A couple of weeks later, when reviewing the party with Captain Frank C. White, who was the ramrod for the local Fourth Army Rifle Team, we disagreed on the length of the snake. Frank thought it was five feet long, and I was sure it was six feet. To settle the matter, I sent a note to Mr. Jordan asking him to verify the snake's length. He sent me a copy of his book with the answer written on the inside cover page. His remarks are pretty smart and a diplomatic answer when settling the dispute between two good friends. Here is what he wrote:

Western Music and the Swagger Stick

Growing up in Southern California in middle and high school, none of us would ever have Western music playing on the radio. There were two reasons: One was that rock 'n' roll and Beach Boy-type music were becoming the favorites. That had to be your favorite music to be hip. The second reason was we thought Western was the music of the underclass, such as those who came to California during the Dust Bowl. My folks listened to Benny Goodman, Tommy Dorsey, and Lawrence Welk. They loved to dance, and that music suited them so that's what I heard on the radio as a little kid. I didn't fully appreciate it until much later, but my Air Force rifle team was a little treasure of talented singers and guitar pickers. The leaders were Paul Stamper, Emmett Adkins, and Barney Bernard. After matches, we would often have a beer bust, and the guys would play Western music. It wasn't my thing, but I was part of the team and soon began to enjoy Western music. I even went to a couple of Western shows with the team.

At one major show in San Antonio, the announcer made a big deal out of the Air Force team, and we were asked to stand. Of course, after his introduction we got a big ovation. It's doubtful the audience knew or cared who we were, and I was a little embarrassed. At another show, Little Jimmy Dickens, who knew some of our guys, came over and shook our hands. I can't remember who he was playing with, but it could've been Hank Williams or maybe Roy Acuff, one of the big stars. San Antonio was getting some big-name Western performers in the 1960s. I have to say, it wasn't long until I was selecting radio stations that played Western, and I still do. About the same time, I met Lt Col Bailey, the uncle of my good high-school buddy Wayne Bailey. He and his wife were patrons of the San Antonio Symphony, and they took me to my first-ever symphony performance. Of course, I'd heard classical music on the radio, but live music at a symphony is captivating. Between Western and classic, my musical appreciation jumped to new heights and expanded even wider in both realms when we moved to Washington, D.C. We still enjoy the fine performances of the San Antonio Symphony.

After leaving the team and preparing for Vietnam, I was training at Lackland Air Force Base when some of the team shooters called me over to a picking and singing session and to have a beer with them. Turned out it was a little more than that. They presented me a swagger stick with a silver butt on the tip. The butt was engraved as follows: USAF, National Rifle Team, OIC, 1963-1966. For those not familiar with a swagger stick, it resembles a pointer used by a professor. In the time of Roman centurions, it was an emblem of office. For British officers it was a substitute for a riding crop and a symbol of authority. At the 1943 Tunis victory parade celebrating the North African campaign, General Eisenhower carried one. Gen Patton often carried a swagger stick, and I've read Gen William J. Livsey carried one carved from poplar when he was commander of Eighth Army in Korea. Some of the Marine field-grade officers were still carrying them when I first came into the service. All the officers in charge (OICs) of the various military rifle teams were lieutenant colonels or at least field-graders. I was only a lieutenant, and it certainly never hindered me. But with this swagger stick, symbolic but clear, the team was promoting their lieutenant to field grade. It was both an honor and humbling.

Air Force Shotgun Team

The shotgun team described here was the Air Force team that shot international trap, often referred to as bunker or Olympic trap. It's a similar discipline to American trap with the clay target going away from the shooter; however, the target goes faster, travels farther, and flies at wider angles and at varied elevations.

It is a tough sport that requires solid concentration and is not for those with oversized egos. Two shots are allowed at each target with shooters moving after firing at one target from the station (shooting position) and then moving to the next station for the next shot. The shooters are constantly moving until all have fired at 25 targets.

The trap house is flat with the ground (hence, called a bunker) and contains 15 trap machines, launching the clay targets, with three machines for each shooting station. In American trap, the trap house is elevated and contains only a single machine to launch the targets. While American trap is very popular in our country, most of the world shoots only international (bunker) trap.

My initiation to bunker trap shooting came in Germany in 1968 when my friend Frank White took me to a small country match. My name was at the bottom of the scoring card in that match, but it piqued my interest. There was no high-power military rifle competition, and it was time to try something else. Needless to say, I'm still trying it, unsuccessfully chasing better scores. It did bring me into a whole different world of shooters and many new friendships. The icing on the cake was becoming team captain for the Air Force Trap Team. In 1971, the Air Force gathered a makeup team for the Pan-American Game tryouts in Phoenix. Somehow, I was called back from Germany on temporary duty status and was captain of that team. The four shooting members of the team were young guys from 20 to 22 years old. They all had more shotgun experience than I did. They had joined the Air Force to shoot bunker trap not long before the marksmanship school was closed and were now assigned to other Air Force duties. We trained together and competed in the tryouts without much success. They were good young guys, and I liked them; we got along well. Retired Chief Master Sergeant Herman Mashburn was our coach. I tell of that training and shooting in my recount of "You Are Under Arrest." After the tryout, we all went back to our normal Air Force assignments.

In 1979, I returned from Germany and was assigned to the Pentagon. Once again, I became captain of the little Air Force volunteer team. Understand, this was all extra duty, and for the most part we had to pay our own expenses, including travel. It was managed as part of the Air Force Morale and Welfare (MWR) program. As part of the program, we were allowed to travel in a permissive travel status, meaning it was authorized, but at our own expense. The best part was we did not get charged leave time. That was a big plus, particularly for guys who were married and had kids, so they didn't burn up all their vacation time.

We had a bunker trap range at Lackland to train on, which was built in the '60s when the Air Force had full-time shooting teams. There were very few bunkers in those days, fewer than 10 in the United States (that number doubled by the late 1990s), so we were fortunate to have one of our own for training and matches. The bunker itself and the topside shooting stations were fine. However, the trap machines were ancient, in poor repair, and single loaders, meaning someone had to be in the bunker to load the machines for each shot. It was simply impossible for two or three guys to try to train. It took two people and sometimes three to keep the machines fully loaded during a competition or to even train. I explained the problem to my friend Gen J.B. Davis. And wonder of wonders, $35,000 appeared for new automatic loading machines. The shooters were all volunteers and could quit anytime they wanted. We had to furnish our own guns, but sometimes ammo would be available for matches. As the overall MWR shooting program developed under the leadership of Col Steve Richards and Mr. Steve Ducoff, we were able to get more assistance and eventually airline tickets and ammo.

Terry Howard had a short period of shooting with the full-time Air Force trap team before that program ended in 1969. He was a Technical Sergeant in the weather forecasting field by the time I met him, but he could shoot and was already competitive. Additionally, he could coach, and we badly needed coaching. As an aside, I will tell you he is still coaching and has developed more Junior All-American skeet shooters than anyone in the world. He became our coach and was by far the best shooter on the early team. Some of the early shooters were Master Sergeants Tom Price and Chuck Bautista. Airman John Staub and Paul Bobby were younger shooters. Majors Woolace and Don Berry shot with us for a short period. We were not a powerhouse, but the other top teams, the Army, the Army Reserve team, and Marines took notice, as did top civilian individuals. They could no longer win matches cheaply. At one major championship held at Fort Benning, we managed to beat all comers. That shooting team consisted of Terry Howard, Chuck Batista, John Staub, and me. Terry Howard qualified for the Olympics in 1980 to be held in Moscow. As a result of the Russians invading Afghanistan, the United States canceled participation in Moscow and joined 65 other nations in an alternate Olympics for the free world held in Beijing,

China. Terry won the gold medal and was shooting so well at that time I would've bet on him winning in Moscow also. Terry retired in the late 1980s, but three new young guys came to the team: A1C Mike Herman, 2d Lt Dominic Grazioli, and 2d Lt John Linn. These guys were what you would call "lean and mean." By that I mean young, strong, and ready to take on the world. It took a couple years to get them really going, but they became the team core and were a constant threat to full-time Army, Marine Corps, and top civilians on the USA Shooting Team in Colorado Springs.

In those days a qualifying score was required by USA Shooting (Olympic shooting authority) for travel to world cups and world championships. The number was based on scores required to win in international competitions. That score was set at 192 out of a possible 200. It happened that in 1992, all three of the young guys and I fired that score. I knew then they were on their way. When the student outperforms the teacher, the teacher has been successful. I do like to remind them (Lt Grazioli and Airman Herman) of the 1993 Central Region Trap Championship at Lackland Air Force Base. Conditions were poor, and scores were low. They thought they would surely win first and second place. Their scores were the same at 180 going into the shoot-off. They didn't realize I had a 183 and by then it was too late.

We all shot 23s in the shoot-off, which made me the winner. It was a fluke but taught them a lesson. Grazioli won medals in 10 world cups; four were gold. He also won a bronze at a Super World Cup, which is limited to only World Cup winners. Mike Herman shot in many world cups and won the gold medal in the Brazil World Cup and a bronze in China. They represented the United States in more than 20 World Cups. They were both shooting well and were top candidates for the two spaces the U.S. was allowed for the Beijing Olympics. Mike broke his foot just before the final selection. Grazioli won the final shoot-off, and I am proud to say was part of our U.S. Olympic team in Beijing. What makes me just as proud was Mike's acceptance of not making the team. It was apparent to all of us watching that he couldn't shoot well with a heavy cast on his foot, but he never blamed the cast or whined about not making the

Olympic team. He was so close, and I felt bad for him. He should have been on our Olympic team with Grazioli.

Two people who were not in the Air Force but were of conside-rable help to the team were Dr. Steve Holtzclaw and Mr. Lucio Sosta. Steve was a medical student who loved to shoot bunker trap. He started shooting with me about the time the three young Air Force guys, John Linn, Mike Herman, and Dominic Grazioli, joined the team. I like to tease them and say they all grew up together. Now they have wives and kids, and two even have grandkids. I don't know if we adopted him, or he adopted the team, but Steve stayed with us the whole time. Even after I retired, the two of us would hang out with the Air Force shooters. Steve always had medications, bandages, and the medical knowledge to ease any hurts or pains. Plus, he is excellent company; we became close personal friends.

Lucio was president of Perazzi USA and a superb gunsmith. Some consider him to be the best gunsmith in the world and won't let anyone else touch their guns. He could certainly fix a Perazzi with his eyes closed, but I've also seen him repair a Fabbri. If one of my guys needed help on his gun, it was overnighted to Lucio, and he would have it shipped back to us the same day he received it. He treated us like family, and we felt the same of him. Al Kondak is now head of USA Perazzi, and we have become friends.

Other good shooters who helped make up the team were: MSgt James, A1C Bollinger, Lt Col Bill Adair, and SSgt P.D. Parker. All were valued members and contributed to our success. P.D. took the extra duty as custodian of our bunker at the Lackland Rod and Gun Club. Once he got on the team, I never had to worry about it. It was always ready and in good shape. He was assigned to the team in late 1990, and I retired in 1992 so we did not have as much time together as the other team members. Fast forward 13 years after assignment to the team and his retirement: P.D. became manager of the San Antonio Gun Club (SAGC), a skeet and trap facility. He took over a failing club that was in the red financially and had been managed poorly by several of his predecessors. The SAGC is a private club on city property with the public invited to shoot. We have 500 members, but more than 3,000 non-member guests shoot at the club each year. It is used for several charity shooting events.

The club grosses nearly $700,000 per year. They have moved from being in the red to having a sizable reserve. Under P.D.'s leadership, a first-rate five stand and an excellent bunker trap have been added to the facility. He runs the club like a first-rate business. The grounds are trimmed, it is clean, the skeet and trap houses are loaded, and there are no errant hulls cluttering up the area. His superb staff is made of Brian Roberts, Michael Calzada, David Escobedo, and Louis Hernandez. The fields are always ready to go. His matches are run to perfection and are well attended. The SAGC is arguably the best trap and skeet club in the nation. If there were a club manager of the year award, P.D. Parker would win it hands down.

I was the Air Force team leader for 17 years. The team traveled for matches at:

- Prado, California, where the 1984 Olympics were held
- Miramar Naval Air Station in California
- Marine Corps base at Quantico, Virginia
- Pachmayrs (now Triple B), California
- Martinez, California
- Shelley Gitman's bunker in Pennsylvania
- Paul Bobby's bunker in New Jersey
- The Strodtman Ranch in Jackson, Montana
- The Renton Fish and Game Club bunker in Washington State
- USA Shooting Range in Colorado Springs
- Missoula Trap and Skeet Club, Montana
- Prince George's Gun Club, Maryland
- Fort Benning, Georgia
- The Barn, Tennessee
- Fairfield Sportsman Club, Ohio

And finally, as sort of a retirement tour in August 1992, I took the three top team shooters, Linn, Herman, and Grazioli, to Belgium and Germany. From there they traveled the world representing the United States in bunker trap. Several generals helped me in promoting the Air Force trap team. Gen J.B. Davis gave us the most assistance, but others included our Air Force Chief of Staff Gen

Long Shots — Teams

Merrill A. McPeak, Gen Robert C. Oaks, Lt Gen John L. Pickett, Lt Gen Robert D. Beckel, and Maj Gen Keithe Nelson. We had a last shoot with me as the boss at Lackland Air Force Base with a few of my civilian friends and all the Air Force shooters. The team gave me a fine fly rod with my name printed on the shaft as a retirement gift; it is cherished. It was a most pleasurable additional duty, and I enjoyed the shooting, but most rewarding was being around the young guys and watching them progress. They won more than their fair share of medals and were perfect sportsmen. It made me proud just to stand with them. I'd love to do it again.

Teams have always intrigued me, and I have been a long-time observant student of what makes a team successful. I must report that the secret still eludes me. Some elements are essential, such as knowing the mission/objective, team leadership, the training, and equipment/resources necessary, and the strong will of the players. But in what mix, and who plays these parts? Who is the driver? Is it the commander, the coach, a senior sergeant, the top athlete/soldier? Or maybe a lower ranking person or just a couple of spark plugs? Again, in what combination? The San Antonio Spurs lead all NBA teams in making the playoffs for 22 years straight. Why and how? Great athletes - the trident of Manu Ginobili, Tony Parker, and Tim Duncan, for sure, but how did they come together? In addition to having arguably the finest NBA coach, Mr. Greg Popovich, they have a superb general manager in Mr. R.C. Buford and, above that, a smart businessman in Mr. Peter Holt. Holt let Pop coach, Buford managed, and he stayed very low-key behind the scenes. Each of these three men run in their proper lanes and do their jobs well, which sets the stage for athletes to succeed. The team dynamic is the same in business, the military, fraternal organizations, schools, etc. But again, the question is in what mix and who plays what part?

Perhaps another example could be the story of Seabiscuit, the famous racehorse. The main players were Charles Howard, the owner, a gregarious outgoing person, and a super salesman; Tom Smith, the trainer, a very focused and reserved person, maybe even anti-social; and Johnny (Red) Pollard, the determined jockey who didn't really fit in with Howard or Smith. And then you have

Seabiscuit, probably the strangest and sometimes laziest racehorse in history. Each of these players was different. Howard called Smith "Tom," and Tom called Howard "Mr. Howard." He would not even go up to the big house where Howard and others went to celebrate wins. None of them socialized together. Of course, they were in quite different levels in life. Howard was wealthy, ran the Marquis and selected the matches, but he didn't tell Tom how to train. Neither one of them told Pollard how to be a jockey, each did their own thing without the others interfering. And Seabiscuit pretty much ran the way he wanted. Naturally, you need to get the best people you can find and tell or show them what is needed. They must have authority and be held responsible, then give them guidance and turn them loose.

    Being a part of the team also means including team members in decision-making when the situation allows. You might be surprised at some of the good ideas /advice that comes from the junior staff working at lower levels. Again, the question is who/what is the catalyst for the right mix that produces the synergy that makes the team rise above statistically individual contributions? Getting that right makes the team successful. We understand the recipe and know the ingredients, but I must admit, after studying teams for 70+ years, preparing the stew is still opaque. Even if you get it right once, don't fool yourself into thinking you can use the process to develop a different team. One size certainly does not fit all, and there is no magic bullet.

    A huge part of my life has been as a team leader, which has given me unmeasurable joy. To see many fine young guys come together as a team and succeed even beyond their individual talents at the highest levels is more than rewarding. Winning is a goal, but the coming together of a team is the real magic. The alchemy of the championship team comes from pulling their inner strengths together, and that can't be coached. That also makes the U.S. Navy Seals, USA Delta forces, and USAF Para-Rescue such magnificent units. This is going to be a bit of bragging, but I'm not smart enough to dress it down and still show the success that should be recorded. I had the honor and privilege of being an integral part of several state, national, world championship, and world military games teams. I was either an athlete, a coach, a team captain, or chief of mission. Some of my guys went on to the Olympics. None of these great wins were just because of me—success was due to the many hard-working people who supported me, and of course to those tough, determined athletes who were with me in the many struggles to the top. They can be lauded without moderation. My policy was to never interfere with the coaching, and neither did I try to be one of the boys. I set goals and long-term objectives, but on the firing line or in the field, the coaches ran the show. The teams knew this and understood we were all in the fight together. No rah, rah, Notre Dame, give me one for the Gipper, speeches from me—it was not my style. There is no shortage of studies and books on leadership, and many styles work in different situations. You can intimidate or inspire, but you can't do both—the latter being desirable and more successful in the long haul. For sure, the leader must have integrity and courage. By courage, I mean the fortitude to do the right thing no matter how painful that might be. That could include cutting a personal friend off the team or speaking truth to power when it could jeopardize your career. In discussing moral values, Mark Twain said, "it is curious that physical courage should be so common in the world and moral courage so rare." If integrity is honesty and sincerity, and you combine that with courage, it could best be described as character.

A statement by General Norman Schwarzkopf highlights the critical value of courage. He said, "Leadership is a potent combination of strategy and character. But if you must be without one, be without strategy." Of course, my teams were made up mostly of military personnel who were already highly motivated and disciplined before coming on a team. Mostly, I tried to steer them mentally by telling them they could and would win, and, in some cases, showing them by example. Much of the time, it was just showing them they had my full and enthusiastic support of their efforts. Naturally, I cheered them on in competitions when it was appropriate, but there certainly was no hugging in my day. There is a fine line between professionalism and personal relationships, and that line must be maintained. Only a couple of times did I ever have to pull ears, and even then, the guys respected me and understood there was nothing personal against them. One must remember that leadership is not about being the best, it's about making everyone better—but it doesn't hurt to be the best. What is really important is competence to get the job done. Naturally, the leader must have the courage to do things right every time. That creates reliability and continuity, which is essential. Often overlooked, but of equal importance, is compassion and empathy. Team members have to know their leaders, other members of the team, and care for them in order to build trust. The cavalry phrase, "Horses first, men second, officers last," or maybe the more modern version, "Mission, men, and last me," comes to mind. The athletes or troops can't be fooled; charisma is nice but does not make a leader.

I had attended the National U.S. Shooting Championship at Camp Perry, Ohio, in 1960 and 1961 as an individual competitor. Earning a position on the California State high-power rifle team in 1962 allowed me to travel to the national championship as a team member. I was really a junior member in the sense of team experience but gained much from the older guys who coached and supported me in those championships. I was able to witness the enthusiasm and discipline of individual champions, and more particularly, the military teams from the Army and Marine Corps. The military teams inspired me, for sure. I was blessed and honored to be the leader of several shooting and modern pentathlon teams at national and international levels, which I will describe separately.

The first team I could really call my own was an eighth-grade boys, .22-caliber rifle team at the California Cadet Corps Championship held in Sacramento in 1962. I was teaching eighth-grade social studies at Hamilton Junior High School in Fresno, California. We had a middle-school Cadet Corps, which is a state-funded program of the California National Guard. I was commissioned in 1961 as a second lieutenant, which was my first-ever win in military uniform. As the Assistant Commandant, my job was to coach and train the kids for the state rifle championship. We won, and it was most gratifying as I had the boys in my social studies class in addition to Cadet Corps training. We practiced our shooting indoors on the auditorium stage, using reduced targets and bullet traps to catch the .22-caliber lead bullets after they passed through the paper target.

Another fun team of kids was the Air Force dependent highschool boys at Ramstein Air Force Base. We trained at night in a Quonset hut converted to a makeshift indoor range. A Postal Match (targets certified and mailed to Heidelberg Army headquarters) was conducted for all service dependents, Army, Air Force, and Navy in Europe. It was surely a long shot. It pleased me no end when our boys won. Witnessing the synergy of effort, involving morale, cohesion, affection, and trust, come together to make winning teams has brought me great satisfaction.

By good fortune I became team captain for the U.S. team at the German National Hunters Championship (DJV) five times and three times at the European Hunters Championship. Another honor was being captain of the Air Force International Trap Team for 17 years. A major challenge and great success came after my retirement when I was brought back into the service to lead the Modern Pentathlon Team at the World Military Championships and World Military Games 12 times. These teams allowed me to proudly wear a military uniform on official business for 42 years, from 1961 to 2003.

Modern Pentathlon

Although little-known in the United States, modern pentathlon is a wonderful and very challenging Olympic sport.

Because of my upcoming Air Force retirement at the end of December in 1992, I was losing all my good young guys on the USAF International Trap Team. Losing a team is difficult, but it was much more than that. They had been with me for many years. Several started with me when they were brand-new lieutenants or young airmen. I was retiring and would no longer be their team captain. I hated losing those fine young guys I had become very close to. It was in August of 1992, and I had just returned from a 17-day overseas "retirement" trip. The purpose was to give my top three young shooters, Capt Grazioli,

1st Lt Linn, and A1C Herman, a taste of European competition. A call came in from Mr. Steve Ducoff on a Friday afternoon. Steve was the Chief of Air Force Sports. He along with then-Lt Steve Richards had revitalized Air Force competitive shooting after the closure of the marksmanship school in 1969. Ducoff wanted me to take a joint military team to a CISM world volleyball championship in China the next week. The Pentagon certainly would not miss me, and my staff could handle about everything, but I wasn't too keen on being out of the office again so soon and had little interest in volleyball. However, it is not easy to say no to Steve, a Vietnam veteran and a friend. He was in a bind and told me he needed two Chiefs of Mission, one for China and one for Russia, and they had to be full colonels. Then he told me the world championship in Russia would be for Modern Pentathlon. That sparked my attention.

While serving at Randolph Air Force Base in 1973, I was asked if the Air Force could find a full colonel to attend a modern pentathlon competition and final banquet. In those days, the Army sponsored athletes to train full-time in modern pentathlon. The training was conducted at Fort Sam Houston, Texas. My boss, Col Albert D. Audette, agreed to represent the Air Force. That was the only time I was around modern pentathlon, but I recognized it as being a superb sport requiring exceptional athletes. Ducoff needed the help, so I signed on. It started a great and most enjoyable journey with a whole new group of fine young men, building championship teams. Pentathlon brought me back to the young guys, which gave me so much satisfaction. My thanks went out to Steve Ducoff. I was saddened by his passing three years ago.

Steve had just inherited this requirement from Armed Forces Sports. Why it was so late was not revealed to me nor did I care; it was what it was. But we had to leave the next Friday to reach Russia for the opening ceremony. Steve arranged a telephone conference call for me to speak with the athletes on Monday morning. I introduced myself and made clear what I expected of them. After that telephone meeting, I called the Armed Forces Sports office to find out what had been done. It was rather shocking to hear nothing had been done other than notifying the athletes of the event. Travel needed to be arranged along with visas for Russia. The wheels started turning rapidly with overnight mail for passports being sent to Washington. I turned my efforts to the travel itinerary and getting the visas. It sounds easy, but the first trip to the Russian Embassy for visas failed when our courier, who was next in line, had the door shut in his face as they closed for the afternoon and the rest of the day. The airline tickets were purchased, and the visas approved on Wednesday. Late that afternoon, Armed Forces Sports called me to report the trip would be canceled because the Secretary of Defense (Sec Def) had restricted all travel to Russia without his approval. They had the proper forms but had just realized it required a lengthy process through several layers of reviewing authority before it could be presented to the Sec Def. Needless to say, I was livid and did not contain my bad temper.

I had already told the young troops we were going, and by now had set my mind on it. It seemed incompetence reigned. Remember, this was late Wednesday afternoon, and we were scheduled to fly out on Friday. After the air cleared a bit, a runner appeared at my office with the form, which sure enough required the secretary's approval. It happened that in the preceding months the Sec Def's military aide, a Maj Gen, had stopped in and asked me how a particular situation involving NATO and my four-star boss might best be approached. Things went well with my advice, and he later thanked me. Now I called him for help. I explained we were merely a goodwill sports team. Apparently, the secretary was disturbed by too many military, retired military, reservists, and DOD civilians muddying up what he wanted done in Russia. Remember, Russia was in considerable turmoil in 1992. The general agreed to help and told me that Sec Def Dick Cheney was on travel for the week, but his deputy Mr. Donald J. Atwood could grant approval. Mr. Atwood was at a formal dinner but expected to be out by 9 p.m., when the general would get his signature. I waited in my Pentagon office and true to his word, at 10 p.m. the approval was delivered to my office. Sometimes you're lucky enough to know just the right guy. The Armed Forces Sports Staff was flabbergasted on Thursday morning when I told them to come pick up the Sec Def approval. We were on our way, and the team met me in Frankfurt, Germany, before our last leg to St. Petersburg.

CISM stands for Conseil International du Sport Militaire or in English, International Military Sports Council. It was started after World War II and originally was composed of a few European nations. The United States soon joined, and eventually most of the free world became members. Its purpose was to engage Armed Forces of the free world in friendly sporting competitions. Their motto was: "Friendship through sports." The official languages agreed upon were French and English. Those countries behind the Iron Curtain established their own sports organizations.

After the Berlin Wall fell in 1989, Russia, her previous Eastern European allies, and the new nations springing from the old Soviet Union petitioned for entry in CISM. After acceptance, Russia was granted approval to hold a modern pentathlon World Championship as their first CISM event. It is a premier military sport in Europe, Russia, and the countries of the former Eastern Bloc.

The Baron Pierre de Coubertin, a Frenchman, is credited with bringing back the Olympic Games originally held in ancient Greek times as early as the eighth century BC. His new modern Olympic games were first held in Athens in 1896. The Baron was still in charge in 1912 when the games were held in Sweden. It was then that he introduced what he conceived as being the most difficult of all Olympic sports. It would reflect what an athlete or warrior should be. Remember, he was a Frenchman, so he went back 100 years to the Napoleonic Wars to depict this perfect warrior/athlete: a soldier charged with delivering an urgent message. The soldier would start out on an unknown horse drawn from the stables. He would ride the horse until it fell from gunshot or exhaustion, fight off the enemy with a pistol, and then battle assassins with a sword. He would be forced to swim a river and finally race on foot to deliver the important message. This was depicted at the opening ceremonies in St. Petersburg, Russia. It was done dramatically, after two marching bands, skydivers, martial arts demonstrations, charging Cossacks on horseback, dancers, and jugglers. The Chiefs of Mission for the 12 countries attending the world championship were sitting on a high dais in a field that resembled a football stadium. Suddenly, a horse and rider appeared at the far end on a dead run down the middle of the field. When they got even with

Long Shots — Teams

the dais we were sitting on, the horse tripped, which threw the rider, who did a perfect somersault and landed on his feet. For a nanosecond when the horse went down, I thought the rider and horse would be hurt. Then I realized it was planned and no doubt practiced because it went off perfectly. I immediately recognized the rider was wearing a three-cornered hat (that stayed on his head) and a long tailcoat. He then ran forward on down the field, and two gunmen firing pistols popped up from the lawn. He fired and both fell. On he ran, and then another enemy jumped up with a sword. They dueled, and the enemy went down. He then ran to the end of the field where what looked like a huge fire hydrant was spewing water. He charged through the gusher, turned, and ran directly back to the dais where he whipped a paper out of his pouch and handed the message up to us. Pretty dramatic, and I doubt it could be repeated except in Hollywood.

Competition started with 20 shots from the .22-caliber pistol in a timed sequence. Pistol shooting involves hand and eye coordination, but it also requires very steady nerves and a low pulse rate. The second discipline is fencing, which is exactly the opposite of the low pulse rate and settled nerves demanded in pistol shooting. The fencing event, using the epee, looks and sounds more like a bar fight. Of course, it requires skill and finesse, but there's a lot of excitement and adrenaline flowing. Swimming 300 meters is the third event. The fourth event is riding an unfamiliar horse in the arena on a timed course of obstacles, requiring jumps, double jumps, and triple jumps. The rider has only 20 minutes to practice and get familiar with the horse he has drawn before his turn to ride him. The final event is a cross-country run of 4,000 meters, and after the ride, it is the most fun to watch. Distances have since been reduced to 200 meters for the swim and 3,000 meters for the run. Pistol shooting has changed from .22 to pellet gun. Points are awarded in the preceding events, and the athlete with the highest score starts the run, followed by the second highest scoring athlete, then the third, and so on.

The first runner has the gold if he can stay in front, but Number Two knows that if he can pass Number One, he gets the gold. And Number Three knows if anyone passes him, he won't get a medal. Those following can see who they have to pass for a medal or to help

487

their team. It's a hard-fought event. Many collapsed at the finish line, and some collapse before. Some vomit at the end. I told my guys they better collapse or be puking at the end, or we didn't need them on our team. One of my favorite troops, PFC Chad Senior, puked nearly every time at the end of his run. Problem was, I usually took the team to dinner after the championship, and he was often still puking. Chad was rated as the Number One pentathlon athlete in the world for a couple of years, is a two-time Olympian, and is one of the fiercest competitors I have ever known. You can understand why.

My trip to St. Petersburg sold me on pentathlon, and I was hooked. It is such a great sport, and I had the good luck to have a world champion and Olympic gold medalist, Janusz Peciak, to guide me and coach our athletes. He had won his gold in 1976 at the Montréal Olympics. The athletes were Capt Paul Messenger, 2d Lt Dirk Bouma, SPC 4 Dale Brynstead, and 2d Lt Andrew Miltner. Messenger and Brynstead had been in international competition previously, but never in Russia. Miltner and Bouma were on their first run. I had given them all a rather stern lecture about what I expected on our first telephone meeting the week before. They no doubt expected some harsh treatment. It certainly wasn't forthcoming. My charge face-to-face was simply, "We don't have a bunch of chicken rules, you can do anything you have balls big enough to do, just remember two things: do not embarrass me or our flag."

Capt Messenger was smart and knew his way around. He made an excellent team leader, looked right, and acted right. The team followed his lead. Before the trip, they asked me if they could leave their wheel caps home and bring only their flight or garrison caps, which fold flat and are much easier to pack. I was required to carry the wheel cap and understood the difficulty in packing it, so I agreed with their request. After all, they were carrying riding boots, dress uniforms, swords, fencing suits, and other athletic uniforms. I was traveling in a civilian coat and tie in case an occasion called for it, but they assured me they did not need a coat and tie. As it turned out, all the teams were invited to a Russian ballet, and the word was to dress accordingly, which meant civilian coat and tie. The team looked at me rather anxiously. I told them without any rancor to just dress as best they could, using a sweater as a substitute for a sport coat. Of course, they only had military shirts and ties. When all the teams were assembling for the bus ride to the opera, the other teams showed up in coat and tie. Most countries heavily subsidize their teams. The Italians showed up in beautiful, matched silk sport coats. My guys arrived wearing their Class A uniforms. Those who have not served in the military should understand that troopers would much prefer being in civilian clothes rather than their uniform for a fun outing. They were the only team in uniform, and I could not have been prouder. I didn't require it, nor did I suggest it. They simply rose to the occasion. In all the following years when I was chief of mission, the team never failed to rise to the occasion.

We were received and treated very well by the Russian military conducting the competition. The barracks room our team was assigned was sparse, simply a bed for each athlete. The floors were wood and had just been refinished, leaving a heavy pine odor. But the rooms and halls were clean as a pin. The heads (bathroom) were also clean, but a little primitive. There were no toilet seats, and in place of showers there were large wash basins used for bathing. My quarters were a little better as I had a lamp, a closet for hanging uniforms, a couple of chairs, and a shower. Needless to say, the guys had a key to my room so they could take showers. The civilians I encountered were all polite and accommodating.

What they continually said was, "You were with us in the Great Patriotic War." Many veterans from that era attended our competitions, and all wore military decorations and medals on their civilian suits. I was assigned a car and driver plus two interpreters, both young lieutenants in the Russian intelligence service. Their second language was Chinese, and their third was English. No restrictions were placed on me, and I could take the car and driver anywhere I wanted any time I wanted, with or without my interpreters. Our coach, Janusz Peciak, was fluent in Russian, and I didn't need the interpreters, but I liked them, and they liked our guys, so I generally took them with me in the car, which they loved. My question to them was: "Is it better now or before the wall fell?" Both answered, "It was better before."

When I asked why, they told me that their fathers were colonels. One was still on active duty, and the other recently retired. The one on

489

active duty had come from East Germany and was now quartered with his family in a tent. The boy of the recently retired colonel told me his father did not have enough money to buy his wife a new dress for their anniversary. They loved to hear jazz and pop music on the car radio, so I asked them if they were able to listen to that previously and they both said, "No." Both had recently graduated from military schools, so who knows what restrictions had applied.

The competition was divided in two locations. Pistol shooting, fencing, and swimming were conducted at a barracks in St. Petersburg. The equestrian portion and the cross-country running course were located at a country barracks. After the completion of the first competitions, we were advised to pack our gear and be prepared to move to the second location and barracks the next morning. One of my Russian interpreters had a girlfriend near the second barracks, and he was clearly anxious and excited about seeing her. After some thought, it seemed to me only prudent to send someone in advance to ensure our quarters were acceptable and properly prepared for our arrival. I ordered a car and driver to take my interpreter to the new location that evening. The Russian motor pool was not happy, and no doubt figured what was up, but they were not about to turn down a request from the American Colonel. The Russian kid could not believe I could and would send him ahead. A small favor and a little goodwill build solid relations. Besides, he was a young guy doing a good job for us. When he met us the next day, he was as happy as a pet skunk.

The Russians had a full cultural program as is required by CISM for all competitions. One day, we visited Peter the Great's summer palace. Another day, the Chiefs of Missions were given a tour of St. Petersburg on a Russian Navy ship. I was surprised to learn of the many channels throughout St. Petersburg, sort of the Venice of the North except with deep channels that allow Navy ships. The ship we were on had a Greek Orthodox priest assigned, and he went with us and gave a prayer before our departure. Vodka was flowing heavily on the ship, and my glass was kept full. I kept looking for place to ditch the drink, but it was difficult. The priest kept up glass for glass with the heavyweights. I'm talking about large water glasses. Another social activity for the Chiefs was a visit to the Hermitage Museum. The team was having a fencing practice, and I thought they might need me, and I wanted them to know they came first so I skipped the Hermitage. Huge mistake, the team didn't need me, but I considered it duty.

The tournament was organized and run exceptionally well. Maybe because it was the first CISM hosted by the Russians, but for whatever reason, they went out of their way in doing everything possible to make it a successful competition. Our athletes performed reasonably well in competition, considering their short training time and the fact that most of the other competitors were full-time athletes. Many had just returned from the Barcelona Olympics. We did set the military standard for other nations to follow, and our team did an extraordinarily good job in building friendships with the other athletes. It was very important to the Russians for the U.S. to have a presence at their first competition open to the free world. It was clear after the competition and during the final banquet that the Americans were the favored team of the championship.

Apparently, there was considerable uncertainty whether the U.S. was going to send a team to this competition, which was certainly not helpful to our athletes being called upon at the last minute. Our team suffered jet lag as we arrived in Russia Sunday evening with scheduled training on Monday and competition on Tuesday. As you might imagine, I fixed that on future trips. Our team did as well as the coach expected. We won the silver medal in individual fencing and a fourth place in swimming. Our scores earned sixth place in the team event, far from outstanding but still respectable. The Russian team took top honors on the podium, which was no surprise. Russia has been a strong competitor in modern pentathlon for many years.

The closing banquet was held in the Leningrad officers mess and required class A uniforms. It was a real celebration with caviar galore and champagne flowing. Each team was seated at a round table with four or five bottles of champagne already on the table. It was plenty for three to four glasses per person. You might think athletes would not drink to excess. Think again! This crowd was finished with the match and maybe competition for the year, the Olympics were over, and now CISM was finished. We drank our champagne, but the party was going strong, and I suspect many of the younger enlisted athletes, particularly in the Eastern Bloc, had never been in an officers' club or any club like this one. A pay-as-you-go bar was open, but most athletes had no money. I thought it would show great sportsmanship if I bought champagne, and we took a bottle to each table and toasted that country including Russia, Germany, Switzerland, Austria, Holland, Finland, Italy, France, Greece, Czechoslovakia, and Ukraine. I bought 11 bottles, one at a time. The athletes were hugging each other, trading caps, and singing. Someone made a film cassette of the dinner, and I have a copy which was not shared with my chain of command. One of my boys said, "A Russian colonel kissed me, but I think they're just trying to embarrass me." I sure hope so. I had that cassette converted to a CD, but few have seen it. My flight cap was traded for an Austrian's beret. The next day was a free day, thank goodness. No one saw me until after lunch, which I certainly didn't want to eat.

After seeing these athletes partying with each other at the banquet, it's hard to imagine them as adversaries. The CISM motto, "Friendship through sports," certainly happened in Russia. I felt sorry for the Russian athletes. They simply had no money and were selling anything they could, including uniforms and items like binoculars, which I suspect were government property. One young married captain whose wife had just had a baby was trying desperately to sell a collection of coins that were so worn I doubt any collector would want them. It was a sad sight.

I probably spent more time with my two young Russian interpreters than my own team since they followed me everywhere like ducklings. They were enthusiastic and energetic just like our 2d Lts. One of them said something about American Levis and that one day he would get a pair. I asked him if they were available on the market. He told me they were, but the cost was a month's salary. It happened that Capt Messenger, who had been at international competitions before, had brought a pair to trade. The Russian and he were about the same size. Our team was driven to the airport for departure in a small bus. We said goodbye to our driver and then handed the Levis to our young second lieutenant interpreter. He was spellbound, looked at us, and started crying. We all sort of looked the other way for a moment or two so he could regain his composure. We patted him on his back as we got in the ticket line, but his eyes were still leaking. Besides representing the United States in the first CISM championship held in Russia, we may have made history as being the first to fly an American flag in Russia (barring the U.S. Embassy) since the Polar Bear Expedition in 1918 and 1919 when United States Army troops were sent to fight the Bolsheviks in northern Russia. The 339 Infantry Regiment, referred to as Polar Bears, suffered terribly in the bitter winter months while battling the Bolsheviks. They lost 232 men before being evacuated. The after-action report of my trip was given to my boss, Admiral Smith, with copies to the Chiefs of Staff of the Air Force and the Army, and to the Chairman of the Joint Chiefs of Staff. All showed interest in the trip.

In earlier times, the U.S. Army ran a very good training program for modern pentathlon, but that has long since been discontinued.

It was clear our athletes now needed help to be competitive. The U.S. Modern Pentathlon Association, which was headquartered in San Antonio, was the center for civilian training and had the jumping horses needed. Army athletes used them at no cost, but there was no permanent facility for a fencing salle or indoor shooting range. Since Army personnel were getting the use of horses and coaches at no cost, I thought perhaps the Army could help us with a building at Fort Sam Houston. Of course, the best way to get things done is to get support from the very top, which in this case was the Chief of Staff of the United States Army. I had retired and was no longer in the Pentagon. One doesn't just walk into his office, but I had previously worked for Army four-star General Jack Merritt who arranged an audience with Gen Gordon R. Sullivan, the 32nd Chief of Staff of the Army. Gen Sullivan received me warmly and was interested and enthusiastic about our Russian competition and Armed Forces sports. He told me to grab the general who oversaw Army sports and get back on his schedule so we could have a three-way meeting to get things rolling. it was a huge help, I can tell you.

I told the General the Army was getting free coaching and use of horses from the U.S. Modern Pentathlon Association, but they needed a permanent building to conduct fencing and indoor pistol shooting. I suggested Fort Sam Houston would be a good location. Gen Sullivan said, "Why don't you go down and visit with Lieutenant General Jaco, commander of Fifth Army and see what he can do?" Then the general said, "Tell him I said he was a good guy." We were sitting catty cornered from each other, and he reached over and tapped me on the knee and said, "Tell him I said he was a really good guy." With those instructions I was finally able to get past the palace guards at Fort Sam Houston and get an appointment with Lt Gen Neal T. Jaco, but only after telling his executive officer I had a private message from the Army Chief of Staff for General Jaco. Fortunately, I was able to meet with the General 15 minutes before a joint meeting with his staff and key base management and security personnel. I gave him Gen Sullivan's regards and repeated his comments that Gen Jaco was a good guy and then reached over and tapped his knee and told him Gen Sullivan had done that to me and instructed me to change from a good guy to a really good guy. Gen Jaco laughed at that. We went into a conference room for the staff meeting. As I recall, there were at least a dozen officers and senior civilians present, including the Brigadier General who was the Garrison commander. All were adamant that a building should not be furnished to the U.S. Modern Pentathlon Association even if some Army troops would be using the facility. There were comments like, "We would have to give a building to the Girl Scouts and who knows who else?" Base security said, "We can't have civilians bringing guns on the installation." Lots of negative remarks were offered. Gen Jaco thanked me for coming and closed the meeting by thanking the staff and saying, "Let's look really hard at what we can do." Two days later, a call came to me with the building number of a base gym. It was perfect: a big locker room, a large gang shower, which could handle 20 guys at a time, and the upstairs area for the .22 pistol shooting. And best of all, a basketball gym floor big enough for five fencing lanes. We were in business. As an aside, I knew Gen Sullivan's Secretary, Lil, from my previous Pentagon tour when she was Secretary to Major General Charles W. Dyke (known as Wild Bill Dyke), one of my favorite bosses in the Joint Chiefs of Staff. Senior Generals' schedules are furnished to their senior staff to keep them informed as to schedule openings, etc. Lil told me there was a lot of interest by the Army staff, wondering who this Air Force Col visiting the Chief could be and what he might be about. She would not tell a soul, so we had a great laugh about the mystery.

Modern pentathlon is dominated by the military. The CISM world championship mirrors most participants in the regular world championship, which is open to anyone. Most modern pentathlon athletes who make the Olympic team are either military members or prior military.

Consider the time for training in five different sports, not to mention owning jumping horses, or having access to a fencing salle. It is not a sport that can be trained for in the morning before college classes. To be competitive, it is a full-time occupation. Another reason is tradition and the fact that the Baron de Coubertin fashioned the event after military skills: shooting, fencing, and riding. Although fencing and horseback riding are no longer considered a military skill, tradition holds.

When modern pentathlon was introduced as an Olympic sport in the 1912 Olympics held in Sweden, the United States entered one contestant. Would you like to guess who that might have been? I have a copy of the entry form. It was 2nd Lt George S. Patton. Lt Patton was from a very wealthy Southern California family, so I expect he learned to ride and play polo before starting at the Virginia Military Institute, and he rode and played polo at West Point. Lt Patton ended the Olympic event in fifth place. Strange as it seemed, his pistol shooting brought him down. Patton finished third in the ride, which was then a steeplechase, on a horse he borrowed from the Swedish Cavalry. He claimed another third in the cross-country run but collapsed in a dead faint after crossing the finish line. Two others did the same, and one died. That will give you some idea of the determination and all-out effort made in these competitions. His main competitors were the Swedes, and they loved him. He had great respect for the Swedish Pentathlon Team, and they held him in high regard. Lifelong friendships were established. After World War II he was invited to Sweden. The same athletes he had competed against in 1912 were still alive (Sweden was neutral during World War II), and they put on a mini pistol competition where he earned the silver medal. It brings to mind the motto of CISM, friendship through sports.

Our coach, Janusz Peciak, five-time world champion and Olympic gold medalist, feels the CISM world championship is harder fought than the open world championship. He coaches both the open and the CIMS championships so he should know. Pentathlon has a long military tradition, and the two cannot be separated.

World Championships 1993-2002

After St. Petersburg, our next world championship in 1993 was held in Banska Bystrica, Slovakia, another country with a strong tradition in Modern Pentathlon. Teams represented seventeen countries, including Chile, Italy, France, the Czech Republic, Poland, Austria, Switzerland, the Netherlands, Belarus, Russia, Hungary, Ukraine, Sweden, Korea, German, Slovakia, and the United States. Iran was an observer nation. Capt Paul Messenger and Lt Dirk Bouma returned to the team, and our third team member was a young fireball Army private, Scott Christie, for his first modern pentathlon championship. Air Force Reserve Maj Donald Morley accompanied the team as adjutant and assistant to coach Janusz Peciak.

When we arrived, we were informed there would also be a triathlon event. Major Morley represented the U.S. and won the gold medal. Quite a surprise to us, and I think to him, also. Nevertheless, it was a pleasant surprise. Captain Messenger was again our top performer, and he won an individual silver in the swim, but our team score was discouraging and put us in the bottom half. Again, our team was made up of part-time athletes who were all holding down regular military jobs and had little time to train.

Luckily, we had a stopover at Rhein Main in Germany to catch up on jet lag and train with the German team, but it wasn't enough. Our friends from the Netherlands flew us with them from Germany to Slovakia and back to Germany. Col Novotny, President of the technical committee (competition boss), told me the U.S. athletes were the most military and disciplined of all teams. That's always music to my ears. They were clearly the most watched and most popular among the

496

other athletes. As a matter of interest, I was selected, by unanimous vote of all mission chiefs and CISM officials, to be a member of the jury of appeals, which is quite an honor. The jury of appeals handles all disputes and appeals beyond the rules to ensure fairness on all sides. It is an affirmation of faith in the member's impartiality in reaching just decisions. Naturally I was pleased and held that position in all following championships.

The 1994 world championship was held in Revingehed, Sweden. It was a very enjoyable competition organized and run by the 7th Mechanized Brigade commanded by Col Mats Welff. His Royal Highness, Prince Bertil, sent a welcoming address to all participants. The members of the 7th Mechanized Brigade had spent most of their careers together and knew each other well. It was interesting to see how they worked as opposed to U.S. military units with frequent changes of personnel. The young lieutenants of the 7th were enthusiastic and wanted me to drive their tanks. I had fun with them racing around learning how to operate their tanks. The gun turret on their main battle tank was permanently fixed which only allowed the gun to be adjusted for elevation. Since the gun turret did not allow for rotation, the tank had to be moved to change direction of fire on different targets. Sweden was neutral during World War II, and I believe these tanks were from before that era. They would be only moving steel coffins against a modern army.

The good thing was that Sweden had ordered Panzer tanks from Germany. Still, the young tankers were a proud and gutsy group, and I thoroughly enjoyed them. Our team did a little better in the competition. All three athletes had competed in the previous world championship, Capt Messenger, Lt Bouma, and Private Christie. Our coach was Janusz Peciak. Additionally, I brought Army 2d Lt Jim Gregory, an eager and hard charger who had just graduated from Ranger school, along as team adjutant. Mr. Johnny Russell joined as an assistant coach for riding. I recall the ride was conducted on a rainy day with everything being wet and slick. Private Christie was not yet a great rider, and we were worried about him riding in the rain. He drew a sweet little mare hardly bigger than a pony. She started around the course at a medium gait but seemed to have the course already memorized. The little mare never missed a beat. She ran the course in good time without a fault for a perfect score. We were laughing our tails off watching as Scott did little more than hang on. He won the ride and a gold medal to our great pleasure, although we were still laughing that night at dinner. Capt Messenger took the gold medal in swimming. He and Christie took the first individual gold medals in recent memory, and the first ever in the expanded CISM that now includes the former Eastern Bloc countries. We were also the highest team in the combination of run/swim/ride.

Capt Bouma contributed solid scores, and our team earned fifth place in the overall team standing (ahead of all other nations who were not a part of the former Eastern Bloc). In the individual standing, PFC Christie was 12th, Capt Bouma was 16th, and Capt Messenger was19th after having drawn a very poor horse. The countries represented in this competition were Austria, Belarus, the Czech Republic, France, Germany, Italy, Poland, Russia, Slovakia, Sweden, Switzerland, Ukraine, and the United States.

The Italians sponsored the world championship in 1995 and held the competition in Rome. We had built good relations with their team in the two previous world championships, so they let us come early to get over jet lag and have four days of training, for which they were kind enough to furnish quarters and meals. That time before the competition gave our guys an opportunity to train together. The competing countries were Italy, Ukraine, Russia, Korea, Poland, Belarus, France, Switzerland, Sweden, the Czech Republic, Hungary, Austria, Germany, Slovakia, Holland, Bahrain, Chile, and the U.S. Mexico was represented by observers. As was expected, the Italians did a superb job in organizing and running the events to include the messing and billeting accommodations. Our new team coach was Jan Bartu, who had won an Olympic silver medal in modern pentathlon for the Czech Republic. Team members were Capt Messenger, 2d Lt Jim Gregory, and SPC 4 Scott Christie. Second Lieutenant Glenn Voelz acted as adjutant. I should explain that modern pentathlon teams consist of three athletes. There is no official position for adjutant, but I always attempted to bring an extra athlete or two to cover any unforeseen events, such as sickness or emergency leave, to ensure we could field a team. But it was also to give our new athletes experience and exposure to the nations of Europe and their athletes.

It should also be noted that invitations from those running the competitions often allowed for only three athletes. The host for world championships was obliged to offer free housing, messing, and all event costs. Therefore, I had to get permission to bring extra athletes from the host country and jump a hurdle in getting extra funds from Armed Forces Sports. Phil Cota held the purse strings, but as it turned out he had been an Army captain serving in Vietnam the same time I was there. It took a little cajoling, but he always came up with the extra money. Glenn Voelz was a recent West Point graduate. He was a handsome lad who attracted girls, but important to me was that he was in top shape and clearly a gifted athlete. He fit in well with our guys, and I could see he had potential, so we tried to get him for the next couple of world championships, but he was in jobs or positions where he could not be released. I'm sorry we didn't get him but happy to report he retired as an Army full colonel. Once again, our team did a fine job representing the U.S. military—they looked and acted like the outstanding soldiers they were, and I was proud to be their team chief. We began to be noticed in competition. In the relay event, a team competition, we ended up in fifth place. We had one poor ride on an impossible horse, or we would've made it to the winner's podium. For the first time the team won the swimming event in the relay competition. That was our first for us as a team win, and while it was only in one of the five events it foretold the future.

The world championship for 1996 was delayed as the scheduled host country found they could not sponsor the event. The United States picked up the slack and agreed to hold the modern pentathlon world championship at Fort Sam Houston in San Antonio. Naturally, I became an advisor and was perhaps a little heavy-handed. I had no worries about the actual running of the competition as it would be handled by our San Antonio folks belonging to the U.S. Modern Pentathlon Association. My concern was more about the attention of chiefs of mission and officials representing CISM. All went off exceptionally well, and while we were officially hosted by Maj Gen James B. Peake, the real credit must go to Mr. Edward K. Miller, who

499

acted as Chairman for the organizing committee. Ed's normal job on the post was director of plans, training, mobilization, and security. That alone made him an excellent choice to be chairman, but he also knew modern pentathlon, which made his selection even better. Understand, hosting this event, he was in charge not only of the competition but of all the ceremonies, protocol, logistics, transportation, marketing, public affairs, finance, contracting, security, medical, housing, dining, linguist coordination, and the list goes on.

We had a spectacular opening ceremony hosted by Brig Gen Simmons. In addition to each of the country's athletic teams marching, we had a band, a joint service honor guard and flag detail, and a show by the 1st Cavalry Horse Detachment. They put on a magnificent display of horsemanship with riders shooting balloons and racing with a chuck wagon. For the CISM dignitaries and the chiefs of mission we had dinner hosted by Brig Gen Claypool on a river barge while viewing San Antonio at night. We used the historic Spanish governor's palace for a luncheon with the same group. I knew the San Antonio Mayor, Howard Peak, so we invited him and my friend Capt Jack Dean, the U.S. Marshal for the Western District of Texas, as extra guests. The host was Brig Gen Griffin, but our European guests were more impressed with the mayor and the U.S. Marshal, who was carrying a pistol and looked like a Texas Ranger—which he had been. For the athletes' cultural day, we took them on an Alamo tour and then lunch at the Lone Star brewery, then a visit to the Buckhorn Museum, the Lone Star Museum, and finally shopping at the River Center Mall. The people conducting the competition events were volunteers from the U.S. Modern Pentathlon Association. They were old hands and knew what they were doing. I had no worries there, and the competitions came off like clockwork. Mr. Charles Michaels handled the scoring. The chiefs of the five disciplines were as follows: Mr. Joe Forrester for shooting, Mr. John Moreau handled fencing, Mrs. D. Holler was chief for swimming, Mr. Skip Connors conducted the running, and Lt Col John Russell was chief for riding, with retired Col Gayle O'Rear assisting.

If anyone is the epitome of modern pentathlon, it must be Colonel John Russell. He started his military career in the National Guard and served in the 104th Cavalry. Commissioned as a second

Long Shots — Teams

lieutenant in 1943, he fought from Africa through Italy to Germany and was awarded the Purple Heart at the battle of Monte Cassino. He was a horseman through and through and competed in the equestrian events of the 1948 Olympics and again in 1952 when he won a bronze Olympic medal. After retirement from the military, Col Russell became the coach for the U.S. modern pentathlon team in addition to providing riding and jumping horse lessons to a whole cadre of civilians, both juniors and seniors. I worked with Col Russell, and he was generous with his knowledge and time. At one point when I was filling in as Executive Director for the U.S. Modern Pentathlon and organizing the San Antonio Cup, a major international competition including athletes from the U.S., Italy, Mexico, Great Britain, Peru, Poland, Brazil, Canada, Denmark, and Kazakhsta. We were running low on funds. Col Russell handed me an unsolicited check for $5,000, with no fanfare and without a desire for recognition. No one is in his league in the building and support of U.S. Modern Pentathlon.

It was my honor to wish him well at his 100-year birthday celebrated in 2020. He has since passed, and we shall never see a patron of his caliber again. Another pentathlon stalwart is Danny Steinman who was an athlete in the 80s and then President of the U.S. Modern Pentathlon Association.

Our team members for the 1996 CISM World Championship were Capt Bouma, Capt Fred Eaton, 1st Lt Jim Gregory, and SPC 4 Scott Christie. Other members of our team were Coach Jon Bartu and Mr. Jon Hess as adjutant. Jon was a young real estate agent who liked pentathlon and was a patron. He was always able to find someone with a large, impressive home to act as hosts for a formal reception. For this competition reception, Mr. and Mrs. Marshall Steves were gracious in offering their beautiful home, which was the location for the surprise birthday party every year for Lady Bird Johnson. Dr. Steve Holtzclaw came on board as our medical doctor. Steve is a civilian and a top graduate of Johns Hopkins in emergency medicine. He had accompanied me as team doctor when I was Chief of Mission for the U.S. trap and skeet shooting teams to world championships in Cyprus and Lima, Peru. He also traveled with our Air Force team. I knew he would be perfect for the pentathletes, and he was. They took to him

501

immediately. The Army objected to sending a civilian and wanted to send an Army doctor, but I managed to squelch that. Dr. Steve was with us from then on.

The San Antonio competition hosted 11 teams: Austria, Chile, the Czech Republic, Germany, Hungary, Italy, Russia, Poland, Slovakia, Sweden, and the United States. By now I knew most of the top modern pentathlon athletes in the world, and it was enjoyable to see and host them here in the States. Russia won the team event with the Czech Republic being second and Italy being third. We ended up sixth. In the relay team event, which is more exciting for me, we ended up being fifth. Italy won the relay with Hungary being second and the Czech Republic being third. No great laurels on our part apart from our team surprisingly winning the riding event. The team riders were Capt Eaton, 1st Lt Gregory and SPC 4 Christie. That win caught the attention of everyone. After the awards and formal closing ceremony the athletes, delegates, volunteers, and organizing committee all joined in a huge Texas barbecue and barn dance. The athletes can be viciously serious during the competition, but when it is over, it's over, and they loved to party afterward. It was something to see, the young athletes from all these different European countries, who are sometimes adversaries, dancing and singing together, some in civilian clothes and some still in riding uniforms from the last event, the Carabinieri in riding boots and double red striped pants, some in cowboy hats and others in short pants. Quite colorful, for sure.

Hungary hosted the world championship in August 1997. Our coach Jan Bartu was from the Czech Republic, the next-door neighbor to Hungary. He arranged for our team to train with the Czech team in Prague for a week before moving to Budapest. That training was certainly a big boost to our team, and it was sorely needed. I was chief of mission, Mr. Ed Miller from Fort Sam Houston acted as team captain, and Jan coached. Dr. Steve Holtzclaw was our MD, but he stepped in for any help that was needed. Our athletes were newly promoted Capt James Gregory, SPC 4 Scott Christie, SPC 4 Brett Weatherbie, and SPC 4 Chad Senior. This would be a rather green team. Gregory and Christie were seasoned and were on their third world championship, but not old hats yet. Weatherbie and Senior were just one week out of Army basic training. Our experienced athletes had just returned to training, and neither one was in top shape yet. We had five days training with the Czechs to weld our team together. The training was excellent, and we bonded while enjoying the beautiful city of Prague. Gregory moved in easily as team leader without anything being said and did a superb job in that capacity until he finally left the team after the 2000 world championship in Switzerland. The Czech team put us up at no cost for food and billeting, which was much appreciated as I had scant funds available. They even made lunches for us to carry on our train trip from Prague to Budapest. Sports teams were offered the same fare as students, so we made the trip at little cost and were assigned seats in the first-class cabin. It was an enjoyable trip through the beautiful countryside.

Weatherbie and Senior had made a trip to San Antonio earlier in the year to investigate the sport as both were keen to make an Olympic team. They talked with me, and I encouraged them to join the Army but told them they should first go to officer candidate school (OCS) and become officers since they were both college graduates. I went to Africa on safari for nearly two months, and when I returned, they were both in Army basic training, not OCS—so much for my counseling. The competition was run well, but the food and quarters were rather rugged. Competing teams were: Hungary, the Czech Republic, Belarus, Italy, Austria, Estonia, the Netherlands, Russia, Ukraine, Brazil, Switzerland, France, Latvia, Germany, and the United States. Our team did well, considering their state of training, and we ended up in sixth place in the team event.

Scott Christie had the highest individual score, placing him at Number 13. The real eye-opener for me and the other teams was our guys winning the swim event in the relay team final. They just swam away from all the others—a clear picture of the future. Neither Weatherbie nor Senior was anywhere near ready for a world championship, but I needed to get them seasoned. The competition was officially open to only three athletes, Gregory, Christie, and Weatherbie. Senior would be an extra non-competitor. However, I did manage to get him into a couple of events as a non-scoring entry to give him experience. He did well in the swim, but I noticed as we moved to another area that he had not shaved (all swimmers in those days shaved their entire body before a competition). He answered it wasn't important and did not matter anyway as he wasn't officially in the competition. It's a good thing I didn't have my pistol, or we would've had one dead soldier. Needless to say, I did not talk to him in a mild parental voice. The air turned blue. I wasn't disappointed. I was livid, having begged Armed Forces sports for the extra money needed to bring him. Every practice, training session and competition is important. Additionally, he was a brand-new punk just one week out of basic training and talking to a full colonel in a rather cavalier manner.

From what I could gather, he and Weatherbie, being college graduates, were babied during Army basic training. It was 1997, and the military was going through a ridiculous period of thinking all should be loved. That was the one and only time I ever had to speak with Chad Senior. He became the strongest willed and toughest competitor you can imagine. On top of that, he went to OCS and became an outstanding officer and leader.

The Carabinieri hosted the 1998 World Championship in Rome, Italy. It was a superb competition with fifteen countries competing. Teams competing were: the Czech Republic, Belarus, Russia, Germany, Italy, Poland, Hungary, Sweden, Switzerland, the Netherlands, Ukraine, Estonia, Latvia, Austria, and the United States. I was chief of mission, and Col J. Picariello (from Army Sports) acted as team captain. Janusz Peciak was back as coach and Dr. Steve Holtzclaw was our MD. Competitors were Capt James Gregory, SPC 4 Chad Senior, and SPC 4 Brett Weatherbie. It was an interesting time in Rome as the Italians were very upset with the U.S. military. A Marine aircraft had cut the cable on a gondola in the Dolomite Mountains, sending 20 European skiers to a rapid and early death. The Italian press was calling it the Cavalese cable-car massacre, named after the closest village. The Marine pilot Capt Richard Ashby and navigator Capt Joseph Schweitzer were court-martialed with Ashby being dismissed and sentenced to six months in prison. Capt Schweitzer was also found guilty and dismissed from the service. But that wasn't until many months after the tragedy. As a matter of interest, my friend Chandler P. Seagraves, who was then a young Marine Corps captain, was in the backseat with another captain on that disastrous flight. They were merely riders and were cleared of any culpability. Chandler later flew with the Blue Angels, and I'm happy to report he retired as a full colonel. The anti-U.S. sentiment was running high, and several Carabinieri carrying submachine guns met us at the gate when we deplaned. We picked up our luggage, and they walked us to a waiting van, past checkpoints including customs and immigration without stopping. We had the Carabinieri with us throughout the competition, and I must say they were fun, all young guys full of beans and continually driving way too fast.

I hate to say it, but they reminded me of wild high-school kids. I think they were showing off for my benefit. Dr. Holtzclaw and I were riding in one sedan with submachine guns on the floor, and the driver was cutting corners so sharp and fast those guns would slide from one side of the floor and then back to the other side—just a little crazy. The Carabinieri Commandant, Lt Gen Sergio Siracusa, attended most of the events and was a perfect host. He was dapper and congenial. I enjoyed his company, and he would search me out at the competition sites and social events. I also became friends with Colonnello Dott, Comandante 1 Reggimendo, and many of the Carabineri senior staff. Our athletes, although still quite young and inexperienced, did very well in the competition. Just as important, they carried our flag high and with dignity. And they conducted themselves as gentlemen and professional soldiers, which earned them respect from the Carabinieri and the other teams. High points were SPC 4 Senior winning the individual swimming, and SPC 4 Weatherbie taking third place. Senior was also third in the individual run. In the team event we placed fifth, and in the relay team event we were fourth – not in the winner's circle but respectable. Evidence would show we were moving to the best run/swim team in the world. We were about middle-of-the-road in the ride, but low in shooting and still at the bottom in fencing. Clearly our work was cut out for us, but I had full confidence this team would soon stand on the winner's podium.

Fort Bema in Warsaw, Poland, was the site for the 1999 World Championship. Fifteen nations were represented. They were:

Poland, the Czech Republic, Belarus, Estonia, Latvia, Switzerland, Italy, Germany, Sweden, Slovakia, Austria, Brazil, Lithuania, the Netherlands, and the United States. Our full team composition was Janusz Peciak as coach, Dr. Steve Holtzclaw as MD, and Col Jeannie Picariello, Ad Libitum. Athletes were Capt Jim Gregory, Capt Dirk Bouma, SPC 4 Brett Weatherbie, and SPC 4 Chad Senior. This was a solid team that had been training together full-time courtesy of the Army's world-class athlete program. They were still young in experience, but they were ready to do battle, and battle they did. In the total individual events of all five disciplines, Capt Gregory won the silver. Chad Senior won the individual swimming event for the second year in a row. Capt Gregory's winning the silver medal in the overall competition was the highest ranking for the United States in at least the last 15 years, and we were all pretty excited and joyful about his silver medal. But the crown jewel was the team event. It was won by USA and again, the first U.S. team win in more than 15 years. The team members were Gregory, Senior, and Weatherbie with a score of 15,758. The second-place team was the Czech Republic with a score of 15,560, the Italians took third place with a score of 15,355. It was a solid win with our team 200 points ahead of second place. When I say it was the first team win in 15 years, that is only part of the story. Previous U.S. teams had never faced Russia or the strong teams in the Eastern Bloc. So, ours was the first U.S. team to win over all teams in the world. There was great joy in our camp. At the beginning of this narrative, I credited our coach, Janusz Peciak, as being the gold-medal modern-pentathlon winner in the Montréal Olympics. But he was also five times a world champion. He never bragged or even spoke about it, and I failed to realize what a hero he was in Poland. Janusz and I were in downtown Warsaw and hailed a taxi to take us back to Fort Bema. We got about halfway there when the driver recognized who Janusz was. He became quite excited about having an Olympic gold-medal winner from Poland in his taxi, and he began to veer off course, driving up in front of bars, honking his horn and pounding on his door yelling, "I've got Janusz Peciak! I've got Janusz Peciak!" People would come out and give the high sign or clap, and then we raced off to another bar, and went through the same routine. Janusz finally

Long Shots — Teams

persuaded the driver that we had to get to the Fort. I was thinking for a while we might not ever get there, but I guess that's what one can expect riding with the famous.

The XXXII Modern Pentathlon Military World Championship was hosted by Switzerland. Their competition was held in the City of Aarau, which was founded 750 years ago. I can say it ran like Swiss clockwork. Mr. Adolf Ogi, federal president of the Swiss Confederation, welcomed us to Switzerland. Maj Gen H. Aschmann welcomed us as host for the championship, but it was Col Jean-Jacques Joss who ran the competitions in an exceptional manner. Fifteen nations competed with a total of 55 world-class athletes. Those nations were: the Czech Republic, Switzerland, Sweden, Brazil, Belarus, Slovakia, Italy, Russia, Hungary, Poland, France, Germany, Latvia, Lithuania, and the United States. The last event for the individual competition was the 300-meter cross-country run. Our highest scorer was SPC 4 Chad Senior starting as the sixth man. This is an exciting match to watch as competitors set off at intervals that correspond in seconds to their score in the previous four events. Chad was in sixth place: he knew he had to pass at least three people for the U.S. to gain a bronze medal. It was balls to the wall from the starting gun, with shouting and cheering from all the countries as Chad raced past the 5th place Latvian runner, then the fourth-place Czech runner, then third-place runner, and the second-place runner, and finally trading places with the Number One Swiss athlete to win gold for the race (after which he collapsed), which also gave him the silver medal for the combined scores in all five events. Capt Jim Gregory (who won the silver medal at the 1999 world championship) finished as a very respectable 10th place.

The team relay competition was almost a repeat of the individual competition. Prior to the run in the last event, the U.S. team of Capt Gregory, Capt Bouma, and SPC 4 Senior was in fifth place. It was the last event of the world championship, and all the teams were desperately trying for a medal—all athletes were pushing to the limits for their countries. Capt Bouma was our first runner and did a masterful job in setting the pace, passing Poland, Italy, and Sweden. Other teams were pushing hard from behind, but we had a good handoff to Gregory, who held the pace, and then from Gregory to Senior, who begin challenging the leader. We ended up literally one step behind the Czech Republic for the silver team medal.

The competition was so fierce and evenly matched that we were the only country to win two medals in the overall events—the silver in the run and the silver in the relay team. The highest competitor in each single event of the competition was awarded a gold medal. Chad Senior won the gold medal for his run and for his swim. Again, the U.S. was the only country to win two medals in the single events. This was an exceptionally good, hard-fighting team. They worked together well and were role models for the other countries with their sportsmanship and military bearing. Our team members were Army Capt James Gregory, Air Force Capt Dirk Bouma, and Army SPC 4 Chad Senior. Two new members of the team for their first world championship were cadets Eli Bremer and Luke Chilean from the USAF Academy. Our outstanding coach, Janusz Peciak, who had skillfully guided this team for the past three years, was with us again. Capt Gregory was the team captain and did a superb job, both as an athlete and as a leader. After this championship, he headed off for Special Forces and was a great loss to me and the team. Chad Senior was subsequently rated Number One modern pentathlon athlete in the world. He earned the right and was selected to represent the United States at the Sydney Olympics. One doesn't normally think of Switzerland when considering fine cuisine, but I must report their closing banquet in a dining hall was one of the finest meals I have ever eaten at any military event anywhere.

The 33rd Modern Pentathlon World Championship was held at Warendorf, Germany, in September of 2001. As might be expected, it was run professionally with all things happening as planned. Oberst (Colonel) Christian Kramp oversaw the championship. An opening ceremony was hosted by the Warendorf Mayor, Theo Dickgreber, in front of the City Hall at the center of town. Oberst Jorg Udo Keck, commander of the federal Armed Forces sports school, accompanied the mayor. All teams stood in formation at attention during the opening flag ceremony. The mayor gave a speech welcoming the teams of 18 nations. He also delivered kind words of sympathy and support for the American tragedy of 9/11, asking for a moment of silence to honor those who had died in the horrific event. My Russian colonel friend

Long Shots — Teams

Boris actually had tears in his eyes as he hugged me in Russian fashion at that ceremony. The countries represented were Brazil, Chile, Estonia, Italy, Latvia, Lithuania, Mexico, Poland, Russia, Sweden, Switzerland, Slovakia, the Czech Republic, Ukraine, Hungary, Belarus, and the United States. Sixty-four CISM athletes entered the individual and team events. Our team members were Coach Janusz Peciak, Dr. Steve Holtzclaw as team MD, and Elaine Cheris as fencing coach. Athletes were SPC 4 Brett Weatherbie, SPC 4 Scott Christie, and SPC 4 Kevin Montford. Their finish in the final individual standing was: Weatherbie 13th, Christie 15th, and Montford 23rd, certainly no bragging there. We did have a small amount of success in the individual separate events: Weatherbie placed fourth, just out of medals twice, fourth in the swim and fourth in the ride. This was respectable considering the athletes started training quite late: Weatherbie in July, Christie in April, and our new team member, Montford, in June. While we had not won any of the individual events, their combined scores kept us in the game. The Italian team had tied up first place by a wide margin, but silver and bronze were wide open with Germany, Russia, Czech Republic, Hungary, Sweden, Switzerland, Belarus, and the USA all in the race and very close on scores going into the ride. It was really a cliffhanger with the critical point and deciding factor for us being the last rider. That was SPC Kevin Montford. His ride would either keep us in the race or drop us out of competition. Montford had never been on a jumping horse before the beginning of the year and still had very little experience. He had never been in an arena with four-foot jumps. And to top it off, this was his first international competition. You can imagine what pressure he was under. Everyone was at the fence to watch the new guy in this critical event: team members, the other athletes, coaches, trainers, Chiefs of Mission, CISM representatives, different discipline chiefs, referees, interpreters, support staff, guests, and even the Lord Mayor of Warendorf. It would be a long shot. Montford entered the arena determined and made a perfect ride. We were ecstatic and perhaps a little stunned. We still had one event left, the run, to complete the competition, but everyone knew we had cinched up the silver medal as no one would be able to run past my guys, all three strong runners. Now all the other teams could do was fight over the bronze. Not winning a medal in any of the five single disciplines and then coming back to win silver in the team event says something about our guys. The toughness and grit were there, and they were not about to ever give up. It certainly got attention from the athletes and coaches of the other competing nations.

A social outing conducted for the Chiefs of Mission was watching the conclusion of a fox hunt, where the foxhounds rip into a fox-scented leather hide as the hunters, who have been following the hounds on horseback, appear. The master of the hunt conducted closing ceremonies during which we, along with the riders, were served a fermented liquid presented in crystal glasses from a silver tray. We were in uniforms that looked rather drab compared to the brilliant colors of the impeccably dressed riders.

In 2002, the Czech Republic served as host for the 34th Modern Pentathlon Military World Championship held in Hradec Kralove. Vaclav Havel, president of the Czech Republic, sent greetings of well wishes to all participants. Our male athletes were 1st Lt Eli Bremer, 1st Lt Niul Manske, and SPC 4 Scott Christie. For the first time, female athletes were included. They were 1st Lt Anita Allen, Officer Cadet Laura Hammerich, and SPC Michelle Kelly. Lt Bremer was in the Air Force, and the others were all Army. They were all stationed in Colorado Springs. This was a very young team and inexperienced in their first CISM event for most. Lt Bremer had competed as a cadet two years previously in the CISM semifinal in Switzerland. SPC Christie was our only seasoned veteran. Other team members included me as Chief of Mission, Coach Janusz Peciak, fencing Coach Elaine Cheris, and Dr. Steve Holtzclaw as trainer and physician. Capt James Gregory accompanied the team as the U. S. representative to the CISM Technical Committee for Modern Pentathlon. Jim held that position from 2002 through 2005. He became president of the committee in 2007 and held that post until 2011. His selection for the CISM committee affirms his fine sportsmanship and character. As usual our team did an exceptional job in representing the United States military and demonstrating the CISM motto of "friendship through sports." They set the stage at the opening ceremony with their military conduct and decorum, without question the best marching

Long Shots — Teams

and disciplined team at the formation and parade. Several Chiefs of Mission complimented me on their military bearing. This attitude and conduct prevailed throughout the competition. Our women's team was awarded the sportsmanship trophy for their conduct and display of fairness in competition. Fourteen countries with 49 competitors entered the men's competition. The countries represented were the Czech Republic, Russia, Italy, Ukraine, Belarus, Sweden, Latvia, Switzerland, Slovakia, Hungary, Brazil, Estonia, Bahrain, and the United States.

The semifinal qualifications reduced the competitors for the final from 49 to 32. All our men qualified, but none were high scoring. We placed 6th out of 13 in the team event, and for the team relay we placed fifth, rising far above individual capabilities. While not outstanding, the results pleased me, coming as they were from such a young, inexperienced team. SPC 4 Christie, our most experienced athlete, was a great team leader. Others were senior in grade, but he was clearly the leader. He raised the level of the team with his enthusiasm and exuberance, setting the tone for success, and he was always solid. Lt Bremer was an excellent team member. He set high goals and always went the extra mile. He garnered our only individual medal, silver in swimming. Lt Manske had participated in the pentathlon as a civilian in San Antonio. I knew him from that time, but this was his first CISM, and he had just started training. Nevertheless, his fencing score in the relay event was our highest. He showed considerable potential and a super work ethic, no doubt a strong candidate for future teams. Female athletes representing Latvia, Hungary, Belarus, Russia, Italy, and the U.S. comprised the women's competition. Our women's team went into the final event, the run, in 9th, 11th, and 12th place. The team made a superb effort and ended up 6/7/8. Their combined scores placed them first among the teams. CISM rules require four teams to compete for the award of a medal. Only three of the seven countries had three team members, but our team was high scorer. I call that a winner, and they were presented with a large crystal vase. Later the female athletes presented me with a framed picture of them holding the vase with a little plaque of thanks. I was touched for sure. The organization and conduct of the competition were exceptional. I served as chairman

511

of the jury of appeals, and no appeals were registered—a sure sign of a successful competition. A highlight for the Chiefs of Mission was a glass of wine with the mayor of Hradec Kralove in the old City Hall to celebrate the 34th Modern Pentathlon Military Championship. Col Sotona, Czech Republic, was chairman of the competition. Col Waffler of Switzerland was president of the technical committee. As the senior Chief of Mission, I presented the thank-you remarks for participating nations—all Chiefs of Mission supported the very highest ratings and accolades that I gave to our hosts.

World Military Games

Catania, Sicily, was the site of the 3rd World Military Games in December 2003. The CISM World Games came into being when Russia and its former satellite nations were allowed to join CISM. As a result, the whole world was invited to join in CISM. The Italian military hosted the first CISM World Games in 1995, and 7,000 athletes attended that championship. The world military games are held every four years, the year prior to the Olympics. Competitions were held in the following sports: modern pentathlon, judo, boxing, fencing, track and field, marathon, cycling, swimming, diving, lifesaving, water polo, sailing, football, basketball, volleyball, and gliding. There were 86 nations entered in the 2003 games. Our U.S. athletes for these events numbered 127. Armed Forces sports officials organized and led the delegation. If you're familiar with goat roping, that would be an accurate picture of their efforts. In a previous story, I shared my earliest experience of the U.S. pentathlon team arriving in Russia in 1992, the day before the competition. Our athletes were tired and suffering jet lag from the flights to St. Petersburg. I vowed that would never happen to my guys again, and it didn't, until it did.

  This was a repeat performance, only worse. First, all the athletes were assembled at Fort Belvoir, Virginia. We spent one night on post and vacated the quarters early the next morning for a very boring day of briefings, handing out T-shirts, and orientation of how we would make the trip, etc. We had dinner and then headed to Dulles Airport to arrive five hours early for our flight to Frankfurt, Germany. We flew a normal, scheduled commercial 747 and occupied all the middle rows, seated five abreast, for the overnight flight, which meant the athletes got little rest as they climbed over one another to visit the toilets. The rows on each side of the middle seemed to be saved for civilian passengers.

We arrived in Germany in the early morning for a flight to Rome 12 hours later. Just imagine 127 athletes trying to rest on chairs and on the floor. Fortunately, I was a member of an airline lounge and so was Coach Janusz. After considerable cajoling, we squeezed in all our pentathlon team, exceeding the allowed guest authorization. The next flight took us to Rome, where we had another four hours' wait for a flight to Catania, arriving at midnight. Clearly it was a low-bid transportation deal with little thought or care about the athletes. It took us another two hours to get signed into the games and to our quarters. We got settled in about 0200, finally. To recap, we had a full day in Washington, a full night from Dulles to Frankfurt, a full day in Frankfurt, a four-hour layover in Rome, and then the flight to Catania. Needless to say, I was in a foul mood. Sending men on a mission to win and then giving the opponents an advantage is unconscionable.

Complaining after the fact is pretty much a waste of time, but you can bet a strong message was carried back to Washington. I suspect with a little thought and coordination Armed Forces Sports could've arranged military air directly into Sigonella U.S. Naval Air Station airport, which is less than a 30-minute drive to Catania. However, no imagination was detected. Not a good way to start a serious competition against rested and determined opponents. There was nothing to be done but toughen up and get on with the competition. No complaining from my team; they knew what they were there to accomplish.

Because the military dominates modern pentathlon, this competition would be a preview for the 2004 Olympic Games. The highlight of the opening ceremony and parade of athletes was 1LT Chad Senior leading the U.S. contingent as the flag bearer. Those nations competing in modern pentathlon were Italy, Czech Republic, Russia, United States, Ukraine, Latvia, Korea, Belarus, Lithuania,

Brazil, Slovakia, Chile, Estonia, Bulgaria, Greece, Slovakia, Hungary, Sweden, Switzerland, and the Republic of China. I was Chief of Mission, and our superb coach was Janusz Peciak. Male athletes were USA 1st Lt Chad Senior, USAF 1st Lt Eli Bremer, USA 1st Lt Niul Manske, and USA SGT Scott Christie. Female athletes were USA 1st Lt Lara Hammerich and USA SPC Mickey Kelly. There were only 32 final male contestants from the semifinals of 62 athletes representing 20 nations who were allowed to compete in the finals.

We did not have enough female athletes to post a women's team. There were only 22 female contestants. The highlight for us was SPC Mickey Kelly winning the running event. She was an awesome runner. She had a bad cold during the entire competition, which makes her win even more impressive. The relay team was made up of Lt Manske, Lt Bremer, and SGT Christie. They ended up in fourth place—literally three seconds from the bronze medal team of the Ukraine. In the men's individual competition, we started out poorly in the shooting event, placing us in the lower quarter of the competition. It was always amazing to me, coming from a country of guns and shooting, that we could not do better, but I was not in charge of their yearly training. It was what it was.

Next came the fencing, and we moved up to just below the middle of the pack. Swimming followed, with Senior winning the silver and Bremer coming in fourth, and we moved into the top third. Riding was the fourth event, and now it was nail-biting time as the horses were always a wildcard. Christie led the way by winning a gold medal with 1,200 points, the only perfect riding score of all the 20 nations. Bremer was close behind, taking the bronze medal with 1,172 points and Senior following in fifth place. I was stunned. That was the best combined team score and the first time in my 12 years as Chief of Mission that we put three riders at the top in the riding event. We were still not the leader in points, and the outcome was far from certain, but coaches and Chiefs of Mission for the top contending teams were now worried. They knew I had the best run/swim combination team in the world, and my guys would be fighting like pit bulls. The excitement and the intensity were electric among our team members, not only the athletes preparing to run but the rest of the team, Coach Janusz Peciak,

Long Shots — Teams

Lt Manske, Lt Hammerich, SPC Kelly, and not the least, me. I was less than dignified in my vociferous shouts of support during the run. Senior led the way and took the gold medal in the running. Bremer came in seventh, and Christie came in 22nd but it was enough. We had won the modern pentathlon team event in the 3rd Military World Games. With all odds against us, we still won. An extreme long shot, for sure.

In total individual scores, Senior finished fourth with a score of 5,532, SGT Christie was 11th scoring 5,352, and Lt Bremer ended up in 17th place with a score of 5,208. But we won the team event by a fair margin with 16,092 points followed by Italy with 16,036 points. Ukraine took third place with 15,756 points followed by Belarus, Russia, Hungary, the Czech Republic, Latvia, Switzerland, Korea, Sweden, Chile, and Brazil.

The World Games medal must be ranked just under an Olympic medal in pentathlon. In fact, it is harder to win gold in modern pentathlon at the world games, because it starts with a semifinal match of 62 athletes, where 30 must be eliminated to end up with 32 finalists. So, we really had 62 contestants fighting for the right to compete in the final—a second competition of only the 32 best competitors. The Olympics has no preliminary elimination and only has 32 contestants.

The military games only happen every fourth year, and I don't have to tell you that all heavens must be in exact alignment and in complete harmony for a team to win the gold. First, you must have dedicated, tough, athletes, thoroughly trained to attain perfection. Then you must have them fight their way through the semifinals match where one-half of the competitors are eliminated. If any of your athletes are eliminated in the semifinals, you no longer have a team. Then you must keep the athletes healthy and up mentally for the finals. You must have a master coach who has gained the athletes' confidence as well as the skill to craft and orchestrate their attack. Then you must be lucky enough to draw decent horses. And finally, you must put it all together with athletes who are willing to fight and push themselves to the absolute maximum limits to complete their mission. I am certain these three team members, 1st Lt Senior, 1st Lt Bremer, and SGT Christie, would have rather been on a mission to capture Saddam Hussein, but that was not their mission this time. They were the first U.S. team to ever win the team gold event at the military games.

Think about it—with traditional sports like basketball, swimming, diving, and track and field, the U.S. had won some individual gold medals previously but never a gold team medal. Not only were we the first United States team to ever win a team gold, but we were also the only team to bring back a gold medal of any sort, team, or individual for the United States from this world games that had 87 countries participating in the various sports. That gold medal is worth diamonds for American prestige. We were assigned a mission—and we completed that mission.

The championship trophy was a 4-foot-tall crystal piece enclosed in a beautiful leather container. When the container is opened the crystal piece was highlighted with the red silk lining. In addition, each of the three athletes was presented a large gold medallion like an Olympic medal.

How do you get a 4-foot-high crystal trophy back to the states? Naval Air Station Signorelli was only a short drive away and they had a US Post Office manned by Navy personnel. When boxed for shipment the trophy exceeded the maximum length allowed by the Postal Service. I knew it was too long and there was no sense trying to argue otherwise. I asked to speak with the boss, and a female petty officer came forward. She told me she was the senior supervisor and asked what did I want. I explained my package contained a crystal trophy representing a very significant achievement by an American military team competing against the best from the entire world. It was destined to be presented to the Chairman of the Joint Chiefs of Staff. She eyeballed the package and announced it met all requirements and would be mailed. My kind of trooper, I could've kissed her.

I cannot say enough about our athletes and coach, Janusz Peciak. I was proud to stand with such a team, not only outstanding in sports but also in military bearing and conduct. They will never be topped, and it was a fitting end to my duty as Chief of Mission for modern pentathlon in world championships and world military games. I told the team members they would have an audience and be able to present the crystal trophy to General Richard B Myers, the

Long Shots — Teams

15th Chairman of the Joint Chiefs of Staff. Not an easy thing to do, but I felt they deserved that honor, and it was arranged. The four of us were having lunch together before the Pentagon presentation when the three athletes presented me with a shadowbox containing one of the three gold medallions. I was flabbergasted, didn't really want the medal, and felt bad that one of them had to give up his medal for me but what an honor. it has a permanent home in my living room.

The first year I was Chief of Mission for pentathlon teams I was still on active duty. After my retirement, I was called back to active duty by what is known as invitational orders. That meant I was paid only expenses, which saved cutting off retirement to start active duty pay and then changing back, which can cause a mess. The important part of invitational orders was that it gave me authority and responsibility to fully conduct whatever government business I was charged with, and I can say unequivocally I never needed to exercise authority with any team members, but I used it plenty with whatever was needed to advance our team.

The U.S. teams, starting with the St. Petersburg World Championship, were the first to take on the Eastern European teams, which were strong in modern pentathlon. Previously, modern pentathlon in CISM had been mainly the Western European nations for military world championships, which make our later team's accomplishments even more amazing.

Making me particularly proud was our team's sportsmanlike conduct and military bearing. They set a high bar for others to emulate. Compliments from other Chiefs of Mission and officials conducting competitions were commonplace. Normally, teams were assigned a specific table for dinner, and we usually came together as a team. The team would stand behind their chairs until I took my seat first. If I came late, the team would all stand when I came to the table. Maybe it's a small thing, but it was noticed by other teams and their chiefs. I didn't demand or even suggest they do that, they did it on their own accord. Of course, the good leadership by Capt Messenger, followed by Capt Gregory, set the tone. The team simply rose to every occasion in a military and gentlemanly manner. I was honored to be a part of a team of such fine young men as they grew into the outstanding

517

leaders they became. There is a firm separation in the military between officers and enlisted and even between senior officers and junior officers. There is a reason for that, and it is because it is necessary to conduct our important military business. Teams are a little different, and I became quite close to many of the pentathlon athletes. Colonels do not go around hugging sergeants and lieutenants, even on teams, but regardless of some minor ear pulling, I loved them all. They were certainly a large part of my life and kept me young trying to keep up with them.

There was a great deal of camaraderie among the team members, serving many times together in a very physical sport that requires dependence on each other. I would say we had camaraderie near to those serving together in combat. For those who have never served in the military or on a highly competitive team where success depends not only on you but just as much on your teammates, I recommend reading Sebastian Junger's book *Tribe: On Homecoming and Belonging*. It is an excellent study on bonding and belonging. Many of our athletes developed tight friendships with athletes from the other nations, and it was like old home week when we would meet other teams around the world. Even I became attached to many of the young athletes from other countries. And it was the same for Chiefs of Mission. Most of us developed familiar friendships.

Col Novotny from the Czech Republic was President of the Technical Committee (senior official in CISM modern pentathlon). My good colonel friend from Russia, Boris, met us at many competitions. Col Helmut Gruber from Austria was later president of the technical committee. LTC Wilfred Fluitsma from Holland became another close friend. My closest and my longest-serving comrade was Juerg Waeffler, a reserve colonel from Switzerland. He also became president of the technical committee. All were fine men.

There were many people who helped make our team so successful, but two who were with me the most in the fight were Coach Janusz Peciak and our medical doctor, Steve Holtzclaw. I have already told how lucky we were to have an Olympic gold medalist and arguably the best modern pentathlon coach in the world, so let me tell you about Steve. He was still in college when we first met at a bunker trap shooting range in New Jersey. We became friends and began shooting bunker trap matches throughout the country. He went on to medical school and became a top graduate in emergency medicine at Johns Hopkins University. Steve came from a blue-collar family, and for the most part, worked his way through school by being an emergency responder—my kind of guy.

He had accompanied me as team doctor when I was chief of missions for the United States trap and skeet teams at world shooting championships in Cyprus and Peru. He also traveled with the Air Force trap team when I was in charge of the team. I knew he would be perfect for the pentathletes, and he was. They took to him immediately. Dr. Steve was one of us from then on. Between fencing and riding horses, not to mention cross-country running, there is plenty of opportunity for injury. Steve volunteered to come with our team to world championships and was the perfect guy, not a pretentious bone in his body. He fit in well with all our young athletes and soon had their complete trust. He bandaged up their bumps and bruises and wrapped tape around their toes. They would tell him things they were afraid to tell me. Steve carried everything with him to these events—all the medical drugs, needles, liquids, and paraphernalia he might need in an emergency during travel or on the field.

One case I remember was in Poland when a young German's horse missed a jump and then threw him into a wooden railing. The rider was knocked silly but soon was coherent. He had a nasty cut on his face that Steve cleaned up and then gave him a couple of neat little stitches while he lay on the grass. It wasn't long until all the teams were coming to us for their medical problems. It must be admitted that part of our popularity was due to Dr. Holtzclaw.

However, one incident comes to mind. We were on a flight to Zürich, Switzerland, via an Austrian airline. Several times I was able to have the team upgraded to better seats on transatlantic flights. This time, Steve and I were going in advance of the team. I was dressed in coat and tie, and my sports jacket had a large badge which identified me as Chief of Mission for the United States. It's an impressive, embroidered badge. The airline people gave me an upgrade to business class but would only give out one upgrade. Steve is over six feet tall and while we were boarding, I simply traded tickets with him as a little treat. I didn't realize his original seat was the last one on the airplane next to the toilet. To make matters even worse, that seat did not recline. There was nothing for me to do but tough it out. Then a traveler collapsed, and the stewardess was calling out, "Is there a doctor on board?" Steve always responded immediately to such calls. He identified himself, and Steve and the sick traveler were moved into first-class seating, leaving his business class seat open. While I felt sorry for the stricken traveler, I was delighted for the opportunity to move away from the toilet and its constant business with a light coming on every time the door was opened. No such luck. The stewardess was having no part of me moving into business. I tried to explain it was actually my business seat. She insisted those seats cost money, and no argument could convince the stewardess to let me move, so it was eight hours sitting up straight with the toilet door constantly opening and shutting. As they say, "No good deed goes unpunished." Steve was worth it, but just barely.

Of course, it was the athletes who won the matches, as Teddy Roosevelt so aptly put it, "They were in the ring." Three athletes who were with me the longest were Private Scott Christie, 2nd Lt James Gregory, and SPC 4 Chad Senior.

Christie came to my attention when he was still a teenager not long out of high school and trying to be competitive in pentathlon. His family wasn't wealthy, and he wasn't afraid of work, but one can't hold a full-time job and climb to the top in pentathlon. The best support and a clear avenue for pentathlon training meant joining the Army and being accepted into the Army World Class Athlete Program (WCAP). Fortunately, although I had retired I still had enough juice to get the Army folks to agree that after basic training, he would be sent back to San Antonio. Scott signed up. Of course, going through basic training, his instructors and the normal assignment personnel were not aware of any preset assignments, and he was selected for assignment to Korea through the normal process. That scared Scott and started a firestorm with his mother, who had been told he would be sent back to San Antonio. She reacted strongly and was about to put a contract out on me when, fortunately, my Army contacts worked magic at the proper time, and Scott came to San Antonio. Christie was solid, fearless, tenacious, and always ready—a fine team member. He was small in physical stature, but his big heart and strong desire to be the best made up for it. There was simply no quit in him. In our years together, he went from private (PVT) to PV2, to private first class, to SPC 4, to sergeant. I was delighted to recommend him for OCS. He later became the commander of the Army's World Class Athletic Program—a perfect match. I'm pleased to report he retired as a major. Scott was successful as a private business owner and is now Chief of Protective Service for a major hospital in Florida. You can bet the hospital is safe. He married the right lady, and they have four children. The oldest is serving in the U.S. Space Force.

James Gregory came to pentathlon as a confident, young, enthusiastic, 2d Lt straight from Ranger training, brimming over with piss and vinegar. Good-looking, tall, in super shape, a fine swimmer with an amiable personality, he was a girl's dream. That was, of course, before his wife Bonni and his accomplished daughters Haley and Ashley entered the picture. He became an excellent role model and a superb leader. My guys were great, and I never had any trouble with any of them. But understand, they were young men full of life with lots of energy, often over-exuberant, and prone to taking chances. I didn't have to worry when Jim was along. I never worried much anyway, but with him there, I knew the reins would be pulled in if things got too far out of hand. A better team leader does not exist. Remember, my only rule was not to embarrass our flag or me. When a team comes together, it is better to let them set their own parameters, and they will police themselves better than anyone else could. They never disappointed me.

Gregory was the first alternate and Captain for the United States Modern Pentathlon Team in the 2000 Olympics. Always positive, he went on to join Special Forces and had two deployments to Iraq and three to Afghanistan. I was privileged to be the honored guest at his promotion to Lieutenant Colonel in the Pentagon, by the Under Secretary of Defense. The room was full of Special Forces Colonels in class A uniforms with their trousers bloused. He was in rarefied air, but Jim retired as a Lt Colonel mainly because of his young daughters and not wanting to move them or be gone during their high-school years. He sent me an email from Afghanistan when he was departing. It said that he had just finished working for the finest officers he had ever met. But he was looking down the road toward promotion to full colonel and then serving satisfactorily in that grade for two years. It would take at least five years and probably two or three different moves and another single overseas tour without his family. It would be too much at a critical time for his daughters. I'm certain he would've made at least full Colonel had he stayed. Jim earned a master's degree in public affairs from USC. He put that to good use in retirement and was successful both in the private sector and in government civil service. I suspect he was looking for more challenge and excitement and is now employed by Orbis Operations doing crisis management and security matters for friendly foreign governments. They are lucky to have him.

Senior, today a member of the George Washington University Hall of Fame for swimming, was pretty much still a college boy when we met. But I can tell you that changed. He is one of the most intense competitive athletes I have ever seen. He started his military career as an enlisted man but eventually went to OCS and became an Army officer. I watched him morph into an outstanding leader. After two Olympics, placing 6th and 13th, and promotion to Captain, we talked about his future in the military, and he wondered if he should go to Army Delta Force or Navy Seals? Chad wanted to be challenged, and I suggested Air Force Pararescue. The rest is history. He transferred to the Air Force, and I was pleased to be at his graduation from extremely intense, difficult pararescue training. His class started with 79 candidates at Lackland Air Force Base. The graduating class at Kirkland Air Force Base in Albuquerque two years later had only thirteen members.

They must swim, run, and carry a body over their shoulder. They skydive from heights that require oxygen, and deep-sea dive, parachute into the ocean and recover a zodiac (large rubber raft) dropped with them. They must become proficient in combat shooting and be able to amputate an arm or perform a tracheotomy. They end up a heavily armed and deadly dangerous "medic on steroids," figuratively speaking.

On a visit to meet Chad's newborn daughter, he took me out to Patrick Air Force Base to meet his boss and look over pararescue equipment. I put on his gear, including a flak vest, ammo, and helmet. I was already weighted down when he brought over a 70-pound backpack of medical gear. Be assured pararescue airmen are not the Red Cross. They carry guns and will kill anyone who interferes with their mission of saving the wounded. Chad has had five combat tours in the Middle East so far. If you're going into combat, you couldn't have a better man at your side. Come hell or high water, he would stick with you. He has recently completed a year's sabbatical studying in the Harvard University program.

His selection in 2021 for full colonel was well deserved and attests to his proven leadership. General John W. Raymond, the first Chief of Staff of the United States Space Force, our newest branch of the Armed Forces, officiated at his promotion ceremony. That might tell you something.

These are only three of the many outstanding young men I was privileged to be with as their Chief of Mission for 12 years; there were so many others. During my last six years of being chief, the athletes brought home gold or silver team medals from each competition. No other country in the world can match that record. Talk about rewarding. Few are afforded the honor given to me.

Looking back, I realize it was not the winning — it was the team vitality, energy, style, and honesty- - win or lose. It was them coming together with an esprit de corps that made me proudest. I loved them all — still do.

Hamilton Junior High School Rifle Team—winners of the 1962 California Cadet Corps Championship. L-R Pete Olinger, Jim, Dennis Nelson, Richard Davies, Jim Burkson, 2d Lt Dennis Behrens (coach), Capt Richard Ramacher. Note I'm in an Army uniform.

With my friend and mentor Robert Simmons at Camp Perry in 1961

California State Team at Camp Perry in 1962. The 1,000 yd team champions. DDB kneeling with the scoped rifle. Mr Stevenson standing on right with Martin Hull standing next to him

Colonel George H. Van Duesen and his wife along with their famous peeing dog Endless, and 2d Lt Behrens

The 1966 Carrot Match at Fort Benning, Georgia — Air Force and Army Teams. Col Joseph Peot, Commander of the Army Marksmanship Training Unit, in the top row wearing a wheel cap. 1st Lt Beherens on the right.

A smiling 1964 Air Force Team — but not really happy. Their score tied with the Army for the National Championship but we lost fair and square by V count.
L- R Kneeling: DDB, TSgt Frank Tossas, SSgt Bobby Smith, SSgt Robert (Barney) Bernard. Standing: MSgt Leon Linscott, TSgt Ken Horst, Col Thomas Kelly, SSgt James Patrick, SSgt Henry Evans

Air Force Team at the Albany NY 1,000 yard match.

Coming off the firing line at Quantico Marine Corps Base—weather was foul but we set a new four-man team record.

Winning the General Thomas White Trophy

Winners of the Commandant of the Marine Corps Schools Match—first time for the Air Force. L-R sitting: DDB, MSgt James Carter, SSgt David Thompson, A1C Aldo Frascoia. standing: SSgt Kurt Degerlund, TSgt Frank Tossas, TSgt Fred Dean, SSgt Bobby Smith

Brig Gen Lewis W. Walt presenting a gold medal for the 1,000 yard match.

Winner and tying the record of the 1,000 yard Service Rifle Championship

On the firing line at Camp Perry for the National Trophy Match. Note our flag—try shooting off hand in a 30 mile per hour wind

General John P. McConnell, Air Force Chief of Staff presenting a Commendation Medal to 1st Lt Behrens. Maj Gen H.K. Mooney, Commander of Lackland AFB at left

Champions with the United States National Rifle Trophy—awarded to the top team since 1903. L-R kneeling: DDB, MSgt Leon Linscott, SSgt David Thompson, A1C Aldo Frascoia. Standing: TSgt Fred Dean, TSgt Frank Tossas, SSgt Kurt Degerlund, SSgt Bobby Smith

My Distinguished Badge surrounded by Excellence in Competition Badges donated to the National Firearms Museum. Three were solid gold.

Winners of the American Dependent Schools in Europe Rifle Championship. Shooters L-R John Toeplitz, Robert Zellmer, Gregory Wheat. Coaches Capt Behrens, MSgt Alvord, SSgt Rowan

The 1994 World Championship in Sweden. L-R Capt Dirk Bouma, Capt Paul Messenger, Col Behrens, PFC Scott Christie, and 2d Lt James Gregory, on his first trip. He later became our longest running team captain.

The best Modern Pentathlon run/swim team in the world. L-R SPC Chad Senior, Lt James Gregory, Col Behrens, SPC Brett Weatherbie

Decked out for dinner in Rome L-R SPC Brett Weatherbie, Capt Gregory, Col Behrens, SPC Chad Senior

Who do we put in for the World Championship team event in Poland? L-R Dr Steve Holtzclaw, Col Behrens, Coach Janusz Peciak. We won.

My Carabinieri body guard in Rome—furnished because of the resentment of American military due to the 1989 Cavalese Cable Car disaster

First American athletes to win a team medal In the World Military Games.
L-R Sgt Scott Christie, 1st Lt Chad Senior, Col Behrens, 1st Lt Eli Bremer

Presenting the winning team trophy from the World Military Games to General Richard B. Myers, Chairman of the Joint Chiefs of Staff.
L-R Col Behrens, 1 Lt Chad Senior, the Chairman, Sgt Christie, 1 Lt Eli Bremer

*The US Shotgun Team at the World Championship in Cyprus.
Col Behrens on the left and renowned Coach Lloyd Woodhouse on the right*

Winners of the Nebraska One Box Pheasant Hunt. L-R Sgt Mark Weeks, SSgt Mike Agee, Col Behrens, Capt Mike Herman, SFC Lance Dement

Grand National Quail Club team winners. L-R Mike Molak, Harold Kronseder, Dennis Behrens, Doug Ward

One of the later Air Force Trap Teams. L-R Maj John Linn, SSgt Mike Agee, Dr Steve Holtzclaw, Col Behrens, Capt Mike Herman, Maj Dominic Grazioli

The Air Force trap team. L-R MSgt Bautista, SSgt Parker, A1C Herman, 2d Lt Linn, SMSgt Howard, 1st Lt Grazioli, Col Behrens. Grazioli is obviously working his way back down to 2d Lt

Brig Gen William K. Jones presenting the grand aggregate championship trophy at the Masters Invitational Hi-Desert, High-Power Rifle Match. A first-class gentleman, he served in three wars and was highly decorated, earning the Navy Cross, a Silver Star, a Bronze Star and the Purple Heart. He retired as a Lt Gen.

Admiring the Navy cup at Quantico at the Interservice Championship. I won this trophy 25 years earlier. L-R Maj Gen Keithe E. Nelson, Col Behrens, Dr Akio Mitamura

V

FAMILY AND FRIENDS

Family Tree

If you are looking for a family coat of arms or family crest worn on one's pinky finger, I must disappoint. Not "to the manor born," and good or bad, none of those accouterments are hung on my family tree. Family history known on my mother's side (Sykes), dates back earlier than the Behrens side. To review the Sykes history, I will start with Owen Thomas Senior, my great-great-great-great-great-grandfather. His son Owen Thomas was born in 1754 and died in 1838. He served in the American Revolution and was awarded a pension for that service. His Bible is in the Valley Forge Museum. His male descendants, Evan Thomas Senior, my great-great-great-grandfather, and Evan Thomas, my great-great- grandfather, married women from the families of Henderson, Simmons, and March. My great-grandmother Eva Celestia Sykes (nee) Thomas was born in 1864 and died in 1954 in Pocahontas, Iowa. My great aunt Irma Consuella Elbert (nee) Sykes and my aunt Irma Lucille Wagner (nee) Sykes were members of the Daughters of the American Revolution. My cousin Melva Wagner, daughter of Aunt Lucille, has carried on that tradition. It was Melva who tutored me in the Thomas and Sykes family history. I was fortunate to be around my great-grandmother in her last years (she lived to be 90) and hear her stories of living in Kansas in a sod house in the early 1870s.

In those days, some Indian tribes were friendly, and others were hostile. One story she told was how afraid she was when her parents were away, and Indians came to the house. They were friendly but came into the house and looked all around—fortunately, they were just curious. Evan Thomas served in the Civil War, and James Thomas, the son of Evan, was killed in the Spanish American War.

The Sykes history I know starts with John Sykes. He was my great-great-great-grandfather. History follows with the wedding of his son George Sykes who at 25 years of age, condition listed as widower, married Elizabeth Clarke, 20 years of age, condition described as spinster. George's profession was listed as printer, and his father John's profession was joiner. Elizabeth's father was George Clarke, profession listed as farmer. Their marriage was solemnized at the church in the parish of Leeds in York County on May 23, 1850. He was my great-great-grandfather. The marriage of my great-grandfather, Charles Clark Sykes (note the E is dropped from Clarke), born in 1862, and Eva Celestia Thomas, my great-grandmother, born in 1864, brought the Thomas and Sykes families together.

One of their sons was Clarence Edward Sykes, my grandfather. His first wife was Grace Ewing who died in 1912. They had two children, a boy named Roy Glen, born in 1907, and my Aunt Irma Lucille (named after my grandfather's sister), born in 1909. In 1914, my grandfather married again. He chose Marie Abels from Holland who had come to the United States through Ellis Island. I'm not sure if that makes me an immigrant by today's definition, but if I am, I'm damn proud of it. My grandmother told me about her mother bringing the family to join their father who was already in Iowa. He had come earlier to the United States at the urging of a friend who told him of the great opportunities and his own accomplishments, counting the animals he owned. It was something like two horses, three cows, some swine, and even a few chickens. It was not much, but apparently it was wealth to the Abels.

Grandmother told me about being hired out while still a small girl to a wealthy family in Holland—more or less like an indentured servant. She can remember telling her mother of the breakfast she received, which was an egg and toast with a spread she did not like. Her mother asked the employer to switch to butter instead of the spread on her toast. They did that, but as a trade-off they took away the egg. Hard times, you could say, or maybe a cruel employer. That family wanted to keep my grandmother when they found out the family was moving to America. They promised to take good care of her and send her later, but her mother, Jantje Jansen (nee) Houwen, would have no part of it. My grandmother remembered being in New York as a young girl, fresh off the boat, and as a new immigrant riding a trolley that was still pulled by horses. Her mother became frantic when her little son went missing. No one could speak Dutch, and she could speak no English, so it was a stressful event. Eventually, the little guy was found—he had wandered to the trolley's upper deck.

My grandfather's marriage to Marie Abels brought him seven more children—my aunts and uncles: John 1916, Eva 1917, my mother Clara 1919, Leona 1922, Jeanette 1925, Joe 1927, and Shirlee 1930. I knew them all well, including my Aunt Lucille, Grandfather's daughter from his first marriage who was a bit older. She married Elmer Wagner, an Iowa farmer, and moved with him to his farm near Duncombe in 1937. I don't remember much of her in my early life. Lucille was a schoolteacher and very popular with her students. Much later, I caught up with her and her children, my cousins: Dale, Larry, Marion, Mary, and Melva and visited with them on trips to Iowa. Tales with Dale and Larry are remembered in my stories of the Lincoln and Iowa days. John William (named after one of my grandfather's brothers) was the oldest of Grandma Marie's children. He was the only one who ever caused the family any grief. His struggle was drinking, which often led to fights that put him into the clink overnight now and then. I didn't like him much as a little kid because I remember one time when he gave my grandfather a bloody nose at the front gate of the Iowa farm. My grandfather did not hit back, but it looked like my Uncle Joe and Uncle John scuffled a bit and then John took off. He became a roughneck in the California oilfields, and in later life, I enjoyed his many stories. He had a boatload of them that were often humorous.

Aunt Eva Ilene (named after my grandfather's mother) was down to earth and a hard worker; she was practical with a good sense of humor. Her husband, Forest Ayers, died early, but she raised three children: Keith, Jimmy, and Sheryl Sue. They lived in San Fernando when we lived there, so we had lots of playtime as little kids. One thing we did together was search for discarded bottles that could be returned for a deposit. Regular-size Coke bottles were returned for a penny, and a big bottle was returned for five cents. Pretty good money for young kids, and it kept us busy. The rule was we had to come home when the streetlights were turned on. We still see each other at our annual Sykes reunion.

My mother, Clara Mae (named after one of my grandfather's sisters), was next in line by birth. Mother was followed by Aunt Leona Bernadine, who had some additional schooling after high school either in business or secretarial training. She lived in Santa Paula during my middle and early high-school years and was my "go-to" for tutoring in English and writing papers. In 1962, her husband Max helped me put a well-used 1955 Lincoln Imperial Sedan back in good driving condition for my drive to Texas for Air Force officer training. Max eventually bought my father's taxi company and tells an embarrassing story on himself. The taxi company had a small office with a glass front butting up to the sidewalk with the taxis parked in front. Located on Mill Street just around the corner, off Main Street, it was just big enough for one couch where the drivers could sit as they waited for calls or, often, walk-up customers. Late one night, Max was exhausted from a full day's work and was waiting for the bars to close at 2:00 a.m. to catch the last customers when he fell asleep on the couch while smoking a cigarette. His hand holding the cigarette rested on his lap and burned through his pants. You can guess what else it burned. He jumped up in pain and ripped open his pants. As he was checking his damaged "hardware," he looked up and saw a couple standing hand-in-hand staring at him through the glass door. All he heard was, "uh-oh" as they walked away. He didn't chase after them. True story—maybe. Max was a good storyteller. They had two children Lorraine and David, but they were much younger than I was, and I didn't get to know them until much later in life. Both are good citizens and raised fine kids. Lorraine married Garry Barron, who gives the prayer at our family reunions.

My Aunt Jeanette Marie (named after my grandmother) followed Leona, and she was a real people person. Jeanette had come to California as a teenager for a visit and stayed with us before taking me back to Iowa with her on the train during World War II. She returned to California and married John Dronsky, who was divorced but had two sons, Jack and Jerry. Jack was about four years older than

Long Shots — Family and Friends

me, and Jerry just a couple years older. They were both far wiser of the world than I was, and being from the Los Angeles area they had street smarts. It was fun to hang out with them on their big city territory. Some of those exploits shall not be exposed. Not in front of adults, but both smoked, and my mother wouldn't let me be with them when they smoked. Of course, you know how far that got. Jeanette and John had more children together, but they were much younger, and I never got to know them well. Joe Dronsky was the oldest. He retired as a Navy Chief Petty Officer.

Jeanette was an extremely hard worker and had many varied jobs. She worked her whole life—never retiring. She was a major success financially. She lived in a mid-level tract house, but she could have had a mansion had she chosen to. At one time, she was a waitress at the Brown Derby somewhere in the LA/Hollywood area. Hard to believe, but she was making more money as a waitress than her husband was making as an engineer at Rocketdyne. But as I said, she was gregarious and likable. She had many loyal customers, several in the entertainment industry with a kaleidoscope of personalities. She told me some crazy stories, but she loved her customers and they loved her. Jeanette was short in stature, and her demeanor reminded me of an elf.

Uncle Willis Joe (named after my grandfather's brother) Sykes was born two years after Jeanette, and he stayed on the farm working with my grandfather. Uncle Joe was there during the three summers I went back to work on the farm. Joe was a perfect son to my grandfather and a great role model for me. All kind of things happen on a farm, particularly when dealing with cranky machinery, not to mention obstinate cattle and hogs. I never heard Joe ever complain, nor did I ever see him in a down mood, no matter the circumstances. He just worked hard every day and got the job done. The only time I can remember him ever taking off from work was when he and a couple of buddies made a fishing trip to Minnesota. I dearly hoped he would take me along and lobbied for that, but it didn't happen. Who could blame him? I was 12 or 13, and he was 22 or 23. Can you imagine him and his buddies taking a little kid on a road trip? Joe married Bernie and took over the farm when my grandfather left. With Bernie came running water in the house and indoor plumbing. The faithful outhouse was retired. Joe bought another smaller acreage and added that to farming the old place. They had two boys and two girls: Mike, Linda, Christy, and Brian. I never got to know them as they were born after my visits to Iowa. The last child born to my grandparents was my Aunt Shirlee Jean, who was just seven years older than I was. Shirlee was already away at nurses' school and training at the University of Iowa when I was visiting the farm during the summers. She did come home now and then, and I always looked forward to her visits. She would give me advice and talk about school. I looked up to her. After all, she was in college. Somehow, Shirlee talked Grandpa into letting her drive his Plymouth to Blairsburg (less than a mile) for what purpose I don't recall, but she took me with her, which was pretty neat, and we even got an ice cream. Shirlee married Dr. Jim Easton and they had three daughters: Jill, Diane, and Lisa. Shirlee, and Jim moved to California, but I didn't see the kids much until they were already grown. They are all married and have children of their own, but I get to enjoy their company each year at the Sykes reunion, which Jill generously and graciously hosts in her San Diego home. Shirlee and I became much closer in later life. She visited me several times in San Antonio, Washington, D.C., Oregon, and Europe.

One time, she visited me near Graz, Austria, where I was team captain of the United States team for the international hunters/shooters championship. She was traveling around Europe, and I thought it was unlikely she would find me since Graz is hardly the center of Austrian tourist attractions, but she found me. I was giving a little speech for the American team and took Shirlee to the championship banquet held in a beautiful little castle with grounds that fenced in abundant fallow deer, Axis, and Reh Deer. The castle was lit entirely by wax candles. It was truly spectacular. The Austrian equivalent to our secretary of the interior hosted the dinner. We talked about that event for years. Another time, we took Shirlee skiing at Mount Bachelor in Oregon. After a day on the slopes and a little wine with dinner, Loretta and I were ready for bed. Not Shirlee; she was still disco dancing into the wee hours.

All my aunts, much more than my uncles, were preeminent and solid influences in my maturation. Understand, in those days, the men worked all day every day and didn't have much time around kids.

Before I leave the Sykes family, I must relate some additional information about my grandmother, whose maiden name was Abels. She was really a remarkable lady, coming to a country where she didn't even speak the language. She lived to be 92 years old (born in 1894/died in 1986), and you have to think of what she experienced in her lifetime— from horse and buggy days to a man on the moon. Her brothers and sisters were named Jantje, John, Cornelious, Trena, Ralph, and Catherine. They married into the families named de Groot, Meyering, Lammers, and Ohden. I met most of these great aunts and uncles as a child and even played with cousins but have a faulty memory of those encounters, and that history is lost to me.

On the Sykes side, my Great Aunt Irma Consuella Sykes married Louis Elbert of Pocahontas, Iowa. They owned the town newspaper, the *Record Democrat*, which was a combination of the Republican paper, the Record, and the Democratic paper, which was the Democrat. They also had a couple farms in the area. My great-grandmother Eva Celestia Sykes (nee) Thomas lived with them. They were the most interesting of my older relatives because it seemed to me they had traveled the whole world and told of experiences that excited my imagination. Uncle Louis had been a guest with other newspaper people on a short cruise aboard the battleship Iowa after WWII. It was always fun when they came to California. I visited them in Pocahontas twice when I was an adult. The first time, I had four-high school buddies on a road trip with me, and one of them asked before arrival in Pocahontas if they still used outhouses. We arrived at a beautiful modern and spacious home—all five of us stayed with them. And they also had a new Buick Roadmaster. My friends were impressed—so was I. No outhouse.

The Behrens family history known to me is not documented as far back as that of the Thomas family. My great-great-grandfather was Ludwig Behrens, born in 1825 at Restock, Germany. He married Louisa Bahras of Doberan, Germany. I do not have records or information on my great-grandfather. My grandfather Bernhart Behrens was born on December 25, 1875, in Williams, Iowa and died in Iowa in 1954. Bernhart had two children, a boy and a girl, from his first wife who died. The boy's name was Myron, born in 1898. I have no recollection of him or his sister. My grandfather then married Joanne Jensen, who was born in Sweden. In any case, if you combine the Sykes and Behrens history, I am part English, part Dutch, part German, and part Swedish—certainly a pure Heinz pedigree. Grandparents Bernhart and Joanne Behrens had five children, three boys and two girls. The oldest was Clifford Bernhart Behrens. His wife was named Velma. They were the parents of Duanne and Vernon, the cousins I spent most time with on my summer visits to Iowa. Their younger brother was named Gene. Duanne and Vernon, and my many adventures with them are covered in other chapters: "Iowa" and "Two Boys and Three Guns."

My father, Harold Francis Behrens, was born on June 22, 1909. His younger brother, Arlo Maurice Behrens, was born on August 11, 1917. He married Iva Reading. They had six children: Earl, Alan, Clifford, Lee Jay, Byrne, and Paula, the only girl. They were all younger than I was, but Earl was close in age, so we played together in pre- and grade-school days. They lived in Vallejo and then Napa in central California, which limited visits as it was a full day's drive from Santa Paula.

I do remember one time they came to visit when we lived on Richmond Road and my dog Whitey was on the little patch of grass in front of our duplex. When they drove up, their dog Buster jumped out of the car and immediately attacked Whitey. It was a dogfight with Buster on top, and I didn't like it. Uncle Arlo said it was just a dogfight until Whitey got on top. That's when he pulled Buster back. Uncle Arlo hunted and fished. All the boys followed him. He wasn't too observant or overly concerned with hunting and fishing regulations, but they ate everything caught or shot. His sons and I have become much closer in the last 40 years—particularly Alan and I. He came to see me one time in Germany in the late 1970s—unannounced, driving a huge Army truck and trailer into Ramstein Air Force Base. I never did find out how he located our government quarters, but there he was parked with that Army truck and trailer blocking the street.

Another time, when I was Deputy Chief of Staff of Personnel for the Air Force Electronic Security Command, he surprised me by walking into my office in the headquarters building. Understand, even persons with top-secret clearance were not allowed to be in the building without a full-time escort, and casual visitors were never allowed. Of course, he had a security policeman with him, but how he talked the security police into bringing him into the building is still a mystery. The security boss was not very happy, I can tell you that much.

Alan and I have hunted chukars together since the mid-1980s, and for the last 25 years I hunted with Alan and his brothers Earl and Clifford each year for the opening day of chukar season in eastern Oregon. It's a pretty barebones hunt, but they have moved their game up and now bring trailers and campers. They bring all the food trailers, campers, and four-runners. Clifford has adopted me to live in his trailer and fixes me up with bedding. In fact, they make it a pretty nice trip for me. Clifford has a dandy Kawasaki Mule made for two people with a windshield and a roof. It's a difficult bird hunt, nearly like hunting sheep because of the steep rough terrain. It has become a Behrens reunion, and all of Arlo's sons have appeared at one time or another. The main hunters remain Alan, Clifford, and Earl. It's a trip I look forward to each year. Their sister, Paula, who is now 70 years old, drives 18-wheelers cross-country. You gotta wonder, but she loves it.

My father's sisters were Neta and Irma. I remember Neta but do not remember her family. Irma Behrens married Leo Evans, an Iowa farmer, and my five cousins from that marriage were girls Bonnie, Roma, and Rosemary, and boys Melvin and Gordon.

All my uncles and aunts grew up during the Great Depression. They no doubt faced hard times, but I never heard any of them complain. When I did hear them talk about the Depression it was joking and laughing about how they made things do or about some of the crazy things they did. None of them whined about it or had any "poor-me" stories. They seemed to take life as it came along and refused to be victims. It is said, "You can choose friends, but have to take family as it is." To my knowledge, none of my family has ever been sued, nor have any been charged with a nefarious crime or served time in prison. A little boring perhaps, but not every family can have a Robin Hood. Looking at my family, I realize what genuinely good luck came my way. They represent the best one could hope for, and I would not trade any of them.

551

Loretta

My wife is a colonel. Not many people can say that. Making full colonel (bird colonel) is highly competitive and never certain. Loretta was 29 years old when she was commissioned as a second lieutenant. This made her nearly 50 when she came into the primary zone for promotion to colonel. Other candidates in her promotion group averaged around 43 years old. All services are cognizant of age and have a distinct prejudice against older candidates. We were not thunderstruck at her selection, but it was unprecedented. Many fine officers never make colonel, so it was wonderful news and capped a highly successful career. She had many outstanding bosses—colonels and generals who recognized her talents and ability. They were mentors. However, what gets one promoted is doing excellent work and completing the tough jobs—and that is what she did. We had a hard rule that neither of us would ever appear in the other's office, and we never violated that rule. She certainly was not hanging on my coattails. Her smarts and dedication to the Air Force carried the day. She was not in the first wave of females joining the Air Force, but she was still in the vanguard and paved the way for others. When she first enlisted in 1963, women made up only 2% of the Air Force. When she retired in 2000, that figure moved to above 20%. If she ever felt she was being held back because of being a woman she never told me. But that wouldn't be her way anyway, she would simply press on. Being a colonel moves one into the VIP arena. It says you have proven yourself, and you have made the grade into the highest levels of leadership and authority.

Loretta served as an enlisted member of the Air Force from 1963 to 1967. She was commissioned from Officer Training School at Lackland Air Force Base in 1974. Her first assignment was as an administration officer at Randolph Air Force Base in the Organizational Maintenance Squadron—she considered it the best possible start for a second lieutenant. Most of her time was spent on the flight line and in the maintenance shop, with people working on lots of airplanes: T37s, T38s, T39s, and even an old C–118 used by the Air Training Command IG. Her squadron commander was Lt Col Julius Jayroe, a returned POW from Vietnam.

In 1975, she was stationed in Seoul, Korea, and counted that as a great assignment. Her duty station was with Headquarters, United Nations Command/US Forces, Korea/Eighth US Army. One of her highlights was escorting congressional delegations by helicopter to the DMZ. Living in a Korean apartment and driving all over the city of Seoul in the midst of thousands of little blue taxis was a new experience. An infamous duty was keeping tabs and reporting the monthly Venereal Disease (VD) rate for the 48,000 troops (mostly young) stationed in Korea. I thought the title Command VD Officer would be rather impressive. Loretta did not agree. She gives credit to Col Lou Herrick in that assignment as an excellent boss and teacher.

Moving to Ramstein, Germany in 1977, she was assigned as the only American member in the Allied Air Forces Central Europe Command Group (AAFCE) front office as the junior executive officer (filling a major's position). She worked for the Commander-in-Chief, United States Air Forces Europe, a four-star general, in his NATO dual role as Commander AAFCE.

However, her day-to-day work was for the Deputy Commander AAFCE, Lieutenant General Ernst-Dieter Bernhard. Gen Bernhard was among the first 20 flyers selected to re-qualify to fly in the West German Air Force after World War II. He graciously accepted having an American woman lieutenant working for him—the German Air Force had no women as line personnel. She enjoyed the constant flow in his office of famous names in military aviation—both European and American. One was retired General Johannes Steinhoff, a famous German fighter ace in World War II who was also a prolific author of flying publications. He was credited with 176 victories. He also served as chairman of the NATO Military Committee. In addition to General Bernhard, mentors and supervisors were American Generals Evans and Pauly, Lt Gen Bellis, English Group Captain Bryant (the senior executive), Col Richard E. Skelton, and Lt Col Barbara King.

After Germany she moved to the Pentagon in 1979 for assignment in the Office of the Air Force Director of Administration. Her primary duty was supervising the U.S. Privacy Act for the

Air Force. Her room number was 4A 1088, which was in poor repair. This same room number will have significance in her 1997 Pentagon assignment. Still in the Pentagon, but moving to a different requirement, she became the first executive to the newly separate 1947th Admin Support Group, the forerunner of the Air Force District of Washington. A special duty was liaison to the Air Force Office of Special Investigation (OSI) for all Air Staff inquiries. The unit was commanded by Col Tex Carey, who became a friend and excellent mentor.

From 1983 to 1985 she was commander of the Headquarters Squadron Section, 3700 Personnel Resource Group at Lackland Air Force Base in Texas. Their mission was to provide support to the base personnel offices, processing airmen in and out of service and testing new airmen for assignment in various technical training courses. Col Andy Stanley was her boss and a mentor. He remains a friend to this day.

It was back to Washington, D.C., in 1985 as Headquarters Squadron Commander for the newly formed Air Force District of Washington, commanded by Brig Gen Ted Giddings. This was a unique setup: Two first sergeants—one each at the Pentagon and Bolling Air Force Base. I don't know of any other commander having two first sergeants, but it was two completely different sets of people/missions, and it worked well. Lots of upgrades to dormitories and offices were needed at Bolling. As building custodian for the multi-story Bolling Headquarters building, she directed the complete renovation. She claims to be the only officer to ever receive a medal for interior decoration—probably it was a little more than that. Looking at Bolling Air Force Base today, she is proud to have been a part of starting the base down the road to full renewal and making it a showcase. That said, she is quick to point out that no one could have made a dent in that vast project without General Giddings' vision and strong leadership.

Loretta considers 1987 a watershed year. With General Giddings' direct and strong support she switched career fields from administration to personnel, opening future opportunities. She became the Deputy Chief of Staff of personnel for the Air Force District of Washington.

Next on her dance card for 1988 and '89 was as a student at the Air Command and Staff College (ACSC) located on Maxwell Air Force Base in Montgomery, Alabama. The class was divided into four sections, each with a designated "student senior officer." She was appointed senior officer for her group, which meant representing the class at faculty meetings, social events, etc. A highlight for her was organizing the visit and then escorting British Army four-star General Sir John Winthrop Hackett when he was hosted at the college. He wrote the book *I Was a Stranger*, which recounts his action as a Brigadier General at the World War II Battle of Arnhem. The British dropped paratroopers to secure a bridge in Holland. Light defense was expected, but they ran head-on into a German Panzer tank division that simply wiped them out. Brig Gen Hackett was severely wounded and taken to a German field hospital. They did not recognize who he was, and he escaped. A Dutch family risked their lives to hide him in their home for four months while he recuperated and gained strength. The Dutch resistance eventually smuggled him back to England. The general's comments on the importance of keeping high military standards are provided: "A man can be selfish, cowardly, disloyal, false, fleeting, perjured, and morally corrupt in a wide variety of other ways and still be outstandingly good in pursuits in which other imperatives bear than those upon the fighting man. He can be a superb creative artist, for example, or a scientist in the very top flight and still be a very bad man. What the bad man cannot be is a good sailor, or soldier, or airman. Military institutions thus form a repository of moral resource which should always be a source of strength within the state." Loretta reports it took a copious amount of Scotch to keep him in high spirits. However, she will allow that she too enjoyed the Scotch. When visiting the Canadian equivalent of ACSC in Ottawa, Canada, she managed to break her wrist while competing in a broom ball match on the ice. With the Canadians as well as with the Brits, one could wonder if Scotch was involved.

Her follow-on assignment from ACSC in 1989 was to Lackland Air Force Base, as Commander of the 3731st Personnel Processing Squadron. This was her third assignment as a commander—once as a captain, once as a major, and now as a lieutenant colonel. Not many female officers have been a commander three times. I like to tease, saying the 3731st was a holding squadron for the sick, lame, and lazy. That's really not true as it also held airmen who fell out of training for sickness, broken legs, or any number of legitimate reasons. Nevertheless, she did discharge more than 7,000 airmen in two years. I know she earned an excellent rating from the supreme nitpicking IG team of the Air Force—the Air Training Command IG team—no small feat, considering the volatile nature of the airmen in her squadron, from mental illness to suicide threats to criminals.

Moving to Randolph Air Force Base and the Air Force Military Personnel Center (MPC) in 1990, she worked for Major Generals McGinty and Davitte who were commanders of MPC as well as a favorite she had known from Pentagon days, Mr. Blanchard. He was the first senior executive civilian to become deputy commander of MPC—a position traditionally held by a Brig Gen. Loretta was pleased to be in charge of Enlisted Promotions for two and a half years—she learned the enlisted promotions inside and out—not something every personnel officer knows. She was also charged with revamping and bringing up to date the primary personnel school at Keesler Air Force Base and the field grade Professional Personnel Course at the Air Force University. A major accomplishment was setting up a worldwide call center manned 24 hours a day by military personnel experts at MPC to provide accurate and timely support for personnel units in the field. That structure proved so successful that it was modified for use in emergencies such as tornadoes and hurricanes. Two of her favorite bosses at MPC were Colonel Ken Roth and Colonel Norm Rathje. Both were shooters, so she recruited them for her MPC teams in the base intramural skeet shooting competitions. I was assigned in Washington, D.C., at the time and later was startled to find out she was loaning my expensive shotguns to all the young airmen on teams. Of course, it was for a good cause and helped the kids out.

Upon promotion to Colonel in 1997, she was assigned to the Secretary of the Air Force Inspector General's (IG's) office in the Pentagon. Guess what? It was back to room 4A 1088, the same room she had occupied in 1979. She claims in the intervening 18 years that the office had not changed for the better. One of her first acts was to maneuver her staff out of room 4A 1088 in the Pentagon to a more suitable environment. It was found just one metro stop away in the City of Rosslyn. Anyone who has been in the Pentagon or the Washington, D.C., area knows that office space and location is the singular battleground among bureaucrats—the one thing that will surely bring mortal combat. That move was a mini miracle. She had a large staff with several other full colonels, including officers assigned to her from the Air Force Office of Special Investigation (OSI). Her authority was as wide as was her responsibility. She could open an investigation into any unit or command, including the OSI, in the entire Air Force. Her oversight responsibility extended to the Air Force Reserve and the Air National Guard IG's of all 50 states—that's 50 more colonels. One accomplishment she was especially proud of was establishing, actually developing, the first Air Force school for IG's. Lt Gen Richard Swope, followed by Lt Gen Nicholas Kehoe, were her bosses. She reported to them, and they reported directly to the Secretary of the Air Force. The IG system is placed under the Secretary to preclude undue influence in the normal Air Force chain of command. It was a challenging but rewarding assignment to complete her 30 years of military service.

Loretta received numerous complimentary citations, certificates, and letters of praise and appreciation. She was formally decorated 11 times as the colorful array of ribbons on her uniform attest. Upon retirement, she was decorated with the Air Force Legion of Merit, befitting her superior service.

And the rest of the story! While her Air Force career was nothing less than outstanding, the rest of the story is equally amazing. Loretta grew up in a blue-collar family living in a small town in East Texas. Her father died when she was 16, leaving her mother alone to raise her and her younger brother Anthony who was only 11. Her older brother and sister, Robert and Lou Ella, had already left home and were married.

Loretta finished high school in three years and managed to read every book in the small school library. Her scholastic standing earned her a one-year, $1000 scholarship from a merchant who owned the Hub, the town department store. Loretta started at East Texas

State College—now Texas A & M in Commerce—when she was 16 years old. She finished her freshman year, and the scholarship ran out. What to do? Examining her options, she decided to join the military service in 1963, and at 17 (with her older sister Lou Ella signing for her) she enlisted in the Air Force.

It would be fair to say she took full charge of her life at 16, and at 17 she pressed on with the best option available. Her assignment after basic training was at Lackland Air Force Base. She continued her education, attending San Antonio College classes at night. Her four-year enlistment was completed in 1967, and we were married. I took off for Vietnam, and she enrolled in the University of North Texas at Denton. Upon my return from Vietnam, we moved to Germany where she again pursued her education, taking night classes from the University of Maryland. In 1973, eleven years and four colleges from her start, she was awarded a bachelor's degree from the University of Maryland, the first one in her family to graduate from college. It took a bit of grit, but she wanted a better life, went after that dream, and would not be deterred. Interestingly, her younger brother Anthony followed in her footsteps, joining the Air Force, and subsequently finishing college to become the first person in her family to earn a master's degree.

Our courtship and marriage were a little unconventional. We started dating in 1966 when Loretta was still at Lackland Air Force Base in San Antonio as an enlisted member. Since I was an officer, we had a very secretive romance. Even my rifle team members, with whom I was very close, had no suspicions. The service has very direct guidance concerning fraternization between officers and enlisted. Our plan was to get married upon my return from Vietnam. Two weeks prior to my scheduled departure I got to thinking what would happen if I didn't come back. We all had an automatic government $10,000 insurance policy if we got knocked off. My folks didn't need the money, and I wanted Loretta to get something. So, the marriage was earlier than planned.

Loretta was finishing up her four-year enlistment, and I was attending personnel school in Amarillo. Time was short, but we could make it work by getting married en route, using my allotted travel days from Amarillo to Travis Air Force Base near San Francisco. Loretta flew to meet me in Amarillo, and we drove straight through to my hometown, Santa Paula, California. Against regulations, of course, which set a travel limit of 300 miles per day.

There was no time for announcements. I just called my family and friends. I can imagine what some people thought about this emergency wedding. My mother set up the wedding, which absolutely filled the First Presbyterian Church. My friend and mentor Charles Leavens (father of my high-school girlfriend) gave the bride away. Her older sister Lou Ella flew out to be the maid of honor. My brother was best man, and four of my very best friends, Doug Udall, Wayne Bailey, Byron Edde, and Jim Gofourth, were ushers. It was not fancy but a fun wedding. We had a reception with punch and cake at the church. Afterward we headed for Travis Air Force Base. How many girls would agree to be married in their fiancé's hometown? I had to leave Loretta and, of course, that was very difficult. She was certainly a great help to me in Vietnam as she sent a constant flow of letters. Upon my return from Vietnam in 1968, I was posted to Ramstein Air Force Base in Germany, and Loretta and I began our real marriage there.

The military service had a highly structured and active social community in those days. Neither Loretta nor I entered the Air Force with any previous exposure to formal dinners and balls, so there was much to learn. Naturally, I had formal dress (black-tie) uniforms, white for day events and black for evenings. I had been to a couple of formal mess dinners and receptions for officers, but Loretta had zero experience. Remember, her previous military service (1963-'67) was as a junior enlisted member, not exposed to officers' formal social events. For ladies, the evening events required formal gowns and even long elbow-length gloves. Loretta had no formal wear, and it was not readily available on the local German economy. We were hardly loaded with money as military pay was quite stingy in the 60s. I had been to Hong Kong during my Vietnam time in Asia and had purchased several reams of high-quality, different-colored silk. Although not an experienced couturier, Loretta soon had patterns and made her gowns. They were nice and also stylish. And, of course, as a young bride, she was beautiful in those long dresses. I must say we made a handsome couple with her decked out in those smart gowns.

It was customary for unit commanders or senior supervisors to welcome new officers to their unit for dinner or at least drinks in their homes. There was always a dish, small tray, or receptacle for the new officer to leave his calling card. Loretta and I learned to navigate the many protocols together. My first boss in Germany was Lt Col William Coleman. He and his wife welcomed us with an invitation to their home for dinner. They were a wonderful couple and were most cordial in receiving us. Less formal dinners were common among contemporaries and sometimes even between junior and more senior officers. This was particularly true in overseas assignments where socializing brought more closeness to the military community. Loretta had never learned to cook, and I was worthless in that department. Again, she pushed forward with cookbooks and experiments and practiced to become a very credible cook, and she laid out a beautiful table. One specialty was a pheasant dinner, which was a favorite of many. Later in life, several generals dined at our table.

In that first assignment of our marriage, Loretta was a civilian dependent wife. The vast majority of Air Force officers' wives did not work. Of course, it was not easy to gain employment off base in Germany either. Unofficially, wives were discouraged from working outside the home. Their job was to take care of the house, raise the kids, fix the meals, and support their husbands' careers. Those duties included lunches and teas at the officers' club or in private residences. However, wives were expected to devote volunteer time for activities at the officers' club, preparing for celebrations, unit dinners, dances, etc. Additionally, they were strongly encouraged to donate time at the thrift shop, base school, the Parent Teacher Association, the Red Cross, or other benevolent agencies that improved or supported the base and its people. Loretta chose to be a Red Cross volunteer, and she took it up with zeal, uniform and all. One day each week she put on her American Red Cross blue/gray dress and cap before reporting to the dental clinic. In a short time, she worked her way up to become chief assistant to the senior dental surgeon, a colonel. He scheduled his major surgeries on Loretta's Red Cross duty day.

Hunting and shooting were my main interests in off-duty time. Loretta had never been exposed to these activities, but she dutifully accompanied me on my many outings. During the shooting events, she would normally drop me off and then visit the local sites and probably saw every cathedral and large church in Germany, Austria, Belgium, Switzerland, and Holland. On the small-game hunts for pheasants, Hungarian Partridge, and hares, she would walk with me, helping to pick up the downed game. Hunting in Germany is more formalized than in the States. It is really a subculture with historical rituals, traditions, and even special words in a hunting language. For instance, the long ear of a hare is called a Löffel (spoon), the round ear of a Russian boar is called Teller (dinner plate), and a rabbit tail is called a Blume (flower). Hunters dressed in green clothes and often wore ties. They were careful who they let into their society, and it was very difficult to obtain a hunting license (Jagdschein). Their hunting course lasted one year, with students attending one night each week. The curriculum is wide and arduous, not only the study of animals, but all the flora and fauna. The course includes proficiency with both shotgun and rifle. In addition to an in-depth written test, candidates must pass a rigorous oral examination. You can see the dedication, and they graduate as knowledgeable hunters and good woodsmen.

Due to the Status of Force Agreements with Germany, Americans stationed in their country were allowed to conduct our own hunting courses and accredit hunters' certificates. That certificate allowed us to purchase the regular German Jagdschein. Our courses were much shorter, usually one or two nights a week, over a two-or three-week period, and a Saturday for shooting. Our course could not be compared with the German course but was quite good compared to hunting courses in the States. Still, not many GIs took the time and effort to get a license. That is really a shame as Germany offered excellent hunting opportunities.

Loretta decided on her own to take the U.S. forces hunting course. She was only the second American woman I know of who obtained the German Jagdschein. She did not hunt at that time, but having a Jagdschein enhanced her status greatly with my German hunting friends. I was never in a hunting field with a German female hunter, so you can appreciate how uncommon it was.

I was eminently proud of my civilian bride on that first assignment in Germany. What is astounding is how she was able to adapt and to avoid all the social and etiquette landmines. Think about it: new marriage, new country, totally new and extensive military social protocol including engraved invitations, even dictating proper seating assignments for dinners, fitting in on German hunts as the only lady, and a complete new social environment with other officers' wives who were older, mostly upper crust, college educated and sophisticated. She managed it with style and grace.

People have asked how we managed to both be in the military. I can tell you it was not planned by me. After nearly running the wheels off our Volkswagen beetle driving to Frankfurt, Darmstadt, and other locations where night courses were offered, she gained enough credits, and her bachelor's degree from the University of Maryland was presented by the education officer at Rhine Main Base Air Force Base in 1973, along with a magnum of champagne.

Loretta had been working as a volunteer at the base school. We hadn't talked much about what she planned to do with her college degree, but I thought it would probably be in teaching. We had returned to the States, my new job at Randolph was taxing, and I was putting in long hours. Our house was not ready, and we were staying in a motel that had sort of a half kitchen with a tall table and two bar stools. I got home around 10 p.m. and was dead tired. Loretta had dinner ready, and I had just sat down to eat when she said, "I went to see a recruiter today." I nearly fell off my bar stool. I was shocked. That was that and she was off to Officer Training School. You know the rest of the story.

For most of our careers, we were assigned to the same base, or at least in the same town, but as Loretta climbed the career ladder, higher-rank positions became scarcer. We were separated for some periods of time, but when I retired in 1993, I happily became the trailing spouse and followed her to her assignments until she retired in 2000.

Another first for Loretta was being the only woman ever voted into the United Nations Closed Mess (private dinner club) in Korea. The club did not look like much—more like two large Quonset huts hooked together—but it was prestigious, and outside petitions for membership were not entertained. Members were the senior representatives of those countries that joined with United States in the Korean War. Loretta was a lieutenant protocol officer supporting the United Nations command, which made her eligible. Some countries did not yet have women in their military. And others, including the British, could not conceive of a woman being allowed as a member of a Closed Mess. Nevertheless, the votes came in making her a member. I could go only as a guest of my lieutenant wife and never on my own. So much for my being an Air Force major. The club was an avenue for us to meet officers and civilian officials from several other countries. Each month, a different country would be in charge of presenting a dinner common to their country. In addition, they would often present a social program. I recall one such event sponsored by the British. We were having drinks before dinner when we heard bagpipes coming our way. We stepped to the veranda to watch the Scottish Highlanders. What did we behold? Not Scottish Highlanders, but short Gurkhas (Nepalese soldiers) playing the bagpipes while marching smartly with their spirally wound cloth puttees and famous curved Kbukuri knives. That was a big surprise. They were part of the British contingent in Hong Kong and had rotated up to Korea for three months. The club was fun, even if I was only allowed in as Loretta's guest.

Loretta became president of the Monte Vista Historical Association, which is where we live today. That was a busy time as she was still on active duty. Being retired by that time, I was unhappily pressed into duty of helping with mailouts and other administrative tasks. She was responsible for monthly committee meetings, dealing with various city agencies and authorities, and events such as our annual Fourth of July parade. Her primary mission was preserving and enhancing the Monte Vista Historical District, so she was in constant discussions with the San Antonio Historic Review Board. It was a big and important job that she handled well. She is a no slacker in civic duties and was a member of the San Antonio Association of non-profits and is a current member of Rotary International.

A job she handled exceptionally well was the United States Senate Youth Program. The title is a bit deceptive, as it is really the Randolph Hearst Foundation program. A U.S. Senator puts his name on the program each year, but the Hearst Foundation funds the program and manages it. I must say, it is an outstanding program designed to educate and expose high school students to national government. Each state education department is allowed to send two high school students to Washington, D.C. The Department of Defense Schools and the District of Washington are also invited to send two students. The Hearst Foundation picks up the tab for everything—airlines, hotels, and meals. It is a high-class operation: the kids stay at the Mayflower Hotel. The Hearst Foundation provides an on-site doctor and security. The kids meet privately with their representative and senators. They also meet with the Secretary of Defense, the Chairman of the Joint Chiefs of Staff, the Secretary of State, other secretaries, and cabinet officials, and, above all, they have the opportunity to visit the White House and the President of the United States. The kids were, of course, awestruck meeting the President. Loretta tells of President Reagan coming down the staircase to meet the kids—like a God descending from on high to meet his flock below. I sat in on a couple of their visits with the Chairman of the Joint Chiefs, and the kids asked tough questions. General Powell took all questions and treated the young students like adults. They seemed to appreciate that. Their visit and education also included attendance at the President's State of the Union Message to the nation. Additionally, each night they had a coat and tie dinner which included an address by a government official, often a United States Senator. Added to all that, each attendee was given a $1000 scholarship. It was truly a program to die for. How do they make a program work that requires corralling and herding 104 high-school students for a week of briefings, lectures, private meetings, and banquets? The Hearst Foundation was smart. They called in the military, and that's where Loretta fits in the story. The Foundation asks the Department of Defense (DOD) to provide personnel for the program. I suspect no one is anxious to turn them down. Lieutenants and ensigns who are closer in age to the students work best. Loretta, as a major, was tapped to be the on-site project officer to supervise and direct the junior officers who would each be responsible for eight or ten students.

Loretta was with the group all day. After the students were in bed, she held an after-action assessment in her hotel suite with her lieutenants and ensigns to keep them fully informed and ensure all was going as planned. She also worked with the very able foundation program director, Rita Almon, and several members of the Hearst family. Millicent Hearst Boudjakdji was president of the Hearst Foundation, but Randolph Apperson Hearst was always on the grounds as well as Mrs. George Randolph Hearst Senior. They all worked well together, and Loretta did such a good job they wanted her back the next year, which was a first for the supervising officer to return a second time. No one in DOD was going to turn Randolph Hearst down. She followed a second year, and then a third, and then a fourth, before moving to her next assignment as a student at the Air War College in Montgomery, Alabama.

The Hearst family was most gracious in inviting me to a couple of the dinners, which included speakers. Loretta and I would sit on the dais along with the Hearst family and other dignitaries. I sat, wearing my mess dress uniform, with William Hearst the night Senator Al Gore spoke to the students. Part of his message was that we should cut the size of our military. I wondered what the dozen or so military escorts thought of his remarks. Another time, I sat with Patty Hearst and her husband Bernard (Bernie) Shaw. I have to say, Patty was a lovely lady by then and very polite, and always called me colonel. She became one of my favorites. On that occasion, I managed to piss in the punch bowl. That is another story. If you're interested, I've listed it in my notes of comeuppance. Randolph Hearst was very low-key but always gave me a warm welcome. But it was Loretta they really liked. On the last day after the students had departed, the Hearst Foundation arranged for the young escort officers to keep their rooms one more night to have breakfast in bed the following morning with their wives, husbands, or significant others. Can you imagine breakfast in bed at the swank Mayflower Hotel for those young military troops? The Hearst family took care of those who took care of them.

After retirement, Loretta became CEO of a nonprofit program known as Any Baby Can. Their focus is assisting families to cope with the challenges of a newborn child having severe physical or mental conditions. It's a fine program as many affected families become completely devastated and don't know where to turn for help. Any Baby Can provides everything from diapers to baby cribs for those in need. Their main assistance is counseling to help families reach the appropriate medical programs and apply for grants and other financial assistance. Loretta supervised a squad of 15 social workers, a receptionist, finance manager, and an administrative assistant. It's heartbreaking to see families and children in such stress, but she led the program for two years. In that time, she supervised the move to a new modern facility, standardized procedures, and organized their fundraising and finances in a more businesslike manner. And, for the organization's first time, she established 401(k) retirement accounts for the staff.

A memorable first must be mentioned. It would be safe to say Lt Generals do not give dinners for young captains. You could bet money on that. But be careful, it did happen. When we departed Germany in 1979, Lt Gen Benjamin Bellis and Lt Gen Ernst-Dieter Bernhard had a private dinner in their homes for Loretta. I was a tagalong. General Bellis was the Vice Commander of U.S. Air Forces Europe, and General Bernhard was Deputy of Allied Air Forces Central Europe. Loretta was assigned to Gen Bernhard's office but also worked with Gen Bellis. They had homes next to each other on the base. We started with hors d'oeuvres and drinks in Gen Bernhard's and then proceeded to Gen Bellis's for the main dinner course, after which we retreated to Gen Bernhard's for coffee, after-dinner drinks, and desserts. It was a lovely dinner with beautiful china, crystal glasses, silver flatware and, of course, butlers serving. We were the only guests. Obviously, they thought a lot of Loretta, and we were truly honored by their gracious and unprecedented dinner gesture.

One of Loretta's great joys is travel. She enjoys seeing the world and meeting new people. I'm not sure of the number, but I believe she may have visited more countries than I, and I have visited more than seventy. Her first visit to China was in 1981 when it was

Long Shots — Family and Friends

just opening up. She went with a group from the Smithsonian, and her pictures reveal drab buildings with people dressed in black and gray. A far cry from what it was when we visited Beijing during the Olympics in 2008. She visited Machu Picchu and went down the Amazon 20 years before me. Loretta has walked the narrow passages of Lamu and the broad Avenue of 9 De Julio. She has seen the mist of Iguazu and Victoria Falls, the deserts of the Sinai, and the wetness of the Faroe Islands, and she has traveled as high as 15,545 feet in Tibet and as low as 416 feet below sea level at the Dead Sea. She has been from Singapore to Greenland, Patagonia to Rajastan, Lisbon to Teheran. It could be suggested she has experienced the world firsthand.

Loretta played golf a bit and even did rock climbing. You won't catch me jumping off a cliff and shimmying down a rope. She learned to shoot shotgun and became quite good, shamelessly beating me a time or two in live pigeon competition. Shotgun shooting led to bird hunting, and she remains an enthusiastic quail and dove hunter. Her enthusiasm has brought many ladies into skeet shooting. Additionally, she is an accomplished skier. She also took up fly fishing, and once again often claims the biggest trout. I think the guides are against me.

She loves animals and has probably been on 20 African safaris. Her interest has moved from the animals to becoming an avid bird watcher. She knows more about dogs than I do and can recognize and name nearly every breed. She has had some wonderful house cats that we have carried around the world on our assignments. Horseback riding is another of her loves, and, in fact, our first date was on a trail ride where we rode double on Gunsmoke, my 16 hands tall gelding. He was not a thoroughbred, more like a Hanoverian, but a faithful and trusty steed. Loretta took English riding lessons and became an accomplished rider, far outdistancing me. Her favorite horses are in Patagonia.

Loretta has been a great help to me in my business, Expedition Adventures, and became the expert in photo and bird shooting safaris to Kenya. She is particularly helpful in preparing couples and single ladies for these trips, with options and advice on itineraries, guides, what to pack, international travel, insurance, immunization, and all manner of things. She has guided photo safaris to Kenya and expeditions to

Argentina. My Expedition Adventures partner, Gordie White (quite frankly the guy who really runs the show), leans heavily on Loretta for help on the Kenya safaris and on couples' trips to Argentina.

Another facet is her interest in business. She is partnered in a North Texas rural real estate development and house building operation with her family members, Tom and Guinn Pingleton. Tom is a CPA who recently sold his very successful accounting business to raise Black Angus and invest in properties. Guinn is an accomplished real estate agent who knows how to sell property. They are excellent to work with. Additionally, Loretta has been my full partner for 28 years in the Bunker Club, a nonprofit, raising money to assist aspiring Olympic shooters. She is a lady of many talents.

Loretta is a good, decent person with compassion and empathy for others. Her demeanor is quiet but confident, not really retiring but seeking neither the spotlight nor center of attention. I would say she handles situations without any panic or showing outward irritation—she's matter of fact without theatrics, but always listening and understanding. Don't confuse that with being weak; she is tough when it is called for.

The following story was told to me by her First Sergeant when she was commander of the 3731st Squadron. It seems the first shirt was having trouble with a young college kid who was leaving the Air Force under a process known as self-initiated elimination (SIE), which is allowed during the very early stages of officer training. Some people just don't fit in the military. A discharge from the military for whatever reason requires medical and legal procedures that take time. During this period, an individual is still a sworn-in member of the Armed Forces. They wear a uniform, live in a barracks, and have duties to perform and rules to follow.

This young man thought he was getting out, so he didn't have to follow rules or orders. The days of taking a nonconformist behind the barracks for some hard counseling were over. The first shirt being unsuccessful with words brought the matter to the commander's attention. According to his story, the commander, Lt Col Loretta Behrens listened to his problem and simply said, "Have the airman report to me at 10 a.m." The time arrived and the airman reported in. Standing at parade rest in her office were two very large Air Force military policemen. She calmly told the airman, who was standing at attention, that he was to straighten up, follow all rules and orders of the First Sergeant. He could either do that or she would have him arrested, handcuffed, and escorted to the brig. It mattered not to her either way; it was up to him to decide. The insubordinate airman could tell she was not bluffing. Problem solved.

She has always been generous and never demanding in our marriage. She frequently urges me to do what I want, and if I'm balking because I think it costs too much, she reminds me that settling for less seldom brings contentment. On one occasion, I was interested in a new pair of Holland and Holland 20 bore shotguns. The price was exorbitant, about the cost of two Mercedes, so I thought perhaps it might be prudent to at least mention my interest and the cost. The guns were being sold at auction by James Julia Auctions in Maine. We were in our in-home office when I told her about the guns and that I wanted to travel to Maine for an inspection before making a bid. She merely turned around to the computer and said, "Let me see if I can find some flights to Maine." Not even a comment about the cost. There was none of "if you get that, I get this" bargaining. She wanted me to have what I wanted, and I wanted her to have what she wanted. Which, by the way, included three 911 Porsches. We worked at it.

Loretta would never affront anyone with complaining or invite them to listen to her problems. We had a little setback in 2018 that caused us to modify our activities and alter our lifestyle. The short story is that she was taking chemo treatments in preparation for a breast cancer operation. All was going well, until it wasn't. I was in Argentina and called her up on Facetime every day just to check in and chat a bit. Facetime allowed me to actually see her to make sure she was okay. On a Thursday she answered from a hospital bed! That scared me, but she quickly assured me it was only an overnight stay for a touch of pneumonia, and she was being released in the morning. Loretta said there was no need for me to rush home since my scheduled flight was only three days out.

Arriving home on Monday, I walked into the house, finding Loretta on the living room couch where she had been since

Saturday. She had no strength and could not climb the stairs to our bedroom. Our neighbor and friend Dr. Clint Polhamus had made an appointment for us to see a pulmonologist that day. He examined Loretta. It was not pneumonia; it was idiopathic pulmonary fibrosis. She was admitted to the hospital immediately and placed in ICU for the next four days. Late on the second night the doctor warned me they would most likely need to put her on a respirator. It was quite serious. She recovered somewhat on the fifth day and spent the next week just one step down from the ICU but still on an oxygen mask with a check of all her vitals every hour. In the end she spent 31 straight days in the hospital, the last few in rehab. After a couple of months gaining strength at home, we went into the cancer surgery with her requiring full-time oxygen. An excellent female surgeon got us through that operation with flying colors.

Not even once through the whole ordeal did she ask, "why me?" or complain. I would have been kicking wastebaskets and punching walls. With her lungs badly scarred she will be on oxygen full-time for the rest of her life, but I'm pleased to report she can drive and lead a robust social life with her many friends. Physical activity is reduced because of her lack of strength, but we have adjusted and are moving on down the road. I must add a special thanks to all our neighbors and friends in San Antonio and around the world for the sterling support they gave Loretta and me in a difficult time. It was marvelous and will never be forgotten.

She has done it all and done it well. Her climb from a hardscrabble beginning through highly successful and rewarding careers is more than notable. She earned respect and gained a stature of eminence in the military and in civilian society. But she is much more than that to me. She is my lover, my confidant, my advisor, my critic—my lifelong partner. I would not be where I am without her by my side. I owe her more than I can ever give. Loretta may not fit the classical model of a Norman Rockwell housewife, but she is a lady all the way and the perfect match for me. I love her.

Long Shots — Family and Friends

Mother

My mother, Clara Mae Sykes, was the daughter of Clarence (Jack) and Marie Sykes. She grew up on a family farm with three brothers and five sisters in central Iowa near the small town of Blairsburg. Today it is a little flyspeck, but back then, it was a hub of activity with feed, hardware, and general stores. There were a couple of lockers where farmers could freeze and store meat (that was before electricity was available on the local farms). The consolidated area school was in Blairsburg, and that's where she graduated from high school. She loved to talk about being on the girls' high-school basketball team.

 Born in 1919, Mother was in her early teens during the Great Depression, and those difficult times shaped her. No one starved on the farm, but there was little cash. People learned to make do with what they had, and they did not waste money on things that were not a necessity. While not frugal, she never wasted money on foolish things. Purchases were made carefully and never by layaway. You had the money, or you didn't buy the item. She dressed well but not expensively and always looked for sales. Her jewelry was never costly. Many years later, she told me she was worried about being poor, which made my father and her work extra hard in the early years. They really started with nothing, but they kept any money worries from me, and I never felt poor or deprived of anything.

 The Depression was easing up in 1940, but jobs that paid cash were hard to find, and even if found, the pay was poor. President Franklin Roosevelt started the Civilian Conservation Corps early in his first administration and the cash pay was only $25 per month. That might give you some perspective. My folks traveled to California, not for the beautiful beaches or magnificent mountains, but to find paying jobs. There was a song at the time that described the move to California. I don't recall all the words, but it went something like this: "Dear Okie, if you see Arkie, tell him Tex is out in California digging oil wells; all he needs is a shovel. And there's orange juice fountains flowing for those kids of his." My parents were not Okies, Arkies, or Texans but were in the same boat. My father had been to a school in

Omaha to learn about aluminum cutting and molding, so he landed a job at Lockheed Aircraft. My mother became a Rosie Riveter. She loved working at Lockheed, and it was the first time she ever got a check for working. She had worked as a housemaid and helper for an older couple, Mr. and Mrs. Oakland, on the neighboring farm but was paid in coins only. After a while, she was selected to carry messages, plans, and orders between work units. She did this riding a bicycle with a large basket carrying her cargo. This was an even better job for her as she traveled all over the assembly plant and interfaced with people from all the work units.

After the war, she helped my father run his Greyhound bus, taxi, and Western Union business. They ran it together with my dad opening up early and closing up late. Mom would generally take over in the afternoon, and then we would all be together for dinner. After dinner my dad would go back to meet the last bus at 8:30 p.m. I don't recall her ever just resting. She and Dad would watch Lawrence Welk on TV and that was about the only rest time. They were a perfect pair and were active in both the business and civic community. It made for long days, but on Sundays they slowed down with my dad only going to the bus station to meet the buses and selling what tickets were required. That allowed them to go to church together. Of course, in addition, Mom cooked, washed the clothes, cleaned the house, and raised my little brother Bob and me. It must be admitted that while my mother prepared the meals, she didn't care much about cooking and wasn't a particularly good cook. That is quite astonishing since my grandmother was a very good cook, and when she baked bread the wonderful aroma would engulf the entire house. I'm always amazed at how working mothers manage to keep all the balls in the air.

My parents eventually sold their business, and my mother became a fulltime teacher's aide for physically and mentally challenged children. The teacher helper pay in those days was quite dismal, but she enjoyed getting a paycheck. She didn't have to work but always counseled us to "be useful," and her disposition would not allow her to remain idle anyway. My brother and I were both happy she was working because it got her out of the house, dressed professionally, and with other people every day. She continued as a teacher's assistant for 30 years. She told me that as she got older, the kids could recognize she was a bit fragile. One kid in an excited and agitated state pushed her over. The rest of the kids did not like that and let the perpetrator know what for. She liked her job and enjoyed working. I'm sure it gave her a sense of self-worth and satisfaction.

When she retired from teaching, she was in her early 80s but continued working as a volunteer at Hospice and for the Santa Paula Chamber of Commerce and was a regular ribbon-cutter at new-business openings. She knew nearly everyone in town, and most often took the tickets and attended to the ledgers of who attended chamber events. One amusing story was about her being mugged when she came out of a drugstore on Harvard Street. The mugger grabbed her purse and, in the struggle, knocked her down. A bystander called the police and EMS. When the fire truck arrived, she knew all the firemen. She was black and blue on one whole side of her body but wouldn't go to the hospital. She was taken to the police station, and the chief of police was called. Mother knew him from his childhood days. Chief Gonzales asked my mother how much money she had in her purse. She told him a dollar and 47 cents. He burst out laughing. It happened that my mother had just purchased a prescription and knew exactly how much money she had left in her wallet. The chief apologized, but my mother could see the humor in it. How many ladies know to the penny what they have in their purse? Then he told her if they caught the guy, he would be charged not with just theft but with the attack and bodily injury of a senior citizen. He would spend many a day behind bars thinking about what one dollar and 47 cents cost him. The chief and EMS folks wanted to schedule Mother for trauma counseling, but she would have no part of it. She said, "The heck with that." All she wanted was for them to catch the crook.

Mother was much more direct than my father and was not shy in giving me advice—mostly good but often not followed. In temperament, I am certainly my mother's son. She loved to organize things, and they had to be right. And she really wanted my brother and me to succeed in life. She taught us to be respectful of others, work hard, and always, "Give the best you can.'

When I was in grade and middle school, she was our chariot to take my friends and me to see interesting things or to play at the beach in Ventura. Alfonso Sandoval, our closest neighbor, was often with us along with Doug Udall, who became my best friend in high school. I remember several times going to the beach in Ventura. One really fun thing was to go to the beach for a grunion run. For those not familiar with a grunion run, it is catching fish by hand when they wash up on the sand. Grunion are a small fish, about seven inches in length. They ride in on a wave to deposit their eggs, and then ride out on the next wave. This happens at high tide with the full moon—usually around midnight—so for us, it couldn't be on a school night. If we were lucky enough to find them, we'd see the whole beach where they were spawning; it looked like shimmering silver. Even if they didn't appear it would be an enjoyable time with big bonfires and roasted marshmallows. We also did Saturday overnight camps on the beaches near Santa Barbara in tents for us and our little teardrop trailer (which was also my bedroom at home) for my mother and father. For you history buffs, that area was attacked by the Japanese in 1942. A Japanese submarine surfaced and shelled an oil processing area, causing little damage and no injuries. However, it did put a scare into Californians.

Mother was a member of the Santa Paula Presbyterian Church for 68 years. She became a deacon, and we used to get a kick out of her driving older friends to church when she herself was entering her mid-eighties. Her disappointment in my brother and me for not attending church more was often voiced. Her most enjoyable time was with people—family, friends, and even those she did not know. She was a member of the Santa Paula Ebell Club, the town's leading women's cultural club. She also was a member of several card clubs for many years. The one she liked the best played only bridge and met only once a month, but it was hosted at a different member's home each time. She really didn't care that much about cards; she just liked visiting with people. She was always happy when relatives came to visit. After my father passed, she bought a condo where several families had kids. They were always welcome at her house and often came to play in her living room, where she kept coloring books and toys. She just loved having company. My father enjoyed travel, particularly road trips. Mother accompanied him on some trips, but it really wasn't her thing. She didn't like long periods in the car and much preferred being with people. After my father died, we took her to Hawaii, and she enjoyed seeing the sights (she even waded in the surf with us) but said she enjoyed the people more. We took her on another trip led by anthropologist Dr. Al Ward and his wife Stephanie to study the Tarahumara Indians at the bottom of the Copper Canyon in Mexico. The travel was by plane, train, and Suburban. We flew from El Paso to Chihuahua, then we took the train to Creel, and from there it was by four-wheel-drive Suburbans to the bottom of the canyon on a narrow, steep, and winding gravel road to the town of Batopilas, 6000 feet below the canyon rim. Our group was only Dr. Ward and his wife, Jim and Jan Gofourth, Loretta and I, and my mother. The town had seen its heyday in the late 1800s and early 1900s as the world center for silver mining. The American, Alexander Sheppard, a previous Mayor of Washington, D.C., pretty much founded and directed the city and silver mining in the area. The town was a very important center at the height of silver mining and was the second city in Mexico to use electricity. Only Mexico City was lighted by electricity earlier. It was a fun, historical, educational, and interesting trip. Mother seemed to enjoy the trip but afterward said the best part was being with the Gofourths and us. The town was pretty well run down and more closely resembled a poor Mexican village. We had dinner one evening at a tidy restaurant in a whitewashed building. A three-member band using guitars, violin, and the trumpet played music for us. One band member was the local cop, still wearing his pistol. The place was pretty basic, but they used linen napkins, and coffee was served from an elaborate silver coffee set by a barefoot waiter wearing a straw cowboy hat. I wondered what that coffeepot had seen in the years gone by.

Mother passed away when she was 96½ years old. She never coveted material things; her wealth was in friends and family. Four of her five sisters and one brother followed her to California, and I remember at least three aunts lived with us at different times. She kept close to all of them and was able to help them in one way or another. I believe she had a full, happy, and satisfying life. To one and all, she often announced that she had the best husband and the best boys ever. The boys may be suspect, but I never once heard an argument or a cross word between my parents. Some may question that, but I bet none can dispute it. She had a life well lived.

My Father Hit Me

People who knew my father say it isn't true, but it did happen. More on that later. Harold Francis Behrens was born in 1909 on a farm in Iowa. The name Francis was appropriate as he loved animals and little kids. Dogs just seemed to come to him and so did little kids. Of course, he bribed the little kids as he always seemed to have gum or candy in his pocket. He came of age at the time of the Great Depression of 1929, and I believe his father lost a section of prime land in that traumatic period. My father quit school after the 11th grade when a friend did him a favor and gave him a job driving a truck. It was considered a favor at the time when there were few money-paying jobs and also quite a shame as dad was quite intelligent. He later went to school in Omaha to learn about cutting metal and aluminum. Like most Iowa farmers, he was a hard worker, and he worked all his life. The idea of debt was abhorrent to him. He believed you saved money and then bought what you wanted, not the other way around.

We moved to California in 1940 and settled in San Fernando. Both my mother and father went to work for Lockheed Aircraft, where his schooling in Omaha brought him a good-paying job. Adding to his day job at Lockheed, he drove a taxi at night. Many people in WW II had a day job and a night job. After the war, he bought a small taxicab company in Santa Paula, California. The influx of people to the West Coast and the return of GIs created a vast shortage of housing in California so he traveled between San Fernando and Santa Paula until we could get housing. We only had one car, so my mother kept the car, and my dad used a motorcycle (an Indian, the size of a Harley-Davidson) for his commute. I can remember all four of us squeezed on the big Indian—my brother Bob (two or three years old) on the gas tank with me and Mom behind Dad. It was only around the block but exciting for me.

The taxi company consisted of three cabs during the week, but he added two more for the weekends, and they were kept busy. Many people used taxis when they bought groceries or just to get around town. Some people ordered groceries and had them delivered by taxi. Few families had two cars. Dad drove taxis himself, often all day and then again at the busiest times at night. The little company was successful for many years. Eventually, he was asked to become the Greyhound bus agent, much like a franchise. Later, he was invited to become the Western Union agent for Santa Paula. Both opportunities came to him when the previous agents proved not to be up to the task. He never said, but I believe he was approached for these positions because of his sterling reputation.

When I say hard worker, I also mean he worked every day, Sundays included. He did take off to accompany my mother to church but then went back to work. Being a Greyhound bus agent meant meeting every bus every day to provide tickets, receive packages delivered by the bus, and to send packages out. This was long before there was a UPS or FedEx service. Trains and the buses were the major modes of transport for people. Airline travel for the masses was in the future. Some people wore a coat and tie on the bus.

Understand, his hard work was not just about money. Of course, money was needed to live, but there was no keeping up with the Joneses in his blood. Maybe his work ethic was from growing up on the farm or perhaps the Depression days, but he always wanted to do the best job he could, and that's what it took in his business. He placed little value on material things. He did have some nice suits for church. When he died, my mother told me to take anything of his that I wanted. But he really had nothing personal of material value. Again, his middle name, Francis, fit.

His only time off was when he took trips, and he did love to travel. It was always by car, and he made yearly trips to Iowa. Not only did he have family in Iowa, but he also kept track of his buddies from high school and work who were still living in the area. They all played tricks on each other, and I remember one time my dad doctored up a newspaper article about a new millionaire who had a uranium mine, with him being the millionaire. He sent it one to of his buddies before a trip to Iowa as a joke. But it backfired on him as his buddy passed it around to everyone, so the joke really ended up being on my dad. I was with him on that trip, and they all had a great time over it, including Dad.

Once, we drove off the beaten path to a tiny town in the Ozark Mountains of Missouri named Ava. We went there to visit his friend who had come up to Iowa as a boy looking for food and work during the Depression. My grandfather took him in, and he was the same age as my dad. They became fast friends working on the farm. Ava was small but had a town square, and for some reason they made it one way, but they sure didn't have any traffic. In fact, it was quite sleepy. My dad didn't realize he was on a one-way street going the wrong way. Three or four guys were sitting on the porch in the front of a feed store and saw us going the wrong way. One of them waved us down and said, "You're going the wrong way but it don't make no difference." There wasn't another car in sight. It was a friendly little town. Their main claim to fame, according to the porch setters, was you couldn't spell their town name backwards.

Some of those trips were to buy a new Plymouth from the factory in Detroit for his taxi company. Picking up a Plymouth was strange because he drove Fords most of his life. He was interested in seeing everything, of course the cities, but even more the wonderful and beautiful parks, forests, and historic sights. Many of the trips followed the famous Route 66 from Chicago to Santa Monica. He took little side trips to show us the sights: the Grand Canyon, the Petrified Forest, Painted Desert, Boulder Dam, Santa Fe, and Las Vegas, we saw it all. He also made several trips around California. We visited Sequoia and Yosemite, Big Bear, saw the Golden Gate Bridge, and drove the famous California Coastal Highway One from San Francisco to Ventura.

We were on a trip camping in Death Valley when we heard over the car radio that Pearl Harbor had been attacked, and we had to rush back to our apartment in San Fernando. I did not know what it meant but realized it must be important. On one trip, returning from a visit to my Uncle Arlo and cousins in Vallejo, California, we turned off Highway 99 to see Yosemite. My father had a .22 rifle in the trunk, and my mother and he were discussing whether a rifle would be allowed in the national park, finally deciding that they would say nothing unless asked when we got to the gate. The park rangers didn't ask much in those days. I was still a little guy, and as we started to drive away I said, "What about the rifle"? Fortunately, my father had rolled his window up. He allowed the .22 would probably be okay. We even visited Tijuana Mexico as a side trip when we traveled to the zoo in San Diego.

Dad was always interested in seeing different parts of the country and meeting new people. While the opportunity was never right for him to travel the world he saw it through others. He especially enjoyed the *National Geographic* magazine, and he saved them all. His passion for travel was passed to me.

He did love cars and driving and was a very good mechanic. It seemed like he could fix anything. Even in later years he still changed his own oil and lubed the car—he wanted it done right. It was too bad he never had an exotic car. But he never had the money when he was young, and, second, I don't believe he would've allowed himself such a luxury later. He would not have considered it good value.

I never heard him use a cuss word or even criticize anyone. Hard to believe, maybe, but I never saw him lose his temper. He just seemed to accept things and didn't need to stir anyone's pot. Certainly, he had opinions, but didn't waste his time arguing. His generosity was appreciated by our family and his friends. He was always there to help. One time he loaned money to one of his taxi drivers to get back East to his wife and kids. I recall my mother saying, "You'll never see that money again," and my father replied, "I expect not, but it's not lost if it gets a family back together."

I remember another time, when an older gentleman, who still had young children, could not find a job. He was Mr. Williams and had white hair so even as a kid I knew he was old. My father was quite worried about him because he was so slow, and as a taxi driver you don't make money unless you make trips. The other drivers were younger, faster, and could make more trips. My father discreetly supplemented his income a bit. Guess what, old Mr. Williams improved and ended up learning the quickest and shortest routes to become the best driver of the bunch. And he never missed work. Another time, a Mexican acquaintance was trying to open a radio station, and no one would lend him the money needed. Dad stepped in and helped him out.

As part of the Greyhound business, my father was involved with the Bracero program. Mexican nationals would be brought up by bus from Tijuana, Mexico. Dad would meet the buses and direct them to the proper locations. That program worked very well in Ventura County. It was designed primarily to help the citrus and avocado farmers pick their fruit and get it to the packing houses. The local program was under the umbrella of Sun-Kissed Fruits, with the braceros being housed together in camps where they took meals and slept. The guys who came up from Tijuana were outstanding workers and absolutely no trouble in town. They wanted to work, make money, and get back to their families in Mexico. The work was on short contract times when the fruit was ripe, and many of them came year after year. My father got to know them well, and although he did not speak Spanish, he became their friend, and they trusted him. Proves you don't need to speak the same language to be friends.

Sounds crazy I know, but sometimes one would come in to send five dollars home by Western Union. I don't recall the exact cost, but it was around 75 cents to send the money order. My father had empathy for these guys and advised them to save money until they had $20, which cost the same amount to send as five dollars. That does not sound like much, but remember these workers were at the low end of the pay scale in the late 1940s and early '50s. In 1950, the minimum U.S wage was only 75 cents an hour. In 1955, I was paid 85 cents an hour working with other field hands. The braceros were paid by the amount of fruit picked, and I doubt it came up to minimum wage.

The one thing the married men really wanted to acquire was the old-style Singer sewing machines. They would not only run on electricity but could also be operated manually by a foot pedal. Many of the guys did not have electricity in their homes so this was a great gift for the wives and a genuine value to their family. At that time in the early 1950s, people were throwing the old Singers out or selling them as pre-antiques. My dad was always on the lookout for the Singers, and I was pledged to do the same. He let the braceros have them at whatever he had paid or for free if we got one at no cost. One week, I found two thrown away in alley trash. Some of them with stands were oversized luggage for Greyhound buses, but my dad was the agent and he loaded them up anyway.

My uncle John Sykes worked in the oil fields as a roughneck, and being from an Iowa farm I'm sure he was a hard worker. However, he was also a very hard drinker and seemed to get in lots of fights—his nose showed, as it went left and then right and then back again. He worked all over the California oilfields, but when he was in Santa Paula or cities close by, my father would go and get him out of jail for fighting or maybe just being drunk. Of course, this would always be in the middle of the night so I'm sure my father was not too happy about it, but I never heard him complain or criticize John. He was my mother's brother and family so that was the way it was.

I can't recall my dad ever verbally lecturing me or giving me fatherly advice about life and what I should do. He showed me how to do things like repair roofs, paint houses, etc., but he never formally counseled me about advancing in life. He passed on the values of working hard, honesty, being a good neighbor, saving money, and being respectful of others by his everyday actions. Neither do I ever remember him hugging me, but I certainly felt his love. Hugging was not so universal as today and certainly not in a reserved German farming family, between men. On the other hand, I don't recall him ever scolding me, either. Having said the above, he always supported me and whatever I did. He often volunteered to be our Boy Scout Troop driver, taking kids to camp and other adventures—we would have a whole carload. Additionally, he was the only driver for the Burro Men (four of us who owned three burros that we used for camping or on long hikes), pulling a horse trailer, dropping us off, and picking us up from trips in the backcountry of the Los Padres National Forest.

After graduating from high school, I wanted a new Ford truck for use in my yard-mowing business and I must admit just to own a brand-new vehicle. Of course, I didn't have the money to pay cash, so I needed to buy the car partly on credit. Being underage, someone had to sign for me. In those days a car loan was for 24 months, and the price tag on a Ford V-8 custom cab was $1,900. Remember how my father felt about debt and buying things only after you had the money. He signed and never lectured me, but I knew it hurt him to see me going into debt. By the way, it was paid off in 12 months. Late summer of 1958 I came back after three months of hitchhiking throughout Europe and was flat broke. Four of us, buddies from high school and Ventura Junior College, were contemplating moving on to Fresno State College to complete bachelor's degrees. I was penniless but knew I could easily get a job if I stayed in Santa Paula. There was a decision to be made, and my mother pushed for me to continue college. My father stepped in and said he would pay for me to go to Fresno State. That settled it; away I went on his dollar. You can laugh, but it was $900, one hundred each month for the nine months of school. Tuition in California State Schools at that time was just about nothing, so the hundred bucks covered books, the rent, and food.

I said my father never lost his temper, but I should have said except once. It is still crystal clear in my mind even though more than 70 years have gone by. The hit took place about the time I was in the sixth or seventh grade, in our kitchen when my dad, mom, and my little brother, Bob were eating at our small kitchen table. I was really mouthing off to my mother, and I guess Dad had enough—he reached over and gave me a flick with his open hand. It was a light glancing blow to my forehead, but I was shocked beyond belief. Really stunned, how could it be? I was being a brat and I knew it. "Don't talk to your mother like that." Nothing else was said, no lecturing, nor did he ever speak of it again. I was mortified and embarrassed—I think he was embarrassed, also.

In the end, my father did quite well in the economic side of life. He started on what you might say the other side of the tracks. Maybe not poverty, but pretty close. No one ever helped him financially. He worked hard in his businesses and also in small real-estate efforts, buying rental houses (where I was often found painting or working on roofs with him). Dad was too kindhearted to get really rich, but when he died, he left my mother very secure for the remaining 30 years of her life.

I told you he was a hard worker. What is amazing is he did that in less than great health. His health began to fail when working at Lockheed in 1943. He went to the doctor without results so my mother went with him the second time, and the doctor could not tell her what was wrong, but he told her that Dad would be in a wheelchair in less than three months. That really scared them, and they decided to go back to Iowa and maybe on to the Mayo Clinic. I can remember the trip but, of course, they did not tell me the reasons, and I was too young to realize my father was sick. They left me on the farm with my grandmother and grandfather Sykes while they went on to the University of Iowa Hospital in Ames.

It turned out the doctor in California did not recognize brucellosis, which comes from cows and can be debilitating with lifetime chronic fever, fatigue, and painful inflammation of the joints. Of course, my father had been around cows his whole life and milked them on the farm. The Iowa doctors diagnosed it immediately. He apparently had had the disease for years. I've read the apostle Paul was said to have contracted brucellosis on the island of Malta. I don't think my father ever fully recovered, but he never once complained. He lived a good productive life, and I believe he was quite content with his accomplishments, family, and good standing in the community. He was a man comfortable in his own skin. No one could have been a better father to me. I cannot measure up to his humanity.

Brother Bob

Robert Harold Behrens, my brother, was born in San Fernando, California, in 1944 when I was seven. Our family moved to Santa Paula in 1947. My bedroom in our first house at 1202 Richmond Road in Santa Paula was a teardrop trailer in our carport. Bob, whose childhood nickname was Robbie, slept in my parents' bedroom. When we moved to the hill at 802 Ojai Road, we shared a room. I remember Robbie just as a cute little towheaded kid. I was always gone working, in school, or off with my school buddies where little kids were not invited. The truth is they were to be avoided. I was in high school by the time he was in the third grade and gone to college before he started high school. As you can understand, we are much closer today than we were growing up. Bob did many of the things I did. He was a Boy Scout in Troop 301 and learned to target shoot under Mr. Marshall's coaching. He had the downtown paper route, and later, when he was bigger, a bicycle route. Being born to the same parents, he inherited and was exposed to the same good work ethics. He was always hustling and looking for other job opportunities. Bob was a year younger and smaller than most of his school mates until he had some growth spurts in his mid-teens. He was popular in school and did more school activities than I did. He even played trumpet in the school band. More importantly, he was smart and particularly good at math—still is.

He graduated at 17, and the tall, good-looking, blonde-headed kid was ready for the challenges of college. The University of California at Berkeley reviewed his application and accepted him as an engineering student. But after reviewing my father's financial records, they determined a scholarship could not be granted as my father made too much money. I believe it was somewhere between $8,000 and $10,000. The average yearly salary in 1962 was $4,291. I think part of it was that my father had no debt, not even a mortgage payment. And it is true my father and mother both worked diligently and did not spend money frivolously. They were savers and had just begun to accumulate some money.

Bob had made it a personal goal not to ask my parents, who certainly could have and would have, to pay for his college education—a goal he intended to keep. Somehow, he discovered the General Motors Institute (GMI), which accepted outstanding students for education in engineering. They had a unique program that did not offer scholarships but offered a five-year combination of education and work experience. Bob was a worker, so that sounded good to him. What is amazing is that at 17 he figured out how he could go to college without our parents paying for it. Acceptance to the program was highly competitive, but he made the grade.

He was off for Flint, Michigan, at age 17 and the beginning of his college education at GMI. The program was six weeks of class study and then six weeks of practical experience working in an assembly plant. His sponsor was the GM Chevrolet plant in Van Nuys, California. It was six weeks in Michigan studying and then six weeks in Southern California working. The work was not sitting behind a desk in a corner office with a view, it was working the line along with all the union employees and doing every job that goes on in a car manufacturing factory/ plant. He got lots of air miles before there were things like frequent flyer clubs. At the end of five years, he was awarded a degree in electrical engineering, but in addition to the normal 120 units required for an undergraduate degree, he had earned another 78 units, giving him a couple of years of extra credits. In the fifth year, the top 10% of the class was awarded pay when they were working normally, but they were also paid when they were attending classes, so his last year he was at full-time pay. I'll take that any day.

In 1967, after graduating, Bob stayed on at his sponsor plant in Van Nuys as a starting electrical engineer with beginning pay at $2.53 an hour. He said he felt like he was rich. Running full bore, the plant produced one car every 60 seconds 24 hours a day. As an electrical engineer, he did not work on cars. He worked on plant operations, the assembly lines, and the new robotics. When he started, Chevrolet had 25% of the total U.S. new car market. I visited him at the plant in Van Nuys to see how it worked and was amazed to find they didn't paint all the black cars and then all the blue cars and then a different color; cars came down the line and when they hit the paint booth, a computer was used to order whatever paint was programmed. He worked at the Van Nuys plant, with the exception of taking a graduate degree in business at the University of Michigan, until 1992 when GM realized the business climate in California was lacking and not likely to get better. Obviously, they had some far-sighted and accurate planners. The permit required for closure cost close to $50,000. Bob was irritated because the city provided zero services for that fee. There was a lot of money in plant infrastructure. As I recall, Bob told me the demolition cost was just a little less than a million with the demo company collecting all the salvage value at about $5 million. It took nearly two years to close the plant with the entire cleanup, which, after running assembly lines that produced a car every minute, was a boring time for him.

General Motors had acquired Hughes Electronics and asked Bob to become the General Motors liaison to Hughes, where he entered a completely different work sphere. He said their operation was more like scientists with their engineers wearing white coats. It was an interesting and educational time for him. In 1993 he was asked to come to Detroit and take on some major worldwide corporate projects. He became the Engineering Group Manager, Corporate Facilities Programs, Worldwide Facilities Group (WFG). His group was responsible for the life extension (maintenance) and/or replacement of major facility systems at all locations. The largest of these were roofing, paving, and HVAC (heating, ventilating, and air conditioning). My friend, Kinsey Robinson, president of the Roofers and Water Proofers of America, was astounded to learn Bob had over 200 million square feet of roofs in his program and double that in parking lots. His WFG programs became a base for standardizing GM systems worldwide. He retired from GM in 2003 with over 40 years of service.

Bob loves cars, and one of his perks was getting a new company car every two months. He loved the fast Camaros and Corvettes but had to take whatever new car they gave him—poor boy. He often kept a personal Camaro just to always have a fast, fun car to drive. To this day he is still buying Corvettes, which will certainly blow your wig off at 0 to 60 in three seconds and 0 to 100 in seven seconds. I was always proud of his academic achievements. He was on a level far beyond my reach. Combine high intelligence with a good work ethic and an amiable personality and you get a good employee. Raising a fine son and now enjoying grandchildren are his best rewards.

Bob was with me on a Kenya big-game hunting safari in 1973. Many years later he brought his son for Kenya photo safaris, and two years ago he brought his high-school sweetheart on a Kenya photo safari. He visited me in Texas when I was a company grade-officer and again just after I was promoted to major, when we floated the Rio Grande River in the spring of 1975. Col Tom Kelly, Maj Doug Forsythe, and Frank White joined us. Doug drove in from Kansas City, Missouri, on a Norton 850 CC motorcycle. We put in at Lajitas and took out three days later when we exited the beautiful Santa Elena Canyon with vertical walls as high as 1500 feet above the river.

Frank White brought along a fully automatic M-16 rifle so we had plenty of firepower for shooting at rocks. Our evening entertainment around the campfire was Col Kelly regaling us with some of his many stories gathered over a lifetime of adventures. We crossed over to the Mexican side whenever we saw anything interesting, and we may have even camped on that side one night, but it was a different time with friendlier borders.

It was a mighty fine trip. We were alone on the river and never saw another person during our float. Bob has also been with me in Argentina, visiting Patagonia. Those trips brought us closer together. He comes to Texas for a visit at least once a year, and we saw him two or three times a year in California when visiting our mother.

I had helped Mom manage her finances for many years after my father died, but once Bob retired and went back to Santa Clarita, California, to live, he took over that obligation and did a magnificent job. Most important of all was the understanding way he shepherded my mother in her senior years when she became a little frail and somewhat forgetful about things such as her meds. Cheryl Armstrong, Bob's longtime companion, was also quite helpful. Bob did the unenviable hard work of taking Mom's driver's license away when she was 92, not an easy task with my mother still very independent. His brilliant job of setting up Mother's affairs according to her wishes allowed her estate to be settled without a flaw or probate, another not-so-easy task in the state of California. I can't thank him enough for all his time, love, and care in our mother's last difficult weeks when her health failed. It is a debt that can never be repaid. He took a great deal of worry off my shoulders. I appreciate Bob not only as my brother but also as a friend. I hope that we can have more time together.

Bunker Club

It is strange how a small thing happens and then morphs into something bigger and often better. USA Shooting (USAS) is the national governing body of the United States Olympic and international shooting effort. I was newly elected to the board of governors and found USA Shooting in bad financial condition. Fund-raising was off, and our shotgun shooting ranges were in tatters. Our international trap machines, which were housed in what are called bunkers, were almost unusable. We could not conduct a respectable competition, nor could our athletes adequately train with the equipment on hand. The director (CEO) and shotgun coach were pleading for help. They needed new trap machines for the four bunkers, which required 15 traps each. Cost for each bunker was estimated at $55,000. Therefore, we needed $220,000. The board agreed we needed the new machines but simply could not accept the fiduciary responsibility.

  I was shooting bunker trap at the time, and I was acutely aware of the need. Not being very smart, I told the board that if they would approve the purchase of new traps, I would raise the money to pay the bill. The deal was that I would bring the money, but every penny would go into the fund for new machines. No one would get paid, and we would pay for no administrative or overhead costs. And no one, including me, would be reimbursed for any expenses. Of course, I wasn't sure how I was going to go about getting the money, but the board agreed.

  I returned home and told my wife we might be in bad trouble, and we better start looking to get a couple of extra credit cards. Two early accomplices in this venture were Dr. Steve Holtzclaw and Mr. Guy Avedisian. Both were bunker trap shooters and well aware of the urgent need for new equipment. With the $220,000 future debt hanging around my neck, we pressed on and hatched the plan to raise funds by soliciting contributions from other shooters. Our little group became known as the Bunker Club. We each put $3000 in the pot and enlisted others to join us. Lt Col Jack Horner had been a top shooter and the officer in charge of the Army shotgun team. He was also a referee for the International Shooting Union and witnessed competitions using trap machines from different countries. It turned out the Nasta machines manufactured in Finland were rated Number One. Guy Avedisian was dispatched to Finland with authority to contract for the needed machines. That was the easy part; now I had to get the money.

Long Shots — Family and Friends

A few good souls became members, but it takes a lot of $3000 bills to reach $220,000. Early on, a good shooting friend of mine, Albert Menefee, who was rather sideways with USA Shooting at that moment, called me, and said he was sending me, not USAS, $55,000. I told Albert if he sent me 55 grand that I would be off to Mexico. He relented and sent the check to USAS, which was a huge jump start, but we still needed $175,000. How do we get new members or raise money?

One very hot afternoon in February some of my hunting friends were with me in Argentina in a swimming pool (a converted stock tank), shooting passing doves, when Tom Held and Paul Facchina came up with the idea of holding a sporting clays match to raise funds. Having seen fund-raisers that cost more to run than the funds raised on more than one occasion, I was less than enthusiastic and didn't think it would work well enough for the effort required. Nevertheless, it was agreed that we do the match, and it was conducted at the Pintail Point Gun Club in Maryland. It turned out to be a bang-up success. Tom did some of the early coordination and arranged for the lunches. Paul brought members of his personal office staff to help run the match. We had 42 teams enter. I brought a team of Bunker Club members, and a second team of Bunker Club members was also assembled. Tom brought a team consisting of himself and his three sons. Mona Robinson brought a ladies' team, and my friends from the Prince George's Gun Club brought a team. Paul Facchina brought 37 teams! It was amazing. He just made them an offer they could not refuse. They were all subcontractors on the many projects Paul was working in Northern Virginia, D.C., and Maryland. His invitation was: send a check for this good cause, and if you want to send a team that's all right, also. I got one check from a paving contractor in California. His team did not show up. Some items were donated, and we held a live auction with Paul acting as auctioneer. It was fun to see him work the crowd. He took the bids and worked those bidding against each other. If one of the contractors was about to walk off with an item, Paul would call out one of the contractor's competitors and say, "Harry, are you going to let Joe beat you out?" And then sometimes he would tease them a little bit and say things like, "Mike, I saw you carry a whole suitcase full of money away from that last job, let's spread some of it around. It reminded me of the Godfather. We cleared over $80,000. Sometimes it's very nice to be wrong. We later made our goal, paid off the machines, and had a few bucks left over.

Several of us Bunker Club members were shooting clays in South Texas at the famous 74 Ranch. I brought up the matter of money remaining in the pot after the new bunker machines were paid off. My question was: "Do we say we've done our duty to God and country and pass the remaining money to the general USA Shooting fund, or should we continue the Bunker Club with the new mission of helping young shooters achieve their dream and maybe become Olympians?"

I'm pleased to say my friends agreed to a man and were enthusiastic about helping young shooters. Our program would be to build an athlete endowment to last in perpetuity. We would build a solid base of investments and spend only a portion of the earnings in order to preserve the endowment principle.

My next comment was, "Get out your checkbooks," and that meant me, also. I wanted some checks to carry with me so I could show a solid commitment of our plan to the USA Shooting Board of Directors. It was important for our program to be officially sanctioned and under the umbrella of USA Shooting. The same rules would apply: 100% of the money contributed would go into the endowment. USAS would cover administrative expenses. No one would get paid or be reimbursed, and the funds distributed could only go directly to individual athletes selected for grants. Our funds could not be used for training camps, clinics, or funding teams. We wanted to help those young deserving athletes not yet funded by USAS. While we started out with just a very small group of hunting friends, it blossomed into a much larger group who are dedicated to our mission of assisting aspiring and talented athletes develop their shooting skills to become high-level competitors and Olympians. Over 95% of the endowment contributions have come from my hunting and shooting friends. I like to tell people there are few places you can write one check that supports your personal interest, hunting and shooting, and also supports our flag and the USA Olympic team. We have 130 Bunker Club members, but many of them are wives, children, and grandchildren who have signed up with their own $3,000 checks. Our original dollar goal for the endowment was set at 1.5 million. After the market crash in 2008, it was apparent that 1.5 million would not be enough to ride out the ups and downs of the market and economy. Therefore, we jumped our goal to $3 million. I caught a lot of friendly flak and kidding from our members about raising the goal, but it was all in good fun, and they kept contributing.

While hunting pheasants in the Midwest with a friend, he said, "I'll help you with a stock." You guessed it – it was Berkshire Hathaway, Class A, worth more than $100,000. I was shocked and no doubt my jaw dropped open. In addition to the many wives signing up to be members, we have several father-and-son or father-daughter combinations. Two families have three generations as members: grandparents, sons and daughters, grandsons and granddaughters. Our project is really building a family legacy. Yay, yay, yay, we reached our goal of $3,000,000 in March 2021, and we had already given grants of $335,469 to more than 100 athletes in the previous five years. USA Shooting now has a permanent base of funds to encourage and support young developing athletes in their quest of joining an Olympic team. Three of the six Olympic medal winners in Tokyo received their first financial support from Bunker Club grants. We have paid out $100,000 in support of USAS in addition to building the $4,000,000 endowment. It has taken 28 years, but the result is worth the effort.

I'm the chairman, but Dr. Gene Bishop is the treasurer and the center fulcrum of the Athletes Endowment Committee for USA Shooting and the Bunker Club. His in-depth analysis and tracking of our finances have been essential to our success. He has been a huge help to me and is most appreciated. Other faithful committee members are: Captain Carl Kilhoffer, Mike Malarkey, Kinsey Robinson, and Butch Eller. Butch's son, Glen Eller, is an Olympic Gold Medal Holder. I was privileged to attend the Olympics when he won his gold.

I can't say enough about Bunker Club members. I didn't raise the money; my friends raised the money. They are nothing less than outstanding. They are not just generous, but dedicated and compassionate about helping young folks and our country. Good Samaritans, for certain. We do a rendezvous each year at a different location usually hosted by one of our members. We don't try to raise money or do raffles at these events. They are simply social and an opportunity to have fun together. It always involves some shotgun shooting, horseback riding, tennis, or other activities for the non-shooters. Many tight friendships have been formed at our gatherings by members who did not know each other before joining the Bunker Club. We have evolved into a real fellowship of friends and will continue together wherever our next challenge takes us.

Three years ago, our rendezvous was in Napa, California. The group surprised me with a plaque in recognition of my work for the athletes' endowment. And they worked with USA Shooting to change the name from Athletes Endowment to the Colonel D.D. Behrens Athletes Endowment. Wow, I was flabbergasted, really without words and most certainly humbled. I've been awarded decorations, commendations, citations, and trophies, won medals, and earned special recognition, but this one given by my peers is really something extra special. They are not simply hunting acquaintances; they are fine and true friends. A more generous and congenial group of fine people does not exist. I would put them up against any club. Space does not allow me to depict the quality of our 130 members, but there is a list of all our fine folks in the appendix.

My Boys, My Guys, My Kids

First, I must explain that none of the individuals in this group were mine, they weren't boys, and only a couple could have been described as kids. I use those descriptions merely as terms of endearment. They were, of course, much younger than I by a bunch. I was older than their fathers and closer to their grandfathers. All the young men described wormed their way into my heart one way or another, although I doubt they realized it at the time. To fit into this group, they had to come into my world when they were in their teens or early 20s, just starting out in their adult life's journey, before they were married and had families of their own. In my mind's eye, I still see them as young, eager guys

Long Shots — Family and Friends

beginning life's adventures. Most of them came to me through the military. I tried to boost them on their journey as their coach, boss, supervisor, or maybe just a friend.

Mentoring from me was accomplished more by my actions than verbal dissertations. Perhaps I could be described as an encourager. Some had their ears pulled, but they knew it was never personal. Let me be clear: all of them were good young men and for the most part came from good parents. I made it a point to meet their parents. I am certainly not a muse, and I wouldn't call these young guys protégés. In most cases I was their boss in the beginning, but later our connection became more avuncular. I certainly felt like they were my nephews or maybe closer. It may be presumptuous of me, but I hope I helped them become better men, and maybe move beyond their own visions. I got to know them well. They all had handsome abilities and have become successes in life.

I described three of my guys, Jim Gregory, Chad Senior, and Scott Christie in my recounting of Modern Pentathlon. Another three young men in our brotherhood, Luciano Fontana, Lucas Buxton, and Isaias Miciu, are included in my chapter on Argentina. Gordie White might be a little embarrassed to find that I included him with my kids. We first came together when he was in his early 20s, and he fits in this group. His many attributes are described in my story of Expedition Adventures. Let me tell you about some others.

Casey Mahon was a 19-year-old Airman Second Class who worked for Loretta as an admin assistant in a Security Police Squadron. Loretta felt he had a lot more potential and asked me to take him in my unit. It was apparent the Air Force was the first time he had ever been away from home. Nevertheless, I arranged for his transfer and put him in my orderly room where he might learn something. I didn't pay a lot of attention to him at first as he was working for a good supervisor, but one day my First Sergeant told me Casey's parents were coming to visit and that Casey had paid for the airline tickets. How does an Airman Second Class save enough money for two airline tickets from the States to Europe? Paying for his parents to come visit Germany sent a clear message to me that he was a pretty good kid. I had his folks in my office for coffee and a croissant and told them what a fine job he was doing for the Air Force. He told me the impetus of joining the service came when he was on a job digging a ditch with his brother and father. That's when he decided he wanted something better. Loretta and I both encouraged Casey, without much success, to get more education. Loretta moved up to an assignment under a three-star German general and had a much better job for Casey than my orderly room offered.

Somehow, she seemed to think she had finder's rights and stole him back from me. He married Karen, a schoolteacher at Ramstein AFB, who got his attention about a college degree. It was a privilege to write a letter of recommendation to the USAF ROTC Selection Board on 30 June 1982 recommending him for duty. Casey graduated from ROTC at Texas State University in San Marcos. I was honored to give the commencement speech and to pin second lieutenant bars on him. You may have seen him on TV: he was the young black-haired kid in fatigues who handed the microphone to reporters when they were recognized by General H. Norman Schwarzkopf at his televised news briefings during the first Gulf War. Casey completed his Air Force career with more than 10 years as an officer and retired as a captain. I'm pleased to say that in his retirement speech he said, "Everyone needs a Major Behrens; he saw something in me that I didn't." You can't get a better compliment. But that's not the end of the story. He went on with a second career in communications as an executive director at a medical center, and then at public schools and community college. He and his wife raised two sons. One, Ryan, is now proudly serving as a lieutenant in the Air Force. The other son, Erik, earned a Ph.D. and is teaching. Casey hasn't quit working, but he has moved on, and is now doing volunteer work by helping needy veterans and in other worthy civic services.

John Linn came to my attention when he was still a young teenager following his father around at shooting matches. I recall watching John shoot in a bunker trap competition at the Quantico Marine Corps Range. He missed one bird on his first shot, and on his second shot a very strong wind gust dropped the bird at least three feet. He missed again, and the bird was lost, which cost him a medal. After the trophies were passed out, I told John I saw the bird he missed. It was too bad the freak gust of wind had cost his lost bird. His answer was, "Yes, I should have hit the bird on the first shot." You

Long Shots — Family and Friends

do or you don't. No crying, excusing, or explaining. I knew he was my kind of kid.

His father, also named John Linn, was a famous basketball coach at George Mason University, and there is even a gym named after him. John the senior had retired from basketball but headed up the George Mason College shooting team, which in those days won not only first place but often second place at the collegiate national championships. They had a great team, and John the junior eventually became team captain, not because his dad was the coach, but because he had good leadership skills even as a young college student. When John graduated, he took a job with the Northern Virginia Regional Parks in managing county parks. I knew his father, who had been a captain in the Army. I told him his son had far too much leadership ability to waste working at a park. John Sr. asked me to talk with John Jr., which I did. It took some doing, but he managed to be accepted for Air Force Officer Training School. The rest is history. I was delighted to have him on the Air Force Bunker Trap Team for many years. He retired from the Air Force as a full colonel after a distinguished career and four combat assignments in the Gulf, Iraq, and Afghanistan, where he was awarded three Bronze Stars. John is a leader, no need to pat himself on the back. His actions speak for themselves. The following are two unsolicited stories told to me by his subordinates. I never told him and don't believe John knows the stories were ever shared with me.

One was from a SMSgt who was sharing a tent with John in Iraq. He told me it was hot. The tent was stifling, and you couldn't get a cold drink of anything. Using NCO ingenuity, he managed to appropriate a mini refrigerator and had it hooked up to a generator. He was going to surprise Maj John Linn, his boss, and the unit commander. When Major Linn was presented with this prize he asked, "Did you get one for everyone?" Of course, the answer was no. Maj Linn said, "Take it out, we're not going to have something better than our troops."

An airman who was in John's squadron told me she was scheduled to be put out of the Air Force because she couldn't make the weight standards. She said Maj Linn told her if she would meet him every morning at the gym at 5:00 a.m., he would help her get her

595

weight to meet the standards. She did and credits him with saving her Air Force career.

He and his lovely wife Michelle have faced momentous challenges and heartbreak but are the strongest couple I know. Loretta and I love them both. Michelle made GS15 before John made colonel, so she ranks him. After military retirement John reverted to his earlier days working at a park and is now the Chief Ranger for the Comanche Grasslands. No doubt several Rangers who now work for him wondered how an outsider who had never been in the forest service could be selected as Chief Ranger. I'm sure that question was answered by his leadership when they found what a class act he is. John is an excellent trap competitor, but I believe an even better shot in the field after game birds. I've had the pleasure of hunting with him and his ugly Drahthaars for many years in Idaho, Oregon, New Mexico, Texas, South Dakota, Colorado, and Oklahoma. We have also hunted many times together in Argentina and have shot birds in Spain. John was still a lieutenant when his father died, and I suppose that pushed me closer to him. Our connection is unbreakable. There simply is no better company.

Dominic Grazioli, "Graz," was straight out of the Air Force Academy when he came to shoot on the Air Force Bunker Trap team. I was able to steer his assignments to keep him in locations where he could continue his shooting. While he was assigned at Bolling Air Force Base in Washington, D.C., Loretta got him assigned to her, helping with Randolph Hearst's Senate Youth Program. She told me how helpful he was, particularly one year when a wheelchair-bound student required extra care. He is solid and dependable. Graz was charming with the ladies, and when I sent him to a bunker competition early to pick up a rental car for the team you can bet it was always an upgrade, usually a Cadillac. I don't know if it was 1st Lt Graz or 2d Lt John Linn who had the car keys (always suspect the gold bar), but they had a Cadillac rental car on the Prado Olympic shooting range in Southern California. Somehow the gates to the club got locked with them still inside the fence. Worse yet, the car was running with keys in the ignition, all four doors locked, and no one inside the car. They were obviously in bad need of a good NCO.

Graz was deadly serious about bunker shooting and worked hard at it. He moved from active duty to the reserves but kept up his shooting to become an Olympian in the Beijing Olympics. He was the most winning World Cup bunker trap shooter to ever represent the Air Force. His record will never be broken. He retired from the reserves as a lieutenant colonel, and I was pleased to speak at his retirement ceremony. Graz was very generous. One occasion I particularly recall was on a high-volume dove hunt in Argentina. I took several of my guys on this trip and a young shooter who was new to "my boys." The young shooter did not have the money for shells to keep up with the others in the high-volume shooting. Graz stepped in and picked up the slack, most generously since he hardly knew the kid. He is a strong family man and became Mr. Mom for his kids. He married a real standout, Tina, who is chief of human resources for HEB. Both their children are now in college.

The only guy who was already married to be included in "my guys" was Mike Herman. He came into the Air Force after he was laid off from his job working in a coal mine. He claims they drove into town and saw a sign that said the Air Force needs you. With his wife Jamie's encouragement, he signed up. As an airman, a one striper, he came over to try out for Bunker Trap. Mike had shot American trap before joining the Air Force and soon worked his way onto the Air Force Bunker Trap Team. He had the drive, was ambitious, and showed leadership skills. It was obvious he had qualities to be an officer, and I encouraged him to get a college education. I told him if he earned a college degree that I would get him into officer training school (OTS). Maybe more important was that Jamie fully supported him in this endeavor. It took him seven years, but he earned that college degree. Be warned, making long-range promises to people is fraught with danger.

He applied for OTS and was turned down. He was a Staff Sergeant, and Air Force regulations required enlisted candidates for OTS who had served seven years to be Technical Sergeants. Instead of studying for promotion, he spent his time studying college courses and in his Air Force specialty it took seven years to make TSgt anyway. What a stupid rule—one size does not fit all. I found myself in a bind. I had promised him, and now I had to make it happen and went in for

597

a waiver. It was turned down, which got me hot under the collar. How could the yo-yo-headed bureaucrats turn me down? Obviously, they had given his case only a cursory review. A third and broader analysis discovered a much more favorable disposition. Then, guess what? He couldn't pass the officer physical. You have to be kidding me! He was already in the Air Force, but he had to take another physical for OTS. He couldn't pass because his hearing had deteriorated. And why was that? Because of all the shooting. I thought, "Is this a never-ending struggle?" I knew the only way to get this settled successfully was to go to the very top, Lt Gen Murphy A. Chesney, the Surgeon General of the Air Force. I had met the general before, but didn't have any real personal connection. We met in his office on Bolling Air Force Base where he took medical appointments one day every week. He was gracious and invited me to sit down. I explained the problem and stressed what a great troop Mike was. I told him what a monumental injustice the Air Force was inflicting on this poor young airman with a wife and three children. How he'd worked his tail off for his dream to become an officer only to find out he could serve our country as an enlisted man with less-than-perfect hearing but not serve as an Air Force officer. It occurred to me this would not be a suitable time to mention any other required waivers, so I stuck strictly to the medical dilemma. Gen Chesney listened intently, cracked what appeared to be a very slight smile, and said, "Get the 'expletive' out of my office. Your tears are ruining my shoeshine." Mission accomplished, I exited quickly.

  Thirteen years later, Mike retired from the Air Force as a major. And again, that's not the end of the story. He owns Shoot the Moon, a company specializing in shooting paraphernalia, particularly shooting vests, which are all custom-made to fit the individual shooter. They are in high demand by college teams and our Olympic athletes. Mike became active in American trap shooting and worked his way up the ladder to become President of the Amateur Trap Shooting Association (ATA). That is a big deal. They have 75,000 members, and Mike held the position during the pandemic of 2020. They lost the use of their normal range that year, and he had to work with politicians, including the governor of Missouri, to arrange a location for the ATA National

Championship. His efforts were rewarded, and the match with over 1,800 contestants was a success without any major hitches. ATA was indeed fortunate to have him as president during such a critical time. He and Jamie raised three kids who are all successful. One is a warrant officer in the Army reserves flying helicopters. Another is a nurse studying to be a nurse practitioner, and his daughter is learning her way in the retail business world. From coal miner, to airman, to major, to a successful business owner. A very good climb, I would say. A long shot, for sure.

Zane Kuenzler was 16 years old when we met but could have passed for 19 or 20. He was a big kid with a goatee and a solid handshake. I was shooting in the U.S. Bunker Trap Championship in Colorado Springs, and he was one of the competitors. I hadn't paid any attention to him, but Mike Herman came to me and said, "This kid is driving back and forth every day from Denver, an hour and half drive each way, where he's staying with an aunt." Mike, knowing what a pigeon I am for helping young shooters, wondered if I couldn't help him out.

He was driving what looked like an old ranch pickup so I figured he could use some help. I was staying in VIP quarters at the Fort Carson Army post adjacent to the shooting range. My quarters were a large two-bedroom, two-bath, kitchen, and combination dining/living room. Dr. Steve Holtzclaw was staying with me, and his bedroom had two beds so I told Mike, "Sure, the kid can stay with us."

A cocksure kid, but he was a little hesitant, probably thinking it would be like an Army or Marine Corps barracks he had seen in the movies. The VIP quarters obviously surprised him. He turned out to be the right kid. I liked him and found out that he had won the high junior award at the American Trap Shooting Championship in Vandalia, Ohio. I invited him to an annual antelope hunt with my friends, who were more than three times his age, but he fit in well and became a permanent member of that hunt. We became friends, and I met his parents, followed his progress through college at the Colorado School of Mines, where he played on the school baseball team, and through his early days with ConocoPhillips, where he was one of the fair-haired boys. He was a drilling engineer at age 23 and ran a drilling rig at 27 years old—a young pup in the eyes of many in the oil patch, but Zane has always been able to handle about anything. He left ConocoPhillips to become an entrepreneur. He wanted to be his own boss and now spends his time searching for oil and minerals. When he started his company, he needed a board of directors, so my name was put to paper. Only smoke and mirrors, of course. I went to his outdoor wedding in New Mexico and nearly froze to death, but he and his beautiful bride, Heidi, were radiant and not bothered by the cold. He has been on several hunts with me in the States, and I took him to Argentina for his college graduation gift. Since then, he has been with me several times, and in May of 2022 we hunted quail together in Patagonia.

Zane is a marvelous shot in trap competition or with his 20-gauge Model 21 Winchester used for shooting sporting clays and hunting. He is a southpaw but seems to be able to shoot any gun he picks up. His trap guns were made for right-handed shooters but his Model 21 was factory-made with a cast-on stock and he shoots it like gang busters. He generally outshoots everyone. He has two young boys who are both athletes and who will probably outshoot him soon. He is a veritable entrepreneur and just closed a major project involving two states, city and county governments, and numerous private landowners in the development and sale of a major gravel pit. Some thought it couldn't be done. He knows how to work with people to bring satisfactory solutions to difficult challenges.

It was a cloudy, ugly day with rain spitting on and off. I was trying to test a new shotgun at the Prince Georges Gun Club in Maryland. There was only one skeet field open that afternoon and only one person shooting. He was a big kid and why he was shooting in the rain was beyond me. Never mind that, I also wanted to shoot, but only to try out a gun. We were on a public range so I could have stepped up and shot with the kid any time I wanted. I preferred not to shoot with someone I didn't know, especially someone obviously too stupid to get out of the rain. He finished a round of skeet, and I thought, Good, I can get on the field and quickly shoot. This was important because at that time in the afternoon, I could get back to my apartment in Alexandria in 30 minutes. A half hour later in the day it would take me 45 minutes, and an hour later in the rush hour it would take an hour and half to two hours for the same trip. I just wanted this kid to get off the range. To keep dry, I sat in my Tahoe and waited for him to finish. But then he went to station one and started another round. After he finished that one, it was apparent he was going to shoot another round. Gad, is this dumb head never going to stop?

Finally, I was forced to go out and shoot with him. He introduced himself as Derek Hotchkiss. I was putting my gun away in my Tahoe after shooting when he walked by me to his car. He noticed a small eagle on my windshield that signified I was a colonel. He said, "Sir, are you a Navy Captain?" I told him I was a retired Air Force Col. Then he blurted out, "I'm a midshipman at the Naval Academy."

Derek was in civilian clothes in the middle of the week, shooting sporting clays at a civilian club. Fortunately, I had mellowed a bit from my active-duty military days, and I didn't say what I was thinking: What the hell are you doing in the middle of the week out of uniform away from your duty station playing with shotguns? It turns out he hurt his back playing on the Navy football team and was going for therapy at the Bethesda Naval Hospital. He still should have been in uniform, but I figured if this kid was smart enough to get in a little shooting it was a good thing. I invited him to shoot with me again.

He got out of the Academy on Saturday afternoon and didn't have to be back till Sunday, so he was soon spending Saturday night with my wife and me in Alexandria. I'm not sure if he liked me that much or just came over because he knew I'd take him down for dinner on King Street. He met my friends and shot with Best Guns on the Eastern Shore. I introduced him to John and Denise Freitag, who also adopted him. They had a perfect place for hunting on the Eastern Shore, not far from the Naval Academy. That ugly rainy afternoon started a fine friendship. I met his family and attended his graduation after which he gave me his first salute as an officer, which is quite an honor and includes a silver dollar. I still have that silver dollar. I was pleased to attend his wedding held at the Naval Academy chapel to Jennifer, a wonderful, supportive wife. They now have three kids, one starting college this year. Amazing how time flies. He retired from the Navy right at 20 years as a Commander (equivalent rank to Lt Col in the Army or Air Force).

I'm confident he would've been selected for captain (colonel in the other services) and could very well have gone on to admiral. He had all the bona fides: Academy graduate, played on the Academy football team, a part of the Blue Angels team, two tours on carriers in the Gulf, and working in the Pentagon on the JCS Senior Staff. Plus, he has a pleasing and open personality. He retired in large part because of his family, to keep his kids from having to skip around at different schools. I was honored to be one of two speakers at his retirement ceremony. The other speaker was Rear Admiral Duke Heinz. He spoke first and I wanted to kill him. The admiral was a longtime friend and knew Derek very well. His speech was absolutely elegant. I thought, "This guy should be in DOD public affairs." There was simply no way anyone could have followed his performance. I had to immediately regroup and rather than pile praise on Derek, I gave him a mild roasting. Then I presented him with the Defense Superior Service Medal, which is higher in precedence than the Legion of Merit. That happens to be my highest decoration as a colonel after 30 years' service. It is almost unheard of for a Navy commander to receive such a high award. It attests to his outstanding abilities, dedication, and achievements. He is a take charge and get it done guy. I was hardly surprised when Jeff Bezos hired him at Amazon after outbidding Schultz at Starbucks. At last count, Derek was responsible for over 10,000 employees at Amazon. He has now moved on to Abercrombie and Fitch as a group vice president to direct their worldwide supply and distribution system. As a graduation gift from the Naval Academy, I took him to Argentina, and he has been there two more times with me, one as his retirement gift. We have had several hunts in the States together, and he is always favored company. I'm looking forward to many more hunts together.

A bit of a hybrid, but who also belongs in this group is Steve Holtzclaw. I met him at a bunker trap competition when he was still in college. By the time we started shooting, he was in medical school, but he fit in well with my Air Force shooters, particularly John Linn, Dominic Grazioli, and Mike Herman. He became a part of our group and hung out at matches with us. He and I became fast friends and often roomed together at civilian bunker trap competitions. Dr. Steve also came with me as team doctor when I was Chief of Mission for USA Shooting Team at the 1995 World Championship in Cyprus. On that trip we were run off the road by a bus, which caused us to hit an embankment hard enough tear off a wheel. It's hard to find a good chauffeur.

He was with me again in 1996 when I was leader of the U.S. Shooting Team at the World Championship in Lima, Peru. That was an interesting trip. We went a few days early to visit Machu Picchu. The first stop was Cuzco with an elevation of nearly 12,000 feet where we were taking a city tour when Steve got sick and puked. Fortunately, he'd stepped to the gutter, but he was not looking good. We called a taxi and sent him back to the hotel and I continued with the tour. When I returned to the hotel, I found him in bed, and he said he needed oxygen, which scared me. I thought, He's supposed to be my doctor, taking care of me and, of course, the team. But here he is in bed and calling for oxygen. I scurried down to the front desk, thinking I needed to call 911. The manager was at the counter, and I told him I needed some oxygen fast. He just reached under the counter and started setting small oxygen bottles with face masks attached on the counter. "How many do you want?" he asked.

I was relieved and said one would be enough, then I rushed back to our room. Steve was looking better after 10 minutes on oxygen and asked me if I wanted to try it, which I did. It was quite pleasant. On that trip, the team was staying at the Sheraton Hotel in Lima. Kim Rhode, who later became famous for earning medals in six consecutive Olympics, was on our junior team. She was staying a couple of floors below us and fell out of bed and cut her head, which produced a lot of blood and left a tiny scar. The hotel called the local paramedics, who rushed to her room. Fortunately, Dr. Holtzclaw intercepted them at Kim's doorway, or we would've had Kim in a local hospital.

Steve went with me several times to the World Military Championships for Modern Pentathlon. He was immensely helpful as another adult in the room but also as a doctor. Athletes get beat up and hurt in those pentathlon competitions. They got to really know Steve. They would tell him things they were afraid to tell me. Armed Forces Sports was paying for the transportation and expenses on those trips and always wanted to send military doctors. I'm sure they would've been good, but the athletes knew and trusted Steve, and I threatened the bureaucrats enough that they gave in and published orders for me to take my civilian doctor. He was not only popular with our guys, but athletes from all the other countries would also come to us for medical attention. Steve carried all kind of drugs and fluids with him to cover most anything. He is absolutely unflappable, a perfect attribute for an emergency doctor.

Steve was not a hunter but did come with me on a bird shooting trip to Argentina. He and his bride, Laurie, went on a bird shooting and photo safari in Kenya for their honeymoon. They repeated that same trip with me 20 years later, bringing their son Daniel and daughter Maria. Both are now in college. Daniel was a rower—both sculling and sweeping. He is a handsome lad, 5-foot 11inches of tightly packed muscles. Steve graduated as a top student at Johns Hopkins and then came to San Antonio to work as an emergency room doctor in the Baptist Hospital and became the medical director of their Airlife unit. He lived with us for the first three months until he got settled in. He moved on from the Baptist Hospital to Team Health where he became president of hospital-based services with supervision responsibilities for over 500 emergency rooms. He is now CEO of Alteon Health, one of the largest physician-owned and physician-led medical groups in the United States. He still teaches emergency medicine at Johns Hopkins at least one weekend a month.

For fun, he loves to fly airplanes. First, it was just small single-engine, then he was certified for dual engine, and finally he got a license for multiengine aircraft, learning to fly the Boeing 737. That certification, he told me, took a couple of months of very hard work, and only half the class earned a license. He also holds a jet license for the Russian L-39 light attack fighter jet. When he lived with us, I didn't need to call an electrician or a plumber. He is a licensed electrician and can also fix any plumbing, which he most graciously demonstrated by working on my historic (OLD) home. He is also a good carpenter.

The rest of the story is at his beginning. He graduated from high school but only in the bottom half of his class and then went on to trade school. One would think him unlikely to become the successful

CEO of a major corporation. He first became a licensed electrician but started moonlighting at a hospital on their paramedical ambulance staff while also taking courses at a junior college. What a long shot he was! Steve is multitalented, smart, congenial, and skilled in many fields, with good common sense. He is just super company and we've had some wonderful times together. Those fun times together continued as he and his wife joined Loretta and me in Patagonia in May of 2022.

Mark Taishoff is included in this group of my boys. My best American hunting friend from Germany, Maj Charlie Weaver, learned I was escaping the Pentagon and going to Germany for a couple of weeks of pheasant hunting. He asked me to take a Lt Taishoff, who was now stationed in Germany, hunting with me. I wasn't keen on this, first because I didn't know the lieutenant, and second because I was a guest and would be bringing an uninvited guest with me. However, I don't turn down friends and Charlie was the best, so I chased Mark down and took him with me on a marvelous pheasant hunt near the Danube River. Then we followed up with a visit to my friend René Haillez for another outstanding pheasant hunt in Belgium. Charlie picked the right guy. Mark just beams when he picks up a shotgun. I don't know anyone who enjoys hunting as much as Mark. It's not just enjoyment, it's satisfaction. He's an excellent woodsman, and although we had many wonderful hunts in the States, I must tell you he took me on the best float trip of my life in Alaska.

That trip was a seven-day float, fly fishing for silver salmon and hunting black bear. We used his small self-bailing raft. Mark had all the gear, food, fly rods, guns, and equipment for the trip. We would be in dangerous bear country competing for the same salmon, so Mark was carrying a stainless steel .44 Magnum revolver. He had a .357 Smith & Wesson for me, but I knew he had a parkerized short-barreled Remington 870 pump shotgun, and I told him I'd carry that on a sling. He brought a .338 Winchester Magnum stainless steel rifle with a synthetic stock for the black bear hunting. I had used Alaska Bush Carrier for the fly-in on previous hunts and liked the owner. We were using him again. We had all our gear loaded into one of his Beaver float planes when the owner told me he couldn't make the trip with us. Instead, his 19-year-old son, who was a superb pilot, would fly us to the lake, which was the headwaters of the Talachulitna River. I'd seen debris of too many bush pilot wrecks to be happy flying with a 19-year-old, but we weren't going over any major mountains and it was a good weather day. The flight was uneventful, and we landed on the lake. The kid said he saw something coming in, but he thought it was just a moose. We unloaded our gear on the only sandbar on the lake. The shore was covered in brush right up to the water. There was a sandbar because a tiny little stream emptied into the lake at that point, and salmon were migrating up that little stream. Our gear lay all over the sandbar as we pumped air into the little raft.

We were busying ourselves with the hand pump when I looked up, and there in a slight ditch was a large grizzly bear not 10 yards from us. It stood on its hind legs to get a better view of us. Holy Toledo! We were backed up directly to the lake, not five yards behind us and it was deep. A bear 10 yards from you is already past the danger zone. I grabbed up the 870 that had a little sock-type shell holder on the stock from which I snatched a 12-gauge slug and slammed it into the chamber. As I was doing that, I was quickly saying to Mark, "Get The Rifle, Get The Rifle, Get The Rifle." I had the bear covered, but with only one round in the chamber and none in the magazine; my comfort level was rather low. Mark finally found ammo, got his rifle loaded, and also covered the bear. I wasn't about to lower the shotgun until Mark had him covered with a rifle.

Finally, the bear went back to all four feet and ambled away. And we both gave a sigh of relief. Thoughts raced through my mind: Just how stupid could we be? We are on a sandbar next to a tiny stream full of migrating salmon in bear country and were fooling around with our gear before getting our guns ready for any possible contingencies? I could just picture the Anchorage newspaper headlines: "Two Cheechakos present themselves on a beach as part of a surf and turf lunch for a grizzly bear." We had both hunted Alaska before and knew better. Complacency is not successful in Alaska. Mark hunted with me in Africa, Argentina, Germany, Belgium, and Mexico. In the U.S. he hunted with me in California, Arizona, Idaho, Oregon, Montana, Maryland, Virginia, Wyoming, Texas, and Georgia. We had wonderful hunts together, but I believe our most enjoyable were in the rugged Owyhee area of Eastern Oregon, hunting chukars with my cousins.

Loretta retired from the Pentagon in January of 2000, and we returned to San Antonio. Many of my boys, kids, and guys were well on the way doing whatever they did—shooting, pentathlon, marriage, and kids. I was still in touch with them as I am pleased to be today, but they were all blossoming out. Now and then I'm even flattered by being asked my opinion or advice, but we don't have daily or even weekly contact. Then along came Max Jungk, who brought me out of my funk of not having the young guys around.

It was a chance meeting. Jon Hess, who was involved with Modern Pentathlon, called me and asked if I would give some money to a German kid who didn't have a green card and couldn't get a job. The boy had been in junior pentathlon and was living with Jon. I said, "Heck no. I'm not going to give a kid money, but he can come over and work for me." I didn't really have much work at the house, but Germans had been very good to me in my assignments in Germany, so I thought I owed them a little payback. This blonde-headed German kid came bouncing over with the exuberance of youth and we worked in the yard. Loretta made some sandwiches for lunch, so I invited Max into the house, and he was quite interested in my African trophies and the European trophies that were mostly from Germany and displayed in the kitchen. He didn't know anything about shotgun shooting but wanted to learn and was a good student. He had excellent hand/eye coordination and listened when I gave him instruction. I only let him shoot one box of shells a week on the skeet range, which kept him hungry for more. It was my gun, my shells, and I was paying for the rounds so I made the rules. He became competent in skeet after about six boxes of shells, and it took him less time to become proficient in trap shooting.

He wanted to learn to fish so I started him on casting with a fly rod in my yard. We had an Orvis store, as best I recall, on the north side of San Antonio. Maybe they just had Orvis equipment, but in any case, they had a young man in the store who gave fly rod casting lessons, and, of course, by the time Max finished the first lesson, he could double haul and outcast me. I had the young guide take us on a couple of afternoon float trips for fly fishing, and Max can now get by rather well with a fly rod.

Max came to my house to read books I selected for him, and he really read them. I would give him a little test to see if he picked up important points. In Robert Ruark's *The Old Man and the Boy*, I asked, "When did the hunt end?" Answer: When the boy took the safety off before the flush. "What was the one item the 300 Spartans at Thermopylae could never be without?" Answer: Their shields. He was a good student. Max figured out how he could get things done and picked up a driver's license when he was traveling through Alabama with the school group he had joined from Germany. In San Antonio, he acquired a Volkswagen, but it didn't work in reverse gear so he had to be careful to always park where he could pull straight out. I started taking him around with me and let him drive my Blazer. He had to drive with both hands on the wheel, but otherwise I had no rules, except I made it clear he had to pay the ticket if he got one.

Max wasn't on an organized student exchange program and was pretty much on his own. Through the pentathlon community he had found Jon Hess, a bachelor real estate agent who drove a new Jaguar and lived in a mini mansion in Olmos Park. That allowed him to go to school in Alamo Heights, which is considered to be the best school district in the San Antonio area. He started as a sophomore but was far ahead of the class, so they moved him into the junior class. Finally, he was moved to the senior class. Here was a 16-year-old, with English as a second language, competing with older kids whose parents were doctors and lawyers who stressed education. I stressed education also and made him a deal: If he graduated as an honor student (top 10%), I'd take him on a fly-fishing trip to Montana. You guessed it, he graduated in the top 10%, but then we had some scheduling problems. He couldn't go, and then I went to Africa for two months. Max went back to Germany, where they wouldn't accept his high-school diploma and made him do a final year in Germany.

I went to Germany for a modern pentathlon championship and scheduled time to meet Max's parents. They were gracious enough to take me to dinner, but I'm not sure how happy they were to see me. At that time, German boys were required to spend a year in the military or to take another approved public service job after high school, and I was lobbying for Max to go into the military and become a part of the German military sports program. I knew the German military sports leaders and was certain Max would be an excellent addition to their program. Max loves little kids and is very good with them. In fact, he has a daughter now, and I think he is also godfather to two or three of his friends' kids—he and his wife have twins on the way. In any case, he elected to take a 13-month community commitment at a Catholic orphanage in Nicaragua.

I still owed him a fishing trip in Montana, but we changed that to meeting at the Belize River Lodge. I flew to Belize, and he took a bus from Nicaragua. It was a fun time catching barracuda with hardware and then fishing for bonefish with fly rods. It was in Belize that I made another deal and told him if he could get a master's degree, I would reinstate the Montana trip. He got a Master's in Physics, and we turned the Montana trip into a 30-day road trip, meeting my friends for hunting and fishing. It was so much fun we did it again two years later, and then did a couple repeats of shorter duration. It was those trips that woke up whatever gene it is that hunters carry. He caught the thrill of the chase, and it sparked his passion for hunting.

Obviously, I became very fond of Max. We think alike and he could nearly read my mind and finish my sentences. We just seemed to be on the same wavelength, which is rather strange considering our mismatched ages. Maybe we shared some intuitive power with each other. Sometimes, just a look would convey a meaning or understanding. Max didn't have a very high opinion of German hunters and didn't understand their traditions. Additionally, hunters had killed his cat as they do with all feral cats found in the wild. We made a 10-day trip in Germany together to meet my German hunting friends. Not long after that, Max earned a German hunting license, which is no small thing and takes considerable study, including practical shooting. Some might accuse me of creating a hunting monster. I'm pleased to say he may get in more hunting time than I do. For his birthday in 2017 I took him on a red stag hunt in Austria. In 2019, for another birthday we did a mini road trip for a chamois hunt that took us from Germany to Austria, Slovenia, Croatia, Serbia, and Bosnia. I wanted to visit Sarajevo where the Archduke Franz Ferdinand was assassinated by Gavrilo Princip (using an FN Browning Model 1910 pistol), igniting World War I. We hunted together in November 2021 in Germany and France. We hunted boar, fallow deer, and ducks in Germany. In France we shot pheasants and partridge. Max engineered an invitation for me to shoot at the very prestigious flighted duck hunt hosted by Baron Martin von Jenisch. It was a traditional German hunt with drinks and snacks mid-hunt, and after the evening hunt, dinner with the Baron was most enjoyable.

Max tested and was interviewed by McKenzie Consulting. He turned down their offer and went to work for the Boston Consulting Group. Max completed a Ph.D. program in engineering. His dissertation was judged the best, winning him a 3,000 Euro award. He moved to Nordex, where he was the project officer leading 200 engineers in developing and producing the largest wind turbine ever built for land use. He married the lovely Elena who became a medical doctor. They had a large and really fun wedding celebration with family and friends at his grandfather's factory. Each guest was introduced by either Max or Elena taking turns. I was totally surprised and honored when Max introduced me as his mentor. It really touched me. By the way, I have become close to his parents and consider them, along with his brother Paul and sister Lina, as my extended family members. Starting at 16, he was a very long shot. He is now a vice president of the Nordex Group.

All these young men have brought me joy and enriched my life beyond measure. Many developed distinguished talents, but above all, they have integrity and character. Perhaps Proverbs 27:17 applies, "As iron sharpens iron, so one person sharpens another." It wasn't perfect, but I did my best for each one. While I may have offered some steppingstones, at the end of the day they made themselves. I probably got more from them than they got from me. They will do the right thing every time. And yes, even if no one else is looking. They are superb blueprints for their children. No veil can screen the immense pride I have in them. If God had granted me a son—any of "my boys" would do nicely. They are under my tent.

Long Shots — Family and Friends

The Big Three

They were gentlemen who came into my life after I was already a Colonel. They were at least 10 years older than me and were all different, but we became good friends. I learned something from each of them and they contributed to my life. As you might expect, we met through bunker trap shooting. I introduced them to each other, and they became friends. Who were they? George, Albert, and Akio.

George Revitz was a real-estate and land developer in the Maryland, Washington, D.C., and Virginia area. He owned Westchester Construction and was well-known and respected in the business community. George didn't care much for skeet or pigeon shooting, but he loved to shoot international trap (also called bunker or Olympic trap). We competed in matches together on the East Coast at Prince Georges, Quantico, and Fort Benning, and we shot together in Los Angeles. His wife Laura was a skilled skeet shooter and a world champion at live pigeon shooting. She and I hunted pheasant, quail, and dove, but George had little interest in hunting. Laura and my wife Loretta became good friends and remain so to this day. We would often go to dinner together, and it seemed George knew every maître d', manager, and owner in the top Washington, D.C., restaurants. We were always guaranteed a good table and fawning service. Those dinners often caused friction because George always wanted to pay. I didn't want to look like a cheapskate or a moocher and insisted on paying my half. Looking back, it was a mistake for me to be so stubborn. I should've let George pay more. It was something he could do and wanted to do. I did things for him he couldn't do, like introducing him to the Commandant of the Marine Corps and taking him on military installations, which was always a pleasure for me and enjoyable for him. George had a wonderful sense of humor, mostly at his own expense, and kept the group in smiles. He was generous to a fault. I had two young military friends, one in England and one in Germany, coming back to the States with assignments in Maryland. Both were hunters and, unlike the Western states where huge areas of public land are available for hunting, the East Coast, particularly

611

around the Washington area, is more limited. Many of the best hunting areas are on private property and leased to hunting clubs. My friends were young and of junior grades, so they had no money to join a private club. I asked George if he had some property that he might let us use. His right-hand man was standing with him when I asked the question. George asked him, "What about the thousand-acre property on Kent Island?" The assistant said it wasn't available and was leased out to Bethlehem Steel. George said, "Just tell Bethlehem that we want to have these three guys join their hunting group." The assistant told him that Bethlehem Steel might not like that idea. George said, "Tell them anyway." When his assistant then said they might sue, George answered in a strong and annoyed tone, "Let them sue." Never before and not after did I ever see or hear George show annoyance. That wasn't his way. Nevertheless, a week later I was informed the Bethlehem Steel folks would be delighted to have us join them. We had a good goose hunting season, and the following year George kicked them off the lease and we had a thousand acres of prime farmland to ourselves for goose hunting. I was a little embarrassed because the hunting lease had to be worth thousands of dollars, but George was generous, and he wanted to do it.

George served in the Navy as an enlisted man and had a soft spot in his heart for the military. When we were assigned to the Pentagon for the second time, I went to Washington to look for an apartment and was shooting with George at Quantico. When he learned I was looking for a place, he said, "Follow me after the match, I know of a nice apartment complex." It was quite a large complex with very nice apartments right off Shirley Highway, a super location for anyone assigned at the Pentagon. As we walked to the office, he told me that they probably would not know him, but he was a major partner. He was mistaken. When we walked in the door it was apparent that they knew who he was and nearly jumped to a military attention. We looked at a two-bedroom, but I needed a three-bedroom unit. George asked when a three-bedroom unit would be available, and the manager said they had a waiting list for those. George said, "That's fine, put Col Behrens at the top of the list." I asked George what the rent was, and he became a little upset, saying the price was right. When I pressed him on it, his answer was, "Do you think I need money? The price is right." It was zero. He was a generous and special friend, but that was too much and I couldn't accept it.

It is always interesting to me to learn how people become successful in whatever they do. George told me, "There's a lot of money in the world, and if you're doing business make sure it is good for everybody. If it's good for you and not the other party, you will not do further business together. And if it's good for them and not for you, you will not do more business. Let everybody make a fair amount of money and you will continue to do business together. If the people on the other side of the deal are in trouble or having a hard time, don't take advantage, help them out a bit and they'll remember it." I thought that was excellent advice coming from a good person. I noted that's the same advice given by Frank Bennett, former CEO of Hearst Corporation, in his book, *Leave Something on the Table.* He said, "Nobody else has to lose in order for you to win. It's important to leave something on the table for the other parties to do a business deal. Doing so is not just good manners, it's good business."

One time when I was traveling with a couple of junior officers from the USAF Electric Security Command (ESC) headquarters in San Antonio for a meeting at the National Security Agency in Maryland, George learned I was headed his way and invited us to dinner. It turned out he could not join us, but he arranged a dinner in Georgetown. The maître d' explained that everything was paid for including the tip for whatever we ordered. George was overly generous. John Allgood joined me at George's funeral where I was honored to be a pallbearer.

My friend from Nashville, Tennessee, Albert Menefee, was a noted skeet competitor. I believe he held some National Skeet Shooting Association records in the .410 category. He lived on the highest hill in Brentwood, a high-end Nashville community. Albert also owned a two-thousand-acre ranch one hour south of Nashville. He had built a very large barn for horses when he was riding on fox hunts. It also contained sleeping quarters, a kitchen, and a combination living/dining room. He had put in a trap and skeet range on the property that he simply called the "Barn." After hearing about bunker trap, he was intrigued and went down to Fort Benning, Georgia, to enter a competition and see what it was about. That hooked him, and he went back to Tennessee and built a bunker trap at the Barn. He put on a couple of two-day regional matches for USA Shooting. His matches were open to all comers. And he would accept no entry fees, which means he paid for the whole deal. As I recall, we had 30 competitors from all across the United States at each one of those 200 clay bird matches. He also served lunch and dinner in the dining room of the Barn. The shooters wore whatever they had, but the waiters were in tuxedos, very classy indeed.

Albert had been very successful in the road-building business, and he owned a quarry among other things. His demeanor could be described as rough and ready, which was probably just a reflection of the often-rugged construction business. He often did jobs in other states and internationally, and then would sell all the equipment when the job was finished rather than bring it back to Nashville. He told me that one time he sold a large Caterpillar to a company in Argentina. Apparently, the engine gave out shortly after the equipment arrived in Argentina. There was no guarantee on any of the equipment in the sale, but the company owner in Argentina called Albert more to tell him about it than to complain. Albert told me he was in one of his large machine shops when he received the call. He realized during the call he had a new engine still crated up sitting right in front of him. So, even though there was no guarantee, he told the Argentine folks he would ship them a new motor. Albert said from then on South Americans bought all the equipment from jobs he completed when he didn't want to drag the equipment back to Nashville.

The Nashville entertainment people were drawn to him, probably because he was bigger in the financial world and was not a groupie. Some would fly down to his farm by helicopter for his shooting lessons. Louise Mandrell sponsored a huge annual Boy Scout benefit shoot. But behind the scenes, who was conducting the event? Albert.

Once, Albert called me and said, "I want you to meet me in Vegas. Louise Mandrell is opening a new show and I want her to meet you." So, Vegas it was. I was surprised that Louise was such a small lady, but what a performer. One of his stories that was quite amusing involved Reba McIntyre, who was performing at a venue that offered free entry for guns turned in. That all changed when Reba came down to the Barn and learned to shoot skeet. She is claimed to have said, "Shooting skeet was the next best thing to ---," according to Albert. By the way, she is a first-class lady. I met Barbara and Louise Mandrell and Reba McIntyre through Albert. Another time he called me and said he needed some help and wanted me to come to the Barn. He was hosting some high-flyers from the NRA convention for lunch and a round of sporting clays on his range. If Albert asked, I would never say no, so off I was for Nashville.

Albert asked me to lead the team of singer Lee Greenwood, Bob Allen, owner of Bob Allen Sporting Goods, and Prosser Mellon, the philanthropist. It was a privileged group, but they were good, and we won the match. Of course, it was just a fun match, but Albert wanted us to win. Other visitors to the barn were the governors of Tennessee, Alabama, and Arkansas.

Later, I learned I had prostate cancer. When he found out about it, he said, "Don't worry about anything, get the very best doctors, and I will pay for everything." I didn't take him up on it but what a beautiful offer. How many people could or would do that? He was also a major contributor to the Bunker Club.

When making moves between San Antonio and Washington, D.C., we let professional movers handle everything except my shotguns, which traveled with Loretta and me in my Tahoe, along with our two house cats. We were welcomed and stayed with Albert and his wife Valere at the Barn and in Brentwood. The world championship for FITASC sporting clays was being held in South Africa at a time when I was between safaris, and a friend of mine, Dr. Steve Wilhite, was a shooting team member. I was not on the team but thought there might be an extra spot to shoot just as an individual and I mentioned it to Albert. His immediate response was, "You are the honorary team captain!" I didn't want to push myself on anyone. It was just that if there was an empty spot, I'd take it. Then I get a call from Hal DuPont, the U.S. team captain, saying how delighted he was that I would join them as honorary team captain. Delighted, my foot, but he was a gentleman and put a positive spin on it. I was embarrassed and felt sorry for Mr. DuPont being strong-armed, but he was very pleasant, and I stayed out of the team's way in South Africa. Albert had a lot of pull in the shooting community.

Dr. Steve Holtzclaw and I went to visit Albert when he was in Hospice. He was in bed, but his mind was sharp. He asked how I was doing with my travel business, and I told him we were working on trips to Kenya. He said right away, "I know some people who should go with you, I'll make some calls." Here he was on his death bed but still trying to help me. An amazing friend.

A book could be written and should be written about Dr. Akio E. Mitamura. We met at a Grand Prix bunker trap match in Alberta, Canada. My friend Colonel Rip Sewall and I had driven up from Missoula, Montana. After one day's competition we were doing some fun shooting at ZZ birds (simulated live pigeons). Competitors were taking turns shooting from a designated position. I noticed Akio studying the ground behind the shooting position apparently looking for something. I asked him what he was looking for and he told me the front red bead off his shotgun barrel. Colonel Sewell and I joined the search. I spied it in the grass, picked it up, and handed it to him. He was pleased and offered us each a Cuban cigar. That started a wonderful relationship that blossomed into a fine friendship. His shotgun looked like a Perazzi, which I was shooting. Thinking his just had side plates and some engraving, I said, "That's a fine-looking Perazzi." Come to find out he was shooting a Fabbri. My Perazzi cost ten grand. A Fabbri starts at $100,000 before the selected engraving is added. He had the best, but he never touted it or tried to show off in any way. He wouldn't even correct me by saying his shotgun was a Fabbri, not a Perazzi. But that was Akio, always reserved and understated.

Akio and his entire extended Japanese family were interned (locked up and guarded) during World War II. He was 15 years old. Before going to the Heart Mountain concentration camp in Wyoming, he was secured with his family behind chain-link fences at the Santa Anita racetrack. He could see a Coca-Cola sign flashing on and off and he desperately wanted one. He didn't get a Coca-Cola until many months later. He tells the story of the FBI arresting his uncle in a hotel, and as they walked through the lobby the proprietor asked, "What about the rent money?" His answer was, "Ah, the fortunes of war," and out they went. His family lost everything as did most of the interned Japanese—buildings neglected, banknotes overdue, accounts depleted, and properties forfeited. His immediate and extended family were all bankrupt; they had nothing. He was drafted into the Army out of the internment camp either just before or just after the end of World War II. After completing Army service, he took advantage of the G.I. Bill to earn a college degree from UCLA. He wanted to become a doctor, but that's not an easy task when you have no money. What to do? For the first time in his life, he traveled to Japan to study medicine where he had support from family members and their friends. He graduated from medical school at Kyoto University and was the first doctor to come from Japan after World War II and be accepted for residency in the United States. His specialty was clinical pathology. Eventually, several doctors were working for him in Los Angeles area hospitals.

His home was in a secluded area on the top of a hill in Hacienda Heights, California. The house was white stucco, built in the 1930s, and looked like something Rudolph Valentino or a movie star from that era would own. The grounds were beautiful, and he had over a thousand bird-of-paradise plants. It took two full-time gardeners to keep the grounds immaculate. He had so many interesting things in his house, and it was always a pleasure to take my boys and friends to his place. He never complained about his internment or bad treatment during World War II and was a solid patriot. After all, he was born in the United States and was an Army veteran. Whenever I took my military boys to a shoot in Southern California, he would take all of us to dinner. We would often go to the Akasaka, an upscale Japanese restaurant not far from his house. He wanted people to have whatever they wanted, and we received menus without prices. At the end of dinner, we would all leave together, and never stop to pay the bill. It was evident that he ruled the entire restaurant. Later I found out he was an investor. And there were always Cuban cigars for my boys.

Akio played in several movies and was a member of the Screen Actors Guild. He told me it cost him around $10,000 to play in each film, considering the difference in doctor's pay and what he was paid as a minor actor, but he loved it. It was strange to me because he was quiet and always shied away from the limelight. The movies he played in were

Indiana Jones and the Temple of Doom (Harrison Ford), 1941 (John Belushi), Flight of the Intruder (Danny Glover), Conan the Barbarian (Arnold Schwarzenegger), Matlock (Andy Griffith), Motorcycle Gang (Carla Gugino), and Wind and the Lion (Sean Connery). I had met Robert Stack earlier at a shoot, but Akio re-introduced me along with another star, Andy Griffith. The director and producer John Millius was a close friend of his and often accompanied us to dinner. John's story in the *Shooting Sportsman* issue of May/June 2001 tells of shooting pigeons in Spain, where the great Dr Akio Mitamura and the legendary John Huston conspired to get him addicted to Cuban cigars.

He had all the toys: an airplane, a 56-foot three-bedroom, two-bath fishing boat in Santa Monica, and a 42-foot fishing boat at Cabo San Lucas in Mexico. We took the boat from Santa Monica out one time for an afternoon of fishing with 10 of my civilian friends from Washington, D.C. He had a nice selection of shotguns, including five Fabbris. Akio found out I was bringing the Air Force boys to the annual California Golden Bear Bunker match. He called me and asked what I was driving. I told him a Rent-a-Wreck or the cheapest thing we could get. He said, "I want you to drive my Ferrari." I told him the boys could drive the Rent-a-Wreck and follow me in the Ferrari. When I showed up at the shooting range, he came to me saying, "Mea culpa; mea culpa. I just sold the Ferrari yesterday." I didn't know what to think, but then he said, "I brought you my Aston Martin." Wow, it was a James Bond special—a silver gray coupe. When you put the hammer down it would leap forward like a cheetah after a tommy. He also had a Lamborghini. But he mostly drove a small Mercedes sedan or sometimes a beat-up Dodge pickup.

I learned a lot from Akio. When he walked into a fine restaurant the first thing that he did was hand the maître d' a $100 bill. You can't believe what a wonderful aura that produced. When traveling with others, he did whatever the group did and never asked for anything better. We were on a fishing trip to Belize that was far below his standards, but he never complained or hinted in any way that things weren't perfect. My friend Roger Bain was with us, and we barely got back to Key West on that trip, flying in a storm across the Gulf in George Silvernail's airplane, but that's another story.

Long Shots — Family and Friends

My civilian friends in Washington loved him. Cecelia Harding, wife of my friend Bob Harding, prepared a marvelous paella dinner for Akio and a group of our hunting friends. Akio declared it the best he ever had. And I think he meant it, and not just as a compliment for Cecelia. When I was stationed in the Pentagon he would often fly to Washington from Los Angeles on the redeye. I would pick him up at the airport on Friday morning and bring him back to my Pentagon office to sleep on one of my bosses' couches until noon when we'd take off for a weekend of shooting. I was staying at Motel 6 in those days and we would share a motel room. He was just easy to be with and rolled with the punches, never asking for something better than what was provided. We did have a fun visit to Tokyo together. He taught 2nd Lt John Linn and me how to eat Chinese noodle soup with chopsticks. Akio wanted to fly in a military jet and my friend Lt Gen J.B. Davis, who was stationed in the Tokyo, made it happen. Not an easy thing to arrange, and it required approval from the Commander, Pacific Air Forces, Gen Merrill McPeak, whom I knew well from AAFCE at Ramstein AFB, Germany. The flight was scheduled where F-16 fighter jets were located at Misawa Air Base in northern Japan. His pilot was an ace from Vietnam. I didn't fly in a fighter jet, but we had a marvelous view as we completely circled Mount Fuji on our way to Misawa in the general's plane.

When he visited us in San Antonio, he loved to visit Luby's cafeteria and enjoyed picking out the dishes he liked or wanted to try. He also relished the pies at the old Earl Abel's on Broadway. Dr. Steve Holtzclaw and I sat with John Millius at Akio's memorial service. Buddhist priests conducted the service in English and Japanese. We learned one of his grandfathers was mayor of Tokyo in 1908 when it was the largest city in the world. The other grandfather was surgeon to the emperor. Again, that was Akio, he never told us about his powerful ancestors or tooted his own horn.

All the Big Three are gone. Sadly they are only shadows now. I miss each one of them but cherish the memories of the fine times we shared. I thank my lucky stars for bringing those men to me. How lucky I was to know and count them as friends.

Goofs, Comeuppance, Stupid, and Other Embarrassing Moments

The Air Force Marksmanship School and competitive shooting teams were dismantled in 1969 as a result of Vietnam and budget constraints. In my opinion, this was a shortsighted move and a bureaucratic decision that saved little money and caused a significant decline in the basic war skill of marksmanship. No racquetball courts or golf courses were closed. In any case, I was serving in Germany in 1971 when the Air Training Command invited me to return to the States and be part of the Air Force team for the Pan-American Games tryouts. Capt Steve Richards and Mr. Steve Ducoff undertook the task of building an Air Force shooting program under the Air Force Morale and Welfare (MWR) umbrella. Which, by the way, turned out to be an excellent program that neither one of the Steves ever received enough credit for building. The team would not be made up of full-time shooters but volunteers who still wanted to compete in marksmanship events.

The Pan-American Games tryouts for shotgun events were being held near Luke Air Force Base in Phoenix, Arizona. The two Steves were recruiting prior Air Force team shooters for these tryouts. It was a two-month permissive, temporary duty assignment (TDY) to train and then shoot in the tryout for a spot on the United States team. Permissive means exactly what it sounds like—you had to have permission from your boss, and it was an official assignment, but not officially funded. The Air Force Morale and Welfare funds provided support—usually about one half of the normal Air Force rate. Still, it was a good deal. The program was great for morale of the troops and good for the Air Force public image.

I was all in for this program and flew back to the States. Ammo was furnished but we had to have our own personal firearms. The volunteer makeup shotgun team did not have standard shooting vests, hats, coats, or any other standardized items so we looked a little poor compared to the Army and Marine Corps full-time shooters who had proper team uniforms. Our shotgun team was made of three airman

620

first class (three stripers), who would be equal to corporals in the Army and Marine Corps. We had one other officer, Second Lieutenant DeFilippi and me. The stripers had all been new members to the full-time shooting teams when they were dismantled and had good training and experience. They were Wally Zobel, Phil Wright, and Bob Green. Chief Master Sergeant Herman Mashburn was our coach—he had been with the full-time teams and was accomplished as a coach and team organizer.

Lt DeFilippi had a car but the rest of us rode with Chief Mashburn. We trained at Lackland Air Force Base and then made the trip to Arizona. Once at Luke Air Force Base, the Chief was our only transport to the range other than a shuttle bus, which was infrequent and could leave you stranded at the shooting range for a couple hours after your event. Food was available at the chow hall or the NCO and officers club. The Army and the Marine Corps brought their own transportation. Being new to the shotgun world, I did not know officers from the other services and was not keen on asking for rides or invitations to go off base for dinner. Sometimes cars were available from the motor pool so I sauntered into their office and asked if I could check out one of their cars. The motor pool cars could be used for regular duty or MWR activities. Luckily, they had one available, which made my life much easier, and I could also help my teammates.

That same afternoon, Pearlie White, a friend from Germany, showed up at the tryouts. He was a retired Staff Sergeant and was the manager at the Ramstein Air Force Base Rod and Gun Club in Germany. We shot together often in Germany. He helped me many times arranging dinners and competitions at the Rod and Gun Club. I wanted to do something nice for Pearlie, so I invited him to dinner. He was not really eligible to use the officers' club and would not have been comfortable there—and I was not welcome at the NCO club. However, a Mexican restaurant was recommended and that became our destination for dinner. It was called Rosie's and was not a bad joint, although it was quite a way out in the middle of nowhere, just off the highway but without any paved parking. It was all gravel with one light on a telephone pole for the parking area. I parked under the light in an effort to keep the government car in the safest possible area. In those days, kids were still stealing hubcaps, so I didn't want to take any chances. The food was good, and it was a better place than we expected. It was one large room without a divider, more or less set up as a restaurant on one side and the other half as a bar. The bar was loaded with a large group of German officers in flight suits. And they were celebrating big time—lots of drinking and lots of noise. Some might say it was wild but mostly it was just loud, not really hurting anything. We finished dinner, and because I was driving a government car, I didn't even have a beer. We drove back to the base without incident. Mission completed!

I got back to my room and hit the sack early. I was in a deep sleep and woke up abruptly. I heard very loud banging on my door—and I mean loud. I thought it must be a fire or one of the boys in bad trouble, or some dire emergency. I jumped out of bed and did not take time to put anything on. I opened the door and there stood two very large strapping Air Force military policemen. I was standing there completely naked, my dingdong hanging down, when one of the police asked if I had driven a government car that evening. I answered in the affirmative. His response was, "Come with us; the wing commander wants to see you."

"Let me take a quick shave, and I'll hustle right over to the commander's office," I said.

"No! Consider yourself under arrest, Captain, you are coming with us right now."

I'm thinking, "What for? Criminy Sakes, it is 4:30 in the morning." The wing commander, a colonel, is the head man on base, everyone reports to him, including the base commander, Director of Operations, the chief of every department, every colonel on base—they all worked for the wing commander, and he wanted to see me. That got my attention—he could end my career in two seconds. One of the cops radioed someone that they had me and were taking me directly to the wing headquarters. It sounded like they had captured a dangerous desperado. I suspect he was talking to the Chief of Police who could relay the news to the wing commander's executive officer.

We went to the headquarters and straight to the commander's office. His executive officer, a lieutenant colonel, was in the outer office. He motioned me toward the commander's office and told me to report in—no time lost. I knocked and was told to enter. To admit that my pulse was highly elevated might be an understatement. I entered, reported in, saluted, and said, "Capt Behrens reporting as ordered, sir."

"Did you use an Air Force car last night?" he asked me.

"Yes, sir," I replied.

"Were you drinking and partying at Rosie's last night?" he pressed.

"No, sir."

"Were you drinking last night alone?"

"No, sir."

"Were you with others who were partying and drinking?"

"No, sir."

"Did you see anyone partying and drinking last night at Rosie's?"

"Yes, sir."

"Who were they?" he asked.

"Civilians and German officers in flight suits," I said, still standing at rigid attention.

"Was anyone with you?"

"Yes, sir."

"Who was it?"

"Mr. Pearlie White."

"Who is he?"

"Sir, he is the manager of the Rod and Gun Club at Ramstein Air Force Base, Germany."

"Take a seat, Captain."

I did so gladly, thinking I might get through this. My shirt was sweated through so maybe that was a sign of guilt. Taking an Air Force car off base for dinner was a gray area and I knew this.

Then he told me, "Senator Barry Goldwater in Washington, D.C., was told Air Force officers were drunk and disorderly last night at Rosie's and were driving an Air Force car."

He asked if I saw any disorder.

I answered, "Heavy drinking and loud talk, but no disorder that I saw."

"Why did you park under the light?" he asked me.

"Sir, I thought it was the safest and most secure spot to protect the Air Force car."

He answered, "Maybe next time you shouldn't park the car under a light. Turn in the car. Dismissed."

What a sigh of relief. It was bad enough that I had to turn in the car, but then the Air Force cops told me that several field-grade officers on the Army and Marine Corps team were rousted out of bed to find out who in their unit might have checked out a government vehicle. It was very embarrassing. The next day, I sidestepped any inquiry, saying it was a mistake and had been cleared up. This was really true. No one seemed to notice I no longer had a car. I only had the car for one day and one night. Even with the time change, someone having dinner at Rosie's had contacted the senator or his staff in the very wee hours for the complaint to get back to Phoenix in the early morning. I guess if they didn't put the handcuffs on, then I didn't have to report being arrested. You can bet this incident was not shared with my teammates or anyone else.

We were shooting a bunker trap match at Jack Burch's place, the Hilltop Range in Kerrville, Texas, when I noticed a man wearing a turban, obviously a Sikh, at the other end of the range. I went down to welcome him, and it turned out he was there with the Indian National Trap Team. Their leader was a tall Indian officer with a handsome mustache. He was introduced as "Chilly," but his name was Rajyavadhan Singh Rathore. He told me he was an Army colonel, and this was his first trip to the United States. He was in good physical shape and still had the exuberant look of youth about him, so I assumed he meant Lt Col. Later, I asked him when he would be eligible for promotion to full colonel, and he told me he was a full colonel. It turned out he had taken over the regiment his father commanded as a colonel. But now he was having a hard time shooting because of pain and stiffness in his lower back. Of course, he had no medical insurance that would help him in the United States, and I didn't know when or if I could get him into the hospital at Fort Sam Houston. So, I asked my friend Dr. Gene Bishop, who was practicing medicine at the Fredericksburg hospital, for help. Gene took care of him, and Chilly and I became good friends. He's been in my home twice, once with his wife. And I've also met him for shooting in Colorado Springs and in Italy.

Long Shots — Family and Friends

Later we met Chilly in Delhi, India. I had a group of 18 friends who were traveling with Loretta and me to see parts of India. The Palace on Wheels was our base for lodging and transportation. It was a great way to see India, I must tell you. We were staying one night in Delhi after the train trip at the classic and historic Imperial Hotel. The walls were adorned with many large photographs of Imperial days under British rule. Several were of troop parades and many included elephants. Some recorded visits of the English Royal family members and Lord Mountbatten. It is also the site where Hindu extremists tried to assassinate Mohammad Ali Jinnah in the turmoil of the British leaving India in 1947. Jinnah had insisted the old India under the British be partitioned, developing the two countries of India and Pakistan. He is considered the father of Pakistan and was their first governor general.

Col Rathore was well known in India. He was not only a colonel, but he was also a sports champion who earned a silver Olympic medal in double trap shooting. Winning an Olympic medal in shooting is a much bigger thing in India than it is in the United States, and he was known in nearly every jewelry or high-end carpet store we visited. He had been featured several times on national television, and the Prime Minister had also decorated him. Chilly called me at the hotel and invited Loretta and me to dinner. He offered to come and pick us up, and I asked him how long it would take to get to our hotel. He said it would be two hours. I'm thinking—two hours to pick us up, two hours to take us back to his house, two more hours to bring us home, and then two hours to get back to his house—far too much. It was a bit more than the call of duty, so I called him back and said we would take a taxi. Thinking that over and not knowing the safety of taxis in Delhi, I thought it would be prudent to take a car and driver that belonged to the hotel. That was arranged and sure enough it took two hours to get to his quarters, which were not on post but in a military housing area. It was a cinderblock house much like our military housing but comfortable. His wife, Gayatri, was a medical doctor and a little scamp with a fine sense of humor. I always enjoy her company. They had staff to cook and serve the dinner. We had a most enjoyable evening with them and their two children. He walked us to our car when we were ready to leave and shook hands with the hotel's driver.

The next day, Loretta and I were going down to breakfast and noticed how polite the staff was, standing back when we walked by, and some maids nearly curtsying. People were nearly falling all over themselves trying to be courteous. I thought, Wow, they must know I'm a colonel and must have high respect for the military and maybe the American military, too. I told the hotel senior manager, who was English, that we were supremely impressed with his courteous staff. He said, "You know why?" I was still thinking it had to be because I was a colonel, but I said, "No, why?" He replied, "Because you are friends with Col Rathore." It turns out the driver came back and blabbed that he had dinner with Col Rathore's staff, and the colonel even shook his hand. Talk about having your bubble burst. They didn't care about me one bit; it was only because we knew Col Rathore. When you think you are important, you'd better be ready for some comeuppance. Chilly is now retired from the military and a member of the Indian Parliament.

In August 1992, I was Chief of Mission for the U.S. Military Modern Pentathlon Team competing in St. Petersburg, Russia. This was a new sport and a new team for me. I had a captain, two second lieutenants, and a Spec 4 as athletes, plus a civilian as the coach. We did not win, but the athletes had done reasonably well in the competition and more importantly they carried our flag proudly. They were excellent representatives of the United States by both their bearing and behavior. I was proud of the team.

There were some rules about how much caviar could be carried out of Russia per person, and my guys felt they might have exceeded those limits. In any case, they were hoping I would wear my uniform and sort of hustle them past any customs inspection. As it turned out, a couple of Russian army colonels were at the airport as escorts to make sure we had no problems. We looked like a small pack train dragging our equipment. The athletes had fencing suits with helmeted masks, swords, pistols, running shoes, riding boots, athletic attire, civilian clothes, military shoes, and uniforms. It was a real bag drag. Everything was settled with luggage checked when we moved over to the gate for boarding with the two Russian colonels still with us. When boarding was announced, the Russians motioned us over, and they started pushing those in line out of the way. I didn't want them to do that and felt very conspicuous with my uniform, including my wheel cap with darts and farts (silver trim) on the bill. The athletes in civilian clothes could have been from anywhere, but I stood out like a neon light and was embarrassed about crowding in front, certainly not a good image for America.

Suddenly, a booming voice sounded out, "God damn you, Behrens," loud enough that it was probably heard in the Kremlin. I was stunned. Who would know me in a Russian airport? It was retired Gen Chuck Yeager. He was with Paul Volcker, who had been chair of the Federal Reserve, and a couple of big players from Washington. Gary Loomis, who manufactured superb fly-fishing rods, was also with them. Imagine yourself in a Russian airport when someone singles you out and shouts such an announcement. The general was smiling, but the Russian colonels continued to shove and pull us along with them through the first-class passenger line. That was embarrassing enough, but the attention from Gen Yeager made it even worse. I was certainly red-faced. The good part was that the flight was on Delta Airlines, which flew between St. Petersburg and Frankfurt, Germany. The plane was only a quarter full. Paul Volcker is a large, tall (6 feet, 7 inches) man and he sat in first class along with the Washington crowd. Gen Yeager and Gary Loomis sat in the back with us. They had all been on what the general described as a magnificent Atlantic salmon fishing trip, along with some hunting in Russia. Someone in the group killed a very large brown bear, and Gen Yeager was offered a moose. Never mind that bear season was probably not open.

The six of us, along with Gen Yeager and Gary Loomis, made our own little section on the plane and had a marvelous time. Gen Yeager entertained everyone with his stories, and he had pictures that he autographed for the athletes. He and I talked about our fun days at the gun club in Germany. Gary Loomis added some business and fishing stories. And I'm happy to report, I'm still fishing with a Gary Loomis rod he gave me. Capt Messenger was one of the athletes and it was his birthday. I had a very nice tie that the team planned to give him, but we decided to have a little fun and asked Gen Yeager if he would present a gag gift from all of us. The gift was an especially ugly lamp that had been given to me as a souvenir from a Russian general. It was a copy of one of their missiles with the huge red lightbulb on top. Pure ugliness, but Gen Yeager played his part well as he handed the gift to Messenger and told him all his teammates would be pleased when they visited his home to see this reminder of a great trip on his coffee table. Messenger fell for it but looked like a deer caught in the headlights. We couldn't contain ourselves and burst out laughing. He took the missile lamp with him, but I doubt it made it to his home.

The stewardesses treated us like we were champion gladiators, and they must've broken the rules because we had all the booze we could drink, and GIs never miss a good opportunity like that. It was after the competition, and they deserved it. The question remains, Did I deserve the St. Petersburg air terminal embarrassment?

I take a lot of people on hunts. My friends are an eclectic group. Some are blue-collar, and some are senior executives, but they all mix well, and we have fun together. Every now and then a member of the group leaves early to handle business matters, and we all give them a little trouble just in fun for leaving early. Normally, remarks include something about leaving a fine group of friends just to make more money, or "How can you trade our golden friendship for golden nuggets?"

One group from Washington, D.C., was headed up by my longtime friend retired TSgt John Allgood. He brought along a hunter who was new to his group and I did not know, but I was told he was like a second son to President Ronald Reagan. And of course, I'm his third cousin, right? His name is Fred Ryan and he proved to be an excellent addition to John's group. I liked him, but he was leaving the hunt a day early. So, I sort of slipped the knife to him as he was settling up the bill prior to his departure, saying, "Why would you leave such a great group early?" He feigned a little remorse and said Chief Justice Roberts was making his first public appearance. I said, "So what?" He told me the Chief Justice was making his appearance at the Ronald Reagan Presidential Library. Again, I said, "So what?" Then he said in an almost embarrassed tone, "I am the Chairman of the Reagan Library." I was shocked. Why didn't one of those dodo heads in the group tell me that? In any case, now I was embarrassed. A comeuppance if there ever was one. Be careful of being a smarty-pants. Later, Fred not only got us into the library, but he also arranged a tour conducted by the curator, who took us into the basement, which holds thousands upon thousands of gifts given to the President. We also got to visit Nancy Reagan's private quarters at the museum. And all because someone was chided for leaving our group early. Being a smart aleck can backfire, but this one turned out well.

My boyhood friend Harold Barker and I played cowboys and Indians together in grade school. His father was a sergeant in the Ventura County Sheriff's Department, so he was kind of a big shot in our small world. He always had a few nice pistols for us to handle. Harold was one grade ahead of me in school so when he got to high school he migrated more to friends in his own grade. We remained friends. He went to work for the Santa Paula Police Department, then moved to the Ventura Police Department and eventually to the Santa Barbara Police Department. A friend of his became Sheriff of San Mateo County adjacent to San Francisco and he hired Harold on as Under Sheriff.

Loretta and I visited Harold in the late 1970s and learned that he was developing helicopter and SWAT teams. In the conversation he mentioned that one of the largest U.S. magazine companies had attempted to bribe him by offering $10,000 for a photo of Patty Hearst behind bars. She happened to be locked up in the San Mateo County jail awaiting her trial. It had to be a shot showing her behind bars. If there ever was a straight arrow it was Harold Barker. He was not amused and threw the offending messenger out of his office. I forgot about the incident.

As a little background for those of you who may not know, Patty Hearst was kidnapped from college by the Symbionese Liberation Army in 1974 when she was 20 years old. She claimed to have been raped and threatened with death. Whether it was coercion, Stockholm syndrome or not, she was convicted of bank robbery and sentenced to 35 years in prison, later reduced to seven years. President Jimmy Carter commuted her sentence, and finally she was pardoned by President Bill Clinton. Her grandfather was the famous newspaper magnate William Randolph Hearst.

Fast forward 10 years from that event, when Major Loretta Behrens was selected by the Office of the Secretary of Defense to assist the Senate Youth Program by "honchoing" some junior officers. Those officers were chaperoning a group of high-school students who were brought to Washington for a program promoting good government. She dealt directly with the Hearst organization and Randolph Hearst, Patty's father. I was invited to some of the dinners and got to know Randolph Hearst, his sister Melissa, William Hearst, and Patty Hearst. Patty was a nice-looking blondish brunette and, of course, dressed to the nines. She was extra polite and always addressed me as Colonel. She was easy to talk to and down to earth. I liked her. The Hearst family invited Loretta and me to join them at the major dinners. The dinners were held in the Mayflower Hotel with all the kids and the escort officers dressed in coat and tie.

On the night in question, Loretta and I were sitting on the dais with the Hearst family and dignitaries in front of the kids. Senator Al Gore was the speaker that night, and I recall it was highly political with him pushing an agenda to reduce our military. Patty Hearst married Bernard Shaw (Bernie), a cop, who had been a part of her security detail. Bernie was a good guy, at least 10 years younger than I was, and like Patty, easy to talk to. He and I were sitting next to each other on the dais and were talking between dinner and dessert, discussing pistol shooting, when I thought he must know Harold Barker. So, I asked him if he knew my friend Harold Barker. When I said Harold Barker, Patty, who was sitting on the other side of Loretta, heard me. She looked over at me and said, "Harold Barker!" In less than a nanosecond, I recalled Harold's story of having her locked up in his jail and could hardly believe how stupid I was to mention him. What in the world was I thinking? I wanted to pull a napkin over my head and pull a Houdini. It wasn't being uncaring; it just hadn't come to mind. All these thoughts raced through my mind. And then she said, "Harold Barker saved my life." You have never in your life seen anyone as relieved as Dennis Behrens was at that moment. Apparently, her incarceration and pending trial were so highly charged politically that the U.S. Marshal in San Francisco had ordered that no one could take or move Patty out of the county jail without his permission, or the permission of the County Sheriff in his absence. Patty had a severe medical emergency on a weekend. In any case, the jail infirmary recognized it was something beyond their capability, but they could not move her without approval of the U.S. Marshal or County Sheriff. Neither one could be found or contacted. Harold was the Under Sheriff and is a man of action. He wasn't about to ask anybody's permission. He ordered them to immediately transfer her to the hospital, and he was on the way to meet them there. I didn't know this until many years later when Harold related the full story to me. But I'm still wondering how I could have forgotten Harold had her locked up in his jail. A really dumb mistake.

You are fired and retired! Failing your mission is worse than an embarrassment, but that's what happened to me. It was not my fault, but in the military, we're not looking for fault. Either you complete the mission or you don't and pointing the finger or explaining is a waste of time. General Wolfgang Altenburg was visiting Washington and I was acting as his guide and escort. We had meetings in the U.S. Capital in the morning with lunch to follow at the Pentagon. The invitation read: In honor of General Wolfgang Altenburg, The Chairman of the NATO Military Committee, The Vice Chairman of the Joint Chiefs of Staff, requests the pleasure of your company at Luncheon on Tuesday, Thirteenth of June at half past twelve o'clock, Chairman's Dining Room, The Pentagon. A pretty simple and clear plan: do our office calls and get to the Pentagon for lunch. Things started well with the capital police meeting us at the curb and escorting us into the building and to the proper offices. They were good and took no security chances. When we got to the elevator there was a capital policeman waiting and he rode it up with us to the correct floor. When the elevator door opened, there was another capital policeman waiting for us. Security was tight for this visiting general but, he was really a visiting dignitary. We kept fairly close to schedule and were just a few minutes behind when we reached Congressman Les Aspen's office, our last call of the morning. He was a very powerful Congressman and Chairman of the House Armed Services Committee. This was, of course, before he became Secretary of Defense. The meeting was held in a separate small board room and was running just slightly over time, but we had a little built-in slack, and I

631

thought we were still going to be fine. Then they got into a controversial subject, which turned into an animated discussion with them taking strong opposite positions. It was finger-pointing in vigor but with both still smiling as they made points for their separate opinions. We were now running over time, and I knew it, but what could I do? The general knew our schedule but continued. Congressman Aspin's meeting was probably the most important of his Washington visit. There was no way I was going to interfere and remind him we were scheduled for lunch. It was before the days of cell phones, and I kept thinking, He'll be finished in a minute. When the meeting was concluded, we exited the building as quickly as possible, but it still took nearly 15 minutes. Our driver and bodyguards from the Naval Investigative Service had our car and the chase car on the street right at the walkway. It was by then past the luncheon time. I told the driver to step on it, we were late for a meeting with the Vice Chairman and members of the Joint Chiefs of Staff. We were flying across the Arlington Memorial Bridge at about 90 with the red and blue lights flashing (no siren). It was a little too fast for the Gen Altenburg, and he leaned up and said politely, "Slow down a bit." It still took nearly 15 minutes from the U.S. Capitol to the Pentagon, so it was close to one o'clock.

    Understand, military protocol for General Altenburg required that he be met at his car upon arrival. And the officer meeting him would be the senior general present in the Pentagon. General Powell was gone that week so Air Force General Robert Herres, the Vice Chairman of the Joint Staff, was waiting for us and opened the car door for Gen Altenburg. We hustled up to the Chairman's dining room. The Chief of Staff of the Air Force, Gen Larry D. Welch, the Chief of Staff of the Army, Gen Carl E. Vuono; the Commandant of the Marine Corps, Gen Alfred M. Gray, Jr., and the Chief of Naval Operations, Admiral Carlisle A. H. Trout, were waiting for us. All were very cordial and even made a point of talking to me, except for Gen Welch, Chief of Staff of the Air Force. We sat next to each other at the luncheon, and he never said a word to me. I was thinking, He probably wants to say, "You're fired and retired." Think about it, five four-star generals, that's 20 stars total, being kept waiting and wasting 30 minutes of their valuable time. It was mission failure on my part, but I never heard a word about it. Perhaps Gen Welch couldn't figure out how to find me. No doubt the Colonel's Group had already burned my records. Or maybe they figured it just couldn't be helped. Who knows?

Honorables

I am one of the luckiest people in the world to have such a myriad of wonderful friends. Some will be recorded in history, others maybe not. But in my mind they are all honorable. Many have been mentioned in stories and remembrances in this book. A few who are still among the living deserve a bit more elaboration. I am only including here those who have known me for more than 45 years.

Friends for 70 years from the 1940s and '50s would include Perry (Buddy) Foster, Manny Vanegas, Jim Gofourth, and Byron Eddie. Buddy lived on Richmond Road about 300 yards down the street from where we lived in 1947. He, Butch Moore, who lived just a couple houses down from Buddy, and I made up the Richmond Road Gang. It really wasn't much of a gang. We played cowboys and Indians, trick-or-treated, and just hung out together. Buddy was a good athlete and lettered in football, track, and basketball. He was a high-school star as quarterback on our football team. He married Joan Fulton. Joan was a cheerleader and active in about every kind of school activity. She was a favorite of everyone. They were married right out of high school and are still going strong together with five great-grandchildren. Bud served in the Army, then finished college, and became a schoolteacher in Clovis, California. Buddy and Joan keep tabs on our classmates and organize our yearly reunion.

Byron Edde wasn't an athlete, but he was a top student. He was a Boy Scout, and we shot on the .22 rifle team together. Byron's folks had a middle-income house just off W. Main St., but it was small. Since his sister got the second bedroom, Byron lived in a 14-foot trailer in the backyard. It wasn't a little teardrop like my bedroom on Richmond Road; it was a camping trailer that you could stand up in with a table and sink. Byron worked after school delivering papers, at first by bicycle and then by car when he got a driver's license. His route covered a wide area, nearly to Fillmore. Rather than buying an older "cool car" he bought a newer 1950 Studebaker Champion for the same money. He was practical and needed reliability. Byron was smart enough he could've gone to any college but got a scholarship from the U.S. Navy and started in Ventura Junior College, later choosing the University of California at Berkeley. He graduated with a degree in electrical engineering and went to work for the Navy. When that commitment was completed, he taught at both Moorpark Junior College and then Ventura Junior College. After his teaching, he went back to work for the Navy where much of his work was in electronic jamming systems and other classified government projects. He did contract work for the Air Force in Colorado Springs and at Edwards Air Force Base, California. To this day, at 83 years old, he is still consulting with the Navy at Point Mugu, California. Byron tutored me in algebra when we were together at Ventura Junior College. I was honored to be best man at his wedding when he married Martha, who was one of the twins featured in the billboard ad for Double Mint Chewing Gum: "Double your flavor, double your fun, with Double Mint, Double Mint, Double Mint Gum." Her father ran an ad agency. Byron has taken up trap shooting, and we plan to get together for a little mini-reunion on the shooting range here in San Antonio.

My high-school partner in the grass-cutting business was Manny Vanegas. We went to high school, Ventura Junior College, and Fresno State College together. Manny was always good company. He was not judgmental and rolled with the tide. Obviously, I liked him, and he was a good worker. It was his mother who gave us the fancy Lincoln car for our cross-continent trip, and his grandmother who owned the Carmelita Café (really a bar) and treated us to huevos rancheros. Manny liked to dance, and he had rhythm that would make Lawrence Welk jealous. One might not expect it as he was short and overweight, but he could tear up the dance floor. He kept up with all the rock 'n' roll singers and in 1955 wanted to go see Little Richard, the up-and-coming rock 'n' roll singer who put out the songs, "Long Tall Sally" and "Tutti-Frutti." Little Richard was appearing in Oxnard, only 30 minutes' drive from Santa Paula. This was before he appeared on The Ed Sullivan Show. His show was in a rough part of the city and Manny thought he needed someone to go with him. I wasn't into rock 'n' roll music much but put on a coat and tie and went along. The audience was at least 95% black and dressed to the nines. The show was not held in a theater but just a large room with no stage. Little Richard appeared gaudily dressed with huge hair piled up in a pompadour. He put on an electrifying performance that was raucously outrageous—we loved it. Some people couldn't see him well, so he jumped on top of the piano. It was not a grand piano, only one that you would see in a private house pushed up against the wall. That's a picture still etched in my mind. I thought, Oh no, he's going to scratch the piano, not realizing nobody cared. He did the full performance dancing on top of that piano. The crowd was lively, noisy, and jumping around. We were offered drinks by many people but were still juniors in high school and too chicken to accept. Another time, Manny was riding with me when six of us in two cars went down to Hollywood to see a 3D movie. I think it may have been at Grauman's Chinese Theater. On the way back, when we turned off Highway 99 onto Highway 126 at Castaic Junction, we got into a race. It was late and there was no traffic. I had my dad's 1955 Ford V-8 and was racing against a '56 Ford, which, for some reason, I think George Dabney was driving. It was raining and Manny, who was riding in the backseat, was scared and cautioning me to slow down. He got down on the floor—this was before seatbelts. Neither one of us driving were giving up, but when we hit 100 mph, we both came to our senses. Manny was mad at me for a week. Don't trust your kids with a fast car.

  Jim Gofourth lived with his brother on the back porch of his father's small house adjacent to nursery/hothouses where his father had started a business raising avocado trees for sale to ranches. Both our fathers, neither one of whom had finished high school, were self-made men and just beginning to be successful in business. Jim and I mirrored each other in backgrounds (figuratively on the wrong side of the tracks). We took high-school classes in agriculture as our main study. We were both in the Boy Scouts, and our interests were camping, shooting, and hunting. And he was one of the four Burro men. He played football all four years of high school and got a very racy black 1950 Chevrolet Coupe his senior year. School wasn't Jim's thing, but he did start at Ventura Junior College. Tragically, his dad died and Jim, being the oldest son, quit school to take care of his mother, sisters, and brother. Jim married Jan Reed, and they make a perfect couple.

After selling the avocado tree nursery, he went to work at Reed and Lang, an earthmoving and trucking company that also operated a large machine shop. Jim became a master at operating Caterpillars and backhoes. Eventually, along with his partner George Dabney, he bought the Reed and Lang Company. They, along with Jan, built it into a very successful company.

I said school was not Jim's thing, but he became self-educated by reading and studying those subjects that interested him, particularly Western U.S. history. He became a master pistol shooter and could take me on any time. Not only could he shoot pistols, but he also became a very credible gunsmith and could accurize a 1911 Colt with the very best of them. He could put a perfect trigger on a 1911. Jim didn't just study how to do things. He has the hand skills to make them. He makes beautiful knives and replicas of famous knives. One that I coveted was a replica of a knife made in San Francisco with ivory grips set off with brass nail heads. He also made exact replicas of Kentucky rifles, and his meticulous work shows. Anything he makes, I guarantee you, it will be perfect. In addition to being a master pistol shooter and superb gunsmith, he was not to be challenged in a pool game for money. Secondary to his normal work, he was raising cattle on leases that were too small for big numbers of cattle. He learned horsemanship and became a good cowboy. That led to roping. He learned to be a header in team roping at age 40 and became a champion with several presentation saddles to prove it. His dad taught him, as mine did, that your word is your bond, and a handshake seals an agreement. He is a man of his word and can be counted on no matter how difficult or painful it might be to him. One of his many honors was becoming a member of the prestigious California Rancheros Visitadores and he never misses their annual historic 60-mile horseback ride. Jan and Loretta became compadres, and we have had many happy days together.

Long Shots — Family and Friends

Many friendships of 50 and 60 years were started in the 1960s when I entered the military. Those still alive with whom we are actively involved are described in the following brief sketches.

In 1963 as a second lieutenant, I was assigned on temporary duty to the Air Force Marksmanship School at Lackland Air Force Base in San Antonio. It was for duty shooting rifles, or maybe just being looked over as a possible permanent team member. The high-power rifle team trained on the rifle ranges at Camp Bullis. The Fourth Army rifle team also used Camp Bullis, and that is where I encountered Army Capt Frank C. White. He was a graduate of the University of Texas, but before that, he was a student at Wentworth Military Academy. He was experienced, knew the Army, had served in Korea and Germany, and really knew guns and shooting. A field-grade officer oversaw the Fourth Army rifle team, but Frank really led the team. He was certainly a fountain of knowledge for me. He started my shotgun education with his Krieghoff three-barrel set, and today he owns the most beautiful 20-gauge Piotti shotgun I have ever seen. We shot many matches together in the States, including the Masters Hi-Desert Invitational at Twentynine Palms, where I was lucky enough to win the thousand-yard match, and where my Air Force team beat the Army and Marine Corps, a long shot for sure.

He served in Vietnam before me, and when I moved from Vietnam to Ramstein, Germany, I was pleased to find Frank assigned at an Army military police unit in Frankfurt, Germany. He got me started in international (bunker) trap shooting, hunting, and in the German Hunters Association Sport Shooting (DJV). We had enjoyable days in Germany hunting and shooting in competitions. We even shot in the German National DJV championship. Frank left the Army but went into the Army Reserves and retired as a lieutenant colonel. When he first left the Army, he went to work in federal civil service supervising a sky cop program. This was at a time in the 1970s when airlines were being hijacked and flown to Cuba. Frank's duty station was the Houston International Airport, and he had numerous amusing stories. Many of them involved taking guns away from little old ladies who thought they should be able to travel with their pistols or just forgot them in their purses. In those days, it wasn't a big deal, and most people just turned their guns over for safekeeping or took them home and came back for another flight. Today, of course, the bureaucrats want to prove they're working, so the culprits will be handcuffed and carried away to jail and the courts—arrested for making an honest mistake.

Frank's father had been one of the original investors in the Ozona Bank in 1906. He was on the Board of Directors when he died, and the other owners and board members wanted Frank to come back to Ozona and take his father's place on the Board of Directors. That created a quandary as Frank needed to work, and Ozona is a very small city. A solution was discovered with Frank being on the Board of Directors but also serving in the bank as a loan officer. Frank moved back to Ozona and worked in the bank until retirement, but he is still on the Board of Directors. We have had great times in shooting sporting clays at the many competitions in South and West Texas. He learned to fly and bought an airplane that we used on occasion. Frank introduced me to his good friend Cal Sugg and the three of us shot sporting clays and hunted together along with our wives, Helen, Donna, and Loretta. I shot my first Whitetail deer with Frank on Cal's ranch in West Texas, and we hunted turkeys there many times. When I was recovering from a radical prostatectomy surgery, Frank came to visit. He brought a wrapped gift and left it in a bag with a bottle of wine. The wrapped gift looked about the size of a book, and I didn't open it for a couple of days. What a surprise—it was a Colt Woodsman pistol in the original box. The enclosed note read: "Anyone can get by without a prostate, but no man can live without a Woodsman." Frank is a stalwart, and a truer friend cannot be found. As they say in West Texas, "A man you could go to the well with," and they don't get better than that, my friends.

It all started with a ring. Col Tom Kelly, my commander in 1965 when I had the Air Force Rifle Team, told me to go out and get an officer to travel with me on a three-month training and shooting competition that would include the Interservice Rifle Championship at Quantico, Virginia, and the U.S. National Championship at Camp Perry, Ohio. Looking back, I suspect he thought I was getting too close to my enlisted team members. He was right; the camaraderie was tight. I was the team officer in charge (OIC) and had the team going well, so I was not about to share decision-making with anyone senior to me who might compromise the team. However, I was only a first lieutenant, which caused a dilemma—how do I find an officer junior to me? It was late springtime, and we were holding the All-Air Force Rifle Championship at Camp Bullis, which brought in rifle shooters from all over the Air Force, representing the major Air Force commands. The Strategic Air Command (SAC) team had a large contingent, and they were shooting well. My team members were spread out among the command teams to help in training and coaching. One of my team members, MSgt James Carter, was a Mason and was helping the SAC team. He told me 2d Lt Rolf Smith was wearing a Masonic ring. That settled any ethics or character questions I might have to worry about, so I watched how Rolf handled his teammates and was impressed. He was precocious and clearly the boss, but not a martinet. He fit the bill and jumped at the chance of shooting on the big Air Force team for three months. Col Kelly had him snatched out of SAC and assigned for duty with my team. We traveled, roomed, and shot together, which started a lifelong friendship. I like to tell him that he just followed me around, but kidding aside, I was able to help him on a couple of assignments and was pleased to do so.

Rolf was in my unit at Ramstein, Germany, as a Maj and Lt Col, and then followed me to the Electronic Security Command (ESC) in San Antonio where he served as a colonel. When we were assigned together in Germany, he got a German hunting license and began hunting. After I became chairman of the Rhineland Pflaz Land Council, I appointed him chairman of shooting for the 11 rod and gun clubs in our council. I selected him to be on the U.S. team, competing in the European Hunters Shooting Championships held in Graz, Austria. Rolf was a superb rifleman, but a shotgunner he was not. I coached him through the shotgun portion, and he managed to shoot a quite respectable score, which both surprised and delighted me. We hunted in Germany and Austria while we were on active duty. Later, we hunted stags in Patagonia, and he's been with me on 13 African safaris. He can shoot and even set some national long-range rifle records — always nice to have a real marksman on safari. Rolf's last Air Force assignment was developing and overseeing the first Air

Force office of innovation in ESC. It became a showplace and template for other commands.

When Rolf retired from the Air Force, he went to Exxon, still working on innovation and thinking out of the box. He then moved on with establishing his own very successful company in solving problems and teaching innovation. His book, *The Seven Levels of Change,* a field guide for thinking expeditions, explores thinking differently and moving through levels of change. The book is in its fourth edition and sixth printing and is catalogued in the Library of Congress. His classes or thinking expeditions are literally life-changers for many. He is a busy guy and always involved in many activities. He's 83 years old and now running classes at the county jail in rehabilitating inmates by challenging them to change and expand their horizons. His house is full of pets – cats, dogs, and a very smart parrot. He is raising sheep and longhorns. They keep horses while also nursing a pecan orchard back to health. He is always positive and has the gift of being cheerful and optimistic, which is a great strength. He and his artistic wife Julie are some of our oldest friends, and we cherish them. Friends for 58 years. *Waidmannsheil* Rolf.

In the spring of 1968, I met Joseph Donald Berry (Don) on the skeet range at Ramstein AFB in Germany. I was a rank beginner, and he was already an accomplished shotgun competitor. Don was a good badminton and tennis player. He knew how to keep his eye on the shuttlecock, giving me a good, thorough thrashing every time we played. He still plays tennis. Getting me to see the target and forget my rifle shooting discipline of concentration on the sights was a tough task but he managed it. His interest in guns, hunting, and shooting matched mine. We were both young junior captains, enjoying life to the fullest with as much hunting and shooting as we could squeeze in. Ramstein had a rod and gun club with excellent facilities: rifle range out to 100 yards, a running boar range, plus skeet and trap ranges. The clubhouse dining room was large enough for banquets and served both lunch and dinner. Their sales room was well supplied with sporting goods including firearms, and they even had an in-house stock maker, Herr Fuchs, who also prepared wall plaques for skull-mounted trophies.

Long Shots — Family and Friends

The club was good for socializing, but other than skeet shooting they lacked programs for hunting and shooting. Don and I made a perfect pair to liven things up. We developed a champion junior rifle team and started a monthly trap match bringing in German, Belgian, and French competitors. We also started DJV (German Hunters shooting), which was a big hit with German hunters and brought them into the club. Hardly a month went by without an event. I believe it is fair to say we got the place jumping, provided good recreation to many more GIs, and gave them an opportunity to socialize with a much larger community. We had marvelous hunts and memorable times together. He is a collector and expert on Browning Superposed shotguns. Don retired as a major and went on to another successful career with Sacramento County in California. He and his wife Barbara are gracious and generous hosts. Barbara makes the very best lasagna in the world. His son Brian retired as a lieutenant colonel from the Air Force and brought him two fine grandsons. We formed a solid friendship at Ramstein that has survived 54 years and will continue until we are no more.

A couple of F-4 flyers just back from Vietnam came out to the rod and gun range at Ramstein to see if they could shoot some trap. It was 1969, and one of them was a navigator, Tommy Brown. Naturally, I fixed them up with guns and ammo. Tommy and I became friends. Tommy slipped back into his F-4 flying life and we lost touch. The next time I saw him he was a pilot, which is quite unusual, but he was one of the few navigators to be retrained as a pilot and had completed his second tour in Vietnam. Tommy had grown up around fishing, and apparently his father took him fishing so often he was simply sick of it. But he loved to hunt anything from big game to bird hunting. He hunted with me in Kenya and Argentina for birds. He along with Tom Riffe started me hunting antelope and introduced me to Bart and Gay Byrd (who became valued friends). We hunted antelope for many years.

Tommy inherited a section of property in the sagebrush country west of Spokane on Rocky Ford Creek and turned it into a nice retreat of duck hunting for his friends. The only rule was you had to take the ducks home that you killed. He bought a railroad train caboose and had it brought to the ranch. It was no small task to clear a makeshift road to have it delivered, but it made an excellent clubhouse.

    Tommy had many interesting assignments, one of which was as a member of the Air Force Inspector General's evaluation team. Another was as squadron commander as a lieutenant colonel for pilot training at Vance Air Force Base, Oklahoma. His last Air Force assignment was as director of operations for the Air Force survival school. Tommy hadn't had survival training since he was a lieutenant in his Vietnam days, and he decided to go through the course again as a student, not telling them that he would be their new boss. He wanted to see how realistic their training was. One of his (simulated) prison guards slapped him hard enough to knock him out of his chair, so he found it was pretty realistic. Tommy saw black-and-white and not much gray in the world, particularly when integrity was in question.

    I always enjoyed hunting with Tommy and never failed to learn something. He taught me how to skin antelopes clean as a whistle without any nicks by using a rope tied to the antelope hide and to the back of a pickup or car that was used to pull the hide off. He managed to get his car, pickup, or SUV stuck more than anyone I've ever known. If there was a mud puddle in the area, we'd be stuck in the middle of it. One time, we were shooting prairie dogs miles from anywhere in the Malta area of Montana. It was hot and dry, and we were buzzing along at a good speed on a dirt trail when we came upon a patch of water. Tommy plowed right through, but we didn't get through. We were a foot deep in water and two feet deep in mud. We couldn't even open the car doors. Tommy was always prepared with a tall farm bumper jack and shovels but had neither on this hot summer afternoon. Some hunts are best forgotten. Another thing you could count on with Tommy was getting a speeding ticket or at least being stopped. He drove cars as fast as they would go, forgetting he was no longer in an F-4. After not fishing for many years, he took it up again and even got a boat with, naturally, a big outboard engine. Tommy passed recently and we miss him. His wife Mary Jane became good friends with Loretta, and they're still in touch with each other nearly weekly.

Long Shots — Family and Friends

Another F-4 pilot, Robert (Rip) Sewall, assigned to Ramstein from Vietnam in 1968, drove as fast as Tommy Brown. He loved cars and owned 166 in his lifetime up to now. The fastest I've ever been in a car was in his Ferrari when we topped out at 157 miles an hour (it was in clicks but figured out to 157 MPH) on the Autobahn. At the same time Rip owned the Ferrari, he owned a blue-colored front-wheel-drive Oldsmobile Toronado, which looked quite similar to the Ferrari. Believe it or not, when we went to matches people would come up and look at the Toronado but paid little attention to the Ferrari.

Of course, we were in Europe when they didn't have a lot of American cars. We met at Ramstein and began shooting trap and the DJV matches together throughout Germany and trap in Belgium and France. We shot together at the German national DJV championship. He married Josie, a delightful lady from France. I visited him on my way to Korea when he was base commander at Murphy Dome in Alaska. He later served as base commander of Zweibrucken Air Force Base in Germany. He retired in Great Falls, Montana, and had a very successful second career in real estate. For several years I would join him in Montana and travel with him in his motorhome to shoot bunker trap matches in Jackson and Missoula, Montana. We had great fun on those many road trips. He and Josie have two sons and two daughters. They now live in Phoenix, Arizona, and Rip at 93 years old still golfs and goes to the gym twice a week. I'm wondering what his 167th car will be.

Capt Doug Forsythe, a C-130 pilot, came to Ramstein in 1968 following an assignment in Vietnam. He was a superb pilot, and I mentioned flying with him in my remembrances of Ramstein. He was already a good skeet shooter and had shot some competitions when I met him. He could shoot rings around me with his 28 gauge. Doug was an enthusiastic bird hunter and had little interest in hunting other game. I was able to take him on some pheasant hunts in Bavaria. We became friends and have since hunted together in the States and Argentina. We had a hunt this last November in Eastern Oregon and just completed a dove and pigeon hunt in March 2022 in Argentina. Doug is always good company and more interested in the hunt than the number of birds killed. He and his lovely wife Joanne are dog people. They had a bloodhound when they first came to Germany.

Later Joanne got interested in Newfoundlanders, which they had for many years. Joanne eventually bought a young Portuguese Water Dog named Beamer and started showing her in competitions. Beamer turned out to be quite a good dog, winning numerous ribbons.

Portuguese Water Dogs are certainly not in the hunting dog category, but Doug took Joanne's show dog hunting, where she showed zero interest in birds initially. Not giving up, Doug coaxed her into retrieving a Hungarian partridge, and the light bulb came on. Once Beamer knew what he wanted, she turned into a superb retriever and flushing dog. It was lights out for any wounded bird that tried to get away. She tracked them down, including a couple for me. He wrote a nice tribute to Beamer that I've added to my notes on hunting. The die was cast: Joanne took Beamer as a show dog in spring and summer and Doug got possession in the fall, but they often sparred over who owned the dog in September. Joanne can pick 'em. Her next show dog was Caeli, a prolific winner of ribbons culminating in second place at the Westminster Dog Show in New York. Caeli, like Beamer, only had to find out what Doug wanted to become a bird dog. I have accused Doug of trying to have Portuguese Water Dogs listed in the hunting division.

Doug and I share the same birth date, including the year. He came into the Air Force before me, and while we both retired as colonels, he very happily points out that his date of rank is earlier than mine, ranking me. Doug had many challenging and interesting assignments, but I think his proudest was in the 21st Air Force as Deputy Chief of Staff Operations (DCS). Combat control units had been consolidated into three squadrons to make sure they got support and supervision that had been lacking for years. Doug decided he needed to see it firsthand to ensure they got the training needed. That led to jumping with the teams. The hierarchy was not convinced a 49-year-old full colonel should be learning how to jump out of airplanes. Nevertheless, Doug got instruction and qualified more or less through the back door. He did tell me that he questioned the wisdom of that decision after jumping at night in the Gulf of Mexico and then not being able get the Zodiac outboard engine to start. He had a heck of a time paddling against the tide to reach shore. After retiring from the Air Force, his second successful career was at Boeing. You can be sure any time he was in charge things worked. Doug has opened his home in Gig Harbor to me and my friends and I always enjoy visiting with Joanne. They've been our friends for 54 years.

Lt Bob Robertson showed up at Ramstein after just finishing a tour in Southeast Asia and started shooting and hunting with us. Bob married a German lady and still lives in Germany. He went to work for Ford Motor Company and transferred to the Air Force reserves. Bob keeps me abreast of hunting in Germany.

Another young guy who I helped get started in German hunting in 1968 was Roger Green, an Army lieutenant. When Roger completed his Army commitment, he first went into teaching in Wyoming and eventually became a talented gunsmith. Visiting his gun shop in Glenrock, I saw a photograph of Roger in the Oval Office with President George H.W. Bush. He told me about telling a retired U.S. Senator that it was a shame the President of the United States was shooting a foreign-made shotgun. Roger had forgotten about that conversation when the phone rang in his gun shop. The caller said, "This is John Sununu. The President wants to talk with you." Thinking his friends were pulling a joke on him, he said (expletive) you and hung up. The phone rang again, and the caller said more firmly, "This is John Sununu, and the President wants to talk with you." Roger said he could hear the thump, thump, thump of helicopter blades in the background and realized the caller might be John Sununu. The next thing, President Bush came online and said, "I'm told you think I should be shooting an American shotgun; why don't you get me one?" Roger told me he was so surprised and overwhelmed that he could hardly talk. What to do? He picked a 20-gauge Winchester Model 21, had it engraved, and went to work preparing it for the President. The Secret Service gave him the appropriate stock dimensions. He had it all completed and ready to go 30 days before the proposed presentation when the Secret Service told him, for the first time, the President was left-handed. That of course changed everything, and Roger says he worked 30 days night and day to get the gun adjusted. How many people can claim the title "Gun Maker to the President?"

Roger was president of the Deutscher Drahthaar of America and of course knew my close hunting friend Joe Kelly, who has superb Drahthaar hunting dogs and is a judge of Drahthaar training, testing, and certification. Roger kept close ties with Germany, ensuring the dog breed remained pure. It's amazing how small the world is sometimes. Neither Roger, Joe, nor I realized our mutual connection for a long time. But then again, I knew Roger in 1968 and didn't know Joe until 1990.

Although not assigned at Ramstein, my roommate from Vietnam, Mark Siefert, arrived at Wiesbaden Air Force Base, Germany. His Air Force specialty had been intelligence, but he transitioned into Systems Acquisition. He was a contract negotiator on the B-1A development program and stayed in the acquisition/systems procurement for the rest of his career, retiring as a colonel. He then went to work with Martin Marietta, first on their staff for 12 years and then another nine years as an independent contractor. He and his wife Lynne live in Colorado Springs but are avid skiers and have a house in Vail. They have hosted Loretta for skiing many times, and recently visited us in San Antonio.

A delightful couple, Tom and Ruthellen Riffe, came into our lives when we reported in at Rhein Main Air Force Base, Germany. Tom was a captain, as was I, and Ruthellen was a first-grade teacher at the base school. Loretta became a teachers' aide in her classes. We skied together in Austria and later at Vail. Tom transferred to the reserve and retired as a colonel. In civilian life he worked for FlightSafety and retired as a vice president. He started me on antelope hunting, and both Loretta and I also had the pleasure of shooting birds with him. They were with us in Argentina, and we had many fun times together. They now divide their time between homes in Colorado and Florida, which always includes some crazy house cats for entertainment.

Four friends must be mentioned who have known me for 45 years or more. They are Steve Richards, Gen J.B. Davis, Kelly Beckley, and Maxey Brantley. They have been briefly mentioned in other sections of this narrative. But with their long friendships, I would like the reader to know them better.

Steve Richards was a young captain when I met him in 1971. He had been a pistol shooter in college and was shooting on the Air

Force pistol team for a short period before the marksmanship school was closed. Steve loved shooting and wanted to keep it going in the Air Force at least as a recreational sport with the hope that some shooters would rise to a level that would give the Army and Marine Corps competition. He started by wrapping it into the Air Force Morale, Welfare, and Recreation (MWR) program with a budget of $2,000, which of course would provide little more than a T-shirt and a ball cap for the pistol, rifle, and shotgun teams. Shooters came together to support the program, but they had to pay their own way and supply their own guns and ammo. But if their duties allowed, they could attend shooting competitions on permissive TDY orders (government time), which means time off without being charged for leave. That was at least a start. Steve teamed up with Mr. Steve Ducoff, who was in charge of MWR recreation, and together they grew the program over the years to a budget of $700,000, with an additional $200,000 in ammunition provided by the Air Force Logistics Command. In addition, they added a full-time program administrator along with a full-time gunsmith by the time Steve Richards retired. It was a remarkable achievement done basically on a part-time basis without any real program authority. Steve simply moved it expertly through the various bureaucratic stages until it became an officially recognized program. Without Steve's dedicated and enthusiastic leadership it never would've happened. Think about it, he started with nothing and no senior patron and developed it into a major recreational program. And remember, he conducted all that as an unofficial extra duty. Steve never came close to receiving the credit he is due. He had demanding jobs in the Air Force in the personnel field and then in command and director positions and retired as a colonel. Following retirement, he became the general manager of the Dominion Country Club, arguably the most prestigious country club in San Antonio. He held that position for 12 years until the country club was sold. Steve is an excellent leader and takes the time to know his employees and let them know he appreciates their contributions. Even today when we visit the Dominion Country Club with him, employees come over to say how much they appreciated his mentorship and help when he ran the club 20 years ago.

We started our relationship as shooting friends, but it grew into a much broader friendship. After leaving the country club, Steve had several other major and challenging positions. But just as important have been his contributions of time and energy to several nonprofits. He was president of USA Shooting, and later served as president of USA Modern Pentathlon. He also served on the Olympic Foundation Board. Additionally, he was president of "Any Baby Can," a charitable organization caring for children with long-term illnesses. He has given much in support of these worthwhile organizations. His wife Sue has been a perfect partner in supporting him, raising their two children and teaching school. Both of their children are highly accomplished. Glen retired from the Air Force as a lieutenant colonel with 21 years in the service as an F-16 and F-22 pilot and instructor before moving to a second career. He is a captain and senior instructor for Delta Airlines. Their daughter Cristy retired from the Air Force Reserve as a lieutenant colonel having served as a flight test engineer for the F-16, flying in the back seat to evaluate the tests. She is now the Executive Director of Strategic Missile Defense Systems at Raytheon. And, the best part is that they each brought Steve and Sue two grandchildren. Teachers are classified as community "givers" in my mind, and Sue is certainly a giver. Steve knew the Olympics and organized a perfect visit for Loretta and me along with him and his wife to the Beijing Olympics. It was one of the best trips we've ever taken, and we added a visit to Tibet as a little icing on the cake.

Steve and Sue are marvelous hosts and are real foodies. Steve is a budding chef, and I don't miss any invitations to his house. They are positive and optimistic thinkers and are always up and enthusiastic. They see the glass as half-full and strive cheerfully to fill it up. We have become very close, and better friends can't be found.

It was a chance comment in 1973 that led to a wonderful friendship. Some of us from Randolph Air Force Base were on a Saturday afternoon dove hunt in South Texas. I was just a captain, and the others were all field-grade officers. Lt Col James B. Davis was part of the group and happened to hear me mention René Haillez, who I hunted with in Belgium. Small world that it is, Lt Col Davis knew and had hunted with René. The friendship started on that hunt is about to reach the half-century mark.

Lt Col J.B. Davis was a graduate of the Naval Academy. Upon graduation he transferred to the Air Force, which proved to be an excellent move as he retired as an Air Force four-star general. He had a distinguished career, and there is no need here to review his military record. It stands by itself. His decorations and awards were many, including decorations from three foreign countries. He was a fighter pilot, and his flight record reveals 270 combat hours.

But I want to tell you about my friend Gen J.B. Davis, not his military record. The first thing one would notice is the ease with which he meets people. He has certainly "been there and done that," but he never brags about himself, and in fact most of his jokes are self-deprecating. I've never seen him pull rank on anyone and he fits in with any crowd. There just isn't any "stuck up" in him at all. He comes from a small farming town, but it would be a mistake to say he was just a Nebraska farm boy. He has seen the world and played with its leaders. One classmate at the Naval Academy was John McCain, and he knew many other senators and high government officials, but you would not know that unless you asked. Of course, with his many experiences in life he can mesmerize a dinner party or entertain a whole hunting camp. One of his experiences, which I like to remind him of, was his coming face-to-face with a picture of himself on a wanted poster when he was in Belgium. It had been tacked on a telephone pole near his home by terrorists. It offered a reward for his killing. He said not to worry about him, the reward money was far too small for the trouble. Few of my friends have been on wanted posters.

Although it is in plain sight, he was the first to point out to me the social value of Air Force rod and gun clubs where enlisted and officers could freely mix without rank or privilege souring the occasion. One of my favorite memories was attending the opening of a new trap range at Yokota Air Force Base in Japan. Gen Davis was commander of U.S. Forces in Japan, and he wanted a trap range to broaden off-duty recreation for his enlisted troops. Land in Japan is very limited. Gen Davis wouldn't give up and put the trap range right next to the golf course! My kind of general. He is a superb traveler and takes whatever is happening in stride without a complaint. One incident I vividly recall was walking down Florida Street in Buenos Aires side-by-side with Gen Davis. I was walking on the general's left when I felt a pickpocket reaching into my left pocket from behind me. Grabbing his hand, I started shouting "Police! Police!" Gen Davis grabbed the culprit around the neck, and we soon had him on deck with both of us on top of him. He looked to be about 14 and was certainly no professional. Our car for the airport was arriving in one hour, and, realizing we would be in the police station at least four hours, we released our wide-eyed prisoner. You could still see him running like a gazelle two blocks away.

We have hunted or shot together in Virginia, Texas, California, Nebraska, Florida, Georgia, Argentina, Japan, and Bolivia. He is a fellow member and a favorite at the Grand National Quail Club, and we still shoot pheasants every October in Nebraska. We've had many fun experiences with shotguns in the field. In addition to our personal friendship, he has been the most generous and continuous booster of the Air Force trap team. We certainly would not have been the success we were without his chaperoning through the years. Getting a bunker trap and training area at Lackland Air Force Base got us started, and he continued to assist me in getting team members assigned near areas where they could train. He attended some of our matches and even did some fun shooting with the team, surprisingly scoring well in a foreign and very difficult game. His help for the team was simply invaluable. I've been honored by Gen Davis and his gracious wife Carol with dinners in their homes in Texas, Japan, and Belgium. A superfine friend—we need to organize a 50-year reunion.

Kelly and Connie Beckley came to Ramstein Air Force Base in 1976. It was only Kelly's second Air Force assignment. He was a lawyer in the Base Judge Advocate office. They were 12 years younger than I and still radiated the excitement of youth. We hit it off immediately and they certainly became favorites. They were inquisitive and anxious—ever willing to see and experience everything Europe could offer. We took them under our wing and had many fun weekends exploring Germany, Luxembourg, and Belgium. We had a wonderful week skiing in Italy and were very fortunate to find a private one-car garage where we could park Kelly's new 300 Mercedes. Like all guys, me included, he wanted to protect his new car from weather and theft.

Connie skied with us the whole time, but she did look a little comical. She was a small woman, and she must've been eight months pregnant, so she was quite a sight on the ski slopes. Kelly is not a hunter, but I hunted antelope successfully with his father. He and Connie went on a trip to Kenya with Loretta and me to see the animals and swim in the Indian Ocean. Many years later, they came with us to Córdoba and then Mendoza to tour wineries. We also journeyed to the top of the Andes Mountains west of Mendoza to see the statue of Jesus and step into Chile without visas or border guards.

Kelly became the judge advocate for my unit, and we ran together nearly every day over the lunch hour, sometimes deliberating politics, sometimes discussing history, often examining options open to me in imposing corrections or punishment of offenses committed by members or dependents in my unit. The daily runs made me think about running a marathon. Kelly readily agreed, and we decided if we were going to do one it would be the original marathon to Athens. He was 29 and I was 41. Taking Connie and his mom and dad with him, he drove to Greece. I flew down to meet them. Our goal was, first, to finish the marathon, second, to complete it without walking or resting, and third, to run it in less than four hours. Marathon is a very small little village on the coast, and to get the proper Olympic mileage we had to run around the city twice before heading to Athens. We were training in Germany in 60° and 70° weather, but it was over 80° in Greece, something we hadn't planned on. It was a pleasant run for the first 20 miles with people cheering and clapping as one would see in a sports event. Many older ladies dressed in black were waving palms like fans as we ran by. We hit what runners describe as the dreaded wall at the 20-mile point, which was also the beginning of the uphill grade into the city of Athens. Now we had traffic with car, truck, and bus exhaust to hamper us. If a traffic light changed, we simply had to run in place until we had a chance to cross the street or road. My legs were really giving out at that stage, and if it hadn't been for Kelly, I would've gone to walking. I was slowing him down and waved him on, but I don't think he pushed as hard as he could have. He ran into the

Olympic stadium only two minutes ahead of me, but we were three or four minutes over the four-hour goal. He could have been under four hours for sure if he hadn't slowed for me.

Kelly also traveled with me to my outlying military units, some as many as 200 miles from Ramstein, to write wills for my people and give legal advice. We had fun traveling together, but I appreciated him giving this extra service to my folks stationed on mountaintops. After his active-duty commitment, Kelly transferred to the Air Force Reserves and became the Reserve Judge Advocate for Europe, eventually retiring as a full colonel. He graduated from the University of Oregon in Eugene and returned to Eugene to start his own legal practice. He is still there, and one of his sons has joined him as an attorney. Connie started her own business as an investment advisor and built up a large clientele. Both were highly successful.

We became business partners in real-estate ventures. I was still on active duty and did not have time for an outside business, so Kelly carried the ball, and I was a very silent partner doing little more than sending a check when it was needed. Loretta and I went out to Eugene once a year to look at the properties, but also to ski with Connie and Kelly at Mount Bachelor. The partnership accumulated a good number of rental properties, including a small apartment house we eventually traded for mini storage. I wish we still owned those properties today. Connie and Kelly traveled more than anyone I know, including me, and I have traveled quite a bit. Kelly was too far along in life when we met him for me to call him one of my kids. But I hold him in that same very special circle.

Army First Lieutenant Maxey Brantley met me on the trap range at Ramstein Air Force Base in 1977. He was assigned to babysit nukes near Dortmund, Germany, and came to Ramstein for one of my monthly trap competitions. I remember that match and can clearly remember buying a Browning 32-inch trap gun from Maxey after a very cursory "look over" under the car lights. After a more thorough inspection in good light the next day, the gun revealed considerably more hard use. I remind him often of that sale in the dark. We met at matches on and off through the years, and he was on the Army International Trap Team from 1982 to 1986. He is still shooting matches and is quite competitive in the senior class. He organizes and runs the Senior Open along with Dave Senter. That match is quite popular and is sold out to maximum capacity of 30 shooters every year. I shot in matches with Maxey from Fort Benning, Georgia, to Los Angeles, California. He was an intelligence officer when he retired in 1995 at Fort Meade, Maryland. He moved to Fort Huachuca, Arizona, as an Army civil service intelligence officer. We did have a fine desert quail hunt with him in Arizona.

He finally got smart and moved from Department of Defense (DOD) Army to DOD Air Force at Randolph Air Force Base here in San Antonio. That was super good for me because I have a constant partner for shooting bunker trap. The one bad thing about him moving here is he is a gun nut like me and keeps finding nice shotguns that I can't turn down. That's my story anyway; someone must take the blame. We still shoot bunker trap together. Maxey learned to hunt the German way and hunted all game available in Germany. Today he is mostly a bird hunter, but he did connect with a beautiful trophy quality white tail last year. We hunt dove together here in South Texas and do a quail hunt every November in the Panhandle. He has also shot doves with me in Argentina.

Maxey and his delightful wife Blanche are both foodies and search out the best restaurants. I can attest that they are excellent cooks and lay out a beautiful table. They have three sons: Travis is the bunker shooter, Casey is the gun nut and hunter, and Nicholas is the pistol shooter. I have enjoyed shooting with all of them. Travis is CFO of McDermott International. Maxey and I have shot and hunted together for many years, but it wasn't until 2002 when he moved to San Antonio that we became really close friends. He is a fine companion, and I hold him in high regard. To have a good friend you must be a good friend—stick with them forever.

Reflections

Life has been good to me. I don't pretend to be a fount of knowledge or wisdom. I can only offer what my 89 years of life contained.

Life's travels and experiences make a long hike in learning. One doesn't become smarter with age, maybe less ignorant, but not smarter. It's to be hoped that experiences will make one wiser and perhaps lead to a more thoughtful life. "I know a thing or two because I've seen a thing or two." Integrity is black-and-white and does not change; it makes your character. I've told more than one new young lieutenant that he already owns the most valuable thing he will ever own—and that is his name. You sully that, and it is a bell you cannot un-ring. If you are ever in doubt on an issue, ask yourself if your mother would be proud of you? That will settle the question. Life's experiences allow one to view things and see situations with a different set of eyes. My travels and adventures have created a wealth of memories from different cultures and experiences.

Much of the world is gray, and viewed through different prisms, light produces different shades. The Texas educator and historian J. Frank Dobie wrote in a *Guide to Life and Literature of the Southwest*, "If during a decade a man does not change his mind on some things and develop new points of view, it's a pretty good sign that his mind is petrified and that he need no longer be counted among the living." It's also been said that if you're not wrong sometimes, you are probably thinking too small.

Warren Buffett said, "Pick your associates whose behavior is better than yours, and you'll drift in that direction." Remember, of course, you are no better than what you will tolerate. Some, including me, are intolerant and too quick to criticize. I love Pope Francis saying, "Who am I to judge?" Wow, think about his stature and influence worldwide—what a positive image of humility. It's a strong and meaningful statement for all of us to emulate. We can all do better.

My wife, Loretta, is a Rotarian, and I learned their four-way test: Is it the truth? Is it fair to all concerned? Will it build goodwill and better friendship? Will it be beneficial to all concerned? A pretty good roadmap, I would say. Each year at their Pow Wow, the Chiefs of the California Indians hold a ceremony honoring members who have passed. They recite an Indian prayer that includes my favorite line, "I seek strength—not to be greater than my brother, but to fight my greatest enemy—myself." Hate, grudges, and vendettas destroy those who persist in feelings of ill will.

Winston Churchill said, "You make a living by what you get, but you make a life by that which you give." Albert Pike in his publication ***Morals and Dogma*** wrote, "What we do for ourselves, dies with us. What we do for others, remains and is immortal." When you have a chance to do good—don't delay or postpone those opportunities; they may not come again. It could be financial contributions, volunteer services, or even a friendly hello to a crotchety neighbor. Just do something—don't wait for the ideal occasion. Time becomes more valuable with age; be careful how you use it. It is a thief for certain, so remember *carpe diem*. Don't waste the day; it can't be recovered.

After retiring from the Air Force, I had an epiphany and realized my time was more important to me than making money. However, I ended up working my tail off for nonprofits and to make Expedition Adventures successful. Figure out what you want to do in life, and then go for it. Don't waste time on what might have been or worry about previous wrongs. Do the best you can with what you have, be it athletic ability, brains, personality, disposition, whatever life's given you. Michelangelo is supposed to have said (translated to something like) "Most people aim too low and therefore don't achieve much." Aim high and even if you fail you have at least been in the ring fighting. Life really depends on you. It is your choice to be happy or not, to succeed or not. To borrow from John Wooden, "Things turn out best for people who make the best out of the way things turn out." I did the best I could with the life given me and have no objections and few regrets. I do wish I had been a better leader, better husband, and better friend. What I regret most are things I didn't do when I had the opportunity. But I consider my life to be the best possible of any life I could have had. In addition to the experiences, adventures, and seeing the wonders of the world, I've owned the finest shotguns and some of the best cars ever manufactured. I've won awards, trophies, and accolades. But the best things in life are not things. I caught the perfect wife for me and have more wonderful friends than any man should be allowed. Success to me is measured by family, friends, good deeds, and precious memories. If the angels aren't jealous, there's something wrong with them. I'm content with life but not satisfied. The songwriter and entertainer Dave Stamey sings, "If your trail's been a good one, you don't mind looking back," but maybe more importantly, he sings, "the windshield is bigger than the mirror." There are projects, challenges, travels, and adventures ahead. I'm anxious to meet them.

> The content of your character is your choice. Day by day, what you choose, what you think, what you do—is who you become. Your integrity is your destiny...it is the light that guides your way.
>
> —Heraclitus

Loretta as an Airman First Class in 1966.

Our wedding – Feb 1967

Easter Sunday in Germany with our new (used) 1966 VW.

Decked out for a Dining Out at Ramstein in 1968. Loretta in her homemade gown.

Loretta in her newly decorated 18th floor penthouse 1986.

Running the marathon with Kelly Beckley in Oct 1978—Marathon to Athens.

My cousin Donald Hurt. I had him on weekends in 1992 when he was a buck private going to Diesel Mechanic School at Aberdeen. A spark was lit and I'm proud to report he is now a Lt Col helicopter pilot.

Loretta with Midshipman Derek Hotchkiss in 1996

Traveling with Loretta in India

In Tibet with Loretta

Pinning gold bars on 2d Lt Casey Mahon in 1987.

Promoting John Linn to Lt Col in 2008.

Annual Secret Santa Shoot. Dec 11, 2021 was our 35th consecutive year.

*Annual Children's Shelter Shoot in San Antonio on 18 Dec 2021.
L-R Jeff Julig, Larry Trick, Maxey Brantley, Gordie White, Judy Trick, Blanche Brantley, Gene Bishop, Shelly Jewett, Art Aiken, Loretta, Roberta Aiken, Bob Hayes, Larry Petty, P.D. Parker, DDB*

Chiefs of the California Indians. They honor American Indians with poems and prayers.

California Indians who are also Bunker Club members. L-R DDB, Mike & Tana Gallagher, Mike & Leslie Sloan, Doug & Carolyn Jensen, Jeri & Bob Herold, Gail & Steve Jeffress

Bunker Club visiting the Olympic Training Center

Laura Revitz with her pigeon shooting World Championship Trophy

On the range used for the Los Angeles Olympics with two of the Big Three.
L-R George Revitz, DDB, Dr Akio Mitamura

Max with Antelope taken on the Allemand Ranch

In Patagonia with Isaias Miciu examining the ranch house owned by Butch Cassidy and the Sundance Kid.

Jim Gregory's Promotion to Lt Col in 2011

Retirement of Commander Derek Hotchkiss in 2018.

Gordie White & me in a rifle match with my .458

In Austria for Max's first red Stag

With Doug Forsythe and his faithful Portuguese Water Dog Beamer. A super bird finder

Two friends through thick and thin for 57 years – Rolf Smith & DDB

In Belize with Max

On a scaled quail hunt in New Mexico

Bird shooting in France with Max in 2021.

Brother Bob and me with Mom

Mother at 92 still working as a volunteer for the Chamber of Commerce — be useful

Married 56 years

At the California Indians annual Pow Wow

Loretta with her favorite cat Felix

VI

BACKWORD

Flashbacks from 'DDB's Boys'

"Nice shooting, sir!" MSgt. Carter said as I finished the 600 yards stage in a Leg Match. He was scoring me. "Lt. Behrens is looking for another officer for the National Rifle Team. Would you be interested?" I was at Camp Bullis, San Antonio, Texas, at the annual Air Training Command High Power Rifle Championships, June 1965. While in Communications Officer Tech school at Keesler AFB, I had organized the base High Power Rifle Team. I had placed in the top 10% of the individual "Leg" match, earning a Bronze "Leg" medal. After the team matches, MSgt Carter introduced me to DDB. That led to my shooting with him and the AF National High Power Rifle Team every summer for the next three years. I earned my Distinguished Air Force Rifleman Badge in 1966 while shooting with Dennis and the National Team.

After that, we were stationed together often. He knew my father and knows all of my children. In 1975 we were in Stuttgart, Germany, together and later at Ramstein AFB. He coached me into getting a Jagdschein, and I hunted with him in Germany and Austria from 1975-1983. In 1995 he introduced me to African big-game hunting. We have been on 13 safaris as well as stag hunting twice in Argentina.

In 1983, leaving Ramstein and reporting in for a new assignment in San Antonio, my wife and I showed up at his front door. Dennis greeted me with: "Congratulations! You made Colonel." After that promotion he and I spent two more years together in Electronic Security Command. He and Loretta now live 62 miles from us, so we try to get together for lunch or dinner every month or so.

I've known, shot with, hunted with, adventured with, and been stationed with DDB for 60 years. He's been my older brother since I met him … and my only Air Force mentor.

A real raconteur par excellence, he simply cannot not tell stories. And I pushed him for years to gather all of them into a book. He has attacked the project with his typical fervor.

Since I've known Dennis longer than anyone else, he asked me to help with the editing. After reading a draft, I suggested that he include some "backward glances," flashbacks and stories from his friends, especially those in his chapter "My boys, my guys, my kids." Dennis agreed. I chased down as many of "his boys" as I could—and knew some of them personally. I invited them to contribute some stories of memorable times with DDB. Only his boys were allowed to contribute, and requests from others were not entertained. The boys all delivered!

Rolf C. Smith, Jr,
Colonel USAF (Ret)
Air Force Distinguished Rifleman

"You need to address a full Colonel with 'Colonel … yes sir'." This was the first of many valuable lessons I learned from Colonel Dennis Behrens, just 5 minutes after I met him in San Antonio, Texas, as a 16-year-old boy. Since that first meeting 23 years ago, we have done countless hunting and fishing trips together in different areas of the world, where I benefited greatly from his generosity and support and never-ending dedication to teach me, a young German boy in his twenties. One of the most memorable trips for me was for sure our very first road trip through the U.S. It was for me the first time to see the "Wild West" and to meet many of his lifelong friends. Many of them have become good friends for me by now. Each destination, each friend we met, and each hunt we did offered invaluable experience and lessons in life for me that I would have never made without the mentorship of Colonel Behrens.

Two truly life-changing pieces of advice are worth highlighting in particular. During our second U.S. road trip in 2015, we stopped by to see his good friend Frank White in Ozona, Texas. The "old" friends started talking about guns and the great hunting experiences that they had in Germany in the 1960s and '70s. I had great interest in hunting, but until that time had absolutely no connection with German hunting —even quite some prejudice about the "old-timey" German hunting culture.

Dennis and Frank challenged me hard. "If you really want to become a hunter, take the German hunting classes, pass the exam and get exposed to German hunting—one of the best hunting traditions in the world." I was too stubborn to understand at that time. But some months later, when I was back in Germany, I signed up for a German hunting course, which included twelve months of extensive studying and practice before you are allowed to get a German hunting license. I passed the challenging exam and entered a new episode of my (hunting) life.

I have been a very passionate hunter since then in Germany and all over the world, have met many astonishing people and great friends, and I have truly discovered a hidden passion that I would have probably never discovered if not for Colonel Behrens.

The second piece of advice formed along many hours of talking on our road trips and sharing thoughts about life and career planning. Without ever telling me what to do, Colonel Behrens guided me with his many years of experience and his strong values. Many career steps, like consulting, Ph.D. in Engineering, or others were greatly supported by him.

But the most valuable piece of advice that he passed on to me was: "Take time to do things now and don't get too busy chasing after your career." With this great advice in mind, I decided to take one or two months every year to go on extraordinary trips and gain rich experiences in life. Even more important now with family and soon three kids, this helps me to balance a challenging management position and to be the father I always hoped I could be. This would have been impossible without the mentorship I have enjoyed during the past 20+ years by Colonel Behrens. He is much more than a mentor. He is one of my closest friends and almost like a father to me.

Colonel, you have been such an incredible tutor and mentor to me. You made me look differently at many things. I hope to get many more chances to learn from you.

Deepest gratitude, respect and love—sir.
Dr. Max Jungk Bad Oldesloe,
Germany

June 1979, Quantico Marine Base Virginia, Weapons Battalion, Marine Corps Marksmanship Training Unit, 80 °F and sun. Earlier in the day I manage to hitch a ride from Fairfax, Virginia, with my not-so-trusty Franchi shotgun to one of the handful of Olympic-style bunkers in the U.S. I manage, at the age of 14, to gain entry into Quantico with no formal ID, said not-so-trusty shotgun, requisite ammunition, and all the cash money I had in the world for entry fees.

I meet the tough Range Gunnery Sergeant with a repaired hole through his leg and a number of bunker shooters from the service teams, and for the first-time lay eyes on but do not speak with Col DDB. I don't think the good Colonel, as-always fully pressed and square shouldered, even noticed the 14 year old with the cheap Italian shotgun, a mouth full of braces, long hair, and a 98-lb wrestling weight (really). Had DDB known what this relationship would bring—he would have grabbed his trusty Superposed and never looked at this kid.

July 1986, Southern California—U.S. Olympic Trials for International Shotgun. Sun warm on my shoulders, 80 °F, light inland breeze blowing my shoulder-length hair bleached from the sun. Col DDB joins me on the ready bench.

Had I but known the challenge, toil, heartache, loneliness, and overall gut-check resultant from our next conversation, I would have grabbed my trusty Winchester and run in another direction. "John, what are you planning career-wise after graduation?" came as the question, and as the short conversation progressed, "Do you have any interest in officership in the Air Force"—with those eleven words the die was cast.

Long Shots — Backword

July 1988, Washington, District of Columbia, "Lieutenant, you are an officer first, all things, (that including shooting, in our circle, a pretty close equivalent to religion) are secondary to your officer oath." DDB administered that oath to me on occasion for the next three decades.

April 29, 2016, Camp Phoenix, Kabul, Afghanistan, sun warm on my shoulders, 80 °F, light breeze through my now thinning hair, I load up in the Apache gunship, I turn on the headset beneath my helmet, my ear-set clicks from the pilot's microphone, "Colonel, you buckled in and ready? We're about to have a good ride with the doors open…we'll be on our side for a while and don't want to lose you out the door." I click my mic, "Roger" I reply "appreciate the lift, I believe this is my fini flight after 16 years bouncing around in this AOR." In a few moments I was on the deck, Bagram Air Base, ready for that final ride home where my beautiful bride, and dutiful Drahthaar would welcome me home once again, and for the last time, from far-away deserts.

In the interim, and since, DDB has been a rock for me to lean on when John D., John R., John W., and a pretty good dog named Ginger went on to the next realm. DDB awarded Ginger "The Air Force Commendation Medal" for valorous field performance on the Owyhee's volcanic rock.

I honestly don't believe Colonel DDB held much hope for my military career; however, he continued to set the finest example of officership for my emulation and continued his mantra of officership and service before self before it was a "core value."

I was perhaps the lowest performing and highest demerited officer trainee ever to graduate on the hallowed parade field of Medina Air Base. However, with a little help and tutelage from DDB, and despite many shortcomings, his student had some rather unique opportunities to represent our great nation on the Tomb of the Unknown Soldier and at the White House. He helped me convince the smartest, most beautiful, and perhaps most fierce, engineering officer in the Air Force that marrying me was not too far a step down. His patient preparation allowed me to assume the solemn responsibility of leading our national treasure of young airmen in combat service support operations throughout S.W. Asia.

Not all was work with DDB—we've played just as hard, and I owe a debt of pure fun. A Turkey hunt South of San Antonio (story for another day), crazy cousin Chukar hunts, dove in Cordoba, driven partridges in Spain, California Quail in Patagonia on DDBs 80th birthday, and perhaps most unique: An honest-to-goodness truffle hunt over dogs in Italy. DDB and I have shot competitions the world over and hailed our brethren at The Grand National Quail Club. We even had the opportunity to help recognize the sacrifice of a true American patriot with a flight in a fighter jet in his homeland of Japan —I'll never forget the slim smile post F-16 flight from Dr. Akio M. (survivor of our country's imprisonment of Asian Americans during WWII). Akio loved anything that went fast, and I'll bet he's described better elsewhere in this treatise.

DDB dragged me and a few others of my ilk by the ear into becoming better citizens. He selflessly provides his most valued treasure—time. His investment, both literally and figuratively, in this motley crew of a future generation of leaders and their loved ones, continues to pay dividends of safety, prosperity, and perhaps a little fun to lives of people the world over.

Thanks, DDB.
John Linn
Colonel USAF (Ret)

Growing up in the white suburbs of Detroit was one thing but growing up directionless in a dysfunctional family is another. My dad was an alcoholic. He also was a racist. My mom was loving and caring, but woefully ignorant (not in a mean way) of the world around her. Educationally, neither made it past the sixth grade. And there are the kids. A total of seven survived. All in some form or another followed in their parent's footsteps. I did not.

At 18, a year after graduating from high school (the second in the family), but with no direction in life I had an epiphany of sorts. My future was my present, and I saw no positive path forward. I was not smart, disciplined, or organized enough to be a college student. Instead, I did menial work for my dad. In an eight-foot-deep ditch that was collapsing on my father, older brother, and me, I recognized I had to leave to have a future. Little did I know at the time that months later I would be serving our country in Germany. My future had begun without me even realizing it.

I started as an Airman Basic, and as I later found out I was succeeding. Yet, I needed to grow up. I needed someone to make me realize I had a future unlike any dream I could imagine. Little did I know that I had not only one, but two true parent figures watching over me. They saw my future when I did not. They saw in me something I did not know existed.

They were Dennis and Loretta Behrens. They are the parents I wished I had. I am beyond proud to be one of their "kids."

Loretta was a first lieutenant in my first assignment as an administrative specialist. To me she was the Executive Officer, and I never put any thought to anything other than supporting her. She, unbeknownst to me, also was supporting me. When she transferred to be an aide to a four-star general, she told her husband Dennis, a major and commander of a NATO support group, "You need to hire this kid."

And so, my life began to change.

Dennis hired me. Like Loretta, I was there to fully support him. Then one day my life changed. He unexpectedly sat down at my desk and proceeded to tell me I needed to go to college and earn a degree. He set about creating a new life for me, and he was determined to succeed.

And he did.

Despite a fear of failure, I took college courses at night, and to my shock I was passing my classes … with good grades. My enlisted career was succeeding. I was on the staff of a four-star general, later to be the Air Force Chief of Staff. I was married, and my wife Karen confidently said, "You can earn a college degree, and you can be an officer." By this time the Behrens' transferred to the Pentagon where he became the Director of Personnel for the Joint Chiefs of Staff. One day, nearly seven years still in Germany, I realized that taking night courses was an endless game plan. I called Dennis and explained that I needed to earn my college degree faster than taking night and weekend classes. Now a full Colonel he said, "I will call you back in a couple of days." And a couple of days later he did and told me he had two Air Force ROTC jobs, one at San Diego State University and the other at Southwest Texas State University. "You're not going to San Diego," I remember him telling me in that Colonel voice. "You're going to San Marcos." I asked why not SDSU and, he replied "because it is San Diego."

Instantly realizing beaches conflicted with studies, I did as I was told.

For two years I served as a NCOIC while simultaneously taking nearly a full course load. Finally, I had enough credits, and with a passing officer qualifying test I was accepted into officer training. Two years later, with that cherished bachelor's degree in hand, the time had come to become an officer. My Professor of Aerospace Studies (PAS) asked the six future lieutenants if they had suggestions for a keynote speaker.

Without hesitation I offered Colonel Dennis Behrens. The PAS agreed, and on a "cold" December Texas day (probably in the 50's) Dennis spoke to all of us, but I knew he was speaking to me specifically. Shortly after, with him smiling proudly, Loretta pinned on one of my second lieutenant bars. I was now Lieutenant Casey Mahon.

Dennis and Loretta succeeded where it took me years to understand their determination, perseverance and, yes, even love, to help make me who they knew I was and what I would become. After becoming a commissioned officer, I was fortunate to be successful in ways I would never have imagined. I earned my master's degree, served on the Public Affairs staff of General H. Norman Schwarzkopf during Operation Desert Storm, and after retiring from the USAF I reinvested my "second career" in public education.

Through all the years going back to 1977 the influence of the Behrens is indescribable in the most positive way. In large part because of their belief in my needing to be formally educated, that impression carries with our sons, Erik who earned his doctorate and is now a professor, and now Air Force Lieutenant Ryan, earning a master's and being one of only 12 applicants worldwide to be selected to an Aspen Institute Security Forum. More so with Ryan, there is no question in my mind his acceptance to Officer Training School was because someone who cared enough for his dad cared enough to help the next generation. That person was Dennis Behrens.

This incredible couple were and are the parents who I wished I had. The Behrens never had children of their own, but I know they have quite a few "kids." I am lucky enough to be one of them. I will always love them for helping me become what they knew I could be.

What is really important is what you gave me to get me to this point. You inspired me and had faith in me when even I wasn't sure I had the right stuff. Through the past nearly 50 years you have continued to be there providing counsel, wisdom, and strength. This to me is truly the gift I have and do cherish. It was an honor serving under and supporting you. I became who I am because of you. You're both role models, but most importantly you're good people. I'm thankful you came into my life.

Casey Mahon
Captain USAF (Ret)

I've certainly been surrounded by the best. Pretty damn grateful for the friends and support I've had. Really wish you could have been at my promotion. Like I said, I sure do appreciate, and respect, everything you've done for me. Always, relentlessly, in my corner.

One incident that comes to mind would have occurred around September 1997. I was just out of college and just out of basic training. We were traveling back from a pentathlon competition (CISM, I believe). Col Behrens ALWAYS made us travel in slacks and a sport coat, and he put that to good use when he got us upgraded to business class seats.

So, it was my first-time flying business class, next to Col Behrens. Towards the end of the flight, he had me pull out my travel voucher and walked me through how to fill it out (again, I had been in the military for about 14 weeks at this point). We got to the end of the voucher, and his tone turned very serious. I was at the section where you signed your name. He reiterated what that meant: when you sign your name, you always ensure you are honest. Your word is your bond-type of speech. He was VERY serious about it and wanted to ensure that I understood.

Twenty-four years later, I still remember that when I sign something.

Chad Senior
Colonel USAF
Olympic Team 2000 & 2004

The Colonel is one of those characters who likes to talk, but also doing everything he plans! He doesn't drop any details on his way!

I was visiting Tipiliuke lodge (in Patagonia, where I used to live since a kid) when an old man said hello from the other corner and said: "You must be the kid I'm looking for." I didn't understand very well what he meant, and we just kept talking. Later I just realized he was looking for the young photographer recommended by our common friend Marcos Furer.

I later met Loretta. It is so nice to see the great team they make together. You would ask yourself how they can live together, being super active, and she is so peaceful and quiet. They make such a balanced team!

That was the kick-start of our great friendship that we built with our dear Colonel Dennis Behrens. Not only good experiences were shared in hunting trips where I used to join as a photographer, but we always crossed paths here and there, (mostly in the USA and-or Patagonia). One day in Dallas (at the Dallas Safari Club) he said "Boy, you must come to Africa, and get to know it in the real way, not in just a simple touristic boring tour. You will come with my friends on a real and authentic hunting and safari trip" and we kept talking about so many other things.

Years later my phone rings, it is the Colonel! "Come on stupid boy, get ready! We'll meet at Nairobi, and we'll drive all around Kenya and Tanzania, the real deal!" Joining more and more of the Colonel's great adventures, I could see how he is always giving some life lessons. But that particular trip to Africa was no doubt a before and after in my photography!

More years later Dennis writes: "I'm planning to go to Patagonia! Not for hosting anyone, just to go hunting, fishing, and traveling with my good friend Max from Germany!" I thought it was another great opportunity to spend some good time out there with them and give back at least a little part of that wonderful experience in Africa.

I was planning, a bit nervous seeking to make sure everything turned out good. Picked them up to start the trip, and the first thing dear Colonel says is: "How the hell a stupid boy like you can get a truck like this?" (a phrase that only those who know the Colonel will understand it well). With Max we couldn't stop laughing! Starting there a joke battle between Dennis, Max, and me, another great adventure began.

We were on a fishing trip where I was supposed to be the guide. We found ourselves stuck in a swamp by the early rains that year which I had not foreseen. Max was walking with the Colonel —it was not easy to move around. I went forward to find the way out, hearing cracking sticks and whining. Suddenly I hear a strong and broken voice from a real "Colonel" saying "Boys, this reminds me a lot of Vietnam!" Stunned along with Max, we didn't know if it was just a joke or a nightmare recalled by Dennis. He had to scream: "Move on, you stupid boys, we've got to get out of here!" Once more he made us laugh, that was so him!

As I always say, it is not only the good moments that I enjoy being with Dennis, but his ambition to educate, teach and help is what makes him such a great person! One day he knew I was working on my *Wild Trout* book project (which I later published in 2018) so Dennis showed up with a check to promote the publishing. I said, "OK Colonel, you have bought X quantity of books, and as soon as they are sold, you will have your profit." Of course, he never heard me. When I tried to do it, he was offended because I was refunding more than he loaned! He tried so hard to convince me to put that money in an investment so that one day it would pay for the school of Ilya and Amadeus (my children).

Today I'm not in Patagonia anymore, I live thousands of miles away, in the NW of Argentina, and even being that far, away from any of his hunting destinations, our dear Colonel is planning a road-trip driving hundreds of miles through the countryside just to come visit us in our new life project we just began with Mariel (my wife), our kids, and me. I can't wait to meet him again and keep all our talks and discussions continuing, which luckily seems to be never-ending. Like our friendship!

Isaias Miciu
Juan Pablo, Los Altos, Argentina

My first meeting with Colonel Behrens occurred in the summer of 1995 at the Olympic Training Center in Colorado Springs. Between rounds, I was sitting alone on a dilapidated couch in the clubhouse reading an edition of the NRA's *American Hunter* magazine. As a new shooter to international trap, I didn't know many of the contestants at that year's U.S. Championship.

A well-dressed gentleman walked in, noticed the article I was reading, and proceeded to ask if I was a hunter. Eager to visit with someone, I affirmed that hunting was part of life in my hometown. We visited for a minute and introduced ourselves with a handshake.

"I'm Colonel Behrens," he said with a smile.

"Zane Kuenzler, nice to meet you." Thinking back, I didn't punctuate it with a "sir" because my education in manners wasn't complete at this stage in my life.

"What do you think of that article you're reading?" he had asked.

I glanced down at the story. It was a well-written article by a famous professional hunter from Africa and had held my interest throughout.

"It's pretty good."

"The author's a friend of mine; we've hunted together a few times," the Colonel had remarked.

Sure he is, I thought to myself. Cornered by another blowhard

Long Shots — Backword

trap-shooter with made-up stories for the clubhouse. My interest in continued conversation had definitely diminished.

"Really? You'll have to tell me some of those stories. But it looks like my squad's about up. I'll catch you after?"

"Sounds good. Nice to meet you," the Colonel remarked.

I had hustled out of the clubhouse and turned my mind to shooting. It was my first international trap shoot, and the five most successful shooters in my age group would be named to the Junior Olympic team. That was heady stuff for a seventeen-year-old and seemed like the most important thing in the world at the time.

Somewhere mid-round I noticed the Colonel spectating the shooting. He seemed to be keeping an eye on me. I had remembered thinking he must be bored and lonely, as watching a round of any kind of trap is like watching paint dry. Afterwards he approached and waved me over.

"Zane, this is Dr. Holtzclaw. He's one of my friends and is bunking with me in the Officers Quarters at Fort Carson."

"Nice to meet you," I said. No "doctor" and no "sir" made it into my limited dialect.

"I hear you are driving back and forth to Denver for this shoot?" he had asked.

"Yep, my aunt has a loft there. Saves me a hotel and food."

"Well, if it's all right with your folks, there is an extra bed at the base, and I'll spring for dinner."

"Sound's good." I could at least listen to this Colonel's embellished hunting stories if it saved me three hours of driving and upgraded me from standard McDonald's fare.

We had loaded my junk in the Colonel's rental and passed an enjoyable sit-down dinner at a local Italian restaurant. If memory serves, the Doctor and I had even gotten several words in between hunting and military stories of the Colonel's exploits across the globe. I went to bed in the comfortable Officers Quarters thinking this Colonel Behrens had gotten an advanced degree at an Ivy League Storytellers University.

The shoot had gone well, and I headed home with a new vest and some fine memories of friends spread across the country. Life turned back to high school and the routine of academics, baseball, and trying to find someone to pay for college. Little thought or time was allocated to shooting, and so when graduation rolled around I was surprised to receive a gift from Colonel Behrens in the mail.

The accompanying note read, "Congratulations on your graduation. I wish you continued success. Colonel Dennis Behrens, May 1996."

I opened the small parcel included. It was a book by the same author of the articled I had been reading at the clubhouse in Colorado Springs, and was entitled *Aagaard's Africa, A Hunter Remembers*. Opened to the frontispiece an inscription was revealed which read, "For Zane Kuenzler, Congratulations on your wins at the Grand American in Vandalia, and very best wishes for great successes in the future. Salaam, bwana, Finn Aagaard April 1996."

That was the last time I questioned the Colonel's attention to detail or doubted his claims of knowing a particular luminary in the shooting or hunting pantheon. I immediately phoned the Colonel to thank him for such a thoughtful gift.

"Would you like to go hunting with him?" the Colonel asked. And so, my adventures with the Colonel have spanned continents and continued for twenty-five years. I have met more interesting people and seen more of the world through my association with him than with any other person in my life. He has opened windows to the world that were simply not available to a farm kid from rural Colorado.

For that I say simply, "Thank you, sir." My education has progressed, and you deserve an honorific.

Zane Kuenzler Cortez,
Colorado

When I first joined the AF Shooting Team, Col Behrens was the man in charge, and we were both stationed in Washington, D.C., at the time. The team was operated on a shoestring budget so any cost saving we could find would go a long way in providing more support for the entire team. One of the big-ticket items was airfare. Both the

Col and I were flying out of National Airport in D.C. (now known as Reagan.) I was always getting reprimanded for spending more than the Col on tickets that were to the same place from the same airport. I'm sure he had a magician working his tickets because I was never able to get down to the fares he was paying. Then came that trip. I spent hours in the travel office working all the angles I could, perhaps even bringing my travel agent a box of chocolates. She assured me there was no possible way anyone could get this same trip for less money. I was a lock. Right, you know what happened, don't you? I submitted my expenditure report and soon received a call from the Col, once again berating me for the high cost of my airfare. And what was the difference you ask? **Three dollars!**

Along those same lines in saving money, in the early years we tended to stay in places that we could pack in lots of people at the lowest cost. Some of those hotels were, how do you say, less desirable than any normal Air Force person would stay. Let me tell you about the Camilia Hotel just outside Fort Benning, Georgia (at least I believe that was the name). It was the late 1980s, and the Camilia was a 5-star location ... sometime in the '60s. It didn't enjoy many upgrades since then. Inside the main lobby were hundreds of signed pictures from the Miss America Pageant, all looking happy and beautiful. Clearly, they had not been back to this place in quite a while. Outside in the courtyard was a pool that I had never seen with clear or blue water in it. It was always some beautiful shade of algae, mostly green. But the price was right. We could put the whole team in there for something like $20 per night. To give you a picture of the place, it was almost directly across the street from a liquor store and just one block over from the "gentleman's club." No, that makes it sound almost respectable, it was indeed a strip club. So there we stayed, saving all kinds of money, until the night of the shooting. Drug deal/bust gone bad right across the street in the liquor store parking lot. Can't say that I'll miss that place.

Dom Grazioli
Lt Col USAF (Ret)
2008 Olympic Team

I learned from The Colonel that the best stories include detail, enthusiasm, humility, and copious amounts of time! I'm certain that this excerpt will fall short of expectations, but here's a try! Thank you again for including me in telling the story of the life of a gentleman who I deeply respect and admire (Sitting here in a coffee shop in Ohio with tears in my eyes as I write this). Including my wife on this note. As you will see below, she too has been impacted by Colonel Behrens.

Many have heard the story about how Colonel Behrens and I met. It's a mildly interesting tale of the meeting of a recently retired Air Force Colonel and a young Naval Academy Midshipman at a skeet range in Maryland. Unbeknownst to me, the introduction would be the single most consequential in my life. By consequential, I mean impactful and life-changing.

At every milestone in my life, Colonel Behrens was there, bearing gifts and advice. Colonel Behrens was my first salute as a Naval Officer, he attended my Naval Academy graduation, my wedding, and presided over my retirement from the Navy. We hunted together countless times, and his generosity is unmatched. Argentina hunt for graduation, a Merkel 20 for retirement, and a few other worldwide hunting trips for good measure (he will not be happy that I exposed his gifts. Sorry, sir!). On my first trip to Buenos Aires, we roomed together at the Claridge Hotel. I desperately wanted to give him a gift, and I agonized over what to get him. I bought him a cheap green necktie with ducks on it. Many years later he wore it to a very nice dinner in San Antonio. He taught me that the value of a gift was based on the giver, not the price tag. There is no single person on this earth who has taught me more about life, people, humility, chivalry, and the importance of friends.

The Colonel is a humble gentleman through and through. My wife and I once met him at Taverna Cretekou, our favorite Greek Restaurant in Alexandria, Virginia, and he presented a beautiful box of chocolates to my wife Jen. The simple gesture became the gold standard for Jen and me. The chocolates represented more than a gift, but rather an example of how to make people feel like they are the center of the universe. This is a quality that few possess and ever fewer master. Colonel Behrens always reminded me that chivalry never goes out of style.

The Colonel's actions and words imprinted on me. He taught me that two $50 bills aren't as impactful as one $100 bill. I learned to shoot at the target and always know what's beyond it. I learned through his annual Toys-for-Tots shoot that we have all an obligation to give back, no matter how small. I learned that friends trump money every day. He taught me that a tight squeeze and shake of the arm is worth a thousand words. He taught me that a handwritten letter is much more effective than "liking" someone on Facebook or Instagram. He taught me the power of stories, that age is just a number, and the fountain of youth comes from friends. I am humbled to be called one of them! Constant reminder of the respect and admiration I feel for you and all you have done to help me learn and grow. I'm a better man because of you, sir.

Love you, Sir. Thank you for who you are and the impact you continue to make on me!

Derek Hotchkiss
Commander USN (Ret)

Colonel B: I first met Colonel Behrens at a bunker shoot in north Jersey in the fall of 1984. A blue Mercedes pulled up, a man jumped out and immediately took control, giving directions to everyone he saw. I remember thinking he must be the guy in charge. Little did I know that he was just a competitor like me, and he had never even been to this range before. Several years later, I moved to Maryland and started shooting at the bunker in Prince George's County. Dennis was there as often as I was. Most of the other shooters were military or ex-military, and they were deferential to his comments and opinions. He was not a fan of my casual conversations and my not standing at attention when speaking to him. One day he barked at me, stating, "You can't talk to me that way. I am a Colonel in the U.S. Air Force." That began a 37+ year friendship that continues to this day.

For years Colonel B and I traveled the world as officials and team doctor for the U.S. shooting team and the military modern pentathlon team. He was famous for his strong black-and-white views. During these trips, athletes and officials from other countries learned that if they wanted to change the Colonel's mind about something, the best plan was to come to me with their position and ask me to intervene. Some people are horse whisperers. I became a Colonel whisperer.

Dennis has taught me many things, but the most important lesson is that you should live your life to its fullest extent, travel often, and maintain good friendships along the way.

Dr. Steve Holtzclaw, MD
Davie, Florida

> *"Pursue some path, however narrow or crooked,*
> *in which you can walk with love and reverence."*
> —Henry David Thoreau

When I look back across time, I see many people, places, and the winding, twisting trail that brought me to my current place in life. It is often said of people being self-made that they did it on their own merit with little or no help of others. This individualistic notion is one I don't fully believe. We have agency, we clutch opportunity, and there is luck, randomness, and determinism. But I believe our life's path is primarily directed by the influence of others, by chance or intent. Today I live in a little Texas Hill Country town. It is home, and I have no desire to live anywhere else. My work has allowed me to travel, meet fascinating people, and make great friends all over the world. The path I do continue to walk is with love and reverence, and there is no doubt Col Behrens is largely responsible for my passage and outcome. It was the Colonel who put me on the finest path of my life. From my diary:

Long Shots — Backword

16 July 1995
Gowke Camp, Zimbabwe

The clients in camp are very good. A Colonel Dennis Behrens is leading them. He is good friends with Finn Aagaard. He hunted with him three times in Kenya ... A couple of the guys want to hunt leopards. I have a few feeding.

    I remember that July day when the Colonel walked into the dining area of the safari camp. He was joined by his good friends Rolf Smith, Roger Bain, George Gammon, Bart Byrd, and Charlie Weaver. While eating a meal, he told me about his Kenya safaris—hunting buffalo and elephant with my mentor Finn Aagaard. I was captivated. It didn't take much time to realize that I'd never met anyone like the Colonel.

    The Colonel also told me he lived in San Antonio, and I could visit him any time. He offered to take me to meet Finn Aagaard at the Aagaard home in Llano Texas. Well, I did. I flew from Montreal to San Antonio. It was an impactful trip. I not only met Finn and Berit Aagaard, but I also met Loretta!

    It was in September 2007 that the Colonel introduced me to Argentina with a team of "his boys." And it was in the hills of Cordoba while shooting dove that the Colonel told me I should consider being his business partner in Expedition Adventures. He thought it best I resettle my family from a remote far South Texas ranch to a good community in closer to San Antonio, to a better place to raise my family. Well, I did. I left the South Texas ranch and moved to the Hill Country. At the time of this writing, we've been business partners for fifteen years, and it's been better than I imagined.

    The road the Colonel put me on continues to provide me a life of gratitude and without regrets. I owe much to the Colonel for the far and wild places I've seen and the great many friends I have made. He's been a superb business partner but a better friend and mentor. Thank you, Colonel.

    Winston Churchill once said, "We make a living by what we get, but we make a life by what we give."

The Colonel has selflessly given so much to me and to so many others that have the great fortune to be part of his remarkable life. After all the years, I still have not met anyone quite like the Colonel.

Gordie White
Professional Hunter
Wimberley, Texas

Colonel Dennis Behrens was instrumental in my becoming a commissioned officer in the U.S. Army. He wrote a wonderful letter of recommendation for me that must have put me over the top as I was selected to attend Army OCS! However, Dennis' positive influence with my athletic and military career started long before with his recruiting me into the Army's World Class Athletic Program (WCAP) in 1993. I enlisted in the Army in November 1992 with orders in hand to report to Fort Sam Houston, Texas, upon completion of my basic and AIT training. Before I completed my initial training, my follow-on orders read, "Soldier is assigned to Fort Sam Houston, TX in order to train and prepare for the 1996 Olympic Games in the sport of Modern Pentathlon."

What a fantastic first assignment in the U.S. Army!

I clearly remember Colonel Behrens being the consummate professional military team leader, as he was our Conseil International du Sport Militaire (CISM) Team Leader for many CISM Championships and a couple of Military World Games, always leading from the front with his actions, appearance (sharp in uniform), discipline, and speech. He was especially proud of his uniform and would inform us that the uniform he was wearing was the same one he wore on active duty during his Air Force career. He would also advise if your haircut needed a touch-up or your facial hair needed a shave.

As a real leader, Colonel Behrens would always be the first to offer support before, during and after training and competition. He would always have a positive angle on your performance. Most importantly, if you didn't compete up to expectation, Colonel B was

Long Shots — Backword

right there with you in the trenches, lifting you up and preparing you to continue the fight! He was first-rate with his team leader responsibilities. He was constantly fighting for his team logistically, ensuring we had all the support we could get, from upgraded airline travel (always giving up his business class seat to one of our boys), getting the team into the business lounges during international flight stops, and getting us better meals and accommodations once on-site at the competition.

Colonel Behrens embodied the professional "American Military" Officer and Leader. He continually motivated "his boys" through action and words to maintain their military bearing at all times, regardless of the situation. This was critical for his young soldiers and officers on the U.S. Team as we were almost always competing internationally. The majority of the other countries we trained and competed with were athletes first and didn't have much if any professional military training. Under Colonel B, the U.S. team members were always soldiers and military first and displayed this professionalism at all times.

Colonel B fought an uphill battle to get us into the 2003 CISM Military World Games in Catania, Italy, (it cost him greatly personally). I'm glad he pushed for us as we won the Gold in the team event at the military games. Colonel B's boys won the only Gold for the U.S. military (in all of the sports) at those Military Games. He brought the Gold Medal Team to the Pentagon a few months after the games to meet the Joint Chiefs of Staff, Air Force General Richard Myers and some of his staff. What an incredible honor!

On a funny note, after one of the championships, the head coach, Janusz, and some of his coaching buddies from different countries wanted Colonel B to give a speech. He was trying his best to not give any remarks and just enjoy the closing ceremony with "his boys!" However, after plying the good Colonel with a few extra strong drinks, Colonel B gave a remarkable and humorous speech! He played along and had a great time with the entire ceremony, and a blast was had by all!

He was an exceptional military team leader! Colonel B always commanded respect through his lead-from-the-front bearing and positive attitude. As a young soldier, I could not have asked for a better example of what right looked like! He was a mentor, teacher, and leader. Colonel B's support as our CISM Team Leader was unprecedented and provided us with the unique opportunity to thrive!

Colonel Dennis Behrens left an indelible mark on my professional military career as an Army officer!

Scott M. Christie
Major U.S. Army (Ret)

I received a special Christmas surprise opening your card. You know that list of some of my special times are a direct result of an ornery young man meeting one very special colonel many years ago.

My wife saved my life, but you showed me a life I never imagined. You managed to make me better in every way. In fact, that continues today. Every day I ask myself "What would Col B, do?" and it's right every time.

I am proud to be a "Colonel Behrens Kid," and especially proud and humbled to have met you and to be able to call you my friend. I often wonder how you described your mentorship, but thanks for everything you've done for me and my family. In fact, I see a little bit of you in each of my kids. That's a legacy that will last for many years to come.

Some stories …

"You have to Bomb them Sons o' Bitches!" During a "Humanitarian Mission" in Argentina, the after-dinner conversation strayed off to U.S. Foreign Policy. You can imagine the point of view from a group that is tasked with these important missions. Military action was definitely a first option in all foreign policy decisions. This evening, I was occupied by a side conversation when a sudden "BOOM!" echoed through the room. By the time I landed securely back in my chair and my heart rate returned to near normal, Col B loudly exclaimed, "There comes a point where you have to Bomb Them Sons o' Bitches!" I realized that the room had become eerily silent. A sense of discomfort was thick in the air. After what seemed like an eternity, but likely only a few seconds, someone chimed in, "I Agree!" That quickly brought back the typical spirited conversation, and all was normal until the next, "You have to Bomb Them Sons o' Bitches!" It was another great night of laughter, camaraderie and a few adult beverages with our leader, mentor, and friend Col Dennis Behrens.

"Mike, I think you need to take the boys out tonight." "Yes sir!" Normally, Col B never roomed at the same hotel as the other members of the AF Shooting Team. That was either to give us room to unwind or mortal fear that he'd see how we were when he wasn't watching. During an Interservice Trap Championship at Fort Benning, Georgia, he was not only at the same hotel, but he was also on the same floor. This made the children nervous, so we were on the best behavior. With one day left in the match, the Air Force Team was shooting well, but not quite to what was expected. That evening, the team including Col B. were on the balcony staring into nothingness. Mostly looking pitiful and out of sorts. After several minutes, Col B quietly said, "Mike, why don't you take the boys out tonight." In perfect harmony we responded with "Yes Sir!" and disappeared into the night. Needless to say, when Col B tells us to do something, we're "All In."

In this particular case, at about 2:00 a.m., our "All In" was waning. The next morning, we didn't particularly feel at top form. Somehow, after several cups of coffee, we recovered and started to show some life in time for the last day's start. I don't know what scared us the most, the wrath of a very disappointed Colonel or puking on the line in front of the Army. We dug deep, somehow endured, and managed to perform. We came back with one individual medal and a team medal. The boys were out of sync and needed to blow off some steam. Col B knew what they needed, and as usual it was the right thing to do at the exact right time.

Mikey! I've been called a few different names and titles over the years. Mike, Herman, Mr. Herman, Airman, Sergeant, Lieutenant, Captain, Major just to name a few that don't include profanity. It's been said that I have a tendency to get myself in trouble from time to time, so Col B has used all of these and some that I'm sure he's never uttered out loud. However, there is one name that stops me in my tracks and sends chills down my spine. "Mikey." When Col B calls me "Mikey," there is no question that I'm in trouble. I either didn't do something I was supposed to or simply did something wrong. I never crawled up into a fetal position, no matter how much I wanted to. I always took my medicine like a man. Usually followed by fixing whatever I did wrong, then some pouting and hoping I never have to go through that again! I'm happy to report, it's been a few days since I've heard, "Mikey!" Col B, the treatments are helping.

Mike Herman
Major USAF (Ret)

I probably would not have stayed in the AF for a 20-year career if not for Dennis and Charlie, who I worked for as a 2d LT. It allowed me to comfortably retire at age 43. Certainly, his help with assignments allowed me to know Montana, where I settled for good. The friends in Germany I met thru him are still friends to this day. I am sure he was frustrated by my hard-headedness at times. He advised me years ago to invest. I took that advice and now have enjoyed financial success that I could have never, ever, dreamed of. I never thanked him for that, but I do now. And of course, the great trips over the years, Alaska, Chukar hunting in Oregon, pigeons in Argentina, and a cape buffalo in Zimbabwe. More trips than I can remember. But now I have enough great memories to last the rest of my days.

Mark Taishoff
Major USAF (Ret)

I met Colonel Dennis a little over 15 years ago. I was a young guide eager to work hard and to learn from others. I always admired the sense of respect and admiration he always showed towards Patagonia, its nature, and its people. Listening to his hunting, shooting, and fishing anecdotes and stories were always my favorite during the long lunches at Tipiliuke.

I feel lucky to have visited Colonel Dennis and Loretta at their home in San Antonio. They treated me like a son, showed me around town, even had me dress up in a tie for dinner at a beautiful venue one night, not something a country boy, fishing guide from Patagonia is used to!

Colonel Dennis was one of the few that reached out and offered help and support during the pandemic. That shows the heart Colonel Dennis and Loretta have.

Luckily, we've been in touch over the last few years, we drop a few lines every once in a while to check on each other. This upcoming May Colonel Dennis and Loretta are planning on visiting us, and I can't wait to see them!!
Muchas gracias y Saludos!!

Lucas Baxton
San Martin de los Andes, Patagonia

I remember most is simply his pride in the team and that he always wanted the best for us. We had some pretty good successes, winning team gold in Warsaw, Poland, in 1999, for example, but Col. Behrens was far more proud of us (or at least equally proud) when we earned the sportsmanship or "Fair Play" award at the CISM World Championships. I had the opportunity to serve as the Team Captain on multiple occasions, and while I am biased, I believed we always had the best military bearing of all the teams while also maintaining and exuding friendship through sports, which is the CISM motto. And we won that award several times. Much of our success came because of the expectations that Col. Behrens had for the team. We came together not just because we had great people, but also because we never wanted to let him down.

I'll add that it is probably because of a decision Col Behrens made that I am married to my wife today. During the Rome World

Games in 1995, Col. Behrens convinced the Italians that Bonni, my girlfriend at the time (now wife), was the team's athletic trainer, which enabled her to get a credential and gain access to the athlete areas during the competition. The times we spent on that trip together really got me thinking that she might be the one, plus all the guys were ribbing me the entire time about how I needed to ask her to marry me. Because of her credential, she was allowed to attend the final dinner (party) following the competition, and it was on that hour-long bus ride back to Velletri, a small village southeast of Rome (with a restaurant that had the most amazing gnocchi by the way) that I asked Bonni to marry me. I was slightly tipsy at the time, so she conditionally accepted, but insisted that I asked her again when I was completely sober! I followed up shortly after we returned back to the U.S., and we got married in San Antonio on June 29, 1996, at the Fort Sam Houston Chapel.

Jim Gregory
Lt Colonel US Army (Ret)
Olympic Team 2000

> Man is the sum of his actions, of what he has done, of what he can do, nothing else.
> —Andre Malraux

Appendix

Bunker Club Plaque

USAF Chief of Staff Letter

DEPARTMENT OF THE AIR FORCE
OFFICE OF THE CHIEF OF STAFF
UNITED STATES AIR FORCE
WASHINGTON, D.C.

9 September 1965

Lt General W. W. Momyer
Commander
Air Training Command
Randolph AFB, Texas

Dear Spike

General Greene, Commandant of the Marine Corps, has asked me to convey his congratulations on the fine performance of the Air Force team in winning the Commandant, Marine Corps School's Six Man Team Match at the Sixth Annual Interservice Rifle Championships, held at Quantico, Virginia in August 1965. In doing so, I would like to express my congratulations to you, as the Commander of Air Training Command, and to the coaches, team captains, team members, and support personnel who contributed to the outstanding showing made by the Air Force in both the Interservice High Power Rifle and National Rifle and Pistol Matches, just completed, at Camp Perry, Ohio.

While individual excellence in competition is always commendable, the real test of unit capability is in team competition. Members of the USAF Marksmanship School's competitive teams, who participated in these award winning National championship competitions have brought credit upon themselves, Air Training Command, and the United States Air Force.

Sincerely

J. P. McCONNELL, General, USAF
Chief of Staff

Official Match Bulletin— 1,000 YD Match

FIFTH ANNUAL INTERSERVICE RIFLE CHAMPIONSHIP
WEAPONS TRAINING BATTALION
Marine Corps Schools
Quantico, Virginia

9 August 1964

OFFICIAL BULLETIN

MATCH NO. 8 DIVISION "A" THE INTERSERVICE 1000 YARD MATCH

WEATHER: Temperature 80 degrees, clear, with wind from 11 o'clock 8 to 10 mph
COMMENCED FIRING: 0730 - CEASED - 1630
COURSE OF FIRE: 2 sighting shots and 20 shots for record, slow fire prone, one minute per shot

ARM ALLOWED: SERVICE RIFLE, M-1 or M-14

INTERSERVICE MATCH RECORD: 100-14V, GYSGT LEROY F. GROSS, USMC, 1963

PLACE	COMP. NO.	NAME	GRADE	SERVICE	SCORE
WINNER	36	BEHRENS, D. D.	2NDLT	USAF	100-14V
2	22	ANDERSON, C. J.	SGT	USMC	100-12V
3	261	GRAY, J. S.	SGT	USA	99-13V
4	467	TOBALDO, L. D.	SFC	USA	99-12V
5	415	BLAKELY, G. G.	LCPL	USMC	99-10V
6	610	DAHL, P. G.	SP4	USA	99-9V
7	548	LABERGE, L. L.	PFC	USA	98-12V
8	468	WARD, R. A.	SSGT	USAF	98-10V
9	483	PANZER, G. E.	SGT	USA	98-10V
10	69	HUISKINS, R. K.	SP4	USA	98-9V
11	259	SORIANO, S. D.	SSGT	USA	98-9V
12	345	MIRMAK, K. W.	ENS	USCG	98-9V
13	158	TACK, J. R.	SP4	USA	98-8V
14	402	WILLIAMS, E. M.	E6	USA	98-8V
15	442	DINNAN, R.	MSGT	USMC	98-7V
16	281	CZIKORA, B.	SGT	USA	98-7V
17	648	CHAPMAN, A. W.	E6	USA	98-6V
18	370	PRICE, J. L.	SSGT	USA	98-5V
19	498	FAIRWEATHER, D. L.	SGT	USA	98-4V
20	743	SCHILL, M. M.	SP5	USA	97-12V
21	628	EASLEY, T. F.	GYSGT	USMC	97-12V
22	68	FISHER, D. D.	SSGT	USMC	97-11V
23	664	COOK, L. L.	SGT	USMC	97-11V
24	427	BURT, H. W.	SGT	USMC	97-10V
25	374	WEBSTER, H.	SFC	USA	97-10V

8A-1

Commandant of the Marine Corps Letter

DEPARTMENT OF THE NAVY
HEADQUARTERS UNITED STATES MARINE CORPS
WASHINGTON, D. C. 20380

8 SEP 1965

General J. P. McConnell
Chief of Staff
United States Air Force
Washington, D. C. 20330

Dear J. P.:

Accept my heartiest congratulations on the excellent performance of the Air Force Rifle Team in winning the National Trophy Team Match at Camp Perry.

The score of 1455-102Vs under such adverse weather conditions is evidence of the great marksmanship skill and coaching ability of the Air Force Team.

Please convey my congratulations to the coach, team captain and firing members for their outstanding victory.

Sincerely,

WALLACE M. GREENE, Jr.
General, U. S. Marine Corps
Commandant of the Marine Corps

News Release— Air Force wins the National Trophy

USAF NATIONAL RIFLE TEAM CAPTURES HIGHEST AWARD AT NATIONAL MATCHES

The most highly coveted Team Trophy, the National Trophy, was won August 28 by the USAF National Rifle Team at Camp Perry, Ohio. The six man team fired a 1455-102V over the National Match Course to defeat 804 other competitors and 134 teams on the last day of the matches. The Army Eastern Team was runner up with a 1451.

The National Trophy was established in 1903 by the same act of Congress which created the National Matches and is awarded for excellence in team competition to the highest scoring team of all the Regular service, Reserve, National Guard and State Civilian teams.

Members of the Air Force Team were 1/Lt Dennis D. Behrens, OIC of the Team; MSgt Leon Linscott, Team Captain; SSgt David A. Thompson, coach; TSgt Frederick P. Dean; TSgt Franklin J. Tossas; SSgt Kurt J. Degerlund; SSgt Bobby E. Smith; and A1C Aldo E. Frascoia.

The matches were marred by 25 mph winds, rain and very low temperatures throughout the team competitions. The Air Force seized the lead with their first pair of shooters in the offhand stage of the match and maintained at least a three point edge throughout the match. This was the first time that an Air Force Team has ever taken home the National Trophy. Last year the Marine Corps Team squeezed out the Air Force Blue Team by V-count only.

Major General H. K. Mooney, Commander Lackland AFB, and Colonel Thomas C. Kelly, Commander of the Marksmanship School, were present during the firing of the team matches helping spur the team on to victory.

In the individual portion of the National Matches, TSgt Kenneth Horst, USAF, placed second with a 795-64V. Match Winner was 1/Lt David Meredith, USA, with a score of 796-79V. Both scores broke the old record of 792-76V.

Within 45 minutes after winning the Team Match, the Chief of Staff USAF, General J. P. McConnell, sent a personal congratulatory message to the Team. "General McConnell, Chief of Staff United States Air Force, congratulates the United States Air Force National Rifle Team for winning the National Trophy Team Match. Each individual is to be singularly congratulated on his outstanding performance. They collectively have enhanced the marksmanship posture of the United States Air Force and have set a precedent that will be hard for their successors to follow."

Rhein-Pfalz Land Council Patch

Listing of African Safaris and Some of Those Who Were with Me

Kenya Feb 1971 Gofourth Joe Cheffings
(Big Game—buffalo and elephant hunting) Bateleur

Kenya Dec 1971 Loretta Joe Cheffings
(Plains Game hunting)

Kenya 1973 McCausland, Bob Behrens Finn Aagaard
(Big Game—buffalo and elephant)

Kenya 1976 Master's Degree-Troy State Joe Cheffings
(Photo) Barry Borgiet, Bobby Kuhlo, Loretta

Kenya 1979 Kelly and Connie Beckley, Loretta Joe Cheffings
(Photo)

Zimbabwe 1984 Tommy and Mary Jane Brown, Mark Taishoff, Loretta
(Big Game—lion, leopard, buffalo) Travor Landry Lou Hallamore

Kenya 1987 Loretta, Jan & Lesa Gofourth, Joe Cheffings
(Birds and photo) Scotty Cameron, Tom and Mary Jane Brown

Kenya 1994 Rolf Smith, Roger Bain Joe Cheffings
(Birds and photo) Bateleur

Kenya 1995 Armstrong, Trick, Bierbaum Joe Cheffings
(Bird Shooting and photo)

Zimbabwe 1995 Weaver, Byrd, Bain, Gammon, Smith Dudley Rogers
(Big game—buffalo, leopard and Plains Game) Tshabezi

Kenya 1995 II Wilhite, Johnson, McAllister, & Molly Joe Cheffings
(Birds and photo)

Kenya 1996 Odom, Cushman, Susan, Joe Cheffings
(Birds and photo) Bob & Brent Behrens

Tanzania 1996 (Big Game—buffalo)	German Clients Selous	PH was Phil PD Lozano Tanzania Trophy Expeditions
South Africa 1997 (Bird Shooting)	Steve Wilhite	David Fowler Wild Wings Africa
Zimbabwe 1997 (Big Game buffalo)	Charlie Weaver, Col. Cameron, Barry Borgiet	PH Dudley Rogers
Kenya 1997 I (Birds and photo)	Bell, Trick, McAlister	Michael Cheffings Bateleur
Kenya 1997 II (Birds and photo)	Dr Larry Trick, Dr Steve Holtzclaw, Ray Gentry	Michael Cheffings Bateleur
Kenya 1998 I (Photo)	Vickie Heigel, Palmer, Steve & Sue Richards, Denny & Pinkie Rudolph	Michael Cheffings
Kenya 1998 II (Birds)	Dr Bishop, Col Jack Wood, Robinson, Loretta	Michael Cheffings
Tanzania 1998 (Big Game—buffalo)	Charlie Weaver, Rolf Smith, Jim Gofourth	PH Bill Isemonger Selous
Kenya 1999 I (Birds and photo)	John & Pam Kern, Fred von Bergen	Michael Cheffings
Kenya 1999 II (Birds and photo)	Ron Hill, Robert Thompson	Michael Cheffings
Kenya 1999 III (Photo)	Tom Veitch, John Harris	Michael Cheffings
Namibia 1999 (Plains Game)	Barry Borgiet, Roger Bain, Weaver & Charles Weaver	Dr Peter von Seck
Kenya 2000 (Photo)	Julie Oriet, Byrd, Pam Allemond, Tom Holland, Loretta	Michael Cheffings
Kenya 2001 (Birds)	Potter, Miller	Michael Cheffings
Namibia 2000 (Plains Game)	Smith/Weaver	Dr Peter von Seck
Kenya 2001 (Bird hunt)	Ziegler, Tucker, Jeffress, Herold	—
Namibia 2001 (Plains Game)	Facchina/Bering/Smith	Dr Peter von Seck
Tanzania 2002 (Lion/Buffalo)	Facchina	PHs Chris Trent & Tom Dawn Danny McCallum

Kenya 2002 (Birds)	Kinsey Robinson, Dr Trick, Martin	Michael Cheffings
Kenya 2002 (Photo)	Oriet, Kurani, TD Kelsey	Anthony Cheffings
Namibia 2003 (Plains/leopard)	Himmerich/Smith	Christoff Deikmann
Zimbabwe 2004 (Big Game—elephant and leopard)	Facchina, Hotchkiss	Dudley Rogers
Namibia 2004 (Plains Game)	Johnson, Kinsey & Mona Robinson	Christoff Deikmann
Namibia 2004 (Plains Game)	Don Berry	Christoff, Dr von Seck
Kenya 2004 (Birds)	Snyder, Herold, and Frederick Reardon	Michael Cheffings Bateleur
Kenya 2004	Bryce Potter, Suman, Emory, Miller	Michael Cheffings Bateleur
South Africa 2005 (Birds & plains game)	Rolf Smith	Kas Van Vuuren, Shozaloza
Zimbabwe 2005 (Buffalo, Leopard and Plains Game)	Himmerich, Smith, Williams, Burt Miller	Lou Hallamore H&K
Namibia 2005	Kilhoffer, Suhanin, Smith	Dirk Rohmann/Dr von Seck
Kenya 2006 (Photo)	Richards, Rudolph, Stuart Walker	Michael Cheffings Bateleur
Kenya 2006 (Birds)	Trick, Hofamann, Robinson, Berry, Crossley, Loretta	Michael Cheffings Bateleur
Tanzania 2006 (Plains Game)	Paul Facchina	PH Tom Dawn Danny McCallum
Kenya 2007 (Counts birds)	Bishop, Kilhoffer, Googe, Meints	Michael Cheffings
Namibia 2007 (Plains Game)	Braach, Scott Long	Dirk & Rita Rohmann PH
Kenya 2007 (Photo)	Tucker Family 25 people	Michael Cheffings Bateleur
Kenya 2008 (Birds)	Brown, Peveto, Sloan, McElroy, Thornton	Michael Cheffings Bateleur

Rwanda 2008 *(Mountain Gorillas)*	Brown, Sloan, McElroy, Thornton	Anthony Cheffings OnSafari
Kenya 2008 *(Birds)*	Ritchie/Rymer	Anthony
Kenya 2009 *(Birds)*	Thompson, Van Heel, Lee Seemann, Noel Adams	Michael Cheffings Bateleur
Namibia 2009 I *(Plains Game)*	Himmerich, Kendal, Smith, Gammon	Dr von Seck
Namibia 2009 II *(Plains Game)*	Tom Held, Kyle Miller	Helgaard van der Vyver
Kenya 2012 I *(Birds)*	Jeffress/Melarkey/Vopat July	Michael Cheffings
Kenya 2012 II *(Birds)*	Bishop/Irv Gerrow/Noel Adams, Hetrick, Rob Quist	Michael Cheffings
Mozambique 2013 *(Big Game—buffalo)*	Smith, Kilhoffer, Held, Himmerich	Haldane PH Craig Hammon
South Africa 2016 *(Big Game—buffalo)*	JP Lavalleye—	Jaco de Jager PH El Zulu
South Africa 2016 *(Birds & Blue Train)*	Karl Finkelnburg, Carl Kilhoffer, Doug Ward. PH Mike Currie, Robbie Ralton/Bird Hunters Safari	
South Africa 2016 *(Plains Game)*	Rolf Smith, Carl Kilhoffer, Dan Himmerich	Andries van Wijk Safaris
Kenya 2017 *(Photo)*	Robert Behrens, Dr Holtzclaw, Dr Bishop, San Angelo Group	Anthony Cheffings
Zimbabwe 2018 *(Buffalo & Rovos Rail)*	Rolf Smith, Bobby Dobson, Dan Himmerich	Clive & Lou Hallamore
South Africa 2022 *(Plains Game)*	Dan Himmerich, Rolf Smith PHs Dave Edgcumbe, Radcliffe Robinson	Crusader Safari
Namibia 2026 **(Plains Game)**	Linn, Kuenzler, Jungk, Himmerich, Miciu	Twilight Safaris Mare van der Merwe

My letter attempting to improve small arms policy and training in Vietnam.

```
Major Floyd Smith
6608 Fargo St
Springfield, Va 22150                                   11 July 1968

Dear Major Smith;

        I have been meaning to write you about my tour in Vietnam per our
conversation in 1967, but you know how it goes - put it off until
tomorrow, and tomorrow never comes.

        As you know, my job was in personnel. Our Wing had personnel
located on ten different bases in SEA, so I managed to cover quite a
bit of territory for a nonrated type. My general observation of the
753 situation was that number one, we need more in SEA. Number two,
these personnel should be used as 753s and not just as custodians of
Security Police weapons rooms, as was most often the case. Marksman-
ship training is almost nonexistent in SEA, while OJT, Base Beautification,
and Junior Officer Councils flourish and in fact become almost life and
death programs to commanders that must compare their programs to others
in SEA and PACAF.

        At one period of time, HQ 7th AF directed that no government
weapons could be kept off base and that any private weapon must be
registered and kept in storage by the security police. Our Base
Commander added that he would court-martial any person violating this
directive. Thus, Air Force personnel were effectively disarmed through-
out SEA. It seemed that everyone but Air Force personnel had weapons
in Nha Trang - VC, South Vietnamese military, South Vietnamese civilians,
US Army, US Marine Corps, and US Navy personnel.

        This infamous program was in effect during the "Tet" attack of 1968.
I turned in my weapon in accordance with the directive and was caught in
downtown Nha Trang during the "Tet" without even a pistol. We were
trapped in our Villa for two days and I will assure you that we had an
anxious moment or two. Our next door neighbor was killed by the VC,
and they took over a Villa three houses down the street from us. At
one time we had a gun battle going on between the VC/North Vietnamese
Regulars and the Koreans, South Vietnamese Rangers, the National Police
and Vietnamese civilians. Anyone of these groups could have eliminated
all the personnel in our villa with only a pistol. Of course we had two
knives and several bricks, but none of us were really very efficient with
these "weapons". After "Tet" the weapon policy changed and by the time
I left SEA the senior man in each villa was authorized a weapon.

        It would seem to me that we have certainly reached a sorry state
of affairs when military personnel are denied the use of weapons in a
war zone. Air Force officers have about as much status in Vietnam as
the lowest beggar in Saigon - these are the only two groups that are not
carrying weapons. The Air Force officer because he is a military man
and follows orders, the beggar because he is too poor to buy a weapon
and if he manages to steal one he is too poor to afford to keep it. A Vietnamese
```

Lieutenant, who lived close to us could not understand how an officer could be without a weapon in a war zone. I did all I could to convince him of the "official word" that one is safer without a weapon because he does not have a false sense of security and is less likely to get in trouble etc. etc, but after many hours of explaining, the poor Lieutenant still could not understand. I wonder why? He even pointed out that the VC probably would have taken our Villa had it not been for his protection. Of course, I explained that he was talking about an isolated case and after all there were only thousands of similiar situations in Vietnam. Another good friend of mine from Lackland had a similiar experience in Saigon and even after "Tet" could not get a weapon because there were not enough to go around. I could go on bitching for several volumes, but since you and I probably agree I will save you any further torture. No one can convince me that General McConnell would permit such a sorry situation to exist if he knew of it. My personal feeling is that each man in the Air Force should first be a fighting man (who must keep proficient) with small arms, and second a pilot, personnel officer, candlestick maker, etc. I also feel that there is a definite place in the Air Force for a sniper team made up of our personnel from the Marksmanship school. This team should not be utilized like the present Marine Corps Team in Vietnam, but should be maintained in ready status for situations like Panama, Santo Domingo and future "hot spots." I have not made much progress trying to sell my ideas, but am sending along a sniper program that I started in 1964 in case it might be of interest. I feel strong enough about the value of a sniper program that I would again be a volunteer for SEA or anywhere else that such a program would be developed.

Actually, my tour in Vietnam was really great. I worked every day and usually for at least 12 hours. I had the manning and assignments business and we really had a job with all our operating locations. We worked hard and really accomplished something, even if the base beautification program did steal some of my people at critical times. I was well rewarded for my efforts with a genuine feeling of self satisfaction - even felt a little bad about leaving.

Please drop me a note when you can and let me know how everything is going at your end of the struggle.

                                        Yours Truly,

                                        Dennis D Behrens, Captain, USAF
                                        Det 6, 1141 SPACTRON
                                        Box 9136
                                        APO New York 09012

Bunker Club Donor List

THANK YOU TO OUR GENEROUS DONORS

OLYMPIC LEVEL $25,000+

Colonel Dennis and Mrs. Loretta Behrens
Mr. Robert Behrens and
Mrs. Cheryl Armstrong
Dorothy B. Davis Foundation
Mr. Willard Dow
Mr. Tom and Mrs. Ann Dunham
Mr. Paul and Mrs. Melissa Facchina
Mr. Michael and Mrs. Tana Gallagher
Mr. John and Mrs. Virginia Groendyke
Mr. Steve and Mrs. Gail Jeffress
Mr. Douglas and Mrs. Carolyn Jensen
Mr. Michael and Mrs. Karen Melarkey
Mr. Albert Menefee
Mr. Kyle and Mrs. Lisa Miller
Mr. Clinton Rasberry
Mr. W.C. Rasberry
Mrs. Laura Revitz
Mr. Kinsey and Mrs. Mona Robinson
Mr. Lee and Mrs. Vickie Seemann
Anonymous
Mr. Mike and Mrs. Leslie Sloan
Westchester Foundation

WORLD CHAMPIONSHIP LEVEL $10,000+

Dr. Gene and Mrs. Leslie Bishop
Mr. Walter and Mrs. Darci Broich
Mr. Robert and Mrs. Susan Claytor
Friends of San Antionio Gun Club
Mr. Robert and Mrs. Jeri Herold
Mr. Brian and Mrs. Missy Huntley
Capt. Carl Kilhoffer
Mr. Jim and Mrs. Connie Meeks
Mr. Jacques and Mrs. Regina Pare
Perazzi USA
Anonymous
Mr. Gerald and Mrs. Joyce Suman
Mr. Doug and Mrs. Shara Ward
Anonymous
Mr. John Webster
Mr. Anthony Meier

WORLD CUP LEVEL $3,000+

Mr. John Allgood
Mr. Russ Arnold
Mr. Guy Avedisian
Mrs. Clara Behrens
Mr. Joe Bernolfo
Major Maxey Brantley
Mr. Brad and
Mrs. Linda Brock
Mr. John and
Mrs. Linda Browning
Mr. George Calomaris
Colonel Robert Cameron
Mr. Charles Coble
Mr. H.P. Cohen
Mr. Robert Drickey
Mr. Thomas and
Mrs. Vanessa Dunkin
Mr. Matt and
Mrs. Jennifer Eggley
Mr. Ryan Eggley
Mr. Butch Eller
Mr. Bruce Evans
Mr. Lee Evans
Mr. Karl and
Mrs. Margie Finkelburg
Mr. Casey Gallagher
Mr. Ryan Gallagher
Mr. John Googe
Dr. Paul and
Mrs. Cynthia Googe
Mr. Fred Hawkins
Mr. Thomas Held
Mr. Steve Herold
Mr. Michael Herman
Ms. Alexis Hibbs
Mr. Brandon Hibbs
Dr. Dabney Hofammann
Mr. Tom Holland
Dr. Stephen Holtzclaw
Mr. Denny Iker
Mr. Michael Jeffress
Mr. Doug Jett
Mr. Joseph Kelly
Mr. Christopher and
Mrs. Judith Kinsey
Dr. Kenneth Krueger
Mr. Zane Kuenzler
Dr. James Lally
Mr. Patrick Laux
Colonel John Linn
Colonel Gary Mahan
Mr. Tim Maier
Mr. Tim Markel
Mr. Tim McGill
Mr. William McNutt
Mr. Len Mertz
Dr. Richard Miles
Mr. Robert Mitchell
Mr. Michael Molak
Mr. Tom Nichols
Mrs. Stefani Perez
Dr. Donald Posner
Mrs. LuAnn Rannals
Mr. John Richardson
Dr. Charles Rockwood
Mr. James Rogers
Mr. Armand Roos
Mr. Eduardo Sardina
Mr. Scott Steger
Mr. E.C. Stone
Anonymous
Mr. William Tilley
Dr. Lorence and
Mrs. Judy Trick
Drs. Daniel and
Patricia Valdez
Mr. Gordon White
Mr. Theodore Whitehouse
Dr. Steve Wilhite
Mrs. Dorothy Williams
Mr. Robert and
Mrs. Barbara Zeigler

714

JOHN McCAIN
An American icon who devoted a lifetime of service to our country

Notable & Quotable: 'The Most Wonderous Land'

From Sen. John McCain's remarks at the 2017 Liberty Medal ceremony, Oct. 16:

Some years ago, I was present at an event where an earlier Liberty Medal recipient spoke about America's values and the sacrifices made for them. It was 1991, and I was attending the ceremony commemorating the 50th anniversary of the attack on Pearl Harbor. The World War II veteran, estimable patriot and good man, President George H.W. Bush, gave a moving speech at the USS Arizona memorial. I remember it very well. His voice was thick with emotion as he neared the end of his address. I imagine he was thinking not only of the brave Americans who lost their lives on December 7, 1941, but of the friends he had served with and lost in the Pacific where he had been the Navy's youngest aviator.

"Look at the water here, clear and quiet..." he directed, "One day, in what now seems another lifetime, it wrapped its arms around the finest sons any nation could ever have, and it carried them to a better world."

He could barely get out the last line, "May God bless them, and may God bless America, the most wondrous land on earth."

The most wondrous land on earth, indeed. I've had the good fortune to spend 60 years in service to this wondrous land.... I've tried to deserve the privilege as best I can, and I've been repaid a thousand times over with adventures, with good company, and with the satisfaction of serving something more important than myself, of being a bit player in the extraordinary story of America. And I am so very grateful.

What a privilege it is to serve this big, boisterous, brawling, intemperate, striving, daring, beautiful, bountiful, brave, magnificent country.

With all our flaws, all our mistakes, with all the frailties of human nature as much on display as our virtues, with all the rancor and anger of our politics, we are blessed....

We are blessed, and we have been a blessing to humanity in turn. The international order we helped build from the ashes of world war, and that we defend to this day, has liberated more people from tyranny and poverty than ever before in history. This wondrous land has shared its treasures and ideals and shed the blood of its finest patriots to help make another, better world. And as we did so, we made our own civilization more just, freer, more accomplished and prosperous than the America that existed when I watched my father go off to war on December 7, 1941.

To fear the world we have organized and led for three-quarters of a century, to abandon the ideals we have advanced around the globe, to refuse the obligations of international leadership and our duty to remain "the last best hope of earth" for the sake of some half-baked, spurious nationalism cooked up by people who would rather find scapegoats than solve problems is as unpatriotic as an attachment to any other tired dogma of the past that Americans consigned to the ash heap of history.

We live in a land made of ideals, not blood and soil. We are the custodians of those ideals at home, and their champion abroad. We have done great good in the world. That leadership has had its costs, but we have become incomparably powerful and wealthy as we did. We have a moral obligation to continue in our just cause, and we would bring more than shame on ourselves if we don't. We will not thrive in a world where our leadership and ideals are absent. We wouldn't deserve to.

715

Pentathlon Farewell Letter

Military Modern Pentathlon Team

Dear Team Members,

As I depart from active travel as Chief of Mission for the team, each of you should know your Herculean efforts produced the most outstanding teams ever to represent the United States in Modern Pentathlon. In the last five years, the men have won a World Championship gold team award, two World Championship team silver awards, and two individual silver awards. The women did an unbelievable job in winning the top spot in the first Military World Championship to include women. Additionally, you have won numerous individual events of Modern Pentathlon at these World Championships. And, you have represented the United States three times in the Olympics. To top it off, you won the first and only gold team medal for the United States at the World Military Games. What a record! Poland in 1999, Switzerland in 2000, Germany in 2001, the Czech Republic in 2002 and Italy in 2003. No country in the world can match you. You are simply giants. Whether you were a participating member in these events or a supporting member, all your combined efforts built this magnificent record.

Your conduct and military bearing set the standard for other teams to emulate. You have risen to the occasion every time and have never disappointed me. Your true sportsmanship has reflected the CISM motto of "Friendship Through Sports" and has earned you the respect and admiration of your peers. It was no surprise to me when the American team, of all the 86 visiting nations, clearly received the most applause and cheering at the Third World Military Games pass and review. You are magnificent athletes and superb representatives of the Armed Forces.

One of the best things to ever happen to me is the privilege and indeed the honor of having some small part in this team.

Please accept my congratulations on your success. Your loyalty to the mission and continued devotion to duty have brought credit upon you, the Army, the Air Force, and the United States. I am proud of you.

Dennis D. Behrens, Colonel, USAF, Retired

Index

Aagaard, Berit and Finn, 251, 342, 370-73, 377, 392, 395, 403, 692, 697, 708
Abels, Marie, 544-45
Adams, Col James, 65, 258
Adkins, Emmett, 228, 472
Agee, SSgt Mike, 265-66, 537-38
Aiken, Art and Roberta, 228, 663
Alonso, Adolfo 330
Allemand Ranch, 262, 400, 666
Allen, 1st Lt Anita, 510,
Allgood, John, 204, 220-24, 310, 329, 380, 400, 613, 628
Almon, Rita, 565
Altenburg, Gen Wolfgang, 215, 217-18, 631-32
Anderson, Col Robert D., 175-76, 187, 235
Anderson, Gary 444
A Tear for Somalia (Collins), 353, 368
Any Baby Can, 566, 648
Army at Dawn, The (Atkinson), 133
Atwell, Rich, 63
Audette, Col Albert D. Jr., 117-18, 171, 189-90, 484,
Bailey, Wayne, 36, 49, 68, 84, 559
Bailey, Lt Col, 472
Bain, Roger, 203, 380, 382, 386, 400, 618, 697, 708-09
Baden-Powell, Lord Robert, 356-57
Baker, Secretary of State James, 222
Barker, Harold, 629-30
The Battle for Saigon—Tet 1968, (Nolan), 132

Bauer, Barry and Rosemarie, 230
Bays, 1st Sgt Chief, 177-79, 184
Beckley, Capt Kelly, 184, 189, 646, 650, 659, 708
Behrens, Allen, 261-62, 399
Behrens, Arlo, 95, 261, 550-51, 578-79
Behrens, Bernhart, 549-50
Behrens, Clifford (Cliff), 27, 37-39, 261, 399, 550-51
Behrens, Duane, 27
Behrens, Clara Mae Sykes, 90, 92, 95, 545-46, 571-76
Behrens, Earl, 550-51
Behrens, Harold Francis, 550, 576-82
Behrens, Ludwig, 549
Behrens, Neta (Evans), 27, 95, 551
Behrens, Robert (Bob), 71, 92, 95, 572, 576-77, 582-87, 673, 708
Behrens, Velma, 27, 37-38, 550
Behrens, Vernon, 27, 37-39, 550
Bellis, Lt Gen, Benjamin N., 190, 241, 553, 566
Benavidez, MSgt Raul (Roy), 200
Bernard, SSgt Robert, (Barney), 228, 432-33, 448-50, 472, 527
Bernhard, Lt Gen Ernst-Dieter, 190, 232, 553, 566
Berry, Maj Don, 152-54, 161, 163-65, 318, 475, 640, 710
Best, Randall, 36, 68-70, 93
Bice, Don and Susan 260

717

Bishop, Dr. Gene, 228, 387, 591, 624, 663, 709-11

Blackstone, Bill, 204, 224

Bodle, Mike, 84

Bone, C.H. , 311

Bonelli, Laura and Pedro, 335

Booker Ambulance, 73

Botke, Jessie Arms, 89

Boren Senator David, 217

Borgiet, Barry, 188, 387, 708-09

Bouma, Capt Dirk, 488, 496-98, 501, 506-08, 533

Braach, Dave, 306

Braach, Rob, 221, 267, 306, 710

The Brady Gang, 441-42

Branson, Richard, 175

Brantley, Maj Maxey, 228, 646, 652, 663

Bremer, 1st Lt Eli, 508, 515, 536

Brennan, Chris, 377

Brezhnev, Leonid, 218

Bristow, Whitney, 221

Brock, John, 36, 104, 303

Brooks Mrs. 196, 238

Brown, Dr. J Cudd, 255-56

Brown, Capt Tommy, 154, 365, 393, 641, 643, 708

Bryant, Group Captain, 232, 553

Bunker Club, 17, 446, 568, 587-92, 664, 705, 714

Burton, Tony, 311-12

Bush, President George H. W., 224, 317, 645

Bush, President George W., 369

Bustamante, Fernando, 317

Buxton, Lucas, 330, 337, 593, 703

Byrd, Bart and Gay, 262, 400, 641, 708-09

California Cadet Corps, 99-100, 482, 524

California Indians, 17, 229, 329, 654, 664, 674

Cameron, Col Robert (Scotty), 189, 204, 390, 708-09

Capstick, Peter Hathaway, 359

Carey, Col Tex, 554

Carter, Jack, 345, 371

Carter, MSgt James, 458, 529, 639, 679

Carter, President James (Jimmy) E., 224, 629

Carter, Admiral Powell F. Jr., 210, 242,

Casteel, Bruce, 259

Cataldi, Adrian, 330

Cheffings, Anthony, 402, 410

Cheffings, Joe, 342, 377, 402, 708

Cheffings, Michael, 359, 402, 709

Cheney, VP Dick, 217, 485

Chesney, Lt Gen Murphy A., 598

Chester, Capt, 128

Christie, Maj Scott, 496-98, 501, 509, 514, 520, 533, 536, 700

Churchill, Winston, 139, 357, 655, 697

Chuchupati Fire, 53

Celiz, Emiliano, 336

Clark, Lt Col Al, 204, 254,

Clark, Andrew Bessemer, 315

Clark, John, 377

Clark, Ken, 377

Clarke, Elizabeth and George, 544

Clements, Gov Bill, 65

Cleveland, President Grover, 252

Clinton, President Bill, 259, 629

Coby, Scott, 225, 313, 398, 409

Cochran, Jacqueline, 156

Coleman, Renata, 315

Coleman, Frank, 341
Coleman, Lt Col William, 116, 148, 560
Collins, Douglas, 353-54, 368
Crowe, Navy Admiral William J., 196, 211, 217
Cozzani, Jose, 336
Crespo, Felipe and Octavio, 329, 331
Curtis, Tom, 254, 295
Dabney, George, 36, 49, 84, 86, 63
Dalton, Lt Gen James E., 119, 196-97, 238
Daly, Sgt Maj Dan, 59
Dames, Tom, 380
Davey, Peter, 342
Davis, Gen James B., 65, 171, 225, 240, 248, 262-64, 278, 318, 324, 408, 475, 478, 619, 646-50
Davis, Linda, 213
Davies, Richard, 524
Davison, Nadyne, 36
Dean, TSgt Fred, 529, 532
Dean, Capt Jack, 63, 259, 263, 500
De Gaulle, Gen Charles, 81
Degerlund, SSgt Kurt, 455, 458, 462, 464, 529
Del Campo, Lily, 224
Dement, Joetta, 320-21
Dement, SFC Lance, 265, 320, 537
Dewitt, Terry, 321
Dickens, A1C Bob, 289
Jimmy Dickens, 472
Diem, Ngo Dihn, 122
Director of Civilian Marksmanship (DCM), 42, 101, 428, 443
Dobie, J. Frank, 654
Dobson, Bobby 383
Dow, Willard, 411
Downs, Frederick, 145

Dronsky, John, 546
Duncan, Tim, 479
Duncan, Col Wayne M., 119, 196
Ducoff, Steve, 475, 484, 620, 647
Dyke, Maj Gen Charles W., 119, 196, 216, 494
Edde, Byron, 36, 40, 83, 559, 633,
Edward, Col Dick, 219
Eisenhower, President (Gen) Dwight, 42, 156, 425, 462, 473
Elbert, Irma and Louis, 68, 74, 543, 549
Ellis, Mary Ann, 36
Ellis, Gen Richard H., 173
Ellis, Brig Gen Robert, 164
Emmons, Matt 444
Enzenberger, Robert, 230
Erickson, Dick, 188
Evans, Gordon, 27
Evans, SSgt Henry, 228, 433, 449, 454
Evans, Leo and Neta, 27, 551
Evans, Melvin, 27
Evans, Roger, 230
Evans, Gen William J., 176, 192, 553
Ewing, Grace, 544
Facchina, Paul, 220, 368, 380, 388, 406, 589, 709
Falaschi, Robert, 230
Farris, Lt Col J. D., 116
Fechner, Col Bob, 204
Fisher, Maj Bernard, 146
Fisher, Paris, 204, 223
Fladausch, Paul, 161-62, 187, 397
Fletcher, Allen, 311
Fontana, Luciano, 336, 593
Foster, Buddy (Bud) 36, 77, 633
Forsythe, Capt Doug, 154, 159, 163, 183, 253, 336, 586, 643, 670
Frascoia, A1C Aldo, 448, 458, 460, 529, 532

719

Freed, Lynn, 51, 54
Frontera, Tomas and Clarita, 332
Fry, Lt Col Joe, 122
Fuchs, SSgt, 232
Fulton, Joan, 36, 77, 633
Furer, Marcos, 336, 687
Gagarin, Yuri, 158
Galtieri, Gen Leopoldo, 224
Gallagher, Tana and Mike, 230, 664

Gaylie, Col, 185
Gephardt, Carol, 221
Giap, Gen Vo Nguyen, 121, 128
Giddings, Gen Ted, 221, 237, 398, 554
Gill, Col Bob, 219
Gitman, Shelley, 221, 478

Gofourth, Jan and Jim, 36, 41, 56, 302, 341-46, 379, 575, 559, 633, 635, 708-09
Goldwater, Senator Barry, 623
Gonzales, George, 66
Goodman, Art, 221
Googe, Dr. Paul, 306, 316, 411, 710
Gorbachev, Mikhail, 218
Gore, Vice President Al, 565, 630
Gray, Gen Alfred, 632, 218, 222, 440
Grazioli, Capt Dominic, 221, 247, 408, 476, 483, 538, 596, 693
Green, Bob, 294, 621
Greene, Gen Wallace M., 458, 466
Gregory, Lt Col James (Jim), 497, 501-10, 520, 533, 668, 704
Greve, Lt Gen Carl-Heinz, 173, 193
Grivetti, Lou, 36, 83
Groendyke, John, 263, 297, 329, 409
Grover, Capt Melvin, 169
Guide to Life and Literature of the Southwest (Dobie), 654
Guerinau, Diego 329
Gurd, Capt Roy, 128, 234
Habbick, Joan, 36
Haillez, René, 187, 226, 278, 413

Hallamore, Lou, 252, 365, 383, 708-11
Hamilton, Carl, 28
Hancock, Vincent, 446
Harding, Bob (Robert), 203-05, 380, 619
Hathaway, Chuck, 228
Hathcock, LCpl Carlos N., 102, 460
Hawthorne, Kathleen, 36
Hayes, Alex and Zeke, 332
Hayes, Bob, 663
Hearst Family and Foundation, 564, 629
Held, Tom, 711, 714
Henneke, David, 263
Hennessey, Col Tom, 219
Herman, Maj Mike, 222, 247, 265, 476, 537, 597, 701
Herold, Bob and Jeri, 229, 361, 664, 710
Herres, Gen Robert T., 218, 632
Herrick, Col Louis E.,118
Herrick Trophy Match, 102, 105
Himmerich, Dan, 383-88, 407
Ho Chi Minh, 121
Hogg, Admiral James R., 211 243
Holdridge, Doyle (Dolly), 258
Holland, Tom, 204, 709, 380
Hollingsworth, Lt Gen James, 284
Holtzclaw, Dr. Steve, 501, 602, 696
Horst, TSgt Ken, 425, 433, 449, 460, 527
Hoover, J. Edgar, 441
Hoover, Robert, 157
Hotchkiss, Derek, 307, 601, 660, 668, 671, 695
Howard, Terry, 475
Hunt, Capt Reid, 61
Hunter, Col James, 122
Huntley, Brian, 297
Hurt, Donald, 660
Hurt, Robin, 353
Huyser, Gen Robert E., 191
Hyde, Richard, 36, 68, 93
Iliev, Velizar 320

Jayroe, Lt Col Julius, 553
Jeffress, Gail and Steve, 229, 664, 709, 711
Jensen, Carolyn and Doug, 230, 664, 714
Jewett, Shelly, 663
Johnson, Gen Harold K., 466
Johnson, Pres Lydon Baines, 128, 133, 156, 296
Jones, Alejandro, 330
Jones, Gen David C., 117, 196
Jones, Gloria, 36
Jones, Robert (Bob), 195, 238
Jones, Brig Gen, William K., 452, 539
Jordan, Bill 470
Julig, Ashley and Jeff, 13, 228, 663
Jungk, Dr. Max, 13, 300, 307, 413, 607, 682
Kausch, Dr. Heiner, 159
Keating, Gov Frank, 408
Keil, Kelly, 366
Kelly, Joe, 261, 307, 399, 646
Kelly, SPC Michelle (Mickey), 510, 514
Kelly, Col Thomas C., 116, 122, 145, 273, 291, 427, 434, 470, 527, 586, 638
Kennedy, President John F, 112, 122
Kern, John, 204, 224, 316, 709
Kiehl, Otto, 153
Khan, Mir, 221
Kilhoffer, Carl 329, 388
Killing Zone, The (Downs), 145
King, Lt Col Barbara, 187, 553
Kissinger, Dr. Henry, 134
Khrushchev, Nikita, 112, 122
Knapp, Capt Rosalyn, 169
Knob, Col Dick, 219, 324
Kondak, Al, 477
Krcmar, Tom, 228, 431
Kronseder, Harold, 538
Krueger, Dr. Ken and Patricia, 228
Kuenzler, Zane, 300, 307, 599, 671, 690
Kuhlo, Bobby, 187
Lainez, Manuel 331

Landrey, Trevor, 365
Leavens, Charla and Charles, 33, 36, 83, 559
Lee, Brig Gen Jong Tae, 2nd Marine Brigade, 285
Lehr, William, 9
LeMay, Gen Curtis E., 128, 131, 156, 300, 426, 467
Leone, Roger, 230
Liberty, Col Gail 319
Linn, Col John, 221, 247, 300, 306, 476, 538, 594, 602, 619, 682
Linscott, MSgt Leon, 273 433, 449, 466, 527, 532
Lix, Terry, 263
Longmore, Col, 118
Loomis, Gary, 627
Lorch, Col John H. V., 116, 168
Lozano, Phil, 377, 709
Lumpe, Lt Col Ron, 163, 188
Mack, Dr. Manfred, 160, 187, 384 Mahon, Casey, 593, 662, 686
Mahon, Col Gary, 221
Man-Eaters of Kumaon (Corbett), 356 Man-Eaters of Tsavo (Patterson) , 358 Mann, Brian, 311
Mansfield, Lt Col, 124-25
Marchioli, Col Alexander, 154
Markel, Tim, 262
Marks, Maj Gen, 119
Marshall, Albert, 42
Marshall, Gen George C., 76-77
Marshall, Chief Justice John, 435 Mashburn, CMSgt Herman, 293-94, 474, 621 Mason, Gale, 41
Mason, Kirk, 383, 386
Masons, Masonic, 17, 24, 55, 189, 639
Mattis, Gen James, 133
McCain, Senator John, 134, 218, 649, 715
McCallum, Danny, 379-80, 709-10
McCartan, Col Robert O., 118, 187, 194, 235

McCausland, SmSgt, James, 154, 232, 395, 398, 708
McClaugherty, Priscilla "Pris", 259
McConnell, Gen John P., 444, 466-67, 531
McCormack, Kevin, 220
McCormick, Mike, 263
McElvany, Richard, 230
McHugh, Col John J., 117
McKee, Tom and Jill 548
McKinnerney, Deryl, 254
McNamara, Sec Def Robert S., 128
McPeak Gen Merrill A., 107, 182, 478, 619
McRaven, Admiral William H., 112
Meissner, Kurt, 36, 77
Melarkey, Karen and Mike, 230, 711
Menefee, Albert, 225, 589, 613
Merrit, Gen Jack, N., 207, 213, 217, 241, 493
Messenger, Capt Paul, 488, 492, 496-98, 517, 533, 627-28
Michelangelo, 79, 655
Miciu, Isaias, 307, 336-37, 593, 667, 690
Miller, Burt, 188, 300, 302, 710
Miller, Kyle, 329, 711
Miller, Moose, 41
Mitamura, Dr. Akio, 247, 540, 616, 618, 666
Molak, Janet and Mike, 228, 260, 538
Moller, Richard, 353, 377
Mooney, Maj Gen H. K., 452, 463, 466, 531
Moore, Andy, 284, 402
Moore, Butch, 36, 55, 633
Moore, Roy, 55
Morals and Dogma (Churchill), 655
Momyer, Lt Gen William W., 129, 132

Muehle, Count (Graf) von de, 152
Murray, Sheriff Ben "Doc", 258
Murtha, Congressman John P., 216
Myers, Gen Richard B., 196, 516, 536, 699
Naumann, Gen Klaus, 324
Nelson, Dennis, 504
Nelson, Maj Gen Keith E., 439-40, 479, 540
Nelson, Willie, 203
Nersesian, John, 137
Nessel, Volker, 187
Nixon, President Richard, 42, 134
No Second Place Winner, (Jordan), 471
Nolan, Keith, 132
Nonte, Maj George, 471
Norman, Barbara and Les, 204-05
Nunn, Senator Sam, 217
Oaks, Gen Robert C., 479, 239, 325
O'Brien, Father Denis Edward, 147 Odom, John, 188, 329, 708
Olinger, Pete, 524
Oliver, George, 311
Orange, Maj Bill, 124
Outland, Lawrence, 61-62
Owings, Jackson, 333
Owings, Jimmy, 204
Parker, P. D., 228, 288, 477-79, 539, 663
Pare, Jacques 329
Patterson, Lt Col John Henry. 357-58
Patton, Gen George S., 59, 164, 473, 495
Patrick, SSgt James, 449, 527
Pauly, Gen John W., 182, 185, 192 Peciak, Janusz, 488, 497, 504, 514-18, 535 Peot, Col Joseph J., 447-48, 526
Pétain, Marshal Philippe, 77
Petty, Dr. Larry, 663
Phillips, Mel, 263
Pike, Albert, 655

Pike, Col Vernon, 219
Pingleton, Tom and Guinn 568
Pizzagalli, Sergio, 335
Pope Francis, 654
Powell, Gen Colin L, 196, 222, 225-27, 244, 564, 632
Powell, Capt Willie, 469
Pullum, Lt Col Bill 469
Presley, Maj Bobby, 12
Randall, John, 36, 40, 56-58, 60, 66, 73, 302
Randolph Hearst Foundation, 564, 630
Rathie, Rance, 306, 330, 728
Reagan, President Ronald, 156, 200, 224, 564, 628
Reidy, Beth, 224
Revitz, George and Laura, 200, 203, 221-22, 260, 316, 322, 409, 611
Reynolds, Carl, 230
Rhode, Kim, 319, 445
Rhodes, 2nd Lt Sammy, 218,
Richards, Capt Steve, 228, 475, 484, 620, 646-47
Richardson, Travis, 294
Rieger, Diane, 36
Riffe, Tom and Ruthellen, 169, 641, 646
Riley, Col Jim, 219
Robertson, Josh and Jared 297
Robinson, Kinsey, Mona 204, 224, 316, 321, 389, 401, 410, 586, 591, 710
Robinson, Gen Roscoe, 206, 242
Rogers, PH Dudley, 368, 383, 708-10
Roosevelt, President Franklin, 22, 54, 77, 111, 255, 571
Roosevelt, President Theodore, 60, 287, 313, 351, 358, 428, 448
Rostercil, Alex, 377
Rowden, Lt Col, 418
Royal Order of the La Paloma, 224
Ruark, Robert, 252, 351, 359, 608
Russell, Lt Col John 500

Rust, Lillian, 36
Sadler, Brig Gen Thomas M., 116, 170
Salazar, Yolanda, 36
San Antonio Gun Club, 266
Sancomb, Tom, 59
Sandoval, Alfonso, 574
Scholle, David, 84
Schroeder, Patricia, 217
Schorlemer, Johannes & Renate Freiherr von (John), 159, 187, 325, 328
Schwarzkopf, Gen Norman, 225, 317, 481, 594, 686
Schyurievich, Gen Georay, 245
Search, Erik, 224, 307
Seemann, Lee, 262, 267, 318, 329, 711
Seifert, Mark, 137
Selous, Frederick Courtney, 351, 358
Sewall, Lt Col Robert (Rip), 153, 159, 172, 187, 279, 398, 616, 643
Shah, Reza Mohammad, 65
Shearer, Jordan 297
Sheppard, Alexander, 575
Sherwood, 2d Lt John, 128, 130, 137, 234
Shively, Douglas, 89
Senior, SPC Chad, 487, 502-08, 513, 520, 534, 536, 593, 687
Simmons, Robert (Bob), 61, 524
Sirovatka, 1st Lt Lynn, 123, 142, 235
Skelton, Col Richard E., 119, 173, 179, 187, 553
Sloan, Leslie and Mike, 710, 714
Smith, AW, 329
Smith, Bobby, SSgt, 449, 458, 527, 529, 532
Smith, Travis, 306, 330
Smith, Admiral William D., 212, 243
Smith, Maj Floyd, 132
Smith, Lt Col Rolf, 13, 163, 188, 191, 228, 239, 379, 383, 389-91, 407, 414, 454, 466, 639, 670, 680, 697, 708-11
Siracusa, Lt Gen Sergio, 505

723

Snedeker, Lt Gen Edward W., 103-04, 106
Sneidern, Kjell von, 318
Sosta, Lucio, 477
Sommer, Dan, 263
Sparks, Major William, 168
Spencer, Master Sgt Ted, 184
Stamey, Dave, 656
Stanley, Col Andy, 554
Stapper, Paul, 228, 433, 461
Steinhoff, Gen Johannes, 553
Stillwell, Gen Richard, 233, 284, 286
Sugg, Cal, 298, 638
Sullivan, Gen Gordon R, 493-94
Suman, Gerry & Joyce, 710, 714
Swindle, Jon, 204, 224
Swonson, Capt Jack, 124-25
Sykes Family, 21, 25-26, 37, 68, 543, 548-50, 571, 581, 583
Taishoff, Maj Mark, 163, 204, 221, 225, 252, 260, 269, 325, 365, 396, 400, 404, 605, 702, 708
Taft, 1st Lt Gene, 104-05
Taylor, Joe, 60
Teagarden, Brig Gen Claude, 189
Teague, Congressman Charles, 218
Thatcher, Margaret, 225
Thomas, Coy, 86-88
Thomas, Eva Celestia, 17, 543, 549 Thomas, Evan, 543
Thomas, James, 17, 543
Thomas, Owen Sr., 543
Thompson, SSgt David, 432, 448, 464, 529, 532
Throldahl, Capt Bobby, 137, 171
Tiemersma, Kevin & Maria Jose Gahan 330
Trent, Chris, 377, 380, 709
Trick, Dr. Larry, 227, 316, 389, 663, 708-10
Toeplitz, John, 533
Tossas, TSgt, Frank, 449, 458, 527, 529, 532

Trost, Adam Carlisle A., 218
Truman, President Harry, 77, 111, 156, 281
Truscott, Brig Gen, 133
Tucker, Ann and David, 229, 709-10
Udall, Doug, 36, 40, 67, 73, 75, 84, 93, 144, 256, 302, 305, 559, 574
Uffen, Robert, 36, 83
Urschler, Brig Gen Regis F. A., 119-20, 310
Valdez, Dr Danny and Dr Patricia 228
Van Deusen, Col George H., 116, 418
Vanegas, Manny, 36, 49, 67, 84, 86-88, 93, 633
Vessey, Army Gen, John W, 196, 199, 238,
Villa, Alex, 36, 87
Vuono, Gen Carl E., 632
Wade, Gen Horace M., 149, 226, 278
Wagner Family, 27, 69, 93, 543, 545
Wagner Melva & Phil, 543
Walsh, Col Walter R 440
Walt, Brig Gen Lewis W., 439, 529
Ward, Doug, 229, 254, 300, 307, 538, 671, 711
Warner, Senator John W., 216
Weatherbie, SPC Brett, 502-06, 509, 534
Weaver, Maj Charles, 163, 188, 191, 225, 379, 605, 697, 708
Weeks, Sgt Mark, 265, 537
Weeldreyer, Maj Larry, 283
Weinberger, Sec Def Casper 199
Welch, Gen Larry D., 218, 632-33
West, Phil, 377
Westmoreland, Gen William, 133
Wetzel, Charles, 321
Wheeler, Gen Earl G, 133
White, Frank, 150, 158, 163, 281, 298, 398, 471, 474, 586, 637

White, Gordie, 13, 300, 340, 392, 412, 568, 663, 669, 697-98
White, Pearlie, 151, 163, 187, 621, 623
White, Maj Gen Robert M., 119, 173, 179, 237
Whitehead, Lt Col Trusty, 124
Whitlatch, Maj Gen, 173
Wickham, Army Chief of Staff John A., 207
Wigger, Lones 444
Williams, Don, 36, 49,
Williams, Capt Lloyd, 59
Winter, Doris and Klaus, 159, 187
Wittlinger, Dr. Peter and Rosemary, 230
Wooden, John, 655
Wood, Col Jack, 204, 223, 380, 709
Wright, Jim, 263, 408
Wright, Phil, 294, 621
Yarborough, Senator Ralph, 218
Ycong, Ray, 221
Yeager, Gen Chuck (Charles), 155, 232, 305, 627
York, Alvin, 59
Young, Lt Col, 195, 238
Ziegler, Bob & Barbara, 709, 714
Zobel, Wally, 294, 323, 621
Zutavern, Bill, 265, 318

Back cover photos

Top Left - Hunting quail in south Texas with Loretta. She is shooting her Winchester 21.

Right—My ever faithful Masai bird hunting guides - Kisham, DDB, Anyika, and David

Middle—United States Modern Pentathlon Team at the 1995 World Championship held in Rome, Italy.
L-R—2d Lt Glenn Voelz, 2d Lt Jim Gergory, Spec 4 Scott Christie, Col Behrens, Capt Paul Messenger.

Lower—Roger Bain and DDB

www.ingramcontent.com/pod-product-compliance
Lightning Source LLC
Chambersburg PA
CBHW052205090526
44583CB00017BA/2057